FHG

GW00363287

The Original Pets Welcome!

- Guide to Pet Friendly Pubs
- Holidays with Horses
- Boarding your pets
- Preparing your cat or dog for travelling abroad
- All you need to know when taking your pet to France
- 52nd Edition

PURINA winalot

OPEN for dogs
www.openfordogs.org.uk

© FHG Guides Ltd, 2009

ISBN 978-1-85055-417-2

Maps: ©MAPS IN MINUTES™ / Collins Bartholomew 2007

Typeset by FHG Guides Ltd, Paisley.
Printed and bound in China by Imago.

Distribution. Book Trade: ORCA Book Services, Stanley House,
3 Fleets Lane, Poole, Dorset BH15 3AJ
(Tel: 01202 665432; Fax: 01202 666219)
e-mail: mail@orcabookservices.co.uk
Published by FHG Guides Ltd., Abbey Mill Business Centre,
Seedhill, Paisley PA1 ITJ (Tel: 0141-887 0428 Fax: 0141-889 7204).
e-mail: admin@fhguides.co.uk

Pets Welcome! is published by FHG Guides Ltd,
part of Kuperard Group.

Cover design: FHG Guides
Cover Pictures: With thanks to WINALOT, for picture of *Holly* (also p1, p79)

Thanks to HarperCollinsPublishers Ltd for 'Driving in France' section pages 61-70

All the advertisers in **PETS WELCOME!** have an entry in the appropriate classified section and each classified entry may carry one or more of the following symbols:

- 🐕 This symbol indicates that pets are welcome free of charge.
- £ The £ indicates that a charge is made for pets. We quote the amount where possible, either per night or per week.
- pw! This symbol shows that the establishment has some special provision for pets; perhaps an exercise facility or some special feeding or accommodation arrangements.
- ⌂ Indicates separate pets' accommodation.

PLEASE NOTE that all the advertisers in **PETS WELCOME!** extend a welcome to pets and their owners but they may attach conditions. The interests of other guests have to be considered and it is usually assumed that pets will be well trained, obedient and under the control of their owner.

Contents

Foreword

The 52nd Edition of **Pets Welcome!** Is packed full of pet-friendly accommodation so taking your dog on holiday has never been easier. Choices include hotels, B&Bs, self-catering properties caravans and narrowboats. There is also a big selection of French properties for those wishing to travel further afield, together with some good advice on driving on French roads, and some practical advice about the Pets Travel Scheme.

All of our proprietors are happy to welcome pets, in fact many of them have pets of their own, but they do expect owners to be responsible. Pets should therefore be kept under control at all times and discouraged from jumping on beds and seating. They should never be left unattended, especially in a strange bedroom – a lonely or unhappy pet is very likely to misbehave. Please remember that a little consideration and common sense now will ensure that you and your pets are welcome to return another time.

Most of our entries are of long standing and are tried and tested favourites with animal lovers. However as publishers we do not inspect the accommodation advertised in Pets Welcome! and an entry does not imply our recommendation. Some proprietors offer fuller facilities for pets than others, and in the classified entry which we give each advertiser we try to indicate by symbols whether or not there are any special facilities and if additional charges are involved. However, we suggest that you raise any queries or particular requirements when you make enquiries and bookings.

If you have any problems or complaints, please raise them on the spot with the owner or his representative in the first place. We will follow up complaints if necessary, but we regret that we cannot act as intermediaries nor can we accept responsibility for details of accommodation and/or services described here. Happily, serious complaints are few. Finally, if you have to cancel or postpone a holiday booking, please give as much notice as possible. This courtesy will be appreciated and it could save later difficulties.

Boarding your Pet (Page 10), Preparing your Dogs and Cats for Travel Abroad (Page 12), French Properties (page 17), Readers' Offer Vouchers (Page 433), Holidays with Horses (Page 419), and The Guide to Pet Friendly Pubs (Page 424) are now regular features, and on page 77 you will find some useful information on keeping your pet happy in warm weather. Our latest selection of Pets Pictures starts on page 79. A useful supplement of dog-friendly walks starts on page 90.

We would be happy to receive readers' suggestions on any other useful features. Please also let us know if you have had any unusual or humorous experiences with your pet on holiday. This always makes interesting reading! And we hope that you will mention **Pets Welcome!** when you make your holiday inquiries or bookings.

Anne Cuthbertson, **Editor**

Pets Welcome Free

A small specialist agency with over 40 years experience letting quality cottages.

Enjoy unashamed luxury in traditional Welsh Cottages. Situated near safe sandy beaches and in the heart of Wales — famed for scenery, walks, wild flowers, birds, badgers and foxes.

Pets welcome FREE at most of our properties

Leonard Rees, Quality Cottages, Cerbid,
Solva, Haverfordwest, Pembrokeshire.
SA62 6YE

Telephone: (01348) 837871
for our FREE Colour Brochure

QUALITY COTTAGES
CERBID

www.qualitycottages.co.uk

100s of pictures of quality cottages and beautiful Wales

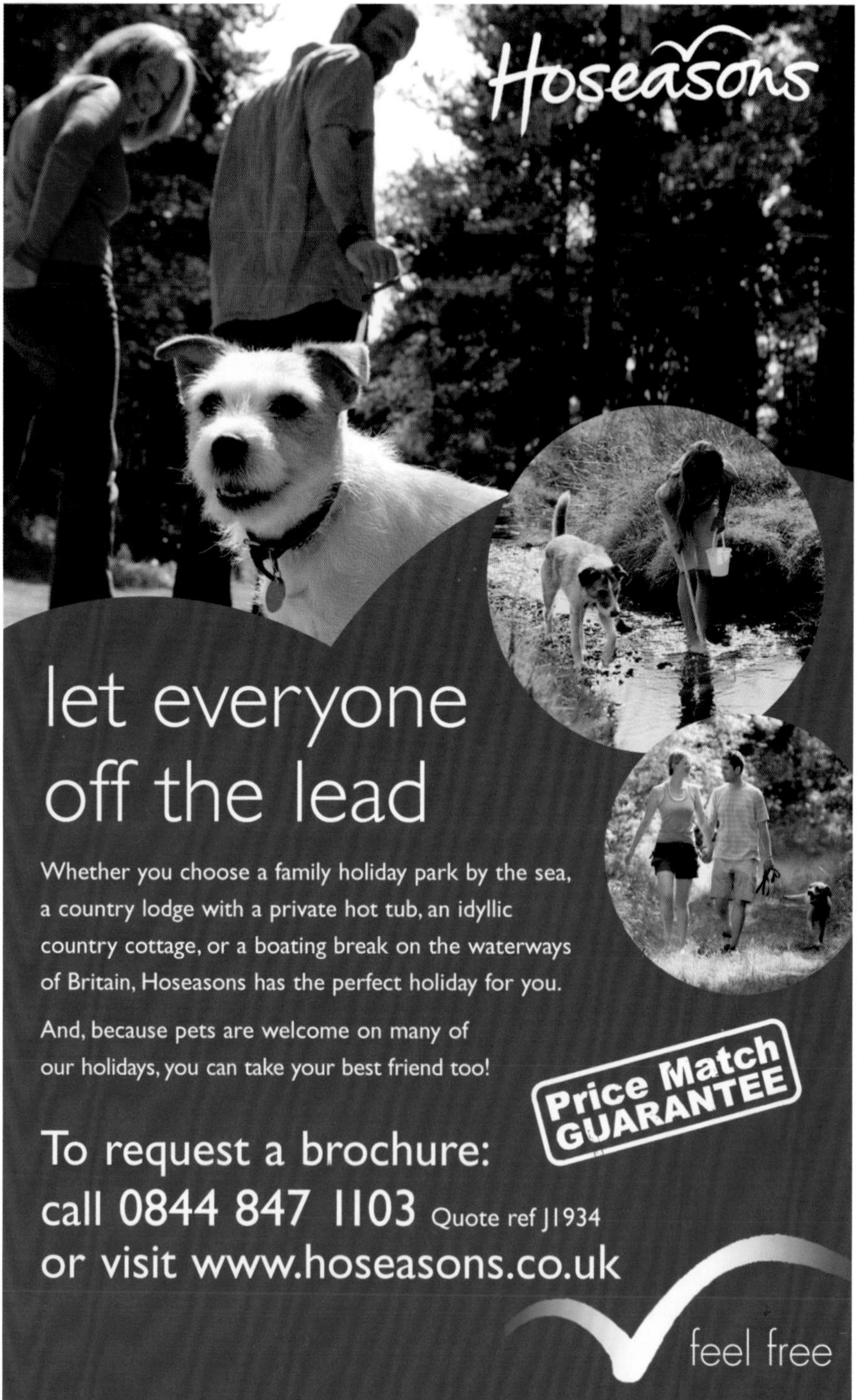
Hoseasons
let everyone off the lead
Whether you choose a family holiday park by the sea, a country lodge with a private hot tub, an idyllic country cottage, or a boating break on the waterways of Britain, Hoseasons has the perfect holiday for you.
And, because pets are welcome on many of our holidays, you can take your best friend too!
Price Match GUARANTEE
To request a brochure:
call 0844 847 1103 Quote ref J1934
or visit www.hoseasons.co.uk
feel free

Dales Holiday Cottages

Everything you could need for a great cottage holiday

- Over 500 cottages to choose from
- Stay anywhere from the Yorkshire Dales to the Highlands of Scotland
- Every cottage is personally inspected
- Pets welcome

Dales Holiday Cottages

Get your FREE brochure today

call 0870 909 9500 or visit www.dalesholcot.com

The Four Seasons Hotel

St Fillans, Perthshire PH6 2NF

Tel: 01764 685 333

e-mail: sham@thefourseasonshotel.co.uk

AA ★★★ HOTEL

Scottish Tourist Board ★★★ SMALL HOTEL

INVESTOR IN PEOPLE

Scotland's Hotels of Distinction

Johansens Recommended

BEST LOVED HOTELS

See Advertisement under Perthshire, St. Fillans

THE INDEPENDENT TRAVELLER

for a wide choice of quality cottages & apartments throughout

* Heart of England, South West, South East
* Scotland
* City apartments in London, Edinburgh and many UK cities
* Pets welcome in many country cottages
* Minimum stay from 3 nights in some properties

Contact: Mary & Simon Ette,
8, The Glebe, Thorverton, Exeter EX5 5LS
Tel: 01392 860807
E-mail: help@gowithit.co.uk • Website: www.gowithit.co.uk

the Independent traveller

Dogs Monthly **is now even bigger, brighter and better than ever before!**
116 pages packed with keeping your best friend happy and healthy, with expert advice on all the aspects you want to know about how to make the most of your partnership with your pet.

Subscribe today, get 3 issues for £1

Subscription Freefone 0800 612 8733

www.dogsmonthly.co.uk

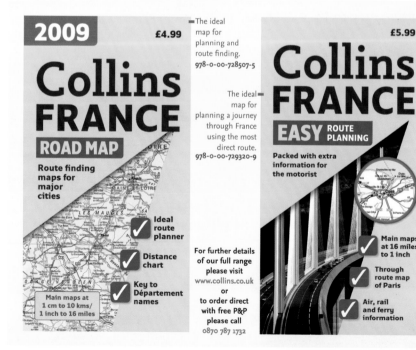

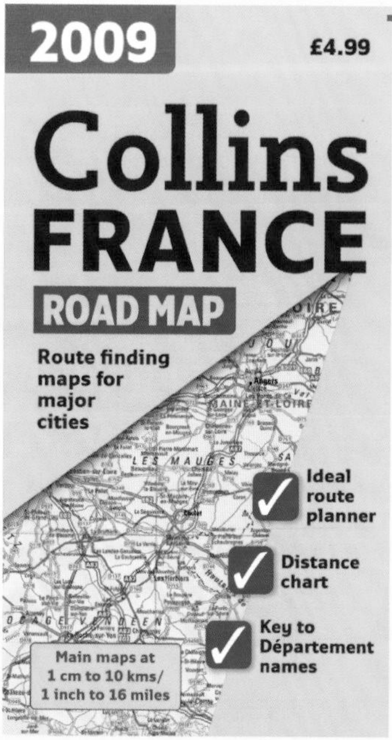

The ideal map for planning and route finding.
978-0-00-728507-5

The ideal map for planning a journey through France using the most direct route.
978-0-00-729320-9

For further details of our full range please visit www.collins.co.uk
or
to order direct with free P&P please call
0870 787 1732

Six months from the taking of a successful blood test you will be able to enter or re-enter the UK from Western Europe and 28 other countries including Australia, Japan and Singapore.

Pets must be treated for ticks and for the echinococcus parasite by a qualified vet who will record this on an official UK certificate not less than 24 hours and not more than 48 hours before entry into the UK. We are trying to secure changes in this very awkward timetable, which is being rigidly enforced.

On entering the UK you must therefore have two official certificates; one for the microchip, rabies vaccine and blood test; the second for treatment against ticks and parasites. You will also have to sign a residence declaration form - provided by the travel operator who is carrying out the checking. It simply confirms that the pet has not been outside the approved countries in the previous six months.

From Europe to the UK

As above, you must microchip your pet, vaccinate against rabies and approximately 30 days later your vet will take a blood test sending it to one of the laboratories from the list of those approved by MAFF. SIX MONTHS after a successful blood test your pet will be allowed to travel to the UK providing it has been treated against ticks and worms.

Costs:

- Microchip: Should be in the region of £25.00
- Vaccine: Varies according to vet but again approximately £30.00
- Blood test: We know that the blood testing laboratory at Weybridge (VLA) charge £49.50 per test.

Therefore anything in addition is that levied by the vet. Providing the rabies vaccination is kept up to date the blood test will not have to be repeated. Should there be a break between rabies vaccines a further blood test would have to be taken and then a period of 6 months allowed before re-entry to the UK would be permitted.

Therefore: Microchip and blood-test are one-off costs but the rabies vaccination is a yearly or 3 yearly cost depending on the vaccine used.

More information can be obtained from

Department of Environment, Food and Rural Affairs PETS
website: www.defra.gov.uk/animalh/quarantine/index.htm

Scottish Executive Environment and Rural Affairs Department
website: www.scotland.gov.uk/AHWP

PETS Helpline:
0870 241 1710 (Monday to Friday – 08.30 to 17.00 UK time)
E-mail:
pets.helpline@defra.gsi.gov.uk (enclose your postal address and daytime telephone number)

Current ports of entry are Dover (from Calais by ferry), Portsmouth (from Caen, Cherbourg, Le Havre or St Malo by ferry) and Folkestone (from Calais or Cheriton by Eurotunnel). London Heathrow is the authorised port-of-entry for : British Midland Airlines from Amsterdam-Schiphol, Brussels, Madrid, Palma Majorca, and Paris (Paris for guide dogs only); Finnair from Helsinki; and Lufthansa from Frankfurt.

The laboratories approved by MAFF for blood testing:

Veterinary Laboratory Agency New Haw, Addlestone Surrey KT15 3NB UNITED KINGDOM	Tel: (+44) 01932 357 840 Fax:(+44) 01 932 357 239 Costs: £49.50
BioBest Pentlands Science Park Bush Loan Penicuik Midlothian EH26 0PZ SCOTLAND	Tel: (+44) 0131 445 6101 Fax: (+44) 0131 445 6102 Costs: £32.50
Agence Francaise De Securite Sanitaire des Aliments Nancy Domaine de Pixerecourt BP9 F-54220 Maizeville FRANCE	Tel: (+33) 3 83 298950 Fax:(+33) 3 83 298959 Costs: 425ff = approx £42
National Veterinary Institute Commission of Diagnosites Section of Diagnostic Department of Virology S-75189 Uppsala SWEDEN	Tel: (+46) 1867 4000 Fax:(+46) 1867 4467 Costs: 500K=approx £40
Danish Veterinary Institute for Virus Research Lindholm DK-4771 Kalvehave DENMARK	Tel: (+45) 72 34 60 00 Fax:(+45) 72 34 79 01 Costs: 252K=approx £25
National Veterinary and Food Research Institute Mustialankatu 3 FI - 00790 Helsinki FINLAND	Tel: (+35) 20 77 24 576 Fax:(+35) 20 77 24 363 Costs: 396.50 Fmark = approx £26.00
Institut fur Virologie Frankfurter Strasse 107 D35392 Giessen	Tel: (+49) 641 99 38350 Fax: (+49) 641 99 38359

GERMANY Costs: 72.60DM= approx £25

Dept. for Equine, Pets and Vaccine Control Virology Unit
Federal Institute for the Control of Viral Infection in Animals
Robert-Koch-Gasse 17
A-2340 Modling
AUSTRIA
Tel: (+43) 2236 46 640 909
Fax:(+43) 2236 46 640 941
Costs: 600 schillings= approx £30

Instituto Zooproftilattico Sperimentale delle Venezie
Via Romea 14/A
1-35020 Legnaro
ITALY
Tel: (+39) 4980 84 259
Fax:(+39) 4988 30 530
Costs: price unknown

Laboratorio central de veterinaria de Santa Fe
Camino del Jau s/n
E-18320 Santa Fe (Granada)
SPAIN
Tel: (+34) 958 44 03 75
Fax:(+34) 958 44 12 00
Costs: price unknown

Institute Pasteur of Brussels
642, Rue-Engeland-Straat
B 1180 Brussels
BELGIUM
Tel: (+32) 2 373 32 56
Fax:(+32) 2 373 33 86
Costs: 1,500BF- approx £25

Institute of Veterinary Virology
Schweizerische Tollwutzentrale
Langgass-Strasse 122
CH-3012 Bern
SWITZERLAND
Tel: (+41) 31 631 2378
Fax:(+41) 31 631 2534
Costs: 96.75 SF= approx £40

What we musn't forget?

✔ *Medicine, if needed* ✔ *Toys* ✔ *Health certificates* ✔ *Food and drink dishes*

✔ *The dog's basket or blanket – it is extremely important that your dog has something to make him feel at home* ✔ *A thermometer* ✔ *A bell to hang around the dog's collar*

✔ *A can opener if you have canned food*

✔ *A deodorant for the hotel room* ✔ *Paper towels* ✔ *Brushes to brush your dog*

✔ *A towel to dry the dog in case of rain or when you get back to the hotel room*

Who benefits from your Will – the taxman, or the ones you love?

This year over £2 billion from Wills went to pay inheritance tax in the UK. Those Wills could easily have been made more tax efficient by leaving something to a charity such as the RSPCA.

Nobody does more for animals than the RSPCA and its branches.

And for every £10 we need to spend, £6 comes from people's Wills.

Our simple guide in plain English could help your Will be more tax efficient.

For a free copy, simply phone the number below, (quoting reference 08NL010140).

0300 123 0239

or e-mail jcurtis@rspca.org.uk

RSPCA

Registered charity no: 219099

Holidays in France

For you and your pets

Since the advent of the pet's passport scheme more and more owners are opting to take their 'best friend' on holiday to other countries.

With that in mind, we have included in this edition of **Pets Welcome!** a small selection of holiday properties in France.

You will find details of each property, plus some very useful practical information and a brief description of the regions.

Enjoy your stay!

AQUITAINE

This region of wide open spaces includes Europe's largest forest and offers a long list of outdoor activities. There are many quality golf courses which makes this France's leading region for golfers. For those interested in the past, there are a number of prehistoric sites and a fascinating variety of artefacts. Visitors should make a point of seeing the many cave paintings and engravings found in the Dordogne Valley. Enjoy the bustling towns, peaceful countryside and villages, and sample the fine wines of Bordeaux and the gastronomic specialties of the region, which include Foie Gras and truffles.

The Farmhouse

Gurs • Pyrénées Atlantique 64190 • Tel: 01622 747840
e-mail: sam@mountains-2-coast.co.uk

Delightful Bearnaise farmhouse, recently renovated to a very high standard with all modern conveniences, yet retaining many original features. The accommodation sleeps up to 8 people, plus 2 cots, and full baby facilities are available. There is a newly fitted kitchen with plenty of workspace, sitting/diningroom with wood burning fire, comfortable seating, TV and DVD. Two double and one twin bedrooms, plus sleeping area for 2 on mezzanine floor. The half-acre grounds have outdoor table and chairs and a barbecue area. Plenty of holiday attractions within an hour, including golf, fishing, tennis, paragliding and sightseeing.

Gurs (Pyrenees Atlantique)

Village near the town of Oloron-Ste-Marie with town lovely Romanesque churches.

THE FARMHOUSE, GURS, PYRENEES ATLANTIQUE 64190 (01622 747840). Farmhouse, recently renovated to a very high standard, sleeping up to 8, plus 2 cots. Newly fitted kitchen. Two double and one twin bedrooms, plus sleeping area for 2 on mezzanine. Half-acre grounds. e-mail: sam@mountains-2-coast.co.uk

Family outings in Dordogne

Bergerac Aquapark – four swimming pools with water chutes and other activities.

Prehisto Parc, Les Eyzies – cavemen, mammoths and everything prehistoric.

Jacqou Park, Le Bugue – three parks on one site, an animal park, and aqua park and an amusement park.

Le village du Bournat, Le Bugue – a reconstructed village showing life in 1900. With animals on a working organic farm, crafts, and a working windmill.

Airparc Perigord, St-Vincent-de-Cosse – a treetop adventure park on the river, one of the most exciting parks for children.

Three period cottages with fenced pool in South Dordogne, set in 65 acre private estate with fishing lake.

- **Kiwi** sleeps 2/3. One double bedroom. Separate shower room.
- **Wren** sleeps 4/6 Two double bedrooms. Separate shower room.
- **Honeysuckle** sleeps 6.Two separate shower rooms.

Great countryside for walking. 10 minutes to the nearest shops/restaurants and convenient for Sarlat and Bergerac.

Local English-speaking vet to assist with formalities for pets' return to UK.

Please visit our website for details/photos - www.lessarrazinies.com - or telephone Mike/Lindy Crowcroft on 0033 (0) 553 03 23 20 (summer) • 020 8340 2027 (winter) e-mail: mikecrowcroft@onetel.com

Le Bugue (Dordogne)

The pretty town of Le Bugue provides an excellent range of shops, including supermarkets, banks, chemists, post office and English-speaking doctor. There is a colourful and busy market every Tuesday, offering a wide selection of local produce, poultry, meats, pates and cheeses. Further afield you can visit prehistoric caves, some with world-famous cave drawings.

SOUTH DORDOGNE. Three period cottages with fenced pool on 65-acre estate with fishing lake. Sleep 2/6. Great countryside for walking. Local English-speaking vet. Contact Mike/Lindy Crowcroft 0033 (0) 553 03 23 20 (summer); 020 8340 2027 (winter). [🐕]
e-mail: mikecrowcroft@onetel.com website: www.lessarrazinies.com

Sleeping up to six people, La Blottière is ideal for couples, yet it is also suitable for families and small groups of friends. There is a well-equipped kitchen/diningroom with wood-burning stove (logs provided). Comfortable sitting room with French doors to private terrace with table and chairs. Laundry room with washing machine etc. One double bedroom, and one room with four single beds. Shower room with shower, washbasin WC and bidet. Cot available. Swimming pool. Non-smoking. Pets welcome.

St Crèpin d'Auberoche 24330 Dordogne • Tel 0033 553 048619
www.holiday-cottage-in france.co.uk

St Crèpin d' Auberoche (Dordogne)

Town with shops and all facilities, approximately 10 miles east of Périgueux, the centre of the Perigord region. Around an hour's drive from the airports at Bergerac and Limoges, and less than 2 hours drive from Bordeaux and Angoulême airports.

LA BLOTTIERE. St CREPIN D' AUBEROCHE, 24330 DORDOGNE (0033 553 048619). Sleeps up to six in one double and one room with 4 single beds. Well-equipped kitchen/diningroom with wood burning stove. Comfortable sitting room. Private terrace. Laundry room. Swimming pool. Non-smoking.
website: www.holiday-cottage-in-france.co.uk

Symbols

🐕 Indicates that pets are welcome free of charge.

£ Indicates that a charge is made for pets: nightly or weekly.

pw! Shows some special provision for pets; exercise facility, feeding or accommodation arrangement.

⌂ Indicates separate pets accommodation.

Le Manoir de St Marcel, Dordogne

PETS WELCOME

5 high quality, attractively restored and well equipped properties.
Sleep 2 to 12 (people).
Resident owners: committed to ensure that you have a wonderful stay.
Even if you are not bringing your dog or horse: Still come!
You will appreciate a warm welcome from fellow animal lovers.
Our vet speaks English and can help with formalities.
Telephone (from Britain) 020 7617 7115 • in France +33(0)5 53 61 06 17
www.LeManoir.org **e-mail: reservations@LeManoir.org**

St Marcel du Perigord (Dordogne)

St Marcel is situated off the D32, 12 miles from Bergerac and 6 miles from St Alvere. There is a good restaurant and bar in the village. The nearest large town is Lalinde, 7 miles, which has one of the prettiest markets in the area. Market day is Thursday.

LE MANOIR DE ST MARCEL. 5 high quality, attractively restored and well equipped properties, sleep 2-12. Resident owners. You will appreciate a warm welcome from fellow animal lovers. Our vet speaks English and can help with formalities. Tel: 020 7617 7115 (UK), +33(0)5 53 61 06 17 (France).[🐕]
e-mail: reservations@LeManoir.org website: www.LeManoir.org

Le Mascaret Farmhouse & Cottage

Located within a short reach of the famous wine regions of Bordeaux, and centrally located for both touring the region and for the perfect holiday French holiday. Surrounded by vineyards, it has a mature garden providing privacy and tranquillity.

Both Farmhouse and Cottage enjoy lovely views and are comfortably equipped including all essential appliances such as dishwashers and washing machines. The **Farmhouse** sleeps up to 9 persons and the **Cottage** sleeps 5. They are separated by trees and a hedge for total privacy, and can be rented separately or together. Beautiful garden with flowers and fruit. There is a swimming pool for warm and sunny summer days and shaded areas throughout the garden where you can relax with a book and a drink or just take a nap. Pets welcome.

Le Mascaret, St Romain La Virvee. Gironde 33240 • inquiries@lemascaret.com

Visit the FHG website

www.holidayguides.com

for details of the wide choice of accommodation

featured in the full range of FHG titles

La Chimere

La Chimere is set behind a 16th Century converted monastary in grounds of approx 10 acres of field and woodland, on the outskirts of the pretty village of St Romain La Virvee.

The apartment is comfortable and well furnished with living / dining / kitchen area, one bedroom, utility room with washing machine, and shower room. Sleeps up to 4, with cot available. Facilities include barbecue, games and bikes and there is a highchair, cot, pushchairs etc for babies/toddlers.

Set in its own private partly walled garden with plenty of room for a game of boules or badminton - or to enjoy a barbecue. Pets welcome Winter lets available.

375 Route de la Virvee, St Romain la Virvee, Gironde 33240
Tel: 0033 (0)557 582899 • Fax: 0033 (0)557 582899

St Romain La Virvee (Gironde)

Pretty village with shop and bars. Good selection of eating places within a five-minute drive and supermarkets in nearby towns of St Andre and de Cubzac. Bordeaux tramway park and ride10 minutes away, 25 minutes from picturesque St Emillion.

LE MASCARET. ST ROMAIN LA VIRVEE, GIRONDE 33240. Surrounded by vineyards, with mature garden. Lovely views. Comfortably equipped including all essential appliances such as dishwashers and washing machines. The Farmhouse sleeps 9 and the Cottage sleeps 5. Pets welcome.
e-mail: inquiries@lemascaret.com

LA CHIMERE. ST ROMAIN LA VIRVEE, GIRONDE 33240 (Tel & Fax: 0033 (0) 557 582 899). Comfortable and well furnished. Well equipped, one bedroom apartment. Sleeps up to 4, with cot available. Pets welcome. Short Breaks and winter lets available.

Looking for Holiday Accommodation?

FHG
K·U·P·E·R·A·R·D

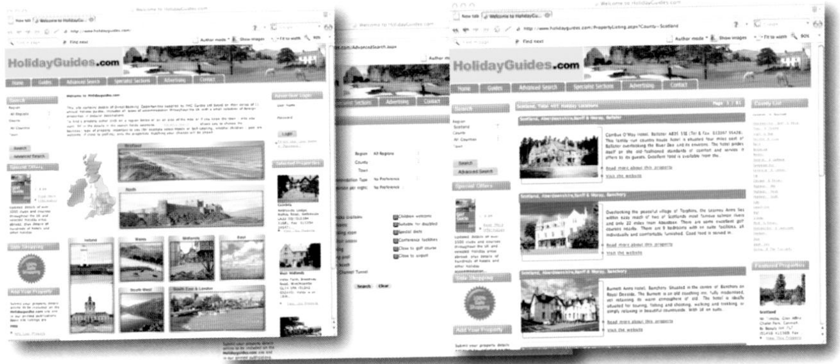

for details of hundreds of properties throughout the UK, visit our website

www.holidayguides.com

AUVERGNE

Lying in the heart of France only an hour from Lyon or three hours from Paris the Auvergne region has a volcanic terrain with a natural beauty and dramatic landscapes. The area is ideal for sporting activities, including skiing, golfing, hiking and hang-gliding, and for the watersports enthusiast, there are excellent opportunities for canoeing, fishing, swimming and sailing.

Gîtes du Château de Coisse ❖ Auvergne

Situated in a small hamlet in the heart of the Livradois Forez Regional Park, get away from the stress and grind of daily life in this tranquil, beautiful part of France.
★★ **2 person gîte** is on the ground floor of this recently converted 18th century barn.
★★★ **6 person gîte** forms the first and second floors and has its own south-facing terrace.
Both have been carefully restored to keep many original features but are also modern, fully equipped and child/pet friendly.

Fiona & Graham Sheldon, Gîtes du Château de Coisse, 63220 Arlanc, France • Tel: 04 73 95 00 45
e-mail: gitereservation@chateaudecoisse.com • www.chateaudecoisse.com

Coisse (Puy-de-Dôme)

Tiny village in the rolling hills of Monts du Livradois, an area of outstanding natural beauty. Town of Arlanc, 2km away, has all amenities.

FIONA & GRAHAM SHELDON, GITES DU CHATEAU DE COISSE, 63220 ARLANC (04 73 95 00 45)
Two restored gîtes in this tranquil, beautiful part of France. 2 star/2 person gîte on ground floor of 18th century barn. 3 star/ 6 person gîte on first and second floors with its own south-facing terrace. Child/pet friendly.
e-mail: gitereservation@chateaudecoisse.com website: www.chateaudecoisse.com

Things to do and see in Puy-de-Dome

Parc Naturel Régional du Livradois-Forez – an area of outstanding beauty with a volcanic region to the north west and many mountains. A rambler's paradise.

Rock climbing and paragliding at Job – for the more adventurous.

The Plan D'Eau near Arlanc – for those who love being beside the water. There is also an open air swimming pool, and tennis courts. Nearby is the Jardin pour la Terre, which is a large map of the world planted with trees and flowers from their native countries.

Comfortable • Spotless • Pretty
Exclusively for non-smokers

Laquairie • Auvergne

At the edge of the tiny hamlet of Laquairie, this cottage was built in 1820 and completely restored in 2000. Perched high above Condat and the Rhue gorge.

Large living room with huge fireplace, fitted kitchen plus a cellar. Main bedroom en suite, and a pretty little second bedroom. Oil-fired central heating.

Stylish, spotlessly clean, and equipped to a very high standard throughout. Comfy beds made up ready when you arrive, and all those little things that you need for a relaxing holiday.

Laquairie is wonderful walking country and one of France's famous national footpaths, that runs from the Atlantic to the Med, is about 20 minutes away - on foot of course!

Plenty of information in English, to get the most from your holiday.

Tel: 00334 7178 6357
From UK Tel: 0844 5553123 (5p/min)
e-mail: discott@auvergnehols.co.uk
www.auvergnehols.co.uk

Laquairie, (High Auvergne)

In a tiny hamlet perched high above Rhue Gorge, one hour from Clermont Ferrand. At the heart of Europe's largest national park, 5 minutes from bakers, butcher, café, supermarket and garage in Condat. A beautiful yet little known part of France.

Comfortable, spotlessly clean cottage at the edge of the tiny hamlet perched high above the Rhue Gorge. Large living room, huge fireplace, fully fitted kitchen (plus cheese cellar). Main bedroom en suite, small second bedroom. Exclusively for non-smokers. Contact DI SCOTT (00334 7178 6357). [Dogs 20 euros (£15) per week, to SPA].
e-mail: discott@auvergnehols.co.uk website: www.auvergnehols.co.uk

Visit the FHG website
www.holidayguides.com
for details of the wide choice of accommodation featured in the full range of FHG titles

Chantagrele, Auvergne

Two beautifully restored stone Gites, in a stunning location within the Livradois Forez National Park, with undisturbed valley views.

Light and spacious, these pretty stone cottages are bright, clean and comfortable, and tastefully decorated, with exposed beams , stone walls and wooden floors. Fully equipped, with three bedrooms, sleeping 4/5; log burners; central heating.

Secluded spacious garden with plunge pool, summer house and BBQ area.

Sauxillanges, 6km away, has all amenities, including convenience shopping and quality restaurants.

Mountain biking, walking, horse riding and fishing are all popular in the area, and skiing is available a short drive away. Open all year.

Contact:

Richard and Elaine Clements
Chantagrele
63490 Condat les Montboissier
Auvergne, France
Tel: 0033 (0) 4 73 72 18 95
e-mail: elaine-clements@hotmail.co.uk

Sauxillanges (Puy-de-Dôme)

Small village with all amenities, including convenience shopping, 2 highly acclaimed restaurants, 4 bars and a weekly market. Ambert and Issoire, two historic towns, and Clermont Ferrand are within easy reach.

RICHARD & ELAINE CLEMENTS, CHANTAGRELE 63490, CONDAT LES MONTBOISSIER, AUVERGNE (0033 (0) 4 73 72 18 95). Two beautifully restored stone Gites, in a stunning location within the Livardois Forez National Park, with undisturbed valley views. Light and spacious. Fully equipped. 3 bedrooms, sleep 4/5. Plunge pool, summer house and BBQ area. Mountain biking, walking, horse riding and fishing in the area, and skiing a short drive away. Open all year. [🐕]
e-mail: elaine-clements@hotmail.co.uk

Things to do and see in High Auvergne

Vulcania – a science oriented Theme Park dedicated to volcanoes.

Haras National d'Aurillac – one of the world's largest studs of heavy breed stallions.

Ecomusée de la Margeride near St Flour - several sites, telling the past and present story of the people of the area, includes houses, gardens, objects, sounds and smells.

Lioran Aventure at Le Lioran – an adventure playground claiming to be a cross between Tarzan and Indiana Jones.

Le Train Touristique running from Bort Les Orgues to Lugarde – a relaxing way to explore the countryside.

BRITTANY

This is a region steeped in tradition, and has maintained its Celtic traditions throughout the centuries. Mont Saint-Michel is reputed to be Brittany's best-known attraction. The beautiful bay of the Gulf of Morbihan is dotted with dozens of little islands, and you can visit fairy tale woods in the Ille aux Moines. Inland is the medieval forest of Merlin the Magician, where it is said that the Knights of the Round Table searched for the Holy Grail. The coast is a great attraction for tourists, who enjoy such activities as wind surfing, water skiing and underwater diving and, as you would expect, there is a wonderful variety of seafood available, including lobsters, oysters salmon and trout.

Les Cheminées

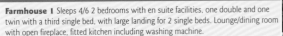

Gite Accommodation in Baud, Brittany

Beautiful 300 year old Farmhouse and Longeres set in 2 acres in a quiet location, Easy walking distance to the town of Baud. The Morbihan beaches are easily accessible together with many other activities including horse riding and golf tours.

Farmhouse 1 Sleeps 4/6 2 bedrooms with en suite facilities, one double and one twin with a third single bed, with large landing for 2 single beds. Lounge/dining room with open fireplace, fitted kitchen including washing machine.

Longere 1 Sleeps 4, up to 6 with sofa bed. Very spacious accommodation, one double and one twin bedroom. Bathroom with shower over. Large open- plan lounge, diningroom and fitted kitchen

The Stable Sleeps 2/4 comfortably. Very pretty house with one double bedroom, and bunk bed plus cot on the large landing. Open plan ground floor accommodation includes lounge/dining area and fitted kitchen.

Longere 2 Sleeps 6 (or 8 with sofa bed). Very spacious house with one double en suite and two twin bedrooms. Family bathroom. Spacious ground floor open-plan with lounge, dining area and fitted kitchen

All accommodation includes:
- Swimming pool • All linen provided • BBQ & Patio furniture.
- Kitchens include fridge, washing machine, microwave.
- Games area with swings, slide and table tennis.

Open all year including Christmas.

Please contact: Jackie or David Giles
Les Cheminées, Baud 56150 France
Tel: 00 33 2 97 39 14 61

Bed & Breakfast available from October to May. E-mail: info@baud-gites.com • www.baud-gites.com

Baud (Morbihan)

Small town overlooking the picturesque Eivel Valley, located within easy reach of the major towns of Vannes amd Lorient. Well supplied with shopping facilities, including two supermarkets, four boulangeries and eight restaurants to suit all tastes.

JACKIE & DAVID GILES, LES CHEMINEES, BAUD 56150 (00 33 2 97 39 14 61). Beautiful 300 year old Farmhouse and Longeres set in 2 acres in a quiet location on the edge of Baud. Sleep 2-8. Morbihan beaches easily accessible; horse riding and golf tours. All linen provided. Swimming pool, BBQ, patio and games area.
e-mail: info@baud-gites.com website: www.baud-gites.com

Cottage situated in one the most beautiful areas of Brittany, 10 minutes from the towns of Pontivy and Baud. Ideal for exploring the region, or for visiting the numerous sandy beaches along the Morbihan coast. Boat trips, horse riding, walking and cycling are available locally The cottage sleeps six, plus cot and there is a pool and summerhouse, large decked terrace with patio table and chairs, a barbecue and a large barn with table tennis, pool table and darts. The garden area has swings and football goal. The ground floor has lounge/diner with log fire, Satellite TV and DVD; fully equipped kitchen; shower room. Upstairs there are three bedrooms and a bathroom.

Tel: 0033 (0) 297 518974

Bieuzy Les Eaux (Morbihan)

Village with restaurants and bars. Golf 3 miles away.

BLAVET RIVER COTTAGE, BIEUZY LES EAUX, MORBIHAN 56310 (0033 (0)297 518974).Cottage sleeping six, plus cot. Pool and summerhouse. Large decked terrace. Ground floor has lounge/diner with log fire. Fully equipped kitchen; shower room. Three bedrooms and a bathroom upstairs.

Auberge du Bon Cidre

37 rue de Cornouaille 29170 FOUESNANT
Tél: 02.98.56.00.16 • Fax : 02.98.51.60.15
www.aubergeduboncidre.com
E-mail: contact@aubergeduboncidre.com

Small family-run hotel in a charming small town famous for its production of Brittany's finest cider. The dining room in the main house serves excellent local cuisine and the comfortable, simply furnished bedrooms are in a modern, quiet annexe overlooking the pleasant garden. The town of Quimper is within easy reach, as are the beautiful sandy beaches of Bénodet and Pont l'Abbé for sailing, diving and sea angling, or take a relaxing boat trip along the river Odet. Leisure centre nearby with tennis courts and an indoor pool; golf courses 8 kilometres.

Fouesnant (Finistere)

Town with grocers, restaurant and Leisure Centre.

AUBERGE DU BON CIDRE, 37 RUE DE CORNOUAILLE (02.98.56.00.16; Fax: 02.98.51.60.15) Small family-run hotel serving excellent local cuisine. Comfortable, simply furnished bedrooms in a modern, quiet annexe overlooking the pleasant garden.
e-mail: contact@aubergeduboncidre.com website: www.aubergeduboncidre.com

Publisher's note

While every effort is made to ensure accuracy, we regret that FHG Guides cannot accept responsibility for errors, misrepresentations or omissions in our entries or any consequences thereof. Prices in particular should be checked.
We will follow up complaints but cannot act as arbiters or agents for either party.

Delightfully situated by the quiet towpath of the Vilaine, 25 kilometres south-west of Rennes, the accommodation sleeps up to 4/5 in 2 bedrooms; 1 double, 2 single beds and travel cot. A spare bed is available. There is an open plan lounge/kitchen/diner fully equipped and comfortably furnished. The bathroom has over-bath shower and a hairdryer is provided. TV, DVD and CD player are provided and there is also a Nintendo GameCube with a selection of games. The garden has a barbecue and garden furniture plus a hammock and tree swing. Bikes are also provided. Swimming, boat hire, golf and fishing locally, beaches are within 80 kilometres. Pets welcome.

Riverside Chalet

30 Rue de l'Ecluse, Guipry, Ille et-Vilaine 35480
Tel: 02380 905569

Guipry (Ille et Vilaine)

Village with bars, restaurants, hotels, supermarkets and chemist shops. Josselin 66 kilometres, Rennes a short car or train ride away.

RIVERSIDE CHALET, 37 RUE DE L'ECLUSE, ILLE ET VILAINE 35480 (02380 905569).Delightfully situated accommodation sleeping up to 4/5 in 2 bedrooms; 1 double, 2 single beds and travel cot. Open plan lounge/kitchen/diner, fully equipped and comfortably furnished. Pets welcome. No Smoking.

Hotel du Château • Josselin

Phone: 02 97 22 20 11 • Fax: 02 97 22 34 09
www.hotel-chateau.com

Guests can be sure of a warm welcome and comfortable accommodation in this hotel situated opposite the fine Chateau de Josselin.

Excellent food is served in the medieval diningroom and, in summertime, meals are served on the terrace with its panoramic views of the castle and river. The 36 bedrooms are well decorated and have TV, direct-dial telephone and bath or shower room. Minimum stay of 3 days. Enclosed garage.

Josselin (Morbihan)

Picturesque medieval town with cobbled streets, cafes, wide range of shops, restaurants, banks and an English Bookshop. Weekly market Saturdays. Chateau de Josselin and Doll's Museum to visit. Two supermarkets outside town..

HOTEL DU CHÂTEAU, JOSSELIN (02 97 22 20 11; Fax: 02 97 22 34 09). A warm welcome and comfortable accommodation in this hotel serving excellent food. Terrace with panoramic views. 36 well decorated bedrooms. Minimum stay of 3 days. Enclosed garage.
website: www.hotel-chateau.com

www.holidayguides.com

La Ferme de la Baie

1 La Rue, 35610 Roz-Sur-Couesnon
Tel: 0033 (0)2 99 80 23 90 • Ruth George & Henry Maisey
e-mail:welcome@fermedelabaie.com

Perfect location for a relaxing holiday, with easy access to coast, historic towns and many tourist attractions and sporting facilities. There are three self-catering properties available, each with its own small garden and outdoor furniture.

The cottages are comfortable and fully equipped, and a cot and other baby equipment is available. Bed and Breakfast accommodation is available in the main farmhouse, and we can provide Evening Meals with 24 hours notice, or provide a home-cooked 'takeaway' to be eaten in your own cottage.

La Rue (Ille et Villaine)

Quiet hamlet near the village of Roz-sur-Couesnon. Good choice of shops in nearby town of Pontorson.

RUTH GEORGE AND HENRY MAISEY, LA FERME DE LA BAIE, 1 LA RUE, 35610 ROZ-SUR-COUESNON (0033 (0)2 99 80 23 90). Three self-catering properties available, each with its own small garden and outdoor furniture. Comfortable and fully equipped. Bed and Breakfast accommodation is available in the main farmhouse.
e-mail: welcome@fermedelabaie.com

Clair de Lune

Le Hazay • Caulnes • Côte d'Armor 22350
Tel: 0033 (0) 296 838284

Set in rolling countryside, this gite has been fully refurbished to provide a cosy and welcoming interior. There is an attractive garden with comfortable garden furniture and barbecue. Swings and see-saw for children and plenty of parking adjacent. The property sleeps up to five in two bedrooms, and all essentials are provided. Just 30 minutes from the glorious beaches of Rennes, and the Port of St Malo is just 45 minutes.

Great diversity of rural pursuits, lovely beaches with many leisure activities in Côte d'Armor as well as stunning coastlines and dramatic inland landscapes.

Le Hazay (Côte de Armor)

Small hamlet two minutes' drive from the towns of Caulnes and Broons, perfect for your every day needs. Dinan 20 minutes north.

CLAIR DE LUNE, LE HAZAY, CAULNES, COTE D'ARMOR 22350 (0033 (0) 296 838284)Refurbished Gite in rolling countryside. Attractive garden. Sleeps up to five in two bedrooms, and all essentials are provided.

FHG Guides

publish a large range of well-known accommodation guides.
We will be happy to send you details or you can use the order form at the back of this book.

Oak Tree Cottages

35 Brenugat • Lizio • Morbihan 56460

Phone: (0033) 297749715 (UK) • 0297749715 (France)
Mobile (0033) 666243753 (UK) • 0666243753 (France)
or E-mail : mark.sample@wanadoo.fr

Two self-catering cottages on the outskirts of Lizio, ideally situated for exploring coast and beaches, the towns of Josselin, Ploermel, Rennes and Malestroit, and for enjoying many local attractions. The gites have private enclosed gardens and patio area with garden furniture and BBQ, plus access to large open garden with boules and table tennis and ample space for sports and activities, and also have a 5mx8m swimming pool in the large garden.
All bedding, towels and electric central heating and gas are included in the price. Accommodation also available on the edge of Le Roc St Andre, in an area of outstanding natural beauty.

Lizio (Morbihan)

Charming town with many interesting places to visit, shops, bars and restaurants.

OAK TREE COTTAGES, 35 BRENUGAT, LIZIO, MORBIHAN 56460. [(0033) 297749715 (UK); 0297749715 (France); Mobile (0033) 666243753 (UK); 0666243753 (France)]. Two self-catering cottages ideally situated for exploring coast and beaches. Private enclosed gardens and patio area, access to large open garden, swimming pool. All bedding, towels, electric central heating and gas included.
e-mail: mark.sample@wanadoo.fr

Things to do and see in Brittany

Parc L'Ange Michel, Saint Martin de Landelles – More than 30 water and land based activities such as waterslides, boats, quad bikes, trampolines, mini-golf and much more.

Oceanopolis, Brest – Marine life centre on the seafront in Brest. Three different climatic zones offering many opportunities for hands on experience of sea creatures. Reasonable prices.

Odet Loisirs, between Quimper and Coray – Park with games for children: trampolines, bouncy castles, slides, mazes, water features and activities for older children.

Le Parc des Grands Chenes – Tree-top assault course, featuring 3 adult courses and a children's course.

Coëtarlann Aventures – A fantastic adventure park beside the river Vilaine, offering pony rides, kayaking, orienteering and tree top adventures

The Manoir de L`Automobile, Loheac – Displaying more than 300 vehicles with a section featuring transport from the age before the automobile and well reconstructed street scenes from 100 years ago.

dogswelcome.fr

Looking for a comfortable cottage for your holiday in Brittany?

We have several specially selected cottages sleeping two, four, six and eight people. Prices from £120 pw.

Tel: Nicola Harrington on 01342 322272
E-mail: nicola@frenchgites.com
www.harrington.fr

Malestroit (Morbihan)

This beautiful medieval town located on the river Oust has shops, restaurants, bars and banks. The Museum of the Resistance to the Second World War is located in nearby St Marcel.

FRENCH GITES. Looking for a comfortable cottage for your holiday in Brittany? We have several specially selected cottages sleeping two, four, six and eight people. Prices from £120 pw. Contact Nicola Harrington (01342 322272). [Pets £15 per week].
E-mail: nicola@frenchgites.com www.harrington.fr

Visit the FHG website
www.holidayguides.com
for details of the wide choice of accommodation featured in the full range of FHG titles

Riverside Cottage

17 Rue de l'Ecluse, Malon, Ille et Vilaine 35480

This spacious detached riverside cottage has stunning views of the river from every room. There is a large mature garden with garden furniture. Ideal for barbecues. Accommodation consists of two double bedrooms and there is a double bed-settee in the lounge. Fully equipped kitchen/diner; lounge with inglenook fireplace and woodburner, plus TV/video/DVD player and radio/CD player. Separate laundry room. This is an ideal area for a relaxing holiday, or for exploring Brittany. Local activities include cycling, walking, fishing, riding, golf, swimming, tennis and boating, and safe beaches are within easy driving distance. The towns of Rennes and Nantes offer sightseeing opportunities, shopping and eating places and there is something of interest for all ages.

Pets Welcome • **Tel: 01707 694173** • **Short Breaks available** **No Smoking**

Malon (Ille et Vilaine)

A quiet, rural hamlet 25 kilometres SW of Rennes. Local villages of Guipry and Messac, 2 kilometres, have bars, restaurants, supermarkets and chemists. Market day Thursday.

RIVERSIDE COTTAGE, 17 RUE DE L'ECLUSE, MALON, ILLE ET VILAINE 35480 (01707 694173). Spacious detached riverside cottage with stunning views. Large mature garden. Two double bedrooms and fully equipped kitchen/diner; lounge with inglenook fireplace and woodburner. Short Breaks available. Non-smoking.

Hôtel de l'Europe

1 Rue d'Aiguillon
29600 Morlaix

Tel. 33 (0)2 98 62 11 99 • Fax 33 (0)2 98 88 83 38
e-mail : reservations@hotel-europe-com.fr

Close to the imposing viaduct in the centre of this sheltered yacht haven, the stylish yet homely Hôtel de l'Europe offers good value for money. Guests will find warm welcome and comfortably furnished bedrooms offering old fashioned elegance; internet access available. Good, modern restaurant next door. There are charming villages in the countryside around Morlaix and 31 challenging golf courses within easy driving distance; tee times can be arranged. Other activities nearby include horse riding, hiking tours, tennis, swimming, fishing, bowling, and deep-sea diving. There is also a casino, cinema, discotheque and amusement park.

Morlaix (Finistere)

Breton city and port with cobbled streets and medieval buildings. There are lots of good shops and a wonderful Saturday morning market selling everything from meat, vegetables, fish and cheeses to clothing, books and bric-a-brac.

HOTEL DE L'EUROPE, 1 RUE D'AIGUILLON, 29600 MORLAIX (33 (0)2 98 62 11 99; Fax: 33 (0)2 98 88 83 38). Stylish yet homely hotel offers good value for money. Warm welcome and comfortably furnished bedrooms. Good, modern restaurant next door.
e-mail: reservations@hotel-europe-com.fr

Please mention **Pets Welcome!**
when making enquiries about accommodation featured in these pages

Dog-Friendly Holiday in Brittany, Northern France

- A cosy yet luxurious detached stone cottage in the beautiful Bay du Mont St Michel. Sleeps 2 adults and 2 children (+ baby), and we welcome pets by prior arrangement.
- Near beaches, golf, shops, fantastic restaurants, St Malo, Dinan, Combourg, it's pretty and has a compact practical kitchenette, lounge/diner with sofa bed and a shower room. Upstairs (open staircase) there is a mezzanine bedroom with twin beds and space for a travel cot.
- Ideal dog-walking country, along canal paths, through country lanes and for long runs on open beaches; along with our enclosed secure garden it's an ideal canine holiday!.
- Garden with BBQ, table and chairs, parking for two cars.
- Heated in winter and can arrange appointments with a local vet for passport appointments. Contact the owners:

Jo and Steve Sanders • 0033 2 99 48 71 30 • joandsteve@free.fr • www.lepinholidays.com

Pleine Fougeres (Rennes)

In a picturesque valley between the historical town of Dol-de-Bretagne in Brittany, and Pontorson in Normandy, and an excellent base for exploring the D-Day Beaches, the Bayeaux Tapestry, Chateaux and zoos. 15 minutes from the unique Bay of Mont-St-Michel. Good shopping, hypermarkets, golf and riding are virtually on the doorstep.

A cosy yet luxurious detached stone cottage in the beautiful Bay du Mont St Michel. Sleeps 2 adults and 2 children (+ baby), and we welcome pets by prior arrangement. Garden with BBQ, table and chairs. We can arrange appointments with a local vet for passport appointments. Contact the owners:JO AND STEVE SANDERS (0033 2 99 48 71 30) [🐕]
e-mail: joandsteve@free.fr website: www.lepinholidays.com

Two ★★★★ gites with pool on Normandy/Brittany border.

Fully furnished and fitted to high standard.
La Grange: Sleeps 8. Four double bedrooms (2 en suite). Family bathroom.
La Pommeraie: Sleeps 8. Two bedrooms (king-size); one with twin beds; one with bunk beds, and 2 bathrooms.
Idyllic rural countryside. Woodland and country walks. Less than 90 minutes from Caen, St Malo, Cherbourg, Rennes, Dinard; 2km from village.

Off-season prices from £400/week;
in season from £550/week
E-mail: info@kingswell.net
Tel: +33 (0)2 99 97 04 91 • Fax: +33 (0)2 99 97 04 92

St Georges de Reintembault (Ille-et-Villaine)

Quiet hamlet on the Brittany/Normandy border. It has a quaint market place, shops, post office and cinema. Small town of St James, with full shopping facilities and large supermarket is four miles away.

ST GEORGES DE REINTEMBAULT, BRITTANY. (+33 (0)2 99 97 04 91; Fax: +33 (0)2 99 97 04 92). Two ★★★★ gites with pool on Normandy/Brittany border, in idyllic rural countryside. Woodland and country walks. 2km from village. Fully furnished and fitted to high standard. La Grange: Sleeps 8. La Pommeraie: Sleeps 8. [🐕]
e-mail: info@kingswell.net

FHG Guides

publish a large range of well-known accommodation guides. We will be happy to send you details or you can use the order form at the back of this book.

Wide range of accommodation on two separate sites, each with a fenced heated swimming pool, only an hour and a half from Saint Malo and Roscoff. Guerledan (largest lake in Brittany) with watersports, restaurants, beaches, etc., 20 minutes, coast 40 minutes. Close to small towns with all amenities.

Kermarc'h: 3 properties (sleep 2/6, 9, 14) set in 4 acres.

Lustruyen: Cottage (sleeps 2/6) and farmhouse (sleeps 9) on one and a half acre site off country lane.

All houses are well furnished and have everything needed for a relaxing and enjoyable holiday. The surrounding countryside is ideal for walking, and close to the Nantes/Brest canal with miles of towpath.

Local helpful English-speaking vet used to complying with the necessary formalities for your pets return to the UK.

Please visit our website for more details and photos • www.holidaysinbrittanyfrance.co.uk or telephone Carolyn Jarman on 00 33 29 63 65 961 • e-mail: jarmankermarch@aol.com

St Nicolas du Pelem/Rostrenen (Côtes D'Armor)

Small town with shops, Tourist Office, supermarket and garage. Many places to eat and drink. Just 15 minutes' drive from large lake offering all kinds of watersports.
Rostrenen is a traditional Breton market town with shops, post office, tourist office and a range of places to eat and drink.

Well furnished accommodation on two rural sites in Central Brittany. Fenced, heated swimming pool. Ideal for walking, watersports; coast 40 minutes. Small towns nearby. Local English-speaking vet. Contact CAROLYN JARMAN (00 33 29 63 65 961) or visit our website. [🐕]
e-mail: jarmankermarch@aol.com website: www.holidaysinbrittanyfrance.co.uk

La Vieille Ferme

Tel & Fax: 0033 2 99 91 20 09

28 Painfaut, St Vincent Sur Oust, Redon, Morbihan 56350

Three cottages set in farmland in an area of designated natural beauty. Each cottage has its own private garden with barbecue and leads to a heated swimming pool. Two of the cottages sleep up to six people, while the third sleeps up to 10. Each has fully fitted kitchen, lounge/diner and bathroom facilities. Internet access. One property is wheelchair friendly. There are beautiful villages just 15 minutes by car, some of which have lakes for swimming and windsurfing. 9-hole golf course is 12 miles away and 18-hole golf course within 30 minutes' drive.

St Vincent Sur Oust (Morbihan)

Small hamlet, in a perfect location for exploring Brittany, has mini-market, butcher and restaurant. Beautiful town of Redon 10 minutes, with busy shopping centre, supermarkets and market. Vannes is 35 minutes' drive and the southern coast of Brittany 45 minutes.

LA VIEILLE FERME, ST VINCENT SUR OUST, REDON, MORBIHAN 56350 (Tel & Fax: 0033 2 99 91 20 09) Three cottages in an area of designated natural beauty. Private gardens with barbecue; heated swimming pool. Sleep 6-10. Fitted kitchen, lounge/diner and bathroom. One property is wheelchair friendly.

Symbols

🐕 Indicates that pets are welcome free of charge.

£ Indicates that a charge is made for pets: nightly or weekly.

pw! Shows some special provision for pets; exercise facility, feeding or accommodation arrangement.

⌂ Indicates separate pets accommodation.

Three 17th century cottages situated in the beautiful Brittany countryside in large garden with a heated swimming pool. The two-acre lawned grounds are ideal for picnics and ball games, and children can play safely. Play area with swings and slide for younger children. All are decorated to a high standard and each has its own private outdoor area complete with high quality wooden garden furniture, parasols and barbecues. The cottages sleep 12, 8 and 4 people and are fully equipped with cooker, fridge, microwave, washing machine and dining table and chairs. Internet access.
The long sandy beaches of Northern Brittany are easily reached.
Cycling, horse riding, walking, swimming, golf and fishing nearby. Pets welcome.
Non-smoking. Short breaks available

LA HAUTE MANCELIERE
Tremblay, Ille et Vilaine 35460 • Tel: 0033 (0)299 977420

Tremblay (Ille et Vilaine)

Village with 11th century church, shops and bars. Supermarket shops and restaurants at St Brice-en-Cogles, 4 kilometres away, the town of St Malo and the port of Concale are only 45 minutes' drive..

LA HAUTE MANCELIERE, TREMBLAY, ILLE ET VILAINE 35460 (0033 (0) 299 977420). Three 17th century cottages in large garden with a heated swimming pool. Decorated to a high standard and fully equipped, own private outdoor area. Sleeps 12, 8 and 4 people. Pets welcome. Short breaks available. Non-smoking.

Looking for Holiday Accommodation?

FHG
K·U·P·E·R·A·R·D

for details of hundreds of properties throughout the UK, visit our website
www.holidayguides.com

LANGUEDOC-ROUSSILLON

The region has a widely varying landscape from mountains and plateaux, to moorlands and coastal plains. The coast is a blend of resorts such as Cap d'Agde and Port Camargue, and old villages and fishing ports. Good beaches offer a variety of watersports and there are many golf courses throughout the region. There are health spas and nature reserves as well as good fishing, cycling and riding, and the area is ideal for walkers. In winter there are good cross-country ski routes and excellent skiing. Markets can be found in towns and villages from early spring until late autumn, and festivals, fetes and concerts can all be enjoyed.

The area is noted for its seafood, including oysters and anchovies, and Sete, the largest Mediterranean fishing port on the coast of France has many excellent fish restaurants. Strong Mediterranean flavours dominate the local dishes, with rich game or beef stews, and, of course, the famed Cassoulet. Other regional specialities include olives, fruit, honey, full fruity red wines and delicious dessert wines.

This old winery lies at the end of a quiet cul-de-sac and has a private garden, safe for children and pets. The house has recently been redecorated to a high standard and sleeps four persons in one double room, and one room with bunk beds. The newly fitted kitchen is fully equipped with all amenities. There is a large terrace opening out from the living room and the garden offers a natural shelter from the sun. The house is situated beside a river which is ideal for swimming. There are also swimming pools locally and the surrounding area is great for trekking and climbing. Pets welcome. Short breaks available.

STONE HOUSE 23 Rue Charles Nel • Camplong Herault 34260 • Tel: 0033 624772546

Camplong (Hérault)

Small, pretty village in the heart of the Languedoc National Park. Four miles from the village of Medieval which has a good restaurant and a market selling local produce, and the nearest town is 7 kilometres away.

STONE HOUSE, 23 RUE CHARLES NEL, CAMPLONG, HERAULT 34260 (0033 624772546). Old winery with safe private garden. Sleeps four in one double room, and one room with bunk beds. Fully equipped kitchen, large terrace. Pets welcome. Short breaks available.

Please note

All the information in this book is given in good faith in the belief that it is correct. However, the publishers cannot guarantee the facts given in these pages, neither are they responsible for changes in policy, ownership or terms that may take place after the date of going to press. Readers should always satisfy themselves that the facilities they require are available and that the terms, if quoted, still apply.

le petit reve ❖

Rue du Commerce • Castelnau d'Aude • Aude 11700

A typical village home with beamed ceilings, shutters and terra cotta tiled floors. Sleeps 4 in two double bedrooms. There is a large kitchen/diningroom with fireplace, stereo/CD player, coffee maker and ample cooking equipment. A plentiful supply of bed linens, towels, pillows etc. is supplied. The mediaeval walled town of Carcassonne, one of UNESCO's World Heritage sites, is easily reached, and has a large number of shops and tourist attractions. Non-smoking. Pets welcome.

Tel 01-510 601-6789 ❖ Fax 01-510- 601-6789
cfhbookings@gmail.com

Castelnau d'Aude (Aude)

Small hillside village near Carcassonne. Easy access to tourist sites, restaurants, beaches and vineyards.

LE PETIT REVE, RUE DU COMMERCE, CASTELNAU D'AUDE, AUDE 11700 (Tel & Fax: 01-510 601-6789). A typical village home; sleeps 4 in two double bedrooms. Large kitchen/diningroom with fireplace. Plentiful supply of bed linens, towels, pillows etc. Non-smoking. Short breaks available. Pets welcome.
e-mail: cfhbookings@gmail.com

Mode d'Artiste

25 Route des Pyrenees
Couiza, Aude 11190
Tel 0033 (0)468 201441

Three apartments in a 17th century riverside house, each tastefully decorated and having large living area with music system, computer and free internet access, fully equipped kitchen; bathroom and separate WC. Children and pets welcome; cot, high chair and toy box available. There is a short path to the River Salz where swimming is available, or the beautiful Mediterranean beaches are just over an hour away. Nearby are thermal spas with outdoor heated swimming pools, and other water sports available locally include canoeing, white water rafting and trout fishing. Ski-ing in Camurac, 30 minutes away. Pets welcome. Short breaks available. Non-smoking.

Couiza (Aude)

Village with all amenities including shops, restaurants and café, just 34 kilometres from Carcassonne. Set in a beautiful area between the Mediterranean Sea and the Pyrenees mountains.

MODE D'ARTISTE, 25 ROUTE DES PYRENEES, COUIZA, AUDE 11190 (0033 (0)468 201441). Three apartments in a 17th century riverside house, tastefully decorated with large living area and fully equipped kitchen; bathroom and separate WC. Pets welcome. Short breaks available. Non-smoking.

Près de la Tour Adelard

Tel 00 32 (0)656 31394
Fax 0032 (0)656 31394

Haut du Village • La Capelle Masmolène • Gard 30700

Villa in quiet, residential area on the edge of a picturesque village and close to an ancient chapel. Ideal for enjoying the sports and activities in the village itself, including tennis, climbing, hiking, cycling, fishing, petanque and walking, or for touring the many towns and villages in the area. The accommodation sleeps up to six in three bedrooms, and there is a lounge, kitchen, hall, conservatory, bathroom and separate toilet. Terrace has barbecue with garden furniture and offers a breathtaking view of the surrounding countryside. Ideal for holidays all year round.

La Capelle Masmolène (Gard)

Typical French village near Uzes, Pont du Gard, Nîmes and Avignon.

PRES DE LA TOUR ADELARD, HAUT DU VILLAGE, LA CAPELLE MASMOLENE, GARD 30700 (Tel & Fax: 00 32 (0)656 31394). Villa in quiet, residential area on the edge of a picturesque village. Sleeps up to six in three bedrooms. Terrace with barbecue. Pets welcome.

10 Rue des Astres
Les Angles, Pyrenees Orientales 66210

Two recently renovated barn apartments with exposed beams. Sleep up to six in two bedrooms and mezzanine floor, cot available. Fully fitted kitchen; lounge with sofas, satellite TV, video and DVD player; shower room/WC. Prices include all linen and towels, electricity and welcome pack of essential groceries. As well as being a good ski area, the village is just 30 minutes from the Spanish border and 90 minutes from the Mediterranean, making it ideal for touring.

Tel 0033 (0)468043728
e-mail: info@pyrenean-trails.com

Les Angles (Pyrenees Orientales)

A Pyrenees mountain village, considered to be one of France's premier ski locations. Ski lifts, shops and a good selection of restaurants locally.

LA VIEILLE GRANGE, 10 RUE DES ASTRES, LES ANGLES, PYRENEES ORIENTALES 66210 (0033 (0)468043728). Two recently renovated barn apartments, sleeping up to six in two bedrooms and mezzanine floor, cot available. Fully fitted kitchen; lounge; shower room/WC. Pets welcome. Short breaks available.
e-mail: info@pyrenean-trails.com

Please mention **Pets Welcome!**
when making enquiries about accommodation featured in these pages

Your Own Private Domaine

Two lovely houses with large pool and tennis court

In a beautiful elevated position overlooking the medieval village of Montagnac, Domaine de l'Hortevieille, a former wine-making property is set in 10 acres of fields, gardens and orchards with its own large, secure pool and tennis court.Two individually designed spacious houses are available for rental - each one well equipped with washing machine, dishwasher, microwave, fridge/freezer, television, DVD player and mini hi-fi. Each has its own private furnished terrace with barbecue facilities. Horse riding is available and mountain bikes are provided for you to explore the beautiful adjacent countryside.

The property is ideally suited for a tranquil summer holiday by the pool or on the beach or if you prefer a more active break in or out of season there are endless possibilities to get to know this rich and historic area. Whatever your interests - wine, good food, golf, fishing, antiques, history, the list is endless - the Domaine's English owners are on hand to help you enjoy your stay to the full.

Weekly rental rates inclusive of maid service, bed linen and towels and a welcome pack when you arrive.

For more information or to make a booking contact Malcolm or Alyson at hortevieille@wanadoo.fr or telephone 00 33 467 24 13 98.

Montagnac (Herault)

Montagnac is within easy reach of Beziers and Montpellier and only a few kilometres from the A75 motorway. The nearest beach is about 10 minutes' drive away. The village centre has been recently renovated and there is a good selection of shops including bakers, general stores and butcher, as well as two bars – one of which serves snacks.

DOMAINE DE L'HORTEVIEILLE, MONTAGNAC. Two spacious houses, each well equipped, with private terrace and BBQ. Horse riding and mountain bikes available. English owners on hand to help you enjoy your stay to the full. Contact Malcolm or Alyson (00 33 467 24 13 98).
e-mail: hortevieille@wanadoo.fr

❖ Le Bau Trinquat ❖

Set in glorious countryside and forests and vineyards, ideal for walkers and cyclists. Recently renovated 17th century property retaining many original features, this fully equipped and comfortable family house has three bedrooms and a secluded roof terrace leading out from the small sitting area. Sunloungers, barbecue and garden furniture are provided. Well equipped kitchen/dining area with gas cooker, dishwasher, microwave, fridge/freezer etc. Bathroom and WC. Ample storage space and laundry room in the stables and cellar. Sleeps 6 plus baby.

Local activities include tennis, horse riding, canoeing and lake and river bathing. Pets welcome.

Hameau de Paguignan • Aigues Vives • Hérault 34210
Tel & Fax: 0033 (0)468911677

Paguignan (Hérault)

Hamlet amidst rolling hills and vineyards, 10 minutes from Minerve. Mobile shops visit the hamlet and there are other shops and restaurants within 10 minutes.

LE BAU TRINQUAT, HAMEAU DE PAGUIGNAN, AIGUES VIVES, HERAULT 34210 (Tel & Fax: 0033 (0)468911677). Renovated 17th century property retaining many original features. Fully equipped and comfortable with three bedrooms and a secluded roof terrace. Sleeps 6 plus baby. Short Breaks available. Pets welcome.

Please mention **Pets Welcome!**
when making enquiries about accommodation featured in these pages

Le Precatalan, Barcares, Perpignan 66420
Tel: 01562 720318

Luxury mobile home on a beautiful landscaped site, 10 minutes' walk from long sandy beaches. There is a lounge area with settee, one double bedroom and one with two single beds, fully equipped kitchen and terrace. The small, friendly site has superb facilities, including swimming pool and smaller pool for children, shop, restaurant, snack bar and take-away, laundry, library and bar with entertainment.
Various water sports are available in the nearby lakes of Salses and Leucate and there is walking in the foothills of the Pyrenees, a short drive away. Sleeps 1-5. Pets welcome.

Port Barcares (Perpignan)

Seaside resort and paradise for water sports enthusiasts and lovers of seafood. Week-long oyster festival in March.

LAURIER ROSE, LE PRECATALAN, BARCARES, PERPIGNAN 66420 (01562 720318). Luxury mobile home on a beautiful landscaped site, near long sandy beaches. Sleeps 1-5. Lounge area, one double and one twin bedroom. Fully equipped kitchen and terrace. Swimming pool. Pets welcome.

5 Rue des Jardins, Ventenac Cabardes
Carcassonne, Aude 11610
Tel 0033 (0)468 240823
www.carcassonne-holidays.com

One, two or three bedroom gites situated in the wine making hamlet of Ventenac-Cabardes Fully centrally heated, they are ideal for both summer and winter holidays. The gites are fully equipped including dishwasher, microwave, freezer, washing machine etc etc, and have TV and DVD; Wifi available. There is a sheltered terrace where you can eat out at most times of the year and a separate swimming pool with gate for safety purposes. Barbecues, sun loungers, tables and chairs provided. Each gite is supplied with an information pack detailing the many places to visit, and the family activities to be found in the surrounding area. Pets welcome. Short breaks available.

Ventenac-Cabardes (Aude)

Typical French village with narrow streets and medieval church, village shop, tennis court and vineyards. Five miles from Carcassonne.

LES JARDINS DU CABARDES, 5 RUE DES JARDINS, VENTENAC CABARDES, CARCASSONNE, AUDE 11610 (0033 (0)468 240823). One, two or three bedroom gites. Fully centrally heated, ideal for both summer and winter holidays. Fully equipped. Sheltered terrace, separate swimming pool. Information pack. Pets welcome. Short breaks available.
website: www.carcassonne-holidays.com

LIMOUSIN

The Limousin region, situated in the centre of France, offers visitors a peaceful and traditional way of life. This is a charming and historic land of hills and valleys, forests and plains, rivers and picturesque ancient cities. The region takes its name from the Capital Limoges, which is renowned for its exquisite enamel and porcelain. This pleasant town has many parks and gardens, and the old quarter with its narrow medieval streets and houses is worth a visit. There are many opportunities to enjoy swimming, sailing, canoeing and water skiing on the numerous rivers and lakes, and there are several golf courses throughout the region. There is good riding country in the south and many riding establishments catering for all standards of rider. Here you will find the National Stud and racecourse at Arnac-Pompadour. There are many fairs and markets in towns and villages on various days of the week, and you can enjoy pates and foie gras, and perhaps even sample the local speciality, an excellent potato pie made with smoked ham and herbs.

Upper Dordogne Valley • Limousine • Corrèze • Near Argentat

Character Cottage, sleeps 2

On the edge of a picturesque village. One bedroom with en suite shower room.

Low Season £140
Mid Season £160
High Season £190
15% off second week booked

Kitchen/diner. Sitting room. Terrace and sun deck. Walk from cottage into amazing countryside.

See other cottages and B&B on www.argentat.co.uk. Contact Jim Mallows e-mail: au-pont@wanadoo.fr

Argentat (Corréze)

This delightful market town is an ideal holiday destination offering peace and quiet, and beautiful scenery. Excellent food and wine can be enjoyed in attractive riverside restaurants and other good eating places. There is a wide variety of cultural and sporting activities to enjoy, and many shows and exhibitions take place during the summer.

UPPER DORDOGNE VALLEY. Character Cottage, sleeps two.On the edge of a picturesque village. One bedroom with en suite shower room. Kitchen/diner. Sitting room. Terrace and sun deck. Walk from cottage into amazing countryside. Contact JIM MALLOWS for details
e-mail: au-pont@wanadoo.fr website: www.argentat.co.uk

FHG Guides

publish a large range of well-known accommodation guides.
We will be happy to send you details or you can use the order form at the back of this book.

Le Chant d'Oiseau, Estivals

Situated in a hamlet on the borders of Corrèze, Lot and Dordogne, four oak-timbered gites provide perfect relaxation in tranquil countryside.

• Fully equipped kitchen with microwave, dishwasher and washing machine • French doors to patio with barbecue and garden furniture. • Pool with alarm • Bed linen • Baby furniture available • Pets welcome.

Close to many attractions of the region, with horse riding, cycling, canoeing, walking, golf and tennis easily available.

Readily connected by motorway, rail (inc. motorail) and regional airports.

Contact Robin or Loraine Cornish • Tel: 00 33 5 55 85 31 28
e-mail: robin.cornish@wanadoo.fr • www.lechantdoiseau.com

Estivals (Corrèze)

The village is centrally located for visiting many places of interest including attractive prehistoric and medieval sites and interesting cave formations, also amusement park for the young and not so young, Brive la Gaillarde. 16km north east offers a variety of supermarkets and shops, and the nearby village of Cressensac has a mini-market and bakery.

LE CHANT D'OISEAU, ESTIVALS. Four oak-timbered gites provide perfect relaxation in tranquil countryside. Fully equipped kitchen with microwave, dishwasher and washing machine. Bed linen. Pets welcome. Close to many attractions, with horse riding, cycling, canoeing, walking, golf and tennis easily available. Contact ROBIN OR LORAINE CORNISH (00 33 5 55 85 31 28) [🐕]
e-mail: robin.cornish@wanadoo.fr website: www.lechantdoiseau.com

Things to do around Corrèze

The Splash Centre In Argentat – an aquatic park incorporating many outdoor activities.

Gouffre de Padirac – a series of underground lakes accessed via a hole deep into the earth – the underground boat ride is an experience not to be missed.

Plan d'eau du Coiroux , Aubazine – Supervised swimming, fishing, children's games. Windsurfing allowed. Other activities: 18-hole golf course, 9-hole pitch and putt, "Mayaventure" adventure park.

Les Aubarèdes, Beaulieu sur Dordogne – swimming and fishing. Canoeing and kayaking centre. Water sports centre. River trips on traditional flat-bottomed gabares.

Vol en Montgolfière, Arnac Pompadour – Ballooning flights from Pompadour and other sites subject to demand.

La Varache

La Varache is situated in the heart of the Limousin countryside, a region filled with trails and footpaths winding their way through lush unspoilt scenery. La Varache offers two self-catering holiday homes (gites), both tastefully converted from a 15th century house, and incorporating many modern facilities, including central heating, alongside original old world beams and open log fireplaces.

Gite 1
Accommodates up to 9 persons.
Two comfortable first-floor bedrooms.
Spacious lounge with original fireplace; queen-sized sofa bed. Full bathroom with shower; well equipped kitchen. Outside deck with BBQ.

Gite 2
Sleeps up to 8.
Large bedroom with bathroom en suite upstairs; mezzanine bedroom. Downstairs comfortable lounge with wood-burning stove, sofa bed; bathroom; large, fully equipped kitchen. Deck area; BBQ.

Contact: Chris & Lori Hill, La Varache Enterprises,
La Varache, 87120 Eymoutiers, FRANCE • Tel: 00 33 555 69 27 47
e-mail: enquiries@limousingite.com • www.lavarache.com

Eymoutiers (Haute Vienne)

On the banks of the River Vienne, approx 40 km from Limoges. Attractive upland town of tall, narrow stone houses crowding round a Romanesque church. Within easy reach of many beautiful places of interest.

CHRIS & LORI HILL, LA VARACHE, 87120 EYMOUTIERS (00 33 555 69 27 47) 2 tastefully converted self-catering gites situated in the heart of the lush and unspoilt Limousin countryside. Sleep up to 8/9 persons. Well equipped and furnished. Excellent base to explore surrounding countryside.
e-mail: enquiries@limousingite.com website: www.lavarache.com

Things to do and see in Haute Vienne

Chateau de Chalus – Final resting place of Richard 1st (Richard the Lionheart) mortally wounded during the siege of the castle in 1199

Les Loupes de Chabrières, Gueret – A variety of wolf species (including the white wolf) being bred in a natural environment.

Parc du Reynou, near Limoges – Walk among the animals at this open Wildlife park with a difference.

Aquarium , Limoges – In the centre of Limoges this aquarium has 300 different species and and more than 2500 fish.

LAKESIDE CHALETS

Dave & Kate Wood
L'Ancien Fournil, 2 Le Joulageix, 19370 Chamberet
E-mail: gites-limousin@orange.fr
Tel: 00 33 555 98 11 53

Charming chalets in an idyllic situation on the hillside, perfect for nature lovers. The chalets sleep up to four people in double/twin bedrooms with en suite bathrooms; livingroom with comfortable seating, DVD and CD players, books games and a few DVDs. Fully equipped kitchen/diner. Laundry facilities nearby. Rates on request. The area is ideal for all outdoor pursuits including swimming, waterskiing, canoeing and windsurfing, and is a walker's

Lake Treignac (Corrèze)

Village 4.5 miles from the town. Good restaurants, and café bars in the area.

Charming chalets in an idyllic situation, perfect for nature lovers. Sleep up to four in double/twin bedrooms with en suite bathrooms; livingroom with comfortable seating. Fully equipped kitchen/diner. Laundry facilities nearby. DAVE & KATE WOOD, L'ANCIEN FOURNIL, 2 LE JOULAGEIX, 19370 CHAMBERET, (00 33 555 98 11 53).
e-mail: gites-limousin@orange.fr

La Grange

6 Puy Japin • Viersat • Creuse 23170
Tel 0033 555 657136 or 07971834337
E-mail: contact@lagrangeencreuse

Detached house, sleeps eight, with private garden, garden furniture and barbecue. Upstairs there are three bedrooms and a shower room with toilet and washbasin. Downstairs there is a lounge with dining area, TV/DVD and CD player, and log fire for winter months; bathroom with toilet and washbasin; well equipped kitchen. Ideal for touring being only a few kilometres from the Auvergne border and convenient for the towns of Aubusson and Clermont Ferrand.

Viersat (Creuse)

Small hamlet 15 minutes' drive from Montlucon where there are shops, supermarkets, restaurants and a castle.

LA GRANGE, 6 PUY JAPIN, VIERSAT, CREUSE 23170 (0033 555 657136 or 07971834337) Detached house, sleeps eight, with private garden. Three bedrooms and a shower room with toilet and washbasin upstairs; lounge with dining area and well equipped kitchen, bathroom downstairs.
e-mail: contact@lagrangeencreuse

Symbols

- 🐕 Indicates that pets are welcome free of charge.
- £ Indicates that a charge is made for pets: nightly or weekly.
- pw! Shows some special provision for pets; exercise facility, feeding or accommodation arrangement.
- ⌂ Indicates separate pets accommodation.

NORMANDY

The region of Normandy, with its lush countryside and a coastline warmed by the Gulf Stream, has long been a favourite destination with holidaymakers. There are many resorts and seaside towns and, inland, magnificent forests, tranquil streams and the many orchards which are indicative of this fruit producing region. There are many delights to discover such as the picturesque harbour of Honfleur, the Bayeux Tapestry and William the Conqueror's birthplace. Normandy promises many gastronomic delights, from seafood and duck, to cream, cheeses and the famous Calvados. Why not explore the 'Cider Road' and the 'Cheese Road', or simply relax on a horse drawn carriage ride.

Country cottage in Normandy

L'Etre Bidault, near Bagnoles de l'Orne

www.propertiesinnormandy.com

L'Etre Bidault is a beautiful detached stone cottage set in its own grounds on the edge of the Forêt des Andaines, which stretches for over ten miles and is full of wildlife including red squirrels and red deer. Medieval towns, chateaux, local markets are close by, as well as opportunities for many outdoor activities.

Sleeps 4 + cot. 2 bedrooms, one double, one twin, large, well equipped kitchen/diner with woodburner, spacious lounge with exposed stonework and beams, open fireplace. Bathroom and separate toilet. Central heating, satellite TV and ADSL, internet. Large, enclosed private garden with furniture and BBQ provided. Mountain bikes for hire. Golf and horse riding nearby. No smoking. Pets welcome. The perfect location for holidays with pets, as forest walks can be enjoyed directly from the cottage.

If you would like to request more information or wish to make a booking, please contact Dave and Lyn on

00 33 6 77 31 80 35 or 07914 190925 • e-mail: info@propertiesinnormandy.com

Bagnoles de l'Orne (Orne)

The spa town and local area offer a diverse selection of activities of interest to all age groups. These include visiting castles, museums or the casino, to more active pursuits such as canoeing, fishing or horse riding.

DAVE & LYN NEWNHAM (00 33 6 77 31 80 35 OR 07914 190925). Pretty detached stone cottage set in its own grounds on the edge of the Forêt des Andaines. Sleeps 4 plus cot. Pets welcome. No smoking. [🐕]

e-mail: info@propertiesinnormandy.com website: www.propertiesinnormandy.com

Normandy Thatched Cottages

Situated in the village of Berville sur mer, La Ferme du Chalet is a charming group of four person and six person thatched cottages converted from a 17th Century stable.

Set in 2 hectares these gites offer a wonderful tranquil holiday destination, only 500 metres from the River Seine.

The beautiful historic port of Honfleur with its picturesque Saturday market is 10 minutes away by car or you can walk along the riverbank which offers spectacular views of the Pont de Normandie. On days out you are well placed to explore the sights of Normandy and Brittany. You can visit the landing beaches after a visit to the museum at Arromanches, or explore the many beautiful beaches of the area.
Berville sur Mer is part of the Natural Park of Brotonne and there are many cycle paths, picnic areas and hiking paths on both sides of the River Seine.

Channel Ports: Le Havre 25 minutes. Caen 1 hour. Calais 2.5 hours. Boulogne 2.15 hours.

TOP SUN

Tel: 01463 717874 • E-mail: info@topsun.co.uk
www.topsun.co.uk
Reservations: Top Sun Ltd.
17 Springfield Gardens, Inverness IV3 5SJ

Berville sur Mer (Eure)

A small Normandy village on the banks of the Seine, about five miles from Honfleur, where there are many shops and restaurants. There is also good shopping at Beuzville, and at the out of town Supermarket on the way to Honfleur.

LA FERME DU CHALET, BERVILLE SUR MER. Charming group of thatched cottages converted from a 17th Century stable, only 500 metres from the River Seine. The beautiful historic port of Honfleur with its picturesque Saturday market is 10 minutes away by car. Le Havre 25 minutes, Caen 1 hour. TOP SUN LTD, 17 SPRINGFIELD GARDENS, INVERNESS IV3 5SJ. (01463 717874).[Pets 20 euros per stay].
e-mail: info@topsun.co.uk website: www.topsun.co.uk

Visit the FHG website
www.holidayguides.com
for details of the wide choice of accommodation
featured in the full range of FHG titles

La Détourbe

Set in 2 acres of beautiful grounds, **La Détourbe** is a stone longère, with a barn conversion providing two gites, which are fully equipped to a very high standard. All bedrooms have en suite facilities.
Gite 1 • ground floor; lounge, corner kitchen, double bedroom (plus double bed-settee in lounge).
Gite 2 • ground floor; as gite 1, plus first floor with 2 double bedrooms, one with additional single bed.
Ideal location for enjoying the peace and tranquillity of the countryside within the Normandy regional park.
See our website for more information.

John and Chris Gibson • La Détourbe • Beauvain • 61600 La Ferté-Macé • Orne• France
Tel: 0033 (0) 2 33 30 12 68 • Fax: 0033 (0) 2 33 30 12 70
e-mail: johnandchrisg@orange.fr • www.normandy-gites.co.uk

La Ferté-Macé (Orne)

Small town with a range of shops and restaurants. Beach offers water sports, fishing and supervised swimming. 10km from the spa town of Bagnoles-de-l'Orne with good shopping, sports facilities, casino and golf.

JOHN AND CHRIS GIBSON, LA DETOURBE, BEAUVAIN, 61600 LA FERTE-MACE, ORNE. (0033 (0) 2 33 30 12 68; Fax: 0033 (0) 2 33 30 12 70). A stone longère set in two acres of beautiful grounds, with a barn conversion providing two gites. Ideal location for enjoying the peace and tranquillity within the Normandy regional park. [🐕]
e-mail: johnandchrisg@orange.fr www.normandy-gites.co.uk

Things to do and see in Normandy

Chateau de Chalus – Final resting place of Richard 1st (Richard the Lionheart) mortally wounded during the siege of the castle in 1199

Les Loupes de Chabrières, Gueret – A variety of wolf species (including the white wolf) being bred in a natural environment.

Parc du Reynou, near Limoges – Walk among the animals at this open Wildlife park with a difference.

Aquarium , Limoges – In the centre of Limoges this aquarium has 300 different species and and more than 2500 fish.

Enchanted Village at Bellefontaine – Large parkland offering a variety of traditional attractions including a miniature railway, electric cars and a fantasy land.

Parc Festyland, Caen – A modern theme park for family entertainment - roller coasters, water flumes, magic roundabouts, 180 degree cinema and many different types of entertainments.

La Cité de la Mer, Cherbourg – A museum devoted to nautical/submariner interests. Here you will learn about the dark oceanic depths and man's underwater adventures, and go on a fascinating journey round the decommissioned submarine The Redoubtable, France's first nuclear powered ballistic missile submarine.

La Petite Maison à La Denillière

Gite finished to exceptional standard with beautiful artwork, lovely rugs and antiques. Sleeps up to 4. Separate fitted kitchen with cooker, microwave, fridge, dishwasher, washing machine and dining area. Comfortable lounge with 3-piece suite, tables and desk. Downstairs shower room and loo. Upstairs two double bedrooms, one with double bed, the other two singles. Hanging space. (There is also a small double sofa-bed in lounge).

Set amidst beautiful countryside just outside the small village of Le Gast, very near the stunning St Sever Forest, and mid way between Vire and Villedieu les Poeles.

We are central enough to tour to Normandy's historic sites including the WWII landing beaches, Bayeux, Mont St Michel and the Swiss Normand. There are local amenities such as swimming baths, golf and horse riding, plus of course wonderful walks in the forest. Miles of lovely sandy beaches are within an easy drive. Once outside the main towns, dogs are allowed on beaches all year round.

We welcome pets and responsible owners to our gite.

Please contact the owners on either 0871 717 4235 or 0033 2 31 66 94 59

E-mail: info@french-holidaygite.co.uk

or visit our website at www.french-holidaygite.co.uk

Le Gast (Calvados)

Small hamlet in a peaceful setting. Easy driving distance to beach and close to many famous attractions. 10km from market town of Villedieu-les-Poeles with restaurants and bars and 35km from the resort town of Granville with Dior Museum.

LA PETITE MAISON A LA DENILLIERE. Gite finished to exceptional standard with beautiful artwork, lovely rugs and antiques. Amidst beautiful countryside just outside the small village of Le Gast. Central for touring Normandy's historic sites. Sleeps up to 4. Pets and responsible owners welcome. Contact owners on (0871 717 4235 or 0033 2 31 66 94 59).
e-mail: info@french-holidaygite.co.uk website: www.french-holidaygite.co.uk

Please note

All the information in this book is given in good faith in the belief that it is correct. However, the publishers cannot guarantee the facts given in these pages, neither are they responsible for changes in policy, ownership or terms that may take place after the date of going to press. Readers should always satisfy themselves that the facilities they require are available and that the terms, if quoted, still apply.

MIDI-PYRENEES

The largest region in France, the Midi Pyrenees lies midway between the Mediterranean and the Atlantic and subsequently enjoys a particularly pleasant climate. The varied landscape and wide open spaces offer all kinds of holiday opportunities such as rafting, canoeing and skiing, as well as hiking, horse riding and cycling. There is also a choice of spas for the health and fitness enthusiast. The fascinating sites of Rocamadour and Padirac in Lot and the medieval village of Cordes-sur-Ciel in Tarn are certainly worth a visit, and don't overlook the must-see museum of Toulouse-Lautrec's work in Albi. On the other hand, whether religious or not, a visit to Lourdes can be inspiring.

Wherever you travel in the region you will be overwhelmed by the friendliness of the people. There is usually some sort of festival being held, and countless local markets will give you the opportunity to sample such culinary delights as Roquefort cheese, cassoulet and foie gras, or to enjoy the wines of Cahors and Armagnac.

A Bertin • Quartier Ricau

32160 Beaumarches • Tel 0033 0562 691734
e-mail: frances.nustedt@gmail.com

Early 19th century farmhouse amidst some of the most beautiful countryside of this region offers a newly converted, light and spacious apartment with its own entrance; shared swimming pool and south-facing terrace. There are double and twin en suite bedrooms, and a large living area with new kitchenette, and a boiler room that houses washing machine, ironing facilities and freezer. Motoring, cycling and walking is really enjoyable on the deserted country lanes and quiet countryside of the region. There are numerous medieval villages within a few miles, with traditional French fruit and vegetable markets, and the food served in the local restaurants is very good, and very affordable.

Beaumarches (Gers)

Village just 10 minutes from the small medieval town of Marciac, famous for its annual Jazz Festival.

A BERTIN, QUARTIER RICAU, 32160 BEAUMARCHES (0033 0562 691734). Newly converted, light and spacious apartment with its own entrance in early 19th Century farmhouse. Shared swimming pool and south-facing terrace. Double and twin en suite bedrooms, and a large living area with new kitchenette.
e-mail: frances.nustedt@gmail.com

Visit the FHG website

www.holidayguides.com

for details of the wide choice of accommodation featured in the full range of FHG titles

Aux Memes
32140 Bellegarde • Gers
Telephone : +33 (0)5 62 66 91 45
Mobile : +33 (0)6 83 63 02 22
Fax : +33 (0)5 62 66 91 45
Email : enquiries@auxmemes.com
The Gite has two bedrooms and sleeps up to five. There is a large shower room, a living/diningroom with wood burning stove, TV, DVD player, CD player; internet access. The attached kitchen has gas cooker, fridge/freezer, dishwasher and washer/dryer. Private gardens with garden furniture, picnic bench and barbecue, and there is a swimming pool which is open from May to September. Towels and bicycles are available for hire. Babysitting can be arranged.

Bellegarde Adoulins (Gers)

Village with beautiful views of The Pyrenees, 4km from the old market town of Masseube which offers all amenities.

AUX MEMES, 32140 BELLEGARDE, GERS (Tel & Fax: +33 (0)5 62 66 91 45; Mobile: +33 (0)6 83 63 02 22). Gite with two bedrooms, sleeping up to five. Large shower room, living/diningroom with wood burning stove. Attached kitchen. Private gardens with garden furniture, barbecue. Swimming pool.
e-mail: enquiries@auxmemes.com

Castelnau de Montmiral • Tarn 81140 • Tel 0033 (0)563 332875
La Greze
Ideal for a leisurely and relaxed holiday, these are luxury gites set in 17 acres of meadowland with beautiful views. The gites are light and airy, with open-plan livingroom/kitchen with dining tables and a full range of units, dishwasher, refrigerator and cooker. The comfortable lounge has a double sofa bed; one double bedroom; luxury bathroom. Private terrace for outdoor eating. Wifi access.
There are many towns and villages to explore in the region, and the Mediterranean coast is easily accessible for a day out.
Pets welcome. Short breaks available.

Castelau de Montmiral (Tarn)

Historic village with good amenities including grocers, bakers, post office and two hotels. Tuesday is market day.

LA GREZE, CASTELNAU DE MONTMIRAL, TARN 81140 (0033 (0)563 332875). Luxury gites in meadowland with beautiful views. Open-plan livingroom/kitchen. Comfortable lounge with double sofa bed; one double bedroom; luxury bathroom. Private terrace for outdoor eating.

Please mention **Pets Welcome!**
when making enquiries about accommodation featured in these pages

Luxurious, spacious self-catering accommodation for two in the annexe to the main B&B, with its own private entrance and offering an open plan living area, with newly fitted kitchen and all amenities. Separate dining area and large living space with TV and DVD player. Wifi available. Double bedroom with fully fitted en suite bathroom. Futon provided for extra guest. Private terrace. Guests may also use the back terrace, as well as the garden. Not suitable for very young children. B&B also available. Ideal base for either a relaxing or an action packed holiday, and within easy reach of peaceful villages and well known tourist attractions.

La Maison Bleu

Girard, Duravel, Lot 46700

Tel 0033 0565238189 • www.lamaisonbleue46.com/home.html

Girard (Lot)

Hamlet situated between the medieval village of Puy L'Eveque and the town of Duravel.

LA MAISON BLEU, GIRARD, DURAVEL, LOT 46700 (0033 0565 238189). Luxurious, spacious self-catering accommodation for two in annexe to main B&B, with own private entrance. Open plan living area, with newly fitted kitchen and all amenities. Double en suite bedroom.
website: www.lamaisonbleue46.com/home.html

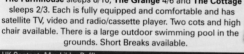

LA BASTIDE • PUYCALVEL 81440 • LAUTREC • TARN

Tel/Fax: (33)(0)5 6370 56 96

Three properties are available in four and a half acres of meadows in the hills of Pays de Cocagne, an unspoilt area between Toulouse, Carcassonne and Albi. They can be rented individually, or all together to accommodate larger family groups. **The Farmhouse** sleeps 8/10, **The Grange** 4/6 and **The Cottage** sleeps 2/3. Each is fully equipped and comfortable and has satellite TV, video and radio/cassette player. Two cots and high chair available. There is a large outdoor swimming pool in the grounds. Short Breaks available.

UK Contact: Mrs Libby Ruffle
Tye Barn House, Barking Tye, Ipswich IP6 8HZ • Tel/Fax: 01473 658 678 • e-mail: ianandjos@tarn-gites.com

Lautrec (Tarn)

The village is the ancient home of Toulouse Lautrec's family; Pink Garlic Festival held in August.

LA BASTIDE, PUYCALVEL 81440 LAUTREC (Tel & Fax: 0033 (0)5 6370 56 96. Three fully equipped and comfortable properties in the hills of Pays de Cocagne. Sleeps 2/3, 4/6, 8/10. Large outdoor swimming pool. Short Breaks available. UK CONTACT: MRS LIBBY RUFFLE, TYE BARN HOUSE, BARKING TYE, IPSWICH IP6 8HZ (TEL/FAX: 01473 658 678)
e-mail: ianandjos@tarn-gites.com

FHG Guides

publish a large range of well-known accommodation guides.
We will be happy to send you details or you can use the order form at the back of this book.

Family House with Pool
Prayssac • Lot 46220

Family house with three double bedrooms, one with en suite bathroom. There is also a separate bathroom and cloakroom. Central heating for colder months. The large kitchen/family room is full equipped. Lounge/ dining area has wood burning fire, TV, DVD, Hi-Fi ADSL (Broadband). Disabled Access and child friendly. Secluded garden with large stone table seating 10; swimming pool with sun loungers, chairs and tables. The towns of Cahors, Puy l'Eveque Luzech, Albas and many more, and a wide range of activities can be found in the area.

Tel & Fax:
0033 (0)565 360188

Prayssac (Lot)

Small, peaceful town with shops and market.

FAMILY HOUSE WITH POOL, PRAYSSAC, LOT 46220 (Tel & Fax: 0033 (0)565 360188). Family house with three double bedrooms, one en suite. Large kitchen/family room, fully equipped. Lounge/ dining area has wood burning fire. Disabled access and child friendly. Secluded garden. Swimming pool.

GITE JEAN LUZENT

L.d. Jean Luzent, St. Bauzeil, Ariege 09120
Tel 0033 (0)561 696045

The traditional farm house in regional style, converted into 3 gites for holiday letting and situated at the end of a quiet village road, surrounded by forests, meadows and an orchard of apple trees. Accommodation consists of two bedrooms; living area with sofa bed, table, chairs and small TV; bathroom. Kitchenette with electric stove, oven, fridge, cabinets. There is also a communal area with TV, allowing you to socialise with the other guests. Ideal for exploring the medieval villages and the many historical and cultural sites of the region, or for visiting the larger towns of Toulouse (65 km), Andorra (95 km), Carcassonne (80 km), and Lourdes (180 km). Pets welcome.

Saint Bauzeil (Ariege)

Quiet, rural village 4 km from shops at both Pamiers and Varhiles..

GITE JEAN LUZENT, L.D. JEAN LUZENT, ST. BAUZEIL, ARIEGE 09120 (0033 (0)561 696045) Traditional farm house converted into 3 gites, surrounded by forests, meadows and an orchard of apple trees. Two bedrooms; living area with sofa bed, and communal area with TV.

www.holidayguides.com

La Brise

Superb riverside holiday cottage

A large, light and airy house divided into two separate areas. Standing in a quiet garden leading down to the edge of the river, with magnificent far reaching views, and 5 minutes' walk down the riverside to the medieval village of Puy L'Eveque, set deep in the heart of the Lot Valley.

Libelulle (sleeps 6)
Well equipped to a high standard. 3 bedrooms with en suite dressing and bathroom. Large lounge, French windows to balcony. Kitchen and dining room. Wood burner.

Papillon (sleeps 4)
Well equipped; 2 double bedrooms with French windows to balcony. Bathroom with separate WC. lounge with woodburner. Laundry room with separate washer and dryer.

Both accommodation areas have private BBQ and seating areas. Riverside seating. Pool overlooking the river; Swedish sauna. Use of canoe, dinghy and evening boat trip up the river.

The valley of the River Lot is one of France's most vibrant and beautiful areas, with limestone gorges, majestic chateaux and ancient villages perched precariously on the side of cliffs. Amazingly this area is still unspoilt and you can find total isolation as well as busy market towns. The climate is excellent and the warm season extends from early April to late October.
Welcome pack with wine offered on arrival.
Prices from £275 inclusive. No hidden extras.

Please contact:
Chris & Edwina Flannery, La Brise,
8, Rue des Balmes, Puy L'Eveque,
46700 Lot, France
Tel: 07801 909850 or 00 33 565 35 20 29
e-mail: chrsfln@aol.com
website: www.labrise.co.uk

Puy L'Eveque (Lot)

Beautiful medieval town on the edge of the River Lot, with ancient timber framed houses and narrow cobbled streets. Several restaurants and bars, bakers, bank and post office, and a small supermarket on the edge of the village. The town of Cahors is thirty minutes away. One and a quarter hour's drive from Bergerac airport.

CHRIS & EDWINA FLANNERY, LA BRISE, 8 RUE DES BALMES, PUY L'EVEQUE, 46700 LOT (07801 909850 OR 00 33 5 65 35 20 29. Superb riverside cottage in quiet garden, with two separate accommodation areas. Sleep 4 and 6, pool, sauna. Both well equipped to a high standard, kitchen, dining room, woodburner. Linen included.
e-mail: chrsfln@aol.com website: www.labrise.co.uk

Please note

All the information in this book is given in good faith in the belief that it is correct. However, the publishers cannot guarantee the facts given in these pages, neither are they responsible for changes in policy, ownership or terms that may take place after the date of going to press. Readers should always satisfy themselves that the facilities they require are available and that the terms, if quoted, still apply.

La Petite Grange

La Petite Grange is ideally situated for exploring this wonderful area with its breathtaking scenery, many interesting villages and towns and plenty of outdoor activities. The house has two large bedrooms and can accommodate up to five people, plus cot. It has been renovated to a high standard including double glazed windows and central heating, yet still retaining many of its original features such as the stone walls and oak lintels. There is an open plan living, dining and kitchen area which is very well equipped comfortable furniture and fridge, dishwasher, washing machine and modern oven and hob. Satellite TV is provided, as well as video player and CD/radio. There is a front terrace with barbecue, ideal for eating out, and the garden provides plenty of space for relaxing or playing.

Lafargue • 46170 Sainte Alauzie • Tel/Fax: +33 (0) 5 65 24 94 52

Sainte Alauzie (Lot)

Village 10 minutes' drive from Montcuq and Castelnau-Montratier where there are plenty of good shops and restaurants.

LA PETITE GRANGE, LAFARGUE, 46170 SAINTE ALAUZIE (Tel & Fax: +33 (0) 5 65 24 94 52) Ideally situated for exploring this wonderful area. Two large bedrooms (sleeps up to 5, plus cot). Open plan living, dining and well equipped kitchen area; original features. Front terrace with barbecue.

Les Pradals • Sainte Croix • 81150 Tarn

David Orchard and Pia Columberg

Tel: 00 33 563 539 490 • Fax: 00 44 870 458 2566 • E-mail: info@lespradals.com

This lovely barn conversion in a beautiful setting has been fully restored and offers a mixture of classic stone and wood architecture together with the modern comforts of satellite TV, internet access, pool and a wellness package. The house is family and disabled friendly and sleeps up to four people. There are two bedrooms, large bathroom and

American-style kitchen area. The organic garden supplies complimentary vegetables and there is a swimming pool in the grounds. There are plenty of outdoor activities in the surrounding area including cycling, golf, potholing and riding and lots of summer festivals to enjoy.

Sainte Croix (Tarn)

Picturesque village just 10 minutes from Albi, famous for its Toulouse Lautrec Museum, winding streets, shops and eating places.

DAVID ORCHARD AND PIA COLUMBERG, LES PRADALS, SAINTE CROIX, 81150 TARN (0033 563 539 490; Fax: 0044 870 458 2566). Barn conversion with all modern comforts, pool and a wellness package. Sleeps up to four. Two bedrooms, large bathroom and American-style kitchen area. Organic garden, swimming pool.
e-mail: info@lespradals.com

Please mention **Pets Welcome!**

when making enquiries about accommodation featured in these pages

POITOU-CHARENTES

Poitou-Charentes is a very unspoilt region with pleasant countryside, bustling ports and harbours, long sandy beaches, islands and marinas. Enjoy 300 miles of Atlantic coast for sunbathing, sailing or windsurfing, take a cruise on the Charente River or discover the secrets of Cognac by visiting its cellars and distilleries. There are numerous vineyards, castles and Romanesque churches to visit, or experience the futuristic universe at Futuroscope Theme Park outside Poitiers. If walking or cycling is your thing the mainly flat agricultural land away from the coastline is ideal. The cuisine of this abundant region includes the famous Marennes Oleron oysters, melons, goat cheeses such as chabichou and Pineau, a mixture of grape juice and cognac.

Fourwinds

Beauregard
Juillac Le Coq
Charente 16130

Self-catering accommodation is offered in this delightful holiday home in the heart of Charente countryside, a very peaceful area with plenty to do and see. The many outdoor activities include tennis, swimming, guided walks and a superb 18 hole golf course. Cruises, canoeing and kayaking are available on the Charente river. The accommodaton sleeps up to 5 in one double and one twin bedroom, plus extra single bed. Travel cot available. There is a fully fitted kitchen, diningroom/lounge, shower room and laundry facilities. Two patio areas, BBQ and swimming pool are all available. B&B can be provided if preferred.

Tel: 0033 545 800259

Beauregard (Charente)

Hamlet on the outskirts of the town of Juillac Le Coq, 12km from Cognac.

FOURWINDS, BEAUREGARD, JUILLAC LE COQ, CHARENTE 16130 (0033 545 800259). Self-catering accommodation in the heart of Charente countryside. Sleeps up to 5. Fully fitted kitchen, diningroom/lounge, shower room and laundry facilities. Two patio areas, BBQ and swimming pool. B&B available.

FHG Guides

publish a large range of well-known accommodation guides.
We will be happy to send you details or you can use the order form at the back of this book.

Set in the heart of beautiful Poitou-Charentes, one of the sunniest regions of France, cosy cottage and two stable conversions positioned around a grassy courtyard with wooden garden table and chairs ideal for enjoying meals outdoors.
All three properties share the courtyard, the games area in the hangar next to the little cottage, the laundry room and the swimming-pool. Each is fully equipped for four people and baby equipment is available. The surrounding countryside is ideal for walking and cycling, and fishing, boating, golf and horse riding are all available.
There are many interesting places to visit, also larger towns with a variety of shops and markets.

La Charronniere

Chaunay, Vienne 86510
Tel: 0033 (0)549 429972
enquiries@lacharronniere.com
www.lacharronniere.com

Chaunay (Vienne)

Town with shops, supermarket, bar, restaurant and post office.

LA CHARRONNIERE, CHAUNAY, VIENNE 86510 (0033 (0)549 429972). Cosy cottage and two stable conversions positioned around a grassy courtyard. Each is fully equipped for four and baby equipment is available. Ideal for walking and cycling.
e-mail: enquiries@lacharronniere.com website: www.lacharroniere.com

La Luque

Courpignac
Charente Maritime 17130
Tel: 01580 765385

South-facing house full of character with large rooms and ancient beams, rustic kitchen with antique farmhouse table, fully equipped with cooker, fridges, washing machine and dishwasher.
Sleeps 2-8 in three bedrooms, one on the ground floor, and the other two on the mezzanine floor. Two sittingrooms, one with open fire, and there is satellite TV, a hi-fi and DVD player plus an extensive library of books, games, DVDs, records and tapes. Separate bathroom and toilet with utility area.
Two acres of gardens with shaded courtyard and garden furniture and barbecue. Pets welcome.

Courpignac (Charente Maritime)

Peaceful area near the small town of Jonzac with its fascinating Medieval section, spa health centre and thermal swimming centre.

LA LUQUE, COURPIGNAC, CHARENTE MARITIME 17130 (01580 765385). South-facing house full of character with large rooms and ancient beams; rustic kitchen, fully equipped. Sleeps 2-8 in three bedrooms. Two acres of gardens; garden furniture and barbecue.

www.holidayguides.com

Logis La Cabane

La Cabane • Breville • Charente 16370
Tel 0033 (0)545 811867
www.logis-la-cabane.com/index.html

Three lovely holiday cottages in a fantastic setting. Ideal for a get away from it all holiday for children and their parents or for couples wanting peace and tranquillity, yet close to many interesting places to visit and with golf, fishing, canoeing, horse riding tennis, karting and swimming in the area. The three properties are set around a courtyard and are furnished and decorated in a simple style. Each has washing machine, TV and DVD player. Sleep 3, 5 and 6. There is a private patio, garden furniture and barbecue for each and a swimming pool, paddling pool and plenty of sun loungers in the grounds. Lots of space for children to play, and a sandpit and selection of toys is provided.

La Cabane (Charente)

Peaceful hamlet with bar, restaurant and cybercafe, just 1km from Breville where there are good shops.

LOGIS LA CABANE, LA CABANE, BREVILLE, CHARENTE 16370 (0033 (0) 545 811867). Three lovely holiday cottages set around a courtyard and furnished and decorated in a simple style. Sleep 3, 5 and 6. Private patio, garden furniture and barbecues; swimming pool, paddling pool.

Chez Bobin

Lathus St Remy • Montmorillon
Vienne 86390
Tel: 07747 794782
or 44 01273 600161

Secluded cottage with secure, fully enclosed garden, swimming pool, trampolines and hammocks, and lovely terrace with barbecue. There are three cycles available for guests' use and there are lovely walks and cycle rides, plus fishing and horse riding just minutes from cottage.
The spacious accommodation has beamed ceilings and tiled floors, fully fitted kitchen/breakfast room, separate utility room, two double bedrooms and a twin room. The sittingroom has wood burning stove and lots of games and toys and the separate mezzanine area has TV and DVD players, selection of DVDs and an extra sleeping area. Wireless broadband and internet radio is available. Pets welcome.

Lathus St Remy (Vienne)

Village with shops, bank and bar. Lake St Pardoux 45 minutes by car.

CHEZ BOBIN, LATHUS ST REMY, MONTMORILLON, VIENNE 86390 (07747 794 782 or 44 01273 600161). Secluded cottage with secure, fully enclosed garden, Spacious accommodation has beamed ceilings and tiled floors, fully fitted kitchen/breakfast room, separate utility room, two double bedrooms and a twin room.

Gite Complex in the idyllic Charente Maritime region

Countryside property situated in the hamlet of La Ville Aux Moines and designed especially for families.

With 3 two bedroomed and 3 three bedroomed gites, we can accommodate family parties of up to 42 people. Each gite is equipped with a fully stocked kitchen, bedrooms have full size wardrobes and include bedding, towels, cots, high chairs. Satellite TV and DVD player and a wide selection of books, videos and DVDs.

On site large solar heated pool plus child's pool, half acre garden, swings, table tennis, children's play fort and football net, garden tennis and badminton. Many activities nearby: tennis, horse riding, golf, water sports. Quality supermarkets, bars, restaurant and banks within 15 minutes. Many beaches and tourist attractions nearby. Communal laundry, Pets welcome in some gites. Bed & Breakfast available.

Contact David Inchboard • Tel: 0033 5 46 32 04 81
E-mail: david.inchboard@wanadoo.fr • www.gitecomplex.co.uk

La Ville Aux Moines (Charente Maritime)

Small hamlet within easy reach of quality supermarkets, bars, restaurants, swimming pools and banks in nearby towns of Surgeres or Jean D'Angely (15 minutes). Many beaches and tourist attractions, including La Palmyte Zoo, nearby.

DAVID & ISABEL INCHBOARD, 17 RUE DES PUITS, LA VILLE AUX MOINES, 17330 DOEIUL SUR LE MIGNON (0033 5 46 32 04 81). Countryside complex of 3 two bedroom and 3 three bedroom gites. Designed for families. Fully equipped. Many activities on site including large pool and child's pool.
e-mail: david.inchboard@wanadoo.fr website: www.gitecomplex.co.uk

Please note

All the information in this book is given in good faith in the belief that it is correct. However, the publishers cannot guarantee the facts given in these pages, neither are they responsible for changes in policy, ownership or terms that may take place after the date of going to press. Readers should always satisfy themselves that the facilities they require are available and that the terms, if quoted, still apply.

Lymerac
Salles Lavalette
Charente 16190

Spacious farmhouses with swimming pool, horse riding facilities, children's play area and panoramic views of the surrounding countryside. Table tennis, badminton, petanque and mountain bikes are provided for guests. The accommodation is fully equipped and sleeps 2-8 in three bedrooms. Large oak beamed lounge and dining area with exposed stone walls feature fireplace, wood burning stove and DVD player. Wet room with wheel-in shower and separate toilet with handrail. Modern fitted kitchen. Baby equipment available. Pets welcome.

Tel: 0033 (0)545 647341

Salles Lavalette (Charente)

Lovely village with bar, restaurant, shops and post office. Many towns nearby provide a wide range of shops, restaurants and tourist attractions.

LYMERAC, SALLES LAVALETTE, CHARENTE 16190 (0033 (0)545 647341). Spacious farmhouses with swimming pool, horse riding facilities, children's play area and panoramic views. Fully equipped. Sleeps 2-8. Large lounge, dining area. Wet room, separate toilet. Modern fitted kitchen.

La Remigeasse
4 Rue de Chez Mesnard, Fleac Sur Seugne
Ile d'Oleron, Charente Maritime 17800
Tel: 0033 546905460

The house is situated on a small site of 38 holiday homes, within five minutes' walk of the beach. Ample car parking. Open-plan lounge/kitchen/dining area and separate bathroom on ground floor. Mezzanine floor bedroom sleeps two people, and there are bunk beds in a small outbuilding, ideal for teenagers or older children. Small back garden. Sleeps 2-4. Disabled access.

Seugne (Charente Maritime)

Small town on Ile d'Oleron, an island with beautiful sandy beaches connected to the mainland by a viaduct.

LA REMIGEASSE, 4 RUE DE CHEZ MESARD, FLEAC SUR SEUGNE, ILE D'OLERON, CHARENTE MARITIME 17800 (0033 546 905 460). Holiday home five minutes from beach. Ample car parking. Open-plan lounge/kitchen/dining area, separate bathroom on ground floor. Mezzanine bedroom sleeps two, small outbuilding with bunk beds. Small back garden. Disabled access.

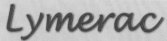

WESTERN LOIRE

This region, with its pleasing warm climate, has long been a favourite holiday destination. The visitor is spoilt for choice as lush countryside, vineyards, long sandy beaches and salt marshes vie for attention with fascinating cities, sleepy villages, ancient buildings and castles with stunning artwork, and cultural festivals galore. The famous 24-hour race is held at Le Mans-Laval, and there are facilities throughout the region for a huge variety of sporting activities, both land and water based. The countryside is easily explored by bicycle or on foot, or you may prefer to spend a day cruising on the tranquil waterways. Explore the Loire Valley vineyards, and enjoy the delicious and famous wines of the area with fresh fruit and vegetables, game, wild mushrooms and generous platters of seafood from the region's rivers and the sea.

Les Augerelles

Vendée/Charentes Border

3 bed house (7/9) and 1 bed gite (2/4)

• Well equipped and recently refurbished • secure garden with sun and shade • part-covered barbeque area with furniture • 4.5m raised pool with removable steps • heating for off-season, thick stone walls • quiet hamlet but with market town nearby • 200 hectares of common land opposite, good walks • ideal location for Atlantic coast, Marais and Bocage • managed by family members resident in the region • available together for main holiday season or separately for longer lets and off-season by negotiation.

For more details contact:

Janet & John Nuthall • 01249 443458

e-mail: jnuthall2@toucansurf.com for brochure

or visit **www.vendee-gites.co.uk/lesaugerelles.htm** for much more information and pictures

Fonteney le Comte (Vendée)

A town of art and history with elegant squares and gardens. Nôtre Dame church and the Vendée museum are worth a visit. Numerous festivals and events take place throughout the year..

LES AUGERELLES, VENDEE/CHARENTES BORDER. 3 Bed house (sleeps 7/9) and 1 bed gite (sleeps 2/4). Well equipped and recently refurbished. Swimming pool. Heating for off season. Quiet hamlet with market town nearby. Managed by family members resident in the region. Contact: JANET & JOHN NUTHALL (01249 443458) [ ]
e-mail: jnuthall2 @toucansurf.com website: www.vendee-gites.co.uk/lesaugerelles.htm

Symbols

- Indicates that pets are welcome free of charge.
- £ Indicates that a charge is made for pets: nightly or weekly.
- pw! Shows some special provision for pets; exercise facility, feeding or accommodation arrangement.
- ⌂ Indicates separate pets accommodation.

La Belle Maison

5 Rue du Moutier
Marsais Ste Radegonde Vendée 85570
Tel 0033 (0)251876353 or 00 0251 876353
E-mail: alfred.stradling@wanadoo.fr

Apartment sleeping from 2-6 people, can be rented out for self-catering, or on a bed and breakfast basis with a minimum of two nights' stay. There are beautiful rooms and a comfortable sitting area, and guests are free to relax in the tranquil garden and make use of the Jacuzzi under the trees. The house is in an ideal position for visiting many attractions in the surrounding area including beaches and historic sites. There is a large swimming pool a few minutes away, open in summer months, and an Adventure Park and zoo are just 10 minutes away.

Marsais Ste Radegronde (Vendée)

Peaceful village near Fontenay Le Comte and the medieval town of Vouvant.

LA BELLE MAISON, 5 RUE DU MOUTIER, MARSAIS STE RADEGONDE, VENDEE 8557 (0033 (0)251876353 or 00 0251 876353) Apartment sleeping from 2-6 people, self-catering or B&B (min. two nights stay). Beautiful rooms and a comfortable sitting area, tranquil garden. In an ideal position for visiting many attractions in the surrounding area.
e-mail:alfred.stradling@wanadoo.fr

Looking for Holiday Accommodation?

FHG
·K·U·P·E·R·A·R·D·

for details of hundreds of properties throughout the UK, visit our website

www.holidayguides.com

Regional map of France

• **Tourist information**

French Tourist Office
178 Piccadilly
London
W1J 9AL

Web address: www.franceguide.com
Tel. no.: 0906 8 244 123

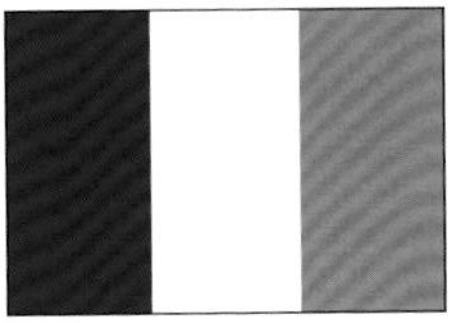

Capital city: **Paris**

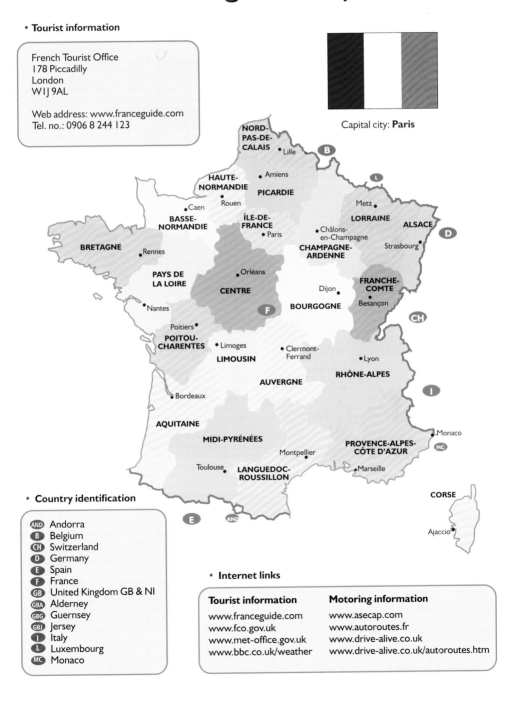

• **Country identification**

- AND Andorra
- B Belgium
- CH Switzerland
- D Germany
- E Spain
- F France
- GB United Kingdom GB & NI
- GBA Alderney
- GBG Guernsey
- GBJ Jersey
- I Italy
- L Luxembourg
- MC Monaco

• **Internet links**

Tourist information	**Motoring information**
www.franceguide.com	www.asecap.com
www.fco.gov.uk	www.autoroutes.fr
www.met-office.gov.uk	www.drive-alive.co.uk
www.bbc.co.uk/weather	www.drive-alive.co.uk/autoroutes.htm

Driving in France

French drivers tend to be quite aggressive and the high incidence of road deaths has become a cause for national concern. There are speed restrictions for drivers who have held their licence for less than 2 years (•10 km/h on motorways, 100 km/h on dual carriageways and 80 km/h on ordinary roads). Seatbelts are compulsory for both front and rear. Children under 10 should travel in the back, if possible. Babies and young children should be restrained appropriately, with a booster seat (**siège réhausseur**) or babyseat (**siège pour bébés**).

• **All routes**

• **Town centre**

built up area	**50** km/h
ordinary roads	**90** km/h
dual carriageway	**110** km/h
motorway	**130** km/h

• **Speed restrictions**

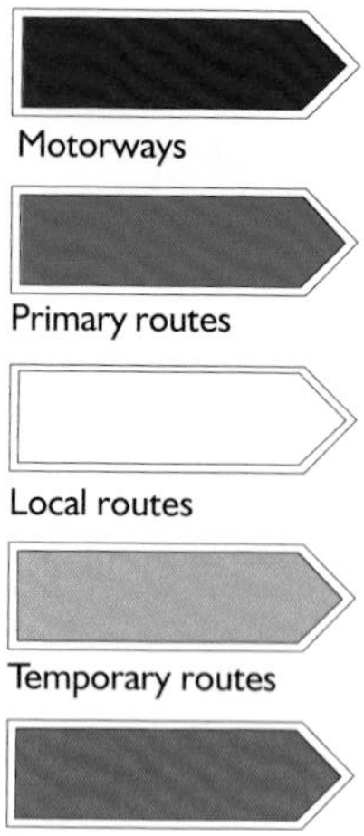

• **French road signs are colour-coded**

NORTH **Nord**

WEST **Ouest**

Est EAST

SOUTH **Sud**

• **Direction indicators**

• **Route for heavy vehicles**

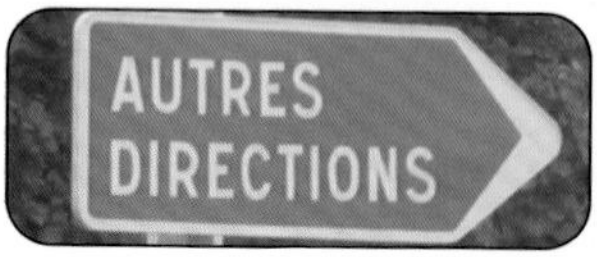

• **Other routes**

Talking

we are going to...
nous allons à...
nooz a-loñ a...

is the road good?
est-ce que la route est bonne?
ess kuh la root ay bon

is the pass open?
est-ce que le col est ouvert?
ess kuh luh kol ayt oo-vehr

which is the best route?
quel est le meilleur itinéraire?
kel ay luh may-yuhr ee-tee-nay-rehr

can you show me on the map?
pouvez-vous me montrer sur la carte?
poo-vay voo muh moñ-tray soor la kart

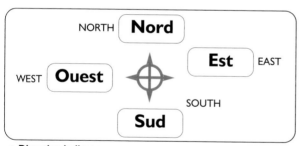

do we need snow chains?
est-ce qu'il faut des chaînes?
ess keel foh day shen

• **Lorry exit**

• **School exit**

Warning that the crossroads (**carrefour**) is a roundabout (in France roundabouts are • fairly new).

• **Slow down**

• **Detour**
Follow the yellow detour signs to rejoin your route.

Road closed •

• **Road liable to flooding**

• **Danger still present**

• **Signs on entering**
• **and leaving town**

• **You do not have right of way.** The traffic on the roundabout has right of way.

• **Give way**

is this the road to...?
c'est bien la route de...?
say byañ la root duh...

I am sorry, I did not know
je suis désolé, je ne savais pas
zhuh swee day-zo-lay zhuh nuh sa-vay pa

do I have to pay the fine straight away?
est-ce qu'il faut payer l'amende tout de suite?
ess keel foh pay-ay la-moñd toot sweet

how do I get to...?
pour aller à...?
poor a-lay a...

Although some portions of motorways are free around cities, you have to pay a toll if travelling over long distances. You get a ticket when you join the motorway. On leaving it you hand the ticket in at the **péage** and the amount to pay is flashed up on an illuminated sign. Remember it is the front passenger who pays if you have a right-hand-drive car. Take care over speeding: limits are lowered in wet weather – by 20 km/h on motorways and 10 km/h on other roads.

• **Motorway emergency phone**

• **Motorway signs are blue; local signs are white**

• **Motorway junction/exit**

The motorway routes sign posted here
• are toll-paying (**péage**).

• **Toll station**

• **Stop**
Toll station

• **Motorway services are located every 30–40 km**

If you break down on the motorway

If you break down on the motorway, first you should put on your hazard lights and place the warning triangle about 30 m behind the car. You should alert the police on emergency number 17 stating your exact location. If you are using an emergency SOS phone (located every 2 km along the motorway) they will know your location. The police will arrange for a recovery vehicle to come to you.

my car has broken down
ma voiture est en panne
ma vwa-toor ayt oñ pan

what do I do?
qu'est-ce que je dois faire?
kess kuh zhuh dwa fehr

I am on my own (female)
je suis seule
zhuh swee suhl

my children are in the car
mes enfants sont dans la voiture
mayz oñ-foñ soñ doñ la vwa-toor

the car is near junction number...
la voiture est près de la sortie numéro...
la vwa-toor ay pray duh la sor-tee noo-may-roh...

it's a blue Fiat Uno
c'est une Fiat Uno bleue
say ooñ fyat oo-noh bluh

registration number...
numéro d'immatriculation...
noo-may-roh dee-mat-ree-koo-las-yoñ...

In Paris, you generally pay to park. In towns outside Paris there may be a weekly market held in the main square on Saturday morning. Parking will be forbidden from midnight of the night before until 3.30pm. Take care not to park or your car may be towed away.

- **Pay at the meter** (below the sign).

Paying
- Most of the time, parking is not free.

- **Parking meter**

insert money

cancel

parking fee payable

press for ticket

- **Only 3 minutes**

- **No parking on the pavement**

no parking

vehicle exit

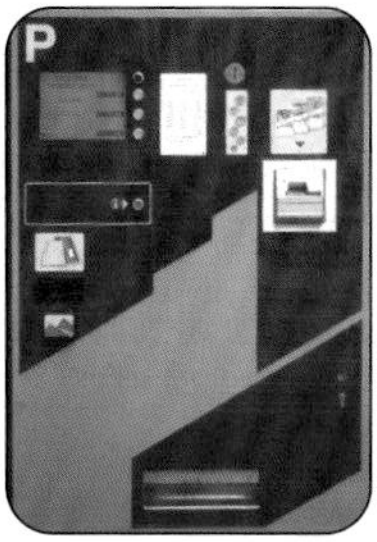

• Newer parking machines take notes and let you choose the language for your transaction.

• No parking on Saturdays, market day

• Don't be fooled: **libre** means there are spaces, not that parking is free.

• **Car park full**

• **Open 24 hours**

• **Disabled parking places** •

I am looking for a car park
je cherche un parking
zhuh shehrsh uñ par-keeng

can I park here?
est-ce que je peux me garer ici?
ess kuh zhuh puh muh ga-ray ee-see

the ticket machine doesn't work
l'horodateur ne marche pas
lo-ro-da-tuhr nuh marsh pa

do I need to pay?
il faut payer?
eel foh pay-ay

how long for?
pour combien de temps?
poor koñ-byañ duh toñ

Petrol stations in small towns are generally manned, but closed Sundays and in the evenings. The big towns have 24-hour petrol stations and you can buy petrol at some large supermarkets.

• **Petrol pumps are colour-coded** You will find the pump number at the side

• Colour-coding matches the pump handle: green for unleaded (**sans plomb**), blue for super and yellow for diesel. The figure to the right (98, 95, 97) refers to the octane rating. Most cars run on the lower rating. The higher one is for powerful cars or towing cars.

• Diesel is also known as **gazoil** or **gazole**.

• **Turn off engine**

Talking

is there a petrol station near here?
est-ce qu'il y a une station-service près d'ici?
ess keel ee a oon stass-yoñ sehr-vees pray dee-see

fill it up please
le plein s'il vous plaît
luh plañ see voo play

40 euro worth of unleaded petrol
quarante euro d'essence sans plomb
ka-roñt uh-roh dess-oñss soñ ploñ

I'd like to wash the car
je voudrais laver la voiture
zhuh voo-dray la-vay la vwa-toor

pump number...
pompe numéro...
poñp noo-may-roh...

how much is that?
c'est combien?
say koñ-byañ

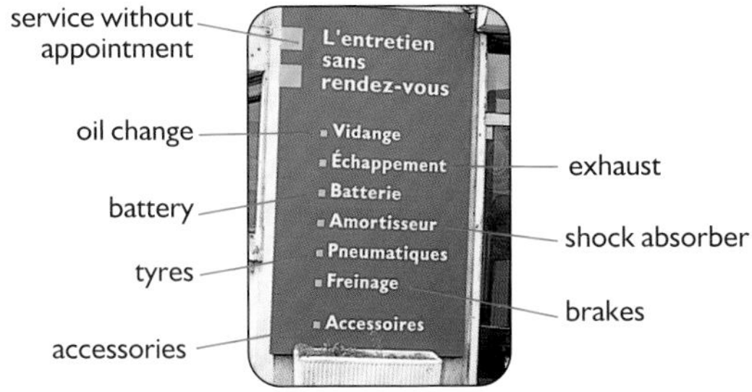

You should carry a red warning triangle in case of breakdown. It is also advisable to carry a first-aid kit in the car. You will have no trouble in France finding a **garage** to do repairs.

I have broken down
je suis en panne
zhuh sweez oñ pan

I have a flat tyre
j'ai un pneu crevé
zhay uñ pnuh kruh-vay

I need tyres
j'ai besoin de pneus
zhay buh-zwañ duh pnuh

where is the nearest garage?
où est le garage le plus proche?
oo ay luh ga-razh luh ploo prosh

the … is not working
le/la … ne marche pas
luh/la … nuh marsh pa

can you repair it?
vous pouvez le réparer?
voo poo-vay luh ray-pa-ray

when will it be ready?
ça sera prêt quand?
sa suh-ra pray koñ

can you replace the windscreen?
pouvez-vous changer le pare-brise?
poo-vay voo shoñ-zhay luh par-breez

the car won't start
la voiture ne démarre pas
la vwa-toor nuh day-mar pa

the battery is flat
la batterie est à plat
la ba-tree ayt a pla

I have run out of petrol
je suis en panne d'essence
zhuh sweez oñ pan dess-oñss

something is wrong with…
il y a un problème avec…
eel ee a uñ pro-blehm a-vek…

the … are not working
les … ne marchent pas
lay … nuh marsh pa

how long will it take?
ça va prendre combien de temps?
sa va proñdr koñ-byañ duh toñ

how much will it cost?
combien ça va coûter?
koñ-byañ sa va koo-tay

please check…
vous pouvez vérifier…
voo poo-vay vay-ree-fyay…

the oil
l'huile
lweel

the water
l'eau
loh

the tyres
les pneus
lay pnuh

Emergency

The emergency number is 17 for the police (15 for an ambulance and 18 for the fire brigade). You will see either **Police** or **Gendarmerie** (in smaller towns and villages). You should report all thefts or crimes to them.

• Police station

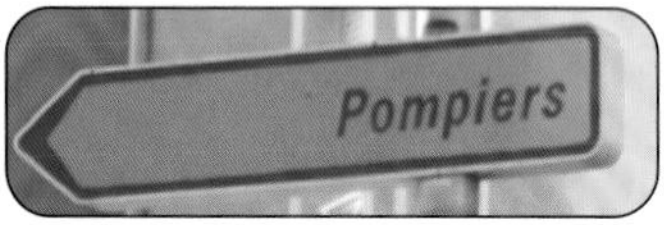

• Fire station

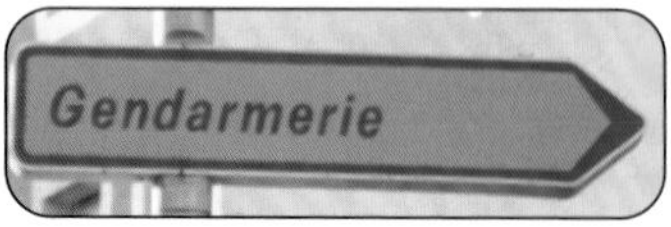

• Local police

help!
au secours!
oh suh-koor

can you help me?
vous pouvez m'aider?
voo poo-vay mah-day

please call...
s'il vous plaît! appelez...
seel voo play ap-lay...

the police
la police
la po-leess

an ambulance
une ambulance
oon oñ-boo-loñss

fire!
au feu!
oh fuh

please call the fire brigade!
s'il vous plaît! appelez les pompiers!
seel voo play ap-lay lay poñ-pyay

my ... has been stolen
on m'a volé mon/ma...
oñ ma vo-lay moñ/ma...

I want to report a theft
je veux signaler un vol
zhuh vuh seen-ya-lay uñ vol

here are my insurance details
voici mon assurance
vwa-see moñ a-soo-roñss

please give me your insurance details
votre assurance s'il vous plaît
votr a-soo-roñss seel voo play

where is the police station?
où est la gendarmerie?
oo ay la zhoñ-darm-ree

I would like to phone...
je voudrais appeler...
zhuh voo-dray ap-lay...

my car has been broken into
on a forcé ma voiture
on a for-say ma vwa-toor

I need a report for my insurance
il me faut un constat pour mon assurance
eel muh foh uñ koñ-sta poor mon a-soo-roñss

Looking for Holiday Accommodation?

FHG
K·U·P·E·R·A·R·D

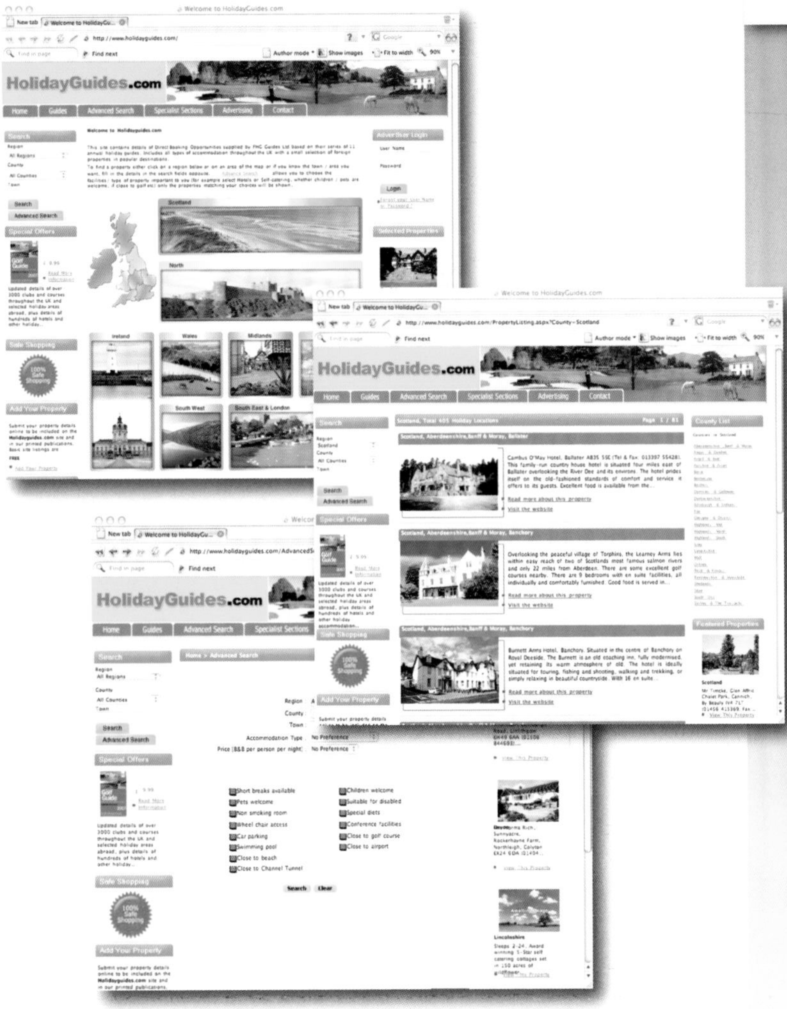

for details of hundreds of properties throughout the UK, visit our website

www.holidayguides.com

DogsTrust
the new name for the NCDL

DogsTrust : A Dog is For Life

Are you thinking of going on holiday in the UK with your dog?

If so, the Dogs Trust has a free factsheet which will be of particular interest.

"Safe travel and happy holidays with your hound in the UK"

For this and any other of our free Dogs Trust factsheets please contact us at:

**Dogs Trust,
17 Wakley St. London EC1V 7RQ.
Tel: 020 7837 0006**

**Website: www.dogstrust.org.uk
or e-mail us, info@dogstrust.org.uk**

Last year Dogs Trust cared for over 11,500 stray and abandoned dogs at our network of 15 Rehoming Centres.
So if you are looking for a companion for your dog or you have a friend who might like a dog, just contact your nearest
Dogs Trust Rehoming Centre.

We care for around 1,600 dogs on any given day, so we are sure we will be able to find your perfect partner.
The Dogs Trust never destroys a healthy dog.

For details of our Sponsor-a-Dog scheme please call **020 7837 0006** or visit **www.sponsoradog.org.uk**

Dogs Trust Rehoming Centres

ENGLAND

Dogs Trust Canterbury
01227 792 505

Dogs Trust Darlington
01325 333 114

Dogs Trust Evesham
01386 830 613

Dogs Trust Ilfracombe
01271 812 709

Dogs Trust Kenilworth
01926 484 398

Dogs Trust Leeds
01132 613 194

Dogs Trust Merseyside
0151 480 0660

Dogs Trust Newbury
01488 658 391

Dogs Trust Roden
01952 770 225

Dogs Trust Salisbury
01980 629 634

Dogs Trust Shoreham
01273 452 576

Dogs Trust Snetterton
01953 498 377

WALES

Dogs Trust Bridgend
01656 725 219

SCOTLAND

Dogs Trust West Calder
01506 873 459

NORTHERN IRELAND

Dogs Trust Ballymena
028 2565 2977

Registered Charity No. 227523

Donate £1 to your favourite Pets Charity

FHG has agreed to donate £1 from the price of this Pets Welcome! Guide to EITHER The Royal Society For The Prevention of Cruelty to Animals, Dogs Trust, The Kennel Club, or the Scottish Society for the Prevention of Cruelty to Animals

RSPCA

DogsTrust the new name for the NCDL

THE KENNEL CLUB *Making a difference for dogs*

SCOTTISH SPCA Living for the day when ANIMAL CRUELTY STOPS

To allow the Charity of your choice to receive this donation simply complete the slip below and return to FHG at

FHG Guides Ltd, Abbey Mill Business Centre
Seedhill Paisley PA1 1TJ
Closing date April 24th 2009

Note: Original forms only please, do not send photocopies.

✂--

Please donate £1 from the price of this Pets Welcome! guide to:

RSPCA ☐ DOGS TRUST ☐ KENNEL CLUB ☐ SSPCA ☐

Name..

Address..

....

Postcode..Date..

FHG Guides may send readers details of discount offers for our holiday guides.
If you do not wish to receive this information please tick here ☐
Your details will not be passed on to any other organisation.

FHG K·U·P·E·R·A·R·D

THE KENNEL CLUB

Making a difference for dogs

Dogs and the Kennel Club

Founded well over a hundred years ago, in 1873, the Kennel Club registers around 275,000 dogs a year. It is the governing body of dogs in the United Kingdom, and its main objective is to promote in every way, the general improvement of dogs, and encourage responsible dog ownership.

From running the largest dog show in the world, Crufts, to giving critical advice to owners, the media and politicians alike, as well as providing educational schemes, such as teaching safety around dogs. It covers both the fun and the serious side of dogs, and dog ownership, and is central to all dogs and dog owners.

The number of breeds recognised by the Kennel Club is ever increasing, with 208 breeds currently eligible for registration. The KC has three registers - the Breed, the Activity and the Companion Dog register – one for every kind of dog and activity, as both the Activity register and Companion Dog register are open for crossbreeds.

The small cost to register dogs ensures that money is being put back into dogs, enabling the Kennel Club to run its schemes, and also to be the voice for dogs in Government on behalf of all their owners. The variety of schemes run by the KC, reflect its diverse role with dogs and their place in society as a whole.

For those wanting to buy a pedigree dog there is access to, and information on, the best breeders through the Accredited Breeder Scheme and the Puppy Sales Register, all easily accessible on the Kennel Club website, as well as breed specific health research. And for those who want a pedigree dog but would prefer an adult dog, there are many breed specific rescue centres. They also offer the support of expert knowledge and advice on specific breeds.

The Kennel Club Charitable Trust raises and disburses funds to a variety of deserving causes, such as canine health research projects, specialist studies and canine charities. Every penny that is raised goes directly to the Trust, ensuring that our dog friends and people within the canine field enjoy the maximum benefit.

The Kennel Club has a role to play for lost dogs through Petlog, the UK's largest national pet identification scheme. The details on Petlog (**www.petlog.org.uk**) are available to local authorities, police and established welfare and rescue organisations. This ensures that lost or stray animals are speedily reunited with their owners when found and scanned for details on a previously inserted microchip, even when abroad.

Safety for children around dogs is another priority for the Kennel Club, which has led to the development of its fun and informative popular online game called 'Safe and Sound' (www.safeandsound.org.uk), which is free to play. Children's lives are enriched by living with dogs, as they learn responsibility and empathy while interaction with a dog can increase their self-esteem.

Ensuring dogs are well behaved means also teaching the owners how to achieve this, which is where the Good Citizen Dog Scheme (GCDS) comes into focus. It is the largest dog training programme in the UK and has four levels of assessment, from Puppy Foundation through to Gold. 190,000 dogs have successfully passed through the scheme, with more than 1,800 training clubs across the UK running the programme. Training your dog helps to create a better bond between a dog and its owner, and it is a responsible dog owner's job to ensure that you have a well behaved and lovable dog.

The Accredited Instructors scheme for dog training and canine behaviour is for anyone training dogs or teaching people to train dogs. It provides a network of instructors, trainers and advisors to help, and is a voluntary scheme, which aims to give a worthwhile qualification, in which scheme members and the public can have confidence.

The Young Kennel Club (YKC) is a vital part of the Kennel Club, ensuring that youngsters have an opening into the world of dogs. The Young Kennel Club is for young members from 6 – 24 years (**www.ykc.org.uk**)

If you are a dog-friendly business then you can benefit by getting on board with the Kennel Club's Open for Dogs sticker campaign. Hundreds of businesses – from hotels and pubs to castles and cafes – are already displaying the stickers to alert the nation's many millions of dog owners that their canine companions are welcome.

To request your free sticker or if you already display one and would like to get your website added to the list of dog-friendly places located at **www.openfordogs.org.uk,** then email **press.office@thekennelclub.org.uk**

For more information about this or any of the Kennel Club's activities visit www.thekennelclub.org.uk or make an appointment at the Kennel Club's headquarters, which also hold the UK's definitive canine library and art gallery, in Piccadilly, London. The press office is available to comment on all canine issues.

Telephone 020 7518 1008

press.office@thekennelclub.org.uk

www.thekennelclub.org.uk

NEW

Purina winalot

Meaty Duos is the delicious new meal from Winalot. Each portion of Meaty Duos has a mix of roasted flavoured meaty pieces and a generous serving of tender meaty chunks. It's packed full of flavours and textures to give your dog a delicious, wholesome meal.

An irresistible taste esperience!

Meaty Duos is available in:

- Chicken & Liver in Gravy
- Chicken & Lamb in Jelly
- Beef & Kidney in Gravy
- Beef & Turkey in Jelly
- Duck & Rabbit in Gravy
- Lamb & Duck in Jelly

In Store NOW!

Trademark owned by Société des Produits Nestlé S.A., Vevey, Switzerland.

[redacted]

PURINA
winalot

www.winalot-dog.co.uk

For many of us enjoying a country holiday also means taking our dogs on scenic walks, or for a journey in the car - often in warm weather, and at these times they may need a little extra care and attention. The following tips could make your pet's life on hot days considerably more comfortable:

WATER!

A normal 20kg dog will drink about one and a half pints of water a day. In the heat this can increase by 200 to 300%. Water should always be available. Make sure you take plenty for your pet, as well for yourself when out walking and in the car. Stabilising non-spill water bowls are great for travel, while handy inflatable bowls are ideal for stowing in your knapsack. You can even buy water bottles that your dog can carry.

SHADE

Encourage your dog to favour shady, cool spots when you stop for a rest - rather than sunbathe with the rest of the family!

CAR

NEVER leave your dog in the car unattended. Placing a dog in the back of any car even with an open rear window is undesirable and may be fatal. Remember - even a car parked in shade in the morning when it's cool could reach over 100 degrees very quickly as the sun moves. Heat stroke can occur within minutes.

EXERCISE

Plan your walk so you avoid strenuous exercise during the hottest part of the day. Some dogs like to paddle or swim - if there is no water around and your dog seems uncomfortably hot, seek a shady spot and provide water.

HEALTH

A dog's heat loss system is dependent on overall health. If your dog is fit, supple and active then walking will be a pleasurable experience, however, if there is any indication of heart or respiratory problems arising, controlled exercise in the cool is recommended. Veterinary advice should be sought if problems persist during heat stressful times.

HEAT STROKE

This is an emergency and potentially life threatening situation. If in doubt take the following action, then seek advice. A chilled dog is better than an overheated one.

- Cease any form of exercise.
- Move the dog into a cool place.
- Sponge the dog with cold water - all over, avoiding water round the mouth or nose.
- Do not offer food or fluids until evident recovery.
- Seek veterinary advice if in doubt.

PURINA
winalot
Have your pet's photo featured in
Pets Welcome!
As the sponsor of Pets Welcome! 2009 Winalot is offering readers a FREE packet of Winalot Healthy Hearts and Winalot Coat Conditioners for every photo featured. The perfect way to reward your best friend.
winalot
Good life
healthy hearts
BEEF FLAVOUR
winalot
Good life
coat conditioners
CHICKEN FLAVOUR
www.winalot-dog.co.uk
Trademark owned by Société des Produits Nestlé S.A., Vevey, Switzerland

Readers' Pets Pictures

Send us your favourite Pet Photo!

On the following pages are a selection of Pets photos sent in by readers of **Pets Welcome!**

If you would like to have a photo of your pet included in the next edition (published in April 2009), send it along with a brief note of the pet's name and any interesting anecdotes about them.

Please remember to include your own name and address and let us know if you would like the pictures returned.

We will be happy to receive prints, transparencies or pictures on disk or by e-mail to **editorial@fhguides.co.uk** All pictures should be forwarded by the middle of January 2009.

Thanks to everyone who sent in pictures of their pets and regret that we were unable to include all of them, pictures not included in this edition will be considered for use in the future.

See the following pages for this year's selection.

Send your Pet photo to: FHG Guides, Abbey Mill Business Centre, Seedhill, Paisley PA1 1TJ

BESSIE
tiptoes through the tulips.
Jennifer & Victor Gibbons,
High Peak, Derbyshire

HOLLY plays peek-a-boo.
Mrs J. Langton,
Bigbury-on-Sea, Devon

A sailor's life for me,
says NIKE.
Miss B. Robinson, Chatham, Kent

Bring on the party food,
say KELLY, LYNDI, BARNEY and OSCAR.
Mrs Sandie Stimson, Crowland, near Peterborough

SNOWY does a spot of sand hopping.
Anne & Gus Azzopardi, St Albans

PADDY enjoys a breath of sea air.
Sharon Symons, Bude, Cornwall

ELLIE'S
Springtime portrait.
Pru Coleman, Wolverhampton

JAKE communes with nature.
Mrs Valerie Stockton, Wolverhampton

PINKY "socks" it to 'em.
John Nilsen, Knightswood, Glasgow

DINO'S
cheesey grin.
Mrs P. Orchard, Chatham

A nice refreshing bath and a lovely warm towel – bliss, says JASPA.
Diana Woolley, Kettering, Northants

Wonder what the " walkies" are like around here, wonder POPPET and PADDY.
Mrs Judy Farnham, Skelmersdale

KELSEA
seeks some creature comfort.
Mrs Julie Davis, Dunstable

IZZY enjoys the joke.
Brian & Pauline Townsend

CAPTAIN in pensive mood.
Christine Remon, Dunstable

MERROW checks out the park.
Judy Zatonski

Yuck, what was in that sandwich, asks MISTY.
Mrs M. Bryan, Paisley

The sand sure gets between your toes, says JADE.
Julie Faulkner, Bexleyheath

Nothing wrong with *my* driving.
Yvonne Baker, Wolverhampton

What's that strange creature, asks POPPET.
Mrs J. Farnham, Skelmersdale

We're a couple of swells, say GEMMA and Bracken.
Mrs Olwen M. Ellam, Chippenham

Flowers just for you.
David Guiterman

FRED enjoying all the fun of the fair.
Yvonne Baker, Wolverhampton

Do you like my cool shades, asks JAKE.
Mrs Valerie Stockton, Wolverhampton

LENNOX proves he's got green paws.
Mrs P. Orchard, Chatham

Making new friends.
David Guiterman

ISLA and ROXY
– travelling companions.
Erin Gorman, Paisley

Ah, the sun at last,
says PEPPER.
Elaine Docherty, Barrhead

OZY going where no dog
has gone before.
Ian Pearson,
Nether Stowey, Somerset

There's nothing like a good gossip
over the garden fence, says POPPY.
Mrs B. Cade, Stirling

Find your own toy, says CHARLIE.
MaryJane & Ian Price,
Wirral, Merseyside

IF YOU LOVE DOGS YOU'LL LOVE YOUR DOG

BRITAIN'S BEST-SELLING DOG MAGAZINE
your dog
September 2008 £3.35
YOUR PROBLEMS SOLVED
20 pages of
DOG ANSWERS
• Road rage • My dog's bored • Leave my trousers alone! • Our neighbour is complaining
page 56
Walk this way
Stop that pulling on the lead!
Top of the classes
Everything you need to know about training school
Get active
Things to do with your dog
Game for anything
Beagle breed profile
From the heart
Understanding heart disease
Victoria's secrets
Tips from the star of 'It's Me Or The Dog'
Home truths
How to work and have a happy dog
DOG STUFF!
page 48
• New products • Tried & tested • Book reviews
OUT & ABOUT
page 86
• We test the UK's first dog activity trail in Yorkshire

MAGAZINE your dog MAGAZINE

Your Dog is Britain's **best-selling dog magazine,** a monthly read that's packed with tips and advice on how to get the best out of life with your pet.

Every issue contains in-depth features on your dog's health, behaviour and training, and looks at subjects such as how to pick the perfect puppy for your lifestyle.

Out & About

Discover ways to keep you and your dog fit, from a stroll in the wood to an energetic ramble.

Dog Answers

Twenty pages of your problems solved by our panel of experts — everything from training, health, behaviour, feeding, breeds, grooming, legal and homeopathy.

Dog Stuff!

All the latest product news plus long and short-term testing of everything from tough dog toys to wellies.

And lots, lots more...

Your Dog Magazine is available from your newsagent; price £3.35. Alternatively, why not take out a subscription? To find out more, contact the subscriptions hotline on tel. 01858 438854 and quote ref PW04.

A dog-friendly walk in...

Loch Lomond and The Trossachs

The first national park we are stopping off at on our dog-friendly tour of the UK is Loch Lomond and The Trossachs.

Balquhidder

This walk, which begins in Balquhidder, takes you along pine-scented forest paths where you will be able to enjoy fine views of the glen and surrounding scenery.
By Mary Welsh.

The lovely view of Loch Voil.

Views of the majestic Loch Lomond.

Pic: Loch Lomond and The Trossachs National Park Authority.

Fact file

Distance: 9km/ 5½ miles.
Time: 3 hours.
Map: Explorer 365.
Start/parking: In Balquhidder; grid ref: 536209.
Terrain: Good tracks throughout, may be muddy after rain.
Nearest town: Callander.
Refreshments: Kings House Hotel, Balquhidder; Monachyle Mhor, Balquhidder.
Public toilets: None en route.
Public transport: Contact Traveline, tel. 0870 608 2608.
Stiles: One.
Suitable for: All the family. Dogs should be on leads if there is livestock about.

These walks have been reproduced from Your Dog Magazine, Britain's best-selling dog magazine. Available from all good newsagents from the seventh of every month. Your Dog is priced at £3.35 and is packed with practical advice on every aspect of caring for and enjoying your pet. For more information, contact the editorial department on tel. 01780 766199; for subscription details contact tel. 01858 438854.

1 Wind left of the new church (built in 1853) to take a tree-lined gravelled track, directing you towards a waterfall. Beside you hurries the Kirkton Burn. Ignore the path to the right, which is your onward route, to walk to a footbridge from where you have a fine view of the delectable fall. Return to the path, you ignored earlier, now on your left, and signposted 'Creag an Tuirc and Kirkton Glen'. The pleasing path climbs uphill, through trees, to go over an easy stile, and then winds steadily through tall conifers. Watch out for the sign on the right directing you to Creag an Tuirc. After 0.5km go through a hurdle gate on the right, descend steps to cross a stream and climb up the other side. Ascend to a cairn and a seat on the top of a crag, with a lovely view of Loch Voil below.

2 Return from the crag and on through the hurdle. Continue, left, down the path to the main track, where you turn right along a way that leads through Kirkton Glen. Go past a track coming in on the left and then another on the right. Go ahead into the glen to walk through an area where young conifers have been planted. Stride on through a fine stand of Scots pine and carry on. Now that much of the forest has been felled it is possible to see the shape of the glen.

3 Follow the track to the head of the glen to reach a signpost. Bear right, still on the forestry track, and return down the glen. Because the track is at a higher altitude you are able to see the glen stretching down below you. About a mile along you have another fine view of Loch Voil. Follow the track as it winds right and joins your outward route. Turn left and follow back to Balquhidder church and the parking area.

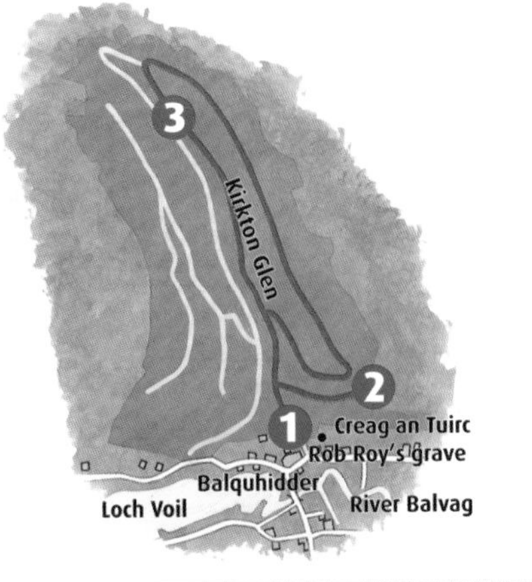

A dog-friendly walk in...
Snowdonia

Looking west over Cyfrwy towards the Mawddach Estuary, Cardigan Bay and the Lleyn Peninsula from the summit at Penygadair.

The national park of Snowdonia is famed for its spectacular mountain ranges and great ancient legends.

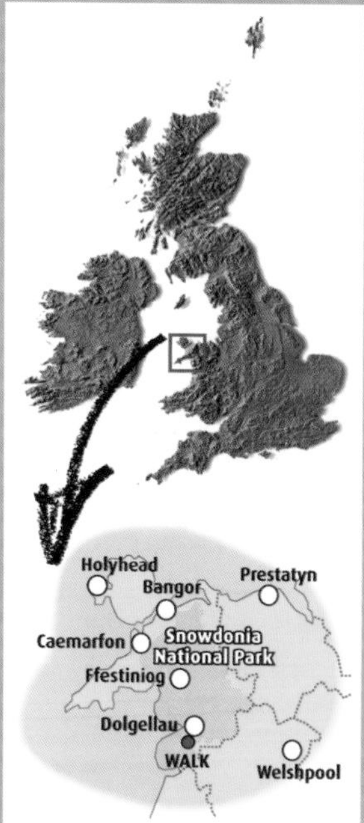

Cadair Idris

The five-peaked massif of Cadair Idris dominates the southern coastal reaches of Snowdonia National Park. Follow the pony track from Ty-Nant, the main footpath up the mountain from Dolgellau, to the summit at 2,927ft (893m) and back, your efforts rewarded by spectacular views in all directions.
By Evelyne Sansot.

Late afternoon over Cadair Idris.

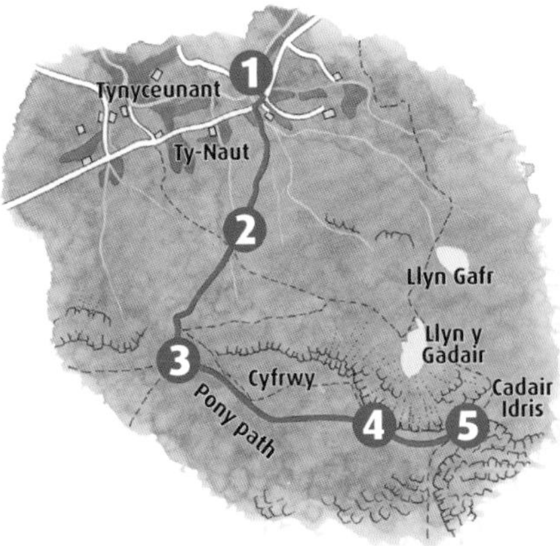

Your Dog Magazine is available from all good newsagents. For more information, contact the editorial department on tel. 01780 766199.

1 As you exit the car park, turn right on to the road. Ty-Nant Farm is across the field on your left, below the Cadair Idris Ridge with, from left to right, Mynydd Moel, Penygadair (the summit) and Cyfrwy (The Saddle). Turn left on to the access track to Ty-Nant Farm, go through a kissing gate to the right of the buildings and continue uphill through some woodland. Go right at a fork in front of a wall, as waymarked. After another kissing gate, bear right over a footbridge and continue along the fence on your right. The path then swings to the left as you leave the woods and you gain your first views over the valley on your right, with Carnedd Lwyd ahead and Cadair Idris on your left. Go through a metal gate and keep along the same rocky track as it veers slightly to the left then becomes a grassy path. You now catch sight of the Mawddach Estuary and Cardigan Bay on your right; Bardsey Island and the Lleyn Peninsula soon become visible too.

2 Keep following this path through two metal gates in total then steeply uphill in a zigzag, before it flattens.

3 Go through a gap at a wall junction and keep straight on, to then go through a gate (or over a ladder stile) and continue along the wire fence on your right. The path soon veers left to go up the western flank of The Saddle and you gain further views over Cardigan Bay south of the Dyfi Estuary and down the Dysynni Valley on your right. The path gets steeper and is marked by a series of cairns.

4 As you reach the top of the rise and finally catch sight of the summit at Penygadair ahead of you, make sure you keep your dog safely under control as you are standing at the top of the cliffs overlooking Llyn y Gadair. Turn right and follow the path round the edge of the cliff then up amid the boulders to scramble to the summit. There is a stone shelter just below the trig point pillar.

5 The safest route back is down the same pony path. Be sure to keep to the right-hand path from the summit though, as the left-hand path would take you down the south side of the mountain!

Fact file

Distance: 8 km (5 miles).
Time: Allow 5 hours.
Map: Explorer OL23 (Snowdonia, Cadair Idris area).
Start/parking: Pont Dyffrydan National Park Car Park, opposite Ty-nant Farm, 3 miles south west of Dolgellau; grid ref: SH697153.
Terrain: Good tracks and footpaths, rocky in places.
Nearest town: Dolgellau.
Refreshments: Tea rooms at Ty-nant Farm; Gwernan Lake Hotel (dog-friendly).
Public toilets: Public facilities at Ty-nant car park.
Public transport: Buses to Dolgellau. For more information, ring Bws Gwynedd or Traveline on tel. 0870 608 2608. Alternatively, visit www.gwynedd.gov.uk/bwsgwynedd or www.traveline.org.uk
Stiles: None.
Suitable for: Fit walkers and dogs.

A dog-friendly walk in... Dartmoor

Dartmoor has wild, dramatic vistas and colourful history steeped in folklore.

Lustleigh Cleave

This exploration of Lustleigh Cleave combines a fine ridge walk with a woodland and riverside ramble through a deep and sequestered valley, with a lovely boulder-strewn waterfall. The views over eastern Dartmoor, including Hound Tor and Haytor Rocks, are superb and there is a good deal of off-lead walking. We start and end at Lustleigh, one of Dartmoor's prettiest villages. By Robert Hesketh.

A Dartmoor mare and foal on Hunter's Tor.

There is plenty to see from Hunter's Tor.

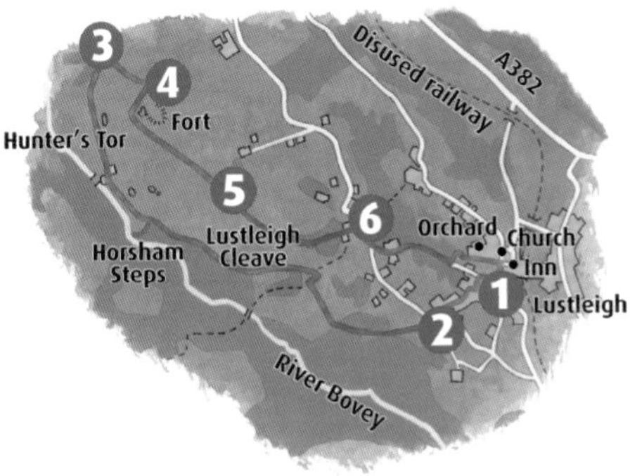

1 From Lustleigh's church, turn left. Follow the lane signed for Rudge. Cross the bridge and keep right when the lane forks. Turn first right at the chapel and walk uphill before turning left by Oakehurst on to the signed path. Follow this uphill past houses and gardens to a group of three stone and thatched houses. Turn left and then turn right at the T-junction. About 50m ahead, turn left on to the bridlepath for Lustleigh Cleave.

2 Continue ahead through Heaven's Gate. At the junction of paths, follow the bridle path ahead signed Manaton via Water. Bear right and uphill when the path forks. Continue uphill for Hammerslake at the next fingerpost. Turn left at the following fingerpost, signed Bridge (originally Foxworthy Bridge but the fingerpost has been damaged). Ignore the side turnings and then about 1.5km (1 mile) ahead divert left for 200m on the path for Horsham to see Horsham Steps, a beautiful boulder-strewn waterfall. Be careful of slippery moss, which grows thickly on trees and boulders in the clean, moist air of the Cleave. Return to the main path and turn left for Foxworthy. Pass behind the house and through a gate. Just beyond the converted barn take the path right signed Peck Farm.

3 When the path meets a concrete track turn right. Bypass Peck Farm, taking the signed public bridlepath through the gate to the right. Carry on to the top of the ridge. Hunter's Tor, a superb viewpoint, includes the eroded ramparts of the Iron Age fort — easily missed unless you look for them.

4 Follow the fine and clearly defined ridge path on to Harton Chest, a massive granite boulder, which can be climbed with care. Looking down nearly 500ft to the floor of the Cleave gives a dramatic impression of its size and steepness.

5 Entering woodland, littered with boulders, the path descends gently at first and then sharply. At the fingerpost, ignore the sign for Heaven's Gate and go straight ahead through the gate in front of you.

6 Turn right on to the metalled lane and first left after 250m. Follow the lane down past Ellimore Farm. At the bottom of the hill, take the signed public footpath left. Walk down through the woods, ignoring the first gated path on the left. Leave the wood by a gate and cross the brook via a wooden bridge. The large boulder in the centre of Lustleigh Orchard is surmounted by a stone seat, the May Queen's throne. Walk straight on through the orchard back to the start of the route at Lustleigh's Church.

Your Dog Magazine is available from all good newsagents. For more information, contact the editorial department on tel. 01780 766199.

Fact file

Distance: 8.5km (5 miles).
Time: Allow 3 hours.
Maps: Landranger 191, Explorer OL 28 or Harvey's Dartmoor.
Start/parking: Roadside parking in Lustleigh; grid reference SX785813.
Terrain: Footpaths, bridlespaths and lanes well-signed; some short but steep ascents and descents.
Nearest towns: Moretonhampstead and Bovey Tracey.
Refreshments: Both Primrose Cottage Tearooms (home-made cakes) and the Cleave Hotel (real ales and a good menu) in Lustleigh welcome dogs.
Public toilets: Lustleigh.
Public transport: Bus no. 178 from Newton Abbot to Moretonhampstead via Bovey Tracey (Monday to Saturday).
Stiles: None.
Suitable for: Anyone who is fairly fit.

A dog-friendly walk in...

The North York Moors National Pa

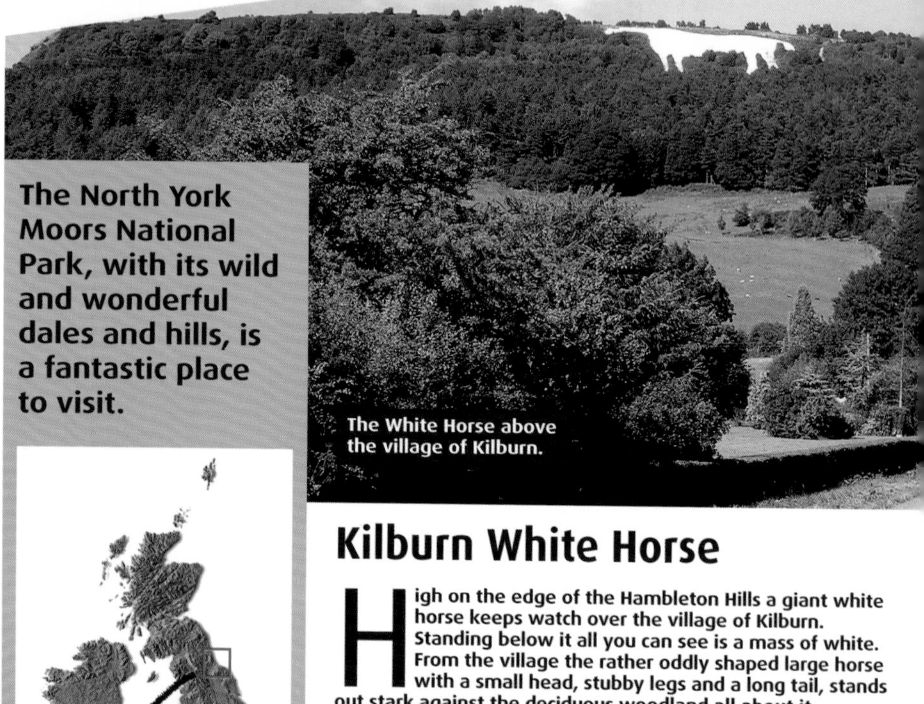

The White Horse above the village of Kilburn.

The North York Moors National Park, with its wild and wonderful dales and hills, is a fantastic place to visit.

Kilburn White Horse

High on the edge of the Hambleton Hills a giant white horse keeps watch over the village of Kilburn. Standing below it all you can see is a mass of white. From the village the rather oddly shaped large horse with a small head, stubby legs and a long tail, stands out stark against the deciduous woodland all about it. **By Mary Welsh.**

The church in Kilburn village.

1 From the car park at Sutton Bank visitor centre, with dogs on the lead, cross the main road, the A170, with care. Turn left along the signposted level footpath to walk along the edge of the escarpment. From here you can see the Vale of York with the Pennines as a backdrop, considered by James Herriot as the 'best view in Yorkshire'. To your left is Kilburn Moor Plantation. Carry on ahead along the delightful way, ignoring the path descending right.

2 Stroll on, now with the Yorkshire Gliding Club's airfield to your left.

The cottage of carpenter Robert Thompson.

Watch out for falling towlines as you go and keep to the path — gliders approach from any direction and are silent, so you will have no warning to get out of the way. Follow the path as it continues above the White Horse. When you reach the top of the tail, take the railed steps down the steep hillside to arrive in a small car park.

3 Here you have a choice. If you wish to visit Kilburn village on foot, join the narrow road (known locally as the Mare's Tail) and turn right to walk for a mile. In summer this can be quite busy but there are several verges you can walk on. Remember that you will have to return up the road (for a mile). To continue with the walk, if you decide not to visit Kilburn, turn right at the bottom of the steps (left through the car park if you have walked from Kilburn), go through the car park and then a gate on to a track into the forest. Where the track divides take the signposted right fork and follow the path below the limestone cliffs of Roulston Scar.

4 When the way forks again, take the right branch, known as the Thief's Highway, and strike steeply uphill through the fine woodland. At the top of the slope, join the path along the escarpment, turning left to walk your outward route.

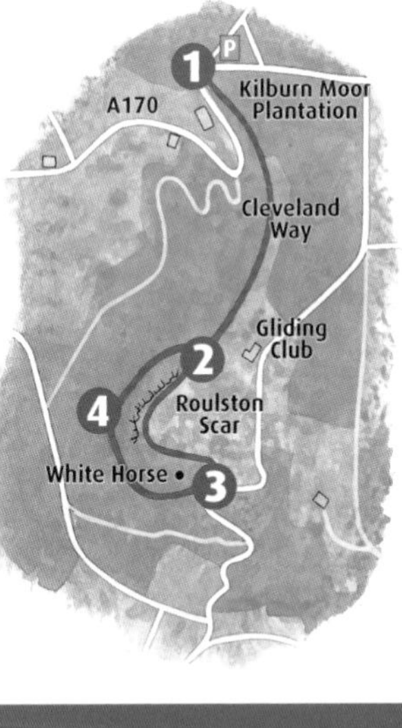

Your Dog Magazine is available from all good newsagents. For more information, contact the editorial department on tel. 01780 766199.

Fact file

Distance: 5km/3 miles or 8km/5 miles.
Time: 2 hours or 4 hours.
Map: OS Explorer OL26.
Start/parking: Sutton Bank national park centre; grid ref; 516831.
Terrain: Mostly on level paths and tracks with a steepish descent of many steps and steepish return ascent to the scarp edge.
Nearest towns: Thirsk and Helmsley.
Refreshments: Sutton Bank national park centre cafe and Kilburn village.
Public toilets: Sutton Bank centre.
Public transport: Moors Bus network. For information contact tel. 01845 597000.
Suitable for: All the family. Dogs on leads on road to Kilburn.

A dog-friendly walk in...

Northumberland National Park

Hadrian's Wall attracts thousands of visitors from all over the world.

Northumberland National Park contains parts of the magnificent Hadrian's Wall as well as simply breathtaking views and huge skies.

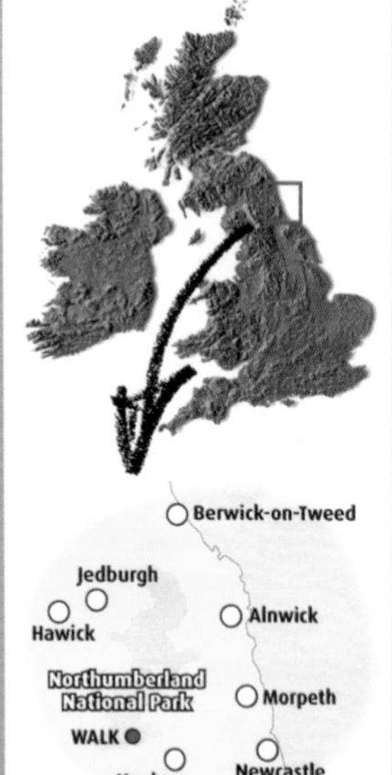

Hadrian's Wall and Vindolanda

Enjoy this splendid walk along Hadrian's Wall. Take your time on its ups and owns. Pause often to appreciate the vast landscape of rolling hills, heather-covered moors, valleys cut by rivers, huge skies and the dense forests of the Northumberland National Park.

By Mary Welsh.

The magnificent crags above Crag Lough.

Pic: The Countryside Agency.

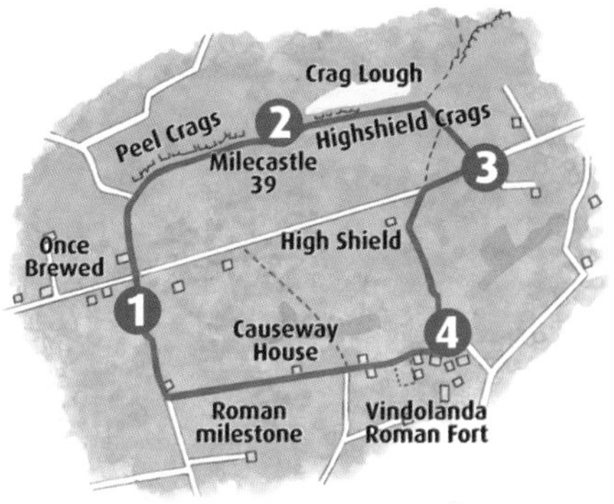

Your Dog Magazine is available from all good newsagents. For more information, contact the editorial department on tel. 01780 766199.

1 Turn left out of the Once Brewed National Park Visitor Centre car park and walk a few steps to the Military Road. Cross and walk uphill to a ladder stile on the right, just beyond a cottage. Walk half-left to the next stile and, beyond, follow the track half right to the foot of the stepped path that climbs steeply to a gap stile and then a ladder stile, on to Peel Crags. Carry on parallel with Hadrian's Wall on your left. After descending steps into the first 'nick', or cleft, in the next one you'll come upon the remains of Milecastle 39, 'Castle Nick'. Climb out of this cleft and go on the continuing roller-coaster way. Then descend a very long, steep flight of steps to the aptly named Sycamore Gap, which achieved fame as a location in the film 'Robin Hood: Prince of Thieves'.

2 Climb more steps out of this 'nick' in the Whin Sill ridge and carry on to Highshield Crags. Pass through Hadrian's Wall and walk on along the magnificent crags above Crag Lough. These are unfenced and there is an immense sheer drop to the lough, so dogs should be under close control. Enjoy the wonderful views as you go and then pass through lofty Scots pine on a descending path. Emerge from the trees, walk on for a short distance to take a stile on the right, and join a wide gravelled track. Turn right and descend to the Military Road once more.

3 Turn right and, using the verge, walk for less than a quarter of a mile to cross what can be a busy road at times to climb a signposted step stile into a hay meadow. Stroll the narrow path that bears steadily half-right to come to a stile which takes you into a small grassy patch beside a house, High Shield. A narrow path leads on to another stile. Descend a pasture to climb the next stile. Beyond, head on down the pathless pasture to reach the bottom-left corner beside woodland. Pass Chesterholm Roman milestone. Go over a stile on to a narrow lane.

4 Here go right and walk down the lane known as Stanegate, which means 'Stone Road', with Vindolanda Roman Fort to your left. There is an entrance fee and no dogs are allowed. Carry on along Stanegate Lane passing Causeway House. Stroll on to the end of the lane where there are the remains of another Roman milestone. Turn right and walk up the road to the car park. A few more steps up the road is the B-road, where you turn left for the Twice Brewed Inn.

Fact file

Distance: 7.4km/ 4½ miles.
Time: Allow 2 – 3 hours.
Map: Explorer OL43.
Start/parking: Car park at Once Brewed Visitor Centre; grid reference 754668, just off the B6318.
Terrain: Good paths but often steep both up and down along the Wall. Field paths are waymarked. Quiet road walking.
Nearest towns: Haltwhistle and Hexham.
Refreshments: Twice Brewed Inn almost next to the visitor centre or Milecastle Inn, 1½ miles west along the B-road.
Public toilets: At the visitor centre.
Public transport: For Hadrian's Wall bus AD122. For other services contact Traveline, tel. 0870 608 2608 or contact Tyne Valley Line, tel. 0845 748 4950.
Stiles: Several — most easy although some dogs might need help.
Suitable for: All the family.

A dog-friendly walk in... The Lake District

The Lake District has high mountains, sweeping views, wonderful woodlands and a myriad of becks and fine lakes.

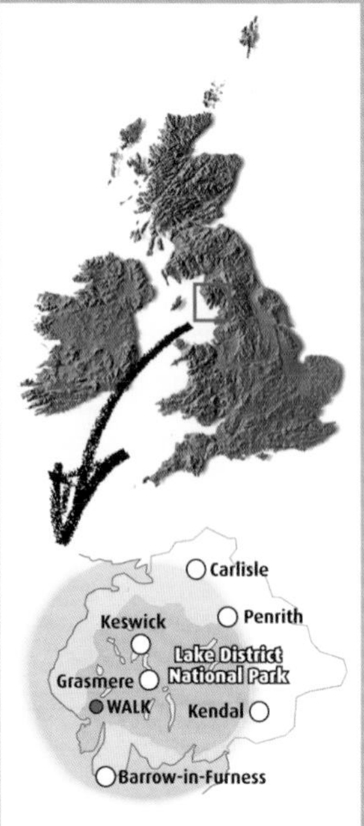

Broughton-in-Furness

In 1859 Coniston village was linked by rail to the main west coast line. This line enabled slate quarried in the fells to be transported. The trains also carried goods, tourists and schoolchildren. In the late 1960s the nine-mile line was closed. In 2003, the national park resurfaced and refurbished the track, and the new trail was officially opened and is a very popular route with walkers. **By Mary Welsh.**

The second lake beside the railway track.

View from the High Cross Inn.

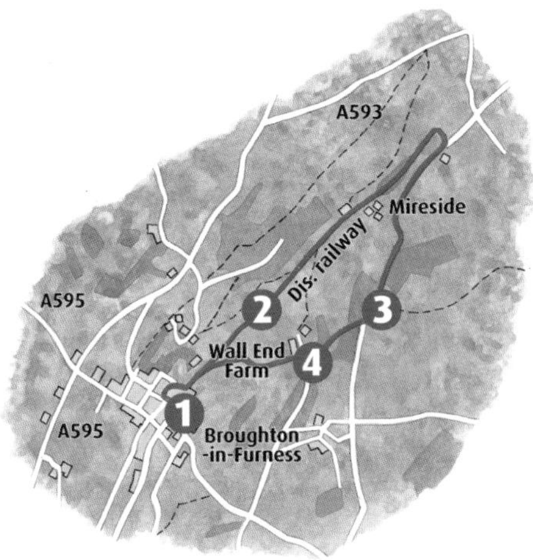

Your Dog Magazine is available from all good newsagents. For more information, contact the editorial department on tel. 01780 766199.

1 Leave Broughton's village square in the direction of the signed public toilets. Follow the track as it bends right to join the trackbed of the railway. Here, wind left, go round the barrier and dogs can start their 1¼ miles of freedom. Walk left, through the deep cutting. Just before the old bridge over the line, on the left, is the first of the two lakes. Go on under the bridge and up the short sloping path, on the left, to a seat overlooking the beautiful second lake.

2 Stroll the lovely way to cross a fine wooden bridge spanning a farm track. Carry on, soon to pass through another cutting shaded by tall forest trees, until you reach a fence supporting a 'no path' sign. Here bear right to descend through two gates on to Five Arches Road, named after a demolished bridge that carried the old railway line. Walk right to pass Mireside Farm and wind on along the narrow quiet road, through pastures and mixed woodland to come to a signposted bridleway on your right.

3 Pass between small plantations of firs, where dogs can have more freedom and then ascend the continuing steepish track that climbs through deciduous woodland to where it divides. Take the short right fork to the side of the access lane to Wall End Farm, which you cross.

4 Climb the stile, ascend a little slope and then descend the ongoing path over rough pasture, where there might be sheep or deer. This path keeps parallel with the wall on your right but keepng a short distance away from it. Press on until you can take the easy to miss gap stile in the wall, a 'fat man's agony'— two stone slabs which you have to squeeze between and that stout dogs may find difficult. Walk ahead beside another wall, also on your right, and go through the next gap stile or use the gate to its left, which is usually open. Walk ahead to the fenced edge of the railway cutting, high above where you walked earlier. Turn left and walk on through a gateless gap and on again to a step stile in the right corner on to the railway track. Cross and walk up the track ahead. Wind left to return to the village square.

Fact file

Distance: 6.5km (4 miles).
Time: 2 – 3 hours.
Map: OS Explorer OL6.
Start/parking: Broughton-in-Furness Square, just off the A595.
Terrain: Level, easy walking along railway track; a little quiet road walking; the track from Five Arches Road to the access track at the top of slope can be muddy in the dip.
Nearest town: Ulverston, Millom.
Refreshments: In Broughton there is a good choice of inns and cafes, and one restaurant, all offering excellent food.
Public toilets: Just off the village square.
Public transport: Stagecoach bus service from Millom and Ulverston. For details, contact Traveline, tel. 0870 608 2608.
Suitable for: All the family.

A dog-friendly walk in...

The South Downs

The undulating green landscape of the downs.

The stunning South Downs, with its chalk hills that afford beautiful views of the coast and nearby beaches, is a must for dogs and their owners.

Houghton Forest

This is very much a walk for the nature lover. There are no picture postcard villages or ancient ruins or other places to explore — just wide open spaces and dappled woodland paths. Leave your troubles at home and enjoy being at one with nature.

By Sylvie Dobson.

In summer poppies adorn the fields around Houghton Forest.

Pic: Countryside Agency/John Tyler SDJC.

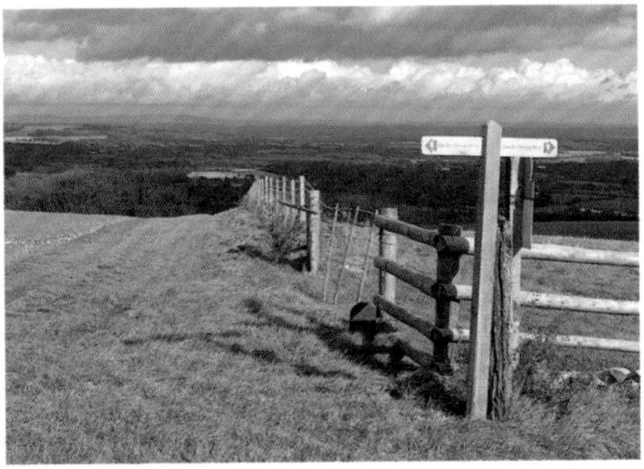

The view from the South Downs Way.

1 Go through the metal gate immediately opposite the car park entrance and head on into the forest. You should look for a side path on the right that will lead you up through the trees to a crossing track. Go left and continue in a clockwise direction around a field.

2 The path ascends quite gently and soon joins a much wider track. Although the walk continues to the left you may like to go right for a short way for some super views over the River Arun towards Amberley. The path you have joined is the South Downs Way and it offers some delightfully easy walking. When you notice the path starting to descend you should get good views down the Scarp to the villages of Bignor and Burton. Keep descending until you pass a trio of barns on your right and come to a junction with paths seeming to go in all directions. Go left as though staying on the South Downs Way but in just a few paces take the narrower track again on the left.

3 Ahead would have taken you to Bignor Hill, a superb viewpoint but requiring quite a demanding climb so perhaps saved for another day. You still face a gentle climb as the path takes you through a gate and on to open pasture. Keep ahead to a crossing track and then go across a field aiming for the woods straight ahead. There may be a crop in this field but the path should be clearly defined.

4 Once into the shelter of the trees the path appears to fork; go left and then stay on this main track until you eventually join a T-junction. The finger post has a sign showing that you have joined the Monarchs Way, another long distance path. Follow it to the left and enjoy a delightful stroll through mainly deciduous woodland. There are various side paths and turnings but by following the Monarchs Way signs navigating couldn't be easier. Having gone over a wide stony crossing track bear right and walk ahead to the car park.

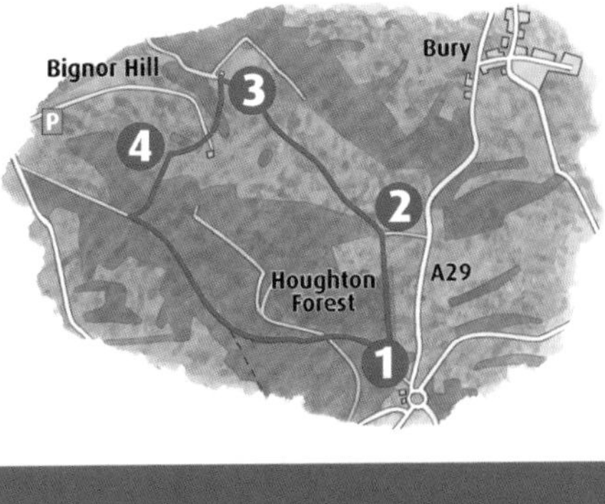

Your Dog Magazine is available from all good newsagents. For more information, contact the editorial department on tel. 01780 766199.

Fact file

Distance: 6.7km (4¼ miles).
Time: About 2 hours.
Map: OS Explorer121, Arundel and Pulborough.
Start/parking: Whiteways Lodge car park on the junction of the A29 and A284 about 2 miles north of Arundel.
Terrain: Undulating rather than strenuous. Paths are well defined and the route easy to follow.
Nearest town: Arundel.
Refreshments: There is a cafe by the car park. Alternatively there is a wide choice in Arundel or the George and Dragon in Houghton.
Public toilets: At the car park.
Public transport: Contact Traveline, tel. 0870 608 2608.
Stiles: None
Suitable for: The whole family. Dogs can be let off the lead apart from the stretch between the three barns and re-entering the forest.

England and Wales • Counties

1. Plymouth
2. Torbay
3. Poole
4. Bournemouth
5. Southampton
6. Portsmouth
7. Brighton & Hove
8. Medway
9. Thurrock
10. Southend
11. Slough
12. Windsor & Maidenhead
13. Bracknell Forest
14. Wokingham
15. Reading
16. West Berkshire
17. Swindon
18. Bath & Northeast Somerset
19. North Somerset
20. Bristol
21. South Gloucestershire
22. Luton
23. Milton Keynes
24. Peterborough
25. Leicester
26. Nottingham
27. Derby
28. Telford & Wrekin
29. Stoke-on-Trent
30. Warrington
31. Halton
32. Merseyside
33. Blackburn with Darwen
34. Blackpool
35. N.E. Lincolnshire
36. North Lincolnshire
37. Kingston-upon-Hull
38. York
39. Redcar & Cleveland
40. Middlesborough
41. Stockton-on-Tees
42. Darlington
43. Hartlepool

Hoseasons
bring your best friend
Over 200 pet-friendly countryside & seaside locations in the best areas of Britain. Peaceful, stylish lodges & lively holiday parks – some with pools, bars and restaurants.
Lowest Price Guaranteed.
0844 847 1103 ref H1935
hoseasons.co.uk
feel free

People-friendly Cottages for Pets!

Lovely locations with superb walks in some of England's most picturesque countryside. From Windsor to the Welsh Borders, with lots to choose from in the Cotswolds and Shakespeare's Country.

Small, friendly company with personal knowledge of the area - why not tell US what your pet likes and we'll do our best for him.....and you!!

Cottage in the Country
Cottage Holidays

e-mail: enquiries@cottageinthecountry.co.uk • www.cottageinthecountry.co.uk
Tel: 01608 646 833 • Fax: 01608 646844

www.classic.co.uk

classic cottages

Featuring 600 hand selected coastal and country holiday homes throughout the West Country

01326 565 555

Visit the FHG website

www.holidayguides.com

for details of the wide choice of accommodation featured in the full range of FHG titles

HOSEASONS. Over 200 pet-friendly countryside and seaside locations in the best areas of Britain. Peaceful, stylish lodges and lively holiday parks, some with pools, bars and restaurants. Lowest price guaranteed. Call 0844 847 1103 Quote H1935 or book on-line.
website: www.hoseasons.co.uk

COTTAGE IN THE COUNTRY COTTAGE HOLIDAYS (01608 646833; Fax: 01608 646844). Lovely locations with superb walks in some of England's most picturesque countryside. We'll do our best to find the right place for you to call 'home'!
e-mail: enquiries@cottageinthecountry.co.uk website: www.cottageinthecountry.co.uk

CLASSIC COTTAGES (01326 565 555). Featuring 600 hand selected coastal and country holiday homes throughout the West Country.
website: www.classic.co.uk

FARM & COTTAGE HOLIDAYS (01237 459897). Over 850 of the finest selection of holiday cottages throughout Devon, Cornwall, Dorset and Somerset in superb rural and coastal locations.
website: www.holidaycottages.co.uk

THE INDEPENDENT TRAVELLER, FORD COTTAGE, THORVERTON, EXETER EX5 5NT (01392 860807 Fax: 01392 860552). For a wide choice of cottages and apartments throughout England, Scotland & the Isles. Pets welcome in many properties. Quality Cottages in coastal, country and mountain location. Property finding service.
e-mail: help@gowithit.co.uk website: www.gowithit.co.uk

THE FOUR SEASONS HOTEL, ST FILLANS PH6 2NF (01764 685333). Ideal holiday venue for pets and their owners. Spectacular Highland scenery, walking, fishing, watersports. Wonderful food. Full details on request. STB ★★★ Hotel, AA ★★★ and 2 Red Rosettes, Which? Hotel Guide, Johansens, Best Loved Hotels. [ ]
e-mail: sham@thefourseasonshotel.co.uk website: www.thefourseasonshotel.co.uk

DALES HOLIDAY COTTAGES. Over 500 personally inspected cottages in sublime locations anywhere from the Yorkshire Dales to the Highlands of Scotland. For couples, groups and families. Full of character, near great walks and country pubs, just right for pets. Call 0870 909 9500 or visit our website.
website: www.dalesholcot.com

'QUALITY COTTAGES', CERBID, SOLVA, HAVERFORDWEST, PEMBROKESHIRE SA62 6YE (01348 837871). Cottages set in all coastal areas, enjoy unashamed luxury, highest residential standards. Log fires. Linen supplied. Pets welcome free. [pw!]
website: www.qualitycottages.co.uk

Go BLUE RIBAND for quality inexpensive self-catering holidays where your dog is welcome – choice of locations all in the borough of Great Yarmouth. Detached 3 bedroom bungalows, seafront bungalows, detached Sea-Dell chalets and modern sea front caravans. Free colour brochure: DON WITHERIDGE, BLUE RIBAND HOUSE, PARKLANDS, HEMSBY, GREAT YARMOUTH NR29 4HA (01493 730445). [pw! First pet free when booking through Pets Welcome!, 2nd pet £10 per week].
website: www.BlueRibandHolidays.co.uk

BLUE BALL INN (formerly The Exmoor Sandpiper Inn), COUNTISBURY, LYNMOUTH EX35 6NE (01598 741263). Romantic coaching inn on Exmoor. 16 en suite bedrooms, extensive menus with daily specials, good wines. Horse riding, walking. No charge for dogs. [ ]
website: www.BlueBallinn.com or www.exmoorsandpiper.com

DALES HOLIDAY COTTAGES. Over 500 personally inspected cottages in sublime locations anywhere from the Yorkshire Dales to the Highlands of Scotland. For couples, groups and families. Full of character, near great walks and country pubs, just right for pets. Call 0870 909 9500 or visit our website.
website: www.dalesholcot.com

THE MANOR HOUSE HOTEL, STUDLAND BAY BH19 3AU (01929 450288; Fax: 01929 452255). National Trust hotel set in 20 acres on cliffs overlooking Studland Bay. Superb food and accommodation. Log fires and four-posters.Tennis, horse-riding, golf and walking. [Pets £5 per night]
e-mail: info@themanorhousehotel.com website: www.themanorhousehotel.com

Pet-friendly
holidays in
Cornwall
Fishing Lakes
Farm Animals
Swimming Pool
Hot Tubs
Call for your FREE colour brochure
Tel: 01726 882540
Luxury Lodge, Caravan and Bungalow accommodation
Motorhome, Tourer and Tent pitches
Trencreek Farm
country holiday park
www.surfbayholidays.co.uk
Hewas Water, St Austell, Cornwall

Cornish Seaview Cottages
14 gorgeous holiday properties on the North Cornish coast.
Sleeping from 2 – 20.
All our properties are in fantastic locations with great views. They are ideal for walking the coastal paths and accessing the local beaches. Pets are welcome at most and we pride ourselves on our personal service and welcome.
The houses are tastefully furnished and are equipped to a high standard with all the comforts required for a relaxing holiday. All have central heating, dishwashers and washing machines.
For full information with photographs and virtual tours please visit our own website
www.cornishseaviewcottages.co.uk
Tel: 01428 723819 • e-mail: enquiries@cornishseaviewcottages.co.uk
We look forward to welcoming you

Classy Cottages
2 cottages just feet from beach in Polperro + 3 other coastal cottages.
Out of season all cottages priced for 2 people. Cottages sleep 2-16.
Access to INDOOR POOL, well equipped GYM and TENNIS COURTS
Very high quality cottages with open log fires. Pets very welcome.
Please contact FIONA and MARTIN NICOLLE on 01720 423000

Cornish Traditional Cottages

Quality Holidays at Competitive Prices

A fine selection of cottages and houses throughout Cornwall

Pets welcome in many.

Tel: 01208 821666
www.corncott.com

Toad Hall Cottages

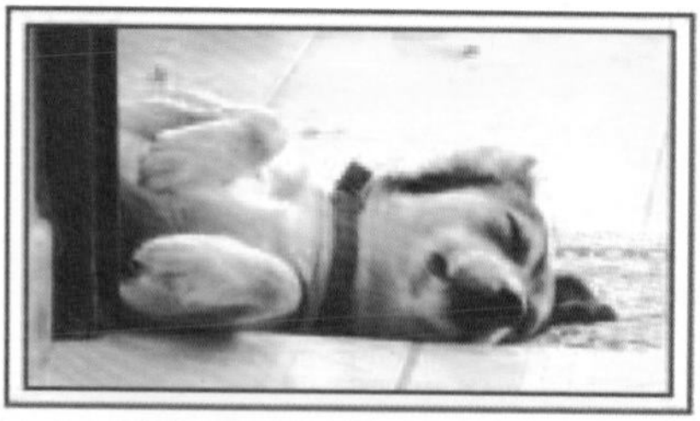

Cottage Holidays for laid back dogs.

300 quality waterside & rural properties in beautiful locations.

People welcome too!

For our fabulous fully detailed brochure

telephone 01548 853089 (24 hours)
www.toadhallcottages.co.uk

Bodmin, Bodmin Moor

St Breward, Bodmin, Cornwall PL30 4LZ

Tel: 01208 850277 / 850617

Fax: 01208 850915

Penrose Burden Holiday Cottages

Set in an area of outstanding natural beauty, sits 'Penrose Burden' surrounded by its 250 acres with breathtaking views overlooking the protected Camel Valley, on the edge of Bodmin Moor. Penrose Burden is a settlement of attractive stone cottages, varying in size, catering for two to seven persons, that have been beautifully converted into holiday homes. Also nestling beside Wenford Bridge are two riverside character cottages, idyllic for the free estate salmon and trout fishing!

NEW IN 2002: "TOAD HALL" a creative concept for today's open-plan living. All bedrooms en suite, enjoy 'patio dining' perched among stunning views, in your own grounds. With the ever-changing seasons, this all year round accommodation is geared to meet all seasonal requirements, including wood burners. All accommodation is suitable for disabled guests.

Paradise for dogs and their owners! Situated midway between north and south coasts, easy access to the new 'Eden Project', 'The Lost Gardens' and 'National Trust' properties. Why not walk or cycle the 'Camel Trail' and end up at "Rick Stein's"? Penrose Burden has received much acclaim including being featured on television and in the national press!

www.penroseburden.co.uk

Close to The Eden Project

Darrynane Cottages

Darrynane, St Breward, Bodmin Moor PL30 4LZ

Tel/Fax: 01208 850885

www.darrynane.com • enquiries@darrynane.co.uk

3 fabulous detached cottages all with private, gated gardens. Situated in a unique moorland valley, with oak woods, waterfalls and the river. The cottages provide a homely base for walking, relaxing or touring Cornwall. Eden Project and Camel Trail close by. Woodburning stoves, four-poster beds. Open all year.

★★★ SELF CATERING

HENWOOD BARNS HOLIDAY COTTAGES

Three stone barns set around original courtyard on the edge of Bodmin Moor, with stunning views. Tranquil, village location, horse riding two minutes' walk. Woodburning stoves; sleep 2/5; within easy reach of North Cornwall and Devon.

HENWOOD, LISKEARD PL14 5BP • 01579 363576/07956 864263

e-mail: henwoodbarns@tiscali.co.uk • www.henwoodbarns.co.uk

FREE or REDUCED RATE entry to Holiday Visits and Attractions – see our **READERS' OFFER VOUCHERS** on pages 433-440

RAC SELECTED SITE

Hedley Wood Caravan & Camping Park

Bridgerule (Near Bude), Holsworthy, Devon EX22 7ED

Tel: 01288 381404 • Fax: 01288 382011

AA

16 acre woodland family-run site with outstanding views, where you can enjoy a totally relaxing holiday with a laid-back atmosphere, sheltered and open camping areas. Just 10 minutes' drive from the beaches, golf courses, riding stables and shops.

On site facilities include: Children's Adventure Areas, Bar, Clubroom, Shop, Laundry, Meals and all amenities. Free Hot Showers/Water. **Nice dogs/pets are very welcome. Daily kennelling facility. Dog walks/nature trail.**

Static caravans for hire. Caravan storage available. **Open all year.**

Visit our website: www.hedleywood.co.uk or write or phone for comprehensive brochure

Give your pet the holiday it deserves

Crackington Haven, Bude, Cornwall

Quality Cornish Cottages sleeping from 1 to 8, at a price you can afford.
Situated in peaceful wooded valley leading to the beach.
Perfect location for walking, touring or just relaxing.
14 acres of fields/woodlands to exercise your dog.

website: www.mineshop.co.uk

or phone Charlie or Jane on **01840 230338**

We are proud that all our properties are inspected by, and featured in,

The Good Holiday Cottage Guide

Five 18th Century converted barns, beamed ceilings, log fires and secluded rural setting. Ideal touring base. Five miles to coast at Crackington Haven. Sleep 2/6. Pets welcome. Open all year. From £90 short breaks, £165 per week.

Lorraine Harrison, Trenannick Cottages, Warbstow, Launceston, Cornwall PL15 8RP • Tel: 01566 781443
e-mail: trenannick-1@tiscali.co.uk • www.trenannickcottages.co.uk

FHG Guides

publish a large range of well-known accommodation guides.
We will be happy to send you details or you can use the order form at the back of this book.

Cawsand

Pet-friendly hotel set in 4 acres of Cornish countryside

Wringford Down

Hat Lane, Cawsand,
Cornwall PL10 1LE
Tel: 01752 822287

AA ★★★ Guest Accommodation

accommodation@wringforddown.co.uk • www.wringforddown.co.uk

Located on the Rame peninsula in an Area of Outstanding Natural Beauty with tiny Cornish fishing villages, dramatic cliff top walks and secluded sandy bays.

- 11 suites, some within main building and others in adjacent chalets. All have private bathrooms.
- Well stocked bar, and restaurant serving excellent home-cooked food.
- Pets are allowed in several of the suites, including our 3 bedroom self-catering cottage.
- Wringford is an ideal base for walking with dogs, being on the edge of the Mount Edgecumbe Country Park and the South West Coast Path.
- Indoor pool kept at a nicely warm 29 deg C. The pool is open from just before Easter until just after the October half term break.
- Television lounge and a playroom with books, board games and a piano.
- Courtyard room with a pool table and an adults-only room off the bar with a bar billiards table and dartboard.

THE LISCAWN

AA ★★★★ Guest Accommodation

AA ★★★★ Guest Accommodation

A 14th Century Country Inn

Crafthole, Near Torpoint, Cornwall PL11 3BD • Tel: 01503 230863

e-mail: enquiries@liscawn.co.uk • www.liscawn.co.uk

Charming, family-run 14th Century Inn in 'The Forgotten Corner of Cornwall'.
A few minutes' walk from the Cornish Coastal Path.

En suite 4* accommodation with colour TV and
coffee & tea making facilities in every room.

Self-Catering Suites available.

Family and Pets welcome.

Fully licensed Bar with cask ale. Bar meals available.
Extensive grounds and beer garden with beautiful views over to Dartmoor.

Cornwall Holiday Cottages • Crantock & Feock

★★★/★★★★ Self-Catering

Luxury cottages, some with spectacular sea views, we have period and modern properties, some with log burners or open fires. Sleeping from 2-8 people in great comfort. All equipped to a very high standard. All have gardens and are within easy reach of a beach. Self Catering. Dogs, where accepted, £25 pw each.

Cornwall Holiday Cottages, PO Box 24, Truro TR1 9AG

Tel: 0845 226 5507 • e-mail: rentals@cornwall-cottages.biz • www.cornwall-cottages.biz

Crantock Bay Hotel a very special place, all year round...

Award-winning hotel AA ★★★

Crantock Bay Hotel is superbly located for a holiday with your dogs. Our gardens lead direct to the Cornish coastal path and within 10 minutes walk of the 'dogs welcome' beaches of Polly Joke and Crantock Bay. Facilities include: comfortable bedrooms - many with sea views, a quality restaurant, indoor pool, spa bath, gym and tennis court. NEW 'Thalgo' Beauty Spa.

Crantock Bay Hotel
West Pentire, Crantock, Cornwall TR8 5SE

Tel: (01637) 830229 Fax: (01637) 831111
Email: stay@crantockbayhotel.co.uk
www.crantockbayhotel.co.uk

CREEKSIDE HOLIDAY HOUSES

Spacious houses sleep 2/4/6/8. Peaceful, picturesque water's edge hamlet. Boating facilities. Use of boat. Own quay, beach. Secluded gardens. Near Pandora Inn. Friday bookings. Dogs welcome.

PETER WATSON, CREEKSIDE HOLIDAY HOUSES, RESTRONGUET, FALMOUTH TR11 5ST • 01326 372722 **www.creeksideholidayhouses.co.uk**

Falmouth, Fowey (near)

Tudor Court

55 Melvill Road, Falmouth TR11 4DF

Strikingly stylish, mock-Tudor family-run guest house, in award-winning gardens. Comfortable, friendly, non-smoking accommodation, a short walk from town and beaches. Sea view rooms.

Business or pleasure, short or long stay, a warm welcome awaits you.

Sue & Dick Barrett • 01326 312807

enquiries@tudorcourthotel.com

www.tudorcourthotel.com

Open all year incl. Christmas

£32- £40ppn

Creekside Cottages

offer a fine selection of individual water's edge, village and rural cottages, sleeping from 2-10, situated around the creeks of the Carrick Roads, near Falmouth, South Cornwall. Set in enchanting and picturesque positions, with many of the cottages offering panoramic creek views. Perfect locations for family holidays, all close to superb beaches, extensive sailing and boating facilities, Cornish gardens and excellent walks. The majority of the cottages are available throughout the year, and all offer peaceful, comfortable and fully equipped accommodation; most have open fires. Dogs welcome.

Just come and relax

For a colour brochure please phone
01326 375972
www.creeksidecottages.co.uk

Penmorvah Manor Hotel and Courtyard Cottages

Falmouth, Cornwall TR11 5ED

- 3 Star Country House Hotel and Self Catering Courtyard Cottages
- Situated in 6 acres of mature gardens and woodland
- Ideal for visiting Cornwall's superb gardens
- Close to Falmouth and Coastal Paths • Well-behaved dogs welcome
- Ground floor bedrooms for easy pet access • Ample car parking

Tel: 01326 250277 • Fax: 01326 250509

e-mail: reception@penmorvah.co.uk

www.penmorvah.co.uk

LANCROW BARN

www.foweyvacations.com
tel: 01726 814263
sarahfurniss@aol.com

Quality barn conversion close to sea with spectacular coastal and countryside views. Furnished to a high standard with Amdega Conservatory and vast open plan sitting room. Well equipped kitchen. 3 en suite bedrooms. Central heating. Sky+ and flat screen TVs. Large enclosed garden with BBQ. Pets welcome. Good walks from property. Close to harbour town of Fowey and few minutes' drive from The Eden Project.

Prices from £650 to £1000.

The Old Ferry Inn

Why not bring your dog for its well deserved holiday to the family-run Old Ferry Inn, close to the edge of the beautiful River Fowey. There are many varied walks from country and riverside to breathtaking views along the Cornwall Coastal Path. The 400-year-old hotel has an excellent à la carte restaurant for evening meals and a comprehensive bar menu for lunch and evening. The Inn has 12 letting rooms with tea and coffee making facilities, colour TV and telephone, most rooms being en suite, some with views of the Fowey river.

Prices are from £85-£120 per night for two people sharing.

Bodinnick-by-Fowey PL23 1LX

Tel: (01726) 870237 • Fax: (01726) 870116

www.oldferryinn.com • e-mail: royce972@aol.com

Two self-contained apartments situated in detached house surrounded by large garden. Both have sea views, double glazing, central heating and are fully furnished. 600 yards from safe, clean, sandy beach, harbour and shops. Superb coastal walks. Ideally located for exploring Cornwall. ***Short breaks available. Sleep 2-4 persons. Pets welcome. Children welcome. Open all year***

Mrs S. Pike, Tregillan, Trewollock Lane, Gorran Haven, St Austell PL26 6NT Tel: 01726 842452 • ★★-★★★ Self Catering
e-mail: tregillanapartment@tiscali.co.uk • www.tregillanapartments.co.uk

---

BOSCREGE
CARAVAN & CAMPING PARK

- ★ Special out of season offers
- ★ Award winning quiet family park close to local beaches and attractions with no bar or clubs

For Brochure Telephone: 01736 762231

- ★ Static caravans available for holidays
- ★ Touring caravans
- ★ Tents & motor homes
- ★ Free showers
- ★ Microwave facilities
- ★ Games room
- ★ Child's play area
- ★ Laundry
- ★ Pets welcome

www.caravanparkcornwall.com
enquiries@caravanparkcornwall.com

---

trevornick
TREVORNICK HOLIDAY PARK, TREVORNICK COTTAGES AND HOLYWELL BAY GOLF CLUB

We welcome dog owners at Trevornick and have a designated dog walking field and dog-friendly pitches. We are only a very short walk away from Cubert Common and the spectacular North Cornwall Coastal Path. Beautiful 5-star graded family Holiday Park overlooking the superb Holywell Bay beach, 5 miles from Newquay. We only accept families and couples. We provide a full programme of free entertainment and a children's club. Superb facilities including club, bar, grill, takeaway, heated outdoor pool, supermarket, hire shop, launderette, play area, 3 coarse fishing ponds and more. Large level pitches, electric hook-ups, superpitches and Eurotents (ready erected, fully equipped six-berth tents with TV, microwave etc). We introduced a limited allocation of dog-friendly Eurotents in 2008. Our 4-Star Trevornick Cottages are also dog-friendly. Also on site are the 18-hole Par 3 links golf course and 18-hole pitch-and-putt course, providing lots of fun for all the family. Well behaved dogs are welcome too.
Everything provided for a fabulous family holiday all in one location. For further information please contact:

TREVORNICK HOLIDAY PARK, HOLYWELL BAY, CORNWALL TR8 5PW

www.trevornick.co.uk
www.trevornickcottages.co.uk
www.holywellbay.co.uk
www.holywellgolf.co.uk

Tel: 01637 830531 • Reservations: (local rate): 0845 345 5531 • e-mail: bookings@trevornick.co.uk

Liskeard

CUTKIVE WOOD HOLIDAY LODGES

Nestling in the heart of a peaceful family-owned country estate are six well-equipped comfortable cedar-clad lodges. Set on the edge of ancient bluebell woods with lovely rural views, you can relax and enjoy yourself in this tranquil and idyllic setting. Help with the animals, explore the woods and fields, fun play area. So much for everyone to see and do – memorable beaches, wonderful coasts, walk the moors, inspiring gardens and Eden, theme attractions, historic gems. Dogs welcome. Ideally situated to enjoy coast and country holidays whatever the time of year.

St Ive, Liskeard, Cornwall PL14 3ND • Tel: 01579 362216
www.cutkivewood.co.uk • e-mail: holidays@cutkivewood.co.uk

Caradon Country Cottages in magnificent countryside

between Bodmin Moor and Looe. Ideal for exploring Devon and Cornwall, Eden Project, coast and countryside. Central heating and log burners for cosy Winter Breaks. 5-acre grounds. Every comfort for you and your pets.

e-mail: celia@caradoncottages.co.uk
East Taphouse, Liskeard, Cornwall PL14 4NH

Butterdon Mill Holiday Homes

Idyllic rural site set in 2.5 acres of mature gardens. Two-bedroom detached bungalows sleeping up to six. Games barn and children's play areas. Ideal for touring coasts and moors of Cornwall and Devon. Located 3 miles from Liskeard, 8 miles from Looe. Discounts for Senior Citizens/couples Sept to June. PETS WELCOME. Brochure available.

Butterdon Mill Holiday Homes, Merrymeet, Liskeard, Cornwall PL14 3LS
Tel: 01579 342636 **e-mail: butterdonmill@btconnect.com**

Hayloft Courtyard Cottages, Menheniot, Liskeard A warm welcome and Cornish Cream Tea await your arrival at our family-run cottages. Lovingly converted from original stone barns and equipped to a high standard with many home-from-home comforts including beautiful new jacuzzi bathrooms in most cottages. An excellent touring base - only a short drive to Looe and Polperro. The Coastal Path, moors and dog-friendly beaches are all nearby. Restaurant on-site offering popular meal delivery service. Children's play area. Short breaks available.

www.hayloftcourtyardcottages.com Michele & Steve Hore • 01503 240879 • e-mail: courtyardcottage@btconnect.com

Boturnell Barns Cornwall

Really dog friendly self catering accommodation Set in 25 acres, no limit on number of pets, Dog crèche

Tel 01579 320880 website: www.dogs-holiday.co.uk e-mail sue@dogs-holiday.co.uk

Hopsland Cottages, Commonmoor, Liskeard PL14 6EJ
Tel & Fax: 01579 344480. A beautiful barn on our farm which has been converted into 3 well-equipped self-catering cottages (all with DVD), which sleep between 4 and 6 persons. Beautiful views and very peaceful. Own exercise fields for dogs, or just 150 yards from Bodmin Moor, with miles of open space. Many ancient monuments to visit.
www.hopslandholidays.co.uk • e-mail: hopslandholidays@aol.com

★★★ HOTEL

AA ★★★ HOTEL

e-mail: relax@polurrianhotel.com • www.polurrianhotel.com

Set in 12 acres with stunning views across Mount's Bay. The hotel has two pools, gym, snooker room, tennis court, sun terraces and secluded gardens. Most of the recently refurbished bedrooms have sea views. Our restaurants offer excellent food in stylish surroundings. Whether it is a more casual atmosphere in the High Point Restaurant or a formal dinner in the main Dining Room, we have something for everyone.

Mullion, Lizard Peninsula, Cornwall TR12 7EN • Tel: 01326 240421 • Fax: 01326 240083

*Dogs stay for **FREE** during Low Season at Mullion Cove Hotel*

MULLION COVE HOTEL

...located on the Cornwall Coast Path in a spectacular position on the Lizard Peninsula. Stunning country and coastal walks. Hotel facilities include a dog-friendly lounge, dog welcome pack, comfortable bedrooms and excellent food. **Tel: 01326 240328**

Email: enquiries@mullion-cove.co.uk
www.mullion-cove.co.uk

Lizard, Longrock, Looe

Gallen-Treath
GUEST HOUSE

PORTHALLOW, HELSTON, CORNWALL TR12 6PL
Tel & Fax: 01326 280400

Friendly guesthouse with spectacular coastal views, comfortable en suite rooms, hearty meals and a warm welcome. Close to coastal path, diving, gardens and more. Traditional breakfasts.

e-mail: gallentreath@btclick.com • www.gallentreath.co.uk

• Mount View Hotel •

A family-run pub with comfortable accommodation, situated 100 yards from Mount's Bay in Longrock village. Three en suite rooms and two with shared bathroom. Breakfast in dining room, lunch and dinner available. Dogs welcome by arrangement. Prices from £20 pppn.

Longrock, Penzance, Cornwall TR20 8JJ • Tel: 01736 710416

Paul & Barbie Higgins
Trewith, Duloe, near Liskeard
Cornwall PL14 4PR

TREWITH HOLIDAY COTTAGES
Self Catering Accommodation Open All Year

Tel: 01503 262184
mobile: 07968 262184

Situated in a superb elevated position of outstanding natural beauty. Just 1½ miles from Looe. Choice of 4 refurbished cottages with 1-3 bedrooms. Fully-equipped and tastefully furnished with full central heating. Use of laundry room. Peaceful location with delightful walks. Many beaches, coves, fishing, shopping close by in Looe. Because of ponds young children need supervision. Well behaved dogs welcome.

e-mail: info@trewith.co.uk • www.trewith.co.uk

COLDRINNICK COTTAGES
Duloe, Near Looe PL14 4QF

Coldrinnick Cottages are attractively converted barns, set in their own large secure, secluded gardens on a working dairy farm. Outstanding views, woodland walks to west Looe valley, close to moors and coast. Excellent locality for walking and relaxing.

Well Meadow sleeps 2 people, **Wagon** sleeps 2/4 and **Rose** 2/6.

Heating, electricity, bed linen etc all inclusive. An ideal place for families and dogs alike. *For a brochure or any information please contact:*

Bill and Kaye Chapman on 01503 220251

www.cornishcottage.net

Talehay Holiday Cottages
Pelynt, Near Looe PL13 2LT

A Quiet Haven in the Countryside near the Sea

Cosy, traditional cottages with many original features retained provide superb holiday accommodation on 17C non-working farmstead. Set in 4 acres of unspoilt countryside offering peace and tranquillity with breathtaking coastal and country walks on your doorstep. This is an ideal location for dogs and their owners alike. Close to the Eden Project.

★★★★ SELF CATERING

Tel: Mr & Mrs Dennett • 01503 220252

e-mail: infobookings@talehay.co.uk • www.talehay.co.uk

Cornish Dream

"For those who enjoy the comfort of a high quality hotel but prefer the freedom of a cottage"
...The Good Holiday Cottage Guide

Idyllic 18th Century 5 Star Country Cottages for romantics and animal lovers, near the sea in the beautiful Looe River valley.
Your own delightful private garden with roses around the door and breathtaking views.
Exclusively furnished, antiques, crackling log fires, candlelit meals, four-posters, crisp white linen.
Riding, heated swimming pool & tennis court. Wonderful walks from your cottage gate. Open all year.
Golf, fishing, sea, coastal walks all nearby. Pets are welcome.

Tel: 01503 262730
www.cornishdreamcottages.co.uk

Secluded traditional cottages set in the grounds of a country estate minutes from Looe and the coast.

- **Private gardens and grounds**
- **Log fires and generous heating**
- **Delicious optional home-cooked food delivery**
- **Coastal path, woodland and moor walking nearby**
- **Well-behaved dogs welcome**
- **Open all year, winter short breaks**

www.trenantcottages.com

e-mail: Liz@holiday-cottage.com **Tel: 01503 263639**

Fox Valley Cottages

Lanlawren, Trenewan, Looe PL13 2PZ

Set in beautiful countryside For a peaceful and relaxing holiday

A warm welcome from Andy & Linda, who are two of the partners who live on site.
• Indoor heated pool, spa and sauna • Cleaned to a high standard, warm, comfortable and well equipped • Log fires for those cosy winter nights • A field where your dog can have a good run around • Just three miles from Polperro, with country and coastal walks nearby • We are open all year round, including Christmas. • Short breaks, long weekends or midweek breaks out of season.

Tel: 01726 870115 • e-mail: lanlawrenfarm@lycos.com • www.foxvalleycottages.co.uk

Looe

TREMAINE GREEN

for MEMORABLE HOLIDAYS

"A beautiful private hamlet" of 11 traditional cosy Cornish craftsmen's cottages between **Looe** and **Polperro.** Clean, comfortable and well equipped, with a warm friendly atmosphere, for pets with 2 to 8 people. Set in award-winning grounds, only 12 miles from the **Eden Project** with country and coastal walks nearby. Pets £18 pw; owners from only £120.

• Towels, Linen, Electric & Hot Water included • Dishwashers in larger cottages • Launderette • Kid's Play Area • Games Room • Tennis Court • TV/DVDs• Cots & Highchairs • Pubs & Restaurants in easy walking distance • Activities Area

Mr & Mrs J Spreckley, Tremaine Green Country Cottages, Pelynt, Near Looe, Cornwall PL13 2LT
www.tremainegreen.co.uk • e-mail: stay@tremainegreen.co.uk • Tel: (01503) 220333

Valleybrook

Peakswater, Lansallos, Looe, Cornwall PL13 2QE

Peaceful 9-acre country site, with 6 superb villas and 2 delightful cottages. 3 miles from coast, Eden Project 11 miles.

- All accommodation dog-friendly - 2 dogs maximum
- Individual fenced gardens
- Day kennelling nearby
- Dog walk and off-lead dog paddock on site
- Many dog-friendly beaches
- Dog-friendly local pubs
- Short Breaks available
- Open all year

Contact Denise, Keith & Brian Holder

www.valleybrookholidays.com

01503 220493

WRINGWORTHY COTTAGES

LOOE

Our 8 traditional stone cottages are set amongst unspoilt Cornish hills in 4 acres of space. Wringworthy is minutes from Looe with its stunning coastal path and sandy beaches. Walks from our door; dog-friendly beaches within a short drive. The perfect base to explore the delights of Cornwall and Devon – hidden gardens, Eden, Bodmin Moor, NT and more.

Sleeping 2-8, each cottage layout is unique but all are fully equipped with fridges, washing machines, DVD/video, microwaves, linen, towels etc. You can't help but relax at Wringworthy – outdoor heated pool, games barn, BBQ areas, lawns, outdoor games and friendly farm animals. Safe fun for children and wide open spaces for everyone.

Whether you take a short break or longer our heated cottages and warm welcome await you all year round.

Green Acorn Award holders for sustainable tourism and commitment to the environment.

Tel: 01503 240685 www.wringworthy.co.uk pets@wringworthy.co.uk

Penquite Country Cottages

Duloe, Near Liskeard PL14 4QG

Four spacious and comfortable one-bedroom cottages for couples, or just one. Set in tranquil surroundings and enjoying outstanding views, Penquite offers real peace and quiet. Woodland walks from your front door, and within easy distance of the moors and coast, we are well situated for all that Cornwall has to offer. Fully equipped; heating, electricity, bedding and towels all included.

Well behaved dogs most welcome. No children.

Please contact Martin and Wendy Welch for further information/brochure on 01503 220260 or e-mail: stay@penquitecountrycottages.co.uk
See us at www.penquitecountrycottages.co.uk

Badham Farm, St Keyne, Liskeard PL14 4RW • 01579 343572
www.badhamfarm.co.uk • e-mail: badhamfarm@yahoo.co.uk

Farmhouse and farm buildings converted to a high standard. Sleep 2-10. All well furnished/equipped; prices include electricity, bed linen and towels. Most have a garden. Tennis, putting, children's play area, fishing lake, animal paddock, games room with pool and table tennis. Separate bar. Laundry. Barbecue.
Well behaved dogs welcome (not in high season). Prices from £120 per week.

★★★★ SELF CATERING

Cottages for Romantics

Old world charm, log fires, antiques, beautifully furnished with the comforts of home. Private gardens, spectacular views, peace ~ for families, friends and couples to enjoy. Nestling on a south-facing hillside, near coast ~ heated pool, tennis, badminton, lake, shire horses, etc. Enchanting 70-acre estate with bluebell wood, walking and wildlife. Delicious fare also available by candlelight 'at home' or in our tiny inn.

O. Slaughter, Trefanny Hill, Duloe, Near Liskeard PL14 4QF
Tel: 01503 220 622
e-mail: enq@trefanny.co.uk
www.trefanny.co.uk

THE COTTAGES AT *Trefanny Hill* Nr. LOOE

A Country Lover's Paradise with an abundance of country walks from your garden gate and coastal walks only 4 miles away.

Discover the magic of Trefanny Hill

St Anthony – Helford River

www.StAnthony.co.uk

Enchanting creekside cottages in a timeless and tranquil hamlet. Springtime bluebell woods and hedgerows banked with primroses, reflections of multi-coloured sails off sandy beaches, the solitary blue flash of a Kingfisher in autumn, smoke grey herons and shining white egrets standing patiently by the shoreline all evoke the atmosphere of this truly beautiful corner of Cornwall.

- Stunning coastal and riverside walks
- Great country inns and local food
- Warm and comfortable with cosy log fires
- Our own sailing dinghies and fishing boats
- Moorings and easy launching
- National Trust and private gardens nearby
- Short breaks, open all year including Christmas

St Anthony Holidays, Manaccan, Helston, Cornwall TR12 6JW
Tel: 01326 231 357 • e-mail: info@stanthony.co.uk

Marazion, Mawgan Porth, Mevagissey, Mousehole, Newquay

THE GODOLPHIN ARMS

West End, Marazion, Cornwall TR17 0EN

Perched on the edge of the sand, directly opposite St Michael's Mount. The Godolphin Arms has 10 en suite bedrooms, most with breathtaking sea views. Relaxing, comfortable bars and terraced beer garden. Perfect for exploring coast and coves.

01736 710202

e-mail: enquiries@godolphinarms.co.uk

www.godolphinarms.co.uk

AA ★★

Highly Commended in Cornwall Tourism Awards "Pub of the Year"

Blue Bay

a secret shared.....

Hotel, Restaurant and Lodges in fantastic location between Padstow and Newquay overlooking Mawgan Porth beach

Hotel prices from £33 pppn
Lodge prices from £50 per lodge per night. Sleeps 4-8

01637 860324

visit our website at:
www.bluebaycornwall.co.uk

Kilbol Country House Hotel & Cottages

'Perfect Peace in Hidden Cornwall'

Polmassick, Mevagissey PL26 6HA

A small, cottage-style country hotel set in 5-acre grounds. Dating back to the 16th century, it has been fully refurbished and offers 8 rooms, as well as two self-catering cottages. Two miles from the Lost Gardens of Heligan and Mevagissey, and close to the Eden Project. Outdoor swimming pool, riverside walk, wooded area. No children under 12 years in the hotel. Pets welcome.

Tel: 01726 842481 • e-mail: Hotel@kilbol-hotel.co.uk • www.kilbol-hotel.co.uk

Traditional cottage, sleeps two to five. Linen, towels, electricity supplied. Beach one mile. Large garden. Central for touring/walking. Near Heligan Gardens and Eden Project. Pets welcome.

MRS M.R. BULLED, MENAGWINS, GORRAN PL26 6HP
MEVAGISSEY 01726 843517

POLVELLAN HOLIDAY FLAT • • • MOUSEHOLE

Fully furnished, self contained flat with full sea view at the entrance to the unspoiled fishing village of Mousehole. Pets are welcome at no charge. Fully equipped kitchen. Sleeps 2. For details contact:

Mr A. G. Wright, 164 Portland Road, Selston, Notts NG16 6AN
01773 775347 • alang23@hotmail.com

Dewolf Guest House **100 Henver Road, Newquay TR7 3BL**

The amenities of Newquay are close at hand, Porth Beach only a short walk from the Guest House. Single, Double or Family rooms including two Chalets situated in the rear garden, ideal for pets. All rooms non-smoking with en suite facilities, colour TV and tea/coffee making facilities. B&B from £25 per person. Licensed. Off-road car parking available. Special breaks available. Suitable for M1 Disabled. Open all year. AA ★★★★

Tel: 01637 874746 • e-mail: holidays@dewolfguesthouse.com • www.dewolfguesthouse.com

Trethiggey Touring Park

Quintrell Downs, Newquay TR8 4QR

Our friendly, family-run park is just minutes by car from Newquay's famous surf beaches and 15 miles from the amazing Eden Project. Beautifully landscaped, the park has panoramic countryside views and is ideal for touring caravans, tents and campervans. We also have luxury holiday homes for hire. Facilities include shop, off-licence, free showers, electric hook-ups, laundry, children's play area, TV/games room, fishing, cafe and take-away food in summer.

Open from March 1st to January 1st including Christmas and New Year. Short Breaks available. Off season rallies welcome.

For more information phone 01637 877672 or see our website: www.Trethiggey.co.uk • e-mail: enquiries@trethiggey.co.uk

Retorrick Mill • *Self-catering accommodation*

Set in 11 acres, Retorrick Mill has two cottages and six chalets, all very well equipped. Licensed bar. It lies in a secluded valley, right next to Cornwall's beautiful beaches. Peace and tranquillity, within easy reach of everything. Pets including horses very welcome.

For a brochure or further assistance contact Chris Williams.

The Granary, Retorrick Mill, St Mawgan, Newquay TR8 4BH

Tel: 01637 860460

www.retorrickmill.co.uk • e-mail: info@retorrickmill.co.uk

On the outskirts of picturesque St Mawgan village between Newquay and Padstow

QUARRYFIELD

Caravan & Camping Park, Crantock, Near Newquay

Superbly situated overlooking beautiful Crantock Bay and the River Gannel estuary, park with fully equipped modern caravans for hire, and separate level camping field.

Contact: MRS WINN, TRETHERRAS, NEWQUAY, CORNWALL TR7 2RE

Tel & Fax: 01637 872792

Bar • Pool

Children's play area

e-mail: gill@raintreehouse.co.uk

Raintree House Holidays

A range of well equipped houses and bungalows near Trevose Golf Club, sandy beaches, scenic walks.

The Old Airfield, St Merryn, Padstow PL28 8PU

Tel: 01841 520228

www.raintreehouse.co.uk

TORWOOD HOUSE HOTEL **01736 360063**

ALEXANDRA ROAD, PENZANCE TR18 4LZ

Torwood is a small, family-run hotel, situated in a beautiful tree-lined avenue 500 metres from the seafront. All rooms en suite, with TV/DVD, tea/coffee makers and radios. Dinner available on request.

For further details telephone LYNDA SOWERBY

e-mail: Lyndasowerby@aol.com • www.torwoodhousehotel.co.uk

Polperro, Perranporth

POLPERRO

Affectionately let for
30 years for good
old-fashioned family
holidays, as well as for
friends and couples to
enjoy, where pets and
children are most welcome.

Comfortable holiday cottages, built around 250 years ago, full of character and charm, sleeping from 2 -14, with sunny terraced gardens, giving a Mediterranean-type setting.

Definltely located in one of the best positions in the village, directly overlooking picturesque harbour, of 16th century origins with smuggling connections, now a conservation area. 14 miles breathtaking panoramic sea views, stretching to Eddystone Lighthouse, with naval shipping, ocean-going yachts, local fishing boats and pleasure craft often forming part of the seascape.

The cottages are only 2 minutes from shops, excellent selection of quality restaurants, tearooms, olde-worlde pubs and the availability of Cornish pasties, ice cream and fish and chips. Close by, there is a small, sandy beach with rock pools, quay, pier and rock fishing and the beginning of miles of unspoilt National Trust cliff walks along stunning coastal paths of outstanding natural beauty, leading to outlying hamlets, with rocky inlets, beaches, coves and 13th century churches. Between Looe and Fowey, on South Cornish coast, 25 miles city of Plymouth, 12 miles A38 and 15 miles Eden Project.

Prices from £175-£595 per cottage, per week.

• PETS COME FREE • PRIVATE PARKING FREE

For brochure, please telephone GRAHAM WRIGHTS OFFICES 01579 344080

Near Perranporth

Greenmeadow Cottages

Highly praised luxury cottages. Sleep 6.
Superbly clean, comfortable and spacious.
Open all year. Short Breaks out of season.
Pets welcome in two of the cottages.
Non-smoking. Ample off-road parking.

For brochure and bookings

Tel: 01872 540483

www.greenmeadow-cottages.co.uk

★★★ SELF CATERING

Pet-Friendly

Pubs, Inns & Hotels

on pages 424-432

Please note that these establishments may not feature in the main section of this book

Step onto The Coastal Path...

Escape the pressures of life. Relax! explore the Cornish Coast from Green Door Cottages in Port Gaverne.

8 comfortable, restored 18th Century cottages set around a sheltered courtyard, plus 2 prestigious apartments with panoramic sea views beside a picturesque cove, directly on the Coastal path, less than half a mile from Port Isaac.

An ideal location for your holiday and short breaks. Well behaved dogs are very welcome.

Call now for a brochure on:
01208 880293

Green Door Cottages
PORT GAVERNE
email: enquiries@greendoorcottages.co.uk
web: www.greendoorcottages.co.uk

PORTHLEVEN *"Kernow agas dynargh" - "Cornwall welcomes you"*

Fishermen's cottages. Harbour, bay or country views.
3 minutes to beach, coast path, harbourside eating places.
Open fires. Pets welcome. **Tel: 01209 860410**

LONG CROSS HOTEL & VICTORIAN GARDENS
TRELIGHTS, PORT ISAAC PL29 3TF

Lovely Victorian country house hotel with four acres of restored gardens set in beautiful tranquil location overlooking the coast. Close to the area's best beaches, golf courses and other attractions. Spacious, comfortable interior, with newly refurbished en suite bedrooms and suites.

Tel: 01208 880243
www.longcrosshotel.co.uk

THE CORNISH ARMS **Pendoggett, Port Isaac PL30 3HH**
Tel: 01208 880263 • Fax: 01208 880335 • www.cornisharms.com

A delightful 16th century coaching inn just one mile from the coast.
Whilst retaining the character of a traditional coaching inn, The Cornish Arms offers all modern amenities in every bedroom. The daily specials board features locally caught seafood and an extensive range of other dishes.

Port Isaac, Portreath, Portwrinkle

The Garden House near Port Isaac, Cornwall

Secure garden for dogs (1 large or 2 small maximum). Doggy shower. Lovely far-reaching view across open countryside. Very warm and cosy for all year round. Full central heating, electricity, bed linen and towels included. One bedroom with twin or double. Lounge/kitchen/dining and shower room all fully equipped to very high standards.

Central location in small quiet hamlet near Michaelstow and within 8 miles of Port Isaac, Boscastle, Tintagel, Polzeath, Rock, Wadebridge, Bodmin Moor and Camel Trail. From £160 pw.

Contact David & Jenny Oldham • 01208 850529
Trevella, Treveighan, St Teath, Cornwall PL30 3JN
email. david.trevella@btconnect.com www.trevellacornwall.co.uk

GULLROCK COTTAGES

Port Gaverne Port Isaac North Cornwall

Personal attention from resident owner ensures your home from home comfort in a tranquil setting just yards from the sea at bygone Port Gaverne.

Tel: Malcolm Lee (01208) 880106 • e-mail: gullrock@ukonline.co.uk

This renowned 17th century inn is situated in an unspoilt fishing cove on the rugged North Coast of Cornwall. The beach is just 50 yards from the front door and the Coastal Path offers miles of breathtaking scenery. For a relaxing break with a friendly atmosphere you need look no further. Golf, fishing, sailing and riding are all nearby.

Pets welcome in the Inn and Self-catering accommodation available.

Port Gaverne Hotel Near Port Isaac, Cornwall PL29 3SQ Tel: 01208 880244 Fax: 01208 880151

Friesian Valley Cottages

For Colour Brochure
Telephone 01209 890901

Luxury Cottages in peaceful rural hamlet on Atlantic coast between Newquay and St Ives, surrounded by fields, beautiful sandy beaches and National Trust Coastal Path.

£130 to £620 per week.

WHITSAND BAY SELF-CATERING

12 cottages sleeping 4-10, all with sea views and situated by an 18-hole clifftop golf course.

Children and pet-friendly

Tel: 01579 345688
e-mail: ehwbsc@hotmail.com
www.whitsandbayselfcatering.co.uk

A venue that is unforgettable and unique

A dog-friendly establishment where well behaved dogs are most welcome.
Our beautifully appointed, character 32 bedroom hotel has stunning sea views plus its own 18 hole cliff-top golf course.
With an award-winning restaurant that offers a unique dining experience, everyone is welcome to come and sample our innovative cuisine.
Complete with indoor heated swimming pool & mini gym, as well as a revitalising Skin Care & Spa Salon, a visit to Whitsand Bay Hotel is a must!
For further information or to make a reservation please contact:

WHITSAND BAY HOTEL
LEISURE AND GOLF

Whitsand Bay Hotel Leisure & Golf, Portwrinkle, Cornwall PL11 3BU
Tel: (01503) 230276 • E-mail: whitsandbayhotel@btconnect.com • www.whitsandbayhotel.co.uk

Wheal Rose Caravan & Camping Park

Scorrier, Redruth TR16 5DD
Tel/Fax: 01209 891496

AA

A secluded, 6-acre family-run touring park, central for all west Cornwall. Adjacent to the park is Mineral Tramway popular with walkers and cyclists. The park consists of 50 level, grassed pitches with electrical hook-ups. Spotlessly clean, purpose-built shower/toilet block, shop, children's play area, TV/games room, laundry and disabled facilities.
HEATED OPEN AIR SWIMMING POOL.
Prices from £8.00 per night. Open March to December.
e-mail: les@whealrosecaravanpark.co.uk
www.whealrosecaravanpark.co.uk

Visit the FHG website
www.holidayguides.com
for details of the wide choice of accommodation featured in the full range of FHG titles

St Agnes

The Driftwood Spars St Agnes

The Eating Place at Trevaunance Cove

www.driftwoodspars.com

'Priding ourselves on serving the best of local produce'

En suite rooms available with seaview or garden view

Restaurant • Pub • B&B
Microbrewery • Live Music
Large Car Park

driftwoodspars@hotmail.com
Tel: 01872 552428

Nominated for Best Small Live Music Venue

Well-behaved dogs welcome

Penkerris **Penwinnick Road, St Agnes TR5 0PA**

Tel & Fax: 01872 552262 *Dorothy Gill-Carey*

Creeper-clad B&B/guest house with lawned garden. A home from home offering real food, comfortable bedrooms. Ample parking. Three sandy beaches and dramatic cliff walks (half-mile). Central for touring. B&B from £20.00 to £30.00 pppn. Open all year. Pets most welcome (preferably not during school holidays). ETC ★★ *Guest House*.

e-mail: info@penkerris.co.uk • www.penkerris.co.uk

Blue Hills **TOURING PARK**

Cross Coombe, Trevellas, St Agnes, Cornwall TR5 0XP

Set in a beautiful rural position close to a coastal footpath, a small site with good toilets. A pleasant location for exploring nearby coves, beaches and villages.
2-acre site with 30 touring pitches

01872 552999 • loo@zoom.co.uk
www.bluehillscamping.co.uk

- Caravan Holiday Homes
- Touring & Camping
- Families & Couples
- Pets Welcome
- Exclusive leisure facility:
- Gym, Sauna & Steamroom
- Shop
- Laundry room • Games room
- Children's play area
- Multi-service hook-ups
- Satellite TV in all units
- No club, bar or disco

Chiverton Park

Set in the heart of Cornish countryside, yet only a short distance from superb beaches, this spacious, well-run park offers peace and relaxation in a delightful rural setting. Holiday homes are fully equipped (except linen, which may be hired)

Chiverton Park, Blackwater, Truro TR4 8HS • 01872 560667
info@chivertonpark.co.uk • www.chivertonpark.co.uk

BOSINVER HOLIDAY COTTAGES

Self-catering Establishment of the Year 2006 & 2007 • Cornwall Tourism Awards

Nestling in a hidden valley near the sea, the Eden Project and Lost Gardens of Heligan, our small farm has friendly animals and ponies. Choose from our 16th Century thatched farmhouse or cottages privately set in their own gardens surrounded by wildflower meadows. Wander down to the fishing lake or village pub, swim in the pool, play tennis, or relax and listen to the birdsong. No pets during Summer school holidays please.

Brochure from: Mrs Pat Smith, Bosinver Farm, Trelowth, St Austell, Cornwall PL26 7DT
01726 72128 • e-mail: reception@bosinver.co.uk
www.bosinver.co.uk

If it's views you want,
this is the place for you!

The Links Holiday Flats

Lelant, St Ives, Cornwall TR26 3HY

Magnificent location alongside and overlooking West Cornwall Golf Course, Hayle Estuary and St Ives Bay. Both flats have lovely views. Wonderful spot for walking. We are five minutes from the beach and dogs are allowed there all year round. Two well-equipped flats which are open all year.

Your hosts are Bob and Jacky Pontefract • Phone or fax 01736 753326

SANDBANK HOLIDAYS

St Ives Bay, Hayle, Cornwall TR27 5BL
www.sandbank-holidays.co.uk

High quality Apartments and Bungalows for 2-6 persons. Peaceful garden setting close to miles of sandy beach, acres of grassy dunes and SW Coastal Path. Dogs Welcome. Fully equipped for your self-catering holiday. Heated, Colour TV, Microwave etc. Spotlessly clean. All major debit and credit cards accepted. **Tel: 01736 752594**

Sea Pink

Near St Mawes, South Cornwall. Nestling in a picturesque setting overlooking the little bay of St Just-in-Roseland, Sea Pink is ideally located for exploring the coast and attractions. Recently refurbished, there is a spacious lounge, dining area opening on to sun terrace and lawned garden; three bedrooms. Brochure available. **Contact Judy Juniper • Tel: 01872 863553**
e-mail: cottageinfo@btconnect.com • www.luxury-holiday-cottages.com

Please note

All the information in this book is given in good faith in the belief that it is correct. However, the publishers cannot guarantee the facts given in these pages, neither are they responsible for changes in policy, ownership or terms that may take place after the date of going to press. Readers should always satisfy themselves that the facilities they require are available and that the terms, if quoted, still apply.

St Mawgan

Dalswinton House

St. Mawgan-in-Pydar, Cornwall TR8 4EZ. Tel: 01637 860385
www.dalswinton.com • dalswintonhouse@tiscali.co.uk

HOLIDAYS FOR DOGS AND THEIR OWNERS

Overlooking the village of St Mawgan, Dalswinton House stands in 10 acres of gardens and meadowland midway between Padstow and Newquay with distant views to the sea at dog-friendly Mawgan Porth.

- Dogs free of charge and allowed everywhere except the restaurant
- 8 acre meadow for dog exercise. Nearby local walks. Beach 1.5 miles
- Heated outdoor pool (May-Sep). Off street car parking
- All rooms en suite with tea/coffee fac., digital TV and clock radios
- Wifi access in public rooms and some bedrooms
- Residents' bar and restaurant serving breakfast and dinner
- Bed and breakfast from £40 per person per night
- Weekly rates available and special offers in Mar/Apr/Oct
- Self-catering lodge sleeps 3 adults
- Easy access to Padstow, Eden Project, Newquay Airport & Coastal Path
- New for 2008: dog-friendly self-catering near Falmouth

Regret no children under 16
Maximum 3 dogs per room at proprietor's discretion

Comfortable end of terrace cottage in picturesque and friendly village. Enclosed garden and parking. Ideal location for exploring all Cornwall. Short Breaks and brochure available. Contact:

MRS R REEVES, POLSTRAUL, TREWALDER, DELABOLE PL33 9ET
Tel & Fax: 01840 213120 • e-mail: ruth.reeves@hotmail.co.uk
www.maymear.co.uk

TREWITHIAN FARM St Wenn, Bodmin PL30 5PH

Comfortable, well equipped wing of farmhouse, edge of Bodmin Moor, central location in Cornwall.
Beautiful countryside, very secluded position.
Sleeps 2 plus sofa bed, satellite TV, central heating.
2 dogs welcome, use of kennels and exercise field. Good walking and dog-friendly beaches nearby. Excellent winter rates.

Tel: 01208 895181 **www.cornwall-online.co.uk/trewithianfarm**

Comfortable, well-equipped, centrally heated cottages sleeping two. Ideal for touring, walking and relaxing. Close to Coastal Path and village amenities. Private parking. Ring for brochure. Pets Free.

MR & MRS N. CAREY, SALUTATIONS, ATLANTIC ROAD, TINTAGEL PL34 0DE • 01840 770287
e-mail: merlin0123@tiscali.co.uk • www.salutationstintagel.co.uk

TRENONA FARM

Ruan High Lanes, Truro, Cornwall TR2 5JS

Enjoy a relaxing stay on this mixed farm, on the unspoilt Roseland Peninsula midway between Truro and the Eden Project at St Austell.

B&B in the Victorian farmhouse in double/family rooms, either en suite or with private bathroom.

Self-catering in two renovated barns, each sleeping 6, both well equipped and furnished. Ample parking with room for boats and trailers.

Pets welcome by arrangement. Wheelchair access.

Tel: 01872 501339 • e-mail:info@trenonafarmholidays.co.uk • www.trenonafarmholidays.co.uk

Higher Trewithen is the ideal centre for your pet and your family. We are surrounded by public footpaths and have 3½ acres of fields.

www.trewithen.com • trewithen@talk21.com

Higher Trewithen, Stithians, Truro, Cornwall TR3 7DR • Tel: 01209 860863

...Cornwall's chic country retreat

A secluded hamlet of 5 star contemporary cottages in a tranquil country valley. Explore stunning beaches, fishing villages and country pubs. The Valley has beautiful gardens and woodland walks, ideal for dogs. Relax in architect designed luxury with leisure facilities and experience exquisite cuisine in the stylish Café Azur.

01872 862194 www.the-valley.co.uk

Truro, Wadebridge

Treloan Coastal Farm Holidays Treloan Lane, Portscatho TR2 5EF

Traditional 1930's working farm on coastal footpath. Open all year. Sea views. Access to three coves (local beaches accept pets). Self-catering mobile homes, touring, camping and camping barn. Shire horses, Jersey milking cows/calves and hens/chicks. Experience farm practices: horse ploughing, harvesting, steam tractor, threshing, milking, feeding, egg collecting. Close to shops, pubs, etc. Half an hour from Truro, Eden Project.

01872 580899/580989 • e-mail: enquiries@coastalfarmholidays.co.uk
www.coastalfarmholidays.co.uk

King Harry Cottages CORNWALL

Two cosy cottages nestled in woodland above the river Fal in Cornwall, both with views over the river. Boat hire. Dogs welcome. Near Truro.

t: 01872 861 917
e: beverley@kingharry.net
w: **www.kingharry.net**

Our three luxury cottages are converted from original farm buildings and feature mellow stone elevations under slate roofs. Sleeping between 2 and 7 and surrounded by open Cornish farmland, Colesent is ideally situated between the coast (Padstow, Wadebridge, Rock & Polzeath) and Bodmin Moor. The inland start of the famous "Camel Trail" is at the end of our drive and provides a traffic free walking and cycling path to Bodmin, Wadebridge and Padstow. Two dogs welcome per cottage.

CORNWALL TOURISM AWARDS 2002 - Self Catering Establishment of the Year - Highly Commended.

GARY & MAUREEN NEWMAN, COLESENT COTTAGES, ST TUDY, WADEBRIDGE PL30 4QX
Tel & Fax: 01208 850112 • e-mail: relax@colesent.co.uk • www.colesent.co.uk

Other specialised holiday guides from FHG

PUBS & INNS OF BRITAIN • **COUNTRY HOTELS** OF BRITAIN

WEEKEND & SHORT BREAK HOLIDAYS IN BRITAIN

THE GOLF GUIDE WHERE TO PLAY, WHERE TO STAY

500 GREAT PLACES TO STAY • **SELF-CATERING HOLIDAYS** IN BRITAIN

BED & BREAKFAST STOPS • **CARAVAN & CAMPING HOLIDAYS**

FAMILY BREAKS IN BRITAIN

Published annually: available in all good bookshops or direct from the publisher:

FHG Guides, Abbey Mill Business Centre, Seedhill, Paisley PA1 1TJ

Tel: 0141 887 0428 • Fax: 0141 889 7204

e-mail: admin@fhguides.co.uk • www.holidayguides.com

TRENCREEK FARM COUNTRY HOLIDAY PARK, HEWAS WATER, ST AUSTELL (01726 882540). Pet-friendly holidays in Cornwall. Luxury lodge, caravan and bungalow accommodation. Motorhome, tourer and tent pitches. Fishing lakes, farm animals, swimming pool and hot tubs. Call for your FREE brochure. ETC ★★★★, David Bellamy Silver Award.[pw! Pets from £1 per night touring; £2 per night accommodation]
website: www.surfbayholidays.co.uk

A fine selection of Self-catering and similar Cottages on both coasts of Cornwall and on Scilly. Pets welcome in many cottages. Free colour brochure from: CORNISH TRADITIONAL COTTAGES, BLISLAND, BODMIN PL30 4HS (01208 821666; Fax: 01208 821766). [Pets £16 per week]
website: www.corncott.com

CORNISH SEAVIEW COTTAGES (01428 723819). Ideal for walking coastal paths and accessing beaches. Pets welcome at most. Furnished and equipped to high standard; all have central heating, dishwashers etc. Visit our website for photos and virtual tours. [Pets £20 per week].
e-mail: enquiries@cornishseaviewcottages.co.uk website: www.cornishseaviewcottages.co.uk

CLASSY COTTAGES – Spectacular cottages feet from beach. Isolated residences on coast, isolated garden cottage. Open log fires. Dog-friendly beaches. Access to indoor swimming pool, gym and tennis courts. Local pubs serving good food and allowing dogs. Contact FIONA & MARTIN NICOLLE (01720 423000). [pw! Pets £12 per week]
e-mail: nicolle@classycottages.co.uk website: www.classycottages.co.uk

TOAD HALL COTTAGES (01548 853089 24 hrs). 300 outstanding waterside and rural properties in truly beautiful locations in Devon, Cornwall and Exmoor. Call for our highly acclaimed brochure. Pets welcome.
e-mail: thc@toadhallcottages.co.uk website: www.toadhallcottages.co.uk

FARM & COTTAGE HOLIDAYS (01237 459897). Over 850 of the finest selection of holiday cottages throughout Devon, Cornwall, Dorset and Somerset in superb rural and coastal locations.
website: www.holidaycottages.co.uk

Bodmin

Quaint county town of Cornwall, standing steeply on the edge of Bodmin Moor. Pretty market town and touring centre. Plymouth 31 miles, Newquay 20, Wadebridge 7.

PENROSE BURDEN, ST BREWARD, BODMIN PL30 4LZ (01208 850277 & 850617; Fax: 01208 850915). Holiday Care Award Winning Cottages featured on TV. Open all year. Outstanding views over wooded valley. Free Salmon and Trout fishing. Daily meal service. Superb walking area. Dogs welcome, wheelchair accessible. [Pets £15 per week]
website: www.penroseburden.co.uk

Bodmin Moor

Superb walking area attaining a height of 1375 feet at Brown Willy, the highest point in Cornwall.

DARRYNANE COTTAGES, DARRYNANE, ST BREWARD, BODMIN MOOR PL30 4LZ (Tel & Fax: 01208 850885). Absolutely fabulous detached cottages. Set in private gated gardens. Unique moorland valley setting. Waterfalls, woods, river. Woodburning stoves, four-poster beds, Eden Project and Camel Trail close by. ETC ★★★ [Pets £15 per week]
e-mail: enquiries@darrynane.co.uk website:www.darrynane.com

HENWOOD BARNS HOLIDAY COTTAGES, HENWOOD, LISKEARD PL14 5BP (01579 363576/07956 864263). Three stone barns set around original courtyard on the edge of Bodmin Moor, with stunning views. Tranquil, village location, horse riding two minutes' walk. Woodburning stoves; sleep 2/5; within easy reach of North Cornwall and Devon. [Pets £15 per week]
e-mail: henwoodbarns@tiscali.co.uk website: www.henwoodbarns.co.uk

A useful index of towns/counties appears at the back of this book

NEAR LOOE. In the picturesque Cornish fishing village of Polperro, comfortable, charming holiday cottages, sleeping 2-14, with terraced gardens and private parking, affectionately let for 30 years for family holidays, as well as for friends and couples to enjoy. Definitely located in one of the best positions in the village, directly overlooking 16th century harbour, with 14 miles breathtaking panoramic sea views. 2 minutes shops, excellent selection quality restaurants, tearooms, olde worlde pubs. Close by sandy beaches, quay, pier and rock fishing, miles of unspoilt National Trust cliff walks, along stunning coastal paths. Located between Looe and Fowey, on the South Cornish coast, 25 miles city of Plymouth, 12 miles main A38 and about 15 miles Eden Project and Lost Gardens of Heligan. Prices from £175-£595 per cottage, per week. Pets come free. For brochure, please telephone Graham Wrights offices (01579 344080). [🐕]

Idyllic 18th century country cottages for romantics and animal lovers. Looe three miles. Wonderful walks from your gate. Cottages warm and cosy in winter. Personal attention and colour brochure from: B. WRIGHT, TREWORGEY COTTAGES, DULOE, LISKEARD PL14 4PP (01503 262730). VisitBritain ★★★★★ Quality Assurance Scheme. [Pets £20.50 per week.]
website: www.cornishdreamcottages.co.uk

TRENANT PARK COTTAGES (01503 263639). Secluded traditional cottages in grounds of country estate. Private gardens and grounds. Open log fires. Open all year, winter short breaks. Well behaved dogs welcome. [Pets £20 per week].
e-mail: Liz@holiday-cottage.com website: www.trenantcottages.com

FOX VALLEY COTTAGES, LANLAWREN, TRENEWAN, LOOE PL13 2PZ (01726 870115). Set in beautiful countryside, just three miles from Polperro. Indoor heated pool and spa. Open all year round. Field for dogs to run around. Contact ANDY & LINDA for details. [pw! Pets £15 per week]
e-mail: lanlawrenfarm@lycos.com website: www.foxvalleycottages.co.uk

TREMAINE GREEN COUNTRY COTTAGES, PELYNT, NEAR LOOE PL13 2LT (01503 220333). A beautiful hamlet of 11 award-winning traditional cosy craftsmen's cottages. Clean, comfortable and well equipped. Set in award-winning grounds with country/coastal walks and The Eden Project nearby. [pw! Pets £18 per week]
e-mail: stay@tremainegreen.co.uk website: www.tremainegreen.co.uk

VALLEYBROOK, PEAKSWATER, LANSALLOS, LOOE PL13 2QE. Peaceful nine acre site with six superb villas and two delightful cottages, all dog friendly. Individual fenced gardens, dog walks, dog friendly beaches nearby. Short breaks. Open all year. 2 dogs max. ETC ★★★/★★★★. Contact DENISE, KEITH or BRIAN HOLDER (01503 220493). [pw! Pets £2 per night]
website: www.valleybrookholidays.com

WRINGWORTHY COTTAGES, LOOE (01503 240685). 8 traditional stone cottages set in 4 peaceful acres offer you and your pet space for the perfect break. A friendly welcome awaits in our fully equipped, centrally heated cottages, sleeping 2-8. Linen included, walks from our door and more! ETC ★★★★, Green Acorn Award. [First pet free, additional pets £18 per week]
e-mail: pets@wringworthy.co.uk website: www.wringworthy.co.uk

MARTIN AND WENDY WELCH, PENQUITE COUNTRY COTTAGES, DULOE, NEAR LISKEARD PL14 4QG (01503 220260). Four spacious one-bedroom cottages within easy reach of coast and moors. Well behaved dogs most welcome. No children. ETC ★★★ [Pets £15 per week]
e-mail:stay@penquitecountrycottages.co.uk website: www.penquitecountrycottages.co.uk

BADHAM FARM, ST KEYNE, LISKEARD PL14 4RW (01579 343572). Farmhouse and farm buildings converted to a high standard. Sleep 2-10. All well furnished/equipped; prices include electricity, bed linen and towels. Well behaved dogs welcome (not in high season). Prices from £120 per week. ETC ★★★★. [Pets £4 per night, £20 per week].
e-mail: badhamfarm@yahoo.co.uk website: www.badhamfarm.co.uk

O. SLAUGHTER, TREFANNY HILL, DULOE, NEAR LISKEARD PL14 4QF (01503 220622). Nestling on a south-facing hillside, near coast. Delicious food. Heated pool, tennis, badminton, lake, shire horses. Enchanting 70 acre estate with bluebell wood, walking and wildlife.
e-mail: enq@trefanny.co.uk website: www.trefanny.co.uk

A useful index of towns/counties appears at the back of this book

Manaccan

Village 7 miles east of Helston.

Enchanting creekside cottages in a timeless and tranquil hamlet. Stunning coastal and riverside walks, country inns, local food, warm and comfortable with cosy log fires. Boat hire, moorings. Short breaks. Open all year. ST ANTHONY HOLIDAYS, MANACCAN, HELSTON TR12 6JW (01326 231 357). [Pets £3 per night, £21 per week].
e-mail: info@stanthony.co.uk website: www.StAnthony.co.uk

Marazion

Quaint little village, the oldest town in Britain. Good beach and splendid fishing, sailing waters..

THE GODOLPHIN ARMS, WEST END, MARAZION TR17 0EN (01736 710202) Perched on the edge of the sand, facing St Michael's Mount. Ten en suite bedrooms, most with breathtaking sea views. Relaxing bars. Perfect for exploring coast and coves. AA ★★ [🐕]
e-mail: enquiries@godolphinarms.co.uk website: www.godolphinarms.co.uk

Mawgan Porth

Modern village on small sandy bay. Good surfing. Inland stretches the beautiful Vale of Lanherne. Rock formation of Bedruthan Steps is nearby. Newquay 6 miles west..

BLUE BAY HOTEL, TRENANCE, MAWGAN PORTH TR8 4DA (01637 860324). Hotel, restaurant and lodges in fantastic location between Padstow and Newquay, overlooking Mawgan Porth beach. ETC ★★ Hotel, ★★★ Self-catering. [pw! Pets £5 per night, max. £20 per visit].
e-mail: hotel@bluebaycornwall.co.uk website: www.bluebaycornwall.co.uk

Mevagissey

Central for touring and walking. Eden project nearby.

KILBOL COUNTRY HOUSE HOTEL & COTTAGES, POLMASSICK, MEVAGISSEY PL26 6HA (01726 842481). 'Perfect Peace in Hidden Cornwall'. Small country hotel set in 5-acre grounds, two miles from the coast. Eight rooms, and two self-catering cottages. Outdoor swimming pool, riverside walk. No children under 12 years in hotel. [pw! Pets £10 per week].
e-mail: Hotel@kilbol-hotel.co.uk website: www.kilbol-hotel.co.uk

MRS M.R. BULLED, MENAGWINS, GORRAN PL26 6HP (MEVAGISSEY 01726 843517). Traditional cottage, sleeps two to five. Linen, towels, electricity supplied. Beach one mile. Large garden. Central for touring/walking. Near Eden Project and Heligan Gardens. Pets welcome. [🐕]

Mousehole

Picturesque fishing village with sand and shingle beach. Penzance 3 miles.

POLVELLAN HOLIDAY FLAT. In Mousehole, a quaint and unspoilt fishing village, a fully equipped self-catering flat with full sea views. Sleeps two. Microwave, cooker, fridge, TV, all bedding and towels provided. Open all year. Apply: MR A.G. WRIGHT, 164 PORTLAND ROAD, SELSTON, NOTTINGHAM NG16 6AN (01773 775347) [🐕]
e-mail: alang23@hotmail.com

Newquay

Popular family holiday resort surrounded by miles of golden beaches. Semi-tropical gardens, zoo and museum. Ideal for exploring all of Cornwall.

MRS DEWOLFREYS, DEWOLF GUEST HOUSE, 100 HENVER ROAD, NEWQUAY TR7 3BL (01637 874746). Single, double or family rooms, two chalets in rear garden. All rooms non-smoking with en suite facilities, colour TV and tea/coffee making facilities. Ideal for pets. AA ★★★★ [🐕]
e-mail: holidays@dewolfguesthouse.com website: www.dewolfguesthouse.com

TRETHIGGEY TOURING PARK, QUINTRELL DOWNS, NEWQUAY TR8 4QR (01637 877672). Friendly, family-run park minutes from surfing beaches. Touring caravans, tent and campervans welcome. Luxury holiday homes for hire. Shop, off-licence, free showers, electric hook-ups, laundry, children's play area, TV/games room, fishing, cafe and take-away food in summer. ETC ★★★★
e-mail: enquiries@trethiggey.co.uk website: www.Trethiggey.co.uk

THE GRANARY, RETORRICK MILL, ST MAWGAN, NEWQUAY TR8 4BH (01637 860460). Set in 11 acres, self-catering Retorrick Mill has two cottages and six chalets, all very well equipped. Licensed bar. Pets including horses very welcome. For a brochure or further assistance contact Chris Williams.
website: www.retorrickmill.co.uk

QUARRYFIELD CARAVAN & CAMPING PARK, CRANTOCK, NEWQUAY. Fully equipped modern caravans overlooking beautiful Crantock Bay. Separate camping field. Bar, pool, children's play area. Contact: MRS WINN, TRETHERRAS, NEWQUAY TR7 2RE (Tel & Fax: 01637 872792). [Pets £1.50 to £3 per night (camping only); £10 to £20 per week in caravan]

Padstow

Bright little resort with pretty harbour on Camel estuary. Extensive sands. Nearby is Elizabethan Prideaux Place. Newquay 15 miles, Wadebridge 8.

RAINTREE HOUSE HOLIDAYS. We have a varied selection of accommodation. Small or large, houses and apartments, some by the sea. All in easy reach of our lovely beaches. Please write or phone for brochure. THE OLD AIRFIELD, ST MERRYN, PADSTOW PL28 8PU (01841 520228). [🐕]
e-mail: gill@raintreehouse.co.uk website: www.raintreehouse.co.uk

Penzance

Well-known resort and port for Scilly Isles, with sand and shingle beaches. Truro 27 miles, Helston 13, Land's End 10, St Ives 8.

TORWOOD HOUSE HOTEL, ALEXANDRA ROAD, PENZANCE TR18 4LZ. Torwood is a small, family-run hotel, situated in a beautiful tree-lined avenue 500 metres from the seafront. All rooms en suite, with TV/DVD, tea/coffee makers and radios. Dinner available on request. For further details telephone LYNDA SOWERBY on 01736 360063.
e-mail: Lyndasowerby@aol.com website: www.torwoodhousehotel.co.uk

Perranporth

North Coast resort 6 miles SW of Newquay.

GREENMEADOW COTTAGES, NEAR PERRANPORTH. Spacious, clean luxury cottages. Sleep six. Open all year. Short breaks out of season. Non-smoking. Ample off road parking. Pets welcome in two of the cottages. ETC ★★★ For brochure and bookings: 01872 540483. [Pets £25 per week].
website: www.greenmeadow-cottages.co.uk

Polperro

Picturesque and quaint little fishing village and harbour. Of interest is the "House of the Props". Fowey 9 miles, Looe 5..

POLPERRO. In the picturesque Cornish fishing village of Polperro, comfortable, charming holiday cottages, sleeping 2-14, with terraced gardens and private parking, affectionately let for 30 years for family holidays, as well as for friends and couples to enjoy. Definitely located in one of the best positions in the village, directly overlooking 16th century harbour, with 14 miles breathtaking panoramic sea views. 2 minutes shops, excellent selection quality restaurants, tearooms, olde worlde pubs. Close by sandy beaches, quay, pier and rock fishing, miles of unspoilt National Trust cliff walks, along stunning coastal paths. Located between Looe and Fowey, on the South Cornish coast, 25 miles city of Plymouth, 12 miles main A38 and about 15 miles Eden Project and Lost Gardens of Heligan. Prices from £175-£595 per cottage, per week. Pets come free. For brochure, please telephone Graham Wrights offices (01579 344080). [🐕]

Port Gaverne

Hamlet on east side of Port Isaac, near Camel Estuary.

GREEN DOOR COTTAGES. PORT GAVERNE. A delightful collection of 18C Cornish buildings built around a sunny enclosed courtyard, and 2 lovely apartments with stunning sea views. Situated in a picturesque, tranquil cove ideal for children. Dogs allowed on the beach year round. Half a mile from Port Isaac, on the Cornish Coastal Path. Traditional pub directly opposite. ETC ★★★/★★★★
For brochure: (01208 880293) [🐕]
e-mail: enquiries@gFages.co.uk website: www.greendoorcottages.co.uk

Porthleven

Small town with surprisingly big harbour. Grand woodland walks. 2 miles SW of Helston.

PORTHLEVEN. "Kernow agas dynargh" - "Cornwall welcomes you". Fishermen's cottages. Harbour, bay or country views. 3 minutes to beach, coast path, harbourside eating places. Open fires. Pets welcome. Please contact: MRS KERNO (01209 860410). [Pets £20 per week]

Port Isaac

Attractive fishing village with harbour. Much of the attractive coastline is protected by the National Trust. Camelford 9 miles. Wadebridge 9.

LONG CROSS HOTEL & VICTORIAN GARDENS, TRELIGHTS, PORT ISAAC PL29 3TF (01208 880243). Lovely Victorian country house hotel with four acres of restored gardenst. Close to the area's best beaches, golf courses and other attractions. Newly refurbished en suite bedrooms and suites. [Pets £5.00 per night.]
website: www.longcrosshotel.co.uk

THE CORNISH ARMS, PENDOGGETT, PORT ISAAC PL30 3HH (01208 880263; Fax: 01208 880335). A delightful 16th century coaching inn just one mile from the coast, the Cornish Arms offers all modern amenities in every bedroom. Daily specials board featuring locally caught seafood and an extensive range of other dishes.
website: www.cornisharms.com

DAVID AND JENNY OLDHAM, THE GARDEN HOUSE, MICHAELSTOW (01208 850529). Secure garden for dogs. Doggy shower. Lovely far reaching views. Full central heating and electric inc. Bed linen and towels inc. One bedroom with twin or double. Central location in small quiet hamlet. From £160 pw.
e-mail: david.trevella@btconnect.com website: www.trevellacornwall.co.uk

Homes from home around our peaceful courtyard garden 100 yards from sea in bygone fishing hamlet. Each sleeps six and has full CH, fridge/freezer, washer/dryer, dishwasher, microwave, DVD, video, computer and broadband. £200 (February), £760 (August) weekly. Resident owner. APPLY:- MALCOLM LEE, GULLROCK, PORT GAVERNE, PORT ISAAC PL29 3SQ (01208 880106). [🐕]
e-mail: gullrock@ukonline.co.uk

PORT GAVERNE HOTEL NEAR PORT ISAAC PL29 3SQ (01208 880244; Fax: 01208 880151). Renowned 17th century inn in an unspoilt fishing cove on the rugged North Coast of Cornwall. Beach just 50 yards away. Pets welcome. Self-catering accommodation available. [Pets £3.50 per night].

Portreath

Coastal village 4 miles north west of Redruth.

Charming, elegantly furnished, self-catering cottages between Newquay and St Ives. Sleep 2 to 6. Fully equipped including linen. Beautiful beaches. Laundry and games room. Ample parking. Colour brochure – FRIESIAN VALLEY COTTAGES, MAWLA, CORNWALL TR16 5DW (01209 890901) [🐕

FREE or REDUCED RATE entry to Holiday Visits and Attractions – see our **READERS' OFFER VOUCHERS** on pages 433-440

Portwrinkle

Village on Whitsand Bay, 6 miles west of Torpoint.

WHITSAND BAY SELF-CATERING (01579 345688). Twelve cottages sleeping 4-10, all with sea views and situated by an 18-hole clifftop golf course. Children and pet-friendly. [Pets £5 per night].
e-mail: ehwbsc@hotmail.com website: www.whitsandbayselfcatering.co.uk

WHITSAND BAY HOTEL LEISURE & GOLF, PORTWRINKLE PL11 3BU (01503 230276). Character 32-bedroom hotel with stunning sea views and own 18-hole clifftop golf course. Innovative cuisine. Health & Fitness facilities. Indoor heated pool. Well behaved dogs most welcome. [Pets £10 per dog per night].
e-mail: whitsandbayhotel@btconnect.com website: www.whitsandbayhotel.co.uk

Redruth

Market town nine miles west of Truro, 12 miles east of St Ives.

WHEAL ROSE CARAVAN & CAMPING PARK, SCORRIER, REDRUTH TR16 5DD (Tel/Fax: 01209 891496) A secluded, 6-acre family-run touring park, popular with walkers and cyclists. Spotlessly clean, purpose-built shower/toilet block, shop, children's play area, TV/games room, laundry and disabled facilities.
e-mail: les@whealrosecaravanpark.co.uk website:www.whealrosecaravanpark.co.uk

St Agnes

Patchwork of fields dotted with remains of local mining industry. Watch for grey seals swimming off St Agnes Head.

THE DRIFTWOOD SPARS, TREVAUNANCE COVE, ST AGNES TR5 0RT (01872 552428). Take a deep breath of Cornish fresh air at this comfortable B&B ideally situated for a perfect seaside holiday. Dogs allowed on beach. Miles of footpaths for 'walkies'. Children and pets welcome. AA ★★★★ [Pets £3 per night].
website: www.driftwoodspars.com

PENKERRIS, PENWINNICK ROAD, ST AGNES TR5 0PA (01872 552262). Creeper clad B&B Guest House with garden. Real food, comfortable bedrooms. Ample parking. Dramatic cliff walks and sandy beaches. Open all year. Pets most welcome (preferably not school holidays). ETC ★★ [£5 per dog per night, £26 per week]
e-mail: info@penkerris.co.uk website: www.penkerris.co.uk

BLUE HILLS TOURING PARK, CROSS COOMBE, TREVELLAS, ST AGNES TR5 0XP (01872 552999). In a beautiful rural position close to a coastal footpath, a small site with good toilets. Pleasant location for exploring nearby coves, beaches and villages. Two-acre site with 30 touring pitches. [🐕]
e-mail: loo@zoom.co.uk website: www.bluehillscamping.co.uk

CHIVERTON PARK, BLACKWATER, TRURO TR4 8HS (01872 560667). Caravan and touring holidays only a short drive from magnificent beaches. Quiet, spacious; exclusive gym, sauna, steamroom; laundry, shop, play area and games room. All amenities. No club, bar or disco. [Dogs £15 per week]
e-mail: info@chivertonpark.co.uk website: www.chivertonpark.co.uk

St Austell

Old Cornish town and china clay centre with small port at Charlestown (1½ miles). Excellent touring centre. Newquay 16 miles, Truro 14, Bodmin 12, Fowey 9, Mevagissey 6.

BOSINVER HOLIDAY COTTAGES, ST MEWAN, ST AUSTELL PL26 7DT (01726 72128). Award-winning individual cottages in peaceful garden surroundings. Close to major holiday attractions. Short walk to shop and pub. Phone for brochure. No pets during Summer School holidays. ETC ★★★★ [pw!, Pets £30 per week].
e-mail: reception@bosinver.co.uk website: www.bosinver.co.uk

St Ives

Picturesque resort, popular with artists, with cobbled streets and intriguing little shops. Wide stretches of sand.

SPACIOUS COTTAGE. Sleeps 7/9. Near beaches, harbour, shops, Tate Gallery. Terms £360 to £758 per week. Dogs welcome. Available all year. Telephone: Carol Holland (01736 793015). [Pets £10 per week]

BOB AND JACKY PONTEFRACT, THE LINKS HOLIDAY FLATS, LELANT, ST IVES TR26 3HY (Tel & Fax: 01736 753326). Magnificent location overlooking golf course and beach. Wonderful spot for walking. Five minutes from beach where dogs allowed all year. Two well-equipped flats open all year. [ ]

SANDBANK HOLIDAYS, ST IVES BAY, HAYLE (01736 752594). High quality Apartments and Bungalows for 2-6 persons. Heated, Colour TV, Microwave etc. Dogs welcome. [Pets £14 to £21 per week]
website: www.sandbank-holidays.co.uk

St Mawes

Village with harbour and two good beaches, excellent for swimming.

SEA PINK, NEAR ST MAWES, SOUTH CORNWALL. In a picturesque setting overlooking the coast, Sea Pink is ideally located for exploring the coast and attractions. Spacious lounge, dining area opening on to sun terrace and lawned garden, three bedrooms. Brochure available. Contact JUDY JUNIPER (01872 863553). [Pets £10 per week, pw!]
e-mail: cottageinfo@btconnect.com website: www.luxury-holiday-cottages.com

St Mawgan

Delightful village in wooded river valley. Ancient church has fine carvings.

DALSWINTON HOUSE, ST MAWGAN, CORNWALL TR8 4EZ (01637 860385). Old Cornish house standing in ten acres of secluded grounds. All rooms en suite, colour TV, tea/coffee facilities. Solar heated outdoor swimming pool. Restaurant and bar. Out-of-season breaks. No children under 16. ETC ★★★★ [pw!]
e-mail: dalswintonhouse@tiscali.co.uk website: www.dalswinton.com

St Tudy

Village 5 miles north east of Wadebridge.

Comfortable end of terrace cottage in picturesque and friendly village. Enclosed garden and parking. Ideal location for exploring all Cornwall. Short Breaks and brochure available. Contact: MRS R REEVES, POLSTRAUL, TREWALDER, DELABOLE PL33 9ET (Tel & Fax: 01840 213120). [ ]
e-mail: ruth.reeves@hotmail.co.uk website: www.maymear.co.uk

St Wenn

Village 4 miles East of St Columb Major.

TREWITHIAN FARM, ST WENN PL30 5PH (01208 895181). Comfortable, well equipped wing of farmhouse, edge of Bodmin Moor. Very secluded position. 2 dogs welcome, use of kennels, exercise field. Good walking and dog-friendly beaches nearby. [pw!]
website: www.cornwall-online.co.uk/trewithianfarm

Tintagel

Attractively situated amidst fine cliff scenery; small rocky beach. Famous for associations with King Arthur, whose ruined castle on Tintagel Head is of interest. Bude 19 miles, Camelford 6.

MR & MRS N. CAREY, SALUTATIONS, ATLANTIC ROAD, TINTAGEL PL34 0DE (01840 770287). Comfortable, well-equipped, centrally heated cottages sleeping two. Ideal for touring, walking and relaxing. Close to Coastal Path and village amenities. Private parking. Ring for brochure. Pets Free. [ ]
e-mail: merlin0123@tiscali.co.uk website: www.salutationstintagel.co.uk

Truro

Bustling Cathedral City with something for everyone. Museum and Art Gallery with interesting shop and cafe is well worth a visit.

MRS PAMELA CARBIS, TRENONA FARM, RUAN HIGH LANES, TRURO TR2 5JS (01872 501339). Enjoy a relaxing stay on the unspoilt Roseland Peninsula between Truro and St Austell. Self-catering in two renovated barns, B&B in Victorian farmhouse. Children and pets welcome. Brochure available. [Pets £5 per stay, ⌂]
e-mail: info@trenonafarmholidays.co.uk website: www.trenonafarmholidays.co.uk

HIGHER TREWITHEN, STITHIANS, TRURO TR3 7DR (01209 860863) The ideal centre for your pet and your family. We are surrounded by public footpaths and have 3½ acres of fields. [🐕]
e-mail: trewithen@talk21.com website: www.trewithen.com

THE VALLEY (01872 862194). A secluded hamlet of contemporary cottages in a tranquil country valley. Beautiful gardens and woodland walks, ideal for dogs. Relax in luxury, with leisure facilities, and experience exquisite cuisine in the stylish Cafe Azur. ETC ★★★★★[Pets £20 per visit]
website: www.the-valley.co.uk

TRELOAN COASTAL FARM HOLIDAYS, TRELOAN LANE, PORTSCATHO TR2 5EG (01872 580899/580989). Traditional working farm on coastal footpath. Open all year. Sea views. Experience farm practices. Close to shops, pubs, etc. [Pets £1 each per night, £12 each per week in mobile homes].
e-mail: enquiries@coastalfarmholidays.co.uk website: www.coastalfarmholidays.co.uk

KING HARRY COTTAGES, FEOCK, TRURO TR3 6QJ (01872 861917). Two comfortable, well equipped cottages in own charming gardens. Dogs welcome. Beautiful woodland walks. Perfect for fishing and bird watching. [🐕]
e-mail: beverley@kingharry.net website: www.kingharry.net

Wadebridge

Town on River Camel, 6 miles north-west of Bodmin

Three barn converted luxury cottage-style self catering homes near Wadebridge. Found along a leafy drive, with wonderful views, beside the lazy twisting Camel River with its "Trail" for walking and cycling. CORNWALL TOURISM AWARDS 2002 - Self Catering Establishment of the Year - "Highly Commended". Sleep 2-7 plus cot. Two dogs per cottage welcome. GARY NEWMAN, COLESENT COTTAGES, ST TUDY, WADEBRIDGE, CORNWALL PL30 4QX (Tel & Fax: 01208 850112). [pw! 🐕]
e-mail: relax@colesent.co.uk website: www.colesent.co.uk

Other specialised holiday guides from FHG

PUBS & INNS OF BRITAIN • **COUNTRY HOTELS** OF BRITAIN

WEEKEND & SHORT BREAK HOLIDAYS IN BRITAIN

THE GOLF GUIDE WHERE TO PLAY, WHERE TO STAY

500 GREAT PLACES TO STAY • **SELF-CATERING HOLIDAYS** IN BRITAIN

BED & BREAKFAST STOPS • **CARAVAN & CAMPING HOLIDAYS**

FAMILY BREAKS IN BRITAIN

Published annually: available in all good bookshops or direct from the publisher:

FHG Guides, Abbey Mill Business Centre, Seedhill, Paisley PA1 1TJ

Tel: 0141 887 0428 • Fax: 0141 889 7204

e-mail: admin@fhguides.co.uk • www.holidayguides.com

PORT LIGHT
Hotel, Restaurant & Inn

As featured in Times, Guardian, Mail, Telegraph, Express, Dogs Today, Your Dog and many pet-friendly internet sites

- Luxury en suite rooms, easy access onto the gardens
- Close to secluded sandy cove (dogs permitted) 20 minutes' walk
- No charge for pets which are most welcome throughout the hotel
- Recognised for outstanding food and service
- Outstanding reputation for superb home-cooked fayre
- Set alongside the famous National Trust Salcombe to Hope Cove coastal walk
- Fully licensed bar - log burner - real ale
- Winner 2004 "Dogs Trust" Best Pet Hotel in England
- Large free car park ◆ Open Christmas & New Year ◆ Self-catering cottages

A totally unique location, set amidst acres of National Trust coastal countryside with panoramic views towards Cornwall, Dartmoor and France.

THE PORT LIGHT
HOTEL INN RESTAURANT
Doggies' Heaven, Walkers' Paradise, Romantics' Dream
WE ARE REALLY, TOTALLY PET-FRIENDLY

Important advice: always check to ensure other so-called 'pet-friendly' hotels really are! Talk to us to find out more.

Bolberry Down, Malborough, Near Salcombe, South Devon TQ7 3DY
e-mail: info@portlight.co.uk • www.portlight.co.uk
Tel: (01548) 561384 or (07970) 859992 • Sean & Hazel Hassall

❖ Bolberry Farm Cottages ❖

Bolberry, Near Salcombe, Devon TQ7 3DY

Luxury two and three bedroom barn conversion cottages
• Private gardens • Shared orchard • Views across valley • Gas, coal, open fires
• Parking • Finished to a very high standard • Linen and towels included
• Central heating • Close to coastal path and pet-friendly beaches
• Dog wash • Superb meals available at our nearby Port Light Inn & Hotel • Credit/Debit cards accepted

Tel: 01548 561384 • e-mail: info@bolberryfarmcottages.co.uk • www.bolberryfarmcottages.co.uk

Hazel & Sean Hassall • *The Pet Holiday Specialist* •

North Devon Holiday Homes

Call for a free colour guide or visit our website now for 100s of the best value cottages around Exmoor and Devon's unspoilt National Trust/dog walking coastline.

(01271) 376322

www.devonandexmoor.co.uk

cottage heaven
The finest holiday cottages in rural and coastal locations throughout the West Country
Farm & Cottage HOLIDAYS
01237 459897
holidaycottages.co.uk
devon
cornwall
somerset
dorset

...and Bertie came too!
Helpful Holidays have a wonderful variety of cottages, houses, apartments all over the West Country - seaside, moorland, farmland and villages. Many of our properties welcome pets and are in ideal locations for countryside rambles!
All properties are inspected, star rated & frankly described by us in our full colour brochure.
01647 433535
Helpful Holidays
www.helpfulholidays.co.uk

Toad Hall Cottages
Cottage Holidays for laid back dogs.
300 quality waterside & rural properties in beautiful locations.
People welcome too!
For our fabulous fully detailed brochure
telephone 01548 853089 (24 hours)
www.toadhallcottages.co.uk

Your first visit won't
be your last adventure.
The largest selection of VisitBritain
inspected holiday cottages in Devon.
Many of our 300 properties welcome pets.
Please contact us to find the best property
for your **whole** family.
www.marsdens.co.uk
for information and 24 hour on line booking
For a free brochure, contact
holidays@marsdens.co.uk,
phone 01271 813777 or write
2 The Square, Braunton, Devon EX33 2JB
MARSDENS
COTTAGE HOLIDAYS

Holiday Homes & Cottages S.W.

www.swcottages.co.uk

Large selection of cottages in Devon & Cornwall. Pets welcomed. ETC rated. Coastal and Rural locations.

Tel: 01803 299677

Fax: 01803 664037

Appledore, Ashburton

CROSS HOUSE

Fore Street, Northam, Bideford EX39 1AN
Tel: 01237 472042
info@crosshouseandcottages.co.uk
www.crosshouseandcottages.co.uk

'Come as a guest leave as a friend'. We can offer you three 'Home from Home' cottages, all with 'Olde Worlde' charm and up-to-date amenities. We are ideally situated for touring with Exmoor, Clovelly, Lynton, Lynmouth, Tarka Trail within easy reach. Relax on one of the many beaches, the nearest one mile away. Well-behaved owners welcome!

ETC ★★★ - ★★★★

Mrs Angela Bell
Wooder Manor, Widecombe in the Moor, Near Ashburton TQ13 7TR
Tel & Fax: (01364) 621391
www.woodermanor.com
e-mail: angela@woodermanor.com

Cottages and converted coach house on 170-acre working family farm nestled in the picturesque valley of Widecombe, surrounded by unspoilt woodland moors and granite tors. Half-a-mile from village with post office, general stores, two good pubs (dogs welcome) and National Trust Information Centre. Excellent centre for touring Devon with a variety of places to visit and exploring Dartmoor by foot or on horseback. Accommodation is clean and well-equipped with colour TV, central heating, laundry room. Children welcome. Large gardens and courtyard for easy parking. Open all year, so take advantage of off-season reduced rates. Short Breaks available. Two properties suitable for disabled visitors. Colour Brochure.

PARKERS FARM COTTAGES

Come and stay on a real 400-acre farm in South Devon

FARM COTTAGES • STATIC CARAVANS

Friendly, family-run self-catering complex with cottages and static caravans surrounded by beautiful countryside. 12 miles from the sea and close to Dartmoor National Park. Perfect for children and pets, with farm animals and plenty of space to roam. Large area to walk your dogs. Laundry, bar and restaurant. Good discounts for couples. A warm welcome awaits you. British Farm Tourist Award • ETC ★★★★

DOGS' PARADISE

PETS WELCOME

THE ROCKERY, CATON, ASHBURTON, DEVON TQ13 7LH • Tel: 01364 653008
e-mail: parkerscottages@btconnect.com • www.parkersfarm.co.uk

Readers are requested to mention this FHG guidebook when seeking accommodation

Ashburton, Ashwater, Axminster

Parkers Farm Holiday Park

STATIC CARAVANS • TOURING SITE

Friendly, family-run touring site and static caravans situated in unspoilt countryside. Genuine farm. Spectacular views to Dartmoor. Two modern shower blocks; electric hook-ups. Bar and restaurant with area for dogs. Large dog-walking fields. Shop, launderette and indoor/outdoor play areas. 12 miles to coast. Short Breaks available.

PETS WELCOME

HIGHER MEAD FARM, ASHBURTON, DEVON TQ13 7LJ
Tel: 01364 654869 • Fax: 01364 654004
e-mail: parkersfarm@btconnect.com
www.parkersfarm.co.uk

Ashwater, North Devon EX21 5DF
Tel: 01409 211224 • Fax: 01409 211634

BLAGDON MANOR
HOTEL & RESTAURANT

Liz and Steve, along with our two Chocolate Labradors, Nutmeg and Cassia, look forward to welcoming you to Blagdon Manor.

Restaurant: Enjoy excellent cuisine using locally sourced produce. Dinner available every night for residents.
Accommodation: 8 en suite bedrooms
Panoramic views of the Devon countryside and Dartmoor. Beautifully restored Grade II Listed building. Enjoy a peaceful location halfway between Dartmoor and Exmoor and only 20 minutes from the North Cornish coast at Bude.

3 acres of gardens and 17 acres of fields. Children over the age of 12 and dogs are welcome. Double/twin rooms £135-£180 per night, based on two sharing. Single occupancy £85. Dogs £7.50 per night.

e-mail: stay@blagdon.com
www.blagdon.com

Lea Hill

MEMBURY, AXMINSTER EX13 7AQ

Tranquil location • Wonderful scenery • Close to World Heritage Coast • Eight acres of grounds and gardens • Walks, footpaths, dog exercise field • Hot tub and barbecue. Comfortable, well equipped self-catering cottages with en suite bedrooms and own gardens

e-mail: reception@leahill.co.uk • 01404 881881
www.leahill.co.uk

Lilac Cottage

Smallridge, Axminster. Detached cottage, carefully renovated, retaining the inglenook fireplace, oak beams, floors and doors. Oil-fired central heating, colour TV, fully-equipped all-electric kitchen. Furnished to a high standard, sleeps six plus cot. Children and pets are welcome. Walled garden and garage. The villages and surrounding countryside are beautiful on the borders of Devon, Dorset, and Somerset. Many seaside towns within 10 miles – Lyme Regis, Charmouth and Seaton. Contact: **Mrs J.M. Stuart, 2 Sandford House, Kingsclere RG20 4PA • Tel & Fax: 01635 291942 • e-mail: joanna.sb@free.fr**

Fairwater Head Hotel

3 Star Accommodation at Sensible Prices

AA ★★★

Located in the tranquil Devon countryside and close to Lyme Regis, this beautiful Edwardian Country House Hotel has all you and your dog need for a peaceful and relaxing holiday.

Dogs Most Welcome and Free of Charge

Countryside location with panoramic views • AA Two Rosette Restaurant

The Fairwater Head Hotel
Hawkchurch, Near Axminster, Devon EX13 5TX
Tel: 01297 678349 • Fax: 01297 678459
e-mail: stay@fairwaterheadhotel.co.uk
www.fairwaterheadhotel.co.uk

Barnstaple

"Valley View" · Guineaford, Marwood, Barnstaple EX31 4EA

Set in 320 acres of farmland which visitors are free to enjoy. The farm, situated 3½ miles from Barnstaple, produces lamb and is home to Helenbrie Miniature Shetland ponies. There are two bedrooms each containing a double and single bed. Bed and Breakfast from £25. Children are welcomed, half-price under 12 years. Babysitting free of charge. Pets by arrangement. Car essential – parking. Open all year.

Tel: 01271 343458 • www.helenbriestud.co.uk

Martinhoe Cleave Cottages

Martinhoe, Parracombe, Barnstaple, Devon EX31 4PZ

Overlooking the beautiful Heddon valley and close to the dramatic coast of the Exmoor National Park, these delightful cottages, equipped to a very high standard throughout, offer perfect rural tranquillity. Open all year. Sleep 1-2. • **Tel: 01598 763313**

e-mail: info@exmoorhideaway.co.uk • www.exmoorhideaway.co.uk

Winner Golden Achievement Award of Excellence for Devon Retreat of the Year

Situated half way between Barnstaple and Bideford, this delightfully modernised 17th Century farmhouse accommodation is part of a working farm. The farm is centrally located for easy access to the many attractions of North Devon, its beautiful beaches, varied walks and sports facilities including golf, surfing, fishing, riding etc. Its proximity to both Exmoor and Dartmoor makes this location perfect for those who wish to explore. Instow with its sandy beach, pubs and restaurants is a just mile away. It lies adjacent to the Tarka Trail, part of the South West Coastal Footpath, and RSPB bird sanctuary. The bed and breakfast accommodation comprises 3 twin/super king-size and 2 rooms with four-poster beds, 1 double room and 2 single rooms; all rooms en suite, with TV and tea/coffee making facilities. Breakfast includes eggs from our free-range chickens, home-made bread, jams and marmalade. The delightful sitting room has a large selection of books for those who want to relax and browse.

Please visit our website for further details **www.loweryellandfarm.co.uk**

Lower Yelland Farm Guest House, Fremington, Barnstaple EX31 3EN
Tel: 01271 860101 • e-mail: peterday@loweryellandfarm.co.uk

Welcome to North Hill – deep in the rolling hills of Devon, a truly pastoral retreat.

17th century farm buildings, sympathetically converted into cottages sleeping 2-6, with exposed beams, wood stoves and central heating. Set in 9 acres of pastures and gardens with a children's play area. Facilities include: indoor heated swimming pool, jacuzzi, sauna, all-weather tennis court and games room.

This area of North Devon offers some of the finest beaches in the country and the National Park of Exmoor offers thousands of acres of moorland to explore.

Terms from £195 to £910

Carol Ann and Adrian Black, North Hill, Shirwell, Barnstaple EX31 4LG

Tel: 01271 850611 • Mobile: 07834 806434 • www.north-hill.co.uk

North Devon & Exmoor

Enjoy Exmoor's rugged natural beauty and spectacular coastline, together with Marwood Hill and RHS Rosemoor. This charming former rectory offers quiet comfort, long views and Aga-based cookery, all set in 8 acres. Ground floor rooms available. Well-behaved dog owners welcome. Also two-person self-catering cottage.

Bracken House Hotel

Pets Welcome Free of Charge

Bratton Fleming EX31 4TG

Tel: 01598 710320 or visit www.brackenhousehotel.co.uk

YOUR PET STAYS FREE

ETC ★★★

Sandy Cove Hotel stands in 20 acres of cliff, coast and garden. The Hotel Restaurant overlooks the sea and cliffs with spectacular views of the bay. Mini-breaks are available as well as special weekly rates, all of which offer a five-course meal including seafood platters with lobster, smoked salmon and steak. Every Saturday there is a Swedish Smorgasbord and Carvery followed by dancing till late. All bedrooms have colour TV, telephone, teamaking and are en suite. There is an unique indoor swimming pool with rolling back sides to enjoy the sun, as well as a whirlpool, sauna, steam-room and fitness area with gym equipment.

Please return this advertisement to qualify for "Pets Stay Free" offer.
Children have free accommodation sharing parents' room.
Children under 5 years completely free, including meals.

You'll love the special atmosphere of Sandy Cove, why not find us on our website at www.sandycove-hotel.co.uk or ring to request a brochure

SANDY COVE
HOTEL

Combe Martin Bay,
Devon EX34 9SR
Tel: 01271 882243
01271 882888

Bideford, Bigbury-on-Sea, Bradworthy, Braunton

Mead Barn Cottages

Welcombe,
North Devon
EX39 6HQ

ETC ★★★-★★★★ Graded Quality Self-Catering Cottages sleeping 2 - 26 people. Set in 1½ acres.
Games Room • Tennis court • Play Area • Swings
Trampoline • Gardens with Barbecue Area
Proprietors: Robert & Lisa Ireton. **Tel: 01288 331 721**
e-mail: holidays@meadbarns.com
Visit: www.meadbarns.com

The Pines at Eastleigh

A Georgian country house set in 7 hilltop acres with magnificent views over the Torridge estuary to Lundy Island. Log-fires, king-size beds, garden room bar with library, maps and a warm welcome await our guests.

Breakfasts use home-produced and prize-winning locally sourced ingredients.

There are ground floor rooms set around the courtyard garden with easy access. All rooms are en suite and have teletext television, well-stocked hospitality tray with tea and coffee making facilities, telephones and hairdryers.

Selected by the AA as "One of Britain's Best in 2008."

Bed & Breakfast from £40pp.
Self-catering from £350 for 4. No Smoking.

www.thepinesateastleigh.co.uk
e-mail: pirrie@thepinesateastleigh.co.uk

Hotel & Cottages
Eastleigh, Near Bideford,
North Devon EX39 4PA
Tel: 01271 860561

AA ★★★★

MOUNT FOLLY FARM

Cliff top position, with outstanding views of Bigbury Bay. Spacious, self catering wing of farmhouse, attractively furnished. Farm adjoins golf course and River Avon. Lovely coastal walks, ideal centre for South Hams and Dartmoor. No smoking.

Always a warm welcome, pets too!

MRS J. TUCKER, BIGBURY-ON-SEA, KINGSBRIDGE TQ7 4AR (01548 810267).
e-mail: chris.cathy@goosemoose.com • www.bigburyholidays.co.uk ETC ★★★

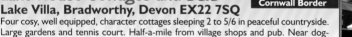

Lake House Cottages and B&B

North Devon/ Cornwall Border

Lake Villa, Bradworthy, Devon EX22 7SQ

Four cosy, well equipped, character cottages sleeping 2 to 5/6 in peaceful countryside. Large gardens and tennis court. Half-a-mile from village shops and pub. Near dog-friendly beaches, coast path and moors. Also two en suite B&B rooms with balcony.

Brochure: Peter & Lesley Lewin on 01409 241962 • e-mail: info@lakevilla.co.uk • www.lakevilla.co.uk

A HAVEN OF PEACE AND TRANQUILLITY
***at Little Comfort Farm, Braunton, North Devon** ETC★★★*

Five spacious self-catering cottages with secluded gardens on organic family farm. Just minutes from golden sandy beaches where dogs are allowed. Well stocked coarse fishing lake. Private 1½km walk. Wood fires for cosy winter breaks. Pets very welcome.
Tel: 01271 812 414 • info@littlecomfortfarm.co.uk • www.littlecomfortfarm.co.uk

Pet-Friendly
Pubs, Inns & Hotels

on pages 424-432

Please note that these establishments may not feature in the main section of this book

Brixham
HOLIDAY PARK

English Tourism Council ★★★★ HOLIDAY PARK

Friendly, comfortable, family-run park offering all you could want from a holiday. Relax under the palm trees, laze by the superb indoor swimming pool , enjoy a drink or meal at the club.

Choose from apartments, chalets in a lawned setting, all fully furnished and equipped – pets welcome in many.

150 yards from beach • 10 minutes' walk from Brixham Harbour • Free Club membership with entertainment • Comfortable bar with meals and takeaway service • Shop and Launderette • Special off-season breaks

BROCHURE HOTLINE

01803 853324

wwww.brixhamholidaypark.co.uk

enquiries@brixhamholpk.fsnet.co.uk

An English Tourism Council Rose award park

**Fishcombe Cove,
Brixham,
South Devon TQ5 8RB**

British Holiday & Home Parks Association

DEVONCOURT
HOLIDAY FLATS

BERRYHEAD ROAD, BRIXHAM, DEVON TQ5 9AB

Devoncourt is a development of 24 self-contained flats, occupying one of the finest positions in Torbay, with unsurpassed views. At night the lights of Torbay are like a fairyland to be enjoyed from your very own balcony.

MasterCard VISA

EACH FLAT HAS:

- Heating
- Sea Views over Torbay
- Private balcony
- Own front door
- Separate bathroom and toilet
- Separate bedroom
- Bed-settee in lounge
- Lounge sea views over Marina
- Kitchenette - all electric
- Private car park
- Opposite beach
- Colour television
- Overlooks lifeboat
- Short walk to town centre
- Double glazing
- Open all year
- Mini Breaks October to April

Tel: 01803 853748
(or 07802 403289 after office hours)
website: www.devoncourt.info

Chittlehamholt, Chudleigh, Chulmleigh, Colebrook, Combe Martin

SNAPDOWN FARM CARAVANS Chittlehamholt, Umberleigh, North Devon EX37 9PF (01769) 540708

6 ONLY – 6 berth CARAVANS with all facilities on small site in beautiful, peaceful, unspoilt country setting - down our quiet lane, on the farm, lots of lovely places to visit nearby . Each with outside seats and picnic table. Field and woodland walks, abundant wildlife. Easy reach sea and moors. Children's play area in small adjoining wood. Well behaved pets welcome. £130 to £330 per caravan per week incl. gas and electricity in caravans. **Illustrated brochure available. (Discount for couples early/late season.)**

Bungalow set well back from the main road into town. One en suite double bedroom, use of large comfortable lounge. Good base for seeing Devon, plenty of places to walk dogs. B&B from £25 per person per night. Dogs welcome FREE of charge.

Tel: 01626 852172

S & G Harrison Crawford, Linden Lea, Parade, Chudleigh TQ13 0JG

Northcott Barton Farm Cottage

Beautifully equipped, spotlessly clean three bedroom cottage with large enclosed garden. A walker's and country lover's ideal: for a couple seeking peace and quiet or a family holiday. Very special rates for low season holidays, couples and short breaks. Near golf, riding, Tarka trail and R.H.S. Rosemoor. Character, comfort, beams, log fire, "*Perfick*". Pets Welcome, no charge.

For availability please contact Sandra Gay,
Northcott Barton, Ashreigney, Chulmleigh, Devon EX18 7PR
Tel/Fax: 01769 520259
e-mail: sandra@northcottbarton.co.uk
www.northcottbarton.co.uk

The Oyster is a modern bungalow in the pretty, peaceful village of Colebrooke in the heart of Mid Devon. There is a spacious garden for children to play around or sit on the patio. Comfortable accommodation with tea/coffee making facilities, with TV in bedroom and lounge. Bedrooms en suite or with private bathroom - two double and one twin. Walking distance to the New Inn, Coleford, a lovely 13th century free house. Dartmoor and Exmoor are only a short drive away. Central heating. Open all year. Ample parking. Terms from £25 per person for Bed and Breakfast. Children and pets welcome. Smoking accepted.

To find us take the Barnstaple road (A377)out of Crediton, turn left after one-and-a-half miles at sign for Colebrooke and Coleford. In Coleford village turn left at the crossroads, then in Colebrooke village take the left hand turning before the church, the Oyster is the second on the right.

Pearl Hockridge, The Oyster, Colebrooke, Crediton EX17 5JQ

Graded ★★★★ **MANLEIGH HOLIDAY PARK**

COMBE MARTIN EX34 0NS (01271 883353)

Quiet family-run site set in beautiful countryside near village, beaches, rocky coves and Exmoor. Chalets, log cabins and caravans tastefully sited on side of Combe Martin valley. Children's play area, laundry. Dog walk. Wine Bar serving delicious home-made food.

Colour Brochure: Lynne & Craig Davey
www.manleighpark.co.uk

Watermouth Cove Cottages, Watermouth, near Combe Martin EX34 9SJ • Tel: 0870 241 3168

Eight beautiful cottages, most with four-poster and log fire, set beside grounds of Watermouth Castle, 200 yards from the harbour/coastal path. Pets welcome all year.

e-mail: watermouthcove@googlemail.com • www.watermouth-cove-cottages.co.uk

---

FOREST GLADE CARAVAN & CAMPING PARK
••FREE INDOOR HEATED POOL••

CULLOMPTON EX15 2DT
01404 841381 (Evgs to 8pm)

A small country estate surrounded by forest in which deer roam. Situated in an area of outstanding natural beauty. Large, flat, sheltered camping/touring pitches. Central facilities building, luxury 2/6 berth full service holiday homes, also self contained flat for 2 persons. Forest walks with dog. **COLOUR BROCHURE.**

Fax: (01404) 841593 • www.forest-glade.co.uk • email: enquiries@forest-glade.co.uk

---

Peaceful woodland setting next to the River Walkham in the Dartmoor National Park. Ideally placed to explore the beauty of Devon. Purpose - built lodges available all year round, sleeping 2-7, tastefully blending into the surroundings. Interior specification and furnishings to a high standard - including fully-fitted kitchen with oven, microwave and dishwasher.

• 3 golf courses a short drive away. • Easy walk to village and shops • Scenic walks. • Fishing • Dogs accepted • Horse riding nearby • Small, select touring area for caravans, tents and motor caravans • Launderette • On A386 Plymouth-Tavistock road.

For Free Brochure:

Dept PW, Dartmoor Country Holidays, Magpie Leisure Park, Horrabridge, Yelverton, Devon PL20 7RY. Tel:01822 852651 or visit our website: www.dartmoorcountryholidays.co.uk

DARTMOOR COUNTRY HOLIDAYS
MAGPIE LEISURE PARK

Walkies on DARTMOOR is FANTASTIC!

The Cherrybrook

Stay at *The Cherrybrook* with your owners and you can step straight from the hotel onto the high moor and walk with them for miles. In the evenings, they can enjoy a drink in our cosy bar followed by our delicious award-winning home-made food.

They must deserve a treat – go on, get them to call!

Two Bridges, Devon PL20 6SP
Call 01822 880260 for details

e-mail: info@cherrybrookhotel.co.uk • www.cherrybrookhotel.co.uk

---

Where else would your dog rather walk?

Walk straight from the hotel... for miles, then relax with our traditional country house hospitality, where dogs are genuinely welcomed. Indulge in our AA Rosetted restaurant with local produce and hearty breakfasts. Country pursuits such as fishing and riding, or golf, and garden or historic house visits are all within easy reach. Tranquillity abounds. No charge for well-behaved dogs.

01822 890403

AA/VisitBritain ★★

Silver
SILVER AWARD

PRINCE HALL *Hotel*
Dartmoor, Devon PL20 6SA
e-mail: info@princehall.co.uk • www.princehall.co.uk

Dartmoor, Dartmouth

The Edgemoor Country House Hotel

Haytor Road, Lowerdown Cross,
Bovey Tracey, Devon TQ13 9LE
Tel: 01626 832466

Charming Country House Hotel in peaceful wooded setting adjacent Dartmoor National Park. Many lovely walks close by. All rooms en suite. Excellent food. Dogs (with well-behaved owners) welcome.

For more information, photographs, current menus and general information about the area see our website :

www.edgemoor.co.uk or e-mail: reservations@edgemoor.co.uk

★★★ HOTEL

Silver SILVER AWARD

TWO BRIDGES HOTEL

Two Bridges, Princetown, Dartmoor PL20 6SW • ETC/AA ★★

To enter the Two Bridges is like stepping back in time. Sink back into the leather chairs around the blazing log fires, with the gleam of copper and brass.The Tors Restaurant serves the very finest West Country cuisine. Premier bedrooms with four-poster bed and jacuzzi bath. A warm welcome awaits all our guests.

Tel: 01822 890581

www.warm-welcome-hotels.co.uk • e-mail: enquiries@warm-welcome-hotels.co.uk

This beachside apartment is situated directly on the beach at Slapton Sands in the unspoilt countryside of the South Hams between the blue waters of Start Bay and the Slapton Ley Nature Reserve. Seven miles from Kingsbridge and Dartmouth. Two bedrooms, one double bedded room with chair bed for child and one twin room, central heating, washing machine, fully equipped kitchen, private parking and balcony overlooking the Ley. Will sleep total of five. Lovely walks on Coastal Path. Send for brochure with pleasure or visit our website on **www.torcross.com**

Torcross, South Devon TQ7 2TQ • 01548 580206 • e-mail: enquiries@torcross.com

Watermill Cottages

Six stone cottages on the banks of a small river, in a peaceful secluded valley a mile inland from Slapton Sands. Wonderful valley walks and freedom for children to explore. Close to dog-friendly beaches, pubs and stunning coastal walks. Home cooking available, log fires and enclosed gardens. Winter breaks offered.

Hansel, Dartmouth, South Devon TQ6 0LN

www.watermillcottages.co.uk

For our colour brochure call 01803 770219 or e-mail: graham@hanselpg.freeserve.co.uk

DARTSIDE *Holidays*

Apartments at Dartmouth, Devon

Comfortable holiday apartments with private balconies – superb river and harbour views. Sailing, boating, fishing, coastal walks within easy reach. Available all year round with colour TV, linen and parking.

Phone for FREE colour brochure

RIVERSIDE COURT, SOUTH EMBANKMENT, DARTMOUTH TQ6 9BH

Tel: 01803 832093 • Fax: 01803 835135 • www.dartsideholidays.com

THE OLD BAKEHOUSE

Tel & Fax: 01803 834585

Mrs S.R. Ridalls, 7 Broadstone, Dartmouth TQ6 9NR

Character cottages with beams and old stone fireplaces, one with four-poster bed. In conservation area, 2 minutes from historic town centre and river. Blackpool Sands 15 minute drive. Free parking. Open all year.

Non-smoking. Autumn/Winter/Spring breaks.

www.oldbakehousedartmouth.co.uk • e-mail: oldbakehousecottages@yahoo.com

Station Lodge, Doddiscombsleigh, Exeter

Comfortably furnished apartment In the beautiful Teign River valley. Excellent location for exploring Devon's moors, coasts and villages. Kitchen, lounge/diner, en suite bedroom with double bed. Private garden, extensive grounds. Pubs, shops and walks nearby, golf, fishing, horseriding, tennis and swimming pools within 10 miles. Central heating. Colour TV. All linen provided. Parking. Non-smokers only. Well behaved dogs welcome. From £200 per week. For further details contact:

Ian West, Station House, Doddiscombsleigh, Exeter EX6 7PW • Tel & Fax: 01647 253104

e-mail: enquiries@station-lodge.co.uk • www.station-lodge.co.uk

THE ROYAL OAK INN

Dunsford, Near Exeter EX6 7DA

Tel: 01647 252256

Enjoy a friendly welcome in our traditional Country Pub in the picturesque thatched village of Dunsford. Quiet en suite bedrooms are available in the tastefully converted cob barn. Ideal base for touring Dartmoor, Exeter and the coast, and the beautiful Teign Valley. Real Ale and home-made meals are served.

Well-behaved children and dogs are welcome

Regular dog Kizzy • Resident dog Connie

Please ring Mark or Judy Harrison for further details.

RYDON FARM

WOODBURY, EXETER EX5 1LB Tel: 01395 232341

www.rydonfarmwoodbury.co.uk

16th Century Devon Longhouse on working dairy farm.
Open all year. Highly recommended. From £32 to £60pppn.

The perfect venue for a quiet get-away break with your beloved pet. Acres of private grounds, mile of driveway for exercise and animals are welcome in guests' bedrooms by arrangement. The hotel stands in its own grounds, four miles south west of Exeter. AA Two Rosette Restaurant, also intimate Lounge Bar which serves bar food. Free hotel brochure on request, or visit our website: ***www.lordhaldonhotel.co.uk***

Best Western Lord Haldon Hotel, Dunchideock, Near Exeter EX6 7YF

Tel: 01392 832483 • Fax: 01392 833765 • e-mail: enquiries@lordhaldonhotel.co.uk

Staghunters Inn/Hotel • Brendon, Exmoor EX35 6PS

A friendly, family-run Exmoor village inn with frontage to the East Lyn River. Beautiful landscaped garden to the rear; 12 en suite rooms. Varied menu of home-made food using fresh local produce. Log fires, fine wines and local cask ales. A walkers' paradise in the Doone Valley, close to Watersmeet, Lynton and Lynmouth. Ample off-road parking. B&B from £30. *New owners: The Wyburn Family.*

e-mail: stay@staghunters.com • www.staghunters.com • Tel: 01598 741222 • Fax: 01598 741352

Exmoor, Hexworthy (Dartmoor), Holsworthy, Honiton

Twitchen Farm

Comfort for country lovers in Exmoor National Park. High quality en suite rooms. Breakfast prepared with local and organic produce. Farm walk through fields to village pub. One dog free, two dogs £5. • *B&B £26–£36.* • ETC ★★★★

Jaye Jones & Helen Asher, Twitchen Farm, Challacombe, Barnstaple EX31 4TT

Telephone 01598 763568 • e-mail: holidays@twitchen.co.uk • www.twitchen.co.uk

THE SPIRIT OF EXMOOR Riding holidays for adults

Exhilarating riding across miles of untamed moorland in small groups. Fit, friendly, forward going, well schooled horses. Non-riders and own horses and pets welcome. Accommodation in secluded, comfortable, 17th century farmhouse or cosy en suite lodges. Delicious home-cooked cuisine; vegetarians welcome. Horse whispering courses. 70% repeat booking says it all.

Please phone Stephany Pettinger for a colour brochure or more information.

stephany@spiritofexmoor.fsnet.co.uk www.spiritofexmoor.com

THE FOREST INN

Hexworthy, Dartmoor PL20 6SD

★★★ GUEST ACCOMMODATION

A haven for walkers, riders, fishermen, canoeists or anyone just looking for an opportunity to enjoy the natural beauty of Dartmoor. We specialise in homemade food using local produce wherever possible. With the emphasis on Devon beers and ciders, you have the opportunity to quench your thirst after the efforts of the day with a drink at the bar or relaxing on the chesterfields in the lounge area, complete with log fire for winter evenings.

Tel: 01364 631211 • Fax: 01364 631515 • e-mail: info@theforestinn.co.uk

Tinney Waters

Coarse Fishing Holidays
Self Catering • Bed & Breakfast
No closed Season

Beautiful setting where you will be able to enjoy peace and tranquillity in the heart of rural Devon. Lots of non-fishing activities.

Telephone: 01409 271362
www.tinneywaters.co.uk

somewhere different **somewhere special**

Combe House Hotel & Restaurant - *You and your dog are most welcome for coffee, lunch or dinner*

Gittisham, Honiton, Nr Exeter, Devon EX14 3AD tel: **01404 540 400** **www.thishotel.com**

HOPE BARTON BARNS

Tel: 01548 561393
www.hopebarton.co.uk

Open All Year

Nestling in its own valley close to the sandy cove, Hope Barton Barns is an exclusive group of 17 stone barns in two courtyards and 3 luxury apartments in the converted farmhouse. Heated indoor pool, sauna, gym, lounge bar, tennis court, trout lake and a children's play barn. We have 35 acres of pastures and streams with sheep, goats, pigs, chickens, ducks and rabbits. Superbly furnished and fully equipped, each cottage is unique, and vary from a studio to four bedrooms, sleeping 2 to 10. Farmhouse meals. Ample parking. Golf, sailing and coastal walking nearby. A perfect setting for family summer holidays, walking in Spring/Autumn or just a "get away from it all" break. Free-range children and well behaved dogs welcome. For full colour brochure please contact: ***Mr & Mrs M. Pope.***

Hope Cove - Near Salcombe - South Devon - TQ7 3HT

WIDMOUTH FARM

Widmouth Farm Cottages

Watermouth, Near Ilfracombe
Devon EX34 9RX
Tel: 01271 863743

Widmouth Farm has 35 acres of gardens, woodland, pastures and a private beach on National Heritage Coastline. There are 11 one, two, three and four bedroom cottages, some early Victorian, some conversions from farm buildings. All are comfortable and well equipped. From £250-£1560 per week. We have alpacas, sheep, goats, chickens, ducks, rabbits, guinea pigs and much wildlife (seals sometimes play off our coast). The surroundings are tranquil, the views superb and access easy (on the A399 between Ilfracombe and Combe Martin). Ideal for walking (the coastal footpath runs around the property), bird watching, painting and sea fishing. Ilfracombe Golf Club quarter of a mile. Pets welcome.

English Tourism Council ★★★ SELF CATERING

e-mail: holiday@widmouthfarmcottages.co.uk • www.widmouthfarmcottages.co.uk

LEAD YOUR MASTER AND MISTRESS TO HERE!

St Brannocks House

Hi! I'm Louis the daxi and my friends can come and stay here free. Look forward to seeing you. I've got:

- ★ Brilliant walks, Exmoor and beaches nearby
- ★ A lovely relaxing home which is open all year
- ★ A level walk to the nearby town shops & harbour
- ★ Great food, cosy Bar and comfy lounge
- ★ A mistress who likes us - and children too
- ★ A large dog-carriage park

★★★★ GUEST ACCOMMODATION

Phone or write to Barbara Clarke
St Brannocks Road, Ilfracombe EX34 8EQ
email: barbara@stbrannockshouse.co.uk
www.stbrannockshouse.co.uk

Tel/Fax: 01271 863873

Ilfracombe, Instow

Varley House, Chambercombe Park, Ilfracombe EX34 9QW

Tel: 01271 863927 • Fax: 01271 879299 • e-mail: info@varleyhouse.co.uk • www.varleyhouse.co.uk

Built at the turn of the 20th century for returning officers from the Boer War, Varley generates a feeling of warmth and relaxation, combined with an enviable position overlooking Hillsborough Nature Reserve. Winding paths lead to the Harbour and several secluded coves. Our attractive, spacious, fully en suite bedrooms all have colour TV, central heating, generous beverage tray, hairdryer and clock radio alarm. Superb food, beautiful surroundings and that special friendly atmosphere so essential to a relaxing holiday. Cosy separate bar. Car Park. Children over 5 years of age. Dogs by arrangement. Bed & Breakfast from £30 per person. Weekly from £189 per person. Low season 3 day breaks from £78pp. NON-SMOKING

Free Wireless Internet Service

Beachside Holiday Park

Relax in one of Beachside's caravans nestled in the hillside overlooking golden Devonshire sands in Hele Bay, Ilfracombe

Call now to request your brochure and to book your holiday or short break

email: enquiries@beachsidepark.co.uk
web: www.beachsidepark.co.uk
tel: 01271 863006

beachside holiday park

A delightful and friendly Victorian Licensed guest house, situated just a 10-minute stroll to both seafront and town centre. 8 individually designed bedrooms, with either en suite shower or bath. Cosy lounge bar and secluded terraced garden. Children and pets are always welcome.

AA Pet-Friendly Accomodation of the Year 2006. Contact Pete and Heather Small

Strathmore • 57 St Brannocks Road, Ilfracombe EX34 8EQ

Tel: 01271 862248 • *e-mail: peter@small6374.fsnet.co.uk* • *www.the-strathmore.co.uk*

The Foxhunters Inn West Down, Near Ilfracombe EX34 8NU

300 year-old coaching Inn conveniently situated for beaches and country walks. Serving good local food. En suite accommodation. Pets allowed in bar areas and beer garden, may stay in accommodation by prior arrangement. Water bowls provided.

Tel: 01271 863757 • Fax: 01271 879313 • www.foxhuntersinn.co.uk

Instow Beach Haven Cottage

Two seafront cottages overlooking the sandy beach. Instow is a quiet yachting village with soft yellow sands and a pretty promenade of shops, old houses, pubs and cafés serving drinks and meals. Beach Haven has extensive beach and sea views from the house and garden, sleeps 5, own parking, gas fired central heating, colour TV, washing machine. Lawned garden overlooking sea with terrace and garden furniture. Coastal walks and cycle trails, boat to Lundy Island. Dog welcome. Other sea front cottages available.

Ring 01237 473801 for prices and vacancies only or send SAE for brochure to Mrs P.I. BARNES, 140 Bay View Road, Northam, Bideford, Devon EX39 1BJ or see www.seabirdcottages.co.uk

beachdown

Relax in a setting so peaceful, you can actually hear the silence! Comfortable and unpretentious. Your pets more than welcome.

Comfortable, fully-equipped, detached cedarwood chalets, most with small enclosed garden for your pet. Car parking alongside. Just 150 yards away from the beach and the South West Coastal Path. We are situated within the beautiful South Hams area of South Devon. Just a 10 minute walk from Burgh Island. Open all year round.

• ***SHORT BREAKS AVAILABLE*** •

Call for a brochure on 01548 810089 or visit our website for more details.
Mobile: 07725 053439

Challaborough Bay, Kingsbridge, South Devon TQ7 4JB • Tel: 01548 810089
e-mail: petswelcome@beachdown.co.uk • www.beachdown.co.uk

BLACKWELL PARK, LODDISWELL, KINGSBRIDGE

Bed, Breakfast and Evening Meal is offered in Blackwell Park, a 17th century farmhouse situated 5 miles from Kingsbridge. Six bedrooms, some en suite, and all with washbasins and tea-making facilities. Large garden, also adjoining 54 acres of woodland/ Nature Reserve. Ample food with a choice of menu.

PETS ESPECIALLY WELCOME • DOGSITTING.
Pets welcome FREE of charge. Dartmoor, Plymouth, Torbay, Dartmouth and many beaches lie within easy reach.

Same family ownership since 1971.

Bed and Breakfast • Evening Meal optional
Proprietress: Mrs B. Kelly • Tel: 01548 821230
Blackwell Park, Loddiswell TQ7 4EA

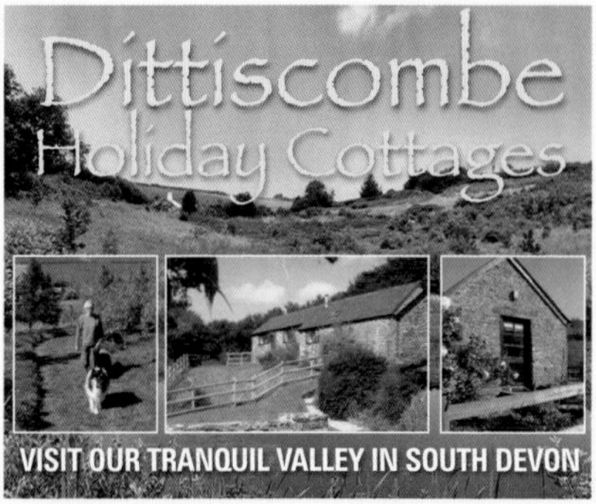
Dittiscombe
Holiday Cottages
VISIT OUR TRANQUIL VALLEY IN SOUTH DEVON

"Dog heaven" says Moses. We humans loved it too!

Perfect location for dogs and their owners.
Six stone cottages with country views.
Wildlife nature trail for 'walkies' on site.
Dog-friendly beaches and pubs nearby.
Woodburners and private gardens.
• Short Breaks off season • Open all Year

For more information, prices and availability, please visit our website:

www.dittiscombe.co.uk

Tel: 01548 521272

Dittiscombe Holiday Cottages, Slapton Near Kingsbridge, South Devon TQ7 2QF

King's Nympton, Lapford, Lynton/Lynmouth

COLLACOTT FARM

Quality Country Cottages

Eight delightful country cottages sleeping 2-12 set around a large cobbled courtyard, amidst twenty acres of tranquil Devon countryside. All are well equipped with wood-burning stove, dishwashers, heating, bed linen, and their own individual patio and garden. A tennis court, heated swimming pool, games room, children's play area, trampoline room and BHS approved riding centre makes Collacott an ideal holiday for the whole family.

Collacott Farm, King's Nympton,
Umberleigh, North Devon EX37 9TP
Telephone: South Molton 01769 572491
www.collacott.co.uk
e-mail: info@collacott.co.uk

Rudge Farm

House built in the 14th Century. Listed as of special historical and architectural interest. Set in beautiful grounds with pond, orchard and woods. Trout fishing and almost 200 acres to wander in. Much wildlife and perfect for watching buzzards and badgers. House very tastefully furnished and fully equipped. Will sleep up to 8. No charge for dogs, linen or fuel. David and Marion Mills look forward to meeting you. Send for our brochure.

LAPFORD • CREDITON • DEVON • EX17 6NG
TEL: 01363 83268

Lynmouth, Exmoor

Bath & Tors

Prices from £39.00 pppn

Prices from £59.00 pppn

Bath Hotel AA ★★ Tors Hotel AA ★★★

Off Season discounts available. Great views of harbour. Quality rooms and service. Ideal for moors. Pets Welcome.

01598 752238 info@bathhotellynmouth.co.uk www.bathhotellynmouth.co.uk 01598 753236

Brendon House is a licensed country guesthouse with five well appointed en suite bedrooms with colour TV and tea/coffee making facilities. There is a residents' lounge with log fire in the winter months, and an award-winning restaurant serving local food and game and home grown seasonal vegetables from the garden.

Sitting in almost an acre of mature gardens, Brendon House provides the ideal location to just relax and unwind or as a base from which to explore the beautiful countryside, walks and views of the Exmoor National Park and the rugged North Devon coast.

BRENDON HOUSE

Brendon, Lynton, Devon EX35 6PS
Tel: 01598 741206 • e-mail: brendonhouse4u@aol.com
www.brendonhouse4u.com

★★★★ GUEST HOUSE

Pet-Friendly
Pubs, Inns & Hotels

on pages 424-432

Please note that these establishments may not feature in the main section of this book

Blue Ball Inn

formerly The Exmoor Sandpiper Inn

is a romantic Coaching Inn dating in part back to the 13th century, with low ceilings, blackened beams, stone fireplaces and a timeless atmosphere of unspoilt old world charm. Offering visitors great food and drink, a warm welcome and a high standard of accommodation.

The inn is set in an imposing position on a hilltop on Exmoor in North Devon, a few hundred yards from the sea, and high above the twin villages of Lynmouth and Lynton, in an area of oustanding beauty.
The spectacular scenery and endless views attract visitors and hikers from all over the world.

We have 16 en suite bedrooms, comfortable sofas in the bar and lounge areas, and five fireplaces, including a 13th century inglenook. Our extensive menus include local produce wherever possible, such as locally reared meat, amd locally caught game and fish, like Lynmouth Bay lobster; specials are featured daily. We also have a great choice of good wines, available by the bottle or the glass, and a selection of locally brewed beers, some produced specially for us.

Stay with us to relax, or to follow one of the seven circular walks through stunning countryside that start from the Inn. Horse riding for experienced riders or complete novices can be arranged. Plenty of parking. Dogs (no charge), children and walkers are very welcome!

Blue Ball Inn *formerly The Exmoor Sandpiper Inn*
Countisbury, Lynmouth, Devon EX35 6NE
01598 741263
www.BlueBallinn.com • www.exmoorsandpiper.com

Lynton / Lynmouth

Jim and Susan Bingham,
New Mill Farm, Barbrook,
Lynton, North Devon EX35 6JR
Tel: (01598) 753341
e-mail: info@outovercott.co.uk

EXMOOR VALLEY

English Tourism Council ★★★★ SELF CATERING

Two delightful genuine modernised XVII Century Cottages by a stream on a 100-acre farm with "ABRS Approved" Riding Stables. Also a Bungalow with fenced garden and panoramic views of Exmoor. All have modernised kitchens, central heating, colour television and video, washing machine, tumble dryers, dishwasher and microwave. Linen available if required. Thoroughly inspected before arrival. Pets welcome at £15 each weekly. Safe for children and pets to play. Horse riding over Exmoor from our own A.B.R.S. Approved stables. Free fishing.

We offer weekend and midweek breaks throughout the year.

Please ask for a brochure.

www.outovercott.co.uk

Situated on the South West Coastal Path with wonderful views, and delicious home cooking, the North Cliff is an ideal base for discovering Exmoor and the North Devon Coast. We welcome pets, children and groups.

Self-catering flat, sleeps 6, also available.

The North Cliff Hotel

North Walk, Lynton, North Devon EX35 6HJ
Tel: 01598 752357
e-mail: holidays@northcliffhotel.co.uk
www.northcliffhotel.co.uk

Two apartments within a family-run guesthouse, sleeping two or three persons.

Our ground floor apartment comprises double bedroom, lounge, kitchen and bathroom with own entrance and private courtyard garden.

The second apartment on the first floor is larger, with two bedrooms, shower room, lounge with screened kitchen and dining area, with views over the gardens and surrounding Exmoor countryside.

Set within the National Park, the spectacular Southwest Coastal Path and Lynton and Lynmouth are within easy reach, all offering excellent walks for you and your dogs. All hotel amenities available on your return.

Moorlands

Where countryside and comfort combine

Woody Bay, Devon EX31 4RA
www.moorlandshotel.co.uk
Tel: 01598 763224

★★★★ GUEST ACCOMMODATION

COUNTISBURY LODGE HOTEL

AA ★★★ Guest Accommodation

Countisbury Hill, Lynmouth EX35 6NB
www.countisburylodge.co.uk

A former Victorian vicarage with magnificent views over the Lyn Valley and sea. Extremely quiet and peaceful yet within 5 minutes' walk of the picturesque village of Lynmouth. Licensed bar. All our bedrooms are centrally heated and en suite. Private parking. Pets welcome free of charge.

❖ ALSO SELF CATERING COTTAGE AND APARTMENT AVAILABLE ❖
Brochure/Tariff with pleasure from Pat & Paul Young (01598 752388)

Self-contained holiday accommodation at
LYNTON AND LYNMOUTH RAILWAY STATION

Ideal for four in two bedrooms (cot available). Sitting room. Bathroom and separate WC. Kitchen/dining room. Children and pets welcome.

W. PRYOR, STATION HOUSE, LYNTON, DEVON EX35 6LB • Tel: (01598) 752275 or 752381 • Fax: (01598) 752475
e-mail: advertise@lyntonadvertiser.com

DOGS WELCOME FREE

Relax and unwind @ the hotel by the sea!

Set directly on the North Devon coastline, the Lundy House Hotel is a small family-run hotel where we aim to give our guests a comfortable, relaxing and truly memorable holiday in idyllic surroundings. Stunning sea views. Terraced gardens lead onto the South West Coastal Path. ***Dogs and dirty boots welcome!***

Lundy House Hotel

Mortehoe, North Devon EX34 7DZ

• Tel: 01271 870372 •
e-mail: info@lundyhousehotel.co.uk • www.lundyhousehotel.co.uk

---

THE SMUGGLERS

Situated in the pretty village of Mortehoe, The Smugglers offers luxury accommodation from twin rooms to family suites. Treat yourselves and your pets to beautiful coastal walks and golden beaches, before you sample our delicious home-cooked meals, real ales and warm, year round hospitality.

The Smugglers Rest Inn, North Morte Road, Mortehoe, N. Devon EX34 7DR • Tel/Fax: 01271 870891
info@smugglersmortehoe.co.uk • www.smugglersmortehoe.co.uk

CRAB COTTAGE, NOSS MAYO, SOUTH DEVON www.crab-cottage.co.uk

• Charming fisherman's cottage, 50 yards from the quay on the River Yealm • Watch the boats on the river from the cottage gardens and window seats • Delightful, quiet village in an area of outstanding natural beauty • Fantastic walks, beaches and dog-friendly pubs on the doorstep • Walk across to village shops in Newton Ferrers at low tide • Close to the South Devon Coastal Path • Sleeps 5 Phone 01425 471372 for a brochure • e-mail: sally.bennetts@btinternet.com

---

Cat lovers' paradise in charming 16th century farmhouse set in lovely Otter Valley. Two acres of beautiful gardens with pond and stream. All rooms en suite, TV and Teasmaids. Pets welcome free of charge. Plenty of dog walking space. Brochure available. Terms from: B&B £25pppn.

FLUXTON FARM, Ottery St Mary, Devon EX11 1RJ
Tel: 01404 812818 • www.fluxtonfarm.co.uk

Paignton, Plymouth

AMBER HOUSE

6 Roundham Road, Paignton, Devon TQ4 6EZ • Tel: 01803 558372

- Overlooks Goodrington Sands. ✻ Ground floor rooms.
- All en suite, some with bath and shower. ✻ Non-smoking.
- Satellite digital TV or Freeview TV and DVD player in all rooms.
- Computer room, wi-fi access in some rooms.
- Good food; special diets catered for. ✻ Large car park.
- English Riviera climate ideal for Spring/Autumn breaks.
- Park and beach 5 minutes' walk. ✻ Walkers welcome.
- We pride ourselves on our high standards.

e-mail: enquiries@amberhousehotel.co.uk

www.amberhousehotel.co.uk *Contact: Christine Clark & Lloyd Hastie.*

The Commodore

Please call **(01803) 553107**

Ideally situated on Paignton sea front, sea view rooms. Luxury en suites, refreshments, sea view guest lounge, bar, gift shop. Dogs allowed on Paignton Green, Fairy Cove, Roundham Head and Goodrington North Beach all year round. Clean and relaxing environment with excellent breakfast. Close to harbour, bus and rail stations. FREE PARKING.

e-mail: info@commodorepaignton.com • www.commodorepaignton.com

The Commodore
14 Esplanade Rd.
Paignton,
Devon
TQ4 6EB

Give your pets a holiday at *Churchwood Valley*

Twelve times David Bellamy Gold Award Winner
Gold in Green Tourism Business Scheme

Relax in one of our comfortable log cabins, set in a peaceful wooded valley near the beach. Wonderful walks in woods and along the coast. Abundance of birds and wildlife. Up to two pets per cabin.

Open April to January including special Christmas and New Year Breaks.

Wembury Bay, Near Plymouth

churchwoodvalley@btconnect.com

www.churchwoodvalley.com

Tel: 01752 862382

Lamplighter Hotel

AA/ETC ★★★

Situated on famous Plymouth Hoe, close to the seafront and the historic Barbican with its cobbled streets and quay. Also close to the city centre, with shops, restaurants and entertainment venues. HMS Raleigh 3 miles (on bus route). Minutes from rail and coach stations, and 850 yards from ferry terminal.
9 bedrooms - 7 en suite and 2 with private facilities.

103 Citadel Road, The Hoe, Plymouth PL1 2RN • Tel: 01752 663855 • Tel/Fax: 01752 228139
e-mail: stay@lamplighterplymouth.co.uk • www.lamplighterplymouth.co.uk

Plymouth, Salcombe, Seaton

The Cranbourne

278/282 Citadel Road,
The Hoe, Plymouth PL1 2PZ
Tel: 01752 263858/661400/224646
Fax: 01752 263858

• Equidistant City Centre and Hoe Promenade • All bedrooms beautifully decorated, heated, with colour TV, tea/coffee facilities • ¼ mile Ferry Terminal • Keys for access at all times • Licensed Bar • Pets by prior arrangement (no charge) • Large secure car park

AA ★★★ Guest Accommodation

Under the personal supervision of The Williams Family

e-mail: cran.hotel@virgin.net • www.cranbournehotel.co.uk

PORT LIGHT Hotel, Restaurant & Inn

As featured in Times, Guardian, Mail, Telegraph, Express, Dogs Today, Your Dog and many pet-friendly internet sites

• Luxury en suite rooms, easy access onto the gardens • Close to secluded sandy cove (dogs permitted) 20 minutes' walk • No charge for pets which are most welcome throughout the hotel. • Outstanding reputation for superb home-cooked fayre specialising in fresh sea food • Set alongside the famous National Trust Salcombe to Hope Cove coastal walk • Fully licensed bar – log burner – real ale • Winner 2004 "Dogs Trust" Best Pet Hotel in England • Large free car park • Open Christmas & New Year • Self-catering cottages

Doggies' Heaven, Walkers' Paradise, Romantics' Dream
WE ARE REALLY, TOTALLY PET-FRIENDLY

Important advice: always check to ensure other so-called 'pet-friendly' hotels really are! Talk to us to find out more.

Bolberry Down, Malborough, Near Salcombe, South Devon TQ7 3DY
e-mail: info@portlight.co.uk • www.portlight.co.uk
Tel: (01548) 561384 or (07970) 859992 • Sean & Hazel Hassall

A totally unique location, set amidst acres of National Trust coastal countryside with panoramic views towards Cornwall, Dartmoor and France.

❖ Bolberry Farm Cottages ❖

Bolberry, Near Salcombe, Devon TQ7 3DY

Luxury two and three bedroom barn conversion cottages
• Private gardens • Shared orchard • Views across valley
• Gas, coal, open fires • Parking • Finished to a very high standard
• Linen and towels included • Central heating
• Close to coastal path and pet-friendly beaches • Dog wash • Short Breaks out of season
• Superb meals available at our nearby Port Light Inn & Hotel • Credit/Debit cards accepted

VISA MasterCard

Tel: 01548 561384 • e-mail: info@bolberryfarmcottages.co.uk
www.bolberryfarmcottages.co.uk • Hazel & Sean Hassall

❖ The Pet Holiday Specialist ❖

MILKBERE Cottage Holidays

Devon/Dorset Border
Seaton, Beer and Sidmouth

3 Fore Street • Seaton • EX12 2LE
Phone: 01297 22925 (brochure)
01297 20729 (bookings)

Look and book online
www.milkberehols.com

Cottages
Bungalows
Houses
Apartments
Caravans

All VisitBritain inspected

Seaton, Sidmouth

Axevale Caravan Park

Colyford Road, Seaton EX12 2DF • Tel: 0800 0688816

English Tourism Council ★★★★ HOLIDAY PARK

A quiet, family-run park with 68 modern and luxury caravans for hire. The park overlooks the delightful River Axe Valley, and is just a 10 minute walk from the town with its wonderfully long, award-winning beach. Children will love our extensive play area, with its sand pit, paddling pool, swings and slide. Laundry facilities are provided and there is a wide selection of goods on sale in the park shop which is open every day. All of our caravans have a shower, toilet, fridge and TV with digital channels. Also, with no clubhouse, a relaxing atmosphere is ensured. Prices from £80 per week; reductions for three or fewer persons early/late season.

www.axevale.co.uk

Oakdown

GOLD

English Tourism Council ★★★★★ HOLIDAY AND TOURING PARK EXCEPTIONAL

SIDMOUTH'S MULTI AWARD-WINNING TOURING & HOLIDAY CARAVAN PARK

Weston - Sidmouth - Devon - EX10 0PT

Telephone: Park/Reservations 01297 680387 • Fax: 01297 680541

e-mail: enquiries@oakdown.co.uk • www.oakdown.co.uk

Welcome to Oakdown, set near the "Jurassic Coast" World Heritage Site, and a winner of "Caravan Holiday Park of The Year" in the Excellence in England Awards 2007 - Sidmouth's multi-award-winning Park. Oakdown is level, sheltered and landscaped into groves to give privacy. Our luxurious amenities include aids for the disabled. Enjoy our Field Trail to the famous Donkey Sanctuary. **Free colour brochure with pleasure.**

The Best of British TOURING AND HOLIDAY PARKS — enjoyEngland Awards for Excellence 2007 SILVER WINNER — LOO OF THE YEAR Awards WINNER

ATTRACTIVE, CAREFULLY SELECTED COASTAL COTTAGES, FARMHOUSES AND FLATS IN SIDMOUTH & EAST DEVON

Please ask for our colour brochure.

SWEETCOMBE COTTAGE HOLIDAYS,
ROSEMARY COTTAGE, WESTON,
NEAR SIDMOUTH, DEVON EX10 0PH

Tel: 01395 512130 • Fax: 01395 515680

e-mail: enquiries@sweetcombe-ch.co.uk • www.sweetcombe-ch.co.uk

ETC ★★★★

LEIGH COTTAGES

WESTON, SIDMOUTH, DEVON EX10 0PH

Eight Cottages150 yards from National Trust Valley leading to Coastal Path and beach. Lovely cliff-top walks and level walks around nearby Donkey Sanctuary fields.

Contact: Alison Clarke • Tel: 01395 516065/514764 • Fax: 01395 512563

e-mail: Alison@leigh-cottages.co.uk • www.leigh-cottages.co.uk

FREE or REDUCED RATE entry to Holiday Visits and Attractions – see our **READERS' OFFER VOUCHERS** on pages 433-440

LANGSTONE MANOR HOLIDAY PARK

Peaceful Holiday Park, offering camping, apartment, cottages, static caravans. Ideal location outside Tavistock with direct access onto Dartmoor. Bar and evening meals. Walks straight onto moor. Excellent location.

Moortown, Tavistock PL19 9JZ

Tel & Fax: 01822 613371

jane@langstone-manor.co.uk

www.langstone-manor.co.uk

TAVISTOCK - EDGE OF DARTMOOR

Comfortably furnished studio cottage five miles from the market town of Tavistock. Ideal for two. Private walled garden. Pets welcome. Private parking, free coal for open fire. All linen provided. Wonderful walking, riding, fishing country with excellent local pubs. Terms £225 per week.

Higher Quither, Milton Abbot, Tavistock, Devon PL19 0PZ

Contact: Mrs P.G.C. Quinton • Tel: 01822 860284.

Cutaway Cottage • Thurlestone, Kingsbridge TQ7 3NF

Self-catering cottage within fenced garden in the middle of the village, on private road. • 5 minutes to pub and shop. • 20 minutes' walk to beaches and sea • Ideal for children, dog walkers and bird watchers.

Pets free of charge ° Phone Pat on 01548 560688

SOUTH DEVON • NEAR TORBAY

6 and 8 berth caravans new in 2007 and other 4 and 6 berths to let. All with toilets and showers. All with electricity, colour TV and fridges. Dogs on lead welcome.

Launderette, shop and payphone.
Also separate area for tourers, motor caravans and tents with modern toilet/ shower block with family rooms. Electric hook-ups and hard standings.

★★★★ HOLIDAY, TOURING AND CAMPING PARK

J. & E. BALL, Dept PW, HIGHER WELL FARM HOLIDAY PARK
Stoke Gabriel, Totnes, South Devon TQ9 6RN • Tel: 01803 782289
www.higherwellfarmholidaypark.co.uk

Red House Hotel and Maxton Lodge

The best of both worlds!...

★ *Indoor and Outdoor Swimming Pools* ★ *Spa Pool*
★ *Licensed Restaurant* ★ *Gym*
★ *Beauty Salon* ★ *Sauna*
★ *Launderette* ★ *Solarium*
★ *Indoor Recreation Room*

We've joined together the friendly service and facilities of the 2 star Red House Hotel for those wanting a traditional hotel atmosphere, with the privacy and freedom of Maxton Lodge's 24 self-contained holiday apartments. Two styles of accommodation sharing the same conveniently located grounds and superb range of facilities, so whether you're a working conference delegate or a fun loving family you'll find a style to suit you.

AA ★★

Red House Hotel, Rousdown Road, Chelston, Torquay TQ2 6PB
Tel: (01803) 607811
Fax: (01803) 605357
e-mail: stay@redhouse-hotel.co.uk
www.redhouse-hotel.co.uk

English Tourism Council ★★ HOTEL
English Tourism Council ★★★ SELF CATERING

Torquay, Torrington, Totnes, Westward Ho!, Woolacombe

Want to wake up to a view like this every morning...?

We do, so why not join us

The Downs Babbacombe

Room with a View ...?

41-43 Babbacombe Downs Road
Babbacombe - Torquay TQ1 3LN
Tel: 01803 328543 / 0845 051 0989
www.downshotel.co.uk

Situated directly above Babbacombe & Oddicombe beaches, we are a fully licensed family run establishment with 12 en-suite guest rooms, 8 have private balconies which enjoy fabulous unobstructed views over Babbacombe Downs and out over Lyme Bay all the way to Portland Bill.

We welcome young and old, couples and singles alike. We can accommodate families in our 4 family rooms, with reduced rates for under 12's, and are Dog friendly.

STOWFORD LODGE
LANGTREE, GREAT TORRINGTON EX38 8NU

Picturesque and peaceful. Four delightful cottages set within 6 acres of private land with heated indoor pool. Magnificent countryside. Convenient North Devon coast and moors. Sleep 4/6. Phone for brochure. **01805 601540**
e-mail: enq@stowfordlodge.co.uk • www.stowfordlodge.co.uk

Downe Lodge

Broadhempston, Totnes, Devon TQ9 6BY

Beautiful, quiet position convenient for Dartmoor and the coast. Woodland dog walking on doorstep. Self-catering cottage available with 3 bedrooms/2 bathrooms. Private garden. No smoking. **Tel & Fax: 01803 812828**
Mob: 07772318746 • e-mail: info@downelodge.co.uk • www.downelodge.co.uk

❖ WEST PUSEHILL FARM COTTAGES ❖

Nestling within the Kenwith Valley, our cottages are set along the beautiful North Devon Coast.

◆ 10 cottages, converted from farm buildings built from traditional local stone in 1854. ◆ 40 ft heated outdoor pool set amongst secluded, sheltered lawns. ◆ Perfectly situated to explore coast and countryside. ◆ Many "award winning" attractions close by. ◆ Pets and children welcome. ◆ Resident proprietors. ◆ Open all year. ◆ Walks, Golf, Riding & Fishing nearby.

West Pusehill Farm, Westward Ho!, North Devon EX39 5AH
Tel: 01237 475638/474622 ◆ www.wpfcottages.co.uk

WELCOME TO THE SURF!
EUROPA PARK
WOOLACOMBE NORTH DEVON
SEE OUR WEBSITE
WWW.EUROPAPARK.CO.UK

PETS FREE IN LOW SEASON (with this advert)

- CLUB
- SAUNA
- INDOOR POOL
- ENTERTAINMENT
- RESTAURANT
- SPAR SHOP
- LAUNDERETTE
- GAMES ROOM

TEL 01271 871425
EMAIL HOLIDAYS@EUROPAPARK.CO.UK

SURFERS PARADISE

Woof!

pet friendly holidays

Holiday Homes & great Camping & Touring

Four award winning Holiday Parks set in Devon's breathtaking countryside next to Woolacombe's 3 miles of golden Blue Flag sandy Beach!

Our Pet Friendly Holiday Homes

are situated with easy access to footpaths or exercise areas, we also include all the little extras that will make your holiday one to remember . . .

"FREE" PET PACK

- Healthy Dog Treat & Rope Toy
- Comfy Dog Bed
- Feeding & Water Bowls
- Lead Hooks Inside/Out
- All-Important Pooper Scooper with Unlimited Refills

PLUS!

WOOF GUIDE to WOOLACOMBE

A guide packed full of useful information including coastal and countryside footpaths, PET FRIENDLY pubs, restaurants and tea houses. Plus maps and access guides for local beaches, details of local vets, pet groomers and pet friendly attractions in the area. You will be spoilt for choice as there's lots to see and do with your best friend!

We love being on holiday with our dogs and know how difficult it can be to find suitable accommodation where both you and your pets can relax and enjoy your well deserved break.

over 40 FREE activities...

- 10 Heated Indoor & Outdoor Pools • Crazy Golf
- Nightly Entertainment & Star Cabaret • Cinema
- Dog Exercise Area • Health Suite • Snooker
- Waterslides • Tennis • Playzone • Kid's Clubs
- Coarse Fishing Ponds • Sauna & Steam Room

... Plus so much more!

...and for just a little more

- 10 Pin Bowling
- 17th Century Inn
- Waves Ceramic Studio
- Affiliated Golf Club
- Indoor Bowls Rinks
- WaterWalkerz
- Restaurants & Bars
- Amusement Arcade
- Activities Programme
- Electric Hook-ups
- Laundry Facilities
- On-site Shop
- Climbing Wall
- Swimming Lessons

REGISTER ONLINE FOR LATEST OFFERS!!

woolacombe.com/fpw

01271 870 343

WOOLACOMBE BAY

*Pets from £10 per week for camping & touring, £20 per week for holiday homes.

Woolacombe

Sunnymeade • Tel: 01271 863668

• *Friendly, comfortable Country Hotel* • *Lovely countryside views*
• *Centrally placed close to Woolacombe's dog-friendly beach, Ilfracombe and Exmoor* • *Off-season special breaks & Christmas*
• *12 en suite bedrooms, 4 on ground floor*
• *Deaf accessible BSL signed* • *Award-winning home-cooked food*
• *Pets welcome* • *Lots of lovely walks from the front door*

www.sunnymeade.co.uk • Fax: 01271 866061

SUNNYMEADE COUNTRY HOTEL
DEAN CROSS, WEST DOWN, DEVON EX34 8NT

CHICHESTER HOUSE HOLIDAY APARTMENTS

Quiet, relaxing, fully furnished apartments.
Opposite Barricane Shell Beach – central seafront position with outstanding sea and coastal views.
Watch the sun go down into the sea from your own balcony.
• Open all year • Free parking • Pets by arrangement.
SAE to resident proprietor, Joyce Bagnall.
Off-peak reductions. Short Break details on request.

The Esplanade, Woolacombe EX34 7DJ
Tel: 01271 870761

Visit the FHG website

www.holidayguides.com

for details of the wide choice of accommodation featured in the full range of FHG titles

PORT LIGHT, BOLBERRY DOWN, MALBOROUGH, NEAR SALCOMBE TQ7 3DY (01548 561384 or 07970 859992). A totally unique location set amidst acres of National Trust coastline. Luxury en suite rooms. Superb home-cooked fare, specialising in local seafood. Licensed bar. Pets welcome throughout the hotel. Short Breaks throughout the year. Self-catering cottages also available. Contact: Sean and Hazel Hassall. [🐕]
e-mail: info@portlight.co.uk website: www.portlight.co.uk

NORTH DEVON HOLIDAY HOMES, 19 CROSS STREET, BARNSTAPLE EX31 1BD (01271 376322). Free colour guide to the best value pet friendly cottages around Exmoor and Devon's National Trust Coast. [Pets £12 per week.]
e-mail: info@northdevonholidays.co.uk website: www.devonandexmoor.co.uk

FARM & COTTAGE HOLIDAYS (01237 459897). The finest selection of holiday cottages throughout Devon, Cornwall, Dorset and Somerset in superb rural and coastal locations.
website: www.holidaycottages.co.uk

HELPFUL HOLIDAYS (01647 433535). Wonderful variety of cottages all over the West Country. Ideal for countryside rambles. Many welcome pets.
website: www.helpfulholidays.co.uk

TOAD HALL COTTAGES (01548 853089 24 hrs). 300 outstanding waterside and rural properties in truly beautiful locations in Devon, Cornwall and Exmoor. Call for our highly acclaimed brochure. Pets welcome.
e-mail: thc@toadhallcottages.co.uk website: www.toadhallcottages.co.uk

HOLIDAY HOMES & COTTAGES S.W, 28 TORWOOD STREET, TORQUAY TQ1 1EB (01803 299677; Fax: 01803 664037). Hundreds of Self-Catering Holiday Cottages, Houses, Bungalows, Apartments, Chalets and Caravans in Devon and Cornwall. Please write or phone for free colour brochure.
e-mail: holcotts@aol.com website: www.swcottages.co.uk

MARSDENS COTTAGE HOLIDAYS, 2 THE SQUARE, BRAUNTON EX33 2JB (01271 813777; Fax: 01271 813664). Over 300 Visit Britain inspected holiday cottages on North Devon's National Trust coastline and Exmoor. Pets welcome at over half our cottages at £15 per week. Online availability and booking.
e-mail: holidays@marsdens.co.uk website: www.marsdens.co.uk

Appledore

Large village on West side of River Torridge 3 miles North of Bideford.

MRS CYMA CASSAR, CROSS HOUSE, FORE STREET, NORTHAM, BIDEFORD EX39 1AN (01237 472042). Three cottages, all with 'Olde Worlde' charm and up-to-date amenities. Exmoor, Clovelly, Lynton, Lynmouth, Tarka Trail within easy reach. Many beaches, the nearest one mile away. [🐕]
e-mail: info@crosshouseandcottages.co.uk www.crosshouseandcottages.co.uk

Pet-Friendly
Pubs, Inns & Hotels
on pages 424-432
Please note that these establishments may not feature in the main section of this book

Ashburton

Delightful little town on southern fringe of Dartmoor. Centrally placed for touring and the Torbay resorts. Plymouth 24 miles, Exeter 20, Kingsbridge 20, Tavistock 20, Teignmouth 14, Torquay 14, Totnes 8, Newton Abbot 7.

PARKERS FARM COTTAGES, THE ROCKERY, CATON, ASHBURTON, NEWTON ABBOT TQ13 7LH (01364 653008). Farm Cottages and Static Caravans to let surrounded by beautiful countryside. Perfect for children and pets. Central for touring; 12 miles Torquay. ETC ★★★★ [pw! Pets £17 per week]
e-mail: parkerscottages@btconnect.com website: www.parkersfarm.co.uk

MRS A. BELL, WOODER MANOR, WIDECOMBE IN THE MOOR, NEAR ASHBURTON TQ13 7TR (Tel & Fax: 01364 621391). Cottages nestled in picturesque valley. Surrounded by unspoilt woodland and moors. Clean and well equipped, colour TV, central heating, laundry room. Two properties suitable for disabled visitors. Colour brochure available. ETC ★★★ to ★★★★ [pw! £15 per week].
e-mail: angela@woodermanor.com website: www.woodermanor.com

PARKERS FARM HOLIDAY PARK, HIGHER MEAD FARM, ASHBURTON TQ13 7LJ (01364 654869; Fax: 01364 654004). Static caravans to let, also level touring site with two toilet/shower blocks and electric hook-ups. Central for touring; 12 miles Torquay. ETC ★★★★, AA Four Pennants. [pw! Pets £1.50 per night touring, £17 per week static caravans]
e-mail: parkersfarm@btconnect.com website: www.parkersfarm.co.uk

Ashwater

Village 6 miles south-east of Holsworthy.

BLAGDON MANOR HOTEL AND RESTAURANT, ASHWATER, NORTH DEVON EX21 5DF (01409 211224 Fax: 01409 211634) Beautifully restored Grade II Listed building in peaceful location 20 minutes from Bude. 8 en suite bedrooms, three-acre gardens. No children under 12 years. AA Three Red Stars, 2 Rosettes. [pw! Dogs £7.50 per night]
email: stay@blagdon.com website: www.blagdon.com

Axminster

Small friendly market town, full of old world charm, set in the beautiful Axe Valley. Excellent centre for touring Devon, Somerset and Dorset. 5 miles from coast.

LEA HILL, MEMBURY, AXMINSTER EX13 7AQ (01404 881881). Tranquil location. Wonderful scenery. Close to World Heritage Coast. Eight acres of grounds and gardens. Walks, footpaths and exercise fields. Hot tub and barbecue. Comfortable, well equipped self-catering cottages with en suite bedrooms and own gardens. Green Tourism Silver Award, VB ★★★★. [pw! Pets £12 per week]
e-mail: reception@leahill.co.uk website: www.leahill.co.uk

LILAC COTTAGE. Detached cottage, furnished to a high standard, sleeps six plus cot. Children and pets are welcome. Walled garden and garage. On borders of Devon, Dorset, and Somerset; many seaside towns within 10 miles. Contact: MRS J.M. STUART, 2 SANDFORD HOUSE, KINGSCLERE RG20 4PA (Tel & Fax: 01635 291942)
e-mail: joanna.sb@free.fr

THE FAIRWATER HEAD HOTEL, HAWKCHURCH, NEAR AXMINSTER EX13 5TX (01297 678349; Fax: 01297 678459). Located in the tranquil Devon countryside and close to Lyme Regis, this beautiful Edwardian Country House Hotel has all you and your dog need for a peaceful and relaxing holiday. Dogs most welcome. Countryside location with panoramic views. AA ★★★, Two Rosettes. [🐕]
e-mail: e-mail: stay@fairwaterheadhotel.co.uk website: www.fairwaterheadhotel.co.uk

Symbols

🐕 Indicates that pets are welcome free of charge.

£ Indicates that a charge is made for pets: nightly or weekly.

pw! Shows some special provision for pets; exercise facility, feeding or accommodation arrangement.

⌂ Indicates separate pets accommodation.

Barnstaple

Market town at head of River Taw estuary, 34 miles north west of Exeter.

"VALLEY VIEW", GUINEAFORD, MARWOOD, BARNSTAPLE EX31 4EA (01271 343458). Set in 320 acres of farmland near Barnstaple, home to Helenbrie Miniature Shetland ponies. Two bedrooms each contain a double and single bed. Bed and Breakfast from £25. Children welcome. Pets by arrangement. Open all year.
website: www.helenbriestud.co.uk

MARTINHOE CLEAVE COTTAGES, MARTINHOE, PARRACOMBE, BARNSTAPLE EX31 4PZ (01598 763313). Perfect rural tranquillity overlooking the beautiful Heddon valley and close to the Exmoor National Park. Delightful cottages, equipped to a very high standard throughout. Open all year. Sleep 1-2. [🐕].
e-mail: info@exmoorhideaway.co.uk website:www.exmoorhideaway.co.uk

LOWER YELLAND FARM GUEST HOUSE, FREMINGTON, BARNSTAPLE EX31 3EN (01271 860101). Delightfully modernised farmhouse accommodation on working farm. Central for North Devon attractions. All rooms en suite, with TV and tea/coffee making. Breakfast includes free-range eggs and home-made bread etc. [Pets £2.50 per night, £15 per week
e-mail: peterday@loweryellandfarm.co.uk website: www.loweryellandfarm.co.uk

NORTH HILL COTTAGES, NORTH HILL, SHIRWELL, BARNSTAPLE EX31 4LG (01271 850611; mobile: 07834 806434). Sleep 2-6. 17th century farm buildings, sympathetically converted into cottages. Indoor heated swimming pool, jacuzzi, sauna, all-weather tennis court and games room. [Pets £20 per week]
website: www.north-hill.co.uk

BRACKEN HOUSE HOTEL, BRATTON FLEMING EX31 4TG (01598 710320). Enjoy Exmoor's rugged natural beauty and spectacular coastline at this charming former rectory, Quiet comfort, long views and Aga-based cookery, all set in 8 acres. Ground floor rooms available. Well-behaved dog owners welcome. ETC ★★★★★. Also Self-catering cottage. [🐕]
website: www.brackenhousehotel.co.uk

Berrynarbor

This peaceful village overlooking the beautiful Sterridge valley has a 17th century pub and even older church, and is half-a-mile from the coast road between Combe Martin and Ilfracombe.

SANDY COVE HOTEL, BERRYNARBOR EX34 9SR (01271 882243 or 882888). Hotel set amidst acres of gardens and woods. Heated swimming pool. Children and pets welcome. A la carte restaurant. All rooms en suite with colour TV, tea-making. Free colour brochure on application. ETC ★★★ [🐕 one dog]
website: www.sandycove-hotel.co.uk

Bideford

Neat port village overlooking the beautiful Sterridge Valley has a 17th century pub and even older church, and is half-a-mile from the coast road between Combe Martin and Ilfracombe.

ROBERT & LISA IRETON, MEAD BARN COTTAGES, WELCOMBE, NEAR BIDEFORD EX39 (01288 331721). 3/4 Star Graded quality, self-catering cottages sleeping 2-26 people. Set in one and a half acres. Games room, tennis court, play area, swings, trampoline and gardens with barbecue area. [Pets £20 per week] ETC ★★★/★★★★
e-mail: holidays@meadbarns.com website: www.meadbarns.com

THE PINES AT EASTLEIGH, NEAR BIDEFORD EX39 4PA (01271 860561). Luxury B&B and cottages. Log-fires, king-size beds, garden room bar with library, maps and a warm welcome await our guests. B&B from £40pp; Cottages from £350 for 4 persons. No smoking. AA ★★★★ [pw! 🐕]
e-mail: pirrie@thepinesateastleigh.co.uk website: www.thepinesateastleigh.co.uk

Bigbury-on-Sea

A scattered village overlooking superb coastal scenery and wide expanses of sand.

MR SCARTERFIELD, HENLEY HOTEL, FOLLY HILL, BIGBURY-ON-SEA TQ7 4AR (01548 810240). Edwardian cottage-style hotel, spectacular sea views. Overlooking beach, dog walking. En suite rooms with telephone, tea making, TV etc. Home cooking. No smoking establishment. Licensed. ETC ★★ HOTEL and SILVER AWARD. AA ★★, GOOD HOTEL GUIDE, CESAR AWARD WINNER 2003, "WHICH?" GUIDE, COASTAL CORKER 2003. [Pets £4.00 per night.]

MRS J. TUCKER, MOUNT FOLLY FARM, BIGBURY-ON-SEA, KINGSBRIDGE TQ7 4AR (01548 810267). Cliff top position, with outstanding views of Bigbury Bay. Spacious, self-catering wing of farmhouse, attractively furnished. Farm adjoins golf course and River Avon. Lovely coastal walks, ideal centre for South Hams and Dartmoor. No smoking. Always a warm welcome, pets too! ETC ★★★ [pw! Pets £15 per week]
e-mail: chris.cathy@goosemoose.com website: www.bigburyholidays.co.uk

Bradworthy

Village to the north of Holsworthy. Well placed for North Devon and North Cornish coasts.

PETER & LESLEY LEWIN, LAKE HOUSE COTTAGES AND B&B, LAKE VILLA, BRADWORTHY DEVON EX22 7SQ (01409 241962). Four well equipped cottages sleeping two to five/six. Quiet rural position; one acre gardens and tennis court. Half-a-mile from village shops and pub. Dog-friendly beaches eight miles. Also two lovely en suite B&B rooms with balcony, all facilities, from £28. [🐕]
e-mail: info@lakevilla.co.uk website: www.lakevilla.co.uk

Braunton

5 miles north west of Barnstaple. To the south west are Braunton Burrows nature reserve, a lunar landscape of sand dunes noted for rare plants, and the 3 mile stretch of Saunton Sands.

LITTLE COMFORT FARM, BRAUNTON, NORTH DEVON EX33 2NJ (01271 812 414). Five spacious self-catering cottages sleeping 2-10 on organic family farm, just minutes from golden sandy beaches where dogs are allowed. Well stocked coarse fishing lake. Private 1½km farm trail. Wood fires for cosy winter breaks. PETS VERY WELCOME [pw! Pets £20 per week].
e-mail: info@littlecomfortfarm.co.uk website: www.littlecomfortfarm.co.uk

Brixham

Lively resort and fishing port, with quaint houses and narrow winding streets. Ample opportunities for fishing and boat trips.

BRIXHAM HOLIDAY PARK, FISHCOMBE COVE, BRIXHAM TQ5 8RB (01803 853324). Situated on coastal path. Choice of one and two-bedroomed chalets. Indoor heated pool, free club membership, comfortable bar offering meals and takeaway service, launderette. 150 yards from beach with lovely walks through woods beyond. ETC ★★★★. [Pets £30 per week]
e-mail: enquiries@brixhamholpk.fsnet.co.uk website: www.brixhamholidaypark.co.uk

DEVONCOURT HOLIDAY FLATS, BERRYHEAD ROAD, BRIXHAM TQ5 9AB (01803 853748 or 07802 403289 after office hours). 24 self-contained flats with private balcony, colour television, heating, private car park, all-electric kitchenette, separate bathroom and toilet. Open all year. Pets welcome.
website: www.devonco.urt.info

Chittlehamholt

Standing in beautiful countryside in Taw Valley. Barnstaple 9 miles, South Molton 5.

SNAPDOWN FARM CARAVANS, CHITTLEHAMHOLT, UMBERLEIGH, NORTH DEVON EX37 9PF (01769 540708). 6 only – 6 berth caravans with flush toilets, showers, colour TV, fridges, cookers and fires. Laundry room. Picnic tables. Unspoilt countryside. Field and woodland walks. Children's play area. Terms £130 to £330 per week incl. gas and electricity. [Pets £1.50 per night, £8.75 per week.]

Chudleigh

Small town 5 miles north of Newton Abbot.

S & G HARRISON CRAWFORD, LINDEN LEA, PARADE, CHUDLEIGH TQ13 0JG (01626 852172). Bungalow set well back from main road into town. One double en suite bedroom, use of large comfortable lounge. Good base for seeing Devon, plenty of places to walk dogs. B&B from £25 pppn. [🐕]

Chulmleigh

Mid-Devon village set in lovely countryside, just off A377 Exeter to Barnstaple road. Exeter 23 miles, Tiverton 19, Barnstaple 18.

SANDRA GAY, NORTHCOTT BARTON FARM COTTAGE, NORTHCOTT BARTON, ASHREIGNEY, CHULMLEIGH EX18 7PR (Tel & Fax: 01769 520259). Three bedroom character cottage, large enclosed garden, log fire. Special rates low season, couples and short breaks. Near golf, riding, Tarka Trail and RHS Rosemoor. ETC ★★★★ [🐕]
e-mail: sandra@northcottbarton.co.uk website: www.northcottbarton.co.uk

Colebrook

Village 4 miles west of Crediton.

PEARL HOCKRIDGE, THE OYSTER, COLEBROOKE, CREDITON EX17 5JQ (01363 84576). Modern bungalow in pretty, peaceful village. Bedrooms en suite or with private bathroom. Dartmoor and Exmoor a short drive. Children and pets welcome. Open all year. Smoking accepted. [🐕]

Combe Martin

Coastal village with harbour set in sandy bay. Good cliff and rock scenery. Of interest is the Church and "Pack of Cards" Inn. Barnstaple 14 miles, Lynton 12, Ilfracombe 6.

LYNE AND CRAIG DAVEY, MANLEIGH HOLIDAY PARK, RECTORY ROAD, COMBE MARTIN EX34 0NS (01271 883353). Quiet family-run site in beautiful countryside near village. Chalets, log cabins and caravans for hire. Children's play area, laundry, wine bar. Graded ★★★★. [Pets £25 per week or part]
e-mail: info@manleighpark.co.uk website: www.manleighpark.co.uk

WATERMOUTH COVE COTTAGES, WATERMOUTH, NEAR COMBE MARTIN EX34 9SJ (0870 241 3168). 8 beautiful cottages, most with four-poster and log fire, set beside grounds of Watermouth Castle, 200 yards from harbour/coastal path. Pets welcome all year. ETC ★★★ [Pets £20 per week]
e-mail: watermouthcove@googlemail.com website: www.watermouth-cove-cottages.co.uk

Cullompton

Small market town off the main A38 Taunton - Exeter road. Good touring centre. Noted for apple orchards which supply the local cider industry. Taunton 19 miles, Exeter 13, Honiton 11, Tiverton 9.

FOREST GLADE HOLIDAY PARK (PW), KENTISBEARE, CULLOMPTON EX15 2DT (01404 841381; Fax: 01404 841593). Country estate with deluxe 2/4/6 berth caravans. All superbly equipped. Many amenities on site. Mother and Baby Room. Campers and tourers welcome. SAE for colour brochure. ETC ★★★★, AA 3 Pennants, David Bellamy Gold Award. [Pets £1 per night, pw!]
e-mail: enquiries@forest-glade.co.uk website: www.forest-glade.co.uk

Dartmoor

365 square miles of National Park with spectacular unspoiled scenery, fringed by picturesque villages.

DARTMOOR COUNTRY HOLIDAYS, MAGPIE LEISURE PARK, DEPT PW, BEDFORD BRIDGE, HORRABRIDGE, YELVERTON PL20 7RY (01822 852651). Purpose-built pine lodges in peaceful woodland setting. Sleep 2-7. Furnished to very high standard (microwave, dishwasher etc). Easy walk to village and shops. Launderette. Dogs permitted. [🐕]

THE CHERRYBROOK, TWO BRIDGES PL20 6SP (01822 880260). In the middle of Dartmoor National Park with seven comfortable en suite bedrooms. Award-winning, excellent quality, home-made food. See our website for details, tariff and sample menu.
e-mail: info@cherrybrookhotel.co.uk website: www.cherrybrookhotel.co.uk

PRINCE HALL HOTEL, DARTMOOR PL20 6SA (01822 890403). Small, friendly, relaxed country house hotel with glorious views onto open moorland. Walks in all directions. Nine en suite bedrooms. Log fires. Gourmet cooking. Excellent wine list. Fishing, riding, golf nearby. Three-Day Break from £100pppn. AA/VisitBritain ★★, AA Rosette for food. []
e-mail: info@princehall.co.uk website: www.princehall.co.uk

THE EDGEMOOR COUNTRY HOUSE HOTEL, HAYTOR ROAD, LOWERDOWN CROSS, BOVEY TRACEY TQ13 9LE (01626 832466; Fax: 01626 834760). Country House Hotel in peaceful wooded setting adjacent Dartmoor National Park. Many lovely walks close by. All rooms en suite. Dogs welcome. See our website for further details. ETC ★★★ Silver Award [pw!]
e-mail: reservations@edgemoor.co.uk website: www.edgemoor.co.uk

TWO BRIDGES HOTEL, TWO BRIDGES, DARTMOOR PL20 6SW (01822 890581; Fax: 01822 892306). Famous Olde World riverside Inn. Centre Dartmoor. Log fires, very comfortable, friendly, excellent food. Ideal walking, touring, fishing, riding, golf. Warning – Addictive. ETC/AA ★★[]
e-mail: enquiries@warm-welcome-hotels.co.uk website: www.warm-welcome-hotels.co.uk

Dartmouth

Historic port and resort on the estuary of the River Dart, with sandy coves and pleasure boat trips up the river. Car ferry to Kingswear.

BEACHSIDE APARTMENT (01548 580206). Seven miles from Kingsbridge and Dartmouth, directly on the beach at Slapton Sands. Two bedrooms, sleeps up to 5. Fully equipped kitchen. Brochure.
e-mail: enquiries@torcross.com website: www.torcross.com

PAM & GRAHAM SPITTLE, WATERMILL COTTAGES, HANSEL, DARTMOUTH TQ6 0LN (01803 770219). Comfortable, well equipped old stone cottages in peaceful riverside setting. Wonderful walks in and around our idyllic valley near dog-friendly Slapton Sands and coastal path. Sleep 3-6. Enclosed gardens. Wood fires. Winter breaks. Brochure. [Pets £15 per week]
e-mail: graham@hanselpg.freeserve.co.uk website: www.watermillcottages.co.uk

DARTSIDE HOLIDAYS, RIVERSIDE COURT, SOUTH EMBANKMENT, DARTMOUTH TQ6 9BH (01803 832093; Fax: 01803 835135). Comfortable holiday apartments with private balconies and superb river and harbour views. Available all year with colour TV, linen and parking. Free Colour Brochure on request. [Pets £50 per week.]
website: www.dartsideholidays.com

MRS S.R. RIDALLS, THE OLD BAKEHOUSE, 7 BROADSTONE, DARTMOUTH TQ6 9NR (Tel & Fax: 01803 834585). Four cottages (one with four-poster bed). Sleep 2–6. Near river, shops, restaurants. Blackpool Sands 15 minutes' drive. TV, video, linen free. Open all year. Free parking. Non-smoking. Green Tourism Bronze Award. ETC ★★★ []
e-mail: oldbakehousecottages@yahoo.com website: www.oldbakehousedartmouth.co.uk

Doddiscombsleigh

Village 6 miles south west of Exeter.

STATION LODGE, DODDISCOMBSLEIGH, EXETER (Tel & Fax: 01647 253104). Comfortably furnished apartment for two people in beautiful Teign River valley. Excellent location for exploring Dartmoor. From £200 per week. For further details contact: IAN WEST, STATION HOUSE, DODDISCOMBSLEIGH, EXETER EX6 7PW. [pw!]
e-mail: enquiries@station-lodge.co.uk website: www.station-lodge.co.uk

Dunsford

Attractive village in upper Teign valley with Dartmoor to the west. Plymouth 35 miles, Okehampton 16, Newton Abbot 13, Crediton 9, Exeter 8.

ROYAL OAK INN, DUNSFORD, NEAR EXETER EX6 7DA (01647 252256). Welcome to our Victorian country inn with real ales and home-made food. All en suite rooms are in a 300-year-old converted barn. Well behaved children and dogs welcome. []

A useful index of towns/counties appears at the back of this book

Exeter

Chief city of the South-West with a cathedral and university. Ample shopping, sports and leisure facilities.

MRS SALLY GLANVILL, RYDON FARM, WOODBURY, EXETER EX5 1LB (01395 232341). 16th Century Devon Longhouse on working dairy farm. Open all year. Highly recommended. From £32 to £60pppn. ETC/AA ★★★★ [🐕]
website: www.rydonfarmwoodbury.co.uk

BEST WESTERN LORD HALDON HOTEL, DUNCHIDEOCK, NEAR EXETER EX6 7YF (01392 832483, Fax: 01392 833765). Extensive gardens amid miles of rolling Devon countryside. ETC ★★★, AA ★★★ and 2 Rosettes. [Pets £5 per night.]
e-mail: enquiries@lordhaldonhotel.co.uk website: www.lordhaldonhotel.co.uk

Exmoor

265 square miles of unspoiled heather moorland with deep wooded valleys and rivers, ideal for a walking, pony trekking or fishing holiday

THE STAGHUNTERS INN/HOTEL, BRENDON, EXMOOR EX35 6PS (01598 741222; Fax: 01598 741352). Family-run village inn with river frontage. Beautiful gardens. 12 en suite rooms. Varied menu, log fires, fine wines and cask ales. A walkers' paradise. [Pets £2.50 per night]
e-mail: stay@staghunters.com website: www.staghunters.com

JAYE JONES AND HELEN ASHER, TWITCHEN FARM, CHALLACOMBE, BARNSTAPLE EX31 4TT (01598 763568). Comfort for country lovers in Exmoor National Park. High quality en suite rooms. Breakfast prepared with local and organic produce. Farm walk through fields to village pub. B&B £26–£36. ETC ★★★★ [One dog free, two dogs £5]
e-mail: holidays@twitchen.co.uk website: www.twitchen.co.uk

THE SPIRIT OF EXMOOR - RIDING HOLIDAYS FOR ADULTS (01598 753318). Accommodation in secluded, comfortable 17th century farmhouse or cosy en suite lodges. Delicious home-cooked cuisine, vegetarians welcome. Non-riders, own horses and pets welcome. Horse whispering courses. Telephone STEPHANY PETTINGER for colour brochure or more information.
e-mail: stephany@spiritofexmoor.fsnet.co.uk website: www.spiritofexmoor.com

Hexworthy (Dartmoor)

Hamlet on Dartmoor 7 miles west of Ashburton.

THE FOREST INN, HEXWORTHY, DARTMOOR PL20 6SD (01364 631211; Fax: 01364 631515). A haven for walkers, riders, fishermen, canoeists or anyone just looking for an opportunity to enjoy the natural beauty of Dartmoor. Restaurant using local produce wherever possible; extensive range of snacks; Devon beers and ciders. ETC ★★★ [🐕]
e-mail: info@theforestinn.co.uk

Holsworthy

Town 9 miles east of Bude.

TINNEY WATERS, PYWORTHY. Self-catering. Three beautiful lakes - carp, tench, bream. No day tickets, no close season. Ideal for birdwatching. Contact: J. MASON (01409 271362).
e-mail: jeffmason@freenetname.co.uk website: www.tinneywaters.co.uk

Honiton

Town on River Otter 16 miles East of Exeter.

COMBE HOUSE HOTEL AND RESTAURANT GITTISHAM, HONITON, Nr EXETER EX14 3AD (01404 540 400; Fax: 01404 46004) Grade 1 Elizabethan Manor set in 3,500 acres of rolling countryside. Fabulous food, generous hospitality and 15 individual rooms. Perfect dog walks.
e-mail: stay@thishotel.com website: www.thishotel.com

Hope Cove

Attractive fishing village, flat sandy beach and safe bathing. Fine views towards Rame Head; cliffs. Kingsbridge 6 miles.

HOPE BARTON BARNS, HOPE COVE, NEAR SALCOMBE TQ7 3HT (01548 561393). 17 stone barns in two courtyards and three luxury apartments in farmhouse. Farmhouse meals. Free range children and well behaved dogs welcome. For full colour brochure please contact: Mr & Mrs M. Pope. [pw! Pets £20 per week]
website: www.hopebarton.co.uk

Ilfracombe

This popular seaside resort clusters round a busy harbour. The surrounding area is ideal for coastal walks.

WIDMOUTH FARM, NEAR ILFRACOMBE EX34 9RX (01271 863743). Comfortable, well equipped cottages in 35 acres of gardens, pasture, woodland and private beach. Wonderful scenery. Ideal for birdwatching, painting, sea fishing & golf. Dogs welcome. ETC ★★★. [pw! Pets £25 per week each].
e-mail: holiday@widmouthfarmcottages.co.uk website: www.widmouthfarmcottages.co.uk

ST BRANNOCKS HOUSE, ST BRANNOCKS ROAD, ILFRACOMBE EX34 8EQ (Tel & Fax: 01271 863873). Lovely relaxing home with level walk to shops and harbour. Brilliant walks, Exmoor and beaches nearby. Great food, cosy bar, comfy lounge. Children and dogs welcome. Open all year. EnjoyEngland.com ★★★★ [🐕]
e-mail: barbara@stbrannockshouse.co.uk website: www.stbrannockshouse.co.uk

VARLEY HOUSE, CHAMBERCOMBE PARK, ILFRACOMBE EX34 9QW (01271 863927; Fax: 01271 879299). Relax with your dog, fabulous walks nearby. Fully en suite non-smoking rooms with lots of thoughtful extras. Superb food, beautiful surroundings. Bar. Car park. Children over five years welcome. Free wifi. Phone about our three day break. ETC ★★★★ [🐕] WE WANT YOU TO WANT TO RETURN.
e-mail: info@varleyhouse.co.uk website: www.varleyhouse.co.uk

BEACHSIDE HOLIDAY PARK, ILFRACOMBE (01271 863006). Relax in one of Beachside's caravans nestled in the hillside overlooking golden Devonshire sands in Hele Bay, Ilfracombe. Call now to request a brochure or book your holiday or short break.
e-mail: enquiries@beachsidepark.co.uk website: www.beachsidepark.co.uk

PETE AND HEATHER SMALL, STRATHMORE, 57 ST BRANNOCKS ROAD, ILFRACOMBE EX34 8EQ (01271 862248) Delightful and friendly Victorian Licensed guest house, 10-minute stroll to both seafront and town centre. 8 individually designed en suite bedrooms. Cosy lounge bar, secluded terraced garden. Children and pets always welcome. [Pets £5 per night]
e-mail: peter@small6374.fsnet.co.uk www.the-strathmore.co.uk

THE FOXHUNTERS INN, WEST DOWN, NEAR ILFRACOMBE EX34 8NU (01271 863757; Fax: 01271 879313). 300 year-old coaching Inn conveniently situated for beaches and country walks. En suite accommodation. Pets welcome by prior arrangement.[🐕]
website: www.foxhuntersinn.co.uk

Instow

On estuaries of Taw and Torridge, very popular with boating enthusiasts. Barnstaple 6 miles, Bideford 3.

BEACH HAVEN COTTAGE, INSTOW. Two seafront cottages with extensive beach and sea views. Sleep 5. Enclosed garden, own parking. Central heating, colour TV, coastal walks. Dog welcome. For colour brochure send SAE to MRS P. I. BARNES, 140 BAY VIEW ROAD, NORTHAM, BIDEFORD EX39 1BJ (01237 473801). [Dog £10 per week]
website: www.seabirdcottages.co.uk

FREE or REDUCED RATE entry to Holiday Visits and Attractions – see our **READERS' OFFER VOUCHERS** on pages 433-440

Kingsbridge

Pleasant town at head of picturesque Kingsbridge estuary. Centre for South Hams district with its lush scenery and quiet coves.

BEACHDOWN, CHALLABOROUGH BAY, KINGSBRIDGE TQ7 4JB (01548 810089; mobile: 07725 053439). Comfortable, fully-equipped chalets on private, level and secluded site in beautiful South Hams. 150 yards from beach and South West Coastal Path. [pw! Pets £15.00 per week].
e-mail: petswelcome@beachdown.co.uk website: www.beachdown.co.uk

MRS B. KELLY, BLACKWELL PARK, LODDISWELL, KINGSBRIDGE TQ7 4EA (01548 821230). 17th century Farmhouse, five miles from Kingsbridge. Ideal centre for Dartmoor, Plymouth, Torbay, Dartmouth and many beaches. Some bedrooms en suite. Bed and Breakfast. Evening meal optional. Dogsitting. Pets welcome free of charge. [ ]

DITTISCOMBE HOLIDAY COTTAGES, SLAPTON, NEAR KINGSBRIDGE, SOUTH DEVON TQ7 2QF (01548 521272). Nature trail and 20 acres of open space. Perfect holiday location for dogs and owners. All cottages have gardens and views of surrounding valley. ETC ★★★★. [Pets £20 per week]
e-mail: info@dittiscombe.co.uk website: www.dittiscombe.co.uk

King's Nympton

3 miles north of Chulmleigh. Winner of CPRE Award for Devon Village of the year 1999.

COLLACOTT FARM, KING'S NYMPTON, UMBERLEIGH, NORTH DEVON EX37 9TP (01769 572491). Eight Country Cottages sleeping from 2 to 12 in rural area; lovely views, private patios and gardens. Well furnished and equipped. Heated pool, tennis court, BHS approved riding school. Laundry room. Open all year. [pw!, Pets £20 per week]
e-mail: info@collacott.co.uk website: www.collacott.co.uk

Lapford

Village 5 miles S.E. of Chulmleigh.

DAVID & MARION MILLS, RUDGE FARM, LAPFORD, CREDITON EX17 6NG (01363 83268). Set in beautiful grounds with pond, orchard and woods. Trout fishing and almost 200 acres to wander in. House very tastefully furnished and fully equipped (sleeps 8). No charge for dogs, linen or fuel. Send for brochure. [ ]

Lynton/Lynmouth

Picturesque twin villages joined by a unique cliff railway (vertical height 500 ft). Lynmouth has a quaint harbour and Lynton enjoys superb views over the rugged coastline.

BATH HOTEL, TORS HOTEL, LYNMOUTH, EXMOOR, NORTH DEVON EX35 6EL (01598 752238). Great views of harbour. Quality rooms and service. Ideal for moors. Pets welcome. Off-season discounts available. [ ]
e-mail: info@bathhotellynmouth.co.uk website: www.bathhotellynmouth.co.uk

MR AND MRS I. RIGBY, BRENDON HOUSE, BRENDON, LYNTON EX35 6PS (01598 741206). Licensed country guesthouse in beautiful Lyn Valley. Ideal walking, fishing, riding. Award winning restaurant serving local food. Weekly discounts and short breaks. VisitBritain ★★★★ [ ]
email: brendonhouse4u@aol.com website: wwwbrendonhouse4u.com

BLUE BALL INN (formerly The Exmoor Sandpiper Inn), COUNTISBURY, LYNMOUTH EX35 6NE (01598 741263). Romantic coaching inn on Exmoor. 16 en suite bedrooms, extensive menus with daily specials, good wines. Horse riding, walking. No charge for dogs. [ ]
website: www.BlueBallinn.com or www.exmoorsandpiper.com

JIM AND SUSAN BINGHAM, NEW MILL FARM, BARBROOK, LYNTON EX35 6JR (01598 753341). Exmoor Valley. Two delightful genuine modernised XVII century cottages by stream on 100-acre farm with A.B.R.S. Approved riding stables. Free fishing. ETC ★★★★. [pw! Pets £15 per week.]
e-mail: info@outovercott.co.uk website: www.outovercott.co.uk

THE NORTH CLIFF HOTEL, NORTH WALK, LYNTON EX35 6HJ (01598 752357). On the South West Coastal Path, the North Cliff is an ideal base for discovering Exmoor and the North Devon Coast. Delicious home cooking. We welcome pets, children and groups. Self-catering flat, sleeps 6, also available. [Pets £4 per night, £20 per week].
e-mail: holidays@northcliffhotel.co.uk website: www.northcliffhotel.co.uk

MOORLANDS. Where countryside and comfort combine. Two self-contained apartments within a family-run guesthouse, within the Exmoor National Park. Hotel amenities available for guests' use. Contact: MR I. CORDEROY, MOORLANDS, WOODY BAY, PARRACOMBE, NEAR LYNTON EX31 4RA (01598 763224). ETC ★★★★ [🐕]
website: www.moorlandshotel.co.uk

COUNTISBURY LODGE HOTEL, COUNTISBURY HILL, LYNMOUTH EX35 6NB (01598 752388). Former Victorian vicarage, peacefully secluded yet only 5 minutes to Lynmouth village. En suite rooms, central heating. Ideal for birdwatching and moors. Parking. Short Breaks. Also available S/C cottage and apartment. AA ★★★ [🐕]
website: www.countisburylodge.co.uk

MRS W. PRYOR, STATION HOUSE, LYNTON EX35 6LB (01598 752275/752381; Fax: 01598 752475). Holiday accommodation situated in the former narrow gauge railway station closed in 1935, overlooking the West Lyn Valley. Centrally placed for Doone Valley and Exmoor. Parking available. [🐕]
e-mail: advertise@lyntonadvertiser.com

Mortehoe

Adjoining Woolacombe with cliffs and wide sands. Interesting rock scenery beyond Morte Point. Barnstaple 15 miles.

LUNDY HOUSE HOTEL, MORTEHOE, NORTH DEVON EX34 7DZ (01271 870372). Quality en suite accommodation in small, friendly hotel. TV & tea-making facilities in all rooms. Stunning views. Write or phone for full details. [🐕]
e-mail: info@lundyhousehotel.co.uk website: www.lundyhousehotel.co.uk

THE SMUGGLERS REST INN, NORTH MORTE ROAD, MORTEHOE EX34 7DR (Tel & Fax: 01271 870891). In the pretty village of Mortehoe. The Smugglers offers luxury accommodation from twin rooms to family suites. En suite rooms, TV, full English breakfast, licensed bar, beer garden, home-cooked meals. Well trained pets welcome. [Pets £5 per week].
e-mail: info@smugglersmortehoe.co.uk website: www.smugglersmortehoe.co.uk

Noss Mayo

Village 3 miles south west of Yealmpton, on south side of creek running into River Yealm estuary, opposite Newton Ferrers.

CRAB COTTAGE, NOSS MAYO. Charming fisherman's cottage, 50 yards from the quay. Fantastic walks, beaches and dog-friendly pubs on the doorstep. Close to the South Devon Coastal Path. Sleeps 5. Phone 01425 471372 for a brochure. [£25 per pet, per week]
e-mail: sally.bennetts@btinternet.com website: www.crab-cottage.co.uk

Ottery St Mary

Pleasant little town in East Devon, within easy reach of the sea. Many interesting little buildings including 11th century parish church. Birthplace of poet Coleridge.

MRS A. FORTH, FLUXTON FARM, OTTERY ST MARY EX11 1RJ (01404 812818). Charming 16th Century farmhouse. B&B from £25. Peace and quiet. Cat lovers' paradise. Masses of dog walks. AA ★★ [🐕 pw!]
website: www.fluxtonfarm.co.uk

Pet-Friendly
Pubs, Inns & Hotels
on pages 424-432
Please note that these establishments may not feature in the main section of this book

Paignton

Popular family resort on Torbay with long, safe sandy beaches and small harbour. Exeter 25 miles, Newton Abbott 9, Torquay 3.

CHRISTINE CLARK & LLOYD HASTIE, AMBER HOUSE, 6 ROUNDHAM ROAD, PAIGNTON TQ4 6EZ (01803 558372). All en suite; ground floor rooms. Good food. Highly recommended. Non-smoking. A warm welcome assured to pets and their families. ETC ★★★★ Silver Award.
e-mail: enquiries@amberhousehotel.co.uk website: www.amberhousehotel.co.uk

THE COMMODORE, 14 ESPLANADE ROAD, PAIGNTON TQ4 6EB (01803 553107). Ideally situated on Paignton sea front, sea view rooms. Luxury en suites, refreshments, sea view guest lounge, bar, gift shop. Excellent breakfast. Close to harbour, bus and rail stations. Free parking. [Pets £5 per night].
e-mail: info@commodorepaignton.com website: www.commodorepaignton.com

Plymouth

Historic port and resort, impressively rebuilt after severe war damage. Large naval docks at Devonport. Beach of pebble and sand.

CHURCHWOOD VALLEY, WEMBURY BAY, NEAR PLYMOUTH PL9 0DZ (01752 862382). Relax in one of our comfortable log cabins, set in a peaceful wooded valley near the beach. Enjoy wonderful walks in woods and along the coast. Abundance of birds and wildlife. Up to two pets per cabin. [Pets £5 per week each]
e-mail: churchwoodvalley@btconnect.com website: www.churchwoodvalley.com

LAMPLIGHTER HOTEL, 103 CITADEL ROAD, THE HOE, PLYMOUTH PL1 2RN (01752 663855; Tel/Fax: 01752 228139). Situated on famous Plymouth Hoe, close to the seafront, historic Barbican, city centre with shops, restaurants and entertainment venues. Minutes from rail and coach stations, and 850 yards from ferry terminal. 7 en suite bedrooms and 2 with private facilities. ETC/AA ★★★
e-mail: stay@lamplighterplymouth.co.uk website: www.lamplighterplymouth.co.uk

THE CRANBOURNE, 278/282 CITADEL ROAD, THE HOE, PLYMOUTH PL1 2PZ (01752 263858/ 661400/224646; Fax: 01752 263858). Convenient for Ferry Terminal and City Centre. All bedrooms with colour TV and tea/coffee. Licensed bar. Keys provided for access at all times. Under personal supervision. Pets by arrangement. AA ★★★ [🐕]
e-mail: cran.hotel@virgin.net website: www.cranbournehotel.co.uk

Salcombe

Fishing and sailing centre in sheltered position. Fine beaches and coastal walks nearby.

PORT LIGHT, BOLBERRY DOWN, MALBOROUGH, NEAR SALCOMBE TQ7 3DY (01548 561384 or 07970 859992). A totally unique location set amidst acres of National Trust coastline. Luxury en suite rooms. Superb home-cooked fare, specialising in local seafood. Licensed bar. Pets welcome throughout the hotel. Short Breaks throughout the year. Contact: Sean and Hazel Hassall. [🐕]
e-mail: info@portlight.co.uk website: www.portlight.co.uk

BOLBERRY FARM COTTAGES, BOLBERRY, NEAR SALCOMBE, DEVON TQ7 3DY (01548 561384). HAZEL AND SEAN HASSALL. Luxury Barn conversion cottages. Private gardens. Close to coastal path and pet-friendly beaches. Dog wash. Short Breaks out of season. The Pet Holiday Specialist. [🐕]
e-mail: info@bolberryfarmcottages.co.uk website: www.bolberryfarmcottages.co.uk

Seaton

Bright East Devon resort near Axe estuary. Shingle beach and chalk cliffs; good bathing, many lovely walks in vicinity. Exeter 23 miles, Sidmouth 11.

MILKBERE COTTAGE HOLIDAYS, 3 FORE STREET, SEATON EX12 2LE (Brochure: 01297 22925 / Bookings: 01297 20729). Specialising in coast/country holidays on the Devon/Dorset border. Cottages, bungalows, houses, apartments and caravans, ideally situated for walking and exploring the Jurassic Coast. [Pets £20 per week.] VisitBritain ★★★/★★★★★.
e-mail: info@milkberehols.com website: www.milkberehols.com

AXEVALE CARAVAN PARK, COLYFORD ROAD, SEATON EX12 2DF (0800 0688816). A quiet, family-run park with 68 modern and luxury caravans for hire. Laundry facilities, park shop. All caravans have a shower, toilet, fridge and TV. Relaxing atmosphere. ETC ★★★★ [Pets £10 per week]
website: www.axevale.co.uk

Sidmouth

Sheltered resort, winner of many awards for its floral displays. Good sands at Jacob's Ladder beach.

OAKDOWN TOURING AND HOLIDAY CARAVAN PARK, WESTON, SIDMOUTH EX10 0PT (01297 680387; Fax: 01297 680541). Sidmouth's multi-award-winning touring and holiday caravan park. Welcome to Oakdown, set near the "Jurassic Coast" World Heritage Site, and a winner of "Caravan Holiday Park of The Year" in the Excellence in England Awards 2007. Oakdown is level, sheltered and landscaped into groves to give privacy. Our luxurious amenities include aids for the disabled. Enjoy our Field Trail to the famous Donkey Sanctuary. Free colour brochure with pleasure. ETC ★★★★★, David Bellamy Gold Award, Loo of the Year Award, Best of British, Excellence in England 2007.
e-mail: enquiries@oakdown.co.uk website: www.oakdown.co.uk

SWEETCOMBE COTTAGE HOLIDAYS, ROSEMARY COTTAGE, WESTON, NEAR SIDMOUTH EX10 0PH (01395 512130; Fax: 01395 515680). Selection of Cottages, Farmhouses and Flats in Sidmouth and East Devon, all personally selected and very well-equipped. Gardens. Pets welcome. Please ask for our colour brochure. []
e-mail: enquiries@sweetcombe-ch.co.uk website: www.sweetcombe-ch.co.uk

LEIGH COTTAGES, WESTON, SIDMOUTH EX10 0PH. Eight cottages 150 yards from National Trust Valley leading to Coastal Path and beach. Lovely cliff top walks and level walks around nearby Donkey Sanctuary fields. ETC ★★★★ Contact: Alison Clarke (01395 516065/514764; Fax: 01395 512563). [pw! Pets £20 per week]
e-mail: Alison@leigh-cottages.co.uk website: www.leigh-cottages.co.uk

Tavistock

Birthplace of Sir Francis Drake and site of a fine ruined Benedictine Abbey. On edge of Dartmoor, 13 miles north of Plymouth

LANGSTONE MANOR HOLIDAY PARK, MOORTOWN, TAVISTOCK PL19 9JZ (Tel & Fax 01822 613371). Peaceful Holiday Park, offering camping, cottages, apartment, static caravans. Ideal location outside Tavistock with direct access onto Dartmoor. Bar and evening meals. Excellent location. ETC ★★★★, AA ★★★[Pets £20 per week.]
e-mail: jane@langstone-manor.co.uk website: www.langstone-manor.co.uk

MRS P.G.C. QUINTON, HIGHER QUITHER, MILTON ABBOT, TAVISTOCK PL19 0PZ (01822 860284). Modern self-contained barn conversion. Own private garden. Terms from £225 inc. linen, coal and logs. Electricity metered. [pw!]

Thurlestone

Village resort above the cliffs to the north of Bolt Tail, 4 miles west of Kingsbridge.

CUTAWAY COTTAGE, THURLESTONE, KINGSBRIDGE TQ7 3NF. Self-catering cottage within a fenced garden in the middle of the village. Private road, 5 minutes to pub and shop, 20 minutes' walk to beaches & sea, Ideal for children, dog walkers and bird watchers. Phone PAT on 01548 560688 []

Torbay

An east-facing bay and natural harbour at the western end of Lyme Bay, midway between the cities of Exeter and Plymouth.

J. AND E. BALL, DEPARTMENT P.W., HIGHER WELL FARM HOLIDAY PARK, STOKE GABRIEL, TOTNES TQ9 6RN (01803 782289). Within 4 miles Torbay beaches and one mile of River Dart. Central for touring. Dogs on leads. Tourist Board Graded Park ★★★★. [pw! Pets £2 per night, £15 per week in statics, free in tents and tourers]
website: www.higherwellfarmholidaypark.co.uk

Torquay

Popular resort on the English Riviera with a wide range of attractions and entertainments. Yachting and watersports centre with 10 superb beaches and coves.

RED HOUSE HOTEL AND MAXTON LODGE HOLIDAY APARTMENTS, ROUSDOWN ROAD, CHELSTON, TORQUAY TQ2 6PB (01803 607811; Fax: 01803 605357). Choose either the friendly service and facilities of a hotel or the privacy and freedom of self-catering apartments. The best of both worlds! AA/ETC ★★ Hotel & ★★★ Self-catering. [in flats; £3 per night in hotel]
e-mail: stay@redhouse-hotel.co.uk website: www.redhouse-hotel.co.uk

THE DOWNS HOTEL, 41-43 BABBACOMBE DOWNS ROAD, TORQUAY TQ1 3LN (01803 328543/ 0845 051 0989). Fully licensed family-run establishment with 12 en suite rooms, eight with private balconies and superb views. Family rooms, reduced rates for under 12s. Dog-friendly. [Pets £5 per night].
website: www.downshotel.co.uk

Torrington

Pleasant market town on River Torridge. Good centre for moors and sea. Exeter 36 miles, Okehampton 20, Barnstaple 12, Bideford 7.

RICH AND DIANA JONES, STOWFORD LODGE, LANGTREE, GREAT TORRINGTON EX38 8NU (01805 601540). Sleep 4/6. Picturesque and peaceful. Four delightful cottages set within 6 acres of private land with heated indoor pool. Magnificent countryside. Convenient North Devon coast and moors. Phone for brochure. VisitBritain ★★★ [Pets £15 per week, pw!]
e-mail: enq@stowfordlodge.co.uk website: www.stowfordlodge.co.uk

Totnes

Town at tidal estuary of River Dart, 7 miles west of Torquay

MRS ANNE TORR, DOWNE LODGE, BROADHEMPSTON, TOTNES TQ9 6BY (Tel & Fax: 01803 812828; Mobile; 07772318746).) Woodland dog walking on doorstep. Cottage available with one or three bedrooms. Private garden. En suite B&B available. No smoking. Beautiful, quiet position convenient for Dartmoor and the coast. [🐕]
e-mail: info@downelodge.co.uk website: www.downelodge.co.uk

Westward Ho!

An excellent resort with 3 miles of golden sands, amusements, pubs, clubs and restaurants. 2 miles N.W. of Bideford.

WEST PUSEHILL FARM COTTAGES, WEST PUSEHILL FARM, WESTWARD HO!, NORTH DEVON EX39 5AH (01237 475638/474622). Nestling within the Kenwith Valley, 10 cottages with heated outdoor pool. Perfectly situated to explore coast and countryside. Many attractions close by. Pets and children welcome. Open all year. [Pets £20 per week].
website: www.wpfcottages.co.uk

Woolacombe

Favourite resort with long, wide stretches of sand. Barnstaple 15 miles, Ilfracombe 6.

EUROPA PARK, BEACH ROAD, WOOLACOMBE (01271 871425). Static caravans, chalets, camping, surf lodges and surf cabins. Full facilities. Pets welcome. Indoor heated swimming pool, sauna, site shop.
e-mail: holidays@europapark.co.uk website: www.europapark.co.uk

WOOLACOMBE BAY HOLIDAY PARCS (01271 870 343). Four award-winning Holiday Parcs set in delightful surroundings, all beside three miles of golden Blue Flag sandy beach in Devon. Pet-friendly holiday homes with pet pack and "Woof" Guide to Woolacombe.
website: www.woolacombe.com/fpw

SUNNYMEADE COUNTRY HOTEL, WEST DOWN, NEAR WOOLACOMBE EX34 8NT (01271 863668; Fax: 01271 866061). Small country hotel set in beautiful countryside. A few minutes away from Ilfracombe, Exmoor and Woolacombe's Blue Flag Beach. 12 en suite rooms, 4 on the ground floor. Deaf accessible. Pets welcome. [pw!]
website: www.sunnymeade.co.uk

MRS JOYCE BAGNALL, CHICHESTER HOUSE, THE ESPLANADE, WOOLACOMBE EX34 7DJ (01271 870761). Holiday apartments on sea front. Fully furnished, sea and coastal views. Watch the sun go down from your balcony. Open all year. SAE Resident Proprietor. [Pets £12 per week, pw!]

DORSET COTTAGE HOLIDAYS

PETS GO FREE.

Self-catering cottages, town houses, bungalows and apartments. All within 10 miles of Heritage Coastline and sandy beaches. Excellent walking in idyllic countryside. Short breaks from £95, weekly from £170 (per cottage). Open all year.

Free brochure tel: 01929 553443
e-mail: enq@dhcottages.co.uk
www.dhcottages.co.uk

Dorset Coastal Cottages

www.dorsetcoastalcottages.com

Tel: 0800 9804070

Carefully selected, traditional cottages in or near villages within ten miles of Dorset's spectacular World Heritage Coast. Many are thatched and have open fires or logburners.

Over half of our cottages welcome dogs.

Full weeks or Short Breaks all year round.
Rents include linen/towels and electricity/gas etc.

Bere Regis, Blandford

Situated in an Area of Outstanding Natural Beauty. A good base for touring; direct access onto heathland and woodland walks. Ideal for nature lovers, bird watching and quiet family holidays. Park facilities include shop, launderette, gas exchange, children's play area, games room, clean, modern facilities, grassy pitches. Tents also welcome. Dogs welcome.

Mr & Mrs R. Cargill, Rye Hill, Bere Regis, Dorset BH20 7LP

Rowlands Wait Touring Park

Tel: 01929 472727
www.rowlandswait.co.uk

ANVIL INN

Salisbury Road, Pimperne, Blandford, Dorset DT11 8UQ

Tel: 01258 453431 • Fax: 01258 480182

A long, low thatched building set in a tiny village deep in the Dorset countryside – what could be more English? This typical Old English hostelry offering good old-fashioned English hospitality, a full à la carte menu with mouthwatering desserts in the charming beamed restaurant with log fire,together with specials of the day and light bites menu in the two bars. All bedrooms with private facilities; wi-fi available in all rooms. Ample parking. **From £75 single, £100 double/twin.**

e-mail: theanvil.inn@btconnect.com
www.anvilinn.co.uk

BOURNEMOUTH HOLIDAY APARTMENTS

16 Florence Road, Bournemouth BH5 1HF • Tel: 01202 304925

Modern well-equipped flats close to sea and shops. Sleep up to ten persons. Car parking. Children and pets welcome. Phone for brochure or e-mail.

website: www.selfcateringbournemouth.co.uk

HOLIDAY FLATS AND FLATLETS 07788 952394

• A SHORT WALK TO GOLDEN SANDY BEACHES • MOST WITH PRIVATE BATHROOMS • CLEANLINESS AND COMFORT ASSURED • LAUNDRY ROOM • FREE PRIVATE PARKING • DOGS WELCOME • COLOUR TV IN ALL UNITS • NO VAT CHARGED •

CONTACT: M. DE KMENT, 4 CECIL ROAD, BOURNEMOUTH BH5 1DU

Langtry Manor

The Country House Hotel in Bournemouth

Built by King Edward VII as a love nest for Lillie Langtry, this is a rare gem of an hotel with the food, service and building steeped in history all blending to create something quite exceptional, from the Four-posters, hot tubs, and complimentary leisure club to the AA Rosette-winning restaurant. Midweek and weekend breaks. As featured on "Holiday" (BBC).

"Best Hotel in Bournemouth" - The Guardian

"By far the best place to stay in Bournemouth" - lonely planet

Derby road, East Cliff, Bournemouth BH1 3QB

0844 371 3705 (Local Rate) **www.langtrymanor.co.uk**

THE VINE HOTEL

22 Southern Road, Southbourne
Bournemouth BH6 3SR
Telephone: 01202 428309

A small, family, award-winning non smoking Hotel only three hundred yards from dog-friendly beach and shops. All rooms en suite; tea/coffee making facilities and colour TV. Residential licence with attractive bar. Full central heating. Forecourt parking. Open all year.

Pets Welcome – Free of Charge •• FHG Diploma

Alum Dene Hotel

2 Burnaby Road, Alum Chine, Bournemouth BH4 8JF Tel: 01202 764011

Renowned for good old fashioned hospitality and friendly service. Come and be spoilt at our licensed hotel. All rooms en suite, colour TV. Some have sea views. 200 metres sea. Parking. Christmas House party. No charge for pets. **www.alumdenehotel.com** • **e-mail: alumdenehotel@hotmail.co.uk**

Southbourne Grove Hotel

96 Southbourne Road, Southbourne, Bournemouth BH6 3QQ • Tel: 01202 420503 • Fax: 01202 421953

Friendly, family-run hotel with beautiful garden and ample guest parking. Close to beach and shops. Excellent food served in spacious restaurant. En suites, four-poster suite, ground floor rooms (one suitable for partially disabled) and large family bedrooms - all with colour TV and tea/coffee making facilities. Senior Citizen and Child discounts. Dogs welcome free of charge. *B&B from £23 per night, from £129 per week.* This is a no smoking hotel. **www.tiscover.co.uk/southbournegrovehotel**

Bournemouth, Bridport

Guests enjoying the lounge

THE *REALLY* DOG-FRIENDLY PLACE

WHITE TOPPS

Small, friendly and catering only for guests with dogs. In a nice quiet position close to lovely walks on the beach (dogs allowed) and Hengistbury Head. Plus the New Forest isn't far away. There's no charge for pets, of course and the proprietor, MARJORIE TITCHEN, just loves dogs.

- DOG(S) ESSENTIAL - ANY SIZE, ANY NUMBER, ANYWHERE
- GROUND FLOOR ROOM FOR ELDERLY DOGS
- ADULTS ONLY (14yrs +)
- GENEROUS HOME COOKING
- VEGETARIANS WELCOME
- NOT SUITABLE FOR DISABLED
- CAR PARKING

WRITE (SAE APPRECIATED) OR PHONE FOR FACT SHEET.

WHITE TOPPS, 45 CHURCH ROAD, SOUTHBOURNE, BOURNEMOUTH, DORSET BH6 4BB
TEL: 01202 428868

No Credit Cards - Cheque or Cash only

e-mail: thedoghotel@aol.com • www.whitetopps.co.uk

IF YOU DON'T LOVE DOGS YOU WON'T LIKE WHITE TOPPS

17th Century

FROGMORE FARM

Enjoy Bed and Breakfast or our delightful Self Catering cottage.

Frogmore is a 90-acre grazing farm situated tranquilly in beautiful West Dorset, overlooking the Jurassic Coast of Lyme Bay, and away from the crowds. En suite shower rooms available.

Ideal for walking, our land is adjacent to National Trust land to the cliffs, (Seatown 1½ miles) and the South West Coastal Path.

Well behaved dogs very welcome • Open all year
Car essential • Brochure and terms free on request.

Contact Mrs Sue Norman • Tel: 01308 456159
Frogmore Farm, Chideock, Bridport DT6 6HT
www.frogmorefarm.com
e-mail: bookings@frogmorefarm.com

Eype House Caravan & Camping Park

Small, quiet family-run park lying on the Heritage Coastal Path, 200 yards from the beach.

Static vans for hire from £180 to £460, tent pitches (all terraced with sea views) £11 to £17.50. Sorry, no touring caravans. **Children and dogs welcome.**

Eype, Bridport DT6 6AL • www.eypehouse.co.uk • Tel: 01308 424903

'DOG DAYS IN DORSET' • DOGS ARE MOST WELCOME AND COME FREE

Wonderful tail-wagging walks from a peaceful small holiday bungalow park (one & two bedrooms). Just a short stroll from the beach on the beautiful Jurassic coast. Our guests may bring more than one dog. For SHORT BREAKS and WEEKLY SUMMER HOLIDAYS

Telephone today for Information Pack and Prices 01308 421 521

Golden Acre Holiday Bungalows, Eype, Bridport, Dorset DT6 6AL • www.golden-acre.com

Lancombes House ~ Holiday Cottages

enjoyEngland.com 3★ - 4★ SELF CATERING

Four individually designed cottages and Farmhouse, arranged around a courtyard and set in 9 acres. Each has its own sitting out area, with garden furniture. Two with enclosed south-facing gardens. Central heating and wood burners/fires in four. In an Area of Outstanding Natural Beauty and surrounded by the beautiful hills and valleys of this unspoiled part of West Dorset, ideal for walking, riding and outdoor pursuits. Children and dogs welcome. Open all year.

Lancombes House, West Milton, Bridport DT6 3TN

Tel: 01308 485375 • www.lancombes-house.co.uk

Two Wings

Granary Lodge

Tamarisk Farm

West Bexington, Dorchester DT2 9DF

1

Please book by phone 01308 897784 • Mrs J. Pearse

On slope overlooking Chesil beach between Abbotsbury and Burton Bradstock.

Four large (Mimosa is wheelchair disabled M3(1) and Granary Lodge is disabled-friendly M1) and two small cottages. Each one stands in own fenced garden.

Glorious views along West Dorset and Devon coasts. Lovely walks by sea and inland. Part of mixed organic farm with arable, sheep, cattle, horses and market garden (organic vegetables, meat and wholemeal flour available). Sea fishing, riding in Portesham and Burton Bradstock, lots of tourist attractions and good markets. Good centre for touring Thomas Hardy's Wessex. Safe for children and excellent for dogs. Very quiet. Terms from £255 to £960.

e-mail: holidays@tamariskfarm.com • www.tamariskfarm.com/holidays

www.foxandhoundsinn.com

FOX & HOUNDS INN

Cattistock, Dorchester DT2 0JH

Set in beautiful countryside, this is a unique 17th century inn with superb accommodation. Excellent home cooked food, fine wines and well conditioned ales.

Tel: 01300 320444

Charmouth, Christchurch, Dorchester, Evershot, Lulworth Cove

MANOR FARM HOLIDAY CENTRE

Charmouth, Bridport, Dorset DT6 6QL (01297) 560226

Two and three bedroomed houses, Luxury caravans. All units for four to six people. Children and pets welcome. Swimming pool and children's pool. Licensed bar with family room. Shop. Launderette. Children's play area. Ten minutes' walk to safe sand and shingle beach. Many fine walks locally. Golf, riding, tennis, fishing and boating all nearby. **SAE TO MR. F. LOOSMORE FOR COLOUR BROCHURE.**

NEW FOREST - Country Holiday Chalet on small, quiet, secluded woodland park, situated within the National Park. Sleeps four. Fenced private garden. Dogs welcome. Car parking. £175 to £350 per week. Write enclosing SAE or telephone:

British Holiday & Home Parks Association

Mrs L.M Bowling, Owlpen Caravans Ltd, Owlpen,
148 Burley Road, Bransgore, Near Christchurch, Dorset BH23 8DB
Tel: 01425 672875 • Mobile: 07860 547391 • www.owlpen-caravans.co.uk

ETC ★★★★ Guest House

CHURCHVIEW GUEST HOUSE

Winterbourne Abbas, Dorchester, Dorset DT2 9LS Tel/Fax: 01305 889296

Our 17th century Guest House, noted for warm hospitality, delicious breakfasts and evening meals, makes an ideal base for touring beautiful West Dorset. Our character bedrooms are comfortable and well-appointed. Meals, served in our beautiful dining room, feature local produce, with relaxation provided by two attractive lounges and licensed bar. Hosts, Jane and Michael Deller, are pleased to give every assistance, with local information to ensure a memorable stay. Short breaks available. Non-smoking.

Terms: Bed and Breakfast: £35–£40; Dinner, Bed and Breakfast: £53–£60.

e-mail: stay@churchview.co.uk • www.churchview.co.uk

GREYGLES Melcombe Bingham, Near Dorchester. Enjoy rural peace in this spacious, well-equipped stone house on the edge of a friendly village, just 10 miles from Dorchester. It comfortably sleeps up to seven in four bedrooms (one on the ground floor). • Sitting room with open fire • Dining room • Kitchen with Aga, dishwasher etc • Garden with patio and Wendy house • Heating, electricity, linen and towels incl. • Short breaks available • No smoking • Ideal for exploring Dorset and the Jurassic Coast

Booking: Tel: 020 8969 4830 • Fax: 020 8960 0069 • e-mail: enquiry@greygles.co.uk
P. SOMMERFELD, 22 TIVERTON ROAD, LONDON NW10 3HL

Summer Lodge Country House Hotel is a secluded escape from the pressures of everyday life. This is a tranquil haven full of Courtesy, Charm, Character, Calm and Cuisine.
Each of our rooms and luxury suites are individually designed.
Superb food and wines in the award-winning restaurant.
A luxury break with little extras that make all the difference.
We make you feel special from the moment you arrive.

Summer Lodge is a pet friendly hotel, for an additional charge of £20 per night we will help to make your dog feel at home.
• Dog towels • Dog biscuits • Water Bowl • Dog basket

AA ★★★★

Fore Street, Evershot, Dorset DT2 0JR
Telephone: 01935 48 2000
E-mail: summer@relaischateaux.com
www.summerlodgehotel.co.uk

Relais & Châteaux

The Castle Inn • Lulworth Cove BH20 5RN

Family-run, dog-friendly inn with good food and B&B accommodation in a wonderful dog walking area. Half a mile from the coast in the heart of the Purbecks. Pets free of charge

Tel: 01929 400311 • www.lulworthinn.com

THE
KNOLL HOUSE
STUDLAND BAY
ESTABLISHED 1931
A peaceful and relaxing holiday for all ages
An independent country-house hotel, in an unrivalled position above three miles of golden beach. Dogs are especially welcome and may sleep in your room. Special diets arranged. Our 100 acre grounds offer nice walks; squirrels and rabbits!
~
Good food and a sensible wine list
Tennis courts; nine acre golf course and outdoor heated pool
Health spa with Jacuzzi, sauna, Turkish room, plunge pool and gym
Many ground-floor and single rooms for older guests
~
Family suites of connecting rooms with bathroom
Separate young children's dining room
Playrooms and fabulous adventure playground
~
Open Easter - end October
STUDLAND BAY
DORSET
BH19 3AW
01929 · 450450
info@knollhouse.co.uk
www.knollhouse.co.uk
ONLY 2 HOURS FROM HEATHROW

Lyme Regis, North Perrott, Poole, Sherborne

WESTOVER FARM COTTAGES

In an Area Of Outstanding Natural Beauty, Wootton Fitzpaine epitomizes picturesque West Dorset. Within walking distance of sea. 4 beautiful cottages sleep 6/8 with large secluded gardens. Car parking. Logs available, Linen supplied, 3 bedrooms. £190-£845. Pets welcome.

Wootton Fitzpaine, Near Lyme Regis, Dorset DT6 6NE

Brochure: Jon Snook & Debby Snook • 01297 560451/561395

e-mail: wfcottages@aol.com www.westoverfarmcottages.co.uk ETC ★★★/★★★★

WOOD DAIRY

WOOD LANE, NORTH PERROTT TA18 7TA

Three well-appointed stone holiday cottages set around courtyard in two and a half acres of Somerset/ Dorset countryside. Area of Outstanding Natural Beauty, close to Lyme Bay and Jurassic Coast. Excellent base for walking, trails and historic properties.

- Pets welcome by arrangement.
- Wheelchair friendly.
- All bookings will receive half price green fees.
- Direct access to Chedington Court Golf Club on the 8th and 9th greens.

Tel & Fax: 01935 891532

e-mail: liz@acountryretreat.co.uk

www.acountryretreat.co.uk

Poole • Harbour Holidays • Quay Cottage and Wychcott

Quay Cottage in quiet area with sea views. Sky TV and DVD. Dogs welcome.
Wychcott - detached bungalow 6 minutes' drive from beaches at Sandbanks.
Fenced rear garden. Barbecue. Safe for young children and dogs. Sky TV/DVD.
Mrs Saunders, 15 White Cliff Road, Poole BH14 8DU (01202 741637)

White Horse Farm

ETC ★★★/★★★★

Self-Catering Barn Cottages

Set in beautiful Hardy countryside, we have five cottages furnished to high standards and are surrounded by two acres of paddock and garden with a duck pond. We lie between the historic towns of Sherborne, Dorchester and Cerne Abbas. Within easy reach of many tourist attractions. Situated next door to an inn serving good food, we welcome pets. All cottages have central heating, colour digital TV and video recorder with unlimited free video-film rental. Electricity, bed linen, towels inclusive. Ample parking. Great value.

The Willows sleeps 4/6; Toad Hall sleeps 4; Badger's sleeps 2; Ratty's sleeps 2/4; Moley's sleeps 2

White Horse Farm, Middlemarsh, Sherborne, Dorset DT9 5QN • 01963 210222

Visit our website: www.whitehorsefarm.co.uk e-mail: enquiries@whitehorsefarm.co.uk

Visit the FHG website

www.holidayguides.com

for details of the wide choice of accommodation

featured in the full range of FHG titles

Studland Bay, Swanage

Manor House Hotel

STUDLAND BAY DORSET

★ ★ ★

"Welcome to one of the most beautiful places in England. I can't take credit for the glorious views and the beaches. But I am proud to provide a comfortable and relaxing hotel with good food and attentive but informal service, to give you the break you deserve."

Andrew Purkis

Manor House Hotel, Studland, Dorset, BH19 3AU • T - 01929 450288 • W - www.themanorhousehotel.com • E - info@themanorhousehotel.com

CALIFORNIA BARN

Swanage BH19 2RS

Tel: 01929 425049 • Fax: 01929 421695

e-mail: delahays@hotmail.com • www.californiacottage.co.uk

A 200-year-old stone barn set in 11 acres of lush meadows with stunning sea views. The beautiful Jurassic Coast, recently designated a World Heritage Site, and the South West Coast Path lie only two fields away. Swanage is only one mile away.

Converted and furnished to a high standard, the three bedrooms and three bathrooms can accommodate up to 10. The location of one bedroom and one bathroom on the ground floor make it ideal for wheelchair users and those with limited mobility. Visitors also have access to a large studio/meeting room. Arts tuition, wildlife and archaeological talks/tours can be arranged. No smoking. Pets allowed; livery available.

Short breaks available September to June (excl. Christmas and New Year).
£275-£575 for 3/4 nights • £475-£1000 per week

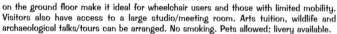

★★★

THE LIMES

A warm welcome awaits all dogs – and their owners – at the Limes, only a few hundred yards from wonderful coastal walks and beach, surrounded by the unspoilt Purbeck Hills. En suite rooms with colour TV and hospitality trays. Pets come free!

• Car Park • Families Welcome •
• Open all Year for Bed and Breakfast •

48 Park Road, Swanage, Dorset BH19 2AE
Tel: 01929 422664
info@limeshotel.net • www.limeshotel.net

Swanage, Wareham, West Bay, West Bexington

SWANAGE BAY VIEW HOLIDAY PARK

4/5/6 BERTH FULL MAINS CARAVANS

COMFORTABLE AND WELL EQUIPPED

*Colour TV * Launderette * Sea Views * Parking space * Pets welcome*
* Fully licensed club with entertainment. * Indoor swimming pool*

EASTER – OCTOBER, REDUCED TERMS EARLY/LATE HOLIDAYS

SAE: M. Stockley, 17 Moor Road, Swanage, Dorset BH19 1RG • Tel: 01929 424154

Cromwell House Hotel

Lulworth Cove, Dorset

Catriona and Alistair Miller welcome guests to their comfortable family-run hotel, set in secluded gardens with spectacular sea views. Situated 200 yards from Lulworth Cove, with direct access to the Jurassic Coast. A heated swimming pool is available for guests' use from May to October. Accommodation is in 20 en suite bedrooms, with TV, direct-dial telephone, and tea/coffee making facilities; most have spectacular sea views. There is disabled access and a room suitable for disabled guests. Self-catering flat and cottage also available. Restaurant, bar wine list.

B&B from £40. Two nights DB&B (fully en suite) from £120 per person. Off-peak mid week breaks all year except Christmas.

Cromwell House Hotel, Lulworth Cove, Dorset BH20 5RJ

Tel: 01929 400253/400332 • Fax: 01929 400566

www.lulworthcove.co.uk **ETC/AA ★★**

Robins • *West Bay, Bridport*

Comfortably furnished bungalow, with attractive garden in a quiet cul-de-sac at West Bay, overlooks open field, only three minutes' walk to the harbour and beach.
Ideal for family holidays, walking, fishing, visiting many places of interest or just relaxing.
Three bedrooms, two double and one twin bedded, sleeping six • Sitting room with TV
Kitchen/dining room • Open all year • Out of season short breaks available

Mrs B. Loosmore, Barlands, Lower Street, West Chinnock, Crewkerne, Somerset TA18 7PT • Tel: 01935 881790

DAVID BELLAMY CONSERVATION AWARD SILVER

GORSELANDS CARAVAN PARK

West Bexington-on-Sea · Dorset

English Tourism Council ★★★★ HOLIDAY PARK

West Bexington-on Sea, Near Bridport, Dorset DT2 9DJ

Peace and Tranquillity

★Small select park with stunning views over Jurassic Coastline

★Excellent beach fishing

★Pets Welcome

★Caravans & Apartments

★ Camping nearby mid July-August

★Shop & Launderette

★Village Pub 100 yards

★Beach & Car Park 1 mile

Tel: 01308 897232 Fax: 01308 897239

www.gorselands.co.uk

e-mail: info@gorselands.co.uk

DORSET COTTAGE HOLIDAYS. Self-catering cottages, town houses, bungalows and apartments. All within 10 miles of Heritage Coastline and sandy beaches. Excellent walking in idyllic countryside. Short breaks from £95, weekly from £170 (per cottage). Open all year. Free brochure tel: 01929 553443. [🐕]
e-mail: enq@dhcottages.co.uk website: www.dhcottages.co.uk

DORSET COASTAL COTTAGES (0800 9804070). Carefully selected, traditional cottages in or near villages within ten miles of World Heritage Coast. Many are thatched; open fires or logburners; over half welcome dogs. Available all year. [Pets £15 per week]
website: www.dorsetcoastalcottages.com

FARM & COTTAGE HOLIDAYS (01237 459897). Over 850 of the finest selection of holiday cottages throughout Devon, Cornwall, Dorset and Somerset in superb rural and coastal locations.
website: www.holidaycottages.co.uk

Bere Regis

Village 7 miles north west of Wareham.

MR & MRS R. CARGILL, ROWLANDS WAIT TOURING PARK, RYE HILL, BERE REGIS, BH20 7LP (01929 472727). Situated in an Area of Outstanding Natural Beauty. A good base for touring; direct access onto heathland and woodland walks. Ideal for nature lovers, bird watching and quiet family holidays. Tents also welcome. Dogs welcome. David Bellamy Gold Award. ETC ★★★.
website: www.rowlandswait.co.uk

Blandford

Handsome Georgian town that rose from the ashes of the 1731 fire; rebuilt with chequered brick and stone. Also known as Blandford Forum.

ANVIL INN & RESTAURANT, PIMPERNE, BLANDFORD DT11 8UQ (01258 453431; Fax: 01258 480182). A typical Old English hostelry offering good old-fashioned English hospitality. Full à la carte menu with mouthwatering desserts in the charming restaurant with log fire, delicious desserts, bar meals, specials board. All bedrooms with private facilities. Ample parking. ETC/AA ★★★★ [Pets £10 per night]
e-mail: theanvil.inn@btconnect.com website: www.anvilinn.co.uk

Bournemouth

One of Britain's premier holiday resorts with miles of golden sand, excellent shopping and leisure facilities. Lively entertainments include Festival of Lights at the beginning of September.

Self-contained two-bedroom apartments in quiet avenue, one minute from clean, sandy beaches and five minutes from shops. Sleeps 2-5. Includes linen. Fully equipped kitchen, cooker, fridge/freezer, microwave, colour TV, washing machine, tumble dryer. Toilet and shower. Central heating. Parking. Terms from £200. Contact: MRS HAMMOND, STOURCLIFFE COURT, 56 STOURCLIFFE AVENUE, SOUTHBOURNE, BOURNEMOUTH BH6 3PX (01202 420698). [Pets £2 per night, £10 weekly]

MIKE AND LYN LAMBERT, 16 FLORENCE ROAD, BOURNEMOUTH BH5 1HF (01202 304925). Modern Holiday Apartments sleeping up to ten persons, close to sea and shops. Clean, well-equipped flats. Car park. Phone or e-mail for brochure. [Pets from £35 per week]
website: www.selfcateringbournemouth.co.uk

HOLIDAY FLATS AND FLATLETS a short walk to golden, sandy beaches. Most with private bathrooms. Cleanliness and comfort assured. Dogs welcome. Contact: M DE KMENT, 4 CECIL ROAD, BOURNEMOUTH BH5 1DU (07788 952394). [Pets £25 per week]

LANGTRY MANOR, DERBY ROAD, EAST CLIFF, BOURNEMOUTH BH1 3QB (01202 553887). A rare gem of a hotel where the building, food, service and history blend to form something quite exceptional. Midweek and weekend breaks. Pets welcome by arrangement. Bournemouth Tourism 'Best Small Hotel'. [🐕]
website: www.langtrymanor.co.uk

ANNE & RICHARD REYNOLDS, THE VINE HOTEL, 22 SOUTHERN ROAD, SOUTHBOURNE, BOURNEMOUTH BH6 3SR (01202 428309). A small, family, award-winning non-smoking Hotel only three hundred yards from dog-friendly beach and shops. All rooms en suite with tea/coffee making facilities and colour TV. Residential licence with attractive bar. Full central heating. Forecourt parking. Open all year. FHG Diploma. [🐕]

ALUM DENE HOTEL, 2 BURNABY ROAD, ALUM CHINE, BOURNEMOUTH BH4 8JF (01202 764011) Renowned for good old fashioned hospitality and friendly service. Come and be spoilt at our licensed hotel. All rooms en suite, colour TV. Some have sea views. 200 metres sea. Parking. Christmas House party. No charge for pets. [🐕]
e-mail: alumdenehotel@hotmail.co.uk website: alumdenehotel.com

SOUTHBOURNE GROVE HOTEL, 96 SOUTHBOURNE ROAD, SOUTHBOURNE, BOURNEMOUTH BH6 3QQ (01202 420503; Fax: 01202 421953). Friendly, family-run hotel with beautiful garden and ample guest parking. Close to beach and shops. Excellent food served in spacious restaurant. En suite, four-poster suite, ground floor and large family rooms available, all with colour TV and tea/coffee facilities. B&B from £23 per night, £129 per week. This is a no-smoking hotel. [🐕]
website: www.tiscover.co.uk/southbournegrovehotel

BILL AND MARJORIE TITCHEN, WHITE TOPPS HOTEL, 45 CHURCH ROAD, SOUTHBOURNE, BOURNEMOUTH BH6 4BB (01202 428868). Situated in quiet position close to lovely walks and beach. Dogs essential. Free parking. [🐕 pw!]
e-mail: thedoghotel@aol.com website: www.whitetopps.co.uk

Bridport

Market town of Saxon origin noted for rope and net making. Harbour at West Bay has sheer cliffs rising from the beach

MRS S. NORMAN, FROGMORE FARM, CHIDEOCK, BRIDPORT DT6 6HT (01308 456159). The choice is yours - Bed and Breakfast in charming farmhouse, OR self-catering Cottage equipped for five, pets welcome. Brochure and terms free on request. [1st dog free, 2nd dog £3 per night, £15 per week]
e-mail: bookings@frogmorefarm.com website: www.frogmorefarm.com

EYPE HOUSE CARAVAN & CAMPING PARK, EYPE, BRIDPORT DT6 6AL (01308 424903) Small, quiet family-run park lying on the Heritage Coastal Path, 200 yards from the beach. Static vans for hire, tent pitches (all terraced with sea views) £11.00 to £17.50. Sorry, no tourers. Children and dogs welcome. [Pets £3 per night, £15 per week.]

GOLDEN ACRE, EYPE, NEAR BRIDPORT DT6 6AL (01308 421521). Private peaceful park. Close to beach. Chalet bungalows (1 or 2 bedrooms), sleep 2-4. Wonderful walks, on the Jurassic Coast.

LANCOMBES HOUSE, WEST MILTON, BRIDPORT DT6 3TN (01308 485375). Four cottages and farmhouse, two with enclosed gardens. Set in 9 acres in an area ideal for walking, riding and outdoor pursuits. Children and dogs welcome. Open all year. ETC ★★★/★★★★ [Pets £12 per week].
website: www.lancombes-house.co.uk

Burton Bradstock

Village near coast, 3 miles SE of Bridport.

MRS JOSEPHINE PEARSE, TAMARISK FARM, BEACH ROAD, WEST BEXINGTON, DORCHESTER DT2 9DF (01308 897784). Self Catering properties sleep 4/7. Overlooking Chesil Beach: four large (MIMOSA FOR WHEELCHAIR DISABLED M3 (1); GRANARY LODGE DISABLED-FRIENDLY M1 and two small Cottages (ETC 3/4 Stars). Part of organic farm with arable, sheep, cattle, horses and market garden with organic vegetables, meat and wholemeal flour available. Good centre for touring, sightseeing, walking. Glorious sea views, very quiet. Lovely place for dogs. Terms from £255 to £960. Please telephone for details. [🐕]
e-mail: holidays@tamariskfarm.com website: www.tamariskfarm.com

FREE or REDUCED RATE entry to Holiday Visits and Attractions – see our **READERS' OFFER VOUCHERS** on pages 433-440

Cattistock

Village one mile north of Maiden Newton.

FOX & HOUNDS INN, CATTISTOCK, DORCHESTER DT2 0JH (01300 320444). Set in beautiful countryside, this is a unique inn with superb accommodation. Excellent home cooked food, fine wines and well conditioned ales. Good dog walking country and just 15 minutes from the coast. [🐕]
website: www.foxandhoundsinn.com

Charmouth

Small resort on Lyme Bay, 3 miles Lyme Regis. Sandy beach backed by undulating cliffs where many fossils are found. Good walks.

MR F. LOOSMORE, MANOR FARM HOLIDAY CENTRE, CHARMOUTH, BRIDPORT DT6 6QL (01297 560226). All units for four to six people. Ten minutes' level walk to beach, many fine local walks. Swimming pools, licensed bar with family room, shop, launderette. Sporting facilities nearby. Children and pets welcome. SAE for colour brochure. [Pets £3 per night, £20 per week]

Christchurch

Residential town near coast, 5 miles east of Bournemouth.

COUNTRY HOLIDAY CHALET on small, quiet, secluded woodland park within National Park. Sleeps four. Fenced private garden. Dogs welcome. Car parking. £175 to £350 per week. BH & HPA Member. Write enclosing SAE or telephone: MRS L.M. BOWLING, OWLPEN CARAVANS LTD, OWLPEN, 148 BURLEY ROAD, BRANSGORE, NEAR CHRISTCHURCH, DORSET BH23 8DB (01425 672875; mobile 07860 547391). [🐕 pw!]
website: www.owlpen-caravans.co.uk

Dorchester

Busy market town steeped in history. Roman remains include Amphitheatre and villa.

CHURCHVIEW GUEST HOUSE, WINTERBOURNE ABBAS, DORCHESTER DT2 9LS (Tel & Fax: 01305 889296). Beautiful 17th Century Licensed Guest House set in the heart of West Dorset, character bedrooms, delightful period dining room, two lounges and bar. Non-smoking. B&B £35–£40pp. B&BEM £53–£60. Short breaks available. ETC ★★★★ [🐕]
e-mail: stay@churchview.co.uk website: www.churchview.co.uk

GREYGLES, MELCOMBE BINGHAM, NEAR DORCHESTER. Spacious, well-equipped house just 10 miles from Dorchester. Sleep 7. Heating, electricity, linen and towels incl. No smoking. ETC ★★★★ Booking: P. SOMMERFELD, 22 TIVERTON ROAD, LONDON NW10 3HL (020 8969 4830; Fax: 020 8960 0069). [🐕]
e-mail: enquiry@greygles.co.uk website: www.greygles.co.uk

Evershot

Village 5 miles North of Maiden Newton.

SUMMER LODGE COUNTRY HOUSE HOTEL, RESTAURANT & SPA, FORE STREET, EVERSHOT DT2 0JR (01935 48 2000). Tranquil haven full of Courtesy, Charm, Character, Calm and Cuisine. Individually designed rooms, superb food and wine. Dogs feel at home with towels, dog biscuits, water bowl and basket. AA ★★★★ [Pets £20 per night].
e-mail: summer@relaischateaux.com website: www.summerlodgehotel.co.uk

Lulworth

Village on coast 4 miles from Wool.

MRS L. S. BARNES, LUCKFORD WOOD FARMHOUSE, EAST STOKE, WAREHAM, NEAR LULWORTH BH20 6AW (01929 463098; Mobile: 07888719002). Peaceful surroundings, delightful scenery. B&B classic farmhouse with style. Breakfast served in conservatory, dining room or garden. Also our camping and caravanning site nearby includes showers, toilets. Caravan and boat storage available. Near Lulworth Cove, Studland, Tank Museum and Monkey World. Open all year. B&B from £30pp per night. Please phone for details. [Pets £5 per night, £30 per week]
e-mail: luckfordleisure@hotmail.co.uk website: www.luckfordleisure.co.uk

Lulworth Cove

Village and Cove on the World heritage Jurassic Coastline. Good beaches and numerous guided boat trips leaving from the cove showing the highlights of the area.

THE CASTLE INN, LULWORTH COVE BH20 5RN (01929 400311). Family-run, dog-friendly inn with good food and B&B accommodation in a wonderful dog walking area. Half a mile from the coast in the heart of the Purbecks. [🐕]
website: www.lulworthinn.com

Lyme Regis

Picturesque little resort with harbour, once the haunt of smugglers. Shingle beach with sand at low tide. Fishing, sailing and water ski-ing in Lyme Bay. Taunton 28 miles, Dorchester 24, Seaton 8.

JON SNOOK AND DEBBY SNOOK, WESTOVER FARM COTTAGES, WOOTTON FITZPAINE, NEAR LYME REGIS DT6 6NE (01297 560451/561395). Within walking distance of the sea. Four beautiful cottages, sleep 6/8, with large secluded gardens. Car parking. Logs available, linen supplied. 3 bedrooms. Well behaved pets welcome. ETC ★★★/★★★★ [Pets £20 per week]
e-mail: wfcottages@aol.com website: www.westoverfarmcottages.co.uk

North Perrott

Village 2 miles east of Crewkerne.

MRS E NEVILLE, WOOD DAIRY, WOOD LANE, NORTH PERROTT TA18 7TA (Tel & Fax: 01935 891532). Three well-appointed stone holiday cottages set around courtyard in two and a half acres of Somerset/Dorset countryside. Adjacent golf course. Close to Lyme Bay and Jurassic Coast, excellent base for walking, trails and historic properties. Wheelchair friendly. Pets welcome by arrangement. [🐕]
e-mail: liz@acountryretreat.co.uk website: www.acountryretreat.co.uk

Poole

Flourishing port and market town. Three museums with interesting collections and lively displays.

HARBOUR HOLIDAYS. QUAY COTTAGE in quiet area with sea views. Sky TV and DVD. Dogs welcome. WYCHCOTT - detached bungalow 6 minutes' drive from beaches at Sandbanks. Fenced rear garden. Barbecue. Safe for young children and dogs. Sky TV/DVD. MRS SAUNDERS, 15 WHITE CLIFF ROAD, POOLE BH14 8DU (01202 741637). [🐕]

Sherborne

Town with abbey and two castles, one of which was built by Sir Walter Raleigh with lakes and gardens by Capability Brown.

WHITE HORSE FARM, MIDDLEMARSH, SHERBORNE DT9 5QN. The Willows sleeps 4-6; Toad Hall sleeps 4; Badger's sleeps 2; Ratty's sleeps 2/4; Moley's sleeps 2. Character self-catering holiday cottages in rural location. Well-equipped and comfortable. Digital TV, video, free films. 2 acres of paddock, garden and duck pond. Inn 100 yards. ETC ★★★/★★★★. AUDREY & STUART WINTERBOTTOM (01963 210222) [pw! 🐕]
e-mail: enquiries@whitehorsefarm.co.uk website: www.whitehorsefarm.co.uk

Studland Bay

Unspoilt seaside village at south western end of Poole Bay, 3 miles north of Swanage.

THE KNOLL HOUSE, STUDLAND BH19 3AW (01929 450450). Country house hotel within National Trust reserve. Golden beach. 100 acre grounds. Family suites of connecting rooms, six lounges. Tennis, golf, swimming, games rooms, health spa. See our Full Page Advertisement under Studland Bay. [Pets £5 per night, including food]
e-mail: info@knollhouse.co.uk website: www.knollhouse.co.uk

THE MANOR HOUSE HOTEL, STUDLAND BAY BH19 3AU (01929 450288; Fax: 01929 452255). National Trust hotel set in 20 acres on cliffs overlooking Studland Bay. Superb food and accommodation. Log fires and four-posters.Tennis, horse-riding, golf and walking. [Pets £5 per night]
e-mail: info@themanorhousehotel.com website: www.themanorhousehotel.com

Swanage

Traditional family holiday resort set in a sheltered bay ideal for water sports. Good base for a walking holiday.

CALIFORNIA BARN, SWANAGE, DORSET BH19 2RS (01929 425049). Luxury stone barn in stunning coast location. Swanage/sandy beach 1 mile. Sleeps 6-10 plus cots. Pets/horses welcome. Non smoking. Wheelchair accessible. Use of large studio/ meetings room. Art/activity/ wildlife holidays. Excellent walking, climbing and wildlife
e-mail: delahays@hotmail.com website: www.californiacottage.co.uk

THE LIMES, 48 PARK ROAD, SWANAGE BH19 2AE (01929 422664). Informal and friendly, with en suite rooms, TV, tea/coffee making facilities. Children and pets welcome. Credit cards accepted. ETC ★★★ [🐕]
e-mail: info@limeshotel.net website: www.limeshotel.net

MRS M. STOCKLEY, SWANAGE BAY VIEW HOLIDAY PARK, 17 MOOR ROAD, SWANAGE BH19 1RG (01929 424154). 4/5/6-berth Caravans. Pets welcome. Easter to October. Colour TV. Shop. Parking space. Rose Award Park [🐕]

Wareham

Picturesque riverside town almost surrounded by earthworks, considered pre-Roman. Nature reserves of great beauty nearby. Weymouth 19 miles, Bournemouth 14, Swanage 10, Poole 6.

CATRIONA AND ALISTAIR MILLER, CROMWELL HOUSE HOTEL, LULWORTH COVE BH20 5RJ (01929 400253/400332; Fax: 01929 400566). Comfortable family-run hotel, set in secluded gardens with spectacular sea views. Heated swimming pool, 20 en suite bedrooms. Restaurant, bar wine list. Self-catering. Disabled access. ETC/AA ★★ [Pets £2 per night]
website: www.lulworthcove.co.uk

West Bay

Seaside location for family holidays, countryside and coastal walks and fossil hunting. One and a half miles from Bridport.

ROBINS, WEST BAY, BRIDPORT. Comfortably furnished bungalow, with attractive garden in a quiet cul-de-sac, overlooks open field, only three minutes' walk to the harbour and beach. Three bedrooms. Parking. Open all year. Personally supervised. MRS B. LOOSMORE, BARLANDS, LOWER STREET, WEST CHINOCK, CREWKERNE TA18 7PT (01935 881790).

West Bexington

Seaside village with pebble beach. Chesil beach stretches eastwards. Nearby is Abbotsbury with its Benedictine Abbey and famous Swannery. Dorchester 13 miles, Weymouth 13, Bridport 6.

GORSELANDS CARAVAN PARK, DEPT PW, WEST BEXINGTON-ON-SEA DT2 9DJ (01308 897232; Fax: 01308 897239). Holiday Park. Fully serviced and equipped 4/6 berth caravans. Shop and launderette on site. Glorious sea views. Good country and seaside walks. One mile to beach. Holiday apartments with sea views and private garden. Pets most welcome. Colour brochure on request. ETC ★★★★, David Bellamy Silver Award. [🐕]
e-mail: info@gorselands.co.uk website: www.gorselands.co.uk

Pet-Friendly
Pubs, Inns & Hotels
on pages 424-432
Please note that these establishments may not feature in the main section of this book

Bibury, Bourton-on-the-Water, Chalford, Cheltenham

HARTWELL FARM COTTAGES **Ready Token, Near Bibury, Cirencester GL7 5SY**

Two traditionally built cottages with far reaching views, on the southern edge of the Cotswolds. Both are fully equipped to a high standard, with heating and woodburning stoves; large private enclosed gardens. Stabling for horses; tennis court. Ideal for touring and horse riding. Glorious walks, excellent pubs. Non-smoking. Children and well-behaved dogs welcome. Sleep 3-4 . • **Contact: Caroline Mann: Tel: 01285 740210**
e-mail: ec.mann@btinternet.com • www.selfcateringcotswolds.com

STRATHSPEY AA ★★★

Lansdowne, Bourton-on-the-Water GL54 2AR

Tastefully furnished bedrooms with TV, refreshment tray, hairdryer, clock radio. Pleasant tranquil garden. Five minutes' walk from centre of village. Open all year. Terms from £27.50pppn. Pets welcome by prior arrangement.

Tel: 01451 810321 • mobile: 07889 491993
e-mail: bookings@strathspey.org.uk **www.strathspey.org.uk**

THE CHESTER HOUSE HOTEL

VICTORIA STREET,
BOURTON-ON-THE-WATER,
GLOUCESTERSHIRE GL54 2BU

TEL: 01451 820286 • FAX 01451 820471
e-mail: info@chesterhousehotel.com
www.chesterhousehotel.com

Chester House Hotel AND BAR

Bourton-on-the-Water - The Venice of the Cotswolds. A haven of peace and comfort tucked away in a quiet backwater of this famous village.

Attention All Dog Lovers! www.doggybreaks.co.uk

Romantic 18th century Coach House in the heart of the beautiful Cotswolds. Close to 600 acres of NT common. Sleeps max. 2 couples + 1 child. Beams, woodburners. Outdoor heated swimming pool and bubbling hot tub. Hillside garden and 20 acres of woodland. Free private kennel facilities (optional). Breaks £125-£635. Brochure:

Ros Smith, The Old Coach House, Edgecombe House, Toadsmoor, Brimscombe, Stroud GL5 2UG
Tel: 01453 883147

NO CHARGE FOR DOGS.

Ideally located for Cheltenham and the Cotswolds.
Wifi access throughout. Friendly resident owners.

CHARLTON KINGS hotel and restaurant

London Road, Charlton Kings,
Cheltenham GL52 6UU
Tel: 01242 231061 • Fax: 01242 241900
www.charltonkingshotel.co.uk • enquiries@charltonkingshotel.co.uk

A historic country hotel whose heritage dates from the 13th Century, situated in the heart of the Forest of Dean, close to the Wye Valley. The hotel retains many of its original features, including beams, timber panelling and oak spiral staircases. 20 en suite bedrooms are located throughout the hotel grounds, including Four-Poster rooms and a Cottage Suite. All bedrooms are en suite and have colour TV, direct-dial telephones and tea and coffee making facilities. Our Two Red Rosette candlelit restaurant is renowned for its quality cuisine and friendliness of service. Tudor Farmhouse is the ideal retreat to relax and unwind.
Please contact us to discuss the availability of our pet-friendly rooms.

GWESTY ★★★ HOTEL

AA ★★★ 72%

Tudor Farmhouse Hotel & Restaurant

Clearwell, Near Coleford, Gloucestershire GL16 8JS
Tel: 01594 833046 • Fax: 01594 837093
e-mail: info@tudorfarmhousehotel.co.uk • www.tudorfarmhousehotel.co.uk

the perfect place...

The Speech House Hotel

A friendly Hotel set in the heart of the Forest of Dean, perfect for walking dogs. Built by King Charles II as a Hunting Lodge and almost completely enveloped by trees, the Speech House is the ideal location for you and your 'four legged friend'.

With 37 en suite bedrooms, several four-poster beds and a beauty salon why not pay us a visit and get away from it all. Courtyard ground floor rooms are available. Pets are welcome.

...for pets

Tel: 01594 822607
relax@thespeechhouse.co.uk www.thespeechhouse.co.uk
The Speech House Hotel, Coleford, Forest of Dean GL16 7EL **AA★★★**

Wharton Lodge Cottages

enjoyEngland.com ★★★★★ SELF CATERING

Two 5* exquisitely furnished and fully equipped, self-catering retreats overlooking Herefordshire countryside, sleeping 2,3 or 4 guests. Just 3 miles from Ross-on-Wye and adjacent to the Royal Forest of Dean, this is an ideal base for exploring this fabulous area designated as an Area of Outstanding Natural Beauty. In addition to the safe, walled, cottage courtyard gardens and the Italianate Garden, guests may also use the 14 acres of parkland. Dog paradise.

GROSVENOR - King-size double and single bedrooom.
HAREWOOD - 2 double bedroooms (master with king-size bed).

e-mail: ncross@whartonlodge.co.uk • www.whartonlodge.co.uk
Weston-under-Penyard, Near Ross-on-Wye HR9 7JX • Tel/ Fax: 01989 750140

The Laurels at Inchbrook

Cow Lane, Inchbrook, Nailsworth GL5 5HA
Tel/Fax: 01453 834021 • e-mail: laurelsinchbrook@tiscali.co.uk
www.laurelsinchbrook.co.uk

A comfortable, rambling house, cottage and garden set beside the Inch Brook and adjoining fields. Lovely secluded garden, with badgers and bats: the stream is an otter route, and many birds come to visit us. Pets are most welcome, and there are dozens of splendid walks and the National Trust's Woodchester Park on our doorstep.

Nailsworth, a fashionable Cotswold town and a centre for excellence when it comes to eating out, is just under a mile away.

Ideally placed for exploring the West Country, Bath and Forest of Dean as well as the Cotswolds, our house is perfect for groups and family gatherings. Brochure on request. Self-catering facilities may be available at certain times of the year.

Rooms from £30 - £60 per night. Rooms: 4 double (one ground floor accessible), 2 twin, 2 family; all en suite. No smoking. Children and pets welcome. Open all year.

Stow-on-the-Wold, Stroud, Thornbury

THE LIMES Large Country House with attractive garden, overlooking fields. Four minutes to town centre. One four-poster bedroom; double, twin or family rooms, all en suite. Tea/coffee making facilities, colour TV in all rooms. TV lounge. Central heating. Children and pets welcome. Car park. Bed and Full English Breakfast from £25.00 to £30.00 pppn. Open all year except Christmas. *Established over 30 years*

Evesham Road, Stow-on-the-Wold, GL54 1EN • Tel: 01451 830034/831056

e-mail: thelimes@zoom.co.uk • www.cotswold.info/webpage/thelimes-stow.htm

THE Old Stocks Hotel **The Square, Stow-on-the-Wold GL54 1AF**

Tel: 01451 830666 • Fax: 01451 870014 • e-mail: fhg@oldstockshotel.co.uk

Ideal base for touring this beautiful area. Tasteful guest rooms including three 'garden' rooms located on the middle terrace of our patio garden. All rooms are in keeping with the hotel's old world character, yet with modern amenities. Mouth-watering menus offering a wide range of choices. Special bargain breaks are also available.

HETB/AA ★★ **www.oldstockshotel.co.uk**

Hyde Crest *Beautiful country house with enclosed acre garden. All rooms on ground floor opening on to patios and lawns. 500 acres of commons, plus country walks nearby.* ***MRS A. RHOTON, HYDE CREST, CIRENCESTER ROAD, MINCHINHAMPTON GL6 8PE***

01453 731631 • e-mail: stay@hydecrest.co.uk • www.hydecrest.co.uk

AA ★★★★ Guest Accommodation

★★★★ BED & BREAKFAST

The Withyholt Guest House

Paul Mead, Edge, near Stroud, Gloucestershire GL6 6PG

Modern guesthouse in Gloucestershire close to Gloucester Cathedral, Tetbury, Stroud. Many lovely country walks. En suite bedrooms, large lounge. Large garden. **Telephone: 01452 813618 • Fax: 01452 812375**

Dear Viva,

Well, we've just got back from our holidays – absolute bliss and what a lovely place the Downfield is – we got a really warm welcome from the owners. Great walks in the Cotswolds, comfy rooms, a bar, delicious food and the Joneses I brought with me were really pleased as well. I made lots of new friends – there were even some cats to chase! Why don't you come with me next year and bring your owners with you – Just call Dina on the dog and bone.

Lots of licks,

Meme and Ru

The Downfield Hotel

134 Cainscross Rd, Stroud, Gloucestershire GL5 4HN

01453 764496

e-mail: downfield@downfieldhotel.co.uk

www.downfieldhotel.co.uk

von Essen hotels
A PRIVATE COLLECTION

THORNBURY CASTLE

Thornbury, Near Bristol South Gloucs BS35 1HH

Tel: 01454 281182 • Fax: 01454 416188

info@thornburycastle.co.uk • www.thornburycastle.co.uk

With a fascinating history, this 16th century building retains many features such as coats of arms, intricate oriel windows, arrow loops and ornate carved ceilings. Three dining rooms offer the finest à la carte menus, using only the finest and freshest ingredients, with a discerning choice of fine vintages and New World varieties from the well stocked cellar. The fabulously atmospheric bedchambers (most with real fires and four-poster beds) have all modern amenities, including opulent bathrooms. The unique surroundings and ambience of Thornbury Castle, together with the excellent and attentive service of the staff, make the Castle a superb venue for those seeking something special.

Bibury

Village on the River Colne, 7 miles NE of Cirencester.

CAROLINE MANN, HARTWELL FARM COTTAGES, READY TOKEN, NEAR BIBURY, CIRENCESTER GL7 5SY (01285 740210). Two comfortable, fully equipped cottages with country views. Ideally located for touring. Stabling available. Glorious walks, excellent pubs. Non-smoking. Children and well-behaved dogs welcome. ETC ★★★★ [pw! Pets £15 per week]
e-mail: ec.mann@btinternet.com website: www.selfcateringcotswolds.com

Bourton-on-the-Water

Delightfully situated on the River Windrush which is crossed by miniature stone bridges. Stow-on-the-Wold 4 miles.

STRATHSPEY, LANSDOWNE, BOURTON-ON-THE-WATER GL54 2AR (01451 810321; mobile: 07889 491993). Tastefully furnished bedrooms with TV, refreshment tray, hairdryer, clock radio. Pleasant tranquil garden. Five minutes' walk from centre of village. Open all year. Terms from £27.50pppn. Pets welcome by prior arrangement. AA ★★★ [Pets £5 per week]
e-mail: bookings@strathspey.org.uk website: www.strathspey.org.uk

CHESTER HOUSE HOTEL, VICTORIA STREET, BOURTON-ON-THE-WATER GL54 2BU (01451 820286). All rooms en suite, all with central heating, colour TV, phone, tea/coffee making facilities. Wheelchair friendly. Ideal for touring Cotswolds. [🐕]
e-mail: info@chesterhousehotel.com website: www.chesterhousehotel.com

Chalford

Village 4 miles south east of Stroud.

ROS SMITH, THE OLD COACH HOUSE, EDGECOMBE HOUSE, TOADSMOOR, BRIMSCOMBE, STROUD GL5 2UG (01453 883147). Romantic 18th century Coach House in the heart of the Cotswolds. Sleeps max. 2 couples + 1 child. Outdoor heated swimming pool and bubbling hot tub. Free private kennel facilities (optional). Breaks £125-£635. Brochure. [[🐕 ⌂]
website: www.doggybreaks.co.uk

Cheltenham

Large residential lown, formerly a spa, 8 miles East of Gloucester.

CHARLTON KINGS HOTEL & RESTAURANT, LONDON ROAD, CHARLTON KINGS, CHELTENHAM GL52 6UU (01242 231061; Fax: 01242 241900). No charge for dogs. Ideally located for Cheltenham and the Cotswolds. Wifi access throughout. Friendly resident owners. [🐕]
e-mail: enquiries@charltonkingshotel.co.uk website: www.charltonkingshotel.co.uk

Clearwell (Forest of Dean)

Village 2 miles south of Coleford in the ancient Forest of Dean.

TUDOR FARMHOUSE HOTEL & RESTAURANT, CLEARWELL, NEAR COLEFORD GL16 8JS (01594 833046; Fax: 01594 837093). Charming 13th Century farmhouse hotel in extensive grounds, ideal for dog walking. 20 en suite bedrooms including Four Posters and Cottage Suite. Award-winning restaurant. WTB ★★★, AA ★★★ and Two Rosettes. [Pets £5 per night].
e-mail: info@tudorfarmhousehotel.co.uk website: www.tudorfarmhousehotel.co.uk

Symbols

- 🐕 Indicates that pets are welcome free of charge.
- £ Indicates that a charge is made for pets: nightly or weekly.
- pw! Shows some special provision for pets; exercise facility, feeding or accommodation arrangement.
- ⌂ Indicates separate pets accommodation.

Forest of Dean

Formerly a royal hunting ground, this scenic area lies between the rivers Severn and Wye.

DRYSLADE FARM, ENGLISH BICKNOR, COLEFORD GL16 7PA (Tel & Fax: 01594 860259). Daphne and Phil warmly welcome you and your dogs for B&B at their 18th century farmhouse on family working farm. Situated in Royal Forest of Dean and close to Symonds Yat with ample walking. Excellent breakfast. Terms from £30-£35. AA ★★★★ Highly Commended. [🐕]
website: www.drysladefarm.co.uk

WHARTON LODGE COTTAGES, WESTON-UNDER-PENYARD, NEAR ROSS-ON-WYE HR9 7JX (Tel & Fax: 01989 750140). Two elegantly furnished, fully equipped self-catering retreats overlooking Herefordshire countryside, sleeping 2, 3 or 4 guests. Fully inclusive rates. Dog paradise. Tourist Board ★★★★★ [Pets £4 per night, £20 per week]
e-mail: ncross@whartonlodge.co.uk website: www.whartonlodge.co.uk

THE SPEECH HOUSE HOTEL, COLEFORD, FOREST OF DEAN GL16 7EL (01594 822607). A friendly Hotel set in the heart of the Forest of Dean. The perfect place for pets. 37 en suite bedrooms. Lavish restaurant. AA ★★★.
e-mail: relax@thespeechhouse.co.uk website: www.thespeechhouse.co.uk

Nailsworth

Hilly town 4 miles south of Stroud

THE LAURELS, INCHBROOK, NAILSWORTH GL5 5HA (01453 834021; Fax: 01453 835190). A lovely rambling house, cottage and secluded garden where dogs and their owners are encouraged to relax and enjoy. Ideally situated for touring all parts of the Cotswolds and West Country; splendid walks. Brochure. [🐕]
e-mail: laurelsinchbrook@tiscali.co.uk website: www.laurelsinchbrook.co.uk

Painswick

Beautiful little Cotswold town with characteristic stone-built houses.

MISS E. COLLETT, HAMBUTTS MYND, EDGE ROAD, PAINSWICK GL6 6UP (01452 812352; Fax: 01452 813862). Bed and Breakfast in an old Converted Corn Mill. Very quiet with superb views. Three minutes to the centre of the village. Field nearby for exercising dogs. Central heating. One double room, one twin, one single, all with TV. £33 single, £63 double or twin, 10% discount for 4 nights or more. ALL ROOMS EN SUITE. [🐕]
e-mail: ewarland@aol.com

Stow-on-the-Wold

Charming Cotswold hill-top market town with several old inns and interesting buildings. Birmingham 45 miles, Gloucester 26, Stratford-upon-Avon 21, Cheltenham 18, Chipping Norton 9.

THE LIMES, EVESHAM ROAD, STOW-ON-THE-WOLD GL54 1EN (01451 830034/831056). Large Country House. Attractive garden, overlooking fields, 4 minutes town centre. Television lounge. Central heating. Car park. Bed and Breakfast from £25 to £30 pppn. Twin, double or family rooms, all en suite. Children and pets welcome. AA ★★★, Tourist Board Listed. [🐕]
e-mail: thelimes@zoom.co.uk website: www.cotswolds.info/webpage/thelimes-stow.htm

THE OLD STOCKS HOTEL THE SQUARE, STOW-ON-THE-WOLD GL54 1AF (01451 830666; Fax: 01451 870014). Ideal base for touring this beautiful area. Tasteful guest rooms (including three 'garden' rooms) with modern amenities. Mouth-watering menus. Special bargain breaks also available. HETB/AA ★★ [Pets £5 per stay]
e-mail: fhg@oldstockshotel.co.uk website: www.oldstockshotel.co.uk

A useful index of towns/counties appears at the back of this book

Stroud

Cotswold town on River Frome below picturesque Stroudwater Hills, formerly renowned for cloth making. Bristol 32 miles, Bath 29, Chippenham 25, Cheltenham 14, Gloucester 9.

MRS A. RHOTON, HYDE CREST, CIRENCESTER ROAD, MINCHINHAMPTON GL6 8PE (01453 731631). Beautiful country house with enclosed acre garden. All rooms on ground floor opening on to patios and lawns. 500 acres of commons, plus country walks nearby. AA ★★★★ [pw!]
e-mail: stay@hydecrest.co.uk website: www.hydecrest.co.uk

MRS UNA PEACEY, THE WITHYHOLT GUEST HOUSE, PAUL MEAD, EDGE, NEAR STROUD GL6 6PG (01452 813618: Fax: 01452 812375) Modern guesthouse in Gloucestershire close to Gloucester Cathedral, Tetbury, Stroud. Many lovely country walks. En suite bedrooms, large lounge. Large garden. ETC ★★★★ [ ]

DOWNFIELD HOTEL, CAINSCROSS ROAD, STROUD GL5 4HN (01453 764496). Easy to find – just 5 miles from M5 – and easy to park. Ideal location for exploring Cotswolds. Comfortable lounges, home-cooked evening meal, cosy bar – all at sensible prices. Dogs and children most welcome. [ ]
e-mail: downfield@downfieldhotel.co.uk website: www.downfieldhotel.co.uk

Thornbury

Market town 12 miles north of Bristol.

THORNBURY CASTLE, THORNBURY, NEAR BRISTOL BS35 1HH (01454 281182; Fax: 01454 416188).The unique surroundings and ambience of 16th Thornbury Castle, together with the excellent and attentive service of the staff, make the Castle a superb venue for those seeking something special.
e-mail: info@thornburycastle.co.uk website: www.thornburycastle.co.uk

Other specialised holiday guides from FHG

PUBS & INNS OF BRITAIN

COUNTRY HOTELS OF BRITAIN

WEEKEND & SHORT BREAKS IN BRITAIN & IRELAND

THE GOLF GUIDE WHERE TO PLAY, WHERE TO STAY

500 GREAT PLACES TO STAY

SELF-CATERING HOLIDAYS IN BRITAIN

BED & BREAKFAST STOPS IN BRITAIN

CARAVAN & CAMPING HOLIDAYS IN BRITAIN

FAMILY BREAKS IN BRITAIN

Published annually: available in all good bookshops or direct from the publisher:

FHG Guides, Abbey Mill Business Centre, Seedhill, Paisley PA1 1TJ

Tel: 0141 887 0428 • Fax: 0141 889 7204

e-mail: admin@fhguides.co.uk • www.holidayguides.com

Bath, Blue Anchor, Brean, Cheddar, Dunster

BATH - TOGHILL HOUSE FARM Cottages and B&B

Luxury barn conversions on working farm just north of Bath. Each cottage is equipped to a very high standard with bed linen provided. You are welcome to roam amongst our many animals and enjoy the outstanding country views. We also provide Bed and Breakfast accommodation in our warm and cosy 17th century farmhouse where all rooms are en suite with TV and tea making facilities. Pets £2 per night, £8 per week.

Brochure - Tel: 01225 891261 • Fax: 01225 892128 • www.toghillhousefarm.co.uk

David and Jackie Bishop, Toghill House Farm, Freezing Hill, Wick, Near Bath BS30 5RT

Primrose Hill offers spacious, comfortable accommodation in a terrace of four bungalows. Private gardens with panoramic views over Blue Anchor Bay, Dunster Castle and Exmoor. A dog-friendly beach is a 10-minute walk away, with other lovely walks from your doorstep. Open all year. Fully wheelchair accessible.

Winner of Exmoor Excellence Awards, Self-Catering Holiday of the Year 2006 & 2007

Primrose Hill Holidays, Wood Lane, Blue Anchor TA24 6LA (01643 821200)

info@primrosehillholidays.co.uk • www.primrosehillholidays.co.uk

Beachside Holiday Park

Coast Road, Brean Sands, Somerset TA8 2QZ

Tel: 01278 751346 • Fax: 01278 751683

- Chalets and Caravan holiday homes on quiet park • Direct access to beach • Full facilities
- Colour television • Cafe/Bar • Golf courses nearby • Free brochure • Pets from £4 per night

FREE BROCHURE • FREEPHONE 08000 190322 • www.beachsideholidaypark.co.uk

WESTWARD RISE HOLIDAY PARK

Brean, Near Burnham-on-Sea TA8 2RD Tel & Fax: 01278 751310

Highly Recommended Luxury 2/6 berth Chalet-Bungalows on a small quiet family-owned Park adjoining sandy beach. • 2 Double Bedrooms • Shower • Toilet • Colour TV • Fridge • Cooker • Duvets and Linen • Open all year • Centrally Heated during winter months • Laundry on Park • Caravan Sales Available • Shops • Clubs • Amusements & Restaurants Nearby • Dogs Welcome

Call now for a FREE BROCHURE www.westwardrise.com

Broadway House Holiday Park

A family friendly touring caravan, camping & lodge park set in an Area of Outstanding National Beauty in Cheddar, Somerset.

Call now to request your brochure and to book your holiday or short break

email: info@broadwayhouse.uk.com
web: www.broadwayhouse.uk.com
tel: 01934 742610

broadway house holiday park

CHEDDAR - SUNGATE HOLIDAY APARTMENTS

Church Street, Cheddar, Somerset BS27 3RA

Delightful apartments in Cheddar village, each fully equipped. Sleep two/four. Laundry facilities. Private parking. Family, disabled and pet friendly. ETC ★★

For full details contact Mrs M. Fieldhouse. Tel: 01934 842273/742264

enquiries@sungateholidayapartments.co.uk • www.sungateholidayapartments.co.uk

In the centre of quaint English village, an ideal location for walking and exploring Exmoor, the surrounding coastline and the many local attractions. Comfortable, family-run hotel which provides a friendly, relaxed atmosphere, home cooking, en suite rooms with colour TV, tea making facilities and a residents' lounge. Packed lunches and drying facilities available. Non-smoking. Well behaved dogs welcome.

Party bookings and mid-week breaks a speciality • Pets Welcome • B&B From £40 • ETC ★★★ Hotel

THE YARN MARKET HOTEL High Street, Dunster TA24 6SF • 01643 821425

Fax: 01643 821475 • e-mail: hotel@yarnmarkethotel.co.uk • www.yarnmarkethotel.co.uk

Exford, Exmoor

Exford, Exmoor National Park, Somerset TA24 7NA ETC ★★★★

Charming, cosy, comfortable centrally heated detached bungalow with enclosed garden and superb views. A short walk from the village of Exford. Ideally located for walking, fishing, riding and exploring Exmoor, and the surrounding coastline. Bring your dog or horse for wonderful trips over the moor. Stabling available. B&B available at Edgcott, Exford, in 18thC cottage. • **Contact: Joan Atkins, 2 Edgcott Cottage, Exford, Somerset TA24 7QG**

e-mail: info@stilemoorexmoor.co.uk

Tel/Fax: 01643 831564 • mobile: 078914 37293 • www.stilemoorexmoor.co.uk

Beside River Exe - Centre of Exmoor National Park -
close to coast. Four charming self-catering cottages.
Dogs and horses welcome. Stabling available.

Riscombe Farm Holiday Cottages
Exford, Somerset TA24 7NH
Tel: 01643 831480 www.riscombe.co.uk

★★★★ SELF CATERING

SIMONSBATH HOUSE HOTEL

Simonsbath, Exmoor, Somerset TA24 7SH
Tel: 01643 831259 • Fax: 01643 831557

Overlooking the River Barle the oldest house on Exmoor Forest offers a peaceful and relaxing location to enjoy the magnificent coastal scenery or to explore the splendour of Exmoor and the spectacular coastline. Surrounded by moorland this is an ideal location for long walks both on and off the lead. The hotel offers large, individually decorated, centrally heated rooms, some with four poster beds, and all with en suite facilities, colour TV and hospitality tray. The comfortable lounge and library have log fires, offering the perfect setting to enjoy drinks before sampling our highly commended cuisine.

The house is situated in three acres of grounds and there is ample off road parking.

Dogs are welcome to stay free of charge. Please contact Andrew or Louise for further detail

www.simonsbathhouse.co.uk B&B / B&B & Evening Dinner

★★★-★★★★ SELF CATERING

Exmoor •• The Pack Horse

Allerford, Near Porlock, Somerset TA24 8HW
Tel/Fax: 01643 862475
www.thepackhorse.net • e-mail: holidays@thepackhorse.net

Our self-catering apartments and cottage are situated in this unique location within a picturesque National Trust village which has local amenities. The Pack Horse sits alongside the shallow River Aller, overlooking the famous bridge. Enjoy immediate access from our doorstep to the beautiful surrounding countryside, pretty villages, spectacular coast, and Exmoor.

Terms from £300 to £545 per week

OPEN ALL YEAR • PRIVATE PARKING • SHORT BREAKS

Very warm welcome assured

WELCOME HOST

West Withy Farm

UPTON,
NEAR WIVELISCOMBE,
TAUNTON, SOMERSET TA4 2JH
Tel: 01398 371 322
e-mail: laurencerye@byinternet.com
www.exmoor-cottages.com
ETC ★★★★ Self Catering

West Withy Farm offers you and your dog a haven of peace and tranquillity in the beautiful, undiscovered Brendon Hills on the edge of Exmoor. The glorious countryside of Exmoor, the Brendons and the Quantocks provides a walkers' paradise. Two well-equipped, detached character cottages, **Upton** and **Stable**, with full central heating and stoves, sleeping 2- 5.

• Private south-facing, enclosed, dog-proof gardens • Panoramic views • Excellent fly fishing locally
• Bed linen and towels provided • Colour TVs • Fully inclusive prices • From £180-£545 per week • Short breaks available

Exmoor, Fitzhead, Langport, Minehead

Brochure from resident owners

Val & Mike Warner, Westerclose House, Withypool, Somerset TA24 7QR

Holiday Cottages – Exmoor National Park

Quality cottages, including bungalows in the grounds of a former hunting lodge. Wonderful moorland location.

Totally peaceful with superb views. Beautiful coast and countryside. Shop and pub 300 metres. Excellent walking straight from your cottage. Log fires. Very well appointed. Dogs & horses welcome. Individual gardens. Sleep 2-6. Internet access. Open all year. Short breaks available.

ETC ★★★★

Tel/Fax: 01643 831302 • www.westerclose.co.uk

Silver

SILVER AWARD

★★★★

North Down Farm

Pyncombe Lane, Wiveliscombe, Taunton TA4 2BL Tel/Fax: 01984 623730

Traditional working farm set in 100 acres of natural beauty. All rooms tastefully furnished to high standard include en suite, TV, and tea/coffee facilities. Double, twin or single rooms available. Dining room and lounge with log fires; centrally heated and double glazed. Drying facilities. Dogs welcome. B&B from £36pppn, 7 nights BB+EM from £299pp. North Down Break: three nights BB+EM from £145pp.

e-mail: jennycope@btinternet.com www.north-down-farm.co.uk

Occupying an unique location with breathtaking views within the National Park. A special place for you and man's best friends.

ETC ★★★★ Telephone or write for colour brochure:

Wintershead

Jane Styles, Wintershead Farm, Simonsbath, Exmoor, Somerset TA24 7LF

Tel: 01643 831222 • www.wintershead.co.uk

FITZHEAD INN

FITZHEAD, TAUNTON SOMERSET TA4 3JP

AA ★★★★ INN

Small, cosy, 250-year old pub offering fresh home-cooked local food, a good selection of wines, real ales and over 40 malts

Tel: 01823 400667 **www.thefitzhead.co.uk**

Thorney Farm Cottages

Four beautiful holiday cottages in the heart of the Somerset Levels. Lovely dog walking from the doorstep and right on the River Parrett Trail. Cottages are furnished to a high standard, a real home-from-home. **Gothic House, Thorney, Langport TA10 0DW**

Tel: 01458 253886 • www.thorneyfarmcottages.co.uk • info@thorneyfarmcottages.co.uk

---

MINEHEAD – 16th CENTURY THATCHED COTTAGES

ROSE-ASH – Sleeps 2 ✦ Prettily furnished ✦ All electric. **WILLOW** – Inglenook ✦ Oak panelling ✦ Electricity, Gas, CH ✦ Sleeps 6. **LITTLE THATCH** – Sleeps 5 ✦ Inglenook ✦ Cosy location ✦ Electricity. Gas, CH.

SAE please to: Mr T. Stone, Troytes Farmstead, Tivington, Somerset TA24 8SU

Private car park – Enclosed gardens – Pets Welcome Tel: 01643 704531

Delightful family-run private guest house only a few minutes' level walking distance from sea front • Delicious home cooking • Full central heating • 8 en suite bedrooms, all with courtesy tray, remote-control TV, hairdryer • Children and well behaved pets welcome • Totally non-smoking

SUNFIELD, 83 Summerland Avenue, Minehead TA24 5BW

Tel: 01643 703565 • www.sunfieldminehead.co.uk

★★★ GUEST HOUSE

THE OLD CIDER HOUSE

4 ★ licensed guesthouse set in the picturesque and historic village of **Nether Stowey** at the foot of the beautiful **Quantock Hills**. The ideal place for walking, sightseeing or just relaxing. **Log Fire. Inclusive D,B&B rates. Guided Walking** also available. Own **microbrewery.**

01278 732228 • info@theoldciderhouse.co.uk

25 Castle Street, Nether Stowey, Somerset TA5 1LN • **www.theoldciderhouse.co.uk**

Sunnybank Holiday Park

Unwind in one of Sunnybank's caravans set at the foot of the stunning Quantock Hills in Doniford, Somerset

Call now to request your brochure and to book your holiday or short break

email: enquiries@sunnybankpark.co.uk
web: www.sunnybankpark.co.uk
tel: 01984 632 237

sunnybank holiday park

Croft Holiday Cottages **• The Croft, Anchor Street, Watchet TA23 0BY**

Tel: 01984 631121 • ETC ★★★★

Courtyard of six cottages/bungalows situated in a quiet backwater of the small harbour town of Watchet. Parking, central heating. TV, DVD, washing machine, fridge/freezer, microwave. Use of heated indoor pool. Sleep 2-6 persons. £170-£675 per property per week. **Contact:** **Mrs K. Musgrave • e-mail: croftcottages@talk21.com • www.cottagessomerset.com**

BIRDWOOD HOUSE *Imposing Victorian house situated on the edge of the Mendip Hills but only 1½ miles from Wells town centre. Two double en suite rooms and one twin room, all with TV and tea/coffee making facilities. Off-road secure parking. Close to a walking trail and cycling route. Groups and parties welcome. B&B from £25pp.*

• Children welcome • Pets by arrangement • No smoking • Open all year • ***AA ★★★***

Mrs Sue Crane, Birdwood House, Bath Road, Wells BA5 3EW (01749 679250) • www.birdwood-bandb.co.uk

Somerset Court Cottages

Wick St Lawrence, Near Weston-super-Mare BS22 7YR • Tel: 01934 521383

Converted stone cottages in mediaeval village. 1, 2 or 3 beds.
Some with four-posters, luxury whirlpool/spa baths. £210-£690 per week.

e-mail: peter@somersetcourtcottages.co.uk • www.somersetcourtcottages.co.uk

Braeside Hotel 2 Victoria Park, Weston-super-Mare BS23 2HZ

Delightful , family-run, 9-bedroom hotel only a two-minute walk from the seafront and sandy beach (dogs allowed all year). All bedrooms en suite.

Tel: 01934 626642 • ETC/AA ◆◆◆◆ (Awarded in 2005)

e-mail: enquiries@braesidehotel.com • www.braesidehotel.com

FARM & COTTAGE HOLIDAYS (01237 459897). Over 850 of the finest selection of holiday cottages throughout Devon, Cornwall, Dorset and Somerset in superb rural and coastal locations.
website: www.holidaycottages.co.uk

Bath

The best-preserved Georgian city in Britain, Bath has been famous since Roman times for its mineral springs. It is a noted centre for music and the arts, with a wide range of leisure facilities.

DAVID & JACKIE BISHOP, TOGHILL HOUSE FARM, FREEZING HILL, WICK, NEAR BATH BS30 5RT (01225 891261; Fax: 01225 892128). Luxury barn conversions on working farm 3 miles north of Bath. Each equipped to very high standard, bed linen provided. Also en suite B&B accommodation in 17th century farmhouse. [pw! Pets £2 per night, £8 per week]
website: www.toghillhousefarm.co.uk

Blue Anchor

Hamlet two miles west of Watchet. Beautiful beaches, and rocks and cliffs of geological interest.

PRIMROSE HILL HOLIDAYS, WOOD LANE, BLUE ANCHOR TA24 6LA (01643 821200). Award-winning, spacious, comfortable accommodation in a terrace of four bungalows. Private gardens with panoramic views. A dog-friendly beach is a 10-minute walk away, with other lovely walks from your doorstep. Open all year. Fully wheelchair accessible. ETC ★★★★ [Pets £15 per week].
e-mail: info@primrosehillholidays.co.uk website: www.primrosehillholidays.co.uk

Brean

Coastal village with extensive sands. To north is the promontory of Brean Down. Weston-Super-Mare 9 miles.

BEACHSIDE HOLIDAY PARK, COAST ROAD, BREAN SANDS TA8 2QZ (FREEPHONE 08000 190322; Tel: 01278 751346; Fax: 01278 751683). Chalets and Caravan holiday homes on quiet park. Direct access to beach (dogs allowed). Full facilities. Colour TV. Cafe/bar. Golf courses nearby. Free brochure. [Pets from £4 per night]
website: www.beachsideholidaypark.co.uk

WESTWARD RISE HOLIDAY PARK, SOUTH ROAD, BREAN, NEAR BURNHAM ON-SEA TA8 2RD (01278 751310). Highly Recommended Luxury 2/6 berth Chalet bungalows. 2 double bedrooms, shower, toilet, TV, fridge, cooker, duvets and linen. Open all year. Call for free brochure. [Pets £15 per week.]
website: www.westwardrise.com

Cheddar

Picturesque little town in the Mendips, famous for its Gorge and unique caves. Cheese-making is a speciality. Good touring centre. Bath 24 miles, Burnham-on-sea 13, Weston-Super-Mare 11.

BROADWAY HOUSE HOLIDAY PARK, CHEDDAR (01934 742610). A family friendly touring caravan, camping and lodge park, set in an Area of Outstanding Natural Beauty in Cheddar, Somerset. Call now to request a brochure or book your holiday or short break.
e-mail: info@broadwayhouse.uk.com website: www.broadwayhouse.uk.com

SUNGATE HOLIDAY APARTMENTS, CHURCH STREET, CHEDDAR, SOMERSET BS27 3RA. Ideally situated for walking, cycling and touring the Mendips and the West Country. Competitively priced for short or longer holidays. For full details contact Mrs M. FIELDHOUSE (01934 842273/742264) ETC ★★ [Quote for Pets].
e-mail: enquiries@sungateholidayapartments.co.uk web: www.sungateholidayapartments.co.uk

Symbols

- 🐕 Indicates that pets are welcome free of charge.
- £ Indicates that a charge is made for pets: nightly or weekly.
- pw! Shows some special provision for pets; exercise facility, feeding or accommodation arrangement.
- ☖ Indicates separate pets accommodation.

Dunster

Pretty village with interesting features, including Yarn Market, imposing 14th century Castle. Priory Church and old houses and cottages. Minehead 3 miles.

THE YARN MARKET HOTEL, HIGH STREET, DUNSTER TA24 6SF (01643 821425; Fax: 01643 821475). An ideal location for walking and exploring Exmoor. Family-run hotel with a friendly, relaxed atmosphere, home cooking, en suite rooms with colour TV and tea making facilities. Non-smoking. Mid-week breaks a speciality – Pets Welcome. ETC ★★★ Hotel [pw!]
e-mail: hotel@yarnmarkethotel.co.uk website: www.yarnmarkethotel.co.uk

Exford

Fine touring centre for Exmoor and North Devon, on River Exe. Dulverton 10 miles.

WESTERMILL, EXFORD, EXMOOR TA24 7NJ (01643 831238; Fax: 01643 831216). Idyllic Scandinavian cottages in grass paddocks by stream, with views across river valley. Heart of Exmoor. Woodburners. Four waymarked walks over 500 acre working farm. Disabled Category 2. Separate campsite by river. VisitBritian ★★★/ ★★★★ David Bellamy Gold Award for Conservation. [Pets £2.50 per night.]
e-mail: pw@westermill.com website: www.westermill.com

CHAPEL COTTAGE, EXFORD TA24 7PY (01788 810275). Enjoy walking or riding on the moors, by the rivers or the beach. Return to our cosy cottage, log fire and beams. Two bedrooms (sleeps 4+2), two bathrooms. Excellent inns within 100 yards. Open all year. [Up to 2 dogs welcome, free of charge]
e-mail: stay@chapelcottage-exmoor.co.uk website: www.chapelcottage-exmoor.co.uk

STILEMOOR, EXFORD, EXMOOR NATIONAL PARK TA24 7NA. Charming cosy centrally heated detached bungalow with enclosed garden, superb views, walking, fishing, riding. Sleeps 6. ETC ★★★★. JOAN ATKINS, 2 EDGCOTT COTTAGE, EXFORD, MINEHEAD TA24 7QG (Tel & Fax: 01643 831564; mobile: 078914 37293) [Pets £2 per night]
e-mail: info@stilemoorexmoor.co.uk website: www.stilemoorexmoor.co.uk

LEONE & BRIAN MARTIN, RISCOMBE FARM HOLIDAY COTTAGES, EXFORD, EXMOOR NATIONAL PARK TA24 7NH (01643 831480). Beside River Exe – centre of Exmoor National Park – close to coast. Four charming self-catering cottages. Dogs and horses welcome. Stabling available. VB ★★★★ [Pets £2.50 per night, £15 per week.]
website: www.riscombe.co.uk (with up-to-date vacancy info.)

Exmoor

265 square miles of unspoiled heather moorland with deep wooded valleys and rivers, ideal for a walking, pony trekking or fishing holiday.

WOODCOMBE LODGES, BRATTON, NEAR MINEHEAD TA24 8SQ (Tel & Fax: 01643 702789). Four self-catering lodges in a tranquil rural setting on the edge of Exmoor National Park, standing in a beautiful 2½ acre garden with wonderful views. [Pets £10 per week]
e-mail: nicola@woodcombelodge.co.uk website: www.woodcombelodge.co.uk

SIMONSBATH HOUSE HOTEL, SIMONSBATH, EXMOOR TA24 7SH. (01643 831259; Fax: 01643 831557). A peaceful and relaxing location. All rooms en suite; comfortable lounge with log fire. Three-acre gardens, ample parking. [pw!]
website: www.simonsbathhouse.co.uk

Pet-Friendly
Pubs, Inns & Hotels
on pages 424-432
Please note that these establishments may not feature in the main section of this book

THE PACK HORSE, ALLERFORD, NEAR PORLOCK TA24 8HW (Tel & Fax: 01643 862475). Self-catering apartments and cottage within picturesque National Trust village. Immediate access to the beautiful surrounding countryside. Stabling available. Open all year. ETC ★★★/★★★★ [Pets £15 per visit]
e-mail: holidays@thepackhorse.net website: www.thepackhorse.net

LAURENCE & CATHERINE RYE, WEST WITHY FARM, UPTON, NEAR WIVELISCOMBE, TAUNTON TA4 2JH (01398 371258). Two cottages sleeping 2-5. Fully inclusive prices. Walkers' paradise in the Brendons and Quantocks. Enclosed, dog-proof gardens. Short breaks available. £180-£545 per week. ETC ★★★★ [Pets £12 per week]
e-mail: laurencerye@btinternet.com website: www.exmoor-cottages.com

WESTERCLOSE HOUSE, WITHYPOOL, EXMOOR NATIONAL PARK TA24 7QR (01643 831302). Stunning views, complete peace, and wonderful moorland location. Five cosy cottages, including two bungalows, all with log fires and individual gardens. Pub/shop 300 metres. Dogs and horses welcome. ETC ★★★★ [pw! Dogs £12 per week]
website: www.westerclose.co.uk

JENNY COPE, NORTH DOWN FARM, PYNCOMBE LANE, WIVELISCOMBE, TAUNTON TA4 2BL (Tel & Fax: 01984 623730). Traditional working farm. All rooms en suite, furnished to high standard. Log fires. Central heating. B&B from £36pppn. BB&EM: 7 nights from £299pp, 3-night B&B and evening meal from £145pp. Dogs welcome. ETC ★★★★ Silver Award. [£8 per pet per visit].
e-mail: jennycope@btinternet.com website: www.north-down-farm.co.uk

JANE STYLES, WINTERSHEAD FARM, SIMONSBATH TA24 7LF (01643 831222). Five tastefully furnished and well-equipped cottages situated in the midst of beautiful Exmoor. Pets welcome, stabling and grazing, DIY livery. Colour brochure on request. ETC ★★★★ [Dogs £15 per week, Horses £20 per week.]
website: www.wintershead.co.uk

Fitzhead

Pretty village 20 minutes from Taunton.

FITZHEAD INN, FITZHEAD, TAUNTON TA4 3JP (01823 400667). Small, cosy, 250-year old pub offering fresh home-cooked local food, a good selection of wines, real ales and over 40 malts. AA ★★★★ [🐕]
website: www.thefitzhead.co.uk

Langport

Ancient market town on the banks of River Parrett, 7 miles NE of Ilchester..

THORNEY FARM COTTAGES. Four beautiful holiday cottages in the heart of the Somerset Levels. Lovely dog walking from the doorstep and right on the River Parrett Trail. Cottages are furnished to a high standard, a real home-from-home. Contact: GOTHIC HOUSE, THORNEY, LANGPORT TA10 0DW (01458 253886). [🐕]
e-mail: info@thorneyfarmcottages.co.uk website: www.thorneyfarmcottages.co.uk

Minehead

Neat and stylish resort on Bristol Channel. Sandy bathing beach, attractive gardens, golf course and good facilities for tennis, bowls and horse riding. Within easy reach of the beauties of Exmoor.

MINEHEAD 16TH CENTURY THATCHED COTTAGES. Rose Ash - Sleeps 2, prettily furnished, all electric. Willow - Inglenook, oak panelling, electricity, gas, CH, Sleeps 6. Little Thatch - Sleeps 5, Inglenook, Cosy location, Electricity. Gas, CH. Private car park. Enclosed gardens. Pets welcome. SAE: MR T. STONE, TROYTES FARMSTEAD, TIVINGTON, MINEHEAD TA24 8SU (01643 704531). [🐕]

SUNFIELD, 83 SUMMERLAND AVENUE, MINEHEAD TA24 5BW (01643 703565). Delightful family-run guest house only a few minutes' level walking distance from sea front. Delicious home cooking. 8 en suite bedrooms. Children and well behaved pets welcome. Totally non-smoking. ETC ★★★ [🐕]
website: www.sunfieldminehead.co.uk

Quantock Hills

Granite and limestone ridge running north-west and south-east from Quantoxhead and Kingston.

THE OLD CIDER HOUSE, 25 CASTLE STREET, NETHER STOWEY TA5 1LN (01278 732228). In picturesque, historic village at the foot of the Quantocks. All en suite; licensed dining. Own car parking, secluded garden. B&B from £30pppn. Wonderful dog-walking country; only 4 miles from coast. EnjoyEngland ★★★★ Guest Accommodation. [Pets £15.50 per week].
e-mail: info@theoldciderhouse.co.uk website: www.theoldciderhouse.co.uk

SUNNYBANK HOLIDAY PARK, DONIFORD (01984 632237). Unwind in one of Sunnybank's caravans, set at the foot of Stunning Quantock Hills in Doniford, Somerset. Call now to request a brochure or book your holiday or short break.
e-mail: enquiries@sunnybankpark.co.uk website: www.sunnybankpark.co.uk

Watchet

Small port and resort with rocks and sands. Good centre for Exmoor and the Quantocks. Bathing, boating, fishing, rambling. Tiverton 24 miles, Bridgwater 19, Taunton 17, Dunster 6.

MRS K. MUSGRAVE, CROFT HOLIDAY COTTAGES, THE CROFT, ANCHOR STREET, WATCHET TA23 0BY (01984 631121) Courtyard of six cottages/bungalows situated in a quiet backwater of the small harbour town of Watchet. Parking, central heating. TV, DVD, washing machine, fridge/freezer, microwave. Use of heated indoor pool. Sleeps 2-6 persons. £170-£675 per property per week. ETC ★★★★ [Pets £15 per week]
e-mail: croftcottages@talk21.com website: www.cottagessomerset.com

Wells

England's smallest city. West front of Cathedral built around 1230, shows superb collection of statuary.

INFIELD HOUSE, 36 PORTWAY, WELLS BA5 2BN (01749 670989; Fax: 01749 679093). Richard and Heather invite you and your dog (if older than one year) to visit England's smallest city. Wonderful walks on Mendip Hills. No smoking. Bountiful breakfasts, dinners by arrangement. AA ★★★★ [🐕]
website: www.infieldhouse.co.uk

MRS SUE CRANE, BIRDWOOD HOUSE, BATH ROAD, WELLS BA5 3EW (01749 679250). Imposing Victorian house on the edge of the Mendip Hills. Two double en suite rooms and one twin room, all with TV and tea/coffee making facilities. Close to a walking trail and cycling route. Pets by arrangement. AA ★★★ [🐕]
website: www.birdwood-bandb.co.uk

Weston-Super-Mare

Popular resort on the Bristol Channel with a wide range of entertainments and leisure facilities. An ideal base for touring the West Country.

MR C. G. THOMAS, ARDNAVE HOLIDAY PARK, KEWSTOKE, WESTON-SUPER-MARE BS22 9XJ (01934 622319). Caravans - De luxe. 2-3 bedrooms, shower, toilet, colour TVs, all bedding included. Parking. Dogs welcome. Graded ★★★. [🐕 pw!]

SOMERSET COURT COTTAGES, WICK ST LAWRENCE, NEAR WESTON-SUPER-MARE BS22 7YR (01934 521383). Converted stone cottages in mediaeval village. 1, 2 or 3 beds. Some with four-posters, luxury whirlpool/spa baths. Superb centre for touring West Country. Short Breaks available. £210-£690 per week. [Pets £2 per night]
e-mail: peter@somersetcourtcottages.co.uk website: www.somersetcourtcottages.co.uk

BRAESIDE HOTEL, 2 VICTORIA PARK, WESTON-SUPER-MARE BS23 2HZ (01934 626642). Delightful, family-run Hotel, close to shops, beach and park. Parking available. All rooms en suite, colour TV, tea/coffee making. November to March THIRD NIGHT FREE. ETC/AA ◆◆◆◆ (Awarded in 2005) [🐕]
e-mail: enquiries@braesidehotel.com website: www.braesidehotel.com

Grittleton, Trowbridge, Westbury

THE NEELD ARMS INN
THE STREET, GRITTLETON SN14 6AP
01249 782470 • Fax: 01249 782358 • e-mail: info@neeldarms.co.uk
17th century inn offering comfortable accommodation and home-cooked food; four-poster available. Children and pets welcome. Convenient for Bath, Stonehenge, Cotswolds. **www.neeldarms.co.uk**

★★★ INN

Ring o Bells Guest House (not licensed)
321 Marsh Road, Hilperton Marsh, Trowbridge BA14 7PL
Warm, friendly environment • Single, double, twin, triple and family en suite rooms, with TV, radio alarm and hairdryer • Wheelchair and disabled accessibility • Pets by arrangement • **www.ringobells.biz** • ETC ★★★ • 01225 754404

Spinney Farmhouse Thoulstone, Chapmanslade, Westbury BA13 4AQ
Off A36, three miles west of Warminster; 16 miles from historic city of Bath. • Washbasins, tea/coffee-making facilities and shaver points in all rooms. • Family room available. • Guests' lounge with colour TV. • Central heating. • Children and pets welcome. • Ample parking. • Open all year. • No smoking. • Enjoy farm fresh food in a warm, friendly, family atmosphere. Bed and Breakfast from £25 per night. Reduction after 2 nights. Evening Meal £14.
e-mail: isabelandbob@btinternet.com
01373 832412

Grittleton

Village 6 miles north west of Chippenham.

THE NEELD ARMS INN, THE STREET, GRITTLETON SN14 6AP (01249 782470; Fax: 01249 782358). 17th century inn offering comfortable accommodation and home-cooked food; four-poster available. Children and pets welcome. Convenient for Bath, Stonehenge, Cotswolds. EnjoyEngland ★★★ Inn.
e-mail: info@neeldarms.co.uk website: www.neeldarms.co.uk

Salisbury

13th century cathedral city, with England's highest spire at 404ft. Many fine buildings.

MR A. SHERING, SWAYNES FIRS FARM, GRIMSDYKE, COOMBE BISSETT, SALISBURY SP5 5RF (01725 519240). Small working farm with cattle, poultry, geese and duck ponds. Spacious rooms, all en suite with colour TV. Ideal for visiting the many historic sites in the area. ETC ★★★ [Pets £5 per night]
e-mail: swaynes.firs@virgin.net website: www.swaynesfirs.co.uk

Trowbridge

County town near Wiltshire, 8 miles SE of Bath.

RING O BELLS GUEST HOUSE, 321 MARSH ROAD, HILPERTON MARSH, TROWBRIDGE BA14 7PL (01225 754404). Warm, friendly environment. Single, double, twin, triple and family en suite rooms, with TV, radio alarm and hairdryer. Wheelchair and disabled accessibility. Pets by arrangement. ETC ★★★
website: www.ringobells.biz

Westbury

Town at the foot of Salisbury Plain, 4 miles south of Trowbridge.

SPINNEY FARMHOUSE, THOULSTONE, CHAPMANSLADE, WESTBURY BA13 4AQ (01373 832412). Enjoy farm fresh food in a warm, friendly, family atmosphere. Off A36, 16 miles from Bath. All rooms with washbasins, tea/coffee making. TV lounge. No smoking. Children and pets welcome. [🐕]
e-mail: isabelandbob@btinternet.com

Pets are Welcome at
WELCOMEBREAK
DAYS INN
Broadband Wifi now available in all rooms
Free Parking • 24hr Reception and all hotels AA Approved and Pet Friendly
for more information visit our website at
www.welcomebreak.co.uk
or you can call the hotel hotline on
AA
01908 299 785

Dorney Self Catering Apartments Wisteria, The Gardener's Bothy and The Smithy

Set in the grounds of a Tudor house • River Thames a short stroll away • Windsor, Eton, Maidenhead 3 miles • London by train 20 minutes • Peaceful, yet well located • Pets welcome • 10 minute walk to Eton Rowing Lake • Book by the night.

Please telephone Jan on 01753 827037 during office hours or book directly online at
www.troppo.uk.com

Membury

Located close to Swindon, Newbury and Reading.

DAYS INN MEMBURY, WESTBOUND JUNCTION 14/15, M4 (Tel & Fax: 01488 72336). Modern, comfortable accommodation in peaceful setting. All rooms en suite, FREE SKY TV, Broadband WIFI, trouser press, hot drinks tray and free parking. Ideally located for visiting Swindon, Chippenham, Bristol, Bath, The Cotswolds, Gloucester and Oxford. AA Approved & Pet Friendly. [🐕]
e-mail: membury.hotel@welcomebreak.co.uk website: www.welcomebreak.co.uk

Windsor

Town on the South Bank of the River Thames, 2 miles south of Slough and 21 miles west of London.

DORNEY SELF CATERING APARTMENTS, THE OLD PLACE, LOCK PATH, DORNEY, WINDSOR SL4 6QQ (01753 827037).Quality accommodation in a unique location set in the grounds of a Tudor house in a rural, peaceful location. The River Thames and Boveney Lock are a short stroll away. Windsor and Eton are less than three miles. Own transport needed. [🐕]
website: www.troppo.uk.com

Visit the FHG website

www.holidayguides.com

for details of the wide choice of accommodation

featured in the full range of FHG titles

Harvey welcomes you to...
49 LOWNDES AVENUE, CHESHAM HP5 2HH
B&B in detached house, 10 minutes from the Underground.
Private bathroom • Tea/coffee • TV.
Good walking country – Chiltern Hills 3 minutes. PAT & GEORGE ORME
Tel: 01494 792647 • e-mail: bbormelowndes@tiscali.co.uk
★★★ BED & BREAKFAST

www.swanrevived.co.uk **Swan Revived Hotel**
High Street, Newport Pagnell, Milton Keynes MK16 8AR
01908 610565 • Fax: 01908 210995 • e-mail: info@swanrevived.co.uk
Delightful 15thC former coaching inn, extensively modernised to provide 40 comfortable guest rooms, two bars, à la carte restaurant, meeting rooms and banqueting facilities. Pets very welcome - no charge is made.

Chesham

Town on south side of Chiltern Hills. Ideal walking area.

PAT & GEORGE ORME, 49 LOWNDES AVENUE, CHESHAM HP5 2HH (01494 792647). B&B in detached house, 10 minutes from the Underground. Private bathroom, tea/coffee, TV. Good walking country - Chiltern Hills three minutes. ETC ★★★ [🐕]
e-mail: bbormelowndes@tiscali.co.uk

Milton Keynes

Purpose-built new city, home to the Open University. Midway between London, Birmingham, Leicester, Oxford and Cambridge.

SWAN REVIVED HOTEL, HIGH STREET, NEWPORT PAGNELL, MILTON KEYNES MK16 8AR (01908 610565; Fax: 01908 210995). Delightful 15thC former coaching inn, extensively modernised to provide 40 comfortable guest rooms, two bars, à la carte restaurant, meeting rooms and banqueting facilities. Pets very welcome. [🐕]
e-mail: info@swanrevived.co.uk website: www.swanrevived.co.uk

Other specialised holiday guides from FHG

PUBS & INNS OF BRITAIN • **COUNTRY HOTELS** OF BRITAIN
WEEKEND & SHORT BREAK HOLIDAYS IN BRITAIN
THE GOLF GUIDE WHERE TO PLAY, WHERE TO STAY
500 GREAT PLACES TO STAY • SELF-CATERING HOLIDAYS IN BRITAIN
BED & BREAKFAST STOPS • CARAVAN & CAMPING HOLIDAYS
FAMILY BREAKS IN BRITAIN

Published annually: available in all good bookshops or direct from the publisher:
FHG Guides, Abbey Mill Business Centre, Seedhill, Paisley PA1 1TJ
Tel: 0141 887 0428 • Fax: 0141 889 7204
e-mail: admin@fhguides.co.uk • www.holidayguides.com

HONEYSUCKLE HOUSE

24 CLINTON ROAD, LYMINGTON SO41 9EA • Tel: 01590 676635
Lovely ground floor double room/single, en suite, non-smoking.
Woodland walk, park, quay and marinas nearby. B&B from £30.00 pppn.
e-mail: paula.farrell@dsl.pipex.com
website: http://explorethenewforest.co.uk/honeysuckle.htm

Efford Cottage

Everton, Lymington, Hampshire SO41 0JD
Tel: 01590 642315 • Fax: 01590 641030
e-mail: effordcottage@aol.com • www.effordcottage.co.uk

Guests receive a warm and friendly welcome to our home, which is a spacious Georgian cottage. All rooms are en suite with many extra luxury facilities. We offer a four-course multi-choice breakfast with homemade bread and preserves. Patricia is a qualified chef and uses our home-grown produce. An excellent centre for exploring both the New Forest and the South Coast with sports facilities, fishing, bird watching and horse riding in the near vicinity. Private parking. Dogs welcome. Sorry no children. **Bed and Breakfast from £25–£35 pppn.** *Mrs Patricia J. Ellis.*

Winner of " England For Excellence 2000"
FHG Diploma 1997/1999/2000/2003 / Michelin / Welcome Host
Awards Achieved: Gold Award / RAC Sparkling Diamond & Warm Welcome
Nominated Landlady of Year & Best Breakfast Award.

AA ★★★★ Guest Accommodation

WELCOME HOST

AA ★★

Ormonde House Hotel

Southampton Road, Lyndhurst, Hampshire SO43 7BT
Tel: (023) 8028 2806 • Fax: (023) 8028 2004
e-mail: enquiries@ormondehouse.co.uk • www.ormondehouse.co.uk

A relaxed blend of professionalism and warm hospitality awaits you at our elegant, family-run, Two Star Hotel, situated opposite the open forest. Ideal for easy walking. 19 pretty, en suite rooms and four luxury self-contained suites, all with CTV, phone and beverage making. 'Superior' rooms have super king zip+link double/twin and sofa; some with whirlpool bath. Suites have super king zip+link double/twin, sofa (double sofa bed) and double whirlpool bath. Each has a full kitchen with washing/dryer machine and dishwasher. Dine with us - our Chefs have an excellent reputation amongst our regular guests for freshly prepared dishes, daily changing specials and wickedly tempting puddings. Close to Exbury Gardens and Beaulieu Motor Museum.

Special 4 night midweek breaks:
From £120pp B&B or from £171pp DB&B.

Readers are requested to mention this FHG guidebook when seeking accommodation

Lyndhurst, New Forest

The Crown Hotel, New Forest

Tired of the same old walks? Enjoy forest, heath and the beach whilst staying at The Crown Hotel. 38 en suite rooms, all individual and recently refurbished.
Our Chef of thirty years, Stephen Greenhalgh, delights us with his imaginative menus using local produce wherever possible, either in the informal bar or the Restaurant overlooking our water-featured garden.

Dogs are welcome to bring their well-behaved owners!

High Street, Lyndhurst, Hampshire SO43 7NF • Tel: 023 8028 2922 • Fax: 023 8028 2751
E-mail: reception@crownhotel-lyndhurst.co.uk • Web: www.crownhotel-lyndhurst.co.uk

GORSE COTTAGE, BALMER LAWN ROAD, BROCKENHURST

Cottage/bungalow on open forest road close to the village in the New Forest. Beautifully decorated and appointed, sleeps 4 in 2 bedrooms. Conservatory, luxury bathroom, log fire, TV/Sky/DVD, secluded sunny garden. Pets welcome.

Contact: MRS E. GILBERT (0870 3210020) or website for details
e-mail: info@gorsecottage.co.uk www.gorsecottage.co.uk

New Forest - charming, secluded cottage

Quiet country hamlet • Great walks
Pets welcome • Sleeps 2+2
Tel: 01425 471372 • www.highfields-cottage.co.uk
e-mail: 07enquiries@highfields-cottage.co.uk

Bramble Hill Hotel

Bramshaw, New Forest, Hampshire SO43 7JG
Telephone: 023 80 813165
www.bramblehill.co.uk

Peacefully located in tranquil surroundings, this country house hotel is only three miles from Junction 1 of the M27 and is set in ancient woodland with 30 acres of glades, lawns and shrubbery to enjoy. Ideal for country walks and horse riding. A short drive from many places of interest including Salisbury, Stonehenge, Winchester and Beaulieu. All bedrooms have en suite bathrooms and some have antique four-poster beds. Cosy public bar and restaurant. Snooker room. A warm friendly welcome and good home cooking assured.

Three day special breaks, weekly terms, daily rates — please phone for details.

In the heart of the New Forest - **THE WATERSPLASH HOTEL**
The Rise, Brockenhurst SO42 7ZP • Tel: 01590 622344

Prestigious family-run country house hotel set in large garden. Noted for fine personal service, accommodation and traditional English cuisine at its best. All rooms en suite. Luxury four-poster with double spa bath. Swimming pool. Short walk to open forest. **AA ★★**. Colour brochure available.

e-mail: bookings@watersplash.co.uk • www.watersplash.co.uk

ST. URSULA

30 Hobart Road, New Milton, Hants. BH25 6EG

Between sea and New Forest, comfortable family home. Excellent facilities & warm welcome for well behaved pets and owners. Ground floor suite suitable for disabled guests plus single and twin rooms.

Mrs Judith Pearce B&B from £27.50 Tel: 01425 613515

Petersfield, Ringwood

LANGRISH HOUSE *Langrish, Petersfield GU32 1RN*
Tel: 01730 266941
e-mail: frontdesk@langrishhouse.co.uk • www.langrishhouse.co.uk

17th century house in idyllic country location.
All bedrooms en suite and non-smoking. Award-winning restaurant; weddings and conferences catered for.

AA ★★★ HOTEL

Little Forest Lodge

Poulner Hill, Ringwood, Hampshire BH24 3HS

A warm welcome to you and your pets at this charming Edwardian house set in two acres of woodland. The six en suite bedrooms are pleasantly decorated and equipped with thoughtful extras. Both the attractive wood-panelled dining room and the delightful lounge, with bar and wood-burning fire, overlook the gardens. The Lodge is in an ideal location for exploring the ancient New Forest, historic Wessex, and the nearby sandy beaches. All well behaved dogs welcome.

AA ★★★★ Guest House

Tel: 01425 478848 • Fax: 01425 473564

The High Corner Inn is set deep in the heart of The New Forest in seven beautiful acres of woodland, ideal for long forest walks. Seven en suite bedrooms; two oak-beamed bars with views across the patio and garden; outdoor adventure playground for children. Good choice of real ales, wines and spirits, quality home-cooked meals, Sunday carvery. Dogs and well behaved owners welcome throughout the inn and in the letting rooms, but horses must use our stables or paddocks.
Linwood, Ringwood, Hants BH24 3QY • Tel: 01425 473973 • Fax: 01425 483052

Lymington

Residential town and yachting centre 15 miles east of Bournemouth.

HONEYSUCKLE HOUSE, 24 CLINTON ROAD, LYMINGTON SO41 9EA (01590 676635). Ground floor double room/single, en suite, non-smoking. Woodland walk, park, quay and marinas nearby. B&B from £30.00 pppn. []
e-mail: paula.farrell@dsl.pipex.com
website: http://explorethenewforest.co.uk/honeysuckle.htm

MRS P. J. ELLIS, EFFORD COTTAGE, EVERTON, LYMINGTON SO41 0JD (01590 642315; Fax: 01590 641030). Outstanding B&B with old world charm in proprietor's own Georgian home. Excellent touring centre for New Forest and South Coast. All rooms en suite with luxury facilities. B&B from £25-£35pppn. No children. AA ★★★★, Michelin. [PW! Pets from £2 per night]
e-mail: effordcottage@aol.com website: www.effordcottage.co.uk

Lyndhurst

Good base for enjoying the fascinating New Forest as well as the Hampshire coastal resorts. Bournemouth 20 miles, Southampton 9.

ORMONDE HOUSE HOTEL, SOUTHAMPTON ROAD, LYNDHURST SO43 7BT (023 8028 2806, Fax: 023 8028 2004). Opposite open forest, easy drive to Exbury Gardens and Beaulieu. Elegant, family-run Two Star Hotel with pretty, en suite rooms with CTV, phone and beverage making. Superior rooms and ground floor suites, all with kingsize bed and some with whirlpool bath. Bar, lounge and delicious dinners available. AA ★★. [Pets £3.50 per night, max. 2 per room]
e-mail: enquiries@ormondehouse.co.uk website: www.ormondehouse.co.uk

THE CROWN HOTEL, LYNDHURST, NEW FOREST S043 7NF (023 8028 2922; Fax: 023 8028 2751). A mellow, Listed building in the centre of the village, an ideal base for exploring the delights of the New Forest with your canine friend(s). Free parking, quiet garden, three star luxury and animal loving staff. [Pets £5.00 per night].
e-mail: reception@crownhotel-lyndhurst.co.uk website: www.crownhotel-lyndhurst.co.uk

New Forest

Area of heath and woodland of nearly 150 square miles, formerly Royal hunting grounds.

MRS E.E. MATTHEWS, THE ACORNS, OGDENS, NEAR FORDINGBRIDGE SP6 2PY (01425 655552). Luxury two bedroomed residential-type caravan. Sleeps 4/6. Maintained to high standard, kitchen, showeroom, sitting/diningroom, outside laundry area, own garden. Lovely New Forest setting. Non-smoking, ample parking. Children over five years. Well-behaved dogs welcome (max. 2). Terms £195 - £375, Easter to mid-October. [pw! Pets £12 each per week].
e-mail: acornshols@btopenworld.com website: www.dogscome2.co.uk

GORSE COTTAGE, BALMER LAWN ROAD, BROCKENHURST. Cottage/bungalow on open forest road close to village in New Forest. Sleeps 4 in 2 bedrooms. Conservatory, luxury bathroom, log fire, TV/Sky/DVD, secluded sunny garden. Pets welcome. Contact: MRS E. GILBERT (0870 3210020.) ETC ★★★★ [Pets £15 per week]
e-mail: info@gorsecottage.co.uk website: www.gorsecottage.co.uk

NEW FOREST - HIGHFIELDS COTTAGE. Charming, secluded cottage. Quiet country hamlet. Great walks. Pets welcome. Sleeps 2+2. Tel: 01425 471372 . [Pets £25 per week]
e-mail: 07enquiries@highfields-cottage.co.uk website: www.highfields-cottage.co.uk

BRAMBLE HILL HOTEL, BRAMSHAW, NEW FOREST SO43 7JG (023 80 813165). Peacefully located in ancient woodland with 30 acres of glades, lawns and shrubbery to enjoy. Ideal for country walks and horse riding. A short drive from Salisbury, Stonehenge, Winchester and Beaulieu. ETC ★★ [🐕]
website: www.bramblehill.co.uk

THE WATERSPLASH HOTEL, THE RISE, BROCKENHURST SO42 7ZP (01590 622344). Prestigious New Forest family-run country house hotel set in large garden. Noted for fine personal service, accommodation and traditional English cuisine at its best. All rooms en suite. Luxury four-poster with double spa bath. Swimming pool. Short walk to open forest. AA ★★ Colour brochure available. [Pets from £4 per night.]
e-mail: bookings@watersplash.co.uk website: www.watersplash.co.uk

MRS J. PEARCE, ST. URSULA, 30 HOBART ROAD, NEW MILTON BH25 6EG (01425 613515). Excellent facilities and warm welcome for well behaved pets and owners! Ground floor suite suitable for disabled guests, plus single and twin rooms. Bed & Breakfast from £27.50. [🐕]

Petersfield

Market town situated on the northern border of the South Downs within an Area of Outstanding Natural Beauty, 11 miles north east of Portsmouth.

LANGRISH HOUSE, LANGRISH, PETERSFIELD GU32 1RN (01730 266941).17th century house in idyllic country location. All bedrooms en suite. Small, cosy restaurant; weddings and conferences catered for. AA ★★★ and Two Rosettes for Fine Dining. [Pets £10 per night]
e-mail: frontdesk@langrishhouse.co.uk website: www.langrishhouse.co.uk

Ringwood

Busy market town, centre for trout fishing, trekking and rambling. Bournemouth 13 miles.

LITTLE FOREST LODGE, POULNER HILL, RINGWOOD BH24 3HS (01425 478848; Fax: 01425 473564). A warm welcome to you and your pets at this charming Edwardian house set in two acres of woodland. Six en suite bedrooms. All well behaved dogs welcome. AA ★★★★ Guest House. [Pets £5 per night].

DAVID SATCHELL, THE HIGH CORNER INN, LINWOOD, RINGWOOD, HANTS BH24 3QY (01425 473973, Fax: 01425 483052). Seven en suite bedrooms deep in the heart of The New Forest. Real ales, home-cooked food, Sunday carvery and log fires. Pets welcome. [🐕]

A useful index of towns/counties appears at the back of this book

ISLAND COTTAGE HOLIDAYS

ETC ★★★ to ★★★★★

Charming individual cottages in lovely rural surroundings and close to the sea. Over 55 cottages situated throughout the Isle of Wight. Beautiful views, attractive gardens, delightful country walks.

All equipped to a high standard and graded for quality by the Tourist Board.

For a brochure please **Tel: (01929) 480080**

e-mail: enq@islandcottageholidays.com • www.islandcottageholidays.com

Open all year (Sleep 1 - 12) £185 – £1495 per week. Short breaks available in low season (3 nights) £155 – £399

Bonchurch, Cowes, Freshwater

ASHCLIFF HOLIDAY APARTMENT

Bonchurch, Isle of Wight PO38 1NT

Idyllic and secluded position in the picturesque seaside village of Bonchurch. Self-contained ground floor apartment (sleeps 2) adjoining Victorian house, set in large south-facing gardens with sea views and sheltered by a thickly wooded cliff. Large, private car park. ETC ★★★. Dogs very welcome. ***For free brochure Tel: (01983) 853919***

ACTUALLY ON THE BEACH

"The Waterfall", Shore Road, Bonchurch, Ventnor, I.O.W. PO38 1RN

Ground-floor self-contained flat. Sleeps 3 adults. Fully equipped. Parking. Sun verandah and Garden.

Brochure from **Mrs A. Evans** **e-mail: benbrook.charioteer@virgin.net** **Tel: 01983 852246**

MEMBER Isle of Wight TOURISM

SUNNYCOTT CARAVAN PARK

COWES • ISLE OF WIGHT

GRADED HOLIDAY PARKS BRITISH

Small, quiet, family-run country park in rural surroundings close to Cowes. All caravans have full cooker, microwave, fridge and colour TV. Shop and laundry room on site. We welcome your pets. Short breaks can be arranged subject to availability.

Phone 01983 292859 for brochure • Proprietors: Jennifer Payne and Jim Payne
www.sunnycottcaravanpark.co.uk • e-mail: info@sunnycottcaravanpark.co.uk

A peaceful and beautiful 19th century rectory set in two-and-a-half acres of lovely gardens, just two minutes' drive from Freshwater Bay. Good area for walking, golfing, sailing, paragliding and bird watching. Close to National Trust areas. Double and family rooms, all en suite. TV lounge, log fires. Children and pets welcome.

B&B pppn: £28-£33 depending on season. Children ½ price.

Mr and Mrs B. Moscoff, Seahorses, Victoria Road, Freshwater PO40 9PP
Tel/Fax: 01983 752574 • e-mail: seahorses-iow@tiscali.co.uk • www.seahorsesisleofwight.com

Seaview

The Country House Hotel by the Sea

THE PRIORY BAY HOTEL

**Priory Drive,
Seaview,
Isle of Wight
PO34 5BU
Tel: 01983 613146
Fax: 01983 616539**

On a site once occupied by medieval monks, Tudor farmers and Georgian gentry, this tranquil retreat now comprises a medley of historic buildings that have been delightfully restored with the requirements of today's discerning holidaymaker in mind.

Set in a picturesque 70-acre estate which incorporates a unique 6-hole golf course, it is a short stroll to the lovely sandy expanse of Priory Bay, whilst in the grounds there is an all-weather tennis court and a croquet lawn. Stylish furnishings feature in the lounges and en suite guest rooms, all of which boast the finest decor.

The excellent chef-inspired cuisine makes full use of local produce, fish being a speciality.

AA ★★★

**e-mail: enquiries@priorybay.co.uk
www.priorybay.co.uk**

**4 Chine Avenue,
Shanklin Old Village,
Isle of Wight PO37 6AQ**

BEDFORD LODGE

Nestled in the heart of the Old Village, we are close to quaint shops and thatched pubs. We have 12 standard en suite rooms and two Premier rooms. We warmly welcome dog owners, and our ground floor rooms have access directly into our private gardens. The park is opposite and the beach is at the end of the road. We have a guest car park and a licensed bar.

AA ★★★ Guest Accommodation

**Tel: 01983 862416 • e-mail: mail@bedfordlodge.co.uk
www.bedfordlodge.co.uk**

❖ HAYES BARTON ❖

7 Highfield Road, Shanklin, Isle of Wight PO37 6PP

Hayes Barton has the relaxed atmosphere of a family home, with well equipped en suite bedrooms and comfortable public areas. Dinner is available from a selection of home-cooked dishes and there is a comfortable guests' lounge. The old village, beach and promenade are all within walking distance. Pets welcome in bedrooms and public areas but not dining room. Parking.

★★★★ GUEST ACCOMMODATION

**Tel: 01983 867747 • Fax: 01983 862104
e-mail: williams.2000@virgin.net • www.hayesbarton.co.uk**

The Country Garden Hotel

Church Hill, Totland Bay, Isle of Wight PO39 0ET

A five minute stroll to the Solent, surrounded by lovely walks and hikes including Tennyson Downs and The Needles, and a short drive to the bustling port of Yarmouth. Set in lovely gardens, this quiet and intimate hotel offers the best of all worlds for your holiday, including making your pet feel welcome! Excellent cuisine from our Chef in our locally popular restaurant overlooking the gardens. Garden, sea view and ground floor rooms available, all en suite with colour TV, fridge, duvets, down pillows, bathrobes, phone, central heating, hairdryer, tea & coffee and ample off-street parking.

ANY DAY TO ANY DAY, B&B or HALF BOARD • **ADULTS ONLY**
Ferry inclusive rates October through April
For brochure, sample menu, tariff, and testimonials from recent guests, please

**Phone/Fax: 01983 754 521
e-mail: countrygardeniow@aol.com
www.thecountrygardenhotel.co.uk**

Totland Bay, Ventnor, Yarmouth

SENTRY MEAD HOTEL

Madeira Road, Totland Bay PO39 0BJ
Tel: 01983 753212 • Fax: 01983 754710
e-mail: info@sentrymead.co.uk • www.sentrymead.co.uk
"....a jewel in the crown of the West Wight"

Westfield Lodges & Apartments

Bonchurch, Isle of Wight • www.westfieldlodges.co.uk

Situated in the peaceful and historic village of Bonchurch on the south west coast of the Island. On a quiet, private site five minutes from the beach. Open all year.

Tel: 01983 852268 • Fax: 01983 853992 • e-mail: mail@westfieldlodges.co.uk

Little Span Farm *Farmhouse B&B and Self-Catering Cottages*

Rew Lane, Wroxall, Ventnor, Isle of Wight PO38 3AU

Arable and sheep farm in an Area of Outstanding Natural Beauty, close to footpaths and holiday attractions. Ideal for family holidays. B&B in farmhouse from £25 pppn or Self-Catering Cottages from £225-£725 per week. Dogs welcome – 2 private kennels with inside and outside runs.

Tel/Fax: 01983 852419 • E-mail: info@spanfarm.co.uk • www.spanfarm.co.uk • Freephone 0800 2985819

ISLE OF WIGHT · Nr YARMOUTH

the Orchards

HOLIDAY CARAVAN & CAMPING PARK

- Indoor pool (open all year)
- Outdoor pool
- Luxury holiday caravans most with central heating
- Dog excercise areas
- 3/4 Day Mini Breaks
- Excellent facilities for caravanners and camp
- Special Ferry Deals
- Excellent walking and cycling from the park.

OPEN CHRISTMAS AND NEW YEAR

AA Premier Park · The Caravan Club Affiliated Site

www.orchards-holiday-park.co.uk t. 01983 531331

ISLAND COTTAGE HOLIDAYS. Charming individual cottages in lovely rural surroundings and close to the sea. Over 55 cottages situated throughout the Isle of Wight. Beautiful views, attractive gardens, delightful country walks. All equipped to a high standard and graded for quality by the Tourist Board. For a brochure please telephone 01929 480080. ETC ★★★ to ★★★★★.
e-mail: enq@islandcottageholidays.com website: www.islandcottageholidays.com

Bonchurch

One mile north-east of Ventnor.

MRS J. LINES, ASHCLIFF HOLIDAY APARTMENT, BONCHURCH PO38 1NT (01983 853919). Self-contained ground floor apartment (sleeps 2) adjoining Victorian house. Large south-facing gardens. Sea views. Large private car park. Pets welcome to use garden. ETC ★★★★ [🐕]

A. EVANS, "THE WATERFALL", SHORE ROAD, BONCHURCH, VENTNOR PO38 1RN (01983 852246). Spacious, self-contained Flat. Sleeps 3 adults. Colour TV. Sun verandah and garden. The beach, the sea and the downs. [🐕]
e-mail: benbrook.charioteer@virgin.net

Cowes

Yachting centre with yearly regatta since 1814. Newport 4 miles.

SUNNYCOTT CARAVAN PARK, COWES PO31 8NN (01983 292859). Small, quiet, family-run park close to Cowes. All caravans have full cooker, microwave, fridge and colour TV. Shop and laundry room on site. We welcome pets. Short breaks arranged. ETC ★★★★ [Pets £20 per week]
e-mail: info@sunnycottcaravanpark.co.uk website: www.sunnycottcaravanpark.co.uk

Freshwater

Two kilometres south of Totland. South-west of Farringford, formerly the home of Tennyson.

MR AND MRS B. MOSCOFF, SEAHORSES, VICTORIA ROAD, FRESHWATER PO40 9PP (Tel & Fax: 01983 752574). Peaceful 19th century rectory set in two-and-a-half acres of lovely gardens. Good area for walking, golfing, sailing, paragliding and bird watching. Double and family rooms, all en suite. TV lounge, log fires. B&B pppn: £28 - £33 depending on season. Children half price. [pw!]
e-mail: seahorses-iow@tiscali.co.uk website: www.seahorsesisleofwight.com

Seaview

Seaside village with sandy beach, narrow streets and white-washed cottages. One and a half miles from Ryde.

THE PRIORY BAY HOTEL, PRIORY DRIVE, SEAVIEW PO34 5BU (01983 613146; Fax: 01983 616539). Set in a picturesque 70-acre estate with a 6-hole golf course, all-weather tennis court and croquet lawn. Stylish furnishings feature in the lounges and en suite guest rooms. Cuisine makes full use of local produce, fish being a speciality. AA ★★★ and Rosette
e-mail: enquiries@priorybay.co.uk website: www.priorybay.co.uk

Shanklin

Resort on Sandown Bay, 7 miles SE of Newport

THE BEDFORD LODGE HOTEL, 4 CHINE AVENUE, SHANKLIN OLD VILLAGE PO37 6AQ (01983 862416; Fax: 01983 868704). Set in delightful gardens with easy access to both the Old Village and the beach. All bedrooms (some ground floor) are en suite with tea/coffee making facilities, central heating and TV. Licensed bar. Private car park. Car ferry crossings can be arranged.
e-mail: mail@bedfordlodge.co.uk website: www.bedfordlodge.co.uk

MRS J. WILLIAMS, HAYES BARTON, 7 HIGHFIELD ROAD, SHANKLIN PO37 6PP (01983 867747; Fax: 01983 862104). Relaxed family home with well equipped bedrooms and comfortable public areas. Old village, beach and promenade within walking distance. Parking. [pw! Pets £3.50 per night, £22 per week].
e-mail: williams.2000@virgin.net website: www.hayesbarton.co.uk

Totland Bay

Small resort 3 miles south-west of Yarmouth Bay.

COUNTRY GARDEN HOTEL, CHURCH HILL, TOTLAND BAY PO39 OET (Tel & Fax: 01983 754521). All en suite, garden and seaview rooms available; TV, phone, duvets, feather/down pillows, fridge, hairdryer etc. Special winter, spring, autumn rates. [pw! Pets £4 per day]
e-mail: countrygardeniow@aol.com website: www.thecountrygardenhotel.co.uk

SENTRY MEAD HOTEL, MADEIRA ROAD, TOTLAND BAY PO39 0BJ (01983 753212; Fax: 01983 754710). This beautiful Victorian villa is set in its own spacious gardens in the tranquil surroundings of West Wight. Just 150 yards from the beach, and with scenic downland walks on the doorstep, this is the perfect place to relax and unwind. All bedrooms en suite. ETC/AA ★★★ Silver Award [Pets £3 per day, £15 per week]
e-mail: info@sentrymead.co.uk website: www.sentrymead.co.uk

Ventnor

Well-known resort with good sands, downs, popular as a winter holiday resort. Nearby is St Boniface Down, the highest point on the island. Ryde 13 miles, Newport 12, Sandown 7, Shanklin 4.

WESTFIELD LODGES & APARTMENTS, BONCHURCH, ISLE OF WIGHT, (01983 852268; Fax: 01983 853992). Situated in the peaceful and historic village of Bonchurch on the south west coast of the Island. On a quiet, private site five minutes from the beach. Open all year. ETC ★★★/★★★★ Self-Catering. [Pets £35 per week]
e-mail:mail@westfieldlodges.co.uk website: www.westfieldlodges.co.uk

MRS F. CORRY, LITTLE SPAN FARM, REW LANE, WROXALL, VENTNOR PO38 3AU (Tel/Fax: 01983 852419, Freephone 0800 2985819). Working farm in an Area of Outstanding Natural Beauty, close to footpaths and holiday attractions. Ideal for family holidays. B&B in farmhouse from £25 pppn or Self-Catering Cottages from £225-£725 per week. Dogs welcome. [Pets £3 per night, £20 per week].
e-mail: info@spanfarm.co.uk website: www.spanfarm.co.uk

Yarmouth

Coastal resort situated 9 miles west of Newport. Castle built by Henry VIII for coastal defence.

THE ORCHARDS HOLIDAY CARAVAN & CAMPING PARK, NEWBRIDGE, YARMOUTH PO41 0TS (Dial-a-brochure 01983 531331; Fax: 01983 531666). Luxury holiday caravans, most with central heating and double glazing. Excellent facilities including indoor pool with licensed cafe. Dog exercise areas. Ideal walking, cycling and golf. Open late February to New Year. located in an Area of Outstanding Natural Beauty. Spectacular views.[Pets £1/£2.50 per night]
e-mail: info@orchards-holiday-park.co.uk website:www.orchards-holiday-park.co.uk

Other specialised holiday guides from FHG

PUBS & INNS OF BRITAIN • **COUNTRY HOTELS** OF BRITAIN
WEEKEND & SHORT BREAK HOLIDAYS IN BRITAIN
THE GOLF GUIDE WHERE TO PLAY, WHERE TO STAY
500 GREAT PLACES TO STAY • **SELF-CATERING HOLIDAYS** IN BRITAIN
BED & BREAKFAST STOPS • **CARAVAN & CAMPING HOLIDAYS**
FAMILY BREAKS IN BRITAIN

Published annually: available in all good bookshops or direct from the publisher:
FHG Guides, Abbey Mill Business Centre, Seedhill, Paisley PA1 1TJ
Tel: 0141 887 0428 • Fax: 0141 889 7204
e-mail: admin@fhguides.co.uk • www.holidayguides.com

Pet-Friendly
Pubs, Inns & Hotels
on pages 424-432
Please note that these establishments may not feature in the main section of this book

Garden of England Cottages

www.goec.co.uk

Accommodation for all seasons

BIG PAWS and LITTLE PAWS ARE WELCOME and GO FREE with every well-behaved owner.

ON-LINE BOOKING & AVAILABILITY Tel: +44 [0] 1892 510117

e-mail: holidays@gardenofenglandcottages.co.uk

All our properties are VisitBritain quality assured.

Ashford, Broadstairs, Canterbury, Chilham, Deal

Luxury pine lodges, superior self-catering accommodation overlooking two lakes in beautiful Kent countryside. Rough shooting and coarse fishing on our farms. Weeks or short breaks. Contact:

ASHBY FARMS LTD, PLACE FARM, KENARDINGTON, ASHFORD TN26 2LZ • Tel: 01233 733332 • Fax: 01233 733326

e-mail: info@ashbyfarms.com • www.ashbyfarms.com

THE HANSON (Lic.) **41 Belvedere Road, Broadstairs CT10 1PF**

A small friendly Georgian hotel with relaxed atmosphere, centrally situated for beach, shops and transport. B&B only or, renowned for excellent food, we offer a 5-course Evening Dinner with choice of menu.

Children and pets welcome • Open all year • Spring and Winter Breaks

Tel: (01843) 868936 www.hansonhotel.co.uk

TREVOR & JEAN HAVE OVER 25 YEARS OF WELCOMING GUESTS

Within four acres of gardens in a delightful rural setting surrounded by orchards. Four converted two-bedroom cottages, sleeping four to five, one suitable for wheelchairs. Ideally situated for touring, cycling, walking, relaxing and exploring the Kent coastline. All bedlinen and towels provided. Children's play field and equipment. Ample parking. Pets welcome by arrangement. Contact **Doreen Ady**.

Hawthorn Farm Cottages • Ware, near Sandwich • ETC ★★★/★★★★

Tel: 01304 813560 • E-mail: hawthornfarmcottages@dsl.pipex.com • www.hawthornfarmcottages.co.uk

★★★★ SELF CATERING

The Smithy, Chilham, Canterbury

Charming Grade II Listed cottage in picturesque village on North Downs Way near Canterbury. Fully furnished to a very high standard, with open fireplace and oak beams. Walking distance to village shop and pubs. Short Breaks available Oct-April. *Contact Christian:*

Tel: 020 8979 2530 • info@smithy-cottage.com • www.smithy-cottage.com

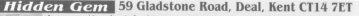

Hidden Gem **59 Gladstone Road, Deal, Kent CT14 7ET**

A serene and luxuriously furnished and equipped one bedroom bungalow, with gas central heating, a secure private garden and off-street parking. Situated in a delightful side street next to Deal Castle, the beach, the lively and picturesque seaside town of Deal and endless beach and country walks. Sleeps 2 • No smoking • Pets welcome FREE

For details please tel Lucy on: 07590 756833 or email via the website www.selfcatering-deal.co.uk

Folkestone, St Margaret's Bay

Wycliffe Hotel • Tel & Fax: 01303 252186

63 Bouverie Road West, Folkestone CT20 2RN

A warm welcome guaranteed at our friendly, family hotel. Clean, comfortable and affordable. Based centrally and are close to all amenities. Conveniently situated just a short distance from the Channel Tunnel and the port of Dover. Off-street parking. Please write or call for our brochure. Pets and Children welcome.

e-mail: sapsford@wycliffehotel.freeserve.co.uk • www.wycliffehotel.com

REACH COURT FARM COTTAGES

REACH COURT FARM, ST MARGARET'S BAY, DOVER CT15 6AQ

Tel & Fax: 01304 852159

Situated in the heart of the Mitchell family farm, surrounded by open countryside. Five luxury self-contained cottages set around the old farmyard, with open views of the rural valley both front and back.

e-mail: enquiries@reachcourtfarmcottages.co.uk

www.reachcourtfarmcottages.co.uk

GARDEN OF ENGLAND COTTAGES IN KENT & SUSSEX, CLAYFIELD HOUSE, 50 ST JOHNS ROAD, TUNBRIDGE WELLS, KENT TN4 9NY (01892 510117). Pets welcome in many of our holiday homes and go free. All properties VisitBritain quality assured. On-line booking and availability. [🐕]
e-mail: holidays@gardenofenglandcottages.co.uk website: www.goec.co.uk

Ashford

Market town on Great Stour River, 13 miles south-west of Canterbury.

Luxury pine lodges, superior self-catering accommodation overlooking two lakes in beautiful Kent countryside. Rough shooting and coarse fishing on our farms. Weeks or short breaks. Contact: ASHBY FARMS LTD, PLACE FARM, KENARDINGTON, ASHFORD TN26 2LZ (01233 733332; Fax: 01233 733326). [Pets £10 per stay]
e-mail: info@ashbyfarms.com website: www.ashbyfarms.com

Broadstairs

Quiet resort, once a favourite of Charles Dickens. Good sands and promenade.

THE HANSON, 41 BELVEDERE ROAD, BROADSTAIRS CT10 1PF (01843 868936). Small, friendly licensed Georgian Hotel. Home comforts; children and pets welcome. Attractive bar. SAE. [pw! Pets £1 per night, £5 per week]
website: www.hansonhotel.co.uk

Canterbury

Cathedral City on River Great Stour, 54 miles east of London..

DOREEN ADY, HAWTHORN FARM COTTAGES, WARE, NEAR SANDWICH (01304 813560). Four converted two-bedroom cottages, sleeping 4-5. Ideally situated for relaxing or exploring the Kent coastline. Children's play field. Ample parking. Pets welcome by arrangement. ETC ★★★/★★★★. [pw! Pets £20 per week]
e-mail: hawthornfarmcottages@dsl.pipex.com website: www.hawthornfarmcottages.co.uk

Chilham

Located in the valley of the River Great Stour, 6 miles east of Canterbury.

THE SMITHY. Charming Grade II Listed cottage in picturesque cottage on North Downs Way. Fully furnished to a very high standard. Walking distance to village shop and pubs. Short Breaks available Oct-April. ETC ★★★★ Contact Christian (020 8979 2530). [Pets £25 each per week]
e-mail: info@smithy-cottage.com website: www.smithy-cottage.com

Deal

Cinque Port and resort on East coast 8 miles N.E. of Dover.

HIDDEN GEM, 59 GLADSTONE ROAD, DEAL CT14 7ET. Luxuriously furnished one bedroom bungalow, with gas central heating, secure private garden and off-street parking. Near Deal Castle, the beach, the town, and endless beach and country walks. No smoking. For details please tel Lucy on: 07590 756833 or e-mail via the website. [🐕]
website: www.selfcatering-deal.co.uk

Folkestone

A traditional holiday resort and channel port, 14 miles east of Ashford.

WYCLIFFE HOTEL, 63 BOUVERIE ROAD WEST, FOLKESTONE CT20 2RN. (Tel & Fax: 01303 252186) Friendly, family hotel. Clean, comfortable and affordable. Based centrally and close to all amenities. A short distance from the Channel Tunnel and Dover. Off-street parking. Please write or call for our brochure. Pets and Children welcome.[Pets £3 per night].
e-mail: sapsford@wycliffehotel.freeserve.co.uk website: www.wycliffehotel.com

St Margaret's Bay

4 miles north-east of Dover

DEREK AND JACQUI MITCHELL, REACH COURT FARM COTTAGES, REACH COURT FARM, ST MARGARET'S BAY, DOVER CT15 6AQ (Tel & Fax: 01304 852159). Situated in the heart of the Mitchell family farm, surrounded by open countryside, these five luxury self-contained cottages are very special. The cottages are set around the old farmyard, which has been attractively set to lawns and shrubs, with open views of the rural valley both front and back.
e-mail: enquiries@reachcourtfarmcottages.co.uk website: www.reachcourtfarmcottages.co.uk

Looking for Holiday Accommodation?

FHG
K·U·P·E·R·A·R·D

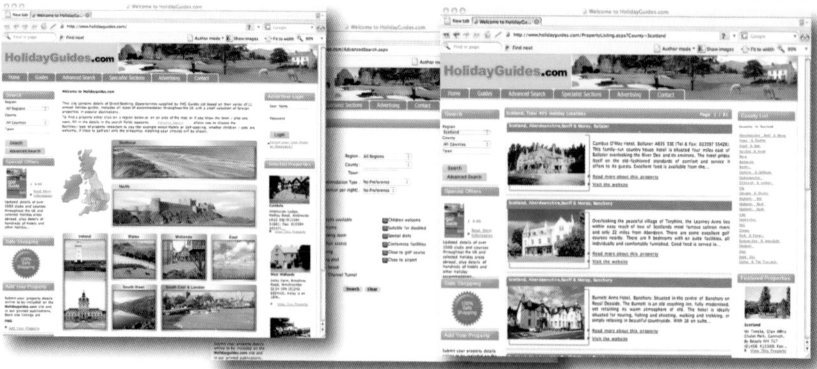

for details of hundreds of properties throughout the UK, visit our website

www.holidayguides.com

Burford, Oxford

The Inn for all Seasons

AA ★★★ AA

Dog owners themselves, Matthew and Heather Sharp extend a warm welcome to others who wish to bring their pets to visit the Cotswolds and stay in a genuinely dog-friendly Inn with dedicated ground floor rooms with direct access to gardens, exercise area and country walks. The Inn for all Seasons is a family-owned and run ★★★ Hotel based on a traditional 16th century English Coaching Inn. Character en suite bedrooms, inglenooks, log fires and a genuinely friendly inn atmosphere provide the perfect setting to enjoy a Rosetted menu prepared by Chef/Proprietor, Matthew, and his English-led kitchen team. An ideal base for touring, walking, garden visiting.

B&B from £65.00pppn • Dinner, B&B from £70.00pppn.

The Barringtons,
Near Burford, Oxfordshire OX18 4TN
Tel: 01451 844324
e-mail: sharp@innforallseasons.com
www.innforallseasons.com

Nanford Guest House *Period guest house located five minutes on foot from the University of Oxford. Wide range and number of rooms, all with private shower and toilet.*

MR B. CRONIN, NANFORD GUEST HOUSE, 137 IFFLEY ROAD, OXFORD OX4 1EJ
Tel: 01865 244743 • Fax: 01865 249596
e-mail: b.cronin@btinternet.com • www.nanfordguesthouse.com

Burford

Small Cotswold Town on River Windrush, 7 miles west of Witney.

THE INN FOR ALL SEASONS, THE BARRINGTONS, NEAR BURFORD OX18 4TN (01451 844324). Family-run and owned Hotel based on traditional 16th century English Coaching Inn. Ideal base for touring, walking and garden visiting. From £70.00pppn DB&B. [pw! Pets £5 per night, £25 per week]
e-mail: sharp@innforallseasons.com website: www.innforallseasons.com

Oxford

City 52 miles from London. University dating from 13th century. Many notable buildings.

MR B. CRONIN, NANFORD GUEST HOUSE, 137 IFFLEY ROAD, OXFORD OX4 1EJ (01865 244743; Fax: 01865 249596). Period guest house located five minutes on foot from the University of Oxford. Wide range and number of rooms, all with private shower and toilet. [🐕]
e-mail: b.cronin@btinternet.com website: www.nanfordguesthouse.com

Tackley/Kidlington

Village 3 miles north-east of Woodstock; approximately 5 miles north of Oxford.

JUNE AND GEORGE COLLIER, 55 NETHERCOTE ROAD, TACKLEY, KIDLINGTON, OXFORD OX5 3AT (01869 331255; mobile: 07790 338225). Bed and Breakfast in Tackley. An ideal base for touring, walking, cycling and riding. Central for Oxford, The Cotswolds, Stratford-on-Avon, Blenheim Palace. Woodstock four miles. There is a regular train and bus service with local Hostelries serving excellent food. ETC ★★★ [🐕 ⌂]
website: www.colliersbnb.co.uk

Please mention **Pets Welcome!**
when making enquiries about accommodation featured in these pages

★★★

Chase Lodge Hotel
An Award Winning Hotel
with style & elegance, set in tranquil surroundings at affordable prices.
10 Park Road Hampton Wick Kingston-Upon-Thames KT1 4AS
Tel: 020 8943 1862 . Fax: 020 8943 9363
E-mail: info@chaselodgehotel.com Web: www.chaselodgehotel.com & www.surreyhotels.com

Pets welcome

Quality en suite bedrooms
Close to Bushy Park
Buffet-style Full Continental Breakfast

Licensed bar
Wedding Receptions
Honeymoon suite
available with jacuzzi & steam area
20 minutes from Heathrow Airport
Close to Kingston town centre & all major transport links.

All Major Credit Cards Accepted

The Hurtwood Inn Hotel
Tel: 01306 730851
Fax: 01306 731390
In the heart of the Surrey Hills, this family-run privately owned hotel is ideally placed to explore some of England's finest countryside. 21 tastefully furnished en suite bedrooms, bar, restaurant. Weddings and functions catered for.
Walking Bottom, Peaslake, Near Guildford, Surrey GU5 9RR
e-mail: sales@hurtwoodinnhotel.com • www.hurtwoodinnhotel.com

Kingston-upon-Thames

Market town, Royal borough and administrative centre of Surrey. Kingston is ideally placed for London and environs.

CHASE LODGE HOTEL, 10 PARK ROAD, HAMPTON WICK, KINGSTON-UPON-THAMES KT1 4AS (020 8943 1862; Fax: 020 8943 9363). Award-winning hotel offering quality en suite bedrooms. Easy access to town centre and major transport links. Licensed bar. ETC/AA ◆◆◆◆ [pets]
e-mail: info@chaselodgehotel.com websites: www.chaselodgehotel.com & www.surreyhotels.com

Peaslake

Village 4 miles north of Cranleigh.

THE HURTWOOD INN HOTEL, WALKING BOTTOM, PEASLAKE, NEAR GUILDFORD GU5 9RR (01306 730851; Fax: 01306 731390). Privately run hotel with 21 en suite bedrooms, bar, restaurant; weddings and functions catered for. In heart of Surrey Hills, with miles of beautiful walks on the doorstep. ETC ★★★. [pets]
e-mail: sales@hurtwoodinnhotel.com website: www.hurtwoodinnhotel.com

Pet-Friendly
Pubs, Inns & Hotels
on pages 424-432
Please note that these establishments may not feature in the main section of this book

Battle, Brighton, Chiddingly, Fairlight, Rye

Beautiful secluded 18th century woodcutter's cottage, nestling in over 40 acres of its own rolling, lush East Sussex land. Surrounded by Forestry Commission woodland.

FOX HOLE FARM, KANE HYTHE ROAD, BATTLE TN33 9QU
Tel & Fax: 01424 772053

AA ★★★★ FARMHOUSE

BEST OF **Brighton & Sussex** COTTAGES

Quality Accredited Agency

+44 (0) 1273 308779
www.bestofbrighton.co.uk

- **Brighton & Hove**
- **Eastbourne**
- **Lewes**

A very good selection of houses, flats, apartments and cottages.

Town Centre, Seafront & Countryside locations – many taking pets (Pets £15/£30 per week)

Chiddingly, East Sussex • *Adorable, small, well-equipped cottage in grounds of Tudor Manor*

• Two bedrooms, sleeps 4-6 • Full kitchen and laundry facilities • Telephone • Use of indoor heated swimming pool, sauna/jacuzzi, tennis and badminton court • Large safe garden

From £410 – £775 per week inclusive • Pets and children welcome • Short Breaks £258-£360

Apply: Eva Morris, "Pekes", 124 Elm Park Mansions, Park Walk, London SW10 0AR

Tel: 020-7352 8088 • Fax: 020-7352 8125 • e-mail: pekes.afa@virgin.net • www.pekesmanor.com

FAIRLIGHT COTTAGE

Warren Road (via Coastguard Lane), Fairlight, East Sussex TN35 4AG

★★★★ GUEST ACCOMMODATION

Peace, tranquillity and a warm welcome await you at our comfortable country house, adjoining 650 acres of country park in an area of outstanding natural beauty – a paradise for dogs and owners. Panoramic sea views from large balcony. Centrally heated en suite bedrooms with beverage trays and colour TV. Comfortable guest lounge. Delicious breakfasts. No smoking. Ample parking. Pets stay with owners (free of charge). Badgers and foxes dine in the garden every evening.

B&B from £32.50pppn. • Single supplement

Janet & Ray Adams • 01424 812545 • e-mail: fairlightcottage@supanet.com

---

BRANDY'S COTTAGE

Mrs Jane Apperly, Cadborough Farm, Rye, East Sussex TN31 6AA
Tel: 01424 814823 • www.cadborough.co.uk • apperly@cadborough.co.uk

★★★★ SELF CATERING

Newly converted and sympathetically restored cottage provides luxurious and spacious accommodation for two people. Located one mile from Rye, close to 1066 Country walks. Facilities include TV/Video/Music Centre, full gas C/H, cooker/hob, microwave, washer/dryer, private courtyard with garden furniture and BBQ. Linen and towels incl. We accept one small well behaved dog and children over 12. Weekly rates from £225 low season to £395 high season. Short breaks available. Four other cottages also available. No Smoking.

★★★ AA & VB ★★★
VB Gold Award
Recommended by Condé Nast Johansens, Signpost and designated a *'Best Loved Hotel of the World'*

"A little Gem of an Hotel"

RYE LODGE

Luxury, elegance and charm in a relaxed atmosphere – Delicious candlelit dinners in the elegant, marbled floored Terrace Restaurant, fine wines and really caring service. Indoor Swimming Pool, Spa and Sauna, plus all the delights of the Ancient Cinque Port of Rye with its picturesque cobbled streets, historic buildings, antique shops, art galleries and old inns.

Short break package: 2 nights dinner, room and breakfast from £160

RYE LODGE HOTEL

'One of the finest small luxury hotels in the country'

HILDER'S CLIFF, RYE, EAST SUSSEX

Tel: 01797 223838 • Fax: 01797 223585
www.ryelodge.co.uk

JEAKE'S HOUSE
Mermaid Street, Rye, East Sussex TN31 7ET
Telephone: 01797 222828 Fax: 01797 222623
e-mail: stay@jeakeshouse.com • www.jeakeshouse.com
Dating from 1689, this beautiful Listed Building stands in one of England's most famous streets. Oak-beamed and panelled bedrooms overlook the marsh to the sea. Brass, mahogany, half-tester and four-poster beds; honeymoon suite; TV, radio, telephone. Book-lined bar. Residential licence. Traditional and vegetarian breakfast served. £45–£63pp. Private car park. Visa and Mastercard accepted.
Gold Gold Award
AA
PREMIER SELECTED
Good Hotel Guide César Award

BEACH COTTAGE • CLAREMONT ROAD, SEAFORD, EAST SUSSEX • BN25 2QQ
Well equipped, three-bedroomed terraced cottage on seafront. Sleeps 5. Central heating, open fire and woodburner. South-facing patio overlooking sea.
Downland walks (wonderful for dogs), fishing, golf, wind-surfing, etc.
Details from: Julia Lewis, 47 Wandle Bank, London SW19 1DW
Tel: 020 8542 5073 • e-mail: cottage@beachcottages.info • www.beachcottages.info

Battle

Town 6 miles NW of Hastings.

FOX HOLE FARM, KANE HYTHE ROAD, BATTLE TN33 9QU (Tel & Fax: 01424 772053). Beautiful secluded 18th century woodcutter's cottage, nestling in over 40 acres of its own rolling, lush East Sussex land. Surrounded by Forestry Commission woodland. AA ★★★★ [🐕]

Brighton

Famous resort with varied entertainment and night life, excellent shops and restaurants.

BEST OF BRIGHTON & SUSSEX COTTAGES has available a very good selection of houses, flats, apartments and cottages in Brighton and Hove, Eastbourne and Lewes. Town centre/seaside and countryside locations – many taking pets. (+44 (0)1273 308779). [Pets £15/£30 per week.]
website: www.bestofbrighton.co.uk

Chiddingly

Charming village, 4 miles north-west of Hailsham. Off the A22 London-Eastbourne road.

Adorable, small, well-equipped cottage in grounds of Tudor Manor. Two bedrooms, sleeps 4-6. Full central heating. Colour TV. Fridge/freezer, laundry facilities. Large safe garden. Use indoor heated swimming pool, sauna/jacuzzi and tennis. From £410 to £775 per week inclusive. ETC ★★★. Contact: EVA MORRIS, "PEKES", 124 ELM PARK MANSIONS, PARK WALK, LONDON SW10 0AR (020 7352 8088; Fax: 020 7352 8125). [2 dogs free, extra dog £7 (max. 4) pw!].
e-mail: pekes.afa@virgin.net website: www.pekesmanor.com

Fairlight

Village 3 miles east of Hastings

JANET & RAY ADAMS, FAIRLIGHT COTTAGE, WARREN ROAD, FAIRLIGHT TN35 4AG (01424 812545). Country house in idyllic location with clifftop walks. Tasteful en suite rooms, comfortable guest lounge. Delicious breakfasts. No smoking. Dogs stay with owners. ETC ★★★★ [🐕]
e-mail: fairlightcottage@supanet.com

Polegate

Quiet position, 5 miles from the popular seaside resort of Eastbourne. London 58 miles, Lewes 12.

MRS P. FIELD, 20 ST JOHN'S ROAD, POLEGATE BN26 5BP (01323 482691). Homely private house. Quiet location; large enclosed garden. Parking space. Ideally situated for walking on South Downs and Forestry Commission land. All rooms, washbasins and tea/coffee making facilities. Bed and Breakfast. Pets very welcome. [pw!]

Rye

Picturesque hill town with steep cobbled streets. Many fine buildings of historic interest. Hastings 12 miles, Tunbridge Wells 28.

FLACKLEY ASH HOTEL, PEASMARSH, RYE TN31 6YH (01797 230651). Georgian Country House Hotel in beautiful grounds. Indoor swimming pool and Leisure Centre. Beauty and massage. Visit Rye and the castles and gardens of East Sussex and Kent. AA ★★★ [Pets £8.50 per night]
e-mail: enquiries@flackleyashhotel.co.uk website: www.flackleyashhotel.co.uk

MRS JANE APPERLY, BRANDY'S COTTAGE, CADBOROUGH FARM, RYE TN31 6AA (01424 814823; Fax: 01797 224097).Newly converted cottage provides luxurious and spacious accommodation for two people. Private courtyard. One small well-behaved dog and children over 12 welcome. No-smoking. Short breaks available. ETC ★★★★ [ ]
e-mail: apperly@cadborough.co.uk website: www.cadborough.co.uk

RYE LODGE HOTEL, HILDER'S CLIFF, RYE TN31 7LD (01797 223838; Fax: 01797 223585). Luxury, elegance and charm in a relaxed atmosphere. Indoor swimming pool, spa and sauna. Delicious candlelit dinners in Terrace Restaurant. Ideal for exploring historic Rye. AA/VB ★★★ Gold Award
website: www.ryelodge.co.uk

JEAKE'S HOUSE, MERMAID STREET, RYE TN31 7ET (01797 222828; Fax: 01797 222623). Dating from 1689, this Listed building has oak-beamed and panelled bedrooms overlooking the marsh. TV, radio, telephone. Book-lined bar. £45-£63pp. ETC/AA ★★★★★ [Pets £5 per night]
e-mail: stay@jeakeshouse.com website: www.jeakeshouse.com

Seaford

On the coast midway between Newhaven and Beachy Head.

BEACH COTTAGE, CLAREMONT ROAD, SEAFORD BN25 2QQ. Well-equipped, three-bedroomed terraced cottage on seafront. CH, open fire and woodburner. South-facing patio overlooking sea. Downland walks (wonderful for dogs), fishing, golf, wind-surfing, etc. Details from JULIA LEWIS, 47 WANDLE BANK, LONDON SW19 1DW (020 8542 5073). [pw!]
e-mail: cottage@beachcottages.info website: www.beachcottages.info

Visit the FHG website

www.holidayguides.com

for details of the wide choice of accommodation

featured in the full range of FHG titles

Spire Cottage, built from the old spire of Chichester Cathedral that collapsed in 1861, is a Grade II Listed country cottage offering stylish bed and breakfast accommodation. Friendly, relaxed atmosphere, excellent facilities, village pub and two golf courses. Also available on a self-catering basis(sleeping 8). Please telephone for further details.

Jan & Andy, Spire Cottage, Church Lane, Hunston, Chichester PO20 1AJ
Tel: 01243 778937 • e-mail: jan@spirecottage.co.uk • www.spirecottage.co.uk

Wandleys Caravan Park

Eastergate, West Sussex PO20 3SE
Telephone: 01243 543235
or 01243 543384 (evenings/weekends)

You will find peace, tranquillity and relaxation in one of our comfortable holiday caravans. All have internal WC and shower. Dogs welcome. The Sussex Downs, Chichester, Bognor Regis, Arundel, Littlehampton – all these historic and interesting places are only 15 minutes from our beautiful, small and quiet country park. Telephone for brochure. New and used holiday homes for sale when available.

ETC/AA ★★★★

ST ANDREWS LODGE

Chichester Road, Selsey, West Sussex PO20 0LX
Tel: 01243 606899 • Fax: 01243 607826
e-mail: info@standrewslodge.co.uk
www.standrewslodge.co.uk

Welcome to St Andrews Lodge, the perfect place for a relaxing break. Situated in the small seaside town of Selsey and well located for Chichester and the South Downs; close to unspoilt beaches and 5 minutes from Pagham Harbour Nature Reserve. Enjoy our delicious breakfast and stay in one of our individually decorated rooms. All equipped with fridge, hospitality tray and ironing facilities. Rooms open on to our large garden to allow your dog to stretch his legs. No charge for dogs but donation to local nature reserve welcome. Licensed bar, wheelchair accessible room, large car park.

Please apply for brochure and details of our special winter offer.

Other specialised holiday guides from FHG

PUBS & INNS OF BRITAIN • **COUNTRY HOTELS** OF BRITAIN
WEEKEND & SHORT BREAK HOLIDAYS IN BRITAIN
THE GOLF GUIDE WHERE TO PLAY, WHERE TO STAY
500 GREAT PLACES TO STAY • **SELF-CATERING HOLIDAYS** IN BRITAIN
BED & BREAKFAST STOPS • **CARAVAN & CAMPING HOLIDAYS**
FAMILY BREAKS IN BRITAIN

Published annually: available in all good bookshops or direct from the publisher:
FHG Guides, Abbey Mill Business Centre, Seedhill, Paisley PA1 1TJ
Tel: 0141 887 0428 • Fax: 0141 889 7204
e-mail: admin@fhguides.co.uk • www.holidayguides.com

Chichester

County town 9 miles east of Havant. Town has cathedral and 16th century market cross.

SPIRE COTTAGE, CHURCH LANE, HUNSTON, CHICHESTER PO20 1AJ (01243 778937). Stylish bed and breakfast accommodation in a friendly and relaxed atmosphere. Excellent facilities. Village pub and two golf courses. [Dogs £5 per night]
e-mail: jan@spirecottage.co.uk website: www.spirecottage.co.uk

Eastergate

Village between the sea and South Downs. Fontwell Park nearby. Bognor Regis 5 miles south.

WANDLEYS CARAVAN PARK, EASTERGATE PO20 3SE (01243 543235 or 01243 543384 evenings/ weekends). You will find peace, tranquillity and relaxation in one of our comfortable holiday caravans. All have internal WC and shower. Dogs welcome. Many historic and interesting places nearby. Telephone for brochure. [🐕]

Pulborough

Town on River Arun 12 miles NW of Worthing.

BEACON LODGE, LONDON ROAD, WATERSFIELD, PULBOROUGH RH20 1NH (Tel & Fax: 01798 831026). Charming self-contained annexe. B&B accommodation, en suite, TV, coffee/tea making facilities. Wonderful countryside views. B&B from £65 per night, family room. Excellent for country walks. No charge for your pets! Telephone for more details. [🐕]
e-mail: gbwingfield@yahoo.co.uk website: www.beaconlodge.co.uk

Selsey

Seaside resort 8 miles south of Chichester. Selsey Bill is headland extending into the English Channel.

ST ANDREWS LODGE, CHICHESTER ROAD, SELSEY PO20 0LX (01243 606899; Fax: 01243 607826). 10 bedrooms, all en suite, with direct dial telephones and modem point, some on ground floor. Dining room overlooking garden; licensed bar for residents only. Wheelchair accessible room. Dogs welcome in rooms overlooking large garden. Apply for brochure and prices. ETC/AA ★★★★ [Pets £3 per stay (donation to local project)]
e-mail: info@standrewslodge.co.uk website: www.standrewslodge.co.uk

Pet-Friendly
Pubs, Inns & Hotels
on pages 424-432
Please note that these establishments may not feature in the main section of this book

THE MEADOW HOUSE • 2a High Street, Burwell, Cambridge CB5 0HB
Magnificent modern house set in two acres of wooded grounds offering superior Bed and Breakfast in spacious rooms, some with king-size beds. Variety of en suite accommodation catering for all requirements. All rooms have TV, central heating and tea/coffee facilities. Car parking. No smoking. Family rate available on request.
hilary@themeadowhouse.co.uk • www.themeadowhouse.co.uk
Tel: 01638 741926 • Fax: 01638 741861

The St Ives Motel London Road, St Ives, Huntingdon, Cambridgeshire PE27 5EX
Family-run hotel with 15 spacious en suite rooms, all non smoking, each with its own patio leading to the garden or orchard. Large bar area, evening meal available.
Tel: 01480 463857 • Fax: 01480 492027
E-mail: stivesmotel@btconnect.com • www.stivesmotel.co.uk

Burwell

One of the largest villages in Cambridgeshire, with over 60 listed buildings of interest, and the 15th century Church of St Mary's. Ideal area for walkers, fishing enthusiasts and nature lovers.

THE MEADOW HOUSE, 2A HIGH STREET, BURWELL, CAMBRIDGE CB5 0HB (01638 741926; Fax: 01638 741861). Modern house in two acres of wooded grounds offering superior Bed and Breakfast. Variety of en suite accommodation. All rooms have TV, central heating and tea/coffee facilities. No smoking. Family rate on request. ETC ★★★★
e-mail: hilary@themeadowhouse.co.uk website: www.themeadowhouse.co.uk

Ely

Magnificent Norman Cathedral dating from 1083. Ideal base for touring the fen country of East Anglia.

MRS C. H. BENNETT, STOCKYARD FARM, WISBECH ROAD, WELNEY PE14 9RQ (01354 610433; Fax: 01354 610422). Comfortable converted farmhouse, rurally situated between Ely and Wisbech. Conservatory breakfast room, TV lounge. Free range produce. Miles of riverside walks. No smoking. B&B from £22.50. [🐕 pw!]

St Ives

Ancient market town on the River Great Ouse, 15 miles north-west of Cambridge.

THE ST IVES MOTEL, LONDON ROAD, ST IVES, HUNTINGDON PE27 5EX (01480 463857; Fax: 01480 492027). Family-run hotel with 15 spacious en suite rooms, all non smoking, each with its own patio. Large bar area, evening meal available.
e-mail: stivesmotel@btconnect.com website: www.stivesmotel.co.uk

Please note

All the information in this book is given in good faith in the belief that it is correct. However, the publishers cannot guarantee the facts given in these pages, neither are they responsible for changes in policy, ownership or terms that may take place after the date of going to press. Readers should always satisfy themselves that the facilities they require are available and that the terms, if quoted, still apply.

*Take a Blue Riband Holiday in beautiful Norfolk and take a pet free**

***One pet stays free when you book through this advert. Extra pet £10**

Inexpensive Self Catering Holidays at ●Caister ●Hemsby ●Scratby ●Winterton ●California and ●Great Yarmouth All year round

Detached Bungalows at Parklands
Hemsby Village, Children's Playground, Digital Freeview TV, Miniature Railway.

Seafront Bungalows
Caister-on-Sea, with enclosed rear gardens leading to the beach.

Detached Chalets on Sea-Dell Park
Quiet location, Beach Road, Hemsby.

Belle Aire Park, Beach Rd, Hemsby
Super Chalets, Free electricity and Clubhouse. Safe children's playground. Pets are allowed on local beaches.

All equipped to very high standard

★ ***Free car parking at all locations***

Open Christmas & New Year

Quality, Value and Service from a family business, since 1955

- ***Popular low season breaks, bungalows from only £85***
- ***Bargain Spring & Autumn breaks, excellent value chalets from £70***

Blue Riband Holidays

☎ Direct Line for Bookings & Brochures
01493 730445 – Call 8am to 9pm 7 days a week
Debit / Credit Cards Accepted

Or browse our full brochure on our website at: www.BlueRibandHolidays.co.uk

For your free colour brochure phone the above number or write to:
Don Witheridge, Blue Riband House, Parklands, North Road, Hemsby, Great Yarmouth, Norfolk NR29 4HA

CASTAWAYS HOLIDAY PARK

BH & HPA approved

Set in the quiet, peaceful village of Bacton, with direct access to fine sandy beach, and ideal for beach fishing and discovering Norfolk and The Broads. Modern Caravans, pine lodges and flats with all amenities. Licensed Club. Entertainment. Amusement Arcade. Children's Play Area.

PETS WELCOME

on-line booking facility available

Enquiries and Bookings to:

Castaways Holiday Park, Paston Road, Bacton-on-Sea, Norfolk NR12 0JB • Tel: (01692) 650436 and 650418
www.castawaysholidaypark.co.uk

the hoste arms

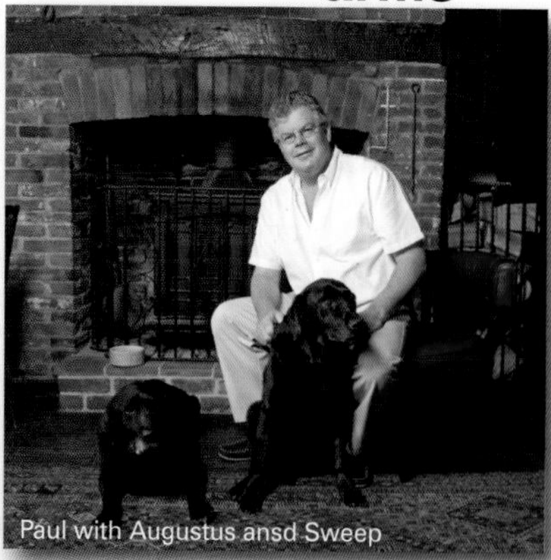

Paul with Augustus ansd Sweep

Situated on the Green in the pretty village of Burnham Market, this stylish hotel provides a relaxing friendly atmosphere, and owner Paul Whittome prides himself on everything being of the highest standard, from the individually designed bedrooms to the fabulous locally-sourced food. There is a cosy bar with log fire, popular with locals and visitors alike and plenty of dogs, a pretty garden, terraced dining area, and comfortable conservatory perfect for coffee or a light lunch.

Amazing value Midweek Dinner, Bed and Breakfast Breaks

The Hoste Arms, The Green, Burnham Market, Norfolk PE31 8HD
Tel: 01328 738777 • Fax: 01328 730103
E-mail: reception@hostearms.co.uk • www.hostearms.co.uk

Caister-on-Sea, Coltishall, Cromer

Elm Beach Caravan Park

Small, select, 4-star Caravan Park with unique, uninterrupted views of the Sea and Caister's golden, sandy beaches. We offer a range of 4-6 berth, fully equipped Heated Caravans, many of which overlook the sea or have sea views. We are a quiet, privately-run park with no entertainment facilities, but enjoy, free of charge, entertainment supplied by neighbouring park, within easy walking distance. Pets very welcome. Open March to January.

Manor Road, Caister-on-Sea NR30 5HG • Freephone: 08000 199 360
www.elmbeachcaravanpark.com • e-mail: enquiries@elmbeachcaravanpark.com

Superior brick-built, tiled roof cottages • Newly fitted double glazing throughout
Adjacent golf course • Lovely walks on dunes and coast
2-4 night breaks early/late season • Terms from £69 to £355.
SAND DUNE COTTAGES, TAN LANE, CAISTER-ON-SEA,
GREAT YARMOUTH NR30 5DT (01493 720352; mobile: 07785 561363)
e-mail: sand.dune.cottages@amserve.net
www.eastcoastlive.co.uk/sites/sanddunecottages.php

★★ SELF CATERING

The Norfolk Mead Hotel

Coltishall • Norfolk • NR12 7DN

Privately owned beautiful Georgian Country House Hotel. Located in 8 tranquil riverside acres, six miles from Norwich and 12 miles from the coast. Recently voted one of the top ten country house hotels in the country, accepting well mannered dogs. Thirteen en suite rooms all quite individual. Lake, boating and birdlife. Award-winning restaurant offering superb cuisine and extensive wine list.

★★ COUNTRY HOUSE HOTEL — Gold GOLD AWARD

Tel: 01603 737531 • e-mail: info@norfolkmead.co.uk
www.norfolkmead.co.uk

CROMER — SELF CATERING COTTAGES

A terrace of four charming almshouses recently modernised and redecorated throughout. Providing either
2 & 3 bedroom accommodation for 4/6 persons plus a 4-Star detached bungalow on Forest Park.
Central heating is included in the letting fee during the low season.
Short breaks available.
Each cottage has its own enclosed garden, ideal for children and **pets always welcome!** Ample car parking in cottage grounds.

Enjoy a walk with your dog on the miles of open uncrowded beaches in North Norfolk. Cromer has a Cinema and Pier with first-rate live shows.

Also included is membership of Forest Park with its beautiful woodland walks, clubhouse and swimming pool open during the high season.
Detailed brochure and tariff (prices from £275 to £620 p.w.)

★★ SELF CATERING

★★★ SELF CATERING

FOREST PARK
Outstanding Natural Beauty

Broadgates Cottages, Northrepps,
Forest Park Caravan Site Ltd,
Northrepps Road, Cromer, Norfolk NR27 0JR
Tel: 01263 513290 • Fax: 01263 511992
e-mail: info@broadgates.co.uk • www.broadgates.co.uk

CLIFTONVILLE HOTEL

Indulge in Edwardian Elegance

AA ★★★ Grade II Listed

30 en suite bedrooms, all with sea views
Executive Suites - A la carte Restaurant
Buttery and Bar - Bolton's Bistro specialising in
Fresh Fish Dishes - Cromer Crabs - Lobsters
Steaks - Pasta and Vegetarian Dishes

Pet-friendly staff - Dog meals available

www.cliftonvillehotel.co.uk Tel: 01263 512543 e-mail: reservations@cliftonvillehotel.co.uk

Kings Chalet Park Cromer, Norfolk

Sleep 2-4

Open March to October

Pet welcome free of charge

Comfortable, well-equipped chalets situated on beautiful, landscaped, quiet site. Ideally placed for walks to adjacent woods, cliffs and sandy beaches. 10 minutes' walk to town. Golf course and local shops nearby. Plenty of local places of interest to visit. One twin, one double room, bathroom, colour TV, microwave, well-equipped kitchenette. Children welcome.

Short Breaks in Spring/Autumn 2 nights or more from £80
Spring/Autumn £140-£210 per week
June-September £230-£305 per week

DETAILS FROM: MRS I. SCOLTOCK, SHANGRI-LA, LITTLE CAMBRIDGE, DUTON HILL, DUNMOW, ESSEX CM6 3QU • TEL: 01371 870482

Scarning Dale

Dale Road, Scarning, East Dereham NR19 2QN
Tel: 01362 687269

A warm welcome awaits you. 16th Century house in 25 acres of landscaped gardens, paddocks and woodland. Excellent home cooking (à la carte and table d'hôte). Indoor heated swimming pool and full size snooker table. Good access Norfolk and Suffolk. Self-catering cottages also available (not commercialised). Dogs welcome in self-catering cottages. Grazing and Stables available.

Tariff: Single £50 – £60; Double £90 – £100.

Bed & Breakfast. En suite rooms in converted dairy.
Central heating, tea/coffee, freeview TV.
Village inn 100 yards for evening meal.

Bartles Lodge, Church Street, Elsing, Dereham NR20 3EA
Tel: 01362 637177
www.bartleslodge.co.uk • e-mail: bartleslodge@yahoo.co.uk

WAVENEY VALLEY HOLIDAY PARK

★ Touring Caravan and Camping Site ★ Licensed Bar ★ Electric Hook-ups ★ Restaurant, Shop, Laundry
★ Self-Catering Mobile Homes ★ Outdoor Swimming Pool ★ Horse Riding on Site ★ Good Fishing nearby

Airstation Lane, Rushall, Diss, Norfolk IP21 4QF • Tel: 01379 741228/741690
Fax: 01379 741228 • e-mail: waveneyvalleyhp@aol.com • www.caravanparksnorfolk.co.uk

4B&B STRENNETH

Country Bed and Breakfast

Airfield Road, Fersfield, Diss, Norfolk IP22 2BP

STRENNETH is well-established and family-run, situated in unspoiled countryside just a short drive from Bressingham Gardens and the picturesque market town of Diss. Offering first-class accommodation, the original 17th Century building has been carefully renovated to a high standard with a wealth of exposed oak beams, with a newer single storey courtyard wing and two converted cottages. There is ample off-road parking and plenty of nice walks nearby.

All seven bedrooms, including a Four-Poster and an Executive, are tastefully arranged with period furniture and distinctive beds. Each has remote-control colour television, hospitality tray, central heating and full en suite facilities. The establishment is smoke-free. Dinners are served by arrangement. There is an extensive breakfast menu using local produce. Ideal touring base. Pets most welcome. Outside kennels with runs if required. Bed and Breakfast from £25.00.

Telephone: 01379 688182 • Fax: 01379 688260
e-mail: pdavey@strenneth.co.uk • www.strenneth.co.uk

Silver SILVER AWARD

★★★★ GUEST ACCOMMODATION

Foxley, Great Yarmouth, King's Lynn, Mundesley-on-Sea

Located on a working farm, a courtyard of 2/3/4 bedroomed converted stables, 3 converted barns and 2 cottages, all fully equipped. Sleeps up to 10. Ideally situated for the beautiful North Norfolk coast, Sandringham, Norwich, and The Broads. 365 acres of mature woodland adjoining farm – private fishing in owners' lake. Indoor heated swimming Pool. Pets welcome at a charge of £10.

MOOR FARM STABLE COTTAGES,
FOXLEY, NORFOLK NR20 4QP • Tel or Fax: 01362 688523
e-mail: enquiry@moorfarmstablecottages.co.uk
www.moorfarmstablecottages.co.uk

Sunwright Holiday Chalets

Sundowner Holiday Park, Newport, Hemsby, near Great Yarmouth. Fully furnished and equipped self catering chalets, sleep up to 6. Two bedrooms, kitchen with all your cooking needs, lounge with TV, bathroom with shower over bath. Close to beach, Norfolk Broads and many attractions. Pets most welcome! **Contact Mrs Michelle Browne, 50 Mariners Compass, Gorleston, Great Yarmouth, Norfolk NR31 6TS • 01493 304282 • e-mail: sunwrightholiday@aol.com • www.sunwrightholidays.com**

A warm welcome for you and your pets. Inexpensive, 'live-as-you-please' self-catering holidays in beautiful Norfolk. Chalets, Bungalows, Caravans and Cottages near Great Yarmouth & Norfolk Broads. SHORT BREAKS AVAILABLE ALL SEASON.

Carefree HOLIDAYS

Colour Brochure : Carefree Holidays, Chapel Briers, Yarmouth Road, Hemsby, Norfolk NR29 4NJ.
Find us on the internet: www.carefree-holidays.co.uk ***BOOKING HOTLINE 01493 732176***

ETC ★★★

HOLMDENE FARM

BEESTON, KING'S LYNN PE32 2NJ

17th century farmhouse situated in central Norfolk within easy reach of the coast and Broads. Sporting activities available locally, village pub nearby. One double room, one twin and two singles. Pets welcome. Bed and Breakfast from £22.50 per person; Evening Meal from £15. Weekly terms available and child reductions. Two self-catering cottages. Sleeping 4/8. Terms on request.

MRS G. DAVIDSON • Tel: 01328 701284

e-mail: holmdenefarm@farmersweekly.net
www.holmdenefarm.co.uk

Pott Row

Detached 2 bedroom bungalow sleeps 4. In quiet rural Norfolk village close to Sandringham and beaches. Facilities include colour TV, video, microwave, fridge/freezer, washing machine, off road parking, dog run. All dogs welcome FREE. Open all year. Please telephone for brochure.

Mrs. J.E. Ford, 129 Leziate Drove, Pott Row, King's Lynn PE32 1DE Tel: 01553 630356

47 SEAWARD CREST MUNDESLEY

West-facing brick built chalet on private site with lawns, flowers and parking. Large lounge/dining room, kitchenette, two bedrooms, bathroom. Beach and shops nearby. Pets most welcome. SAE please for further information.

Mrs Doar, 4 Denbury Road, Ravenshead, Notts. NG15 9FQ
Tel: 01623 798032

KILN CLIFFS CARAVAN PARK

Peaceful family-run site with NO clubhouse situated around an historic brick kiln. Luxury six-berth caravans for hire, standing on ten acres of grassy cliff top. Magnificent view out over the sea; private path leads down to extensive stretches of unspoilt sandy beach. All caravans fully equipped (except linen) and price includes all gas and electricity. Caravans always available for sale or for hire. Within easy reach are the Broads, Norwich, the Shire Horse Centre, local markets, nature reserves, bird sanctuaries; nearby golf, riding and fishing. Facilities on site include general store and launderette. Responsible pet owners welcome. **Substantial discounts for off-peak bookings – phone for details. Call for brochure.**

Mr R. Easton, Kiln Cliffs Caravan Park, Cromer Road, Mundesley, Norfolk NR11 8DF • Tel: 01263 720449

A warm welcome to all pets and their owners at "Whincliff" by the sea. Family/en suite, twin or single room available. Tea/coffee facilities, TV in all rooms, private parking, sea views, unspoilt beach and coastal walks to enjoy. **Anne & Alan Cutler**

WHINCLIFF Bed & Breakfast

CROMER ROAD, MUNDESLEY NR11 8DU

Tel: 01263 721554 • e-mail: cutler.a@sky.com

Dolphin Lodge

Enquiries by telephone only
Tel: 01263 720961 • Mobile: 07901 691084

Friendly-run bungalow accommodation. B&B in village setting just two-and-a-half miles from beaches. Many rural walks. Easy reach of all Norfolk attractions including Norfolk Broads. All rooms en suite, tea/coffee facilities, TVs, hairdryers etc.

Mrs G. Faulkner, Dolphin Lodge, 3 Knapton Road, Trunch, North Walsham, Norfolk NR28 0QE

e-mail: dolphinlodge_@btopenworld.com • www.dolphinlodge.net

64 Earlham Road, Norwich NR2 3DF

Tel: 01603 615599 • Fax: 01603 495599

A family-run guest house where you will receive a warm welcome from Ray and Sue. We are situated only 10 minutes' walk from the city centre. All rooms have en suite facilities and digital TV. We are well known for our excellent breakfasts that set you up for the day.

Edmar Lodge

★★★ GUEST ACCOMMODATION

e-mail: edmarlodge.co.uk

www.edmarlodge.co.uk

AA ★★★ Guest Accommodation

Pet-Friendly
Pubs, Inns & Hotels
on pages 424-432

Please note that these establishments may not feature in the main section of this book

The Lifeboat Inn

16th Century Smugglers' Ale House

Ship Lane, Thornham, Norfolk PE36 6LT

Tel: 01485 512236 • Fax: 01485 512323

e-mail: lifeboatinn@maypolehotels.com

THE LIFEBOAT INN has been a welcome sight for the weary traveller for centuries – roaring open fires, real ales and a hearty meal awaiting. The Summer brings its own charm – a cool beer, gazing over open meadows to the harbour, and rolling white horses gently breaking upon Thornham's sandy beach.

Dogs are welcome in all our bars and we provide the sort of breakfast that will enable you to keep up with your four-legged friend on the way to the beach!

Guests arriving at reception are greeted by our grand old fireplace in the lounge – ideal for toasting your feet after a day walking the coastal path – if you can coax your sleeping dog out of prime position! The restaurant (AA Rosette) opens every evening offering a varied selection of dishes to suit all tastes. Our extensive bar snack menu is also available if guests wish their pets to join them in the bar.

There are numerous and varied walks along miles of open beaches, across sweeping sand dunes, through pine woods or along chalk and sandstone cliff tops. It is truly a walker's paradise – especially if you're a dog.

We hope you will come and visit us. For our brochure and tariff which includes details of breaks please ring 01485 512236 or visit our website

www.maypolehotels.com

HOLIDAY IN OUR ENGLISH COUNTRY GARDEN

Two acres in rural Norfolk. Ten spacious family-run bungalows and 7-bedroom farmhouse. Games room, heated pool, children's play area, fishing, boating, riding and golf nearby. Near River Staithe with access to Broads. Parking. Licensed bar. For details/colour brochure contact: **F.G. Delf, Thurne Cottage, The Staithe, Thurne, Norfolk NR29 3BU**
Tel: 01692 670242 or 01493 844568 • www.norfolkbroads.co.uk/hederahouse

Winterton Valley Holidays

A selection of modern superior fully appointed holiday chalets in a choice of locations near Great Yarmouth. Enjoy panoramic views of the sea from WINTERTON, a quiet and picturesque 35-acre estate minutes from the beach, while CALIFORNIA has all the usual amenities for the more adventurous holidaymaker, with free entry to the pool and clubhouse. Pets very welcome at both sites.

For colour brochure please ring 01493 377175 or write to 15 Kingston Avenue, Caister-on-Sea, Norfolk NR30 5ET • www.wintertonvalleyholidays.co.uk

Readers are requested to mention this FHG guidebook when seeking accommodation

Winterton-on-Sea

Winterton Holidays WINTERTON-ON-SEA • NORFOLK

For a peaceful, relaxing holiday.

1 and 2 bedroom self-catering chalets, furnished and equipped to a high standard

QUIET, PICTURESQUE PARK OVERLOOKING WINTERTON VALLEY WITH PANORAMIC SEA VIEWS

MILES OF WALKS ALONG THE VALLEY, DUNES AND BEACH.

MRS JUNE HUDSON, 42 LARK WAY, BRADWELL, GREAT YARMOUTH, NORFOLK NR31 8SB

01493 444700 • www.wintertonholidays.com

Go BLUE RIBAND for quality inexpensive self-catering holidays where your dog is welcome – choice of locations all in the borough of Great Yarmouth. Detached 3 bedroom bungalows, seafront bungalows, detached Sea-Dell chalets and modern sea front caravans. Free colour brochure: DON WITHERIDGE, BLUE RIBAND HOUSE, PARKLANDS, HEMSBY, GREAT YARMOUTH NR29 4HA (01493 730445). [pw! First pet free when booking through Pets Welcome!, 2nd pet £10 per week].
website: www.BlueRibandHolidays.co.uk

Bacton-on-Sea

Village on coast. 5 miles from North Walsham.

CASTAWAYS HOLIDAY PARK, PASTON ROAD, BACTON-ON-SEA NR12 0JB (01692 650436 and 650418). In peaceful village with direct access to sandy beach. Modern caravans, Pine Lodges and Flats, with all amenities. Licensed club, entertainment, children's play area. Ideal for discovering Norfolk. [Pets £20 per week]
website: www.castawaysholidaypark.co.uk

Burnham Market

Village 5 miles West of Wells.

THE HOSTE ARMS, THE GREEN, BURNHAM MARKET PE31 8HD (01328 738777; Fax: 01328 730103). Stylish hotel with relaxing friendly atmosphere and attentive service. Individually designed bedrooms. Cosy bar with log fire, terraced dining area, conservatory. Locally sourced food. Midweek breaks. AA 2 Rosettes for food. [Pets £7.50 per stay].
e-mail: reception@hostearms.co.uk website: www.hostearms.co.uk

Caister-on-Sea

Historic site with Roman ruins and 15th century Caister Castle with 100 foot tower.

ELM BEACH CARAVAN PARK, MANOR ROAD, CAISTER-ON-SEA NR30 5HG (Freephone: 08000 199 360). Small, quiet park offering 4-6 berth, fully equipped caravans, most with sea views. Entertainment supplied free of charge by neighbouring park. Pets very welcome. [Pets £25 per week]
e-mail: enquiries@elmbeachcaravanpark.com website: www.elmbeachcaravanpark.com

Superior brick-built, tiled roof cottages with double glazing throughout. Adjacent golf course. Lovely walks on dunes and coast. 2-4 night breaks early/late season. Terms from £69 to £355. SAND DUNE COTTAGES, TAN LANE, CAISTER-ON-SEA, GREAT YARMOUTH NR30 5DT (01493 720352; mobile: 07785 561363). ETC ★★ [Pets £15 per week]
e-mail: sand.dune.cottages@amserve.net
website: www.eastcoastlive.co.uk/sites/sanddunecottages.php

Coltishall

Village to the north east of Norwich..

THE NORFOLK MEAD HOTEL, COLTISHALL, NORWICH NR12 7DN (01603 737531). Georgian Country House Hotel with 13 en suite bedrooms. Renowned restaurant offering superb cuisine and a comprehensive wine list. Well mannered dogs welcome. ETC ★★ GOLD AWARD. [Pets £8 per night]
e-mail: info@norfolkmead.co.uk website: www.norfolkmead.co.uk

Cromer

Attractive resort built round old fishing village. Norwich 21 miles.

All-electric two and three bedroom Holiday Cottages sleeping 4/6 in beautiful surroundings, also detached bungalow. Sandy beaches, sports facilities, Cinema and Pier (live shows). Parking. Children and pets welcome. ETC ★★-★★★ Brochure: BROADGATES COTTAGES, NORTHREPPS, FOREST PARK CARAVAN SITE LTD, NORTHREPPS ROAD, CROMER, NORFOLK NR27 0JR (01263 513290; Fax: 01263 511992) [Pets £10 weekly].
e-mail: info@broadgates.co.uk website: www.broadgates.co.uk

CLIFTONVILLE HOTEL, SEAFRONT, CROMER NR27 9AS (01263 512543; Fax: 01263 515700). Ideally situated on the Norfolk coast. Beautifully restored Edwardian Hotel. 30 en suite bedrooms all with sea view. Executive suites. Seafood Bistro, à la carte Restaurant. AA ★★★ [pw! pets £4 per night]
e-mail: reservations@cliftonvillehotel.co.uk website: www.cliftonvillehotel.co.uk

KINGS CHALET PARK, CROMER. Comfortable well-equipped chalets on quiet site; ideally placed for woodland and beach walks. 10 minutes' walk to town, shops nearby. Details from MRS I. SCOLTOCK, SHANGRI-LA, LITTLE CAMBRIDGE, DUTON HILL, DUNMOW, ESSEX (01371 870482). [one pet free]

Dereham

Situated 16 miles west of Norwich. St Nicholas Church has 16th century bell tower.

SCARNING DALE, SCARNING, EAST DEREHAM NR19 2QN (01362 687269). Self-catering cottages (not commercialised) in grounds of owner's house. On-site indoor heated swimming pool and full-size snooker table. B&B for six also available in house (sorry no pets in house). Grazing and Stables available.

BARTLES LODGE, CHURCH STREET, ELSING, DEREHAM NR20 3EA (01362 637177). B&B in en suite rooms in converted dairy. Central heating, tea/coffee, freeview TV. Village inn 100 yards for evening meal [pw! Pets £2 per night, £10 per week]
e-mail: bartleslodge@yahoo.co.uk website: www.bartleslodge.co.uk

Diss

Small market town on the River Waveney 19 miles SW of Norwich.

WAVENEY VALLEY HOLIDAY PARK, AIRSTATION LANE, RUSHALL, DISS IP21 4QF (01379 741228/741690; Fax: 01379 741228). Touring Caravan and Camping Site. Licensed bar, electric hook-ups, restaurant, shop, laundry. Self-catering mobile homes. Outdoor swimming pool, horse riding on site; good fishing nearby.
e-mail: waveneyvalleyhp@aol.com website: www.caravanparksnorfolk.co.uk

PAUL AND YOLANDA DAVEY, STRENNETH, AIRFIELD ROAD, FERSFIELD, DISS IP22 2BP (01379 688182; Fax 01379 688260). Family-run, fully renovated period property with two cottages. All rooms en suite, colour TVs, hospitality trays. Ground floor rooms. Non-smoking. Extensive breakfast menu. Licensed. Bed and Breakfast from £25. ETC ★★★★ Silver Award. [🐕]
e-mail: pdavey@strenneth.co.uk website: www.strenneth.co.uk

Foxley

Village 6 miles east of East Dereham.

Self-catering Cottages (2/3/4 bedrooms) on working farm. All fully equipped, with central heating. 20 miles from coast, 15 from Broads. Mature woodland nearby. Fishing in owner's lake. Indoor heated swimming pool. ETC ★★/★★★★. MOOR FARM STABLE COTTAGES, FOXLEY NR20 4QP (Tel & Fax: 01362 688523). [Pets £10 per week]
e-mail: enquiry@moorfarmstablecottages.co.uk website: www.moorfarmstablecottages.co.uk

A useful index of towns/counties appears at the back of this book

Great Yarmouth

Traditional lively seaside resort with a wide range of amusements, including the Marina Centre and Sealife Centre.

MRS MICHELLE BROWNE, SUNWRIGHT HOLIDAYS,50 MARINERS COMPASS, GORLESTON, GREAT YARMOUTH NR31 6TS (01493 304282) Sundowner Holiday Park, near Great Yarmouth. Fully furnished and equipped self catering chalets, sleep up to 6. Close to beach, Norfolk Broads and many attractions. [Pets £15 per week, discounts available].
e-mail: sunwrightholiday@aol.com website: www.sunwrightholidays.com

CAREFREE HOLIDAYS, CHAPEL BRIERS, YARMOUTH ROAD, HEMSBY, GREAT YARMOUTH NR29 4NJ (01493 732176). A wide selection of superior chalets for live-as-you-please holidays near Great Yarmouth and Norfolk Broads. All amenities on site. Parking. Children and pets welcome. [Pets £20 per week, free in June.]

King's Lynn

Ancient market town and port on the Wash with many beautiful medieval and Georgian buildings.

MRS G. DAVIDSON, HOLMDENE FARM, BEESTON, KING'S LYNN PE32 2NJ (01328 701284). 17th century farmhouse situated in central Norfolk within easy reach of the coast and Broads. Sporting activities available locally, village pub nearby. One double room, one twin and one single. Pets welcome. Bed and Breakfast from £22.50pp; Evening Meal from £15. Weekly terms available and child reductions. Two self-catering cottages. Sleeping 4/8. Terms on request. ETC ★★★ [🐕]
e-mail: holmdenefarm@farmersweekly.net website: www.holmdenefarm.co.uk

MRS J. E. FORD, 129 LEZIATE DROVE, POTT ROW, KING'S LYNN PE32 1DE (01553 630356). Detached bungalow sleeps 4. In quiet village close to Sandringham and beaches. Facilities include colour TV, video, microwave, fridge/freezer, washing machine, off road parking, dog run. [🐕]

Mundesley-on-Sea

Small resort backed by low cliffs. Good sands and bathing. Norwich 20 miles, Cromer 7.

47 SEAWARD CREST, MUNDESLEY. West-facing brick built chalet on private site with lawns, flowers and parking. Large lounge/dining room, kitchenette, two bedrooms, bathroom. Beach and shops nearby. Pets most welcome. SAE please: MRS DOAR, 4 DENBURY ROAD, RAVENSHEAD, NOTTS. NG15 9FQ (01623 798032). [🐕]

KILN CLIFFS CARAVAN PARK, CROMER ROAD, MUNDESLEY NR11 8DF (01263 720449). Peaceful family-run site situated around an historic brick kiln. Six-berth caravans for hire, standing on ten acres of grassy cliff top. All caravans fully equipped (except linen) and price includes all gas and electricity. [Pets £5 per week].

ANNE & ALAN CUTLER, WHINCLIFF BED & BREAKFAST, CROMER ROAD, MUNDESLEY NR11 8DU (01263 721554). Clifftop house, sea views and sandy beaches. Rooms with colour TV and tea-making. Families and pets welcome. Open all year round. [🐕]
e-mail: cutler.a@sky.com

North Walsham

Market town 14 miles north of Norwich, traditional centre of the Norfolk reed thatching industry.

MRS. G. FAULKNER, DOLPHIN LODGE, 3 KNAPTON ROAD,TRUNCH, NORTH WALSHAM NR28 0QE (01263 720961; Mobile: 07901 691084). Friendly-run bungalow accommodation. B&B in village setting two-and-a-half miles from beaches. Many rural walks. Easy reach of all Norfolk attractions including Norfolk Broads. All rooms en suite, tea/coffee facilities, TVs, hairdryers etc. Enquiries by telephone only. [🐕]
e-mail: dolphin_lodge@btopenworld.com website: www.dolphinlodge.net

Symbols

🐕 Indicates that pets are welcome free of charge.

£ Indicates that a charge is made for pets: nightly or weekly.

pw! Shows some special provision for pets; exercise facility, feeding or accommodation arrangement.

⌂ Indicates separate pets accommodation.

Norwich

Historic city with Cathedral, Castle, shops, restaurants and lots to see and do. Many medieval streets and lanes, with attractive timbered houses.

EDMAR LODGE, 64 EARLHAM ROAD, NORWICH NR2 3DF(01603 615599; Fax: 01603 495599). Family-run guest house where you will receive a warm welcome. 10 minutes' walk from the city centre. All rooms have en suite facilities and digital TV. Excellent breakfasts. ETC/AA ★★★ [🐕]
e-mail: edmarlodge.co.uk website: www.edmarlodge.co.uk

Thornham

Village 4 miles east of Hunstanton. Site of Roman signal station.

THE LIFEBOAT INN, SHIP LANE, THORNHAM PE36 6LT (01485 512236; Fax: 01485 512323). A welcome sight for the weary traveller for centuries. Dogs welcome. Restaurant (one AA rosette). Bird watching and walking along miles of open beaches. Please ring for brochure and tariff. [Pets £5 per week.]
e-mail: lifeboatinn@maypolehotels.com website: www.maypolehotels.com

Thurne

Idyllic Broadland village. Great Yarmouth 10 miles.

HEDERA HOUSE AND PLANTATION BUNGALOWS, THURNE NR29 3BU (01692 670242 or 01493 844568). Adjacent river, seven bedroomed farmhouse, 10 competitively priced bungalows in peaceful gardens. Outdoor heated pool. Enjoy boating, fishing, walking, touring, nearby golf, horseriding, sandy beaches and popular resorts.
website: www.norfolkbroads.co.uk/hederahouse

Weybourne

Located in an Area of Outstanding Natural Beauty and part of the Heritage Coastline. Sheringham and Holt 4 miles.

BOLDING WAY HOLIDAYS, THE STABLES, WEYBOURNE, HOLT NR25 7SW (01263 588666). Bed & Breakfast for up to 6 and Self-catering (for 2). In an Area of Outstanding Natural Beauty and on the Heritage Coast. Well behaved pets welcome. Both with fenced gardens. Excellent local walks. Open all year. [🐕]
e-mail: holidays@boldingway.co.uk website: www.boldingway.co.uk

Winterton-on-Sea

Good sands and bathing. Great Yarmouth 8 miles.

WINTERTON VALLEY HOLIDAYS. A selection of modern superior fully appointed holiday chalets in a choice of locations near Great Yarmouth. Enjoy panoramic views from WINTERTON, a quiet and picturesque 35-acre estate, while CALIFORNIA has all the usual amenities, with free entry to the pool and clubhouse. Pets are very welcome at both sites. For colour brochure: 15 KINGSTON AVENUE, CAISTER-ON-SEA NR30 5ET (01493 377175).
website: www.wintertonvalleyholidays.co.uk

WINTERTON HOLIDAYS, WINTERTON-ON-SEA. Privately owned one and two-bedroom chalets, furnished and equipped to a high standard, on picturesque park few minutes' walk from sea. Dogs allowed on beach all year. Ideal for quiet, relaxing break and for exploring Broads, coast, Norwich. Village has pub, restaurant and shops. MRS JUNE HUDSON, 42 LARK WAY, BRADWELL, GREAT YARMOUTH NR31 8SB (01493 444700). [Pets £2.50 per night, £15 per week]
website: www.wintertonholidays.com

WENTWORTH HOTEL

WENTWORTH ROAD, ALDEBURGH, SUFFOLK IP15 5BD

Facing the sea, the Wentworth Hotel has the comfort and style of a country house. 35 bedrooms, many with sea views, two comfortable lounges with open fires and antique furniture, provide ample space to relax. The restaurant serves a variety of fresh produce, including local seafood, and a light lunch can be chosen from the bar menu and eaten "al fresco" in the terrace garden. There are many walks, some commencing from the Hotel. Aldeburgh is the perfect touring centre for East Anglia.

AA ★★★ Two Rosettes 87%

For a reservation, please Telephone 01728 452312 or Fax: 01728 454343

e-mail: stay@wentworth-aldeburgh.co.uk • www.wentworth-aldeburgh.com

ETC Silver Award

Earsham Park Farm

ETC/AA ★★★★ Gold Award

Superb Victorian property overlooking open countryside. Bedrooms attractively furnished; excellent breakfasts. Superb facilities for pets.

01986 892180 • www.earsham-parkfarm.co.uk

Old Railway Road, Earsham, Bungay NR35 2AQ

• Annie's Cottage • Suffolk •

The old wing of Hill Farm farmhouse. Peaceful, rural location in open countryside.
2 bedrooms, sleeps 4. Large lounge/dining room with woodburning stove.
Central heating. Linen and towels provided. Electricity incl. Enclosed private garden.

Well equipped mobile home also available. **www.hillfarmholidays.com**

Contact Lynne Morton, Hill Farm Holidays, Ilketshall St John, Beccles, Suffolk NR34 8JE. Tel: 01986 781240.

AA ★★★

16th century heavily beamed Tudor Hall set in 7 acres of perfect dog walks. Individually furnished en suite bedrooms; renowned restaurant; relaxing inglenook fires.

enquiries@ravenwoodhall.co.uk
www.ravenwoodhall.co.uk

Ravenwood Hall

Country Hotel and Restaurant

ROUGHAM, BURY ST EDMUNDS IP30 9JA

Tel: 01359 270345 • Fax: 01359 270788

Easy access from A14, Junction 45

Edge Hall

www.edgehall.co.uk

2 HIGH STREET, HADLEIGH IP7 5AP • 01473 822458

Truffles invites you to stay in her master's comfortable lodge house. Well behaved owners will enjoy the perfect walks and super breakfasts. Double/twin £85 per night, Single £57.50. Self-catering also available. ETC/AA ★★★★★

Five cottages, each sleeping 1-6, converted from an Old Granary and milking parlour into tasteful, modern accommodation. The owners, Wayne & Sue Leggett, guarantee a warm Suffolk welcome. Step out of your cottage and into beautiful countryside away from the hustle and bustle. The Old Dairy has a high level of accessibility for disabled visitors and three of the other cottages have ground floor bedrooms and bathrooms. Children (and the young at heart) will enjoy the 24′ x 15′ games room with table tennis, pool and table football and there is a large outdoor grass play area. Short breaks are offered out of high season. Less than 2 hours from London and 1 hour from Stansted Airport.

Henley, Ipswich IP6 0RU • www.dameronsfarmholidays.co.uk

FREE or REDUCED RATE entry to Holiday Visits and Attractions – see our **READERS' OFFER VOUCHERS** on pages 433-440

Knights Holiday Homes
at Kessingland

50 Alexandra Road, Lowestoft, Suffolk NR32 1PJ

Kessingland is the most easterly village in the United Kingdom. First to greet the sun. Once known as the richest village in England because of its prolific fishing. Now known for its peaceful, pleasant surroundings, its spacious beach and a place where you can relax and watch the boats sail by. Or perhaps you would like to visit the Suffolk Wildlife Park or wine and dine at the local pubs and restaurants. There is a good local bus service.

• 1-6 persons • Full size cooker • Colour Television • Refrigerator • Video Recorder • Microwave • Bed Linen Supplied • Electricity • Fully equipped Kitchen • Parking • Horse Racing • Power Boat Racing • Golf • Fishing • Bowls • Tennis • Coach Trips • Boating • Art & Film Settings • Concert Hall & Art Centre • Theme Parks

FREEPHONE 0800 269067 • EMAIL : info@knightsholidays.co.uk • FAX 01502 500055

www.knightsholidays.co.uk

Lodge Cottage, Laxfield, Suffolk

★★★★ SELF CATERING

Pretty 16C thatched cottage retaining some fine period features. Sleeps 4. Pets welcome. Fenced garden. 1 mile from village. 30 minutes to Southwold and coast. Rural, quiet and relaxing. For brochure phone Jane: **01986 798830 or 07788853884 or e-mail: janebrewer@ukonline.co.uk**

THE BLACK LION HOTEL & RESTAURANT

The Green, Long Melford CO10 9DN • Tel:01787 312356
e-mail: enquiries@blacklionhotel.net • www.blacklionhotel.net

- The Georgian Black Lion Hotel overlooks the famous green and two of Suffolk's finest stately homes.
- Voted Suffolk's best restaurant, from lunches, dinner and cream teas.
- 10 en suite bedrooms refurbished to luxury status.
- Idyllic dog walks and lots of attention from dog-loving staff.

★★★

Broadland Holiday Village

Discover the delights of the Forgotten Norfolk Broad with your Faithful Friend

Stay in Cosy Brick Bungalows, **some with Private Outdoor Hot Tubs**, or Pine Lodges

Enjoy all the Countryside, Marsh and Beach Walks

And when you've worn him out, you can relax in our indoor heated pool

The perfect holiday for the whole family!

Oulton Broad, Lowestoft NR33 9JY • 01502 573033

www.broadlandvillage.co.uk

Fuschia Cottage, Middleton, Suffolk

Detached cottage fronting onto green. Sleeps 4. Fenced rear courtyard. Pretty quiet village. Lovely walks. Pets welcome. Close to Aldeburgh and Minsmere.
Contact Jane Brewer **01986 798830**
or e-mail: janebrewer@ukonline.co.uk

Gladwins Farm *Cottages in Constable Country*

Set in 22 acres of rolling Suffolk countryside, Gladwins Farm offers a selection of accommodation. Guests staying in any of our 4★ or 5★ self-catering cottages (sleeping 2-8) or the B&B can use the heated indoor pool, sauna, hot tub, the hard tennis court and playground. There is coarse fishing in our lake plus farm animals to entertain the children. Pets welcome in most cottages and loads of dog walking! Riding, golf and beach within easy reach.

If a quiet holiday in a charming area of Olde England is on your agenda, call Pauline or Robert Dossor on 01206 262261 and arrange a memorable stay. See us on the internet at www.gladwinsfarm.co.uk or call for our colour brochure and DVD. Winners, Regional Self-Catering Holiday of the Year 2003 and 2006.

e-mail: gladwinsfarm@aol.com
Gladwins Farm, Harper's Hill, Nayland, Suffolk CO6 4NU

The Crown and Castle

Orford, Woodbridge, Suffolk IP12 2LJ
Tel: 01394 450205

e-mail: info@crownandcastle.co.uk
www.crownandcastle.co.uk

Suffolk Heritage Coast

Now owned by the ex-proprietors of Hintlesham Hall, this comfortable and very dog-friendly hotel is situated close to the 12th century castle in this historic and unspoilt village. Honest good food served in the acclaimed award-winning Trinity Restaurant.

SWEFFLING HALL FARM

Sweffling, Saxmundham IP17 2B
Tel & Fax: 01728 663644

Set well back from the main road in a quiet location • Always a warm welcome • Ideal for walking/cycling and the Heritage Coast • Vintage transport available free for longer stays • One double and one family room with en suite/private bathrooms • Open all year. **e-mail: stephenmann@suffolkonline.net**

Situated in small, picturesque village within 15 miles of Sudbury, Newmarket Racecourse and historic Bury St Edmunds. Bungalow well equipped to accommodate 4 people. All facilities. Car essential, parking. Children and pets welcome. Terms from £74 to £147 per week. For further details send SAE to

MRS M. WINCH, PLOUGH HOUSE, STANSFIELD, SUDBURY CO10 8LT • Tel: 01284 789253

FHG Guides

publish a large range of well-known accommodation guides.
We will be happy to send you details or you can use the order form at the back of this book.

Aldeburgh

Coastal town 6 miles south-east of Saxmundham. Annual music festival at Snape Maltings.

WENTWORTH HOTEL, ALDEBURGH IP15 5BD (01728 452312). Country House Hotel overlooking the sea. Immediate access to the beach and walks. Two comfortable lounges with log fires and antique furniture. Refurbished bedrooms with all facilities and many with sea views. Restaurant specialises in fresh produce and sea food. ETC Silver Award. AA ★★★ Two Rosettes. [Pets £2 per day]
e-mail: stay@wentworth-aldeburgh.co.uk website: www.wentworth-aldeburgh.com

Bungay

Attractive town in the Waveney Valley, with a wealth of historic sites. Town centre has a Roman well, a Saxon church, and the remains of a Norman castle and Benedictine priory. 14 miles south east of Norwich.

EARSHAM PARK FARM, OLD RAILWAY ROAD, EARSHAM, BUNGAY NR35 2AQ 01986 892180 Superb Victorian property overlooking open countryside. Bedrooms attractively furnished; excellent breakfasts. All rooms en suite. ETC/AA ★★★★ Gold Award. [Pets £5 per night]
website: www.earsham-parkfarm.co.uk

ANNIE'S COTTAGE, SUFFOLK. Peaceful, rural location in open countryside. 2 bedrooms, sleeps 4. Large lounge/dining room, woodburning stove. Linen and towels provided. Electricity included. Enclosed private garden. Well equipped mobile home also available. Contact: LYNNE MORTON, HILL FARM HOLIDAYS, ILKETSHALL ST JOHN, BECCLES NR34 8JE. (01986 781240). [ ]
website: www.hillfarmholidays.com

Bury St Edmunds

This prosperous market town on the River Lark lies 28 miles east of Cambridge.

RAVENWOOD HALL COUNTRY HOUSE HOTEL AND RESTAURANT, ROUGHAM, BURY ST EDMUNDS IP30 9JA (01359 270345; Fax: 01359 270788). 16th century heavily beamed Tudor Hall set in seven acres of perfect dog walks. Individually furnished en suite bedrooms; renowned restaurant; relaxing inglenook fires. AA ★★★, AA 2 Rosettes. [pw!]
e-mail: enquiries@ravenwoodhall.co.uk website: www.ravenwoodhall.co.uk

Diss

Town on the Norfolk/Suffolk border. Large number of historic buildings, including early 14 century parish church. 15 miles from Thetford, 23 miles from Norwich.

PAUL AND YOLANDA DAVEY, STRENNETH, AIRFIELD ROAD, FERSFIELD, DISS IP22 2BP (01379 688182; Fax 01379 688260). Family-run, fully renovated period property with two cottages. All rooms en suite, colour TVs, hospitality trays. Ground floor rooms. Non-smoking. Extensive breakfast menu. Licensed. Bed and Breakfast from £25. ETC ★★★★ Silver Award. [ ]
e-mail: pdavey@strenneth.co.uk website: www.strenneth.co.uk

Friston

Village 4 miles from Aldeburgh.

2 FORGE COTTAGES. Traditional Suffolk cottage (the former Forge) retaining some period features. Two minutes pub, one mile shop, Aldeburgh 4 miles. Sleeps 5, secure garden, well equipped. All towels and linen incl. Short breaks available; open all year. Contact: DEBBIE PICKERING (01621 810833). [pw!]
e-mail: forgecottages2@btinternet.com website: www.fristonholidaycottages.co.uk

Readers are requested to mention this FHG guidebook when seeking accommodation

Hadleigh

Historic town on River Brett with several buildings of interest including unusual 14th century church. Bury St Edmunds 20 miles, Colchester 14, Sudbury 11, Ipswich 10.

EDGE HALL, 2 HIGH STREET, HADLEIGH IP7 5AP (01473 822458). Truffles invites you to stay in her master's comfortable lodge house. Well behaved owners will enjoy the perfect walks and super breakfasts. Twin/double £85 per night, single £57.50. Self-catering also available. ETC/AA ★★★★★ [Pets £5 per night, £10 per week]
website: www.edgehall.co.uk

Henley

Vilage 4 miles north of Ipswich.

WAYNE & SUE LEGGETT, DAMERONS FARM HOLIDAYS, HENLEY, IPSWICH IP6 0RU (01473 832454 or 07881 824083). Five cottages, each sleeping 1-6. The Old Dairy has a high level of accessibility for disabled visitors; three others have ground floor bedrooms and bathrooms. Games room with table tennis, pool and table football. Short Breaks out of season.
www.dameronsfarmholidays.co.uk

Kessingland

Little seaside place with expansive beach, safe bathing, wildlife park, lake fishing. To the south is Benacre Broad, a beauty spot. Norwich 26 miles, Adleburgh 23, Lowestoft 5.

Comfortable well-equipped bungalow on lawned site overlooking beach, next to Heritage Coast. Panoramic sea views. Easy beach access. Unspoiled walking area. ETC ★★ MRS L.G. SAUNDERS, 159 THE STREET, ROCKLAND ST MARY, NORWICH NR14 7HL (01508 538340). [Pets £10 per week].

Quality seaside bungalows in lawned surrounds overlooking the sea. Open all year, fully eqipped. Sleep 1/6. Direct access to award-winning beach. Parking Pets very welcome. APPLY– KNIGHTS HOLIDAY HOMES, 50 ALEXANDRA ROAD, LOWESTOFT, SUFFOLK NR32 1PJ (FREEPHONE 0800 269067).
e-mail: info@knightsholidays.co.uk website: www.knightsholidays.co.uk

Laxfield

Village 6 miles North of Framlingham.

LODGE COTTAGE, LAXFIELD. Pretty 16C thatched cottage retaining some fine period features. Sleeps 4. Pets welcome. Fenced garden. 1 mile from village. 30 minutes to Southwold and coast. Rural, quiet and relaxing. ETC ★★★★. For brochure phone: MRS JANE BREWER, LODGE COTTAGE, LAXFIELD ROAD, CRATFIELD, HALESWORTH IP19 0QG (01986 798830 or 07788853884). [Pets £10 per week].
e-mail: janebrewer@ukonline.co.uk

Long Melford

Village in the beautiful countryside of Suffolk, in the River Stour valley, just north of Sudbury, beside the A314 road to Bury St Edmunds.

THE BLACK LION HOTEL & RESTAURANT, THE GREEN, LONG MELFORD CO10 9DN (01787 312356). The Georgian Black Lion Hotel overlooks the famous green, and the cosy bar and restaurant offer a range of innovative dishes. 10 en suite bedrooms refurbished to luxury status. Idyllic dog walks. [🐕]
e-mail: enquiries@blacklionhotel.net website: www.blacklionhotel.net

Lowestoft

Resort town on the North Sea coast, 38 miles north east of Ipswich.

BROADLAND HOLIDAY VILLAGE, OULTON BROAD, LOWESTOFT NR33 9JY (01502 573033). Discover the delights of the forgotten Norfolk Broad with your faithful friend. Stay in cosy brick bungalows, some with outdoor hot tubs, or pine lodges. Indoor heated pool. The perfect holiday for the whole family! [Pets £30 per week].
website: www.broadlandvillage.co.uk

Middleton

Village 3 miles East of Yoxford.

FUSCHIA COTTAGE, MIDDLETON. Detached cottage fronting onto green. Sleeps 4. Fenced rear courtyard. Pretty quiet village. Lovely walks. Pets welcome. Close to Aldeburgh and Minsmere. For brochure phone: Mrs Jane Brewer, LODGE COTTAGE, LAXFIELD ROAD, CRATFIELD, HALESWORTH IP19 0QG (01986 798830)
e-mail: janebrewer@ukonline.co.uk

Nayland

Small town on River Stour, 6 miles north of Colchester.

GLADWINS FARM, HARPER'S HILL, NAYLAND CO6 4NU (01206 262261). Self-catering cottages (sleep 2-8) and B&B set in 22 acres of Suffolk countryside. Indoor heated pool, sauna, hot tub, tennis court and playground. Loads of dog walking. [Pets £20 per week] ETC ★★★★/★★★★★.
e-mail: gladwinsfarm@aol.com website: www.gladwinsfarm.co.uk

Orford

Village on River Ore, 9 miles east of Woodbridge.

THE CROWN AND CASTLE, ORFORD, WOODBRIDGE IP12 2LJ (01394 450205). Comfortable and very dog-friendly hotel situated close to 12th century castle in historic and unspoilt village of Orford. Honest good food served in award-winning Trinity Restaurant. [Pets £10 per night]
e-mail: info@crownandcastle.co.uk website: www.crownandcastle.co.uk

Saxmundham

Small town 18 miles NE of Ipswich.

SWEFFLING HALL FARM, SWEFFLING, SAXMUNDHAM IP17 2BT (Tel & Fax: 01728 663644). In a quiet location. One double and one family room with en suite/private bathrooms. Ideal for walking/cycling and Heritage Coast. Open all year. Always a warm welcome. [pw!]
e-mail: stephenmann@suffolkonline.net

Sudbury

Birthplace of Thomas Gainsborough, with a museum illustrating his career. Colchester 13 miles.

Situated in small, picturesque village within 15 miles of Sudbury, Newmarket Racecourse and historic Bury St Edmunds. Bungalow well equipped to accommodate 4 people. All facilities. Car essential, parking. Children and pets welcome. Terms from £74 to £147 per week. For further details send SAE to MRS M. WINCH, PLOUGH HOUSE, STANSFIELD, SUDBURY CO10 8LT (01284 789253). []

Pet-Friendly
Pubs, Inns & Hotels
on pages 424-432
Please note that these establishments may not feature in the main section of this book

Bring The Whole Family...

Get off on the right foot whether you are a walker, climber potholer, sportsman . . . enjoy a relaxing holiday visiting the many country houses in the Peak District and Derbyshire Dales one of the most beautiful settings in Britain.

- **Choose from over 220 quality self catering properties**
- **Pets welcome in many**

Peak Cottages

Call for a brochure today

0114 262 0777

Or secure bookings on our website

peakcottages.com

Ashbourne, Buxton

DOG & PARTRIDGE

·COUNTRY INN·

Mary and Martin Stelfox welcome you to a family-run 17th century Inn and Motel set in five acres, five miles from Alton Towers and close to Dovedale and Ashbourne. We specialise in family breaks, and special diets and vegetarians are catered for. All rooms have private bathrooms, colour TV, direct-dial telephone, tea-making facilities and baby listening service. Ideal for touring Stoke Potteries, Derbyshire Dales and Staffordshire Moorlands. Open Christmas and New Year. 'Staffs Good Food Winners 2003/2004'.

Restaurant open all day, non-residents welcome

e-mail: info@dogandpartridge.co.uk

Tel: 01335 343183 • www.dogandpartridge.co.uk

Swinscoe, Ashbourne DE6 2HS

Alison Park Hotel **3 Temple Road, Buxton SK17 9BA • 01298 22473**
Situated close to the Pavilion Gardens and within a few minutes' walk of the Opera House. • 17 bedrooms, all with either en suite or private bathroom. • Full English or Continental breakfast, full dinner menu and an extensive wine list; lunches, bar meals & dinner available to non-residents. • Vegetarian and special diets catered for. • Lounge with colour TV. • All bedrooms have tea & coffee makers, colour TV etc. • Wheelchair ramp access. • Ground floor bedrooms. • Lift to all floors. • Conference facilities. • Licensed.
Fax: 01298 72709 • e-mail: reservations@alison-park-hotel.co.uk • www.alison-park-hotel.co.uk

The Devonshire Arms *Peak Forest, Near Buxton, Derbyshire SK17 8EJ*
Traditional inn in the heart of the Peak District. Close to all main attractions. Excellent walking country. All rooms refurbished to a high standard. En suite, TV, tea/coffee facilities. Excellent meals and traditional ales. Warm welcome to all. Dogs free. Prices from £32.50.

Tel: 01298 23875 www.devarms.com ETC ★★★

PRIORY LEA HOLIDAY FLATS. Beautiful situation adjoining woodland walks and meadows. Cleanliness assured; comfortably furnished and well-equipped. Colour TV. Bed linen available. Full central heating. Sleep 2/6. Ample private parking. Close to Poole's Cavern Country Park. Brochure available from resident owner. Open all year. Terms from £105 to £285. Short Breaks available. **ETC ★★/★★★.**

Mrs Gill Taylor, 50 White Knowle Road, Buxton SK17 9NH • Tel: 01298 23737
e-mail: priorylea@hotmail.co.uk • www.cressbrook.co.uk/buxton/priorylea

Draycott, Hope Valley

Hilltop Farm B&B

Hilltop Farm, Nottingham Road, Draycott, Derbyshire DE72 3PD

Overlooking open countryside, Hilltop Farm is an ideal base for those holidaying or working in the area, and is perfect for those travelling with pets. Close to both Nottingham and Derby, the A52 and the MI (Junction 25 is a 3 minute drive).
Two de luxe cabins (sleeping I-5) ensure completely private accommodation, and feel both rustic and comfortable, having timber floors and ceilings throughout, as well as a number of original features such as barn wooden beams and exposed brickwork.
Each cabin has highly modern en suite facilities comprising a luxury steam shower, sauna and whirlpool bath cabin, as well as satellite TV and tea and coffee making facilities.
There is also ample and secure parking as well as space to exercise pets.

Tel: (01332) 874902
info@hilltopfarmbandb.co.uk
www.hilltopfarmbandb.co.uk

THE LITTLE JOHN INN
Station Road, Hathersage
Hope Valley
Derbyshire S32 1DD

This handsome stone building which dates from the 19th century is popular with locals and visitors alike. It has won awards for its ale and carries a good selection of refreshments. This is just the place for a relaxing drink or meal after a day walking on the high moors. Home-cooked food is served in the bar, and there are two plasma screen TVs. The pub is mainly non-smoking. Accommodation is available in five en suite rooms and two charming cottages

Owner Stephanie Bushell offers all guests a warm welcome.

Tel: 01433 650225 • • Fax: 01433 659831

Looking for Holiday Accommodation?

FHG
·K·U·P·E·R·A·R·D·

for details of hundreds of properties throughout the UK, visit our website

www.holidayguides.com

BIGGIN HALL Tranquilly set 1000ft up in the White Peak District National Park, 17th century Grade II* Listed Biggin Hall – a country house hotel of immense character and charm where guests experience the full benefits of the legendary Biggin Air – has been sympathetically restored, keeping its character while giving house room to contemporary comforts. Rooms are centrally heated with bathrooms en suite, colour television, tea-making facilities, silent fridge and telephone. Those in the main house have stone arched mullioned windows, others are in converted 18th century outbuildings. Centrally situated for stately homes and for exploring the natural beauty of the area. Return at the end of the day to enjoy your freshly cooked dinner alongside log fires and personally selected wines.

Well behaved pets are welcome by prior arrangement

Biggin-by-Hartington, Buxton, Derbyshire SK17 0DH
Tel: 01298 84451
Fax: 01298 84681
www.bigginhall.co.uk

English Tourism Council ★★ HOTEL

Wheeldon Trees Farm

Earl Sterndale, Buxton SK17 0AA • Tel: 01298 83219

Relax and unwind with your dog(s) in our 18thC barn conversion. Eight cosy, well equipped holiday cottages sleeping 2-5, total 28.

www.wheeldontreesfarm.co.uk

PEAK COTTAGES (0114 262 0777). Quality self-catering accommodation in the Derbyshire Dales and Peaks. Whether you are a walker, climber, potholer, antiquarian, historian, naturalist, gardener or sportsman – Derbyshire has it all. Pets welcome in many. Telephone for colour brochure. [Pets £12 per week.]
website: www.peakcottages.com

Ashbourne

Market town on River Henmore, close to its junction with River Dove. Several interesting old buildings. Birmingham 42 miles, Nottingham 29, Derby 13.

MR & MRS LENNARD, WINDLEHILL FARM, SUTTON ON THE HILL, ASHBOURNE DE6 5JH (Tel & Fax: 01283 732377). Converted beamed barns on small organic farm - the Chop House sleeps 6 and has a fenced garden, the Hayloft sleeps 2 and is a first floor apartment. Well behaved pets welcome. ETC ★★★★ [pw! Pets £10 per week minimum]
e-mail: windlehill@btinternet.com website: www.windlehill.btinternet.co.uk

MRS M.M. STELFOX, DOG AND PARTRIDGE COUNTRY INN, SWINSCOE, ASHBOURNE DE6 2HS (01335 343183). 17th century Inn offering ideal holiday accommodation. Many leisure activities available. All bedrooms with washbasins, colour TV, telephone and private facilities. ETC/AA ★★ [🐕, pw!]
e-mail: info@dogandpartridge.co.uk website: www.dogandpartridge.co.uk

Buxton

Well-known spa and centre for the Peak District. Beautiful scenery and good sporting amenities. Leeds 50 miles, Matlock 20, Macclesfield 12.

ALISON PARK HOTEL, 3 TEMPLE ROAD, BUXTON SK17 9BA (01298 22473; Fax: 01298 72709). Situated close to the Pavilion Gardens. 17 bedrooms, all en suite or private bathroom. Lunches, bar meals and dinner available to non-residents. Wheelchair ramp access; ground floor bedrooms. Licensed. ETC ★★ [🐕]
e-mail: reservations@alison-park-hotel.co.uk website: www.alison-park-hotel.co.uk

THE DEVONSHIRE ARMS, PEAK FOREST, NEAR BUXTON SK17 8EJ (01298 23875) Situated in a village location in the heart of the Peak District. All rooms en suite with tea/coffee and colour TV. Meals served every day. Excellent walking area. ETC ★★★ [🐕]
website: www.devarms.com

PRIORY LEA HOLIDAY FLATS. Close to Poole's Cavern Country Park. Fully equipped. Full central heating. Sleep 2/6. Cleanliness assured. Terms from £105-£285. Open all year. Short Breaks available. ETC ★★/★★★. MRS GILL TAYLOR, 50 WHITE KNOWLE ROAD, BUXTON SK17 9NH (01298 23737). [pw! Pets £1 per night.]
e-mail: priorylea@hotmail.co.uk website: www.cressbrook.co.uk/buxton/priorylea

Draycott

Suburn 3 miles West of Long Eaton.

HILLTOP FARM B&B, NOTTINGHAM ROAD, DRAYCOTT DE72 3PD (01332 874902). An ideal base for those wanting a quiet and peaceful break, or those travelling with pets. Close to both Nottingham and Derby. Two deluxe cabins (sleeping 1-5) feel both rustic and comfortable with highly modern facilities. Ample and secure parking as well as space to exercise pets. [Pets £10 per night, £25 per week]
e-mail: info@hilltopfarmbandb.co.uk website: www.hilltopfarmbandb.co.uk

Hope Valley

Large valley in Peak District 4 miles from Hathersage.

THE LITTLE JOHN INN, STATION ROAD, HATHERSAGE, HOPE VALLEY S32 1DD (01433 650225; Fax: 01433 659831). Ideal for a relaxing drink or meal after walking the high moors. Popular local pub with award-winning ales and good selection of refreshments. Home cooked food. Five en suite rooms and two charming cottages.

Peak District National Park

A green and unspoilt area at the southern end of the Pennines, covering 555 square miles.

BIGGIN HALL, PEAK PARK (01298 84451). Close Dove Dale. 17th century hall sympathetically restored. Bathrooms en suite, log fires, C/H comfort, warmth and quiet. Fresh home cooking. Beautiful uncrowded footpaths. Brochure on request. ETC ★★ [🐕]
website: www.bigginhall.co.uk

WHEELDON TREES FARM, EARL STERNDALE, BUXTON SK17 0AA (01298 83219). Relax and unwind with your dog(s) in our 18thC barn conversion. Eight cosy, well equipped holiday cottages sleeping 2-5 (total 28). [🐕]
website: www.wheeldontreesfarm.co.uk

Other specialised holiday guides from FHG

PUBS & INNS OF BRITAIN • **COUNTRY HOTELS** OF BRITAIN

WEEKEND & SHORT BREAK HOLIDAYS IN BRITAIN

THE GOLF GUIDE WHERE TO PLAY, WHERE TO STAY

500 GREAT PLACES TO STAY • **SELF-CATERING HOLIDAYS** IN BRITAIN

BED & BREAKFAST STOPS • **CARAVAN & CAMPING HOLIDAYS**

FAMILY BREAKS IN BRITAIN

Published annually: available in all good bookshops or direct from the publisher:

FHG Guides, Abbey Mill Business Centre, Seedhill, Paisley PA1 1TJ

Tel: 0141 887 0428 • Fax: 0141 889 7204

e-mail: admin@fhguides.co.uk • www.holidayguides.com

Hay-on-Wye, Much Cowarne, Pembridge, Ross-on-Wye

BASKERVILLE ARMS HOTEL, Clyro, Near Hay-on-Wye HR3 5RZ
Tel: 01497 820670 **AA ★★★ INN**

Delightfully placed comfortable retreat 1.2 miles from Hay-on-Wye. Run by resident proprietors, the hotel provides tasty, home-cooked food in bar and restaurant, using the best local produce. This little hotel is a fine holiday base and well-appointed en suite bedrooms serve the purpose excellently. See website for Special Rate Breaks.

e-mail: info@baskervillearms.co.uk • www.baskervillearms.co.uk

Cowarne Hall Cottages

Much Cowarne, Herefordshire HR7 4JQ

Tel: 01432 820317 • E-mail: rm@cowarnehall.co.uk • www.cowarnehall.co.uk

Historic, comfortable cottages 'twixt the Malvern Hills and Wye Valley.
In a quiet rural location with wonderful views of fields and hills. Large garden with access to lanes and footpaths. Private enclosed patios. Convenient for nearby towns and attractions.
Free colour brochure and 'planner pack'. Richard and Margaret Bradbury.

Two flats (sleep 4), each superbly equipped, with open plan lounge, fitted kitchen/dining area, bathroom and toilet.The Granary has a wood burner, the Dairy on the ground floor an open fireplace. All linen and towels included. Ideal base for touring; lovely little woodland and riverside walks on the farm itself. Pets welcome under strict control. Terms from £188 per week.

Mrs N. Owens, The Grove, Pembridge, Leominster HR6 9HP
Tel: 01544 388268 • e-mail: nancy@grovedesign.co.uk

ETC ★★★

LEA HOUSE *is a former 16th Century Coaching Inn, beautifully refurbished with antiques, an inglenook fireplace and loads of beams. Home-made breads and preserves complement the excellent home-cooked meals. The area is a doggy paradise - The Royal Forest of Dean, Wye Valley and Welsh hills are close by. £30-£35pppn. Dogs £6 per stay.*

Lea, Ross-on-Wye HR9 7JZ • Tel: 01989 750652
e-mail: enquiries@leahouse.co.uk • www.leahouse.co.uk

Visit the FHG website

www.holidayguides.com

for details of the wide choice of accommodation featured in the full range of FHG titles

Pet-Friendly

Pubs, Inns & Hotels

on pages 424-432

Please note that these establishments may not feature in the main section of this book

Great Malvern

Fashionable spa town in last century with echoes of that period.

KATE AND DENIS KAVANAGH, WHITEWELLS FARM COTTAGES, RIDGEWAY CROSS, NEAR MALVERN WR13 5JR (01886 880607; Fax: 01886 880360). Charming converted Cottages, sleep 2–6. Fully equipped with colour TV, microwave, barbecue, fridge, iron, etc. Linen, towels also supplied. One cottage suitable for the disabled with full wheelchair access. Short breaks, long lets, large groups. ETC ★★★★ [pw! Pets £10 per week.] Also see Display Advert..
e-mail: info@whitewellsfarm.co.uk website: www.whitewellsfarm.co.uk

Hay-on-Wye

Small market town 15 miles north east of Brecon.

BASKERVILLE ARMS HOTEL, CLYRO, NEAR HAY-ON-WYE HR3 5RZ (01497 820670). Delightfully placed comfortable retreat with well appointed en suite bedrooms. Tasty, home-cooked food in bar and restaurant, using the best local produce. Special break rates. AA ★★★ Inn.
e-mail: info@baskervillearms.co.uk website: www.baskervillearms.co.uk

Leominster

Known as "The Town in the Marches", this historic market town is located in the heart of the beautiful border countryside and possesses some fine examples of architecture throughout the ages, such as The Priory Church and Grange Court. Ludlow 9 ½ miles, Hereford 12 miles.

CLIVE & CYNTHIA PRIOR, MOCKTREE BARNS, LEINTWARDINE, LUDLOW SY7 0LY (01547 540441). Gold Award winning cottages around a sunny courtyard. Sleep 2-6. Comfortable, well-equipped. Friendly owners. Dogs and children welcome. Non-Smoking. Lovely country walks. Ludlow, seven miles. Brochure. NAS Level 1 Accessibility. VB ★★★ [🐕] See also colour advertisement page 268
e-mail: mocktreebarns@care4free.net website: www.mocktreeholidays.co.uk

Much Cowarne

Village 5 miles SW of Bromyard.

RICHARD & MARGARET BRADBURY, COWARNE HALL COTTAGES, MUCH COWARNE HR7 4JQ (01432 820317) Historic, comfortable cottages 'twixt the Malvern Hills and Wye Valley. Large garden. Private enclosed patios. Convenient for nearby towns and attractions. Free brochure and 'planner pack'.
e-mail: rm@cowarnehall.co.uk website: www.cowarnehall.co.uk

Pembridge

Tiny medieval village surrounded by meadows and orchards.

MRS N. OWENS, THE GROVE, PEMBRIDGE, LEOMINSTER HR6 9HP (01544 388268). Two flats (sleep 4), each superbly equipped. All linen and towels included. Ideal base for touring; lovely walks on farm. Pets welcome under strict control. Terms from £188pw. ETC ★★★ [Pets £5 per week, pw!]
e-mail: nancy@grovedesign.co.uk

Ross-on-Wye

An attractive town standing on a hill rising from the left bank on the Wye. Cardiff 47 miles, Gloucester 17.

THE KING'S HEAD HOTEL, 8 HIGH STREET, ROSS-ON-WYE HR9 5HL (FREEPHONE: 0800 801098). 14th century Inn. All rooms en suite. Free wifi. Secure car park. Local real ales. Award-winning chef. Relaxed, friendly atmosphere. [🐕]
website: www.kingshead.co.uk

LEA HOUSE, LEA, ROSS-ON-WYE HR9 7JZ (Tel & Fax: 01989 750652). Double/family en suite; twin/double en suite; twin private bath - all individually styled with TV and beverage tray. Secluded garden. Dogs very welcome. £30-£35pppn. AA ★★★★ [Dogs £6 per stay]. See Display Advert.
e-mail: enquiries@leahouse.co.uk website: www.leahouse.co.uk

BROOK MEADOW LAKESIDE HOLIDAYS

* 3 self-catering chalets
* Farmhouse Bed & Breakfast
* Camping & Caravan site (electric hookups)
* Fully Stocked Carp Fishery

Brochure – Mary Hart, Welford Road, Sibbertoft, Market Harborough, Leics LE16 9UJ

Tel: 01858 880886 Fax: 01858 880485

e-mail: brookmeadow@farmline.com • www.brookmeadow.co.uk

SYSONBY KNOLL HOTEL Melton Mowbray, Leics LE13 0HP AA ★★★ ETC

Family-run hotel in rural setting on edge of market town. Grounds of five acres with river frontage. Superb food, comfortable accommodation and a genuine welcome for pets which is rarely found in a hotel of this standard. No charge for dogs, please see our website for further details.

Tel: 01664 563563 • www.sysonby.com

Market Harborough

Town on River Welland 14 miles south-east of Leicester.

BROOK MEADOW HOLIDAYS. Three self-catering chalets, farmhouse Bed and Breakfast, Carp fishing, camping and caravan site with electric hookups. Phone for brochure. ETC ★★★. MRS MARY HART, WELFORD ROAD, SIBBERTOFT, MARKET HARBOROUGH LE16 9UJ (01858 880886). [🐕 camping, £5 per night B&B, £12 Self-catering]
e-mail: brookmeadow@farmline.com website: www.brookmeadow.co.uk

Melton Mowbray

Old market town, centre of hunting country. Large cattle market. Church and Ann of Cleves' House are of interest. Kettering 29 miles, Market Harborough 22, Nottingham 18, Leicester 15.

SYSONBY KNOLL HOTEL, ASFORDBY ROAD, MELTON MOWBRAY LE13 0HP (01664 563563; Fax: 01664 410364.). Family-run hotel on edge of market town. Grounds of five acres with river frontage. Superb food, comfortable accommodation and a genuine welcome for pets. No charge for dogs, please see website for further details. ETC/AA ★★★ [🐕]
website: www.sysonby.com

Please note

All the information in this book is given in good faith in the belief that it is correct. However, the publishers cannot guarantee the facts given in these pages, neither are they responsible for changes in policy, ownership or terms that may take place after the date of going to press. Readers should always satisfy themselves that the facilities they require are available and that the terms, if quoted, still apply.

Barnoldby-Le-Beck, Gainsborough, Grantham, Horncastle, Langton-by-Wragby

Three well appointed cottages and riding school situated in the heart of the Lincolnshire Wolds.

GRANGEFARM
COTTAGES & RIDING SCHOOL

The tasteful conversion of a spacious, beamed Victorian barn provides stylish and roomy cottages, one sleeping 6, and two sleeping 4 in one double and one twin bedroom, comfy sittingroom and diningroom. Fully equipped kitchen. Bathroom with bath and shower.

You don't need to ride with us, but if you do....

The Equestrian Centre offers professional tuition, an all-weather riding surface, stabling for guests' own horses, and an extensive network of bridle paths.

GRANGE FARM COTTAGES & RIDING SCHOOL

Waltham Road, Barnoldby-le-Beck, N.E. Lincs DN37 0AR

For Cottage Reservations Tel: 01472 822216 • mobile: 07947 627663

www.grangefarmcottages.com

★★★★ SELF CATERING

The Black Swan Guest House

21 High Street, Marton, Gainsborough, Lincs DN21 5AH • Tel: 01427 718878

info@blackswanguesthouse.co.uk • www.blackswanguesthouse.co.uk

WELCOME HOST

AA ★★★★

We offer a warm welcome at our former 18th Century Coaching Inn. Fully refurbished to a high standard, the house and stable block now provide very comfortable accommodation. All rooms are en suite, and have digital TV and tea/coffee facilities. There is a guest lounge where our licence enables us to serve a good range of drinks, and you to relax. Our breakfasts are all freshly cooked to order using locally sourced best quality produce. The local area is steeped in history, and the city of Lincoln is only 12 miles away. Single from £45, Double/Twin from £68. We are a non-smoking establishment

WOODLAND WATERS Willoughby Road, Ancaster, Grantham NG32 3RT • Tel & Fax: 01400 230888

e-mail: info@woodlandwaters.co.uk • www.woodlandwaters.co.uk

Set in 72 acres of beautiful woodland walks. Luxury holiday lodges, overlooking the lakes and excellently equipped. Dogs welcome in some lodges. Bar/restaurant on site. Fishing. Golf nearby. Short Breaks available. Open all year. From £435 per week.

WELCOME HOST

POACHERS HIDEAWAY HOLIDAY COTTAGES

FLINTWOOD FARM, BELCHFORD, HORNCASTLE LN9 5QN (01507 533555)

4★-5★ SELF CATERING

Award-winning self catering cottages set in 150 acres of wildflower meadows, fishing lakes and woodland. Sleep 2-24. Miles of private pathways, direct access onto Viking Way footpath. Sauna, jacuzzi and massages available. Linen and towels provided. Stunning views, peaceful and relaxing.

e-mail: info@poachershideaway.com • www.poachershideaway.com

Ground floor accommodation in chalet-type house. Central for Wolds, coast, fens, historic Lincoln. Market towns, Louth, Horncastle, Boston, Spilsby, Alford, Woodhall Spa. Two double bedrooms. Washbasin, TV; bathroom, toilet adjoining; lounge with colour TV, separate dining room. Drinks provided. Children welcome reduced rates. Car almost essential, parking. Numerous eating places nearby. B&B from £25 per person (double/single let). Open all year. Tourist Board Listed. *** PETS WELCOME FREE ***

MISS JESSIE SKELLERN, LEA HOLME, LANGTON-BY-WRAGBY, LINCOLN LN8 5PZ (01673 858339)

Grasswells Farm Holiday Cottages

South Cockerington, Louth • ETC ★★★★

Two single barn conversions - spacious, comfortable and well equipped. Set in three acres of grounds with private fishing lake. Pets welcome. Sleep 2-5. *Contact:* Ms J. Foster, Grasswells Holiday Cottages (Saddleback Leisure Ltd), Saddleback Road, Howdales, South Cockerington, Louth LN11 7DJ • 01507 338508 • www.grasswells.co.uk

MRS GRAVES, GRANGE FARM, MALTBY-LE-MARSH, ALFORD LN13 0JP • 01507 450267

Farmhouse B&B and country Cottages set in 15 idyllic acres of Lincolnshire countryside. 2 miles from beach. Peaceful base for leisure and sightseeing. 2 Private fishing lakes • Many farm animals • Brochure available

••Pets welcome•• **www.grange-farmhouse.co.uk**

FARM • FISHING • FRIENDLY • FUN • Stay on a real farm on the edge of the village of Burgh le Marsh, only 5 miles from Skegness.

• Children's play area, farm animals. • Cottages have their own private fishing waters.
• Tennis court, plenty of space, ample parking, gardens. • Full colour brochure available.
2, 3 and 4 bedroom cottages.

Farm & Country cottages with private fishing

Wainfleet Road, Burgh Le Marsh, Lincs PE24 5AHTel/Fax: 01754 810904
e-mail: macka@freenetname.co.uk • www.thechestnutsfarm.co.uk

Stixwould Road, Woodhall Spa LN10 6QG • Tel: 01526 352411
Fax: 01526 353473 • reception@petwood.co.uk • www.petwood.co.uk

A country house hotel of unique charm, offering a high standard of comfort and hospitality in elegant surroundings. All bedrooms are fully equipped to meet the needs of today's discerning guests, and Tennysons Restaurant offers the very best of English and Continental cuisine. There are ample leisure opportunities available locally as well as tranquil villages and historic market towns to explore. **AA/ETC ★★★**

Barnoldby-le-Beck

Village 4 miles SW of Grimsby.

GRANGE FARM COTTAGES & RIDING SCHOOL, WALTHAM ROAD, BARNOLDBY-LE-BECK DN37 0AR (01472 822216; Fax: 01472 233550; mobile: 07947 627663). Three well appointed cottages and riding school situated in the heart of the Lincolnshire Wolds. Sleep 4/6. ETC ★★★★. Equestrian Centre offers tuition, all-weather riding, stabling. [Pets £20 per week]
website: www.grangefarmcottages.com

Gainsborough

Market town and River Port 15 miles NW of Lincoln.

THE BLACK SWAN GUEST HOUSE, 21 HIGH STREET, MARTON, GAINSBOROUGH DN21 5AH (01427 718878). Former 18th Century Coaching Inn, providing very comfortable accommodation. All rooms en suite, with digital TV and tea/coffee making facilities. Lincoln 12 miles away, many other attractions nearby. Non-smoking. AA ★★★★
e-mail: info@blackswanguesthouse.co.uk website:www.blackswanguesthouse.co.uk

Grantham

Market town 24 miles south of Lincoln.

WOODLAND WATERS, WILLOUGHBY ROAD, ANCASTER, GRANTHAM NG32 3RT (Tel & Fax: 01400 230888). Set in 72 acres of beautiful woodland walks. Luxury holiday lodges, overlooking the lakes and excellently equipped. Dogs welcome in some lodges. Bar/restaurant on site. Fishing. Golf nearby. Short Breaks available. Open all year. [Pets £1 per night camping, £20 per week lodges.]
e-mail: info@woodlandwaters.co.uk website: www.woodlandwaters.co.uk

Horncastle

Market town once famous for annual horse fairs. 13th century Church is noted for brasses and Civil War relic

POACHERS HIDEAWAY HOLIDAY COTTAGES, FLINTWOOD FARM, BELCHFORD, HORNCASTLE LN9 5QN (01507 533555). Sleep 2-24. Award-winning self catering cottages set in 150 acres of wildflower meadows, fishing lakes and woodland. Sauna, jacuzzi and massages available. Linen and towels provided. ETC 4-5 Stars [Pets £10 per week]
e-mail: info@poachershideaway.com website: www.poachershideaway.com

Langton-by-Wragby

Village located south-east of Wragby.

MISS JESSIE SKELLERN, LEA HOLME, LANGTON-BY-WRAGBY, LINCOLN LN8 5PZ (01673 858339). Ground floor accommodation in chalet-type house. Central for Wolds, coast, fens, historic Lincoln. Market towns, Louth, Horncastle, Boston, Spilsby, Alford, Woodhall Spa. Two double bedrooms. Washbasin, TV; bathroom, toilet adjoining; lounge with colour TV, separate dining room. Drinks provided. Children welcome reduced rates. Car almost essential, parking. Numerous eating places nearby. B&B from £25 per person (double/single let). Open all year. Pets welcome free. Tourist Board Listed [🐕]

Louth

Quaint market town with old fashioned architecture. Knwn as the 'Capital of the Lincolnshire Wolds'. 26 miles from Lincoln.

GRASSWELLS FARM HOLIDAY COTTAGES SOUTH COCKERINGTON, LOUTH. Two single barn conversions - spacious, comfortable and well equipped. Set in three acres of grounds with private fishing lake. Pets welcome. Sleep 2-5. ETC ★★★★ Contact: MS J. FOSTER, GRASSWELLS HOLIDAY COTTAGES (SADDLEBACK LEISURE LTD), SADDLEBACK ROAD, HOWDALES, SOUTH COCKERINGTON, LOUTH LN11 7DJ (01507 338508). [🐕]
website: www.grasswells.co.uk

Mablethorpe

Coastal resort 11 miles from Louth.

MRS GRAVES, GRANGE FARM, MALTBY-LE-MARSH, ALFORD LN13 0JP (01507 450267). Farmhouse B&B and country Cottages set in15 idyllic acres of Lincolnshire countryside. 2 miles from beach. Peaceful base for leisure, walking and sightseeing. Two private fishing lakes. Many farm animals. Brochure available. [Pets £4 per night B&B, £30 per week in cottages] *[⌂]*
website: www.grange-farmhouse.co.uk

Skegness

Coastal resort 19 miles NE of Boston.

THE CHESTNUTS, WAINFLEET ROAD, BURGH LE MARSH PE24 5AH (Tel & Fax: 01754 810904) Farm and Country Cottages with private fishing on a real farm, only 5 miles from Skegness. Cottages have private fishing waters. Children's play area, farm animals. Brochure available.
e-mail: macka@freenetname.co.uk website: thechestnutsfarm.co.uk

Woodhall Spa

Edwardian Spa Town 6 miles SW of Horncastle.

PETWOOD HOTEL, STIXWOULD ROAD, WOODHALL SPA LN10 6QG (01526 352411 Fax: 01526 353473). A country house hotel of unique charm, offering a high standard of comfort and hospitality in elegant surroundings. Tennysons Restaurant offers the very best of English and Continental cuisine. Ample leisure opportunities locally. AA/ETC ★★★ [Pets £15 per night.]
e-mail: reception@petwood.co.uk website: www.petwood.co.uk

Long Buckby

Murcott Mill Farmhouse • www.murcottmill.com
Murcott, Long Buckby, Northampton NN6 7QR
Tel/Fax: 01327 842236 • e-mail: carrie.murcottmill@virgin.net
Fabulous location for pets • Off-road, quiet, plenty of walks • Beautiful Georgian mill house • All rooms well appointed • En suite bathrooms newly refurbished • Friendly, animal-loving hosts • Delicious farmhouse breakfast • Separate lounge and dining room

Long Buckby

Village 5 miles NE of Daventry.

MURCOTT MILL FARMHOUSE, MURCOTT, LONG BUCKBY NN6 7QR (Tel & Fax: 01327 842236). Beautiful Georgian mill house, all rooms well appointed. Friendly, animal-loving hosts. Delicious farmhouse breakfast. Off road, quiet, plenty of walks. ETC ★★★★ [Pets £2 per night, £10 per week. pw!]
e-mail: carrie.murcottmill@virgin.net website: www.murcottmill.com

Nottinghamshire

Burton Joyce

Residential area 4 miles north-east of Nottingham.

MRS V. BAKER, WILLOW HOUSE, 12 WILLOW WONG, BURTON JOYCE, NOTTINGHAM NG14 5FD (0115 931 2070 or 07816 347706). Large Victorian house, authentically furnished, in quiet village near beautiful stretch of River Trent. Four miles city. Close to station/bus stop. Bright, clean rooms. TV. En suite. Parking. From £26pppn. Good local eating. Please phone first for directions. [🐕]

Other specialised holiday guides from FHG

PUBS & INNS OF BRITAIN • **COUNTRY HOTELS** OF BRITAIN
WEEKEND & SHORT BREAK HOLIDAYS IN BRITAIN
THE GOLF GUIDE WHERE TO PLAY, WHERE TO STAY
500 GREAT PLACES TO STAY • **SELF-CATERING HOLIDAYS** IN BRITAIN
BED & BREAKFAST STOPS • **CARAVAN & CAMPING HOLIDAYS**
FAMILY BREAKS IN BRITAIN

Published annually: available in all good bookshops or direct from the publisher:
FHG Guides, Abbey Mill Business Centre, Seedhill, Paisley PA1 1TJ
Tel: 0141 887 0428 • Fax: 0141 889 7204
e-mail: admin@fhguides.co.uk • www.holidayguides.com

Bishop's Castle, Bridgnorth, Church Stretton

Broadway House, Churchstoke, Powys SY15 6DU
Tel : 01588 620770 • e-mail: enqs@bordercottages.co.uk
www.bordercottages.co.uk WTB ★★★★★ Self Catering

The 17th century Lodge and 18th century Coach House are located in the grounds of a Regency gentleman's residence with picturesque views towards the South Shropshire hills and Clun Forest. Situated on the Wales/England border, steeped in a colourful history, with historic monuments, wonderful wildlife and country sports and pursuits nearby.

Linen & fuel included.
Minimum price £230 p.w
Sleep 5 and 2. Open all year.

The Granary

The Old Vicarage, Ditton Priors, Bridgnorth , Shropshire WV16 6SP
Tel: 01746 712272 • Fax: 01746 712288

Early 19th century Granary in hill country. Sleeps two/four with view over farmland. Antique furniture complements surroundings. Excellent walking, cycling. Pets welcome. The combined sitting room and dining area has a good quality sprung sofa bed and the Gallery Style kitchen has everything you need for your stay. The library is something we are very proud of, especially if you like antiques, old houses and books on the countryside. The bedroom has two full-size twin beds. Laundry room. The village has a good pub, shops, post office, butcher and surgery. Contact Mrs S. Allen.

E-mail: allens@oldvicditton.freeserve.co.uk • www.stmem.com/thegranary

North Hill Farm *Cardington, Church Stretton SY6 7LL • Tel: 01694 771532*

B&B accommodation in the beautiful Shropshire hills, one mile from Cardington village. Quiet, rural setting with plenty of wildlife. Ideal walking and riding country. Rooms have wonderful views with TV and hot drinks tray. Great local pubs. Well behaved dogs and horses welcome. B&B from £25pp. En suite courtyard room £30pp. Dogs £2 per night. Non-smoking. *Mrs Chris Brandon-Lodge*

e-mail: cbrandon@btinternet.com • www.virtual-shropshire.co.uk/northhill/

Online booking now available

THE LONGMYND HOTEL

CHURCH STRETTON
SHROPSHIRE SY6 6AG
Tel: 01694 722244
Fax: 01694 722718
info@longmynd.co.uk
www.longmynd.co.uk

AA ★★ HOTEL

Perched high above the pleasant town of Church Stretton in grounds of ten acres, this fine hotel enjoys sweeping views over the beautiful Welsh border country. The modern well furnished rooms all have en suite facilities.

Facilities also include an outdoor swimming pool, 9-hole pitch and putt course, and sauna. Riding, fishing, shooting and gliding may also be arranged nearby. The cuisine is noteworthy for its excellence and variety and there are superb facilities for conferences and other functions.

There are also self-catering lodges in the hotel grounds.

Two well-equipped modern caravan holiday homes situated at the head of the Clun valley in South Shropshire's Area of Outstanding Natural Beauty. Perfect for walking, cycling, riding, or just unwinding! Each caravan has three bedrooms, TV, shower room with flush toilet, and kitchen with fridge and microwave. Further shower room and laundry/drying room on site. Well behaved pets and children welcome, horses also accommodated. Open Easter to October.
From £160 per week incl. gas, electricity, bed linen and towels.

The Anchorage, Anchor, Newcastle on Clun, Craven Arms, Shropshire SY7 8PR • 01686 670737

Mocktree Barns Holiday Cottages

Gold Awards: 'Best Value for Money' 2006 • 'Sustainable Tourism' 2007

A small group of comfortable self-catering cottages around a sunny courtyard. Well-equipped. Sleeping 2-6. Two cottages with no stairs. Friendly owners. Open all year. Short breaks. Pets and children welcome. Lovely views. Excellent walks from the door through farmland and woods. Hereford, Cider Country, Black & White villages, Shropshire Hills, Shrewsbury, and Ironbridge all an easy drive. Beautiful Ludlow seven miles. Good food and drink nearby. Brochure available.

Clive and Cynthia Prior, Mocktree Barns, Leintwardine, Ludlow SY7 0LY
Tel: 01547 540441 • e-mail: mocktreebarns@care4free.net
www.mocktreeholidays.co.uk

VisitBritain

Four delightful cottages thoughtfully converted and equipped to the highest standard. All with en suite facilities and garden or seating area. One cottage with disabled access. Situated in a secluded valley and ideally located to explore the beautiful South Shropshire countryside. Sleep 2-6.

SALLY AND TIM LOFT, GOOSEFOOT BARN, PINSTONES, DIDDLEBURY, CRAVEN ARMS SY7 9LB • 01584 861326 **ETC ★★★★**

sally@goosefoot.freeserve.co.uk • www.goosefootbarn.co.uk

THE MOOR HALL

Built in 1789, the Moor Hall is a splendid example of Georgian Palladian style and enjoys breathtaking views over miles of unspoilt countryside. The atmosphere is relaxed and friendly. The gardens, which extend to five acres, provide a perfect setting in which to idle away a few hours, whilst the hills beyond offer wonderful discoveries for the more energetic. B&B from £30 pppn.

Near Ludlow, Shropshire SY8 3EG • 01584 823209 • Fax: 08707 492202
e-mail: info@moorhall.co.uk • www.moorhall.co.uk

AA ★★★★

Warm, comfortable Georgian coach house, friendly informal atmosphere, good traditional English Breakfast; delightful en suite rooms. Easy walking distance from town centre and local inns. Lots of nice local walks. TV, tea/coffee making facilities in all rooms. One double, two twin, and one single room, all en suite. Bed and Breakfast from £28 pppn.

Henwick House, Gravel Hill, Ludlow SY8 1QU

ETC ★★★ *B&B* **Tel: 01584 873338 • Miss S.J. Cecil**

TOP FARM HOUSE Knockin, Near Oswestry SY10 8HN

TELEPHONE: 01691 682582 E-MAIL: p.a.m@knockin.freeserve.co.uk

Grade I Listed black and white house. Bedrooms are all en suite, attractively decorated and furnished. All have tea/coffee making facilities, colour TV, etc. Convenient for the Welsh Border, Shrewsbury, Chester and Oswestry. Bed and Breakfast from £24 to £35 pp. **www.topfarmknockin.co.uk**

AA ★★★★

Oswestry

"JOHANSEN" RECOMMENDED

GOOD HOTEL GUIDE

A WELSH RAREBIT HOTEL

MICHELIN RECOMMENDED

JOHANSENS RECOMMENDED

AA ★★★

Food Award

Pen-y-Dyffryn COUNTRY HOTEL

RHYDYCROESAU, NEAR OSWESTRY, SHROPSHIRE SY10 7JD

This silver stone former Georgian Rectory, set almost a thousand feet up in the Shropshire/Welsh hills, is in a dream situation for both pets and their owners. Informal atmosphere, no traffic, just buzzards, badgers and beautiful country walks, yet Shrewsbury, Chester, Powis Castle & Lake Vyrnwy are all close by. The well-stocked bar and licensed restaurant are always welcoming at the end of another hard day's relaxing. All bedrooms en suite etc; four have private patios, ideal for pets; several have spa baths. Short breaks available from £85 pppd, Dinner, B&B. Pets free.

Tel: 01691 653700

e-mail: stay@peny.co.uk • www.peny.co.uk

Bishop's Castle

Small town in the hills on the Welsh Border, 8 miles from Craven Arms.

BROADWAY HOUSE, CHURCHSTOKE, POWYS SY15 6DU (01588 620770). 17th century Lodge and 18th century Coach House in the grounds of a Regency gentleman's residence on Wales/England border. Picturesque views. Linen and fuel included. Open all year. Sleep five and two. WTB ★★★★★ Self-Catering. [🐕]
e-mail: enqs@bordercottages.co.uk website: www.bordercottages.co.uk

Bridgnorth

Town on cliff above River Severn.

THE GRANARY, THE OLD VICARAGE, DITTON PRIORS, BRIDGNORTH WV16 6SP (01746 712272; Fax: 01746 712288) Early 19th century Granary in hill country. Sleeps two/four with view over farmland. Antique furniture complements surroundings. Excellent walking, cycling. Pets welcome. Contact Mrs S. ALLEN. VisitBritain ★★★.
e-mail: allens@oldvicditton.freeserve.co.uk website: www.stmem.com/thegranary

Church Stretton

Delightful little town in lee of Shropshire Hills. Walking and riding country. Facilities for tennis, bowls, gliding and golf. Knighton 22 miles, Bridgnorth 19, Ludlow 15, Shrewsbury 12.

MRS C.F. BRANDON-LODGE, NORTH HILL FARM, CARDINGTON, CHURCH STRETTON SY6 7LL (01694 771532). Rooms with a view! B&B in beautiful Shropshire hills. TV in rooms, tea etc. Ideal walking country. From £25 per person; en suite available. AA ★★★★ [pw! Pets £2 per night, ⌂]
e-mail: cbrandon@btinternet.com website: www.virtual-shropshire.co.uk/northhill/

THE LONGMYND HOTEL, CHURCH STRETTON SY6 6AG (01694 722244; Fax: 01694 722718). In 10 acre grounds, with sweeping views over Welsh border country. Outdoor pool, pitch-and-putt, sauna. Excellent and varied cuisine. Self-catering lodges in grounds. AA ★★ [Pets £4 per night}
e-mail: info@longmynd.co.uk website: www.longmynd.co.uk

Craven Arms

Surrounded by hills, Craven Arms is home to the Shropshire Hills Discovery Centre where you can experience virtual balloon rides and meet the "hairy mammoth". Beautiful Stokesey Castle lies just outside the town. Ludlow 6½ miles, Shrewsbury 19 miles.

Two well-equipped modern caravan holiday homes in Area of Outstanding Natural Beauty. Each has three bedrooms, TV, shower room with flush toilet, and kitchen with fridge and microwave. Well behaved pets and children welcome, horses also accommodated. Open Easter to October. THE ANCHORAGE, ANCHOR, NEWCASTLE ON CLUN, CRAVEN ARMS, SHROPSHIRE SY7 8PR (01686 670737). [Pets £10 per week].

Ludlow

Lovely and historic town on Rivers Teme and Corve with numerous old half-timbered houses and inns. Worcester 29 miles, Shrewsbury 27, Hereford 24, Bridgnorth 19, Church Stretton 16.

CLIVE & CYNTHIA PRIOR, MOCKTREE BARNS, LEINTWARDINE, LUDLOW SY7 0LY (01547 540441). Gold Award winning self-catering cottages around a sunny courtyard. Sleep 2-6. Comfortable, well-equipped. Friendly owners. Dogs and children welcome. Non-smoking. Lovely country walks. Ludlow, seven miles. Brochure. NAS Level 1 Accessibility. VB ★★★ [🐕] See also colour advertisement page 268.
e-mail: mocktreebarns@care4free.net website: www.mocktreeholidays.co.uk

SALLY AND TIM LOFT, GOOSEFOOT BARN, PINSTONES, DIDDLEBURY, CRAVEN ARMS, SHROPSHIRE SY7 9LB (01584 861326). Four delightful cottages thoughtfully converted and equipped to the highest standard. All with en suite facilities and garden or seating area. One cottage with disabled access. Situated in a secluded valley and ideally located to explore the beautiful South Shropshire countryside. Sleep 2-6. ETC ★★★★ [🐕]
e-mail: sally@goosefoot.freeserve.co.uk website: www.goosefootbarn.co.uk

THE MOOR HALL, NEAR LUDLOW SY8 3EG (01584 823209; Fax: 08707 492202). Built in 1789, a splendid example of the Georgian Palladian style. Breathtaking views, 5 acre garden. B&B from £30 pppn. AA ★★★★ [🐕]
e-mail: info@moorhall.co.uk website: www.moorhall.co.uk

HENWICK HOUSE, GRAVEL HILL, LUDLOW SY8 1QU (01584 873338). Warm, comfortable Georgian coach house, good traditional English Breakfast. Easy walking distance from town centre and local inns. Lots of nice local walks. TV, tea/coffee making facilities. One double, two twin, and one single room, all en suite. B&B from £28 pppn. ETC ★★★ [🐕]

Oswestry

Borderland market town. Many old castles and fortifications. Shrewsbury 16, Vyrnwy 18.

TOP FARM HOUSE, KNOCKIN, NEAR OSWESTRY SY10 8HN (01691 682582). Grade 1 Listed black and white house set in flower-filled gardens. En suite bedrooms. Hearty breakfast. Convenient for the Welsh Border, Shrewsbury, Chester and Oswestry. ETC/AA ★★★★ Guesthouse.
e-mail: p.a.m@knockin.freeserve.co.uk website: www.topfarmknockin.co.uk

PEN-Y-DYFFRYN COUNTRY HOTEL, NEAR RHYDYCROESAU, OSWESTRY SY10 7JD (01691 653700). Picturesque Georgian Rectory quietly set in Shropshire/ Welsh Hills. 12 en suite bedrooms, four with private patios. 5-acre grounds. No passing traffic. Johansens recommended. Dinner, Bed and Breakfast from £85.00 per person per day. AA ★★★. [🐕 pw!]
e-mail: stay@peny.co.uk website: www.peny.co.uk

A useful index of towns/counties appears at the back of this book

One cosy three bedroomed cottage which sleeps six, with four-poster. Also delightful flat which sleeps up to four. Both fully equipped and carpeted throughout; CD and DVD players. Electricity and linen inclusive, laundry room. Ideal base for Alton Towers, Potteries and Peak District. Terms £180 to £350.
EDITH & ALWYN MYCOCK, 'ROSEWOOD COTTAGE and ROSEWOOD FLAT', LOWER BERKHAMSYTCH FARM, BOTTOM HOUSE, NEAR LEEK ST13 7QP
Tel & Fax: 01538 308213 • www.rosewoodcottage.co.uk

WYNDALE GUEST HOUSE 199 Corporation St, Stafford ST16 3LQ
01785 223069 • wyndale@aol.com • www.wyndaleguesthouse.co.uk
Comfortable Victorian Guest House situated quarter mile from Stafford town centre and 3 miles from County Showground. Small nature reserve across the road ideal for dog walking.
★★★ GUEST HOUSE

LITTLE PARK HOLIDAY HOMES
Barn Conversion Units. Full self-catering. Facilities situated near to medieval castle and tourist village. Spectacular views. Near Alton Towers and other theme parks. Ample parking. Please phone for brochure.
Park Lane, Tutbury, Near Burton-on-Trent, Staffordshire DE13 9JQ
Tel & Fax: 01283 812654 • Mobile: 07884 343460

Leek

Village 10 miles from Stoke-on-Trent.

EDITH & ALWYN MYCOCK, 'ROSEWOOD COTTAGE and ROSEWOOD FLAT', LOWER BERKHAMSYTCH FARM, BOTTOM HOUSE, NEAR LEEK ST13 7QP (Tel & Fax: 01538 308213). Cosy three bedroomed cottage with four-poster, sleeps six; also flat, sleeps up to four. Fully equipped and carpeted. Electricity and linen inclusive, laundry room. Ideal base for Alton Towers, Potteries and Peak District. Terms £180 to £350. [Pets £7.50 per week]
website: www.rosewoodcottage.co.uk

Stafford

Town on River Sow 14 miles south of Stoke-on-Trent.

MRS N. ROBINSON, WYNDALE GUEST HOUSE, 199 CORPORATION STREET, STAFFORD ST16 3LQ (01785 223069). Comfortable Victorian Guest House situated quarter mile from Stafford town centre and 3 miles from County Showground. Small nature reserve across the road ideal for dog walking. ETC ★★★ [🐕]
e-mail: wyndale@aol.com website: www.wyndaleguesthouse.co.uk

Tutbury

Village 4 miles NW of Burton-Upon-Trent.

LITTLE PARK HOLIDAY HOMES, PARK LANE, TUTBURY, NEAR BURTON-ON-TRENT DE13 9JQ (Tel & Fax: 01283 812654; Mobile: 07884 343460). Barn Conversion Units. Full self-catering. Facilities situated near to medieval castle and tourist village. Spectacular views. Near Alton Towers and other theme parks. Ample parking. Please phone for brochure. [🐕]

FREE or REDUCED RATE entry to Holiday Visits and Attractions – see our **READERS' OFFER VOUCHERS** on pages 433-440

Warwick

THE CROFT ETC/AA ★★★★

Haseley Knob, Warwick CV35 7NL • Tel & Fax: 01926 484447

- Friendly family country guesthouse • non-smoking
- All rooms en suite or private bathroom, TV, hairdryer, tea/coffee
- Central location for Warwick, Stratford, Coventry and NEC.

e-mail: david@croftguesthouse.co.uk www.croftguesthouse.co.uk

Warwick

Town on the River Avon, 9 miles south-west of Coventry, with medieval castle and many fine old buildings.

DAVID & PATRICIA CLAPP, CROFT GUESTHOUSE, HASELEY KNOB, WARWICK CV35 7NL (Tel & Fax: 01926 484447). All bedrooms en suite or with private bathroom, some ground floor. Non-smoking. Picturesque rural setting. Central for NEC, Warwick, Stratford, Stoneleigh and Coventry. B&B single £40, double/twin £60. ETC/AA ★★★★ [Dogs £3 per night]
e-mail: david@croftguesthouse.co.uk website: www.croftguesthouse.co.uk

Worcestershire

Bishop's Frome, Great Malvern

Five Bridges Cottages

Nestled in the heart of the Herefordshire cider apple and hop growing regions, the cottages are set within the owner's 4-acre garden and smallholding.

Five Bridges Cottages
Near Bishop's Frome,
Worcester WR6 5BX
www.fivebridgescottage.co.uk
Tel: 01531 640340

MALVERN HILLS HOTEL AA ★★ HOTEL

Wynds Point, Malvern WR13 6DW

Enchanting family-owned and run hotel nestling high in the hills. Direct access to superb walking with magnificent views. Oak-panelled lounge, log fire, real ales, fine food and friendly staff. Great animal lovers.

Tel: 01684 540690
www.malvernhillshotel.co.uk

Great Malvern, Worcester

WHITEWELLS FARM COTTAGES

ETC ★★★★

Silver Award Winners 'Heart of England Excellence in Tourism Awards' Self-Catering Holiday of the Year

Ridgeway Cross, Near Malvern, Worcs WR13 5JR

Tel: 01886 880607 • Fax: 01886 880360 • e-mail: info@whitewellsfarm.co.uk • www.whitewellsfarm.co.uk

Seven well-established cottages converted from old farm buildings and a hop kiln, full of charm and character with original exposed timbering. The cottages are exceptionally clean and comfortable and equipped to the highest standards. One cottage suitable for the disabled with full wheelchair access. Idyllically set around a duckpond with two and a half acres of the property being a fully-fenced woodland plantation, ideal for exercising dogs, on or off the lead.

Set in unspoilt countryside with outstanding views of the **Malvern Hills** on the **Herefordshire/Worcestershire border. Ideal base for touring Worcestershire, Herefordshire, the Malverns, Gloucestershire, Welsh mountains, Cotswolds and Shakespeare country**. Electricity and linen included in price. Short breaks and long lets, suitable for relocation. Children and pets welcome. Open all year.

Colour brochure available from: Kate and Denis Kavanagh.

Grrrrrrrrreatest views in England!

Dogs greeted with a Bonio, guests with a smile!....

Superbly located high on the Malvern Hills you'll find this 3★ Country House Hotel.
Accommodation extends over three buildings, so ideal for late night 'walkies'.
Direct access to hills, 2 AA restaurant Rosettes, over 600 wines.

Cottage in the Wood

Holywell Rd, Malvern, Worcestershire, WR14 4LG

01684 58 88 60 www.cottageinthewood.co.uk

Croft Guest House, Bransford, Worcester WR6 5JD

16th-18th Century country house, 10 minutes from Worcester, Malvern and M5.
Close to Malvern Hills for wonderful views and dog walks.
Comfortable, non-smoking house.
B&B from £28 to £38 single, £47 to £65 double.

Ann & Brian Porter • Tel: 01886 832227

e-mail: hols@crofthousewr6.fsnet.co.uk • www.croftguesthouse.com

Harmony House - B&B Accommodation with a difference

Perched on the western side of the Malvern Hills, Harmony House welcomes all who come to stay. Enjoy one of our relaxing therapies, wonderful views, breakfast tailored to your specific desires, and a peaceful night's sleep in one of our three spacious en suite bedrooms. All have tea-making facilities, radio/tape/CD player (but no TV). Non-smoking. Well behaved dogs welcome.

184 West Malvern Road, Malvern, Worcestershire WR14 4AZ • Tel: 01684 891650

e-mail: Catherine@HarmonyHouseMalvern.com • www.HarmonyHouseMalvern.com

MOSELEY FARM BED AND BREAKFAST

Moseley Road, Hallow, Worcester WR2 6NL • Tel: 01905 641343 • Fax: 01905 641416

e-mail: moseleyfarmbandb@aol.com • www.moseleyfarmbandb.co.uk

Spacious 17th Century former farmhouse with countryside views. Rural location four miles from Worcester, 20 minutes from J5 or J7 of M5. Four rooms (two en suite), with colour TV, tea-making facilities and free wifi. Room only weekdays; full English breakfast at weekends. From £25pppn.

Readers are requested to mention this FHG guidebook when seeking accommodation

Bishop's Frome

Village 4 miles south of Bromyard.

FIVE BRIDGES COTTAGES, NEAR BISHOP'S FROME, WORCESTER WR6 5BX (01531 640340). Nestled in the heart of the Herefordshire cider apple and hop growing regions, the cottages are set within the owner's 4-acre garden and smallholding. [Pets £15 per week]
website: www.fivebridgescottage.co.uk

Great Malvern

Fashionable spa town in last century with echoes of that period.

MALVERN HILLS HOTEL, WYNDS POINT, MALVERN WR13 6DW (01684 540690). Enchanting family-owned and run hotel nestling high in the hills. Direct access to superb walking with magnificent views. Oak-panelled lounge, log fire, real ales, fine food and friendly staff. Great animal lovers. AA ★★ [Pets £5 per night].
website: www.malvernhillshotel.co.uk

KATE AND DENIS KAVANAGH, WHITEWELLS FARM COTTAGES, RIDGEWAY CROSS, NEAR MALVERN WR13 5JR (01886 880607; Fax: 01886 880360). Charming converted Cottages, sleep 2–6. Fully equipped with colour TV, microwave, barbecue, fridge, iron, etc. Linen, towels also supplied. One cottage suitable for the disabled with full wheelchair access. Short breaks, long lets, large groups. ETC ★★★★ [pw! Pets £10 per week.] Also see Display Advert..
e-mail: info@whitewellsfarm.co.uk website: www.whitewellsfarm.co.uk

THE COTTAGE IN THE WOOD, HOLYWELL ROAD, MALVERN (01684 588860). High on Malvern Hills. Accommodation over three buildings. 2 AA Restaurant Rosettes, over 600 wines. "Best view in England" - The Daily Mail. Call for brochure. ★★★ [🐕]
website: www.cottageinthewood.co.uk

ANN AND BRIAN PORTER, CROFT GUEST HOUSE, BRANSFORD, WORCESTER WR6 5JD (01886 832227). 16th-18th century country house. 10 minutes from Worcester, Malvern and M5. Non-smoking house. Family Room. Bedrooms have en suite (3), colour TV, tea and coffee tray, hairdryer, radio alarm. Dinners available. Dogs welcome. AA ★★ [🐕]
e-mail: hols@crofthousewr6.fsnet.co.uk website: www.croftguesthouse.com

HARMONY HOUSE, 184 WEST MALVERN ROAD, MALVERN WR14 4AZ (01684 891650). On the western side of the Malvern Hills. Wonderful views, breakfast tailored to your specific desires, and three spacious en suite bedrooms. Non-smoking. Well behaved dogs welcome.
e-mail: Catherine@HarmonyHouseMalvern.com website: www.HarmonyHouseMalvern.com

Worcester

Cathedral city on River Severn, 24 miles south-west of Birmingham.

MOSELEY FARM BED & BREAKFAST, MOSELEY ROAD, HALLOW, WORCESTER WR2 6NL (01905 641343; Fax: 01905 641416). Spacious 17thC former farmhouse in rural location, four miles from Worcester. 20 minutes from M5 J5 or 7. Four rooms, two en suite, with TV, tea/coffee making facilities and free wifi. Microwave, fridge and toaster in dining room for guests' use. Room only or full breakfast available weekends. From £25pppn [🐕]
e-mail: moseleyfarmbandb@aol.com website: www.moseleyfarmbandb.co.uk

Symbols

- 🐕 Indicates that pets are welcome free of charge.
- £ Indicates that a charge is made for pets: nightly or weekly.
- pw! Shows some special provision for pets; exercise facility, feeding or accommodation arrangement.
- ⌂ Indicates separate pets accommodation.

Cottages in Yorkshire

- See the best of the Dales, Coast and Wolds
- A wide range of cottages to choose from
- Personally inspected
- Pets welcome

Dales Holiday Cottages

Get your FREE brochure today

call **0870 909 9500** or visit **www.dalesholcot.com**

DALES HOLIDAY COTTAGES . See the best of the Dales, Coast and Wolds. A wide range of cottages to choose from, all personally inspected. Pets welcome. Free brochure. Call 0870 909 9500 or visit our website. [🐕]
website: www.dalesholcot.com

East Yorkshire

Beverley, Bridlington, Driffield, Grindale

Family B&B • Country location, 18 miles from historic York • Ideal for coast and Moors, racing, Beverley, Cycle Route 66 and Wolds Way • Beautiful country house and gardens • All rooms en suite • For bookings please contact ***Jeanne Wilson***

Robeanne House, Driffield Lane, Shiptonthorpe, York YO43 3PW

AA ★★★ Awards for Comfort & Hospitality

e-mail: enquiries@robeannehouse.co.uk • www.robeannehouse.co.uk

Robeanne House

THE TENNYSON

19 TENNYSON AVENUE,
BRIDLINGTON YO15 2EU
Tel: 01262 604382

Small, non-smoking, family hotel offering all usual amenities. B&B from £24pppn. All rooms en suite. Located within easy walking distance of town centre, North Beach and cliff walks.
Dogs £2.50 per dog per stay. AA ★★★
www.thetennysonhotel.co.uk

The Old Mill Hotel & Restaurant

Friendly country house hotel in tranquil Yorkshire Wolds. Renowned in-house restaurant provides à la carte and bar meal menu. Beautiful walks, Heritage Coastline, golf, clay pigeon shooting and the famous North York Moors all nearby. The hotel is within easy reach of Beverley, York, Scarborough and Bridlington. Why not come and meet our four Labradors?! B&B £48pp, DB&B £70pp
Discount on stays 3+ nights **Mill Lane, Langtoft, Near Driffield YO25 3BQ**
01377 267284 • enquiries@old-mill-hotel.co.uk • www.old-mill-hotel.co.uk

Smithy Cottage **Grindale, East Yorkshire YO16 4XU**

Unique & charming 4-star rated detached single storey 200-year-old former Blacksmiths. Ideal for exploring Heritage Coast, Filey and Bridlington. Spacious, period features, 4-poster bed, log fire, restored to high standard. Parking. Sleeps 4.
Tel: 01904 448933 • e-mail: karen.coman@virgin.net • www.thesmithy.info

PAWS - A - WHILE
Kilnwick Percy,
Pocklington YO42 1UF
Small family B&B set in forty acres of parkland twixt York and Beverley. Golf, Walking, Riding. Pets and horses most welcome. **Brochure available.**
Tel : 01759 301168 • Mobile: 07711 866869
e-mail: paws.a.while@lineone.net • www.pawsawhile.net

Beverley

Popular medieval market and county town in the East Riding of Yorkshire, 8 miles from Kingston upon Hull, 10 miles from Market Weighton and 12 from Hornsea.

ROBEANNE HOUSE, DRIFFIELD LANE, SHIPTONTHORPE, YORK YO43 3PW (01430 873312). Family B&B, country location, 18 miles from historic York. Ideal for coast, Moors, racing, Beverley, Cycle Route 66 and Wolds Way. Beautiful country house and gardens. All rooms en suite. Contact: JEANNE WILSON. AA ★★★ [pw! Pets £5 per night]
e-mail: enquiries@robeannehouse.co.uk website: www.robeannehouse.co.uk

Bridlington

Traditional family resort with picturesque harbour and a wide range of entertainments and leisure facilities. Ideal for exploring the Heritage coastline and the Wolds.

THE TENNYSON, 19 TENNYSON AVENUE, BRIDLINGTON YO15 2EU (01262 604382). Small, non-smoking, family hotel offering all usual amenities. B&B from £24pppn. All rooms en suite. Located within easy walking distance of town centre, North Beach and cliff walks. AA ★★★ [Pets £2.50 per stay].
website: www.thetennysonhotel.co.uk

Driffield

Town 11 miles south west of Bridlington.

THE OLD MILL HOTEL & RESTAURANT, MILL LANE, LANGTOFT, NEAR DRIFFIELD YO25 3BQ (01377 267284). Friendly country house hotel in Yorkshire Wolds. A la carte and bar meal menu. Beautiful walks, Heritage Coastline, golf, clay pigeon shooting and famous North York Moors all nearby. Why not come and meet our four Labradors?! AA ★★ [pw! Pets £5 per night, £30 per week]
e-mail: enquiries@old-mill-hotel.co.uk website: www.old-mill-hotel.co.uk

Grindale

Village 4 miles NW of Bridlington.

SMITHY COTTAGE, GRINDALE YO16 4XU (01904 448933). Unique and charming four-star rated detached single storey 200-year-old former Blacksmiths. Ideal for exploring Heritage Coast. Four-poster bed, log fire, restored to high standard. Parking. Sleeps 4. .
e-mail karen.coman@virgin.net website: www.thesmithy.info

Kilnwick Percy

Located 2 miles east of Pocklington

PAWS-A-WHILE, KILNWICK PERCY, POCKLINGTON YO42 1UF (01759 301168; Mobile: 07711 866869). Small family B & B set in forty acres of parkland twixt York and Beverley. Golf, walking, riding. Pets and horses most welcome. Brochure available. ETC ★★★★ [pw! 🐕]
e-mail: paws.a.while@lineone.net website: www.pawsawhile.net

www.holidayguides.com

Bentham, Bolton Abbey, Clapham, Coverdale, Danby, Denby Dale

HOLMES FARM • **Low Bentham, Lancaster LA2 7DE**

Attractively converted and well equipped stone cottage adjoining 17th century farm house, sleeping 4. In a secluded position surrounded by 127 acres of beautiful pastureland. Central heating, fridge, TV, washing machine, games room. Ideal base for visiting Dales, Lake District and coast.

Tel: 015242 61198 • www.holmesfarmcottage.co.uk • e-mail: lucy@holmesfarmcottage.co.uk

The Devonshire Arms Country House Hotel & Spa

Luxurious comfort, fine food and wines, relaxed and unstuffy
Beautiful setting on the Bolton Abbey Estate in the Yorkshire Dales

Yorkshire Small Hotel of the Year 2007/8 - AA Pets Friendly Hotel 2005

01756 718111 - res@devonshirehotels.co.uk

www.devonshirehotels.co.uk Bolton Abbey, North Yorks, BD23 6AJ ★★★★

New Inn Hotel *Clapham – 'Jewel of the Dales'*

Quality Accommodation in the Yorkshire Dales.

A comfortable hotel in the Yorkshire Dales National Park, The New Inn has been lovingly and carefully refurbished, with a fine blend of old and new to retain the characteristics of this fine 18th Century Coaching Inn. This traditional Village Inn has 19 en suite bedrooms, including ground floor and disabled bedrooms. Resident lounges, Restaurant, two comfortable bars serving a selection of Yorkshire ales, fine wines and a large selection of malt whiskies. Our food offers a mix of traditional and modern cooking.

New Inn Hotel, Clapham, Near Ingleton, N. Yorkshire LA2 8HH

Tel: 015242 51203 ❖ Fax: 015242 51824

e-mail: info@newinn-clapham.co.uk ❖ www.newinn-clapham.co.uk

★★ SMALL HOTEL

Peacefully situated farmhouse away from the madding crowd. B&B with optional Evening Meal. Home cooking. Pets sleep where you prefer. Ideally positioned for exploring the beautiful Yorkshire Dales.

Mrs Julie Clarke,
Middle Farm, Woodale,
Coverdale, Leyburn,
North Yorkshire DL8 4TY
01969 640271
e-mail: j-a-clarke@hotmail.co.uk

The Fox & Hounds Inn ***Ainthorpe, Danby YO21 2LD***

Residential 16th Century Coaching Inn. Freshly prepared dishes served every day. Superb en suite accommodation available. Ideal centre for the moors and coast. Open all year. Pets: £2.50 per night.
ETC ★★★★ *Situated between Castleton and Danby on the Fryup Road.*

For bookings please Tel: 01287 660218

Email: info@foxandhounds-ainthorpe.com • www.foxandhounds-ainthorpe.com

Ivy Holiday Cottage • Denby Dale • Yorkshire

Do you need a cheap holiday break?

Pets free of charge. Lovely walking area, close to moors. Village location and close to craft mills, railway station and good pubs. Fully heated, sleeps 2/4, fully equipped, luxury standard, linen and towels supplied.

£45-£50 per group per night. Short Breaks available all year.

Call Sue on 0121 453 7622

Last of The Summer Wine area

Pet-Friendly
Pubs, Inns & Hotels

on pages 424-432

Please note that these establishments may not feature in the main section of this book

The Foresters Arms

MAIN STREET, GRASSINGTON, SKIPTON
NORTH YORKSHIRE BD23 5AA
Tel: 01756 752349 • Fax: 01756 753633

The Foresters Arms, Grassington, once an old coaching inn, situated in the heart of the Yorkshire Dales. An ideal centre for walking or touring. A family-run business for over 35 years. Serving hand-pulled traditional ales. Home made food served lunchtime and evening. All bedrooms are en suite, having satellite TV and tea/coffee making facilities. Prices £35 single; £70 double. *Proprietor: Rita Richardson*

★★★ GUEST ACCOMMODATION

Fir Tree Farm Holiday Homes - Willow Tree Lodge

Sleeps 4. On a privately owned 100-acre farm in beautiful woodland amidst rolling hills, ideal for exploring the Dales. 10 miles from Ripon and 4 miles from Masham. Short breaks available off-peak. Pets welcome.

High Bramley, Grewelthorpe, Ripon HG4 3DL
Tel: 01765 658727 • www.firtree-farm-holidayhomes.co.uk

★★★★ SELF CATERING

RELAX IN THE HEART OF YORKSHIRE

RUDDING
HOLIDAY PARK

LUXURY COTTAGES AND **TIMBER LODGES**
IN **BEAUTIFUL SURROUNDINGS**

- Deer House family pub
- Children's adventure playground
- Pets welcome • Games room
- Heated outdoor swimming pool and paddling pool
- 18 hole pay & play golf course plus floodlit driving range • 6-hole short course

FOLLIFOOT, HARROGATE HG3 1JH
TEL: 01423 870439 | FAX: 01423 870859
e-mail - holiday-park@ruddingpark.com
www.ruddingpark.com

Holidays for Discriminating Dogs
Yorkshire Dales

- **Sniffing trails**
- **Top paw category**
- **29 acre woodland walks**
- **Area of Outstanding Natural Beauty**
- **David Bellamy Gold Conservation Award**
- **Watch wildlife from quality accommodation**
- **Central: Harrogate, York, Skipton, Herriot/Bronte Country**

WELCOME HOST

★★★★ SELF CATERING

FHG Guides

publish a large range of well-known accommodation guides.
We will be happy to send you details or you can use the order form at the back of this book.

Harrogate, Hawes

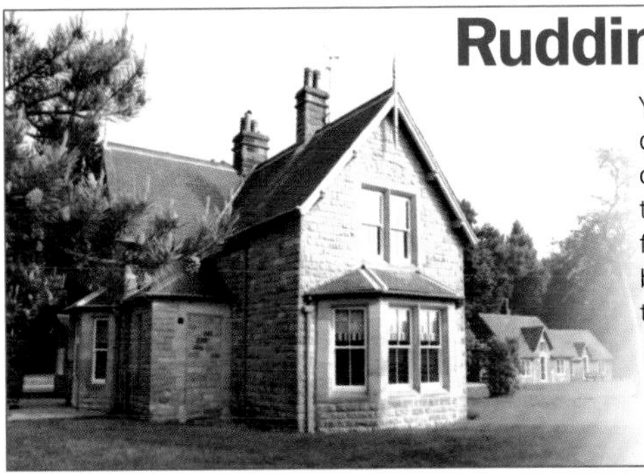

Rudding Estate Cottages

You and your pet can relax in the peace and quiet of a very private country estate in the heart of the Yorkshire countryside. These four traditional country cottages are comfortably furnished, fully equipped and welcome well behaved pets. Towels are provided for dogs and their owners! Please call for a brochure.

Tel: 01423 844844
e-mail: info@rudding.com
www.rudding.com/cottages

STONE HOUSE HOTEL

Licensed Country House Hotel & Restaurant overlooking Magnificent Wensleydale

23 Quality En Suite Bedrooms
(some with private conservatories opening onto Gardens)

Delicious food & Fine Wines

The Perfect Venue for a relaxing break deep in the heart of the Yorkshire Dales.

Dogs genuinely welcome – Short Breaks available now

Sedbusk, Hawes
North Yorkshire DL8 3PT

Tel: 01969 667571
www.stonehousehotel.com

Experience the unique atmosphere and traditional hospitality at...

SIMONSTONE HALL
Simonstone Hall, Hawes, North Yorkshire DL8 3LY

Set in magnificent countryside near the market town of Hawes, Simonstone Hall is a beautifully restored country house hotel with spectacular views over the dale and surrounding fell.

- **Outstanding Bar Meals and Sunday Lunches served in the Game Tavern and Orangery, our Restaurant provides an elegant setting for our wide selection of fine foods and wines.**
- **An excellent base for walking and exploring the Dales.**
- **Pets welcome in most rooms.**

A relaxed, friendly establishment with open fires, four-poster beds and experienced staff to look after all your needs.

Telephone: 01969 667255 • Fax: 01969 667741
e-mail: e-mail@simonstonehall.demon.co.uk
www.simonstonehall.co.uk **AA ★★**

Cocklake House

MALLERSTANG CA17 4JT • 017683 72080

Charming, High Pennine Country House B&B in unique position above Pendragon Castle in Upper Mallerstang Dale offering good food and exceptional comfort to a small number of guests. Two double rooms with large private bathrooms. Three acres riverside grounds. Dogs welcome.

COUNTRY COTTAGE HOLIDAYS

DRYDEN HOUSE ◆ MARKET PLACE ◆ HAWES ◆ N. YORKS DL8 3RA

80 Cottages in the lovely Yorkshire Dales. Our Cottages feature colour TV, central heating, open fires, superb views, gardens, private parking and many allow pets. Sleep 1-10. Short breaks throughout the year - Rents from £120 per Break. Weekly Rents from £200 per week. Brochure / Booking Line open 9.00am - 6.00pm daily (Answer machine out of hours).

Browse/book our properties on www.countrycottageholidays.co.uk

Telephone **WENSLEYDALE (01969) 667 654**

VisitBritain ★★★★ Silver Award

Laskill Grange • Near Helmsley

AA ★★★★

Delightful country house is set in a one-acre garden which has a lake with ducks, swans, peacock and a visiting otter. All rooms lovingly cared for and well equipped. Four bedrooms are in beamed outbuildings and open onto a lawn. All rooms en suite. Generous cuisine using local fresh produce, and vegetarians catered for. Open all year. B&B from £28.50.

Laskill Grange, Hawnby, Near Helmsley YO62 5NB (Contact Sue Smith)
01439 798268 • e-mail: laskillgrange@tiscali.co.uk • www.laskillgrange.co.uk

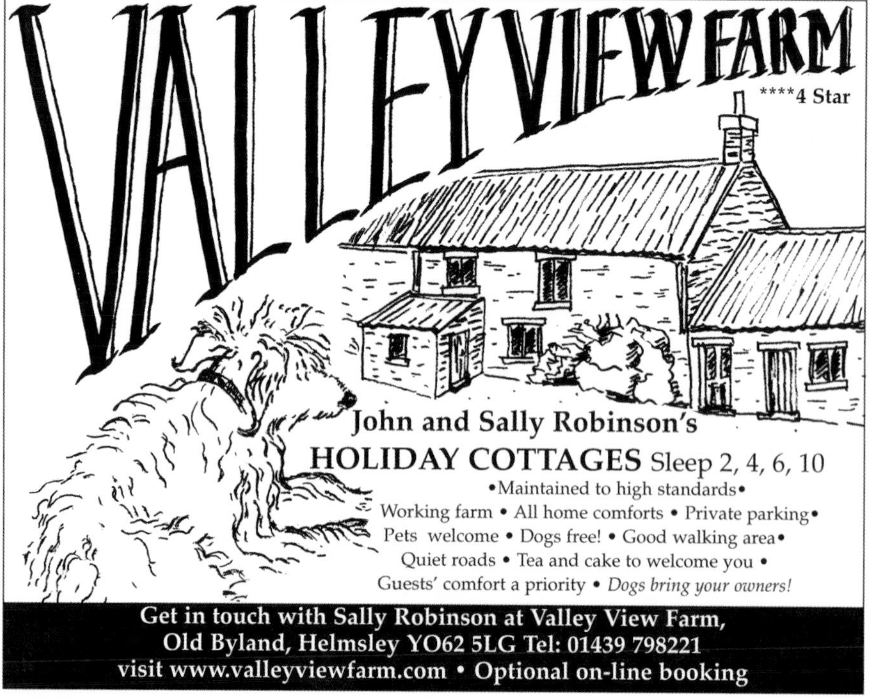

John and Sally Robinson's

HOLIDAY COTTAGES Sleep 2, 4, 6, 10

•Maintained to high standards•
Working farm • All home comforts • Private parking•
Pets welcome • Dogs free! • Good walking area•
Quiet roads • Tea and cake to welcome you •
Guests' comfort a priority • *Dogs bring your owners!*

Get in touch with Sally Robinson at Valley View Farm, Old Byland, Helmsley YO62 5LG Tel: 01439 798221
visit www.valleyviewfarm.com • Optional on-line booking

Kirkbymoorside, Knaresborough, Leeming Bar, Leyburn

Sinnington Common Farm Holiday Accommodation

Kirkbymoorside, York YO62 6NX • Tel: 01751 431719

E-mail: felicity@scfarm.demon.co.uk • www.sinningtoncommonfarm.co.uk

Sinnington Common Farm is a working family farm offering Bed & Breakfast and Self catering accommodation, set in beautiful countryside on the edge of the North Yorkshire moors in Ryedale.

The cottages, "Penny's Place" and "Bruno's Lodge" have been recently renovated to a high standard from original farm buildings. Sleep 2/3.

"Greystones" is a detached bungalow with large, private garden. Sleeps up to 6 people.

GALLON HOUSE ***47 Kirkgate, Knaresborough HG5 8BZ • 01423 862102***

e-mail: gallon-house@ntlworld.com • www.gallon-house.co.uk

Overlooking the beautiful Nidd Gorge, Gallon House offers award-winning accommodation and superb, locally sourced fresh food. Two double and one twin bedrooms, all en suite. Licensed. **ETC/AA ★★★★** *Gold Award*

Newton House, Knaresborough

Delightful Georgian Guest Accommodation. Spacious, tastefully decorated, exceptionally well equipped rooms. Ideal base for exploring Yorkshire.

• Genuine warm welcome • Comfortable sitting-room • DAB radios, TVs, WIFI

• Molton Brown toiletries • Licensed • **Tel: 01423 863539**

www.newtonhouseyorkshire.com newtonhouse@btinternet.com

AA 4 Star Highly Commended • AA Breakfast award

THE WHITE ROSE HOTEL, LEEMING BAR, NORTHALLERTON DL7 9AY

Tel: 01677 422707/424941 • Fax: 01677 425123

Ideally situated for touring the spectacular scenery of two National Parks, Yorkshire Dales, coastal resorts, Herriot & Heartbeat Country. 18 rooms, all private bathroom, 10-channel digital TV/radio, tea & coffee, hair dryer, trouser press and telephone. B&B £49 single, £63 double/twin, £69 family room all including breakfast.

e-mail: john@whiterosehotel.co.uk www.whiterosehotel.co.uk

Tel: 01969 622161

Fax: 01969 623836

e-mail: info@goldenlionleyburn.co.uk

Golden Lion HOTEL

Market Place, Leyburn, North Yorkshire DL8 5AS

At the gateway to Wensleydale, this splendid hotel dates from 1765, although it has been tastefully modernised. Light meals and afternoon teas are served in the bars, and the restaurant with its picture windows and colourful murals is a popular venue. Excellent accommodation is available in rooms with bathrooms en suite, television, telephone, radio and tea and coffee-makers. A lift operates to all floors. Within easy walking distance is the little town of Middleham on the River Ure which is well known as a racehorse training centre.

THE OLD STAR, WEST WITTON, LEYBURN DL8 4LU

Former 17th century Coaching Inn now run as a guest house.
Oak beams, log fire, home cooking. En suite B&B from £26 pppn.

e-mail: enquiries@theoldstar.com www.theoldstar.com

BARBARA & BARRIE MARTIN 01969 622949

Malham - Miresfield Farm • In beautiful gardens bordering village green and stream. Well known for excellent food. 11 bedrooms, all with private facilities. Full central heating. Two well furnished lounges and conservatory for guests' use. ETC ★★★. B&B from £24pppn. **Mr C. Sharp, Miresfield Farm, Malham, Skipton BD23 4DA • Tel: 01729 830414**

BANAVIE ETC ★★★★ **Mrs Ella Bowes, Banavie, Roxby Road, Thornton-le-Dale, Pickering YO18 7SX Tel: 01751 474616**

Large stone-built semi-detached house set in Thornton-le-Dale. Ideal for touring. One family bedroom and two double bedrooms, all en suite. All with TV, shaver points, central heating and tea-making facilities. Open all year. Car park, cycle shed. B&B from £27pppn. Hygiene Certificate held. Your pets are very welcome.

www.banavie.uk.com e-mail: info@banavie.uk.com

The White Swan Inn at Pickering

Market Place, Pickering, North Yorkshire YO18 7AA
Tel: 01751 472288 • Fax: 01751 475554
e-mail: welcome@white-swan.co.uk
www.white-swan.co.uk

AA Rosette since 1996 • ETC ★★★

16th century inn, with a buzz. Relaxed and informal atmosphere with friendly and professional staff. A passion for good food, fine wine and people.

Discover our exclusive meat supply from The Ginger Pig - a top butcher, with fantastic rare breed meat farmed just 7 miles from the inn.

Rooms and Suites beyond expectation but affordably priced. The surrounding countryside offers a thousand and one things to do and places to visit.

NORTH YORKSHIRE MOORS NATIONAL PARK

Stone Cottage with log fire in North York Moors National Park. Sleeps 4.
Near Cleveland Coastal Footpath, sea view. Non-smoking. Whitby 9 miles. Brochure available.
Mrs J. Hiley, 3 Valley Gardens, Stockton-On-Tees, Teesside TS19 8BE
Tel: 01642 613888

EAST FARM COUNTRY COTTAGES, Scalby Nabs, Scarborough, North Yorks • 01723 353635

Single storey, two-bedroom stone cottages (no steps/stairs), set in beautiful countryside within the National Park yet only 5 minutes away from Scarborough. All cottages non-smoking, garden and parking. Ideal base for walking and touring the coastline. Terms £210-£495 per week.

e-mail: joeastfarmcottages@hotmail.co.uk • www.eastfarmcountrycottages.co.uk

Raven Hall COUNTRY HOUSE HOTEL, LODGES & GOLF COURSE
Ravenscar, Scarborough YO13 0ET • 01723 870353 • Fax: 01723 870072
e-mail: enquiries@ravenhall.co.uk • www.ravenhall.co.uk

High above the cliffs where the North York Moors roll down to the sea , this imposing hotel is full of Georgian splendour, and offers outstanding accommodation, superb, typically Yorkshire cuisine and an impressive range of leisure facilities including a 9-hole golf course. A family holiday paradise. AA ★★★ NEW LUXURY LODGES

CAYTON VILLAGE CARAVAN PARK

The very best of coast and country. Luxurious facilities, adventure playground, site shop, dog walk. Seasonal pitches, supersites, hardstanding and storage. Open 1st March - 31st October.
½ mile to beach, adjoining village, 3 miles to Scarborough, 4 miles to Filey.

Cayton Village Caravan Park Ltd, Mill Lane, Cayton Bay, SCARBOROUGH YO11 3NN
01723 583171 • info@caytontouring.co.uk • www.caytontouring.co.uk

Scarborough, Skipton

HARMONY COUNTRY LODGE

ETC ★★★★

Limestone Road, Burniston, Scarborough YO13 0DG (Non-Smoking)

Unique octagonal peaceful retreat in own grounds with superb 360º views of National Park and sea. Two miles from Scarborough. Parking facilities and fully licensed. B&B £29 to £37. Five-berth caravan available for self-catering from £150 to £355. Local dog walks. Pets welcome.

Sue & Tony Hewitt • Tel: 0800 2985840 • www.harmonycountrylodge.co.uk

Humble Bee Cottages

www.humblebeefarm.co.uk
info@humblebeefarm.co.uk

Humble Bee Farm, Flixton, Scarborough YO11 3UJ • 01723 890437

★★★★ SELF CATERING

Relax and unwind in this idyllic rural haven in the heart of the Yorkshire Wolds on our 320-acre farm. Our luxury holiday cottages and unique wigwams offer a fabulous holiday destination. Located close to the East Coast resorts of Scarborough, Whitby, Filey. Ideal for visiting the North York Moors. All our cottages are tastefully furnished and maintained to a high standard. Many original features. Open all year round. **WELL BEHAVED PETS WELCOME BY PRIOR ARRANGEMENT**

Scarborough
Whitby • York

Honeysuckle Cottage

Lovely, stone-built, self-catering cottage in village of East Ayton on River Derwent. Scarborough 4 miles. Sleeps 2-5 + cot. Patio/garden with gas barbecue. Non-smoking. Pets welcome. Private parking. Open all year. EnjoyEngland ★★★★

Tel: David & Jane Beeley •Tel: 01723 882284
e-mail: info@forgevalleycottages.co.uk
www.forgevalleycottages.co.uk

Over 250 super self-catering cottages
IN THE YORKSHIRE DALES, YORK, COAST, MOORS, LANCASHIRE, PEAK and LAKE DISTRICT

Fully illustrated brochure 01756 700872 www.holidaycotts.co.uk
Holiday Cottages Yorkshire Ltd., *Incorporating Red Rose Cottages*
Water St., Skipton, North Yorkshire BD23 1PB

Holiday Cottages

BECK HALL, MALHAM BD23 4DJ

18th century B&B on the Pennine Way, log fires and huge breakfasts. Midweek and 4-night specials.
Ideal for exploring the Yorkshire Dales. Tel: 01729 830332
e-mail: simon@beckhallmalham.com
www.beckhallmalham.com

AA ★★★ Guest House
WELCOME HOST

Situated on the A65 Skipton to Kendal Road, the hotel provides an ideal base for guests wishing to explore the Yorkshire Dales or just get away from it all. Set in a stunning 1400-acre estate with 24-acre lake. The hotel offers 50 en suite bedrooms, a restaurant, with a bar and orangery for more informal meals.

Ten luxury bedrooms now open!

AA ★★★ ★★★ HOTEL Silver

THE CONISTON HOTEL

Clay Pigeon Shooting, Off-Road Driving, Falconry and Fishing available on site. Exceptional location for conferences and weddings. Special rates for Leisure Breaks and family rooms.

Coniston Cold, Skipton, North Yorkshire BD23 4EB

Tel: 01756 748080 • Fax: 01756 749487 • e-mail: sales@theconistonhotel.com • www.theconistonhotel.com

Available for Holiday Letting on a weekly or short break basis. Large Victorian terraced house with 7 bedrooms, sleeps up to 16. Suitable for large groups, extended families or just for the luxury of plenty of space! Dogs welcome by arrangement. Well equipped kitchen with a working Aga, dining room, lounge and cosy basement TV room.

Craven House

56 Keighley Road, Skipton BD23 2NB
Tel & Fax: 01756 794657
info@craven-house.co.uk
www.craven-house.co.uk

Situated on a quiet terrace in the old part of the picturesque, historic village of Staithes, with its artistic and Captain Cook associations, Brooklyn is a solid, red brick house, built in 1921 by a retired sea captain. It has three letting rooms (two doubles, one twin) which are individually decorated with views across the rooftops to Cowbar cliffs. All have a television and tea/coffee making facilities, and although not en suite, do have washbasins. The dining room doubles as a sitting room for guests, and breakfasts are generous, vegetarians catered for, and special diets by arrangement. Pets and children are most welcome.

BROOKLYN B & B

MS M.J. HEALD, BROOKLYN B&B, BROWN'S TERRACE, STAITHES, NORTH YORKSHIRE TS13 5BG
Tel: 01947 841396
m.heald@tesco.net
www.brooklynuk.com

The best B&B in the best village in North Yorkshire

★★★ BED & BREAKFAST

POPLARS HOLIDAY COTTAGES AND BED & BREAKFAST • THIRSK

The Poplars stands in two acres of lovely gardens with a field for dog walking. We have old brick cottages and new lodges, with bed and breakfast in the Poplars House. Contact

AMANDA RICHARDS, THE POPLARS, CARLTON MINIOTT, THIRSK YO7 4LX
Tel: 01845 522712 • www.thepoplarsthirsk.com

Silver SILVER AWARD
★★★★ ★★★★ SELF CATERING

Foxhills Hideaways • Felixkirk, Thirsk YO7 2DS

Quiet, no hassle holidays in cosy Scandinavian log cabins.
Secluded garden setting. Central for the Moors, Dales, York and the coast. Village pub round the corner.
Fully inclusive prices (£250 to £380 per week).
Open all year. Pets welcome.

Out of season short breaks from £120 inclusive. Please write or phone for a brochure

TELEPHONE 01845 537575

FOXHILLS HIDEAWAYS NORTH YORKSHIRE

Whitby 2k • Close to sea and moors

Self-catering two-bedroom cottages, all fully equipped

Central heating • Dogs welcome • Parking • Camping Site

For further information phone
01947 603790
www.swallowcottages.co.uk

MRS JILL McNEIL, SWALLOW HOLIDAY COTTAGES, LONG LEAS FARM, HAWSKER, WHITBY YO22 4LA

Whitby, York

ARCHES GUESTHOUSE *"Just as a Bed & Breakfast should be"*

8 Havelock Place, Hudson Street, Whitby YO21 3ER • *B&B £30-£40pppn*

A traditional seaside B&B, offering outstanding cleanliness, comfort, and great breakfasts. Centrally located, The Arches is the ideal base for experiencing the old world charms of this historic seaside town, exploring the beautiful North Yorkshire moors and coast, or just relaxing. Pets, with well behaved owners, may stay free of charge! Ground floor rooms • Pet-friendly • Family-friendly • Bikers & Hikers welcome.

Ruth & Dick Brew (01947 601880 or 0800 9154256) • e-mail: archeswhitby@freeola.com • www.whitbyguesthouses.co.uk

ASCOT HOUSE **80 East Parade, York YO31 7YH • Tel: 01904 426826**

Fax: 01904 431077 • ETC/AA ★★★★ • ETC SILVER AWARD

An attractive Victorian villa with easy access to the historic city centre by walking or by public transport. Most rooms have four-poster or canopy beds, and family and double rooms are en suite. All rooms have central heating, colour TV and tea/coffee facilities. Singles from £60 to £70, doubles £68 to £80 including Traditional English Breakfast and VAT. Free private enclosed car park.

e-mail: admin@ascothouseyork.com • www.ascothouseyork.com

YORK LAKESIDE LODGES

Moor Lane, York YO24 2QU

Tel: 01904 702346 • Fax: 01904 701631

e-mail: neil@yorklakesidelodges.co.uk

Unique in a city! Luxurious Scandinavian lodges, and cottages in mature parkland overlooking large private fishing lake. Nearby superstore with coach to centre every 10 minutes. Easy access to ring road for touring. Open year round.

ETC 4/5 STARS SELF-CATERING

www.yorklakesidelodges.co.uk

YORKSHIRE & HUMBERSIDE TOURIST BOARD WHITE ROSE AWARDS FOR TOURISM

WINNER

Award – British Holiday Home Parks Association

ST GEORGE'S

6 ST GEORGE'S PLACE
YORK YO24 1DR

Family-run guest house in quiet cul-de-sac near racecourse. All rooms en suite with colour TV, tea/coffee making facilities. Private parking. Pets welcome by arrangement

ETC/AA ★★★

e-mail: sixstgeorg@aol.com
www.stgeorgesyork.com

01904 625056

From £60 per double or twin room

Pet-Friendly
Pubs, Inns & Hotels

on pages 424-432

Please note that these establishments may not feature in the main section of this book

Bentham

Quiet village amidst the fells. Good centre for rambling and fishing. Ingleton 5 miles north-east.

MRS L. J. STORY, HOLMES FARM, LOW BENTHAM, LANCASTER LA2 7DE (015242 61198). Cottage conversion in easy reach of Dales, Lake District and coast. Central heating, fridge, TV, washer, games room. ETC ★★★★. [🐕]
e-mail: lucy@holmesfarmcottage.co.uk website: www.holmesfarmcottage.co.uk

Bolton Abbey

Hamlet 5 miles SW of Ilkley.

THE DEVONSHIRE ARMS COUNTRY HOUSE HOTEL AND SPA, BOLTON ABBEY BD23 6AJ (01756 718111). Luxurious comfort, fine food and wines, relaxed and unstuffy. Beautiful setting on the Bolton Abbey Estate in the Yorkshire Dales. AA ★★★★, Yorkshire Small Hotel of the Year 2007/8, AA Pet Friendly Hotel 2005. [🐕]
e-mail: res@devonshirehotels.co.uk website: www.devonshirehotels.co.uk

Clapham

Village 6 miles NW of Settle.

NEW INN HOTEL, CLAPHAM, NEAR INGLETON LA2 8HH (015242 51203; Fax: 015242 51824). 'Jewel of the Dales'. A comfortable hotel in the Yorkshire Dales National Park. The ideal holiday destination for your pet, be assured of a warm and friendly reception, sit back, close your eyes and soak up the history and atmosphere. ETC ★★ [Pets £5 per night]
e-mail: info@newinn-clapham.co.uk website: www.newinn-clapham.co.uk

Coverdale

Located in the Yorkshire Dales National Park, famous for Middleham Castle, Richard III and the Forbidden Corner..

MRS JULIE CLARKE, MIDDLE FARM, WOODALE, COVERDALE, LEYBURN DL8 4TY (01969 640271). Peacefully situated farmhouse away from the madding crowd. B&B with optional Evening Meal. Home cooking. Pets sleep where you prefer. Ideally positioned for exploring the beautiful Yorkshire Dales. [🐕 pw!]
e-mail: j-a-clarke@hotmail.co.uk

Danby

Village on River Esk 12 miles west of Whitby.

THE FOX & HOUNDS INN, AINTHORPE, DANBY YO21 2LD (01287 660218). Residential 16th Century Coaching Inn. All rooms en suite. Enjoy our real ales or quality selected wines. Freshly prepared food served every day. Winter breaks available Nov-March. Open all year. ETC ★★★★ Inn [Pets £2.50 per night.]
e-mail: info@foxandhounds-ainthorpe.com website: www.foxandhounds-ainthorpe.com

Denby Dale

Town 8 miles west of Barnsley.

IVY HOLIDAY COTTAGE, DENBY DALE. Village location, close to moors, craft mills, railway station and good pubs. Fully heated, sleeps 2/4, fully equipped, luxury standard, linen and towels supplied. £45-£50 per group per night. Short Breaks available all year. Call Sue on 0121 453 7622. [🐕]

www.holidayguides.com

Grassington

Wharfedale village in attractive moorland setting. Ripon 22 miles, Skipton 9.

FORESTERS ARMS, MAIN STREET, GRASSINGTON, SKIPTON BD23 5AA (01756 752349; Fax: 01756 753633). The Foresters Arms is situated in the heart of the Yorkshire Dales and provides an ideal centre for walking or touring. Within easy reach of York and Harrogate. ETC ★★★ [🐕]

Grewelthorpe

Village 3 miles south of Masham.

FIR TREE FARM HOLIDAY HOMES - WILLOW TREE LODGE, HIGH BRAMLEY, GREWELTHORPE, RIPON HG4 3DL (01765 658727). Sleeps 4. On a privately owned 100-acre farm in beautiful woodland amidst rolling hills, ideal for exploring the Dales. 10 miles from Ripon and 4 miles from Masham. Short breaks available off-peak. ETC ★★★★ . [Pets £20 per week.]
website: www.firtree-farm-holidayhomes.co.uk

Harrogate

Charming and elegant spa town set amid some of Britain's most scenic countryside. Ideal for exploring Herriot Country and the moors and dales. York 22 miles, Bradford 19, Leeds 16.

RUDDING HOLIDAY PARK, FOLLIFOOT, HARROGATE HG3 1JH (01423 870439; Fax: 01423 870859). Luxury cottages and lodges sleeping two to seven people. All equipped to a high standard. Pool, licensed bar, golf and children's playground in the Parkland. Illustrated brochure available. ETC ★★★ [🐕]
e-mail: holiday-park@ruddingpark.com website: www.ruddingpark.com

ROSEMARY HELME, HELME PASTURE LODGES & COTTAGES, OLD SPRING WOOD, HARTWITH BANK, SUMMERBRIDGE, HARROGATE HG3 4DR (01423 780279, Fax: 01423 780994). Country accommodation for owners and dogs and numerous walks in unspoilt Nidderdale. Central for Harrogate, York, Herriot and Bronte country. National Trust area. ETC ★★★★, ETC Category 1 for Disabled Access. [pw! Pets £5 per night, £25 per week.]
e-mail:helmepasture@btinternet.com website: www.helmepasture.co.uk

RUDDING ESTATE COTTAGES. (01423 844844). Four traditional country cottages on a very private country estate in the heart of the Yorkshire countryside. Comfortably furnished, fully equipped and welcome well behaved pets. Towels are provided for dogs and their owners!
e-mail:info@rudding.com website: www.rudding.com/cottages

Hawes

12 miles north-west on the Hawes to Kirkby Stephen road.

STONE HOUSE HOTEL, SEDBUSK, HAWES DL8 3PT (01969 667571). This fine Edwardian country house has spectacular views and serves delicious Yorkshire cooking with fine wines. Comfortable en suite bedrooms, some ground floor. Phone for details. [🐕]
website: www.stonehousehotel.com

SIMONSTONE HALL, HAWES, WENSLEYDALE DL8 3LY (01969 667255; Fax: 01969 667741). Facing south across picturesque Wensleydale. All rooms en suite with colour TV. Fine cuisine. Extensive wine list. Friendly personal attention. A relaxing break away from it all. AA ★★ [£12 per stay]
e-mail: e-mail@simonstonehall.demon.co.uk website: www.simonstonehall.co.uk

COCKLAKE HOUSE, MALLERSTANG CA17 4JT (017683 72080). Charming, High Pennine Country House B&B in unique position above Pendragon Castle in Upper Mallerstang Dale offering good food and exceptional comfort to a small number of guests. Two double rooms with large private bathrooms. Three acres riverside grounds. Dogs welcome. [🐕]

COUNTRY COTTAGE HOLIDAYS, DRYDEN HOUSE, MARKET PLACE, HAWES DL8 3RA (01969 667654). 80 cottages in the lovely Yorkshire Dales. Colour TV, central heating, open fires. Gardens, private parking. Many allow pets. Rents from £200 per week. Sleep 1-10.
website: www.countrycottageholidays.co.uk

Helmsley

A delightful stone-built town on River Rye with a large cobbled square. Thirsk 12 miles.

SUE SMITH, LASKILL GRANGE, HAWNBY, NEAR HELMSLEY YO62 5NB (01439 798268). Delightful country house set in 1 acre gardens; all rooms en suite. Generous cuisine of a high standard using fresh local produce, vegetarians catered for. Open all year. ETC ★★★★ Silver Award, AA ★★★★.
e-mail: laskillgrange@tiscali.co.uk website: www.laskillgrange.co.uk

JOHN & SALLY ROBINSON'S VALLEY VIEW FARM, OLD BYLAND, HELMSLEY, YORK YO62 5LG (01439 798221). Fully equipped self-catering cottages on working farm in North Yorks moors. Ideal for touring Yorkshire, or just walking the hills and lanes around. Rural peace and tranquillity. Dogs free. Kennel and run available. ETC ★★★★ [🐕]
website: www.valleyviewfarm.com

Kirkbymoorside

Small town below N.Yorks Moors 7 miles West of Pickering.

MRS F. WILES, SINNINGTON COMMON FARM, KIRKBYMOORSIDE, YORK YO62 6NX (01751 431719). Two newly converted cottages, tastefully furnished and well equipped, on working family farm. Sleep 2/3. Also bungalow sleeps 6. B&B also available. Pets welcome. [🐕]
e-mail: felicity@scfarm.demon.co.uk website: www.sinningtoncommonfarm.co.uk

Knaresborough

Town on escarpment above the River Nidd, 3 miles NE of Harrogate..

GALLON HOUSE 47 KIRKGATE, KNARESBOROUGH HG5 8BZ (01423 862102). Overlooking the beautiful Nidd Gorge, Gallon House offers award-winning accommodation and superb fresh food. Two double and one twin bedrooms, all en suite. Licensed. ETC/AA ★★★★ Gold Award. [🐕]
e-mail: gallon-house@ntlworld.com website: www.gallon-house.co.uk

NEWTON HOUSE, KNARESBOROUGH. Winner of the AA Pet Friendly Award – pets genuinely welcomed and lots of great walks nearby. Spacious and comfortable, newly refurbished ensuite accommodation and great breakfasts. AA ★★★★ Highly Commended, AA Breakfast Award. Contact MARK & LISA WILSON, NEWTON HOUSE, 5-7 YORK PLACE, KNARESBOROUGH HG5 OAD (Tel: 01423 863539). [🐕]
e-mail: newtonhouse@btinternet.com website: www.newtonhouseyorkshire.com

Leeming Bar

Small pretty village 2 miles NE of Bedale.

THE WHITE ROSE HOTEL, LEEMING BAR, NORTHALLERTON DL7 9AY (01677 422707/424941; Fax: 01677 425123). Ideally situated for touring National Parks, Dales, coastal resorts, Herriot and Heartbeat Country. 18 rooms, all private bathroom, 10-channel digital TV/radio, tea and coffee, hair dryer, trouser press and telephone. [🐕]
e-mail: john@whiterosehotel.co.uk website: www.whiterosehotel.co.uk

Leyburn

Small market town, 8 miles south-west of Richmond, standing above the River Ure in Wensleydale.

GOLDEN LION HOTEL, MARKET PLACE, LEYBURN DL8 5AS (01969 622161; Fax: 01969 623836). Excellent accommodation in this splendid hotel at the gateway to Wensleydale. En suite bathrooms, TV, telephone, radio and tea/coffee makers. Lift to all floors. ETC ★. [🐕]
e-mail: info@goldenlionleyburn.co.uk

BARBARA & BARRIE MARTIN, THE OLD STAR, WEST WITTON, LEYBURN DL8 4LU (01969 622949). Former 17th century Coaching Inn now run as a guest house. Oak beams, log fire, home cooking. En suite B&B from £26 pppn. ETC ★★★ [🐕]
e-mail: enquiries@theoldstar.com website: www.theoldstar.com

Malham

Village in upper Airedale, 5 miles east of Settle, across the moors.

MR C. SHARP, MIRESFIELD FARM, MALHAM, SKIPTON BD23 4DA (01729 830414). In beautiful gardens bordering village green and stream. Excellent food. 11 bedrooms, all with private facilities. Full central heating. Two well-furnished lounges and conservatory. B&B from £24pppn. ETC ★★★ [🐕 pw!]

Pickering

Pleasant market town on southern fringe of North Yorkshire Moors National Park with moated Norman Castle. Bridlington 31 miles, Whitby 20, Scarborough 16, Helmsley 13, Malton 3.

MRS ELLA BOWES, BANAVIE, ROXBY ROAD, THORNTON-LE-DALE, PICKERING YO18 7SX (01751 474616). Large stone-built semi-detached house set in Thornton-le-Dale. Ideal for touring. One family bedroom and two double bedrooms, all en suite. All with TV, shaver points, central heating and tea-making facilities. Open all year. Car park, cycle shed. B&B from £27pppn. Welcome Host and Hygiene Certificate held. ETC ★★★★ [🐕]
e-mail: info@banavie.uk.com website: www.banavie.uk.com

THE WHITE SWAN INN AT PICKERING (01751 472288). 16th century inn with a buzz. Dog friendly with excellent: service, rooms, food and wine. "...consistently brilliant.." Please phone or visit our website for a brochure. ETC ★★★, AA Rosette [Pets £12.50 per stay].
e-mail: welcome@white-swan.co.uk website: www.white-swan.co.uk

Port Mulgrave

Located 1km north of Hinderwell.

NORTH YORK MOORS NATIONAL PARK. Stone Cottage (sleeps) 4 in North York Moors National Park. Sea view, near Cleveland coastal footpath. Log fire, non-smoking. Whitby 9 miles. Brochure available (01642 613888). [🐕]

Scalby Nabs (Scarborough)

Small town and suburb 2 miles north west of Scarborough.

EAST FARM COUNTRY COTTAGES, SCALBY NABS, SCALBY, SCARBOROUGH (01723 353635). Single-storey two-bedroom stone cottages (no steps/stairs) in national Park; only 5 minutes from Scarborough. All completely non-smoking. Ideal base for walking or touring. VisitBritain ★★★ [Pets from £10 per week.]
e-mail: joeastfarmcottages@hotmail.co.uk website: www.eastfarmcountrycottages.co.uk

Scarborough

Very popular family resort with good sands. York 41 miles, Whitby 20, Bridlington 17, Filey 7.

RAVEN HALL COUNTRY HOUSE HOTEL, LODGES & GOLF COURSE, RAVENSCAR, SCARBOROUGH YO13 0ET (01723 870353; Fax: 01723 870072). This imposing hotel offers oustanding accommodation, superb, typically Yorkshire cuisine and an impressive range of leisure facilities including a 9-hole golf course. A family holiday paradise. AA ★★★. New luxury lodges. [pw! Pets £5 per night.]
e-mail: enquiries@ravenhall.co.uk website: www.ravenhall.co.uk

CAYTON VILLAGE CARAVAN PARK LTD, MILL LANE, CAYTON BAY, SCARBOROUGH YO11 3NN (01723 583171). Luxurious facilities, adventure playground, site shop, dog walk. Seasonal pitches, supersites, hardstanding and storage. Open 1st March - 31st October. Half-a-mile to beach. ETC ★★★★★, David Bellamy Gold Award. [Pets £1 per night].
e-mail: info@caytontouring.co.uk website: www.caytontouring.co.uk

SUE AND TONY HEWITT, HARMONY COUNTRY LODGE, LIMESTONE ROAD, BURNISTON, SCARBOROUGH YO13 0DG (0800 2985840). A peaceful retreat set in two acres of private grounds with 360° panoramic views of the National Park and sea. An ideal centre for walking or touring. En suite centrally heated rooms with superb views. Non-smoking, licensed, private parking facilities. B&B from £29 to £37. ETC ★★★★
e-mail: mail@harmonylodge.net website: www.harmonycountrylodge.co.uk

HUMBLE BEE FARM FLIXTON, SCARBOROUGH YO11 3UJ (01723 890437). On a 320-acre working farm in the heart of the Yorkshire Wolds, our luxury holiday cottages and unique wigwams offer a fabulous holiday destination. A perfect base for exploring the Yorkshire coast; many local walks in beautiful countryside. [Pets £10 per week]
website: www.humblebeefarm.co.uk

HONEYSUCKLE COTTAGE (01723 882284). Lovely, stone-built cottage, four miles from Scarborough. Sleeps 2-5 + cot in 2 bedrooms. Private parking. Patio/garden with barbecue. Pets welcome. Non-smoking. Open all year. EnjoyEngland ★★★★. Contact DAVID AND JANE BEELEY. [Pets £10 per week]
e-mail: info@forgevalleycottages.co.uk website: www.forgevalleycottages.co.uk

Skipton

Airedale market town, centre for picturesque Craven district. Fine Castle (14th cent). York 43 miles, Manchester 42, Leeds 26, Harrogate 22, Settle 16.

Over 250 super self-catering Cottages in the Yorkshire Dales, York, Coast, Moors, Lancashire, Peak and Lake District. For our fully illustrated brochure apply: HOLIDAY COTTAGES YORKSHIRE LTD (INCORPORATING RED ROSE COTTAGES), WATER STREET, SKIPTON BD23 1PB (01756 700872). [🐕]
website: www.holidaycotts.co.uk

BECK HALL, MALHAM BD23 4DJ (01729 830332). 18th century B&B on the Pennine Way, log fires and huge breakfasts. Midweek and 4-night specials. Ideal for exploring the Yorkshire Dales. AA ★★★, WELCOME HOST [🐕]
e-mail: simon@beckhallmalham.com website: www.beckhallmalham.com

THE CONISTON HOTEL, CONISTON COLD, SKIPTON BD23 4EB (01756 748080; Fax: 01756 749487). Set in a stunning 1400 acre estate, an ideal base for guests wishing to explore the Yorkshire Dales. 50 en suite bedrooms with full facilities. Special rates for leisure breaks and family rooms. ETC ★★★ Silver Award, AA ★★★ & Rosette. [pw! Pets £10 per stay]
e-mail: sales@theconistonhotel.com website: www.theconistonhotel.com

CRAVEN HOUSE, 56 KEIGHLEY ROAD, SKIPTON BD23 2NB (Tel & Fax: 01756 794657). Large terraced house with 7 bedrooms, sleeps up to 16. Suitable for large groups, extended families or just for the luxury of plenty of space! Dogs welcome by arrangement. Well equipped kitchen, dining room, lounge and cosy basement TV room. [🐕]
e-mail: info@craven-house.co.uk website: www.craven-house.co.uk

Staithes

Fishing village on North Sea coast 9 miles NW of Whitby.

MS M.J. HEALD, BROOKLYN B&B, BROWN'S TERRACE, STAITHES TS13 5BG (01947 841396). Situated in the old part of picturesque and historic Staithes. Two double and one twin bedrooms available, generous breakfasts, vegetarians catered for. Pets and children most welcome. ETC ★★★ [🐕]
e-mail: m.heald@tesco.net website: www.brooklynuk.com

Thirsk

Market town with attractive square. Excellent touring area. Northallerton 3 miles.

POPLARS HOLIDAY COTTAGES AND BED & BREAKFAST, THIRSK. The Poplars stands in two acres of lovely gardens with a field for dog walking. We have old brick cottages and new lodges, with bed and breakfast in the Poplars House. Contact AMANDA RICHARDS, THE POPLARS, CARLTON MINIOTT, THIRSK YO7 4LX (01845 522712). ETC ★★★★, Silver Award. [Pets £5 per night B&B, £5 per week SC]
website: www.thepoplarsthirsk.com

FOXHILLS HIDEAWAYS, FELIXKIRK, THIRSK YO7 2DS (01845 537575). 4 Scandinavian log cabins, heated throughout, linen provided. A supremely relaxed atmosphere on the edge of the North York Moors National Park. Open all year. Village pub round the corner. [🐕]

Whitby

Charming resort with harbour and sands. Of note is the 13th century ruined Abbey. Stockton-on-Tees 34 miles, Scarborough 20, Saltburn-by-the-Sea 19.

THE SEACLIFFE, NORTH PROMENADE, WHITBY Y021 3JX (Freephone 0808 1682118). Magnificent seafront position overlooking beach and harbour entrance. Lovely scenic walks. Comfortable bar, sea-view lounge and guests' patio garden. Outstanding freshly cooked breakfast selection. 3-course evening meal (booking required); seafood a speciality. Private car park (8). Dogs by arrangement. Bargain 3-4-2 breaks. VB ★★★★ Guest Accommodation [🐕]
e-mail: stay@seacliffehotel.com website: www.seacliffehotel.com

MRS JILL McNEIL, SWALLOW HOLIDAY COTTAGES, LONG LEAS FARM, HAWSKER, WHITBY YO22 4LA (01947 603790). Discover historic Whitby, pretty fishing villages, way-marked walks. Four cottages, one or two bedrooms. Private parking. Children and dogs welcome. Weekly rates from £195 to £500. Please phone or write for a brochure. ETC ★★★★ [🐕]

ARCHES GUESTHOUSE, 8 HAVELOCK PLACE, HUDSON STREET, WHITBY YO21 3ER. Pet friendly, family-run guesthouse, where a warm welcome and large breakfast is always assured. The ideal base for experiencing the old world charms of this historic seaside town, exploring the beautiful North Yorkshire Moors, or just relaxing. Strictly non-smoking. £30- £40 pppn. RUTH & DICK BREW (01947 601880 or 0800 9154256). [🐕]
e-mail: archeswhitby@freeola.com website: www.whitbyguesthouses.co.uk

York

Historic cathedral city and former Roman Station on River Ouse. Magnificent Minster and 3 miles of ancient walls. Facilities for a wide range of sports and entertainments. Horse-racing on Knavesmire. Bridlington 41 miles, Filey 41, Leeds 24, Harrogate 22.

ASCOT HOUSE, 80 EAST PARADE, YORK YO31 7YH (01904 426826; Fax: 01904 431077). Attractive Victorian villa with easy access to city centre. Family and double rooms en suite. Comfortable residents' lounge, dining room. Single room £60-£70, double room £68-£80. Free private enclosed car park. ETC/AA ★★★★, ETC Silver Award. [🐕]
e-mail: admin@ascothouseyork.com website: www.ascothouseyork.com

YORK LAKESIDE LODGES, MOOR LANE, YORK YO24 2QU (01904 702346; Fax: 01904 701631). Self-catering pine lodges. Mature parkland setting. Large fishing lake. Nearby superstore with coach to centre every 10 mins. ETC ★★★★/★★★★★ [pw! Pets £20 per week]
e-mail: neil@yorklakesidelodges.co.uk website: www.lakesidelodges.co.uk

ST GEORGE'S, 6 ST GEORGE'S PLACE, YORK YO24 1DR (01904 625056). Family-run guest house in quiet cul-de-sac near racecourse. All rooms en suite with colour TV, tea/coffee making facilities. Private parking. Pets welcome by arrangement. From £60 double or twin room. ETC/AA ★★★ [🐕]
e-mail: sixstgeorg@aol.com website: www.stgeorgesyork.com

Please note

All the information in this book is given in good faith in the belief that it is correct. However, the publishers cannot guarantee the facts given in these pages, neither are they responsible for changes in policy, ownership or terms that may take place after the date of going to press. Readers should always satisfy themselves that the facilities they require are available and that the terms, if quoted, still apply.

Wortley

PENNINE EQUINE HOLIDAY COTTAGES Cote Green Farm, Wortley www.pennine-equine.co.uk

An ideal location to spend time with your horse, mountain bike or walking boots. Two comfortably furnished cottages attached to main stable building (each sleeps 6/8). Well equipped, bed linen provided. Non-smoking. Dogs not allowed, but kennels available. Livery and stabling for visitors' horses. 3-mile cross country course within grounds. Riding lessons available. Ample parking for trailers, horse boxes etc.

Contact: Bromley Farm, Wortley, Sheffield S35 7DE (0114 284 7140) • Mobile: 07939 906523

Wortley

Village famous for the Wortley Top Forge, dating back to the Industrial Revolution, and as the birthplace of the notorious highwayman Swift Nick. 2 miles from Stocksbridge.

PENNINE EQUINE HOLIDAY COTTAGES, COTE GREEN FARM, WORTLEY. An ideal location to spend time with your horse, mountain bike or walking boots. Two comfortably furnished cottages (each sleeps 6/8). Well equipped, bed linen provided. Non-smoking. Dogs not allowed, but kennels available. Livery and stabling for visitors' horses. CONTACT: BROMLEY FARM, WORTLEY, SHEFFIELD S35 7DE (0114 284 7140; Mobile: 07939 906523) [Kennels £2 per night, Stabling (not incl. feeding) £40 per week]
website: www.pennine-equine.co.uk

West Yorkshire

Bingley

THE FIVE RISE LOCKS HOTEL & RESTAURANT, BECK LANE, BINGLEY BD16 4DD

Large Victorian house tucked away in tranquil area, but close main roads, tourist sites, cities. Good views, individual decor, informal style. Comfy sofas, interesting artworks. Antidote to chain hotels. Historic canal locks and excellent walking (dogs and humans) close by.

AA/VisitBritain ★★★★ - **Tel: 01274 565296**

e-mail: info@five-rise-locks.co.uk • • www.five-rise-locks.co.uk

Bingley

Town on River Aire 5 miles north-west of Bradford.

THE FIVE RISE LOCKS HOTEL & RESTAURANT, BECK LANE, BINGLEY BD16 4DD (01274 565296). Large Victorian house in tranquil area, but close main roads, tourist sites. Good views, individual decor, informal style. Historic canal locks and excellent walking (dogs and humans) close by. AA/VisitBritain ★★★★ [Pets £5 per night]
e-mail: info@five-rise-locks.co.uk website: www.five-rise-locks.co.uk

Visit the FHG website

www.holidayguides.com

for details of the wide choice of accommodation

featured in the full range of FHG titles

Low Lands Farm

Low Lands, Cockfield, Bishop Auckland, Co. Durham DL13 5AW
Tel 01388 718251 • Mobile: 07745 067754
e-mail: info@farmholidaysuk.com • www.farmholidaysuk.com

Two award-winning, beautifully renovated self-catering cottages on a working family farm. If you want peace and quiet in an area full of beautiful unspoilt countryside packed with things to see and do, then come and stay with us. Each cottage sleeps up to four people, plus cot. Beams, log fires, gas BBQ, own gardens and parking. Close to Durham City, the Lake District and Hadrian's Wall. Pets and children most welcome; childminding and equipment available. Terms from £160 to £340, inclusive of linen, towels, electricity and heating.

Please contact Alison or Keith Tallentire for a brochure.

Category 3 (one cottage)

Charming farmhouse with stunning views. You will be most welcome. Ideal for Newcastle, Durham, Beamish etc. Bed and Breakfast;dinner available, licensed. Great for pets.
IRENE MORDEY AND DAVID BLACKBURN, BEE COTTAGE FARMHOUSE, CASTLESIDE, CONSETT DH8 9HW (01207 508224)

e-mail: beecottage68@aol.com • www.beecottage.co.uk

Bishop Auckland

Town on right bank of River Wear, 9 miles south-west of Durham. Castle, of varying dates, residence of the Bishop of Durham.

ALISON & KEITH TALLENTIRE, LOW LANDS FARM, LOW LANDS, COCKFIELD, BISHOP AUCKLAND DL13 5AW (01388 718251; mobile: 07745 067754). Two self-catering cottages on a working livestock farm. Each sleeps up to 4, plus cot. Prices from £160-£340. Call for a brochure. Pets and children most welcome. ETC ★★★★ ETC CATEGORY 3 DISABLED ACCESSIBILITY (one cottage). [Pets £10 per week]
e-mail: info@farmholidaysuk.com website: www.farmholidaysuk.co

Castleside

A suburb 2 miles south-west of Consett.

DAVID BLACKBURN AND IRENE MORDEY, BEE COTTAGE FARMHOUSE, CASTLESIDE, CONSETT DH8 9HW (01207 508224). Charming farmhouse with stunning views. You will be most welcome. Ideal for Newcastle, Durham, Beamish etc. Bed and Breakfast; dinner available, licensed. Great for pets. VisitBritain ★★★★ [pw!]
e-mail: beecottage68@aol.com website: www.beecottage.co.uk

Please note

All the information in this book is given in good faith in the belief that it is correct. However, the publishers cannot guarantee the facts given in these pages, neither are they responsible for changes in policy, ownership or terms that may take place after the date of going to press. Readers should always satisfy themselves that the facilities they require are available and that the terms, if quoted, still apply.

NORTHUMBERLAND COTTAGES LTD

A local booking agency, with over 25 years of living and loving Northumberland.

Based in the heart of the area between Alnwick and the beautiful sandy beaches of the Heritage Coastline.

Choose from our selection of cottages Telephone 01665 589434 or check availability online at www.northumberlandcottages.com

Allendale, Alnmouth, Alnwick, Bamburgh

FELL VIEW COTTAGE • ALLENDALE

Detached traditional self-catering cottage, rebuilt from original stone barn, situated in a designated area of outstanding beauty. Highest possible standard with unrestricted views and wonderful walks. Sleeps 1-6. Pets welcome.

Contact: Mr C. Verne-Jones, 69 Buckinghamshire Road, Belmont, Durham DH1 2BE
Tel: 0191 386 9045 • e-mail: info@fellviewcottage.co.uk • www.fellviewcottage.co.uk

Saddle Hotel & Grill ETC ★★

24/25 Northumberland Street, Alnmouth NE66 2RA • Tel: 01665 830476

Friendly, family-run hotel situated in Alnmouth, on the Northumberland coast, with miles of white sandy beaches and unspoilt countryside; two golf courses. Fully licensed, home-cooked meals a speciality. All bedrooms en suite. Children and pets most welcome.

Spacious farmhouse in tranquil surroundings • Ideally situated to explore Northumbria • Relaxed and friendly • Large superior bedrooms • Large children's play area • Pets welcome

Rock Farmhouse B&B, Rock, Alnwick NE66 3SE • Tel: 01665 579367
stay@rockfarmhouse.co.uk • www.rockfarmhouse.co.uk

The Mizen Head Hotel

Lucker Road, Bamburgh, Northumberland NE69 7BS

Beautifully refurbished hotel • Locally produced food.

Public bar offers good food and real ales, live music, with an open log fire in winter. Children welcome – family rooms are available with cots if required. Car park. Pets welcome in bedrooms and bar. Local attractions include Bamburgh Castle and Holy Isle. Three-and-a-half mile sandy beach five minutes away. Pets welcome. For golfers discounts can be arranged. Short break details on request.

Tel: 01668 214254 • Fax: 01668 214104
www.mizenheadhotel.co.uk
e-mail: info@mizenheadhotel.co.uk

Bamburgh, Belford, Berwick-Upon-Tweed, Eals

Waren Mill, Belford, Near Bamburgh,
Northumberland NE70 7EE
Tel: 01668 214581 • Fax: 01668 214484
e-mail: enquiries@warenhousehotel.co.uk
www.warenhousehotel.co.uk

Set in six acres of mature wooded grounds, Waren House has been reborn under the talented and loving hands of owners, Anita and Peter Laverack. Beautifully presented food is served in the elegant dining room, and the wine list is a most fascinating read. Probably the icing on the cake is that the beauty of this uncrowded Heritage Coast makes it much like the Lake District was 40 years ago, before it was well and truly discovered.

Please do "discover" Waren House – it will be a choice you will never regret.

Etive Cottage • Warenford, Near Belford NE70 7HZ

Etive is a well-equipped two bedroomed stone cottage with double glazing and central heating. Situated on the outskirts of the hamlet of Warenford with open views to the Bamburgh coast. Fenced garden and secure courtyard parking. Pet and owners welcome pack on arrival - Pets welcome to bring along well behaved owners. *Regional Winner - Winalot 'Best Place to Stay' 2004*

*For brochure contact Jan Thompson • **Tel: 01668 213233 • e-mail: janet.thompson1@homecall.co.uk***

Bluebell Farm enjoys a quiet central position in the village of Belford, three miles from the Heritage Coast and within easy walking distance of all village amenities. Sleep 4-6. Each cottage is equipped with gas cooker, microwave, fridge/freezer or fridge, coffee machine, kettle, toaster and colour television, most with DVD player. All have gas-fired central heating; living/dining/kitchen areas are open plan.

Mrs Phyl Carruthers, Bluebell Farm, Belford, Northumberland NE70 7QE
Tel: 01668 213362• e-mail: phyl.carruthers@virgin.net

Friendly Hound Cottage

Ford Common, Berwick-upon-Tweed TD15 2QD

Set in a quiet rural location, convienient for Holy Island, Berwick, Bamburgh and the Heritage coastline. Come and enjoy our top quality accommodation, excellent breakfasts, and warm welcome. Arrive as our guests and leave as our friends.

Tel: 01289 388554 • www.friendlyhoundcottage.co.uk

★★★★ BED & BREAKFAST

2, THE COURTYARD, BERWICK-UPON-TWEED

Secluded Self Catering Townhouse in heart of old Berwick. Planted courtyard garden and sunny verandah. Historic ramparts 400 yards. Choice of walks. Ideal for exercising pets.

Contact: J Morton, 1, The Courtyard, Church Street, Berwick-Upon-Tweed, TD15 1EE (01289 308737)
e-mail: jvm@patmosphere.uklinux.net • www.berwickselfcatering.co.uk

★★★ SELF CATERING

Stay in stunning Northumberland • • Stonecrop

Nestling in the South Tyne Valley in the small hamlet of Eals is this white-washed cottage with its own orchard. Recently renovated, with modern comforts - a new kitchen and bathroom, a cosy log stove and 3 bedrooms + double sofa bed (sleeps 6-8). Well behaved pets welcome. **Contact: Julie & Richard Parker, Eastgate, Milburn, Penrith, Cumbria CA10 1TN**
Tel: 01768 361509 • www.stonecrop.co.uk

FHG Guides

publish a large range of well-known accommodation guides.
We will be happy to send you details or you can use the order form at the back of this book.

Close to the best parts of Hadrian's Wall • A warm welcome and good food • All rooms en suite • Parking • TV • Central heating. • Children and pets welcome • Open all year • Prices from £30 pppn.

e-mail: info@saughyrigg.co.uk • www.saughyrigg.co.uk

KATH AND BRAD DOWLE, SAUGHY RIGG FARM, TWICE BREWED, HALTWHISTLE NE49 9PT (01434 344120)

Scotchcoulthard • Haltwhistle, Northumberland NE49 9NH

01434 344470 • *Props: A.D. & S.M. Saunders*

e-mail: scotchcoulthard@hotmail.co.uk • www.scotchcoulthard.co.uk

Situated in 178 acres within Northumberland National Park, fully equipped self-catering cottages (sleep 2/7). All bedrooms en suite; open fires. Fridge/freezer, colour TV, microwave; all except one have dishwasher and washing machine. Linen, towels, all fuel incl. Heated indoor pool, games room. Rare breed farm animals. Children and dogs welcome.

Struthers Farm ❖ Catton, Allendale, Hexham NE47 9LP

A warm welcome in the heart of England. Splendid local walks, panoramic views. Double/twin en suite rooms, central heating. Good farmhouse cooking. Ample safe parking. Near Hadrians Wall. Children welcome, pets by prior arrangement. Open all year. Bed and Breakfast from £30; Optional Evening Meal from £12.50.

Contact Mrs Ruby Keenleyside • 01434 683580 • EnjoyEngland ★★★★

Micklewood Park

Self catering houses set within 75 acres at Longhirst, Morpeth, Micklewood is an ideal base from which to explore historic Northumberland. We cater for groups and families who are explorers and sports enthusiasts or simply enjoy relaxing breaks.

Call: 01670 794 530 or visit: www.micklewoodpark.co.uk

NORTHUMBERLAND COTTAGES LTD. A local booking agency, with over 25 years of living and loving Northumberland. Based in the heart of the area between Alnwick and the beautiful sandy beaches of the Heritage Coastline. Choose from our selection of inland and coastal cottages. Telephone 01665 589434 or check availability online. [Pets £10 per week]

e-mail: enquiries@northumberlandcottages.com website: www.northumberlandcottages.com

Allendale

Small town on River East Allen 5 miles South of Haydon Bridge.

FELL VIEW COTTAGE, ALLENDALE. Detached traditional self-catering cottage in a designated area of outstanding beauty. Highest possible standard unrestricted views and wonderful walks. Sleeps 1-6. Pets welcome. Contact: Mr C. Verne-Jones, 69 Buckinghamshire Road, Belmont, Durham DH1 2BE (0191 386 9045). Visit Britain ★★★★.

e-mail: info@fellviewcottage.co.uk website: www.fellviewcottage.co.uk

Alnmouth

Seaside village situated at the mouth of the River Aln.

SADDLE HOTEL & GRILL, 24/25 NORTHUMBERLAND STREET, ALNMOUTH NE66 2RA (01665 830476). Friendly, family-run hotel, on the Northumberland coast. Fully licensed, home-cooked meals. Car park. All bedrooms en suite. Children and pets most welcome. ETC ★★. [🐕]

Symbols

🐕 Indicates that pets are welcome free of charge.

£ Indicates that a charge is made for pets: nightly or weekly.

pw! Shows some special provision for pets; exercise facility, feeding or accommodation arrangement.

☐ Indicates separate pets accommodation.

Alnwick

Picturesque market town in the heart of Northumberland which is famous for its unsspoilt beauty, long sandy beaches, and numerous stately homes and gardens. Berwick-upon-Tweed and the Scottish Border 32 miles, Alnmouth 5 miles.

ROCK FARMHOUSE B&B, ROCK, ALNWICK NE66 3SE (01665 579367). Spacious farmhouse in tranquil surroundings. Ideally situated to explore Northumbria. Relaxed and friendly. Large superior bedrooms. Large children's play area. Pets welcome.
e-mail: stay@rockfarmhouse.co.uk website: www.rockfarmhouse.co.uk

Bamburgh

Village on North Sea coast with magnificent castle. Grace Darling buried in churchyard.

THE MIZEN HEAD HOTEL, BAMBURGH NE69 7BS (01668 214254; Fax: 01668 214104). A warm welcome awaits owners and pets alike at the Mizen Head. Close to the beautiful Northumbrian coastline and just a short drive from many lovely walks in the Ingram Valley. The hotel boasts log fires, live music, good food and real ales.
e-mail: info@mizenheadhotel.co.uk website: www.mizenheadhotel.co.uk

WAREN HOUSE HOTEL, WAREN MILL, BAMBURGH NE70 7EE (01668 214581). Luxurious Country House Hotel. Excellent accommodation, superb food, moderately priced wine list. Rural setting. No children under 14 please. ETC ★★★ SILVER AWARD, AA ★★★ [🐕]
e-mail: enquiries@warenhousehotel.co.uk website: www.warenhousehotel.co.uk

Belford

Village 14 miles south-east of Berwick-upon-Tweed.

ETIVE COTTAGE, WARENFORD, NEAR BELFORD NE70 7HZ. Well-equipped two-bedroomed cottage with double glazing, central heating. Open views to coast. Fenced garden; secure parking. Pet and owners welcome pack. Pets welcome to bring along well behaved owners. Regional Winner, Winalot Best Place to Stay 2004. Brochure: JAN THOMPSON (0168 213233). [🐕]
e-mail: janet.thompson1@homecall.co.uk

MRS PHYL CARRUTHERS, BLUEBELL FARM, BELFORD NE70 7QE (01668 213362). In a quiet central position in the village of Belford, three miles from the Heritage Coast and within easy walking distance of all village amenities. Sleep 4-6. Each cottage is very well equipped, with gas-fired central heating; living/dining/kitchen areas are open plan.
e-mail: phyl.carruthers@virgin.net

Berwick-upon-Tweed

Border town at mouth of River Tweed 58 miles north west of Newcastle and 47 miles south east of Edinburgh. Medieval town walls, remains of a Norman Castle.

FRIENDLY HOUND COTTAGE, FORD COMMON, BERWICK-UPON-TWEED TD15 2QD (01289 388554) Set in a quiet rural location, convienient for Holy Island, Berwick, Bamburgh and the Heritage coastline. Come and enjoy our top quality accommodation, excellent breakfasts, and warm welcome. Arrive as our guests and leave as our friends. VB ★★★★ [🐕]
website: www.friendlyhoundcottage.co.uk

2, THE COURTYARD, BERWICK-UPON-TWEED. Secluded Self catering Townhouse in heart of old Berwick. Planted courtyard garden and sunny verandah. Historic ramparts 400 yards. Choice of walks. Ideal for exercising pets. Contact: J. MORTON, 1, THE COURTYARD, CHURCH STREET, BERWICK -UPON-TWEED, TD15 1EE (01289 308737). ETC ★★★ [pw! 🐕]
e-mail: jvm@patmosphere.uklinux.net website: www.berwickselfcatering.co.uk

A useful index of towns/counties appears at the back of this book

Corbridge

Small town on the north bank of the River Tyne, 3 miles west of Hexham. Nearby are remains of Roman military town of Corstopitum.

MR & MRS MATTHEWS, THE HAYES GUEST HOUSE, NEWCASTLE ROAD, CORBRIDGE NE45 5LP (01434 632010). Stone-built stables in grounds of large country house converted into two self-catering cottages, each accommodating 4/5. ETC ★★★ [Pets £12.50 per week]
e-mail: camon@surfree.co.uk website: www.hayes-corbridge.co.uk

Eals

Village 7 miles from Haltwhistle, 8 miles from Alston.

STONECROP. A white-washed cottage with its own orchard; recently renovated, with modern comforts - a new kitchen and bathroom, a cosy log stove and 3 bedrooms + double sofa bed (sleeps 6-8). Well behaved pets welcome. Contact: JULIE & RICHARD PARKER, EASTGATE, MILBURN, PENRITH, CUMBRIA CA10 1TN (01768 361509)
website: www.stonecrop.co.uk

Haltwhistle

Small market town about one mile South of Hadrian's Wall.

KATH AND BRAD DOWLE, SAUGHY RIGG FARM, TWICE BREWED, HALTWHISTLE NE49 9PT (01434 344120). Close to the best parts of Hadrian's Wall. A warm welcome and good food. All rooms en suite. Parking. TV. Central heating. Children and pets welcome. Open all year. Prices from £30 pppn. ETC ★★★★ [Pets £3 per night]
e-mail: info@saughyrigg.co.uk website: www.saughyrigg.co.uk

A.D. & S.M. SAUNDERS, SCOTCHCOULTHARD, HALTWHISTLE NE49 9NH (01434 344470). Situated in 178 acres within Northumberland National Park, fully equipped self-catering cottages (sleep 2/7). Linen, towels, all fuel incl. Heated indoor pool, games room. Rare breed farm animals. Children and dogs welcome. [🐕]
e-mail: scotchcoulthard@hotmail.co.uk website: www.scotchcoulthard.co.uk

Hexham

Market town on south bank of the River Tyne, 20 miles west of Newcastle-upon-Tyne.

MRS RUBY KEENLEYSIDE, STRUTHERS FARM, CATTON, ALLENDALE, HEXHAM NE47 9LP (01434 683580). Panoramic views, splendid walks. Double/twin rooms, en suite bathrooms, central heating. Good farmhouse cooking. Ample safe parking. Children welcome. Pets by prior arrangement. Open all year. ETC ★★★★.

Morpeth

Market town on River Wansbeck, 14 miles north of Newcastle-upon-Tyne.

MICKLEWOOD PARK, LONGHIRST, MORPETH (01670 794530). Self-catering houses set in 75 acres. An ideal base from which to explore historic Northumberland. We cater for groups and families who are explorers and sports enthusiasts, or who simply enjoy relaxing breaks. [🐕]
website: www.micklewoodpark.co.uk

Pet-Friendly
Pubs, Inns & Hotels
on pages 424-432
Please note that these establishments may not feature in the main section of this book

Balterley, Chester, Macclesfield

Balterley Green Farm

Deans Lane, Balterley, Near Crewe CW2 5QJ
Tel: 01270 820214

Jo and Pete Hollins offer guests a friendly welcome to their home on a 145-acre working farm in quiet and peaceful surroundings. Situated on the Cheshire/Staffordshire border within easy reach of Junction 16 on the M6. Convenient for Chester, Alton Towers and the Potteries. Two family rooms en suite; two double and two twin en suite in converted cottage, also available for self catering. Bed and Breakfast from £25pp. Caravans and tents welcome. Pets £2 per night.

Newton Hall

Tattenhall, Chester CH3 9NE • www.newtonhallfarm.co.uk

Enjoy a quiet, relaxing holiday on our family-run farm. Newton Hall is a part 16thC timbered country house wih lovely gardens and views of Beeston and Peckforton Castles. We are close to the Canal and Sandstone Trail for enjoyable walks. Chester is only 15 minutes by car; also on good bus route. Breakfast consists of fresh, locally sourced produce, served in our elegant dining room overlooking the gardens. Ample secure parking. B&B £30-£45pppn.

Tel: 01829 770153 • Mobile: 07974 745676 • e-mail: saarden@btinternet.com

THE EATON HOTEL CITY ROAD, CHESTER CH1 3AE

Tel: 01244 320840 • Fax: 0870 6221691

Ideally located for you and your dog, in the heart of Chester, with parking, and bordering the Shropshire Union Canal towpath.

www.eatonhotelchester.co.uk

Magic & Romance

A Hotel & Restaurant with a difference, remaining quintessentially English

Not far from the madding crowd, situated in 10 acres of Cheshire countryside 12 miles south of Chester.

8 en suite bedrooms include for pure romance an en suite room in garden tree

A restaurant with a gourmet menu utilising locally sourced beef, lamb and chicken. Fresh fish daily. Food preparation sympathetic to food intolerance.

A relaxed atmosphere with music from the 1930-1940s.

Frogg Manor
HOTEL & RESTAURANT

Fullers Moor, Nantwich Road,
Broxton, Chester CH3 9JH
Tel: 01829 782629/782280 • Fax: 01829 782459
e-mail: info@froggmanorhotel.co.uk
www.froggmanorhotel.co.uk

Astle Farm East. Chelford, Macclesfield SK10 4TA

A warm and friendly welcome awaits in this picturesque arable farm surrounded by a large garden. We offer you a quiet stay in an idyllic setting. All bedrooms en suite, open all year. Pets & Children welcome.

Tel & Fax: 01625 861270 • e-mail: gill.farmhouse@virgin.net

Tall Trees Lodge

Set in the beautiful Cheshire countyside, but just minutes from the motorway. Family-run lodge. All rooms en suite with telephone, tea/coffee, hairdryer. Disabled facilities. Wide range of country pubs within minutes. Pets welcome.

Tarporley Road, Lower Whitley, Warrington, Cheshire WA4 4EZ
Tel: 01928 790824 / 715117 • Fax: 01928 791330
e-mail: bookings@talltreeslodge.co.uk • www.talltreeslodge.co.uk

Balterley

Small village two miles west of Audley.

MR & MRS HOLLINS, BALTERLEY GREEN FARM, DEANS LANE, BALTERLEY, NEAR CREWE CW2 5QJ (01270 820214). 145-acre farm in quiet and peaceful surroundings. Within easy reach of Junction 16 on the M6. Bed and Breakfast from £25pp. Also cottage for self-catering. Caravans and tents welcome. [pw! Pets £2 per night]

Chester

Former Roman city on the River Dee, with well-preserved walls and beautiful 14th century Cathedral. Liverpool 25 miles

MRS ANNE ARDEN, NEWTON HALL, TATTENHALL, CHESTER CH3 9NE (01829 770153; Mobile: 07974 745676). Part 16thC country house on a family-run farm, surrounded by beautiful scenery, with views of Beeston and Peckforton Castles. Ideal for a quiet, relaxing holiday. Chester 15 minutes' drive. ETC ★★★★ Silver Award [🐕]
e-mail: saarden@btinternet.com website: www.newtonhallfarm.co.uk.

THE EATON HOTEL, CITY ROAD, CHESTER CH1 3AE (01244 320840; Fax: 0870 6221691). Ideally located for you and your dog, in the heart of Chester, with parking, and bordering the Shropshire Union Canal towpath. [🐕]
website: www.eatonhotelchester.co.uk

FROGG MANOR HOTEL & RESTAURANT, FULLERS MOOR, NANTWICH ROAD, BROXTON, CHESTER CH3 9JH(01829 782629/782280; Fax: 01829 782459). Quintessentially English Hotel situated in 10 acres of Cheshire countryside. 8 en suite bedrooms include for pure romance an en suite room in garden tree. Gourmet menu. Relaxed atmosphere.
e-mail: info@froggmanorhotel.co.uk website:www.froggmanorhotel.co.uk

Macclesfield

Town 10 miles south of Stockport.

MRS STUBBS, ASTLE FARM EAST, CHELFORD, MACCLESFIELD SK10 4TA (Tel & Fax: 01625 861270). A warm and friendly welcome awaits in this picturesque arable farm surrounded by a large garden. We offer you a quiet stay in an idyllic setting. All bedrooms en suite, open all year. ETC ★★. [⌂ 🐕]
e-mail: gill.farmhouse@virgin.net

Warrington

Town on River Mersey 16 miles SW of Manchester.

TALL TREES LODGE, TARPORLEY ROAD, LOWER WHITLEY, WARRINGTON WA4 4EZ (01928 790824/715117; Fax: 01928 791330). Family-run lodge, just minutes from the motorway. All rooms en suite with telephone, tea/coffee, hairdryer. Disabled facilities. Wide range of country pubs close by. Pets welcome. ETC ★★★
e-mail: bookings@talltreeslodge.co.uk website: www.talltreeslodge.co.uk

Choose from 300 pet friendly cottages

CUMBRIAN Cottages

Superb locations throughout the Lake District and Cumbria. All VisitBritain graded. Contact us for a brochure or visit our website.

www.cumbrian-cottages.co.uk
Tel: 01228 599950
Lines open 7 days 9am - 9pm (5.30pm Sat)

Cottages in Cumbria

- See the best of the Lake District and Eden Valley
- A wide range of cottages to choose from
- Personally inspected
- Pets welcome

Dales Holiday Cottages

Get your FREE brochure today
call **0870 909 9500** or visit **www.dalesholcot.com**

THE EASTERN FELLS, Lake District. ..where dogs stay for *free!*

the greyhound @ shap

Shap, Cumbria
CA10 3PW
01931 716474

www.greyhoundshap.co.uk
info@greyhoundshap.co.uk

the mardale inn @ st. patrick's well

Bampton, Cumbria
CA10 2RQ
01931 713244

www.mardaleinn.co.uk
info@mardaleinn.co.uk

Always open—fresh local produce—open fires—fine cask beers—warm beds

Perfect motorway stop-off on the fringe of the Lake District (M6 J39 only 5 minutes). Coaching Inn dating from the 15th century. Great walks from the door onto the Eastern fells. Fantastic Sunday lunch!

Daily Telegraph '50 Best Pubs'—May 2008. Early 18th century Lake District inn. Fantastic walking around nearby Haweswater. 4 star accommodation.

Special Offer—'Stay for 4 nights pay for 3'!

Children and dogs welcome *(please note that children must be kept on a tight leash at all times!)*

yewtreefarm@reagill
Reagill, near Shap,
Cumbria, CA10 3ER

www.reagill.com
info@reagill.com

Accommodating up to 15. Historical sculpture garden in large grounds and outdoor hot tub. Great walking nearby. Superb facilities, mini football pitch.

tranquillity@knipehall
Knipe, near Bampton,
Cumbria, CA10 2PU

www.knipehall.co.uk
info@knipehall.co.uk

House sleeps up to 12. Huge connecting party barn and outdoor hot tub in private grounds. Beautiful surroundings. Real fires and kitchen Aga range.

Dog friendly accommodation in one of the quietest yet most accessible areas of the Lake District whilst handy for all the major tourist attractions

Luxury 5* self-catering in listed buildings—ideal for family gatherings & groups

NEWBY BRIDGE HOTEL
Overlooking Lake Windermere

RIVERSIDE HOTEL
Overlooking River Kent

DAMSON DENE HOTEL
Tranquil Rural Location

Many rooms feature four-poster beds, some with en suite jacuzzi bath
Seasonal Breaks from £139 per person for three nights including Dinner, Bed and Breakfast.

Newby Bridge Hotel
Newby Bridge
Cumbria
LA12 8NA
Tel: 015395 31222
info@newbybridgehotel.co.uk

Riverside Hotel
Beezon Road
Kendal
Cumbria
LA9 6EL
Tel: 015397 34861
info@riversidekendal.co.uk

Damson Dene Hotel
Crosthwaite
Cumbria
LA8 8JE
Tel: 015395 68676
info@damsondene.co.uk

Stunning Offers... Stunning Hotels... Stunning Locations....
www.bestlakesbreaks.co.uk

Stay Lakeland
Offering a range of high quality self catering holiday accommodations in the Lake District & Cumbria, including Traditional Cottages, Houses, Timber Lodges and Holiday Static Caravans. All our properties are graded at a ★★★ minimum and are inspected annually by VisitBritain.
www.StayLakeland.co.uk
tel: 0845 468 0936

Readers are requested to mention this FHG guidebook when seeking accommodation

Alston, Ambleside

Rock House Estate • **Valley View, Nenthead, Alston, CA9 3NA**

Pets welcome – doggie towel, blanket, water bowl, clean-up bags & a ball thrower provided!
Five luxury cottages sleeping 2, 4, 7, 7, or 14. Undiscovered Cumbria, accessible to the Lakes, Dales and Borders.
The 100 acre estate is surrounded by spectacular views. Ideal for walking and cycling. BBQ and garden furniture. All linen and fuel included. Cots and high chairs available. Each cottage has some of the following features:- four poster bed, spa bath, sauna, flagstone floor, beamed ceiling, real fire. The estate has its own woodland and an adventure play area.
Short breaks available. Pets Welcome at £20 each. Open all year

01434 382 684 • **Info@RockHouseEstate.co.uk** • **www.RockHouseEstate.co.uk**

'Rest awhile in style'

Quality B&B. Tranquil settings in the heart of the village. Own grounds. Car park. All en suite. Kettle, clock/radio, TV, fridge, CD and video players. Heated indoor pool, sauna, hot tub, sun lounge and rooftop terrace. Special breaks. Friendly service where pets are welcome. **www.oldvicarageambleside.co.uk**

Contact Ian, Helen or Liana
The Old Vicarage
Vicarage Road
Ambleside LA22 9DH
Tel: 015394 33364

Lyndale GUEST HOUSE Lake Road, Ambleside LA22 0DN
015394 34244 • www.lyndale-guesthouse.co.uk

Nestled midway between Lake Windermere and Ambleside village, with superb views of Loughrigg Fell and the Langdales beyond. Excellent base for walking, touring, or just relaxing.

Kirkstone Foot

*****AMBLESIDE****

Superior Cottage & Apartment Complex, set in peaceful gardens adjoining the Lakeland Fells & Village centre. Luxury Bathrooms & Fully Fitted Kitchens

ETC FOUR & FIVE STAR RATING
AMONGST THE BEST IN BRITAIN
PETS WELCOME IN MANY UNITS

Brochures & Reservations Tel: 015394 32232
Kirkstone Pass Road, Ambleside, Cumbria LA22 9EH

e-mail: enquiries@kirkstonefoot.co.uk • **www.kirkstonefoot.co.uk**

AMBLESIDE • • • • 2 LOWFIELD, OLD LAKE ROAD

Ground floor garden flat half a mile from town centre; sleeps 4. Lounge/diningroom, kitchen, bathroom/WC, two bedrooms, one with en suite shower. Linen supplied. Children and pets welcome. Parking for one car. Bookings Saturday to Saturday. Terms from £150 to £280 per week.

Contact: MR P. F. QUARMBY, 3 LOWFIELD, OLD LAKE ROAD, AMBLESIDE LA22 0DH
Tel & Fax: 015394 32326 • • • • • • e-mail: paulfquarmby@aol.com

015394 32330
www.smallwoodhotel.co.uk

Smallwood House
Compston Road, Ambleside,
Cumbria LA22 9DH

...where quality and the customer come first

En suite rooms • Car parking • Leisure Club Membership

Greenhowe
Caravan Park
Great Langdale, English Lakeland.

Greenhowe is a permanent Caravan Park with Self Contained Holiday Accommodation. Subject to availability Holiday Homes may be rented for short or long periods from 1st March until mid-November. The Park is situated in the heart of the Lake District some half a mile from Dungeon Ghyll at the foot of the Langdale Pikes. It is an ideal centre for Climbing, Fell Walking, Riding, Swimming, or just a lazy holiday.

Please ask about Short Breaks.
NEW LODGES THIS YEAR

Greenhowe
Caravan Park
Great Langdale, Ambleside
Cumbria LA22 9JU

For free colour brochure
Telephone: (015394) 37231
Fax: (015394) 37464
www.greenhowe.com

Betty Fold, Hawkshead Hill, Ambleside LA22 0PS

e-mail: claire@bettyfold.co.uk • www.bettyfold.co.uk

Situated near Hawkshead and Tarn Hows, large country house in spacious grounds in the heart of Lake District National Park. Betty Fold offers self-catering accommodation in ground floor apartment with private entrance, sleeps 4. One double en suite and one small twin with bathroom and colour TV. Open-plan kitchen/livingroom with electric cooker, fridge, microwave. Terms inclusive of heat, light, power, bed linen and towels.

Our 3-star cottages and snug apartment are the delight of families, couples, walkers, and those seeking me-time in a stunning rural location. With two National Parks on the doorstep, just open the front door of the 1,2 & 3 bedroom cottages for stress-free days in fresh, hillside air and old fashioned family fun. Dogs very welcome and open all year.

Milburn Grange Holiday Cottages

Knock, Appleby, Cumbria CA16 6DR • Tel: 017683 61867
e-mail: petswelcome@milburngrange.co.uk • www.milburngrange.co.uk

Scalebeck Holiday Cottages **Scalebeck, Great Asby, Appleby CA16 6TF • 01768 351006**

e-mail: mail@scalebeckholidaycottages.com **ETC ★★★★**

Comfortable and well-equipped self-catering accommodation in the tranquil Eden Valley, central for the Lakes, Yorkshire Dales, Northumberland and Scottish Borders.

Sleep 2/5 • Ground floor bedrooms • Public telephone • Games room.
Table tennis/pool table • No smoking • Pets welcome • BBQ/Patio area

Skiddaw View Holiday Home Park

Quality self-catering accommodation in the Northern Lake District

Holiday Static Caravans, Timber Lodges and a range of traditional holiday Cottages
Handy for Keswick, Cockermouth etc. 4-acre pet walking field.
Call us on 0845 468 0936 or 016973 20919 or visit: www.SkiddawView.co.uk
Skiddaw View Holiday Home Park, Bothel, near Bassenthwaite, Cumbria, CA7 2NJ

enjoyEngland.com ★★★★ HOLIDAY PARK

Farlam Hall Hotel **Brampton, Cumbria CA8 2NG**

Tel: 016977 46234 • Fax: 016977 46683

Standing in four acres of gardens, with its own lake, Farlam Hall has that indefinable quality that makes a stay here something really special. Fine quality cuisine, individually decorated and well-equipped guest rooms. Ideal touring centre for the Lakes, Borders & Hadrian's Wall.

e-mail: farlam@relaischateaux.com • www.farlamhall.co.uk

Walk your dog straight from the cottages up the hill and on to the fells. 7 cottages on North Pennines farm, sleeping 2-8; excellent base for Hadrian's Wall, Scottish Borders and the Lake District. Local food cooked by Harriet and delivered to your cottage.

Tel: 016977 3435 • e-mail: stay@longbyres.co.uk
www.longbyres.co.uk

Woodend Cottages • between the Eskdale and Duddon Valleys

Visit our website at www.woodendhouse.co.uk or phone 019467 23277

Woodend is remote and surrounded by hills and moorland, with views towards Scafell Pike. The cottages and house offer cosy accommodation for two to six people.

SHORT BREAKS AVAILABLE OUT OF SEASON.

Pet-Friendly
Pubs, Inns & Hotels

on pages 424-432

Please note that these establishments may not feature in the main section of this book

NEW HOUSE FARM

BUTTERMERE/LORTON VALLEY, COCKERMOUTH, CUMBRIA CA13 9UU

www.newhouse-farm.com • e-mail: enquiries@newhouse-farm.co.uk

Tel: 07841 159818

(See Map 5 Ref C3)

SITUATED IN THE QUIETEST AND MOST BEAUTIFUL PART OF THE LAKES, NEW HOUSE FARM HAS 15 ACRES OF OPEN FIELDS, PONDS, STREAMS AND WOODS WHICH GUESTS AND DOGS MAY WANDER AROUND AT LEISURE AND THERE IS EASY ACCESS TO NEARBY LAKES AND FELLS. THERE ARE FIVE LUXURIOUS EN SUITE BEDROOMS, ALL WITH SPECTACULAR VIEWS, AN ELEGANT DINING ROOM AND THREE SITTING ROOMS, ALL WITH OPEN FIRES. GOOD FOOD. WELCOMING HOSTS.

BED & BREAKFAST FROM £75, DINNER, BED & BREAKFAST FROM £99.

Good Hotel Guide | Which? Hotel Guide | **AA ★★★★★**

"THE LORTON VALE — A PLACE FOR ALL SEASONS"

GRAHAM ARMS HOTEL

Longtown, Near Carlisle, Cumbria CA6 5SE

A warm welcome awaits at this 180-year-old former Coaching Inn. Situated six miles from the M6 (J44) and Gretna Green, The Graham Arms makes an ideal overnight stop or perfect touring base for the Scottish Borders, English Lakes, Hadrian's Wall and much more. 16 comfortable en suite bedrooms, including four-poster and family rooms with TV, radio etc. Meals and snacks served throughout the day. Friendly 'local's bar' and 'Sports bar' serving real ale, extra cold lagers, cocktails and a fine selection of malt whiskies. Secure courtyard parking for cars, cycles and motorcycles. Beautiful woodland and riverside walks. Pets welcome with well behaved owners!

Visit our website on www.grahamarms.com • Tel: 01228 791213 • Fax: 01228 794110

e-mail: office@grahamarms.com • www.grahamarms.com

Bed and full traditional breakfast £33– £38. Special rates for weekend and midweek breaks. ETC ★★

Seven cottages sleeping 2-6. Set behind a large Georgian house set in parkland on the side of Hamps Fell. Beautiful garden, great walks. Pets and children welcome. Open all year. Please telephone for details.

Contact: MR M. AINSCOUGH, LONGLANDS AT CARTMEL, GRANGE-OVER-SANDS LA11 6HG • 015395 36475 • Fax: 015395 36172

e-mail: longlands@cartmel.com • www.cartmel.com

THE MANOR HOUSE, OUGHTERSIDE, ASPATRIA, CUMBRIA CA7 2PT

e-mail: richardandjudy@themanorhouse.net • www.themanorhouse.net

Our lovely manor farmhouse dates from the 18th century, retaining many original features and several acres of land. Spacious en suite rooms, tea/coffee making facilities, TV and lots of little extras. Peaceful surroundings, easy access to the Western Lakes and Solway Coast. All pets and children welcome. Bed & Breakfast from £25. Evening meals by arrangement. Inspection Commended.

016973 22420

Cockermouth, Coniston, Crosby-on-Eden, Eskdale

Rose Cottage

Lorton Road, Cockermouth CA13 9DX

Family-run guest house on the outskirts of Cockermouth. Warm, friendly atmosphere. Ample off-road parking. All rooms en suite with colour TV, tea/coffee, central heating and all have double glazing.

★★★★ GUEST HOUSE

Pets most welcome in the house (excluding dining room), and there are short walks nearby. Ideal base for visiting both Lakes and coast.

AA ★★★★ Guest House

Tel & Fax: 01900 822189 www.rosecottageguest.co.uk

The Coppermines & Coniston Lakes Cottages

★★★ to ★★★★

70 unique Lakeland cottages for 2-30 of quality and character in stunning mountain scenery. Log fires, exposed beams. Weekends and Short Breaks.

Book online: www.coppermines.co.uk

015394 41765 Pets very welcome!

BROCKLEBANK GROUND HOLIDAY COTTAGES

TORVER, CONISTON LA21 8BS

Four luxury cottages in a quiet rural setting, sleeping 2,4,7 & 10. Excellent walking from the door. Dog friendly pubs 600 yards. Short breaks available. Prices from £275. ETC ★★★★

info@brocklebankground.com • www.brocklebankground.com

The Wallfoot

www.wallfootco.uk

A popular hotel just 3 miles east of Carlisle, surrounded by fabulous scenery and lovely walks; the Eden Golf Course is on our doorstep. The hotel boasts a newly refurbished bar and restaurant and offers a traditional bar menu and exciting new restaurant menu.

Park Broom, Crosby-on-Eden, Carlisle CA6 4QH
Tel: 01228 573696 • Fax: 01228 573240

Fisherground Farm, Eskdale, Cumbria

Fisherground is a lovely traditional hill farm, with a stone cottage and three pine lodges, sharing an acre of orchard. Ideal for walkers, nature lovers, dogs and children, we offer space, freedom, peace and tranquillity. We have a games room, a raft pool and an adventure playground. Good pubs nearby serve excellent bar meals.

Ian & Jennifer Hall, Orchard House, Applethwaite, Keswick, Cumbria CA12 4PN

017687 73175 • e-mail: holidays@fisherground.co.uk • www.fisherground.co.uk

THE BOOT INN

Boot, Eskdale, Cumbria CA19 1TG • Tel: 019467 23224
e-mail: enquiries@bootinn.co.uk • www.bootinn.co.uk

With walks for all abilities from the front door and a truly warm welcome for you and your dogs, along with good food and clean, comfortable rooms - this is people and doggie heaven! Please call for brochure. B&B from £40ppn. Special breaks available.

(formerly The Burnmoor Inn)

BLENG BARN COTTAGE

Self-catering three bedroom holiday cottage, situated on a family-run mixed working farm in its own secluded valley. Sleeps 6+4. Many traditional features and modern facilities. A perfect base for a leisurely break or a variey of activity holidays. Pets welcome by arrangement.

Mill House Farm, Wellington, Seascale, Cumbria CA20 1BH
Tel: 07801 862237 & 07775 512918 • Fax: 01946 725 671
e-mail: info@blengfarms.co.uk • www.blengfarms.co.uk

CYCLISTS WELCOME · WALKERS WELCOME

★★★★ *Self-Catering*

Hampsfell House Hotel

AA ★★ HOTEL

In two acres of private grounds, just a few minutes' walk from the town centre. Eight well appointed en suite bedrooms. Relax in the traditionally decorated lounges and then enjoy the best of fresh Cumbrian produce in the elegant dining room, where fine wines complement the table d'hôte and à la carte menus. Grange-over-Sands makes an ideal base for exploring the Lake District. Pets welcome, excellent dog walking facilities. Short Break option available.

Hampsfell Road, Grange-over-Sands LA11 6BG • Tel: 015395 32567
www.hampsfellhouse.co.uk • enquiries@hampsfellhouse.co.uk

From £30 per person per night. • 3 nights for the price of 2 from £120, 1st April to 31st March, Sunday-Thursday. • November-March, any 3 nights for the price of 2.

LAKE VIEW COUNTRY HOUSE & SELF-CATERING APARTMENTS

GRASMERE LA22 9TD • 015394 35384/35167

Luxury B&B or 3 Self-Catering apartments in unrivalled, secluded location in the village with wonderful views and lakeshore access. All B&B rooms en suite, some with whirlpool baths. Ground floor accommodation available. No smoking. Featured in "Which?" Good B&B Guide.

Midweek Breaks available in B&B • Winter Short Breaks available in S/C accommodation.

LAKELAND hideaways COTTAGES

Cottages in and around Hawkshead. Great walks and lakes for swimming, dog-friendly pubs, open fires to lie in front of... owners will enjoy it too!

Tel: 015394 42435
www.lakeland-hideaways.co.uk

Hideaways, The Square, Hawkshead LA22 0NZ

THE KINGS ARMS HOTEL

Hawkshead, Ambleside, Cumbria LA22 0NZ
015394 36372 • www.kingsarmshawkshead.co.uk

Join us for a relaxing stay amidst the green hills and dales of Lakeland, and we will be delighted to offer you good food, homely comfort and warm hospitality in historic surroundings. We hope to see you soon!

- SELF-CATERING COTTAGES ALSO AVAILABLE -

Readers are requested to mention this FHG guidebook when seeking accommodation

Kendal, Keswick

Mirefoot Cottages • Self-catering in the Lake District

5 Star, pet friendly, self-catering cottages in a superb rural location in the Lake District National Park. All cottages sleep 2. Fully equipped with TV (Freeview), DVD, WiFi, gas central heating. Tennis court, private parking.

Mirefoot Cottages, Mirefoot, Kendal, Cumbria LA8 9AB

Tel: 01539 720015 • E-mail: booking@mirefoot.co.uk • www.mirefoot.co.uk

2 Modern caravans, fully double glazed, gas central heating. Double and twin bedrooms, kitchen with fridge and microwave, spacious lounge/dining area with TV and video or DVD, toilet and shower. On traditional working farm set in 140 acres of beautiful countryside. Short breaks available out of season.

Mrs L. Hodgson, Patton Hall Farm, Kendal LA8 9DT (01539 721590)

stay@pattonhallfarm.co.uk www.pattonhallfarm.co.uk

RUSSELL FARM Burton-in-Kendal, Carnforth, Lancs LA6 1NN

Tel: 01524 781334 • email: miktaylor@farming.co.uk

Bed and Breakfast • Ideal centre for touring Lakes and Yorkshire Dales, or as a stopover for Scotland or the South • Good food, friendly atmosphere on working dairy farm • Modernised farmhouse • Guests' own lounge • **Contact Anne Taylor for details.**

DERWENT WATER MARINA

DERWENT WATER MARINA, PORTINSCALE, KESWICK CA12 5RF

Lakeside self-catering apartments. Three apartments sleep 2 plus folding bed for occasional use, one apartment sleeps 6. Superb views over the lake and fells. Includes TV, heating and bed linen. Non-smoking. Watersports and boat hire available on site.

Tel: 017687 72912 for brochure • e-mail: info@derwentwatermarina.co.uk • www.derwentwatermarina.co.uk

KESWICK COTTAGES ETC ★★★★ Tel: 017687 78555

8 Beechcroft, Braithwaite, Keswick Cumbria CA12 5TH

Superb selection of cottages and apartments in and around Keswick. All of our properties are well maintained and thoroughly clean. From a one bedroom cottage to a four bedroom house we have something for everyone. Children and pets welcome. Contact us for a free colour brochure.

e-mail: info@keswickcottages.co.uk • www.keswickcottages.co.uk

Tel: 017687 72764
Freephone: 0800 056 6401
Mobile: 07721 957899
e-mail: andy042195@aol.com

SEYMOUR HOUSE

Seymour House is set in a quiet cul-de-sac in Keswick - a beautiful market town in the Heart of the English Lakes, half way between Keswick centre and Derwentwater, both of which offer many attractions.

10 well appointed bedrooms, seven fully en suite.

All rooms have colour TV with video channel, hospitality trays, wash-hand basins and central heating.

Free car parking directly outside.

36 Lake Road, Keswick, Cumbria, CA12 5DQ

www.seymour-house.com

English Tourism Council ★★ HOTEL

MARY MOUNT HOTEL Set in 4½ acres of gardens and woodlands on the shores of Derwentwater. 2½ miles from Keswick in picturesque Borrowdale. Superb walking and touring. All rooms en suite with colour TV and tea/coffee making facilities. Licensed. *Brochure on request.* **BORROWDALE, NEAR KESWICK CA12 5UU**

017687 77223 • e-mail: mawdsley1@aol.com • www.marymounthotel.co.uk

Portinscale, Keswick, Cumbria CA12 5RH

Set within its own garden with private car parking, in the picturesque village of Portinscale near the shores of Lake Derwentwater within walking distance of the market town of Keswick. Ideally situated for exploring all parts of the Lakes. Offering comfort, friendly service, these being the essential qualities provided by the resident proprietor. A well-stocked bar offering local beers; comfortable lounge and elegant dining room where a four course dinner can be enjoyed with a varied selection of wines. All rooms en suite with tea and coffee making facilities, colour TV, telephone.

DB&B from £56. Winter Breaks: 3 nights DB&B £150pp.

★★★★ GUEST HOUSE

Brochure on request, contact Des or Carol Taylorson on 017687 72344
e-mail: stay@rickerbygrange.co.uk • www.rickerbygrange.co.uk

LAKELAND
Cottage Holidays

Self-catering cottages for you and your pets in and around Keswick and beautiful Borrowdale

01768776065
Email: info@lakelandcottages.co.uk
www.lakelandcottages.co.uk

COLEDALE INN

ETC ★★★

Braithwaite, Near Keswick, Cumbria CA12 5TN Tel: 017687 78272

A friendly, family-run Victorian Inn in a peaceful hillside position above Braithwaite, and ideally situated for touring and walking. All bedrooms are warm and spacious, with en suite shower room and colour television. Children are welcome, as are pets. Home-cooked meals, and real ales. Open all year. **www.coledale-inn.co.uk**

Traditional Lakeland hotel with friendly atmosphere. Home cooking, cosy bar, comfortable lounge and some riverside rooms.
Winter and Summer discount rates. Brochure and Tariff available.

ROYAL OAK HOTEL, BORROWDALE, KESWICK CA12 5XB
017687 77214 • e-mail: info@royaloakhotel.co.uk
www.royaloakhotel.co.uk

Overwater Hall

AA ★★★ HOTEL

Hosts: Stephen Bore
Adrian & Angela Hyde

Overwater, Ireby, Near Keswick,
Cumbria CA7 1HH
Tel: 017687 76566
e-mail: welcome@overwaterhall.co.uk
www.overwaterhall.co.uk

Our elegant, family-run Country House Hotel offers you the best in traditional comforts, award-winning food and friendly hospitality. Peacefully secluded yet within only a short drive of the popular centres of the Lake District, this is the ideal place for a real break.

Dogs genuinely welcome in your room, in one of our lounges, the bar, and in our 18 acres of grounds.

Special four-night breaks available all year from £320 per person, inclusive of Dinner and Breakfast.

Please telephone us for a brochure, or refer to our website for further information.

Keswick, Kirkby-in-Furness, Kirkby Lonsdale, Kirkby Stephen

Horse and Farrier Inn

Threlkeld, Keswick CA12 4SQ

★★★★ INN

Situated beneath Blencathra, in an ideal location for walking or touring the Lake District. All 15 bedrooms en suite, with TV, tea/coffee making and hairdryer. Award-winning food and restaurant. Open all year. Pets welcome.

Tel: 017687 79688 • Fax: 017687 79823

info@horseandfarrier.com

www.horseandfarrier.com

Woodside

Ideally situated away from the busy town centre yet only a short walk down the C2C bridle path to the town. All rooms are en suite, and we have ample private parking and large gardens. Being a family-run establishment, you are guaranteed a friendly reception. After a good night's sleep you will be ready for a hearty English breakfast together with cereal, fruit and yoghurt. Dogs welcome by arrangement. B&B from £30.

Ann & Norman Pretswell, Woodside, Penrith Road, Keswick CA12 4LJ • 017687 73522

www.woodsideguesthouse.co.uk

Janet and Peter, 1 Friars Ground, Kirkby-in-Furness LA17 7YB

"Sunset Cottage" is a spacious self-catering 17th century two/three bedroomed character cottage with a large enclosed garden. Original features include inglenook fireplace with logburning stove, oak beams, flagstone floor and oak panelling. Beautiful solid oak and beech fully integrated kitchen with dishwasher, washer/dryer. Panoramic views over sea/mountains; ideal for walking and birdwatching. Coniston/Windermere 30 minutes. Non-smoking. Terms from £150. Open all year. Debit/credit cards accepted.

e-mail: enquiries@southlakes-cottages.com • www.southlakes-cottages.com

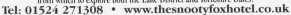

The Snooty Fox • Kirkby Lonsdale

The Snooty Fox is a charming Jacobean Inn, with 9 en suite rooms and a restaurant offering the finest local, seasonal produce. Situated in the heart of the market town of Kirkby Lonsdale and boasting a range of fine cask ales and malt whiskies. The Snooty Fox is the perfect base from which to explore both the Lake District and Yorkshire Dales.

Tel: 01524 271308 • www.thesnootyfoxhotel.co.uk

A warm welcome awaits you at **ULLATHORNS**, a working farm situated in the unspoilt Lune Valley. The farmhouse is dated 1617. One family/twin/double and one double, both en suite, with TV and drink making facilities. Visitors' lounge with log-burning stove. A hearty breakfast is served at individual tables. Ample car parking. An ideal touring base for Lakes and Dales or as a stopover point as situated between M6 junctions. Non-smoking. B&B from £25 (based on two sharing) with reductions for children. Short break offers. **VisitBritain ★★★★**

Pauline Bainbridge, Ullathorns Farm, Middleton, Kirkby Lonsdale LA6 2LZ

Tel: 015242 76214 • e-mail: pauline@ullathorns.co.uk • www.ullathorns.co.uk

Cocklake House

MALLERSTANG CA17 4JT • 017683 72080

Charming, High Pennine Country House B&B in unique position above Pendragon Castle in Upper Mallerstang Dale offering good food and exceptional comfort to a small number of guests. Two double rooms with large private bathrooms. Three acres riverside grounds. Dogs welcome.

FREE or REDUCED RATE entry to Holiday Visits and Attractions – see our **READERS' OFFER VOUCHERS** on pages 433-440

"YOUR PETS & YOUR HOLIDAY"

Combine COMFORT, PEACE AND QUIET, RELAX, FISH, STROLL OR WALK

(SECLUDED COTTAGES with private fishing)

Tranquil, comfortable cottages, set in their own secret valley, overlooking the fishing lakes amidst Lakeland's beautiful Eden Valley countryside, only 30 minutes' drive from Ullswater, North Pennines, Hadrian's Wall and Scottish Borders.

★Well fenced exercise areas for dogs.
★ Clean, well maintained and equipped.
★ Linen provided. ★ Beds freshly made for you.
★ Exceptional wildlife and walking area.
★ Excellent Coarse Fishing for residents only.
★ Golf courses nearby. ★ You & your pets very welcome.
★ Kennel available if required. ★ Open all year – breaks/weeks.

Flexible Terms

Relax and escape to "YOUR" hideaway in the country.

Tel/Fax 01768 898711 24hr Brochure line

e-mail: info@crossfieldcottages.co.uk
www.crossfieldcottages.co.uk

Booking & Availability
01768 898711, 6-10 p.m. or SAE to:

CROSSFIELD COTTAGES, KIRKOSWALD,
PENRITH, CUMBRIA CA10 1EU

RING NOW! It's never too early or too late!

ETC ★★★

PETS – NO PROBLEM!

Owned by Vets

Lake District, Lamplugh (near Loweswater)

"Your own country house in the Lakes"

Two luxury holiday houses available to rent in the Lake District.

Routen House is a beautiful old farmhouse set in 4 acres in an outstanding position with fabulous views over Ennerdale Lake. Fully modernised while retaining the character of the old farmhouse, it has been furnished to a very high standard. Sleeps 12 plus cot.

Little Parrock is an elegant Victorian Lakeland stone house a short walk from the centre of Grasmere with large rooms and a wealth of period features. Lovely private garden. Fully modernised to a very high standard; real log fires. Sleeps 10 plus cot.

Both houses are non-smoking but pets are very welcome. Please contact:

Mrs J. Green • Tel & Fax: 01604 626383 • e-mail: joanne@routenhouse.co.uk

www.routenhouse.co.uk • www.littleparrock.co.uk

Grizedale Lodge **Hawkshead, Ambleside LA22 0QL**

Set in the heart of Grizedale Forest National Park, in a beautiful location, and within easy reach of Beatrix Potter country, Windermere and Coniston.

All rooms en suite, some with four-posters.

Central heating. Residents' licence.

Open all year, from £30pppn.

Tel 015394 36532 • Fax: 015394 36572

enquiries@grizedale-lodge.com

Rose Cottage • Cumbria

Situated just three miles from Loweswater and four miles from Ennerdale, Rose Cottage is very much on the quiet side of the Lake District yet is within easy reach of the hustle and bustle of Keswick & Cockermouth should you desire it. The cottage is lovely throughout with an open plan kitchen and sitting room, cosy coal fire, two bedrooms and enclosed garden. Pets are welcome.

Please contact Sally Fielding on 017687 76836 for more details or visit www.millgillhead.co.uk.

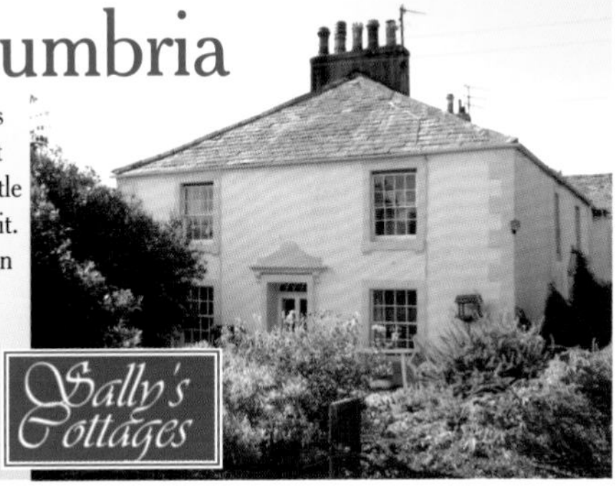

Felldyke Cottage Holidays • "a warm and friendly welcome"

Visiting the Western Lakes? Then why not stay in this lovely 19th century cottage. Sleeps 4, short breaks can be arranged. Pets are welcome.

Open all year, for you to enjoy the Lake District in all its guises.

Mrs A. Wilson • 01946 861151 • dockraynook@talk21.com

www.felldykecottageholidays.co.uk VB ★★★★

FHG Guides

publish a large range of well-known accommodation guides.
We will be happy to send you details or you can use the order form at the back of this book.

Book with this advert and claim a FREE dessert

THE BRITANNIA INN

Elterwater, Langdale, Cumbria LA22 9HP

Tel: 015394 37210

A 500 year-old quintessential Lakeland Inn nestled in the centre of the picturesque village of Elterwater amidst the imposing fells of the Langdale Valley. Comfortable, high quality en suite double and twin-bedded rooms. Dogs welcome. Enquire about our Mid-Week Special Offer of three nights B&B for the price of two. Relax in the oak-beamed Bars or Dining Room whilst sampling local real ales and dishes from our extensive menu of fresh, home-cooked food using lots of Cumbrian produce. *Quiz Night most Sundays.*

www.britinn.co.uk • e-mail: info@britinn.co.uk

Some of the loveliest cottages in the Lake District with stunning scenery on their doorsteps are ready to welcome you and your pets. Prices vary. Please visit our website.

ETC ★★★ - ★★★★★

e-mail: enquiries@wheelwrights.com

www.wheelwrights.com

WHEELWRIGHTS

HOLIDAY COTTAGES, ELTERWATER, NEAR AMBLESIDE LA22 9HS

Tel: 015394 38305

Fax: 015394 37618

HIGHFOLD COTTAGE • LITTLE LANGDALE

Very comfortable Lakeland cottage, ideally situated for walking and touring. Superb mountain views. Sleeps 5. Personally maintained. Pets welcome. Weekly £260–£500. **MRS C.E. BLAIR, 8 THE GLEBE, CHAPEL STILE, AMBLESIDE LA22 9JT • 015394 37686 • www.highfoldcottage.co.uk**

★★★ SELF CATERING

NEAR HOWE COTTAGES

Mungrisdale

NEAR HOWE

An ideal, quiet and tranquil retreat located in the heart of the Cumbrian countryside. Set in an elevated position, all our cottages have spectacular views over the Cumbrian Fells. Our large garden has many relaxation areas. The perfect place to escape to for you and your dog.

Tel/Fax: 01768 779 678 • E-mail: enquiries@nearhowe.co.uk

www.nearhowe.co.uk

Judged to be the '2007 Website of the Year' at the Cumbrian Tourist Awards

A well tended, uncrowded and wooded site set amidst picturesque fells between the Cartmel peninsula and the southern tip of Lake Windermere. On-site facilities: flush toilets • hot showers • laundry facilities • hair dryers • deep freeze • gas on sale • Tourers (30 pitches) £14 per night (incl. electricity & VAT). Tents (30 pitches) £12 - £14 per night. Auto homes £12 (£14 on electricity). All prices for outfit, plus 2 adults and 2 children. Open March 1st to October 31st.

Oak Head Caravan Park, Ayside, Grange-over-Sands LA11 6JA

Contact: Mrs A. Scott • Tel: 015395 31475

Penrith

Your Stepping Stone to the Cumbrian Lake District

ETC ★★★★★

Award-winning Carrock Cottages are four recently renovated stone built cottages set on the fringe of the Lakeland Fells. A quiet rural location near the lovely villages of Hesket Newmarket with its award-winning brewery, Caldbeck and Greystoke. Explore the beauty of the Lake District National Park or head North to historic Carlisle and on to Hadrian's Wall.
Fell walking & other activities close to hand as well as excellent restaurants.
A warm welcome guaranteed.
Accommodation for 1 to 18 people.
On-site games room, home-cooked meal service.
Spa facilities.

Carrock House, Hutton Roof, Penrith, Cumbria CA11 0XY
Tel: Malcolm or Gillian on 01768 484 111 or Fax: 017684 888 50

www.carrockcottages.co.uk • info@carrockcottages.co.uk

LYVENNET COTTAGES Five different cottages (including 5-Star Steel's Mill) in and around the small farming village of Kings Meaburn in beautiful unspoilt 'Lyvennet Valley'. Ideal touring centre for the Lakes, Dales, Hadrian's Wall; superb area for dog walks. Attractively furnished, fuel, power and linen inclusive. All have colour TV, microwave, fridge, washing machine, central heating, parking and private fishing. Children, pets and horses welcome, cots and highchairs on request. Open all year. Terms from £130 to £440.
Contact: Janet Addison, Keld Farm, Kings Meaburn, Penrith, Cumbria CA10 3BS
Tel: 01931 714661/714226 • Fax: 01931 714598 • www.lyvennetcottages.co.uk • ETC 4/5 ★

ETC ★★★

Between Keswick and Penrith and close to the shores of lovely Ullswater, this friendly and well-appointed inn enjoys sweeping fell views and is a haven for a variety of outdoor pursuits. Known for its excellent varied food and real ales. Tastefully furnished bedrooms have en suite facilities, colour television and tea and coffee-makers and there are three self-catering cottages (ETC ★★★★)

The Troutbeck Inn, Troutbeck, Penrith, Cumbria CA11 0SJ • Tel: 017684 83635
Fax: 017684 87071 • e-mail: info@thetroutbeckinn.co.uk • www.thetroutbeck-inn.co.uk

---

Boot & Shoe Inn

Greystoke, Penrith, Cumbria CA11 0TP

16th Century Inn in the heart of the legendary village of Greystoke.
This popular village pub is full of charm, character and history.
Excellent food, en suite accommodation and ambience. Conveniently situated to explore the Lake District, you can always be sure of a warm welcome.

Tel: 01768 483343

• Corner House •

Comfortable, friendly atmosphere with a hearty breakfast to set you up for the day. Secure car and cycle parking. Pets and well-behaved owners welcome!

36 Victoria Road, Penrith CA11 8HR • Tel: 01768 863566

e-mail: doreen@cornerhousepenrith.co.uk

www.cornerhousepenrith.co.uk

★ Seacote Park ★

The Beach, St Bees, Cumbria CA27 0ET

Tel: 01946 822777 • Fax: 01946 824442

reception@seacote.com • www.seacote.com

Adjoining lovely sandy beach on fringe of Lake District, modern luxury holiday caravans for hire, fully equipped to sleep up to 8. Full serviced touring pitches and tent area. St Bees is convenient for touring, with Ennerdale, Eskdale and Wasdale, plus some of England's finest mountain scenery within easy reach. Holiday caravans also for sale.

Tarnside Caravan Park

5 miles from St Bees, own tarn where fishing is available

Seven Acres Caravan Park

small park set among the trees just outside Gosforth

Tanglewood Caravan Park

CAUSEWAY HEAD, SILLOTH-ON-SOLWAY, CUMBRIA CA7 4PE

Tanglewood is a family-run park on the fringes of the Lake District National Park. It is tree-sheltered and situated one mile inland from the small port of Silloth on the Solway Firth, with a beautiful view of the Galloway Hills. Large modern holiday homes are available from March to January, with car parking beside each home. Fully equipped except for bed linen, with end bedroom, panel heaters in both bedrooms and the bathroom, electric lighting, hot and cold water, toilet, shower, gas fire, fridge and colour TV, all of which are included in the tariff. Touring pitches also available with electric hook-ups and water/drainage facilities, etc. Play area. Licensed lounge with adjoining children's play room. Pets welcome free but must be kept under control at all times. Full colour brochure available.

AA ★★★ **TEL: 016973 31253**

e-mail: tanglewoodcaravanpark@hotmail.com

www.tanglewoodcaravanpark.co.uk

FELL VIEW HOLIDAYS, FELL VIEW, GRISEDALE BRIDGE, GLENRIDDING CA11 0PJ

017684 82795 • enquiries@fellviewholidays.com • www.fellviewholidays.com

Sleep 2-5. Lovely, comfortable, well equipped accommodation in an idyllic location between Glenridding and Patterdale. Magnificent views of the surrounding fells. Shared use of gardens.

Short Breaks available out of season. Please look at the website or call for a brochure.

Ullswater, Wasdale, Wigton, Windermere

Land Ends Cabins, Watermillock, Near Ullswater CA11 0NB

Tel: 017684 86438 • Only one mile from Ullswater, our four detached log cabins have a peaceful fellside location in 25-acre grounds with two pretty lakes. Ducks, moorhens, red squirrels and wonderful birdlife. Doggy heaven! Sleep 2-5. **e-mail: infolandends@btinternet.com • www.landends.co.uk**

Cove Park is a peaceful caravan & camping park overlooking Lake Ullswater, surrounded by Fells with beautiful views. The park is very well-maintained. We are ideally situated for walking, watersports and all of the Lake District tourist attractions in the North Lakes. Facilities include clean heated showers and washrooms with hand and hair dryers, washing and drying machines, iron & board, and a separate washing up area and a freezer for ice packs. We offer electric hook-ups with hardstandings, and plenty of sheltered grass for campers.

Cove Caravan & Camping Park

Watermillock, Penrith, Cumbria CA11 0LS

• Tel: 017684 86549 • www.cove-park.co.uk

Bridge Inn

www.santonbridgeinn.com

The Bridge Inn, once a coach halt, is now a fine, comfortable, award-winning country inn, offering hospitality to all travellers and visitors.

The Inn has an excellent reputation for good food, with "real" food served in the Dalesman Bar, or in the Eskdale Room. We serve an excellent selection of Jennings real ales. 16 bedrooms. Weddings and other private and business functions catered for in our function room. Licensed for civil ceremonies, partnerships, naming ceremonies and renewal of vows.

10 minute drive to "Britain's favourite view – Wastwater".

This unspoiled area of the Lake District offers superb walking and climbing.

Bridge Inn, Santon Bridge, Wasdale CA19 1UX

Tel: 019467 26221 • Fax: 019467 26026

e-mail: info@santonbridgeinn.com

A spacious well-equipped, comfortable cottage on a working farm. Superlative setting and views, large kitchen/dining room, Aga, lounge, open fire, TV/video/DVD, three bedrooms, bathroom, separate shower room. Linen, towels, electricity, logs and coal inclusive. Children and pets very welcome. Extensive garden. Storage heaters, washing machine, dishwasher. Easy reach Lake District, Scottish Borders and Roman Wall.

Sleeps 2-8 • Prices from £205–£455

Available all year.

Short breaks by arrangement.

FOXGLOVES COTTAGE. Mr & Mrs E. and J. Kerr,
Greenrigg Farm, Westward, Wigton CA7 8AH • 016973 42676

Langdale Chase Hotel Windermere LA23 1LW

Magnificent country house hotel with over six acres of beautifully landscaped grounds sloping to the edge of Lake Windermere. Panoramic views of lake and fells, log fires, excellent food, and friendly, professional staff all ensure a memorable stay. **015394 32201**

e-mail: sales@langdalechase.co.uk • www.langdalechase.co.uk

THE FAMOUS
WILD BOAR

"Tucked away amongst the gently rolling countryside in the quiet Gilpin Valley, with 72 acres of its own private woodland, this former coaching inn is famed for its traditional atmosphere and the warmth of its welcome."

Complementing the hotel perfectly, bedrooms are cosy and comfortable, and the restaurant offers a menu that makes the very most of Lakeland produce, accompanied by an extensive wine list.

THE FAMOUS WILD BOAR
CROOK, NEAR WINDERMERE
CUMBRIA LA23 3NF
RESERVATIONS: 08458 504604
www.elh.co.uk

English Lakes Hotels

Windermere

CUMBRIAN COTTAGES. Choose from 300 pet-friendly cottages. Superb locations throughout the Lake District and Cumbria. All VisitBritain graded. Contact us for a brochure or visit our website. Tel: 01228 599950 (lines open 7 days 9am-9pm (5.30pm Sat). [Pets £15 per week.]
website: www.cumbrian-cottages.co.uk

DALES HOLIDAY COTTAGES. See the best of the Lake District and Eden Valley. A wide range of cottages to choose from, all personally inspected. Pets welcome. Free brochure. Call 0870 909 9500 or visit our website. [🐕]
website: www.dalesholcot.com

STAY LAKELAND. A range of high quality self-catering holiday accommodation in the Lake District and Cumbria, including traditional cottages, houses, timber lodges and holiday static caravans. All ★★★ minimum and inspected annually by VisitBritain (0845 468 0936) [🐕]
website: www.staylakeland.co.uk

Alston

Small market town 16 miles NE of Penrith.

PAUL & CAROL HUISH, ROCK HOUSE ESTATE, VALLEY VIEW, NENTHEAD, ALSTON CA9 3NA (01434 382 684). Five luxury cottages sleeping 2, 4, 7, 7, or 14. Undiscovered Cumbria, accessible to the Lakes, Dales and Borders. 100 acre estate is surrounded by spectacular views. Short breaks available. Open all year. VisitBritain ★★★/★★★★. [Pets £20 each].
e-mail: Info@RockHouseEstate.co.uk website: www.RockHouseEstate.co.uk

Ambleside

Popular centre for exploring Lake District at northern end of Lake Windermere. Picturesque Stock Ghyll waterfall nearby, lovely walks. Associations with Wordsworth. Penrith 30 miles, Keswick 17, Windermere 5.

THE OLD VICARAGE, VICARAGE ROAD, AMBLESIDE LA22 9DH (015394 33364). 'Rest a while in style'. Quality B&B set in tranquil wooded grounds in the heart of the village. Car park. All rooms en suite. Kettle, clock/radio, TV. Heated indoor pool, sauna, hot tub, sun lounge and rooftop terrace. Special breaks. Friendly service where your pets are welcome. Telephone Ian or HELEN Burt. [🐕]
website: www.oldvicarageambleside.co.uk

LYNDALE GUEST HOUSE LAKE ROAD, AMBLESIDE LA22 0DN (015394 34244) Nestled midway between Lake Windermere and Ambleside village, with superb views of Loughrigg Fell and the Langdales beyond. Excellent base for walking, touring, or just relaxing. [🐕]
website: www.lyndale-guesthouse.co.uk

KIRKSTONE FOOT, KIRKSTONE PASS ROAD, AMBLESIDE LA22 9EH (015394 32232; Fax: 015394 32805). Superior cottage and apartment complex, set in peaceful gardens, adjoining the Lakeland fells and village centre. Open all year. ETC ★★★★/★★★★★ [pw! Pets £5.00 per night.]
e-mail: enquiries@kirkstonefoot.co.uk website: www.kirkstonefoot.co.uk

2 LOWFIELD, OLD LAKE ROAD, AMBLESIDE. Ground floor garden flat half a mile from town centre; sleeps 4. Lounge/diningroom, kitchen, bathroom/WC, two bedrooms, one with en suite shower. Linen supplied. Children and pets welcome. Parking. Terms from £150 to £280 per week. Contact: MR P. F. QUARMBY, 3 LOWFIELD, OLD LAKE ROAD, AMBLESIDE LA22 0DH (Tel & Fax: 015394 32326) [🐕]
e-mail: paulfquarmby@aol.com

SMALLWOOD HOUSE, COMPSTON ROAD, AMBLESIDE LA22 9DJ (015394 32330). Where quality and the customer come first. En suite rooms, car parking, leisure club membership. ETC ★★★★ [Pets £3 per night]
website: www.smallwoodhotel.co.uk

GREENHOWE CARAVAN PARK, GREAT LANGDALE, AMBLESIDE LA22 9JU (015394 37231; Fax: 015394 37464). Permanent Caravan Park with Self Contained Holiday Accommodation. An ideal centre for Climbing, Fell Walking, Riding, Swimming, or just a lazy holiday. ETC ★★★★ [Pets £6 per night, £30 per week]
website: www.greenhowe.com

BETTY FOLD, HAWKSHEAD HILL, AMBLESIDE LA22 0PS (015394 36611). Ground floor apartment sleeping four. Private entrance. Set in peaceful and spacious grounds, ideal for walkers and families with pets. Open all year. [pw! Pets £2 per night.]
e-mail: claire@bettyfold.co.uk website: www.bettyfold.co.uk

Appleby-in-Westmorland

Located in the Eden Valley, ideal for walking, riding, fishing and cycling. Annual events include The Gypsy Horse Fair and the Jazz Festival.

MILBURN GRANGE HOLIDAY COTTAGES, KNOCK, APPLEBY CA16 6DR (017683 61867) 1,2 & 3 bedroom cottages and a snug apartment in a stunning rural location. Two National Parks on the doorstep. Dogs very welcome and open all year. VisitBritain ★★★ Self Catering.
e-mail: petswelcome@milburngrange.co.uk website: www.milburngrange.co.uk

KEITH AND DIANE BUDDING, SCALEBECK HOLIDAY COTTAGES, SCALEBECK, GREAT ASBY, APPLEBY CA16 6TF (01768 351006; Fax: 01768 353532). Comfortable and well-equipped self-catering accommodation in the tranquil and picturesque Eden Valley. Sleep 2/5. No smoking. ETC ★★★★ [pw! £20 per week]
e-mail: mail@scalebeckholidaycottages.com

Bampton

Hamlet 3 miles NW of Shap.

THE MARDALE INN @ ST PATRICK'S WELL, BAMPTON CA10 2RQ (01931 713244). Early 18th century Lake District inn. Fantastic walking around nearby Haweswater. Children and dogs welcome. Daily Telegraph '50 Best Pubs', May 2008. ETC ★★★★ [🐕]
e-mail: info@mardaleinn.co.uk website: www.mardaleinn.co.uk

Bassenthwaite

Village on Bassenthwaite Lake with traces of Norse and Roman settlements.

SKIDDAW VIEW HOLIDAY HOME PARK, BOTHEL, NEAR BASSENTHWAITE CA7 2NJ (0845 468 0936 or 016973 20919). Holiday static caravans, timber lodges and a range of traditional holiday cottages. Handy for Keswick, Cockermouth etc. 4-acre pet walking field. ETC ★★★★ [pw!🐕]
website: www.skiddawview.co.uk

Symbols

- 🐕 Indicates that pets are welcome free of charge.
- £ Indicates that a charge is made for pets: nightly or weekly.
- pw! Shows some special provision for pets; exercise facility, feeding or accommodation arrangement.
- ⌂ Indicates separate pets accommodation.

Brampton

Market town with cobbled streets. Octagonal Moat Hall with exterior staircases and iron stocks.

FARLAM HALL HOTEL, BRAMPTON, CUMBRIA CA8 2NG (016977 46234; Fax: 016977 46683). Standing in four acres of gardens, with its own lake, Farlam Hall offers fine quality cuisine and individually decorated guest rooms. Ideal touring centre for the Lakes, Borders and Hadrian's Wall. AA Three Stars Inspectors' Choice and Two Rosettes, Relais & Chateaux. [🐕]
e-mail: farlam@relaischateaux.com website: www.farlamhall.co.uk

LONG BYRES AT TALKIN HEAD (016977 3435). Walk your dog straight from the cottages up the hill and on to the fells. 7 cottages on North Pennines farm, sleeping 2-8; excellent base for Hadrian's Wall, Scottish Borders and the Lake District. Local food cooked by Harriet and delivered to your cottage. [🐕]
e-mail: stay@longbyres.co.uk website: www.longbyres.co.uk

Broughton-in-Furness

Village 8 miles NW of Ulverston.

PAUL SANDFORD, WOODEND COTTAGES, WOODEND, ULPHA, BROUGHTON-IN-FURNESS LA20 6DY Woodend is remote and surrounded by hills and moorland, with views towards Scafell Pike. The cottages and house offer cosy accommodation for two to six people. Short breaks available out of season.
website: www.woodendhouse.co.uk

Buttermere

Between lake of same name and Crummock Water. Magnificent scenery. Of special note is Sour Milk Ghyll waterfall and steep impressive Honister Pass. Keswick 15 miles, Cockermouth 10.

NEW HOUSE FARM, BUTTERMERE/LORTON VALLEY, COCKERMOUTH CA13 9UU (07841 159818). New House Farm has 15 acres of fields, woods, streams and ponds which guests and dogs can wander around. Luxurious en suite accommodation and fine traditional food. Off season breaks. AA ★★★★★. [Pets £7.50 per night]
e-mail: enquiries@newhouse-farm.co.uk website: www.newhouse-farm.com

Carlisle

Important Border city and former Roman station on River Eden. Castle is of historic interest, also Tullie House Museum and Art Gallery. Good sports facilities inc. football and racecourse. Kendal 45 miles, Dumfries 33, Penrith 18.

GRAHAM ARMS HOTEL, ENGLISH STREET, LONGTOWN, CARLISLE CA6 5SE (01228 791213; Fax: 01228 794110). 16 bedrooms en suite, including four-poster and family rooms, all with tea/coffee facilities, TV and radio. Secure courtyard locked overnight. Pets welcome with well-behaved owners. ETC ★★ [🐕]
e-mail: office@grahamarms.com website: www.grahamarms.com

Cartmel

Village 4 miles south of Newby Bridge.

RATHER SPECIAL COTTAGES. Seven cottages sleeping 2-6. Set behind a large Georgian house set in parkland on the side of Hamps Fell. Beautiful garden, great walks. Pets and children welcome. Open all year. Please telephone for details. ETC ★★★★. Contact: MR M. AINSCOUGH, LONGLANDS AT CARTMEL, GRANGE-OVER-SANDS LA11 6HG (015395 36475; Fax: 015395 36172). [🐕]
e-mail: longlands@cartmel.com website: www.cartmel.com

FREE or REDUCED RATE entry to Holiday Visits and Attractions – see our **READERS' OFFER VOUCHERS** on pages 433-440

Cockermouth

Market town and popular touring centre for Lake District and quiet Cumbrian coast. On Rivers Derwent and Cocker. Penrith 30 miles, Carlisle 26, Whitehaven 14, Keswick 12.

THE MANOR HOUSE, OUGHTERSIDE, ASPATRIA, CUMBRIA CA7 2PT (016973 22420). 18th century manor farmhouse retaining many original features and several acres of land. Spacious en suite rooms, tea/coffee making facilities, TV and lots of little extras. All pets and children welcome. Inspection Commended. [🐕]
e-mail: richardandjudy@themanorhouse.net website: www.themanorhouse.net

ROSE COTTAGE GUEST HOUSE, LORTON ROAD, COCKERMOUTH CA13 9DX (Tel & Fax: 01900 822189). Family-run guest house on the outskirts of Cockermouth. Warm, friendly atmosphere. Parking. All rooms en suite with colour TV, tea/coffee, central heating. Pets welcome. Ideal base for visiting both Lakes and coast. ETC/AA ★★★★ [🐕]
website: www.rosecottageguest.co.uk

Coniston

Village 8 miles south-west of Ambleside, dominated by Old Man of Coniston (2635ft).

LAKELAND HOUSE, TILBERTHWAITE AVENUE, CONISTON LA21 8ED (015394 41303). Village centre guest house, hearty breakfasts, from £27.50 per person. Self-catering cottage also available, sleeping six, with lake views. [Pets at small charge]
e-mail: info@lakelandhouse.co.uk website: www.lakelandhouse.co.uk

THE COPPERMINES AND CONISTON LAKES COTTAGES (015394 41765). Unique Lakeland cottages for 2 – 30 of quality and character in stunning mountain scenery. Log fires, exposed beams. Pets welcome! ★★★ - ★★★★ Book online. [Pets £25 per stay]
website: www.coppermines.co.uk

BROCKLEBANK GROUND HOLIDAY COTTAGES, TORVER, CONISTON LA21 8BS (015394 49588). Four luxury cottages in a quiet rural setting, sleeping 2,4,7 & 10. Excellent walking from the door. Dog- friendly pubs 600 yards. Short breaks available. Prices from £275. ETC ★★★★. [🐕]
e-mail: info@brocklebankground.com website: www.brocklebankground.com

Crosby-on-Eden

Two small villages to the NE of Carlisle.

THE WALLFOOT, PARK BROOM, CROSBY-ON-EDEN, CARLISLE CA6 4QH (01228 573696; Fax: 01228 573240). A popular hotel just 3 miles east of Carlisle, surrounded by fabulous scenery and lovely walks. The hotel boasts a newly refurbished bar and restaurant and offers a traditional bar menu and exciting new restaurant menu.
website: www.wallfoot.co.uk

Crosthwaite

Hamlet 5 miles west of Kendal.

DAMSON DENE HOTEL, CROSTHWAITE LA8 8JE (015395 68676). Tranquil location only 10 minutes from Lake Windermere. Best Lakes Breaks from £139 per person for 3 nights. [🐕 pw!]
e-mail: info@damsondene.co.uk website: www.bestlakesbreaks.co.uk

Duddon Valley

Majestic valley running between Cockley Beck and Duddon Bridge.

COCKLEY BECK FARM COTTAGE, SEATHWAITE, BROUGHTON-IN-FURNESS LA20 6EQ (01229 716480). In the heart of the Lake District National Park, just 4 miles from the summit of Scafell Pike. Self-contained holiday cottage (sleeps 4). Large open-plan kitchen. Well behaved dogs free of charge. Available all year. Private enclosed garden with patio and parking. [🐕]
website: www.cockleybeck.co.uk

Eskdale

Lakeless valley, noted for waterfalls and ascended by a light-gauge railway. Tremendous views. Roman fort. Keswick 35 miles, Broughton-in-Furness 10 miles.

FISHERGROUND FARM, ESKDALE. Traditional hill farm, with a stone cottage and three pine lodges, ideal for walkers, nature lovers, dogs and children. Games room, raft pool and adventure playground. Good pubs nearby. ETC ★★★. IAN & JENNIFER HALL, ORCHARD HOUSE, APPLETHWAITE, KESWICK CA12 4PN (017687 73175) [🐕]
e-mail: holidays@fisherground.co.uk website: www.fisherground.co.uk

THE BOOT INN (FORMERLY THE BURNMOOR INN), BOOT, ESKDALE CA19 1TG (019467 23224). Nine en suite bedrooms. Dogs and their owners made very welcome. Special breaks available all year. Call for a brochure. [🐕]
e-mail: enquiries@bootinn.co.uk website: www.bootinn.co.uk

Gosforth

Small village in Western Lake District, set within the Cumbria National Park, close to the Wasdale and Eskdale Valleys..

BLENG BARN COTTAGE, MILL HOUSE FARM, WELLINGTON, SEASCALE CA20 1BH (07801 862237 & 07775 512918; Fax: 01946 725671. Self-catering 3-bedroom holiday cottage on a large working farm. Sleeps 6+4. Many traditional features and modern facilities. ETC ★★★★ Self Catering.[🐕]
e-mail: info@blengfarms.co.uk website: www.blengfarms.co.uk

Grange-Over-Sands

Resort on the right bank of River Kent estuary 9 miles North of Morecambe.

HAMPSFELL HOUSE HOTEL, HAMPSFELL ROAD, GRANGE-OVER-SANDS LA11 6BG (015395 32567). In two acres of private grounds, just a few minutes' walk from the town centre. The eight en suite bedrooms are well appointed. Enjoy the best of fresh Cumbrian produce in the elegant dining room. Ideal base for exploring the Lake District. AA ★★ [Pets £5 per night].
enquiries@hampsfellhouse.co.uk website: www.hampsfellhouse.co.uk

Grasmere

Village famous for Wordsworth associations; the poet lived in Dove Cottage (preserved as it was), and is buried in the churchyard. Museum has manuscripts and relics.

LAKE VIEW COUNTRY HOUSE & SELF-CATERING APARTMENTS, GRASMERE LA22 9TD (015394 35384/35167). Luxury B&B or 3 Self-Catering apartments in unrivalled, secluded location in the village with wonderful views and lakeshore access. All B&B rooms en suite, some with whirlpool baths. Ground floor accommodation available. No smoking. Featured in "Which?" Good B&B Guide.

Hawkshead

Quaint village in Lake District between Coniston Water and Windermere. The 16th century Church and Grammar School, which Wordsworth attended, are of interest. Ambleside 5 miles.

LAKELAND HIDEAWAYS, THE SQUARE, HAWKSHEAD LA22 0NZ (015394 42435). Cottages in and around Hawkshead. Great walks and lakes for swimming, dog friendly pubs, open fires to lie in front of... owners will enjoy it too. [Pets £20 per week].
e-mail: bookings@lakeland-hideaways.co.uk website: www.lakeland-hideaways.co.uk

THE KINGS ARMS HOTEL, HAWKSHEAD, AMBLESIDE LA22 0NZ (015394 36372). Join us for a relaxing stay amidst the green hills and dales of Lakeland, and we will be delighted to offer you good food, homely comfort and warm hospitality in historic surroundings. We hope to see you soon! Self-catering cottages also available.[🐕, pets £20 per week s/c]
website: www.kingsarmshawkshead.co.uk

A useful index of towns/counties appears at the back of this book

Kendal

Market town and popular centre for touring the Lake District. Of historic interest is the Norman castle, birthplace of Catherine Parr. Penrith 25 miles, Lancaster 22, Ambleside 13.

RIVERSIDE HOTEL, BEEZON ROAD, KENDAL LA9 6EL (015397 34861). Lovely riverside location. Best Lakes Breaks from £139 per person for 3 nights. [🐕 pw!]
e-mail: info@riversidekendal.co.uk website: www.bestlakesbreaks.co.uk

MIREFOOT COTTAGES, MIREFOOT, KENDAL, CUMBRIA LA8 9AB (Tel: 01539 720015). 5 Star, pet friendly, self-catering cottages in a superb rural location in the Lake District National Park. All cottages sleep 2. Fully equipped with TV (Freeview), DVD, WiFi, gas central heating. Tennis court, private parking. VB ★★★★★ [🐕]
e-mail: booking@mirefoot.co.uk website: www.mirefoot.co.uk

MRS L. HODGSON, PATTON HALL FARM, KENDAL LA8 9DT (01539 721590). 2 Modern caravans, fully double glazed, gas central heating. Double and twin bedrooms, kitchen, spacious lounge/dining area, toilet and shower. Traditional working farm set in 140 acres of beautiful countryside. [Pets £10/£15 per week].
e-mail: stay@pattonhallfarm.co.uk website: www.pattonhallfarm.co.uk

ANNE TAYLOR, RUSSELL FARM, BURTON-IN-KENDAL, CARNFORTH, LANCS. LA6 1NN (01524 781334). Bed and Breakfast. Ideal centre for touring Lakes and Yorkshire Dales. Good food, friendly atmosphere on working dairy farm. Modernised farmhouse. Guests' own lounge. [🐕]
e-mail: miktaylor@farming.co.uk

Keswick

Famous Lake District resort at north end of Derwentwater with Pencil Museum and Cars of the Stars Motor Museum. Carlisle 30 miles, Ambleside 17, Cockermouth 12.

LOW BRIERY HOLIDAYS (017687 72044). A peaceful and scenic riverside location just outside Keswick. A choice of cottages, timber lodges and holiday caravans to suit all budgets. ETC ★★★★ [Pets £20 per week]
website: www.keswick.uk.com

DERWENT WATER MARINA, PORTINSCALE, KESWICK CA12 5RF Lakeside self-catering apartments. Three apartments sleep 2 plus folding bed for occasional use, one apartment sleeps 6. Superb views over the lake and fells. Includes TV, heating and bed linen. Non-smoking. Watersports and boat hire available on site. (017687 72912) for brochure. [🐕]
e-mail: info@derwentwatermarina.co.uk website: www.derwentwatermarina.co.uk

KESWICK COTTAGES, 8 BEECHCROFT, BRAITHWAITE, KESWICK CA12 5TH (017687 78555). Cottages and apartments in and around Keswick. Properties are well maintained and clean. From a one bedroom cottage to a 4-bedroom house. Children and pets welcome. ETC ★★★ [Pets £10 per week]
e-mail: info@keswickcottages.co.uk website: www.keswickcottages.co.uk

MR ANDY PETERS, SEYMOUR HOUSE, 36 LAKE ROAD, KESWICK CA12 5DQ (01768 772764; Freephone: 0800 0566401; mobile: 07721 957899). Set in quiet cul-de-sac, short walk to town centre and lake. 10 well appointed rooms, seven en suite, all with colour TV, tea/coffee, shaver points and central heating. Full English breakfast, vegetarians and special diets catered for. Open Christmas and New Year. [Pets £5 per night, £15 per week.]
e-mail: andy042195@aol.com website: www.seymour-house.com

Pet-Friendly
Pubs, Inns & Hotels
on pages 424-432
Please note that these establishments may not feature in the main section of this book

MARY MOUNT HOTEL, BORROWDALE, NEAR KESWICK CA12 5UU (017687 77223). Set in 4½ acres of gardens and woodlands on the shores of Derwentwater. 2½ miles from Keswick in picturesque Borrowdale. Superb walking and touring. All rooms en suite with colour TV and tea/coffee making facilities. Licensed. Brochure on request. ETC ★★ [pw! £6.50 per 2/3 nights , £10 per week.]
e-mail: mawdsley1@aol.com website: www.marymounthotel.co.uk

RICKERBY GRANGE, PORTINSCALE, KESWICK CA12 5RH (017687 72344). Delightfully situated in quiet village. Licensed. Imaginative home-cooked food, attractively served. Open all year. Private car park. VisitBritain ★★★★ Guest House. [🐕]
e-mail: stay@rickerbygrange.co.uk website: www.rickerbygrange.co.uk

Warm, comfortable houses and cottages in Keswick and beautiful Borrowdale, welcoming your dog. Inspected and quality graded. LAKELAND COTTAGE HOLIDAYS, KESWICK CA12 4QX (017687 76065; Fax: 017687 76869). [Pets £15 per week]
e-mail: info@lakelandcottages.co.uk website: www.lakelandcottages.co.uk

COLEDALE INN, BRAITHWAITE, NEAR KESWICK CA12 5TN (017687 78272). Friendly, family-run Victorian Inn in peaceful situation. Warm and spacious en suite bedrooms with TV. Children and pets welcome. Open all year. ETC ★★★ [🐕]
website: www.coledale-inn.co.uk

ROYAL OAK HOTEL, BORROWDALE, KESWICK CA12 5XB (017687 77214). Traditional Lakeland hotel with friendly atmosphere. Home cooking, cosy bar, comfortable lounge and some riverside rooms. Winter and Summer discount rates. Brochure and tariff available. [🐕]
e-mail: info@royaloakhotel.co.uk website: www.royaloakhotel.co.uk

OVERWATER HALL, OVERWATER, NEAR IREBY, KESWICK CA7 1HH (017687 76566). Elegant Country House Hotel in spacious grounds. Dogs very welcome in your room. 4 night mid-week breaks from £320 per person, inclusive of Dinner and Breakfast. Mini breaks also available all year. Award-winning restaurant. AA ★★★ and Rosette. See also advertisement on page 310 [pw! 🐕]
e-mail: welcome@overwaterhall.co.uk website: www.overwaterhall.co.uk

HORSE AND FARRIER INN THRELKELD, KESWICK CA12 4SQ (017687 79688; Fax: 017687 79823). Ideal location for walking or touring the Lake District. All 15 bedrooms en suite, with TV, tea/coffee making and hairdryer. Award-winning food and restaurant. Open all year. Pets welcome.
e-mail: info@horseandfarrier.com website: www.horseandfarrier.com

WOODSIDE, PENRITH ROAD, KESWICK CA12 4LJ (017687 73522). Friendly family-run establishment. All our rooms are en suite. We have ample private parking and large gardens. Non-smoking. Dogs welcome. [🐕]
website: www.woodsideguesthouse.co.uk

Kirkby-in-Furness

Small coastal village (A595). 10 minutes to Ulverston, Lakes within easy reach. Ideal base for walking and touring.

JANET AND PETER, 1 FRIARS GROUND, KIRKBY-IN-FURNESS LA17 7YB (01229 889601). "Sunset Cottage", self-catering 17th century two/three bedroom character cottage with garden. Original features. Panoramic views over sea/mountains; Coniston/Windermere 30 minutes. Non-smoking. Open all year. VisitBritain ★★★★ [Pets £15 per pet]
e-mail: enquiries@southlakes-cottages.com website: www.southlakes-cottages.com

Kirkby Lonsdale

Georgian buildings and quaint cottages. Riverside walks from medieval Devil's Bridge.

THE SNOOTY FOX, KIRKBY LONSDALE (01524 271308). Charming Jacobean Inn, offering 9 en suite rooms, award-winning restaurant and lounge bar, the perfect base from which to explore both the Lake District and Yorkshire Dales. AA/ETC ★★ [🐕]
e-mail: snootyfoxhotel@talktalk.net website: www.thesnootyfoxhotel.co.uk

MRS PAULINE BAINBRIDGE, ULLATHORNS FARM, MIDDLETON, KIRKBY LONSDALE LA6 2LZ (015242 76214). 17th Century farmhouse on a working farm situated in the Lune Valley. B&B from £25. Children and well-behaved pets welcome. Non-smoking. VisitBritain ★★★★ [🐕]
e-mail: pauline@ullathorns.co.uk website: www.ullathorns.co.uk

Kirkby Stephen

5 miles south on B6259 Kirkby Stephen to Hawes road.

COCKLAKE HOUSE, MALLERSTANG CA17 4JT (017683 72080). Charming, High Pennine Country House B&B in unique position above Pendragon Castle in Upper Mallerstang Dale offering good food and exceptional comfort to a small number of guests. Two double rooms with large private bathrooms. Three acres riverside grounds. Dogs welcome. [🐕]

Kirkoswald

Village in the Cumbrian hills, lying north west of the Lake District. Ideal for touring. Penrith 7 miles.

SECLUDED COTTAGES WITH PRIVATE FISHING, KIRKOSWALD CA10 1EU (24 hour brochure line 01768 898711, manned most Saturdays). Quality cottages, clean, well equipped and maintained. Centrally located for Lakes, Pennines, Hadrian's Wall, Borderland. Enjoy the Good Life in comfort. Pets' paradise. Guests' coarse fishing. Bookings/enquiries 01768 898711. ETC ★★★ [pw! £2 per pet per night, £14 per week].
e-mail: info@crossfieldcottages.co.uk website: www.crossfieldcottages.co.uk

Knipe

Rural location 4 miles NW of Shap.

KNIPE HALL, KNIPE, NEAR BAMPTON CA10 2PU. House sleeps up to 12. Huge connecting party barn and outdoor hot tub in private grounds. Beautiful surroundings. Real fires and kitchen Aga range. Ideal for family gatherings and groups. ETC ★★★★★ [🐕]
e-mail: info@knipehall.co.uk website: www.knipehall.co.uk

Lake District

North west corner of England between A6/M6 and the Cumbrian Coast. Fells, valleys and 16 lakes, the largest being Lake Windermere.

LAKE DISTRICT. Two luxury houses available to rent in the Lake District. Routen House, sleeps 12 plus cot. Fully modernised, outstanding position in 4 acres. Little Parrock, sleeps 10 plus cot, short walk from centre of Grasmere with real log fire and private garden. Both houses non-smoking. MRS J. GREEN (Tel & Fax: 01604 626383).
e-mail: joanne@routenhouse.co.uk www.routenhouse.co.uk / www.littleparrock.co.uk

GRIZEDALE LODGE, HAWKSHEAD, AMBLESIDE LA22 0QL (015394 36532; Fax: 015394 36572). In the heart of Grizedale Forest National Park, within easy reach of Windermere, Coniston, Beatrix Potter country and other attractions. All rooms en suite, some with four-posters. Open all year.
e-mail: enquiries@grizedale-lodge.com website: www.grizedale-lodge.com

Lamplugh (near Loweswater)

Hamlet 7 miles south of Cockermouth.

ROSE COTTAGE. Three miles from Loweswater and four miles from Ennerdale, lovely throughout. Open plan kitchen and sitting room, cosy coal fire, two bedrooms and enclosed garden. Pets welcome. Contact SALLY FIELDING (01768 776 836). [🐕]
website: www.millgillhead.co.uk

FELLDYKE COTTAGE HOLIDAYS, LAMPLUGH. Visiting the Western Lakes? Then why not stay in this lovely 19th century cottage. Sleeps 4, short breaks can be arranged. Pets are welcome. Open all year. Contact MRS A. WILSON (01946 861151). VB ★★★★ [pw!🐕] .
e-mail: dockraynook@talk21.com website: www.felldykecottageholidays.co.uk

Langdale

Dramatic valley area to the west of Ambleside, in the very heart of the National Park.

THE BRITANNIA INN, ELTERWATER, AMBLESIDE LA22 9HP (015394 37210; Fax: 015396 78075). 500-year-old traditional lakeland inn. Extensive, home-cooked menu, real ales, cosy bars, log fires. Comfortable, high quality en suite accommodation. Well-behaved pets welcome. ETC ★★★ [🐕]
e-mail: info@britinn.co.uk website: www.britinn.co.uk

WHEELWRIGHTS HOLIDAY COTTAGES, ELTERWATER, NEAR AMBLESIDE LA22 9HS (015394 38305; Fax: 015394 37618). Some of the loveliest cottages in the Lake District with stunning scenery on their doorsteps are ready to welcome you and your pets. Prices vary. Please visit our website. ETC ★★★ - ★★★★★ [🐕]
e-mail: enquiries@wheelwrights.com website: www.wheelwrights.com

Little Langdale

Hamlet 2 miles west of Skelwith Bridge. To west is Little Langdale Tarn, a small lake.

HIGHFOLD COTTAGE, LITTLE LANGDALE. Very comfortable Lakeland cottage, ideally situated for walking and touring. Superb mountain views. Sleeps 5. Personally maintained. Pets welcome. Weekly £260–£500. VB ★★★. MRS C.E. BLAIR, 8 THE GLEBE, CHAPEL STILE, AMBLESIDE LA22 9JT (015394 37686). [🐕]
website: www.highfoldcottage.co.uk

Mungrisdale

Hamlet 8 miles NE of Keswick.

NEAR HOWE COTTAGES, MUNGRISDALE, PENRITH CA11 0SH (Tel & Fax: 017687 79678). An ideal, quiet and tranquil retreat located in the heart of the Cumbria countryside. Set in an elevated postion, all our cottages have spectacular views over the Cumbrian Fells. Our large garden has many relaxation areas. The perfect place to escape to for you and your dog.
e-mail: enquiries@nearhowe.co.uk website: www.nearhowe.co.uk

Newby Bridge

Village 8 miles NE of Ulverston

MRS A. SCOTT, OAK HEAD CARAVAN PARK, AYSIDE, GRANGE-OVER-SANDS LA11 6JA (015395 31475). A well tended, uncrowded and wooded site set amidst picturesque fells. Flush toilets, hot showers, laundry facilities, hair dryers, deep freeze, gas on sale. Tourers (30 pitches) Tents (30 pitches), Auto homes. Open March 1st to October 31st.

NEWBY BRIDGE HOTEL, NEWBY BRIDGE LA12 8NA (015395 31222). Overlooking the southern shores of Lake Windermere. Best Lakes Breaks from £139 per person for 3 nights. [🐕 pw!]
e-mail: info@newbybridgehotel.co.uk website: www.bestlakesbreaks.co.uk

Please note

All the information in this book is given in good faith in the belief that it is correct. However, the publishers cannot guarantee the facts given in these pages, neither are they responsible for changes in policy, ownership or terms that may take place after the date of going to press. Readers should always satisfy themselves that the facilities they require are available and that the terms, if quoted, still apply.

Penrith

Market town and centre for touring Lake District. Of interest are 14th century castle, Gloucester Arms (1477) and Tudor House. Excellent sporting facilities. Windermere 27 miles, Keswick 18.

CARROCK COTTAGES. Four recently renovated, award-winning, stone-built cottages set on the fringe of the Lakeland Fells. Games room, spa facilities. Home cooked meals service. Ideal for fell walking. Excellent restaurants nearby. A warm welcome guaranteed. ETC ★★★★★ Contact MALCOLM OR GILLIAN (01768 484111; Fax: 01768 488850). [Pets £25 per week each].
e-mail: info@carrockcottages.co.uk website: www.carrockcottages.co.uk

LYVENNET COTTAGES. Five different cottages in and around the small farming village of Kings Meaburn in beautiful unspoilt 'Lyvennet Valley'. Ideal touring centre for the Lakes and Dales. JANET ADDISON, KELD FARM, KINGS MEABURN, PENRITH CA10 3BS (01931 714661/714226; Fax: 01931 714598). ETC ★★★★/★★★★★
website: www.lyvennetcottages.co.uk

THE TROUTBECK INN, TROUTBECK, PENRITH CA11 0SJ (017684 83635; Fax: 017684 87071). Close to the shores of lovely Ullswater, this friendly and well-appointed inn enjoys sweeping fell views and is a haven for a variety of outdoor pursuits, Excellent varied food and real ales. Tastefully furnished en suite bedrooms. Three self-catering cottages. ETC ★★★ Inn/★★★★ S/C [Pets £5-£15 per week].
e-mail: info@thetroutbeckinn.co.uk website: www.thetroutbeck-inn.co.uk

BOOT & SHOE INN, GREYSTOKE, PENRITH, CUMBRIA CA11 0TP (01768 483343). Popular 16th Century Inn in the heart of the legendary village of Greystoke. Full of charm, character and history. Excellent food, en suite accommodation and ambience. Conveniently situated to explore the Lake.

DOREEN ROBINSON, CORNER HOUSE, 36 VICTORIA ROAD, PENRITH CA11 8HR (01768 863566). Comfortable, friendly atmosphere with a hearty breakfast to set you up for the day. Secure car and cycle parking. Pets and well-behaved owners welcome! [🐕]
e-mail: doreen@cornerhousepenrith.co.uk website: www.cornerhousepenrith.co.uk

Reagill

Hamlet 5 miles West of Appleby.

YEW TREE FARM, REAGILL, NEAR SHAP, CA10 3ER. Luxury 5★ self-catering, accommodating up to 15. Historical sculpture garden in large grounds; outdoor hot tub. Great walking nearby. Superb facilities. Mini football pitch. Ideal for family gatherings and groups. [🐕]
e-mail: info@reagill.com website: www.reagill.com

St Bees

Village 4 miles south of Whitehaven.

SEACOTE PARK, THE BEACH, ST BEES CA27 0ET(01946 822777; Fax: 01946 824442). Adjoining lovely sandy beach on fringe of Lake District, modern luxury holiday caravans for hire. Full serviced touring pitches and tent area. St Bees is convenient for touring. We also have two other Caravan Parks close by, Tarnside and Seven Acres. ETC ★★★★. Rose Award Park.
e-mail: reception@seacote.com website: www.seacote.com

FREE or REDUCED RATE entry to Holiday Visits and Attractions – see our **READERS' OFFER VOUCHERS** on pages 433-440

Shap

Small town 9 miles South of Penrith.

THE GREYHOUND, SHAP CA10 3PW (01931 716474). Coaching inn dating from 15th century. Perfect motorway stop-off on the fringe of the Lake District. Great walks from the door on to Eastern Fells. Fantastic Sunday lunch! Special offer - stay for 4 nights, pay for 3. [🐕]
e-mail: info@greyhoundshap.co.uk website: www.greyhoundshap.co.uk

Silloth-on-Solway

Solway Firth resort with harbour and fine sandy beach. Mountain views. Golf, fishing. Penrith 33 miles, Carlisle 23, Cockermouth 17.

MR AND MRS M.C. BOWMAN, TANGLEWOOD CARAVAN PARK, CAUSEWAY HEAD, SILLOTH CA7 4PE (016973 31253). Friendly country site, excellent toilet and laundry facilities. Tourers welcome or hire a luxury caravan. Open 1st March - January 31st. Telephone or e-mail for a brochure. AA *THREE PENNANTS.* [🐕]
e-mail: tanglewoodcaravanpark@hotmail.com

Ullswater

Lake stretching for 7 miles with attractive Lakeside walks.

FELL VIEW HOLIDAYS, FELL VIEW, GLENRIDDING, PENRITH CA11 0PJ (017684 82795). Sleep 2-5. Lovely, comfortable, well equipped accommodation in an idyllic location between Glenridding and Patterdale. Magnificent views of the surrounding fells. Short Breaks available out of season.
e-mail: enquiries@fellviewholidays.com website: www.fellviewholidays.com

LAND ENDS CABINS, WATERMILLOCK, NEAR ULLSWATER CA11 0NB (017684 86438). Only 1.5 miles from Ullswater, our four detached log cabins have a peaceful fellside location in 25-acre grounds with two pretty lakes. Doggy heaven! Sleep 2-5. ETC ★★★ [🐕]
e-mail: infolandends@btinternet.com website: www.landends.co.uk

COVE CARAVAN & CAMPING PARK, WATERMILLOCK, PENRITH CA11 0LS (017684 86549). Well-maintained and peaceful park overlooking Lake Ullswater surrounded by Fells. Ideally situated for walking, watersports and all Lake District attractions. Electric hook-ups with hardstandings, sheltered grass for campers. AA 3 PENNANTS.
website: www.cove-park.co.uk

Wasdale

Hamlet 1 mile north east of Wast Water

THE BRIDGE INN, SANTON BRIDGE, HOLMROOK CA19 1UX (019467 26221; Fax: 019467 26026). Award-winning country inn providing good food and accommodation. 16 en suite bedrooms. Ideal for exploring the Western Lakes and fells. Well behaved dogs welcome. [Pets £5 per stay].
e-mail: info@santonbridgeinn.com website: www.santonbridgeinn.com

Wigton

Market town 11 miles SW of Carlisle.

FOXGLOVES COTTAGE, WIGTON. Sleeps 2-8. Spacious, well-equipped comfortable cottage on working farm. Children and pets very welcome. Easy reach Lake District, Scottish Borders and Roman Wall. Available all year. Short breaks by arrangement. MR & MRS E. & J. KERR, GREENRIGG FARM, WESTWARD, WIGTON, CUMBRIA CA7 8AH (016973 42676).

www.holidayguides.com

Windermere

Famous resort on lake of same name, the largest in England. Magnificent scenery. Car ferry from Bowness, one mile distant. Kendal 9 miles.

LOW SPRINGWOOD HOTEL, THORNBARROW ROAD, WINDERMERE LA23 2DF (015394 46383). Millie and Lottie (Boxers) would like to welcome you to their peaceful Hotel in its own secluded gardens. Lovely views of Lakes and Fells. All rooms en suite with colour TV etc. Some four-posters. Brochure available. [🐕 pw!]

LANGDALE CHASE HOTEL, WINDERMERE LA23 1LW (015394 32201). Magnificent country house hotel with grounds sloping to the edge of Lake Windermere. Panoramic views, log fires, excellent food and friendly professional staff all ensure a memorable stay. [Pets £3 per night]
e-mail: sales@langdalechase.co.uk website: www.langdalechase.co.uk

Hundreds of self-catering holiday homes in a variety of wonderful locations, all well equipped and managed by our caring staff. Pets welcome. Free leisure club membership. For brochure, contact: LAKELOVERS, BELMONT HOUSE, LAKE ROAD, BOWNESS-ON-WINDERMERE LA23 3BJ. (015394 88855; Fax: 015394 88857). ETC ★★★ - ★★★★★ [Pets £15.00 per week.]
e-mail: bookings@lakelovers.co.uk website: www.lakelovers.co.uk

THE FAMOUS WILD BOAR (08458 504 604). Nestled in the beautiful Gilpin Valley, former coaching Inn set within its own private 72 acres of woodland. Excellent restaurant with local produce and real ales. Windermere Golf Club and Leisure Club nearby. [Pets £15.00 per night.]
e-mail: wildboar@elhmail.co.uk website: www.elh.co.uk

Looking for Holiday Accommodation?

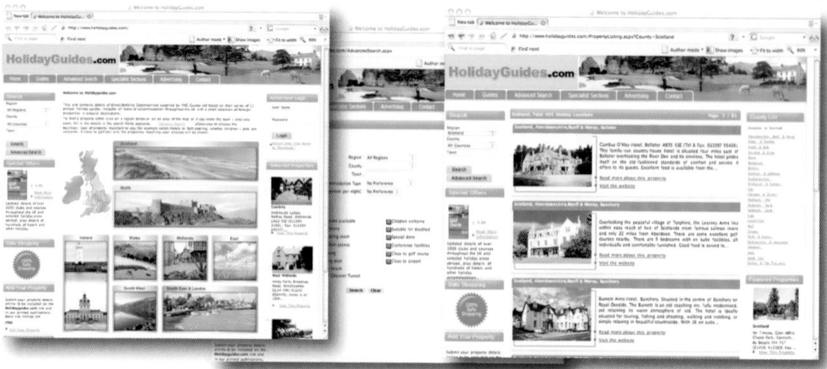

for details of hundreds of properties throughout the UK, visit our website

www.holidayguides.com

Blackburn, Blackpool, Carnforth, Cockerham, Pilling

THE BROWN LEAVES COUNTRY HOTEL, LONGSIGHT ROAD, COPSTER GREEN, NEAR BLACKBURN BB1 9EU • 01254 249523 • Fax: 01254 245240

Situated on the A59 halfway between Preston and Clitheroe, five miles from Junction 31 on M6 in beautiful Ribble Valley. All rooms ground floor, en suite facilities, satellite TV, tea-making and hairdryer. Guests' lounge and bar lounge. Car parking. Pets by arrangement. All credit cards welcome. **www.brownleavescountryhotel.co.uk**

The Brayton

7-8 Finchley Road, Gynn Square,
BLACKPOOL FY1 2LP
www.the-brayton-hotel.com
e-mail: info2@the-brayton-hotel.com

- *Quiet and pleasantly located licensed hotel.*
- *Overlooking Gynn gardens and the promenade.*
- *Short drive or tram ride to all the attractions.*
- *Full 'Restaurant Style' menu served every day.*
- *Dogs most welcome and free. Open all year.*

Phone: 01253 351645

Locka Old Hall Cottage

Arkholme, near Kirkby Lonsdale LA6 1BD

Small cottage with open fire in easy reach of Lake District, Yorkshire Dales and Lancashire coast. Lawned garden with views over fells and Ingleborough. Quiet location. Sleeps 2 (+2 on sofa bed).

Tel: 015242 21561 • E-mail: cottage@locka.co.uk • www.locka.co.uk

A family park situated on an inlet to the Irish Sea. Access to 15 miles of the new Lancashire Coastal Walk. Less than an hour to the Lake District, Morecambe or Blackpool.

There is a heated swimming pool (June to September), shop, amusement arcade, launderette and the wonderful Cockerham Country Club with live entertainment at weekends.

Modern four and six-berth fully equipped caravans for hire.

Controlled dogs welcome. Write or telephone for brochure.

COCKERHAM SANDS COUNTRY PARK

Cockerham, Lancaster LA2 0BB • Tel: 01524 751387

BELL FARM

Beryl and Peter welcome you to their 18th century farmhouse in the quiet village of Pilling. The area has many footpaths and is ideal for cycling. Easy access to Blackpool, Lancaster, the Forest of Bowland and the Lake District. One family room, one double and one twin. All en suite. Tea and coffee making facilities. Lounge and dining room. All centrally heated. Full English breakfast.

Children and pets welcome.
Open all year except Christmas and New Year.
Bed and Breakfast from £27.50.

Peter Richardson, Bell Farm, Bradshaw Lane, Scronkey, Pilling, Preston PR3 6SN

Tel: 01253 790324
www.bellfarm.co.uk

FHG Guides

publish a large range of well-known accommodation guides.
We will be happy to send you details or you can use the order form at the back of this book.

SIX ARCHES CARAVAN PARK,

SCORTON, GARSTANG, NEAR PRESTON PR3 IAL

Situated on the banks of the River Wyre. Modern caravans and self-catering holiday flats for hire, tourers welcome.

Ideally situated for local visitor attractions, Blackpool, Lake District and Trough of Bowland within easy reach.

Facilities include outdoor heated pool, club with live entertainment, children's playground and river fishing. Controlled dogs welcome. Telephone for brochure. **01524 791683**

Loudview Barn • Thornley • Near Preston

Self-catering stone barn conversion in peaceful location in Forest of Bowland.
Exceptional views across unspoilt countryside.
Unit 1: one double, one twin and bunk beds • Unit 2: one double and one twin

Contact: **Mr & Mrs Starkey, Loudview Barn, Rams Clough Farm, Thornley, Preston PR3 2TN**
Tel: 01995 61476 • e-mail: loudview@ic24.net

Blackburn

Industrial town on River Darwen and on Leeds and Liverpool Canal.

THE BROWN LEAVES COUNTRY HOTEL, LONGSIGHT ROAD, COPSTER GREEN, NEAR BLACKBURN BB1 9EU (01254 249523; Fax: 01254 245240). Situated on the A59 halfway between Preston and Clitheroe, five miles from Junction 31 on M6 in beautiful Ribble Valley. All rooms ground floor, en suite facilities, satellite TV, tea-making and hairdryer. Guests' lounge and bar lounge. Car parking. Pets by arrangement. All credit cards welcome. [🐕]
website: www.brownleavescountryhotel.co.uk

Blackpool

Famous resort with fine sands and many attractions and vast variety of entertainments. Blackpool Tower (500ft). Three piers. Manchester 47 miles, Lancaster 26, Preston 17, Fleetwood 8.

THE BRAYTON, 7-8 FINCHLEY ROAD, GYNN SQUARE, BLACKPOOL FY1 2LP (01253 351645). Quiet licensed hotel overlooking Gynn gardens and the promenade. Full 'restaurant style' menu served daily. Dogs most welcome. Open all year. ETC ★★★ [🐕]
e-mail: info2@the-brayton-hotel.com website: www.the-brayton-hotel.com

Carnforth

Town 6 miloes North of Lancaster.

LOCKA OLD HALL COTTAGE, ARKHOLME, NEAR KIRKBY LONSDALE LA6 1BD (015242 21561) Small cottage with open fire in easy reach of Lake District, Yorkshire Dales and Lancashire coast. Lawned garden with views over fells and Ingleborough. Quiet location. Sleeps 2 (+2 on sofa bed)
e-mail: cottage@locka.co.uk website: www.locka.co.uk

Symbols

- 🐕 Indicates that pets are welcome free of charge.
- £ Indicates that a charge is made for pets: nightly or weekly.
- pw! Shows some special provision for pets; exercise facility, feeding or accommodation arrangement.
- ⌂ Indicates separate pets accommodation.

Cockerham

Village 6 miles South Lancaster.

COCKERHAM SANDS COUNTRY PARK, COCKERHAM, LANCASTER LA2 0BB (01524 751387). Family park with access to Lancashire Coastal Walk. Heated outdoor swimming pool, shop, launderette, Cockerham Country Club. Modern 4 and 6-berth fully equipped caravans for hire. [Pets £20 per week]

Pilling

Village 3 miles north east of Pressall.

BERYL AND PETER RICHARDSON, BELL FARM, BRADSHAW LANE, SCRONKEY, PILLING, PRESTON PR3 6SN (01253 790324).18th century farmhouse with one family room, one double and one twin. All en suite, and centrally heated. Full English breakfast is served. Open all year except Christmas and New Year. [🐕]
website: www.bellfarm.co.uk

Preston

Large town on North bank of River Ribble 27 miles NW of Manchester.

SIX ARCHES CARAVAN PARK, SCORTON, GARSTANG, NEAR PRESTON PR3 1AL (01524 791683). Modern 4 and 6-berth caravans, touring pitches; large two-bedroom flats to sleep 6. Blackpool 14 miles, Lake District 30 miles. Licensed club with entertainment. Controlled dogs welcome. [Pets £20 per week]

Thornley

Town 7 miles West of Clitheroe, 4 miles from Longridge.

LOUDVIEW BARN. Self-catering stone barn conversion in peaceful location in Forest of Bowland. Exceptional views across unspoilt countryside. Unit 1: one double, one twin and bunk beds; Unit 2: one double and one twin. Contact: MR & MRS STARKEY, LOUDVIEW BARN, RAMS CLOUGH FARM, THORNLEY, PRESTON PR3 2TN (01995 61476).
e-mail: loudview@ic24.net

Other specialised holiday guides from FHG

PUBS & INNS OF BRITAIN • **COUNTRY HOTELS** OF BRITAIN
WEEKEND & SHORT BREAK HOLIDAYS IN BRITAIN
THE GOLF GUIDE WHERE TO PLAY, WHERE TO STAY
500 GREAT PLACES TO STAY • **SELF-CATERING HOLIDAYS** IN BRITAIN
BED & BREAKFAST STOPS • **CARAVAN & CAMPING HOLIDAYS**
FAMILY BREAKS IN BRITAIN

Published annually: available in all good bookshops or direct from the publisher:
FHG Guides, Abbey Mill Business Centre, Seedhill, Paisley PA1 1TJ
Tel: 0141 887 0428 • Fax: 0141 889 7204
e-mail: admin@fhguides.co.uk • www.holidayguides.com

Ratings & Awards

For the first time ever the AA, VisitBritain, VisitScotland, and the Wales Tourist Board will use a single method of assessing and rating serviced accommodation. Irrespective of which organisation inspects an establishment the rating awarded will be the same, using a common set of standards, giving a clear guide of what to expect. The RAC is no longer operating an Hotel inspection and accreditation business.

Accommodation Standards: Star Grading Scheme

Using a scale of 1-5 stars the objective quality ratings give a clear indication of accommodation standard, cleanliness, ambience, hospitality, service and food, This shows the full range of standards suitable for every budget and preference, and allows visitors to distinguish between the quality of accommodation and facilities on offer in different establishments. All types of board and self-catering accommodation are covered, including hotels,
B&Bs, holiday parks, campus accommodation, hostels, caravans and camping, and boats.

The more stars, the higher level of quality

★★★★★
exceptional quality, with a degree of luxury

★★★★
excellent standard throughout

★★★
very good level of quality and comfort

★★
good quality, well presented and well run

★
acceptable quality; simple, practical, no frills

VisitBritain and the regional tourist boards, enjoyEngland.com, VisitScotland and VisitWales, and the AA have full details of the grading system on their websites

enjoyEngland.com

visitScotland.com

visitWales.com

theAA.com

National Accessible Scheme

If you have particular mobility, visual or hearing needs, look out for the National Accessible Scheme. You can be confident of finding accommodation or attractions that meet your needs by looking for the following symbols.

Typically suitable for a person with sufficient mobility to climb a flight of steps but would benefit from fixtures and fittings to aid balance

Typically suitable for a person with restricted walking ability and for those that may need to use a wheelchair some of the time and can negotiate a maximum of three steps

Typically suitable for a person who depends on the use of a wheelchair and transfers unaided to and from the wheelchair in a seated position. This person may be an independent traveller

Typically suitable for a person who depends on the use of a wheelchair in a seated position. This person also requires personal or mechanical assistance (eg carer, hoist).

Carminish House, Isle of Harris, p380

Scotland

Banks of Orkney, p379

Craigadam, Castle Douglas. p355

Loch Ness, Wilderness Cottages, p365

Scotland • Regions

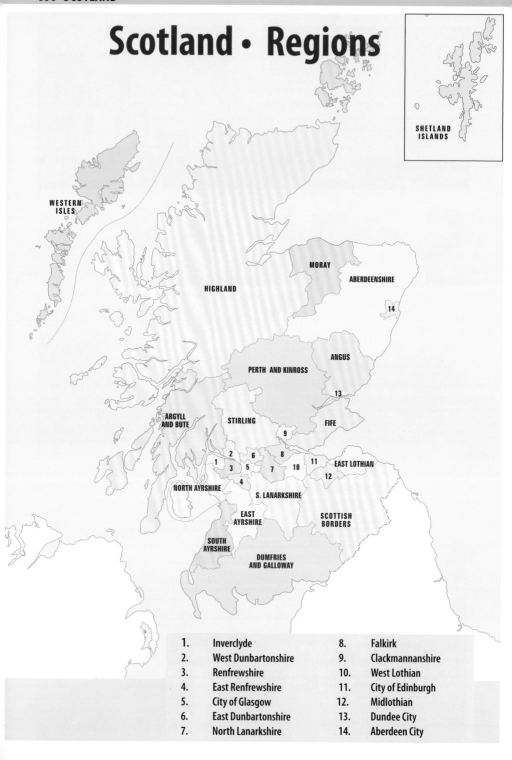

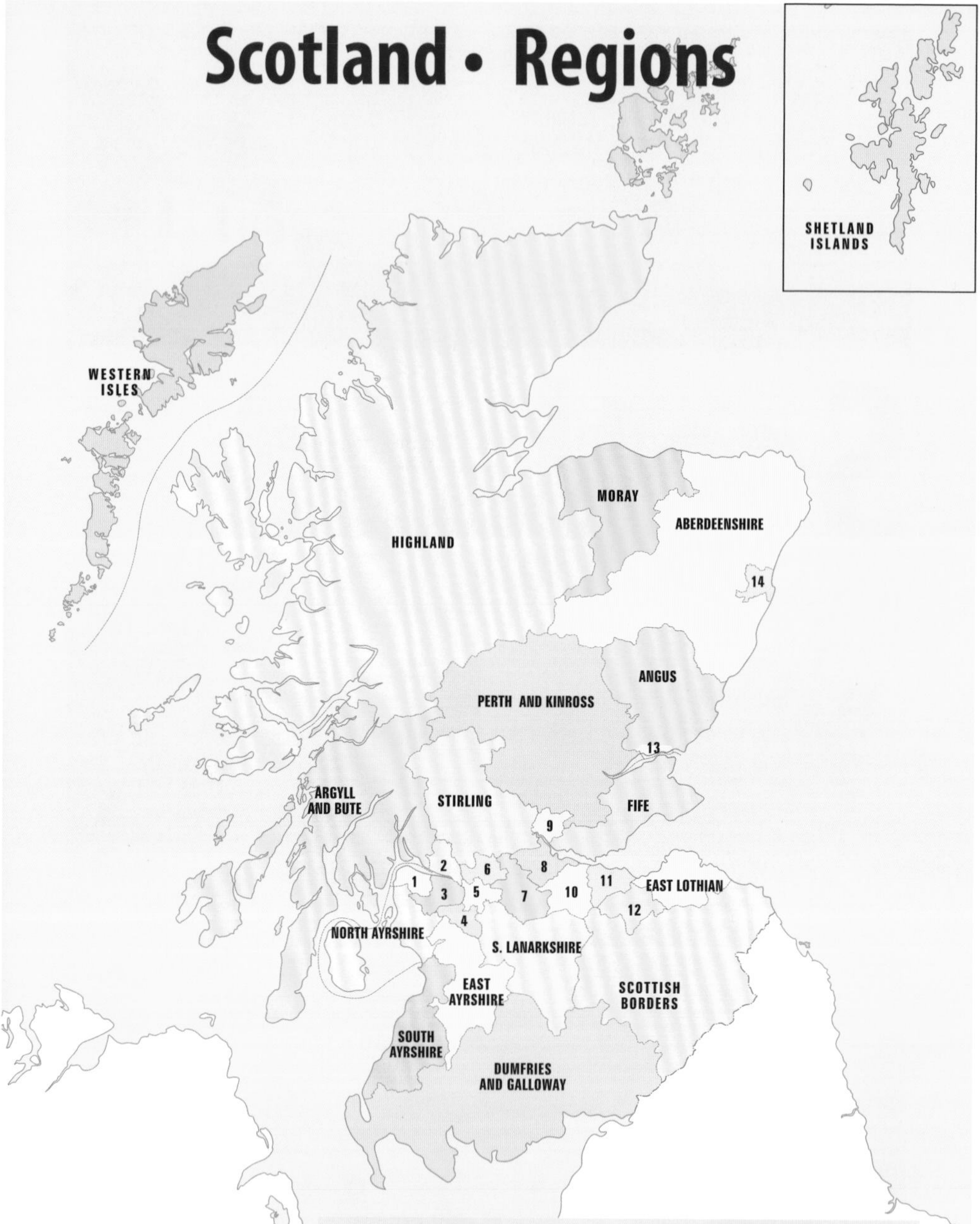

1.	Inverclyde	8.	Falkirk
2.	West Dunbartonshire	9.	Clackmannanshire
3.	Renfrewshire	10.	West Lothian
4.	East Renfrewshire	11.	City of Edinburgh
5.	City of Glasgow	12.	Midlothian
6.	East Dunbartonshire	13.	Dundee City
7.	North Lanarkshire	14.	Aberdeen City

SCOTLAND COTTAGES. See the best of the Highlands, Lochs and Borders. Almost 100 cottages to choose from, all personally inspected. Pets welcome. Free brochure. Call 0870 4059 599 or visit our website.[]
website: www.scotland-cottages.co.uk

Be sure that your money is going to the Scottish SPCA if you want to help animals in Scotland
Welcome to Scotland
the Scottish SPCA starts where the RSPCA finishes ... at the border!
scottishspca.org
03000 999 999
SCOTTISH SPCA
Scotland's Animal Welfare Charity
Scottish Charity No. SC 006467

CAMBUS O'MAY HOTEL

This family-run country house hotel is situated four miles east of Ballater overlooking the River Dee and its environs. The hotel prides itself on the old-fashioned standards of comfort and service it offers to its guests. Excellent food is available from the table d'hôte menu which changes daily and can be complemented by fine wines from the cellar. The 12 bedrooms have en suite facilities and the hotel is centrally heated throughout.

The area affords a wealth of interests such as hill walking, golf, fishing, and shooting, and there are many historic sites including Balmoral Castle.

Ballater
Aberdeenshire AB35 5SE
Tel & Fax: 013397 55428
www.cambusomayhotel.co.uk

This friendly, family-run hotel is set in 2 acres of woodlands with magnificent views across the golf course to the mountains. Pets are welcome in our Pine Terrace rooms which are all comfortable twin rooms. Come to the Glen Lui for a great Scottish experience. Fantastic food and wines. Short breaks available throughout the year.

Glen Lui Hotel, 14 Invercauld Road, Ballater AB35 5PP

013397 55402 • e-mail: infos@glen-lui-hotel.co.uk • www.glen-lui-hotel.co.uk

Idyllically set in 3,500 acres of parkland and forest in beautiful Royal Deeside, but only 20 minutes from Aberdeen Airport and within easy reach of the city centre. The elegant reception rooms are filled with antiques, paintings and flowers, and the beautiful Oval Dining Room is the perfect setting for a leisurely dinner. The 20 bedrooms have every facility for the discerning guest; ground floor rooms are available. In the grounds are many beautiful walks, a Par 3 9-hole golf course, an all-weather tennis court and a summer croquet lawn.

The area is renowned for its golf and fishing, and there are many wonderfully romantic castles to visit.

Raemoir House Hotel & Restaurant

Raemoir, Banchory, Royal Deeside AB31 4ED • Tel: 01330 824884

Fax: 01330 822171 • e-mail: relax@raemoir.com • www.raemoir.com

---

Beechgrove Cottages Glenlivet

Traditional stone cottages set amidst beautiful surroundings near rivers Avon and Livet. All modernised and very comfortable. Fishing available. Ideal for exploring Highlands, Castle & Whisky Trails, walking, skiing, golf. Contact: The Post Office, Tomnavoulin, Ballindalloch AB37 9JA

Tel: 01807 590220 • www.beechgrovecottages.co.uk

Pet-Friendly

Pubs, Inns & Hotels

on pages 424-432

Please note that these establishments may not feature in the main section of this book

MACDONALD
PITTODRIE HOUSE

Macdonald Pittodrie House

One of Scotland's most historic and picturesque hotels, originally built in 1480, still stands amidst the 2500 acre Pittodrie estate, nestling at the foot of the spectacular Bennachie. Stunning views, extensive private gardens and a reputation for culinary excellence and impecccable service combine to ensure your stay will be perfect in every way.

Turrets, spiral staircases, period furniture and ancestral portraits
Make yourself at home in our comfortable surroundings. Dining Room, Drawing Room, Orangery and Patio, Library, Billiard Room, Ballroom, Snug Bar. Log fires in winter, Victorian walled garden.

Luxury accommodation in each unique bedroom
27 rooms/suites, all with private facilities, radio, satellite television, direct dial telephone, wireless broadband internet access, trouser press, iron and ironing board, tea & coffee making facilities, hairdryer, dressing gown and slippers; newspaper deliveries, laundry and dry-cleaning service.

An impressive range of activities around the Estate
Individually tailored – from purely social to teambuilding, from a couple of hours to a whole day, including off-road driving, clay pigeon shooting, archery, shooting, quad-biking, one-man hovercraft, fly casting, family fun days.
Golf, fishing and deer stalking available locally. Also several interesting walks around the Pittodrie estate.

Savour the taste of Scottish country house cooking
Food and drink of the very highest quality in "The Mither Tap" Restaurant, prepared by our award-winning chef, incorporating the freshest of seasonal ingredients. Exceptional international list of over 200 wines, and over 140 malt whiskies on offer in the bar.

Wedding, Conference and Banqueting facilities
Full of period character, and with Bennachie as a backdrop, Pittodrie House is the perfect setting for a truly romantic wedding. Call our management team on 01467 681 744 and arrange to look round the hotel and experience the facilities.

NATIONAL CUSTOMER SERVICE AWARDS 2007 WINNER

AA Hotel Group of the Year Winner 2007-8

MACDONALD PITTODRIE HOUSE

Chapel of Garioch, Near Inverurie, Aberdeenshire AB51 5HS
Tel: 0844 879 9066 • Fax: 01467 681648
e-mail: pittodrie@macdonald-hotels.co.uk

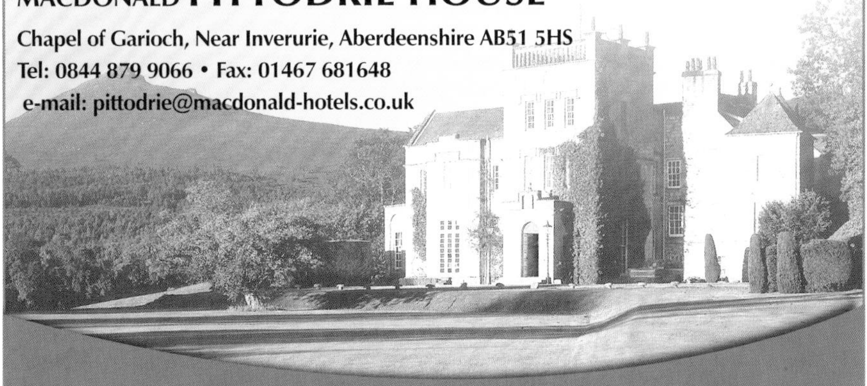

www.macdonaldhotels.co.uk/pittodrie

Turriff

Forglen Cottages......escape to the country

This country estate lies along the beautiful Deveron River and our comfortable secluded cottages all have private gardens, with six miles of our own walks on their doorsteps. Unspoilt sandy beaches only nine miles away, and the market town of Turriff is only two miles. Enjoy Cairngorms, Royal Deeside, picturesque fishing villages and castles. Ideal for top golf courses, free brown trout fishing. Well behaved pets are very welcome to stay free of charge.

Terms: from £209 weekly. Open year round.
5 cottages sleeping 4-9 people.

For a brochure contact: ***Simon Pearse, Holiday Cottages, Forglen Estate, Turriff, Aberdeenshire AB53 4JP***
Tel: 01888 562918 • www.forglen.co.uk
e-mail: reservations@forglen.co.uk

Ballater

Village and resort 14 miles east of Braemar.

CAMBUS O'MAY HOTEL, BALLATER AB35 5SE (Tel & Fax: 013397 55428). Family-run country house hotel 4 miles east of Ballater. Excellent food; 12 en suite bedrooms. Ideal area for hill walking, golf, fishing and visiting Balmoral Castle etc.
website: www.cambusomayhotel.co.uk

GLEN LUI HOTEL, 14 INVERCAULD ROAD, BALLATER AB35 5PP (013397 55402). Friendly, family-run hotel set in 2 acres of woodlands. Pets are welcome in our comfortable Pine Terrace twin rooms. Come to the Glen Lui for a great Scottish experience. Fantastic food and wines. Short breaks.
e-mail: infos@glen-lui-hotel.co.uk website: www.glen-lui-hotel.co.uk

Banchory

Small town on River Dee 11 miles NW of Stonehaven.

RAEMOIR HOUSE HOTEL & RESTAURANT, RAEMOIR, BANCHORY AB31 4ED (01330 824884; Fax: 01330 822171). Elegant hotel set in 3,500 acres of parkland with many beautiful walks, 9-hole golf course, tennis. 20 bedrooms. Ideal for visiting Aberdeen and many castles in the area. [🐕]
e-mail: relax@raemoir.com website: www.raemoir.com

Glenlivet

Located 8 miles north of Tomintoul. Distilleries and State forest.

BEECHGROVE COTTAGES, GLENLIVET. Traditional stone cottages set amidst beautiful surroundings near rivers Avon and Livet. All modernised and very comfortable. Fishing available. Ideal for exploring Highlands, Castle and Whisky Trails, walking, skiing, golf. Contact: THE POST OFFICE, TOMNAVOULIN, BALLINDALLOCH AB37 9JA (01807 590220) [🐕]
website: www.beechgrovecottages.co.uk

Grantown-on-Spey

Market town 19 miles south of Forres.

M. F. TAYLOR, MILTON OF CROMDALE, GRANTOWN-ON-SPEY PH26 3PH. Contact 01479 872565 (Melba Smith). Fully modernised Cottage with large garden and views of River Spey and Cromdale Hills. Golf, tennis and trekking within easy reach. Fully equipped except linen. Two double bedrooms. Shower, refrigerator, electric cooker, colour television. Car desirable. Open March to October. £120 per week. Children and pets welcome. [🐕]

Inverurie

Town 14 miles NW of Aberdeen.

MACDONALD PITTODRIE HOUSE, CHAPEL OF GARIOCH, NEAR INVERURIE AB51 5HS (01467 681744; Fax: 01467 681648). One of Scotland's most historic and picturesque hotels, at the foot of the spectacular Bennachie. Stunning views, extensive private gardens and a reputation for culinary excellence and impecccable service combine to ensure your stay will be perfect in every way.
e-mail: pittodrie@macdonald-hotels.co.uk website: www.macdonaldhotels.co.uk/pittodrie

Stonehaven

Fishing port on east coast, 13 miles south of Aberdeen.

MRS AILEEN PATON, 'WOODSIDE OF GLASSLAW', STONEHAVEN AB39 3XQ (01569 763799). Modern bungalow with six centrally heated en suite bedrooms with colour TV and hospitality trays. Stonehaven two miles. Accessible for disabled guests.

Turriff

Small town in agricultural area, 9 miles south of Banff.

SIMON PEARSE, COUNTRY COTTAGES, FORGLEN ESTATE, TURRIFF AB53 4JP (01888 562918). Estate on the beautiful Deveron River. Sandy beaches only nine miles away, Turriff two miles. 5 cottages sleeping 4–9. From £209 weekly. Open all year. Ideal for top golf courses, free brown trout fishing. Well-behaved dogs welcome. [🐕]
e-mail: reservations@forglen.co.uk website: www.forglen.co.uk

Angus & Dundee

Finavon

Braehead B&B - The Dog-friendly B&B!!
Here at Braehead we offer a very warm welcome to our guests and their four-legged friends. We have 3 guest rooms, all with en suite shower rooms. There is an outside enclosed area and ample car parking. Our two Golden Retrievers and Newfoundland love making new friends, so come and stay with us in the lovely Angus countryside.
Braehead Cottage, Finavon, By Forfar, Angus DD8 3PX Tel: 01307 850715
e-mail: braeheadbandb@btinternet.com www.braeheadbandb.co.uk

Finavon

Located on the River South Esk, 5 miles north east of Forfar.

BRAEHEAD COTTAGE, FINAVON, BY FORFAR DD8 3PX (01307 850715). The Dog-friendly B&B!! We offer a very warm welcome to our guests and their four-legged friends. Three guest rooms, all with en suite shower rooms. Outside enclosed area and ample car parking. Our two Golden Retrievers and Newfoundland love making new friends. [pw! 🐕]
e-mail: braeheadbandb@btinternet.com website: www.braeheadbandb.co.uk

ARDTUR COTTAGES

Two adjacent cottages in secluded surroundings. Ideal for hill walking, climbing, pony trekking, boating and fly fishing. Shop one mile; sea 200 yards; car essential; pets allowed.

MRS J PERY, ARDTUR, APPIN PA38 4DD (01631 730223 or 01626 834172)
e-mail: pery@btinternet.com • www.selfcatering-appin-scotland.com

GO WEST! ESCAPE TO ARDNAMURCHAN & MULL

Steading Holidays
is a family-run business located in Ardnamurchan, Britain's most westerly point. All with superb views, our quality cottages are located throughout Ardnamurchan and Mull and provide a peaceful and unhurried retreat amongst sandy beaches with spectacular sea views to the Western Isles. The area is a true haven for fishermen, birdwatchers, divers, yachtsmen, photographers and hill walkers – as well as a welcome break for those who want to relax and enjoy the "peace and tranquillity".

For details call Steading Holidays
01972 510 262

Stronachullin Lodge

provides pet-friendly self-catering accommodation in Mid Argyll

Three beautifully furnished holiday homes sleeping from 5 to 8 people. Each home has a separate entrance, is centrally heated, and is fully equipped. We are very dog and children friendly. You are free to explore the extensive grounds, which are full of rhododendrons of all sizes and colours. Wellington boots are recommended! Access direct onto the hill behind gives walks of anything from a 10 minute stroll to a 2 hour or more walk, with wonderful views over Loch Fyne. For a change of scene, there are lots of Forestry Commission walks within a 30 minute drive.

Each home has TV, DVD and video; a well equipped kitchen with dishwasher and washer/dryer; and oil fired central heating. All linen is provided, except for towels

For details contact: **Mary Broadfoot, Kenneths of Stronachullin, Stronachullin House, Stronachullin, Ardrishaig, Lochgilphead PA30 8ET**
Tel: 01546 603329 • e-mail: stronachullin@btconnect.com
www.stronachullin.co.uk

FREE or REDUCED RATE entry to Holiday Visits and Attractions – see our **READERS' OFFER VOUCHERS** on pages 433-440

Cairndow, Dalmally

Cairndow Stagecoach Inn

A Warm Scottish Welcome on the Shores of Loch Fyne

Cairndow, Argyll PA26 8BN
Tel: 01499 600286 • Fax: 01499 600220
www.cairndowinn.com

Discounted rates for golfers at Inveraray Golf Club. Tee times available at Loch Lomond

AA ★★★ Inn

★ Historic Coaching Inn on Loch Fyne
★ 18 well-appointed en suite bedrooms
★ 7 de luxe bedrooms; 5 new Lochside rooms
★ Excellent cuisine in Stables Restaurant and lounge meals all day
★ Amenities include lochside beer garden, sauna, and solarium.

Cairndow, Argyll.
At The Head Of Loch Fyne

Two comfortable holiday cottages at the head of the longest sea loch in Scotland. **INVERFYNE** (pictured left), a very spacious cottage with 4 twin bedded rooms, overlooks the estuary. There is a piano in the 32 foot living room and a large utility/drying room. **BRIDGE COTTAGE** (pictured right), is a traditional stone cottage and sleeps four, overlooks the bottom pool of the river Fyne. Linen and electricity are included. Achadunan Estate is set amidst lovely walking country. Golden eagles and deer are your neighbours. Achadunan is home to Fyne Ales micro brewery. Brochures available from:

Scottish Tourist Board ★★★ Self Catering

Mrs Delap, Achadunan, Cairndow, Argyll PA26 8BJ
Tel & Fax: +44 (0) 1499 600 238
www.argyllholidaycottages.com

Rockhill Waterside Country House

Est 1960

Ardbrecknish, By Dalmally, Argyll PA33 1BH • Tel: 01866 833218

17th century guest house in spectacular waterside setting on Loch Awe with breathtaking views to Ben Cruachan, where comfort, peace and tranquillity reign supreme.

Small private Highland estate breeding Hanoverian competition horses. 1200 metres free trout fishing. Five delightful rooms with all modern facilities. First-class highly acclaimed home cooking with much home-grown produce. Wonderful area for touring the Western Highlands, Glencoe, the Trossachs and Kintyre. Ideal for climbing, walking, bird and animal watching. Boat trips locally and from Oban (30 miles) to Mull, Iona, Fingal's Cave and other islands.

Dogs' Paradise! ***Also Self-Catering Cottages***

Home Farm Cottages

Glendaruel, Near Tighnabruaich, Argyll

Beautifully furnished and well equipped, The Byre, The Stables, Dairy Cottage and Home Farm Cottage offer you exceptional comfort from which to base your adventures or indeed to completely chill out. Pets are very welcome and regularly enjoy the many wonderful walks that are on your doorstep and running on the beach (6 miles from cottages). There is a basket area in each cottage (with exception of Dairy Cottage) and also kennels if you prefer.

With Loch Fyne 20 minutes' drive away, you have access to many wonderful restaurants that specialise in seafood.

Tel: 01463 709622 or 01463 238238

e-mail: liz.lowrie@tulloch-homes.com

www.homefarms.co.uk

Dalmally, Isle of Gigha, Kilchattan Bay, Loch Goil, Oban

Set in 20 acres of garden woodland on the south shore of spectacular Loch Awe in the heart of Argyll, Ardbrecknish House dates back to the early – seventeenth century. The house has been carefully converted to provide nine delightful self-catering properties accommodating parties from two to twelve with facilities for larger groups. In the grounds are five custom designed holiday cottages, carefully spaced for optimum privacy and outlook, yet easily accessible to the central facilities. The house and grounds command breathtaking panoramic views over loch, mountain and glen. Boat hire, fishing, golf and walking. Close to Oban, Mull and Glencoe. Bar, meals and games room.

3 night breaks from £80 for 2 persons low season, to £1000 weekly high season rental for 12 person apartment

The community-owned Isle of Gigha (Gaelic: God's Island) is known as The Jewel of the Inner Hebrides. The Atlantic's crystal clear waters surround this six-mile long magical isle, and lap gently on to its white sandy beaches - creating an aura of peace and tranquillity.

The Gigha Hotel caters admirably for the discerning holidaymaker with comfortable accommodation and first class cuisine, including fresh local seafood. There are also holiday cottages available.

A must for any visitor is a wander around the famous sub-tropical Achamore Gardens, where palm trees and many other exotic plants flourish in Gigha's mild climatic conditions.

The Isle of Gigha Heritage Trust retails quality island-related craft products, some of which have utilised the Trust's own tartan. Other activities on offer include organised walks, bird watching, sea fishing, a nine-hole golf course and alternative therapies.

Call us on 01583 505254 Fax: 01583 505244
www.gigha.org.uk

St Blane's Hotel Kilchattan Bay, Isle of Bute PA20 9NW

In one of the most serene and breathtaking locations on Bute, this traditional, family-run, pet-friendly, licensed Hotel offers superior en suite accommodation. It is a perfect base for walking, golf, windsurfing and other water sports. Open to non-residents, and with free moorings for visiting yachts, you can drop by for a meal or drink in the largest beer garden on the island!

01700 831224 • e-mail: info@stblaneshotel.com • www.stblaneshotel.com

Darroch Mhor Chalets

Carrick Castle, Loch Goil, Argyll PA24 8AF

Chill out in Scotland's first national park. Five self catering chalets nestling on the shores of Loch Goil, each with superb lochside views and offering a peaceful and relaxing holiday in the heart of Argyll Forest Park. Each chalet has two bedrooms, living room with colour TV, fitted kitchen with fridge, freezer, microwave, toaster etc. and bathroom with bath and overhead shower. Car parking by each chalet. Great hill walking.

Ideal for pets, genuinely pet-friendly • Open all year – weekly rates £120-£295.
Weekend & short breaks available all year from £70, reductions for 2 persons. One pet free.

Tel: 01301 703249 • Fax: 01301 703348 • chalets@murray-s.fslife.co.uk • www.argyllchalets.com

Small family-run guest house, 10 minutes' walk from train, boat and bus terminal.
A warm welcome awaits you all year round.

MRS STEWART, GLENVIEW, SOROBA ROAD, OBAN PA34 4JF • Tel: 01631 562267

Lagnakeil

HIGHLAND LODGES
VisitScotland
★★★/★★★★ Self-Catering

Our timber lodges and four cottages are set in a tranquil, scenic wooded glen overlooking Loch Feochan, only 3 miles from Oban, **'Gateway to the Isles'**. Equipped to a high standard, including linen & towels. Country pub only a short walk up the Glen. OAP discount. Free loch fishing. Special breaks from £49 per lodge per night, weekly from £225. Lodges/cottages sleep 2-12 comfortably in 1-5 bedrooms.

Contact: Colin & Jo Mossman
Lagnakeil Highland Lodges, Lerags, Oban PA34 4SE
Tel: 01631 562746 • e-mail: info@lagnakeil.co.uk • www.lagnakeil.co.uk

Willowburn

Just half a mile after you cross the Atlantic Ocean over the Clachan Bridge you will find the Willowburn Hotel, a small hotel privately owned and run by Jan and Chris Wolfe. Standing in one and a half acres of garden leading down to the quiet waters of Clachan Sound, the Willowburn offers peace and quiet, good food, fine wines and comfortable homely rooms - all in an informal and friendly atmosphere.

www.willowburn.co.uk

Seil Island, by Oban PA34 4TJ *Telephone: 01852 300276* *willowburn.hotel@virgin.net*

COLOGIN
COUNTRY CHALETS
Oban

All Scottish Glens have their secrets: let us share ours with you – and your pets

Tranquil country glen less than 3 miles from Oban • Free fishing for wild brown trout on our hill loch • Waymarked forest trails for you and your pet • The Barn Country Inn serves food and drink all year round, so you don't have to self-cater if you don't want to • Family-run complex with excellent facilities.

Our cosy chalets, lodges, cottages and private houses are set around an old farm and can sleep from 2-14. Pets are very welcome (2 maximum). Sky TV, wi-fi access and much more. *Call now for our colour brochure or check our website for live availability and secure online booking.*

Scottish Tourist Board ★★★/★★★★ Self Catering
Cyclists Welcome • Walkers Welcome

MRS LINDA BATTISON, COLOGIN FARMHOUSE,
LERAGS GLEN, BY OBAN, ARGYLL PA34 4SE
Tel: 01631 564501 • Fax: 01631 566925
e-mail: info@cologin.co.uk • www.cologin.co.uk

A DOG'S LIFE IN LUXURY AT MELFORT PIER & HARBOUR

Sixteen Luxury Houses, scattered along the shores of tranquil Loch Melfort in Argyll.

Each house has a sauna/spa bath, Sky TV and Wifi.
Private beaches and plenty of hill walking.
Excellent base for touring the Highlands. Family restaurant and bar on site. Prices start from £90 to £235 per night.
Sleep 2-6. Start any day of the week – open all year.

2 Pets very welcome. mention this advert and get one pet for free!

Tel: 01852 200 333 • www.mellowmelfort.com

Self-catering holidays in luxury lodges and new caravans. This immaculate 5-Star park is located on the West Coast of Scotland, near Oban. The wooded surroundings, sandy beach and stunning sea views make Tralee Bay the perfect place for a holiday at any time of year. With a play area, mini golf, fly fishing, woodland walks, boat slipway, and endless supply of RABBITS, the park offers something for everyone. Pets welcome at £15.
DAVID BELLAMY CONSERVATION AWARD GOLD
Scottish TOURIST BOARD ★★★★★ HOLIDAY PARK
Scottish THISTLE AWARDS 2003 WINNER
TRALEE BAY HOLIDAYS
Tralee Bay Holidays, Benderloch, by Oban, Argyll PA37 1QR
Tel: 01631 720255/217
e-mail: tralee@easynet.co.uk • www.tralee.com

ELERAIG HIGHLAND LODGES Near OBAN, ARGYLL

Gateway to the Highlands and Islands. Well-equipped Norwegian chalets on secluded Eleraig Estate 12 miles from Oban. Available April-Oct. Sleep 4-7. PERFECT FOR PETS.
Anne and Robin Grey, Eleraig Highland Lodges,
Kilninver, by Oban, Argyll PA34 4UX • Tel: 01852 200225
www.scotland2000.com/eleraig • e-mail: robingrey@eleraig.co.uk

West Loch Hotel

By Tarbert, Loch Fyne, Argyll PA29 6YF
Tel: 01880 820283 • Fax: 01880 820930
www.westlochhotel.co.uk
e-mail: westlochhotel@btinternet.com

Family-run, 18th century coaching inn of character, well situated for a relaxing holiday. It is renowned for outstanding food. Excellent for hill-walking and enjoying the wide variety of wildlife. Attractions include castles, distilleries, gardens and sandy beaches.

Balinakill

unique beauty and heritage in the heart of Kintyre STB ★★★

Historic award-winning Scottish Hotel on Argyll's Kintyre peninsula. The perfect base for touring or just relaxing. Large en suite rooms, superb cuisine, relaxing therapies, friendly, helpful staff, history, romance, wonderful scenery and a vast range of outdoor pursuits.
Balinakill Country House, Clachan, Near Tarbert PA29 6XL
Tel: 01880 740206 • Fax: 01880 740298 • www.balinakill.com

Taynuilt

Airdeny Chalets - Taynuilt Situated in 3½ acres of peaceful natural habitat. Three 3-bedroom chalets (STB ★★★★) and four 2-bedroom chalets (STB ★★★), all enjoying spectacular views, own privacy and parking area. Furnished to a very high standard. Ideal for walking, cycling, fishing, bird watching, touring the Western Highlands and Islands, or just relaxing. Dogs welcome. Open all year. Prices from £265 to £685. Contact: **Jenifer Moffat 01866 822648 • e-mail: jenifer@airdenychalets.co.uk • www.airdenychalets.co.uk**

Appin

Mountainous area bounded by Loch Linnhe, Glen Creran and Glencoe.

MRS J PERY, ARDTUR, APPIN PA38 4DD (01631 730223 or 01626 834172). Two adjacent cottages in secluded surroundings. Ideal for hill walking, climbing, pony trekking, boating and fly fishing. Shop one mile; sea 200 yards; car essential; pets allowed.[ ]
e-mail: pery@btinternet.com website: www.selfcatering-appin-scotland.com

Ardnamurchan

Peninsula on West Coast running from Salen to Ardnamurchan Point.

STEADING HOLIDAYS, ARDNAMURCHAN & MULL. A family-run business located in Britain's most westerly point. All with superb views, our quality cottages provide a peaceful and unhurried retreat amongst sandy beaches with spectacular sea views. Contact MRS JACQUI CHAPPLE, THE STEADING, KILCHOAN, ARCHARACLE PH 36 4LH (01972 510 262).
website: steading.co.uk

Ardrishaig

Town on west shore of Loch Gilp, 2 miles south of Lochgilphead.

STRONACHULLIN LODGE. Three beautifully furnished holiday homes, each sleeps 5-8. Dog and children friendly. Well equipped, with TV, DVD, dishwasher etc. All linen except towels. Extensive grounds. Contact: MARY BROADFOOT, KENNETHS OF STRONACHULLIN, STRONACHULLIN HOUSE, STRONACHULLIN, ARDRISHAIG, LOCHGILPHEAD PA30 8ET (01546 603329)
e-mail: stronachullin@btconnect.com website: www.stronachullin.co.uk

Cairndow

Village at mouth of Kinglas Water on Loch Fyne in Argyll, near head of Loch.

CAIRNDOW STAGECOACH INN, CAIRNDOW PA26 8BN (01499 600286; Fax: 01499 600220). 18 well-appointed en suite bedrooms. Excellent cuisine in Stables Restaurant and lounge meals all day. Amenities include lochside beer garden, sauna and solarium. AA ★★★ Inn.
website: www.cairndowinn.com

Two comfortable holiday cottages at the head of the longest sea loch in Scotland, in lovely walking country. Sleep four and eight. Linen and electricity included. STB ★★★ Self Catering. MRS DELAP, ACHADUNAN, CAIRNDOW, ARGYLL PA26 8BJ (Tel & Fax: 01499 600238).
website: www.argyllholidaycottages.com

Dalmally

Small town in Glen Orchy to the south-west of Loch Awe, with romantic Kilchurn Castle (14th century). Edinburgh 98 miles, Glasgow 69, Ardrishaig 42, Oban 25, Inveraray 16.

ROCKHILL WATERSIDE COUNTRY HOUSE, ARDBRECKNISH, BY DALMALLY PA33 1BH (01866 833218). 17th century guest house on waterside with spectacular views over Loch Awe. Five delightful rooms with all modern facilities. First-class home cooking with much home-grown produce.

ARDBRECKNISH HOUSE, SOUTH LOCHAWESIDE, BY DALMALLY, ARGYLL PA33 1BH (01866 833223). Self-catering properties and holiday cottages set in 20 acres of garden woodland on the south shore of Loch Awe. Breathtaking panoramic views over loch, mountain and glen. See our website to view properties. [Pets £15 per week]
e-mail: enquiries@loch-awe.co.uk website: www.loch-awe.co.uk

Glendaruel

Village on Cowal Peninsula on West Coast of Scotland.

HOME FARM COTTAGES, GLENDARUEL, NEAR TIGHNABRUAICH (01463 709622 or 01463 238238). Four beautifully furnished and well equipped cottages offering exceptional comfort. Many wonderful walks (beach 6 miles from cottages). Loch Fyne 20 minutes drive away, with access to many wonderful seafood restaurants. [🐕]
e-mail: liz.lowrie@tulloch-homes.com website: www.homefarms.co.uk

Isle of Gigha

A tranquil island, one of the Inner Hebrides just of the west coast of Scotland. A haven for birds and wildlife.

GIGHA HOTEL, ISLE OF GIGHA PA41 7AA (01583 505254; Fax: 01583 505244). Beautiful, tranquil island. Explore the white sandy bays and lochs; famous Achamore Gardens. Easy walking, bike hire, birds, wildlife and wild flowers. Dog-friendly. Holiday cottages also available. [🐕]
website: www.gigha.org.uk

Kilchattan Bay

Quiet seaside village with wide bay on the East coast of Bute.

ST BLANE'S HOTEL KILCHATTAN BAY, ISLE OF BUTE PA20 9NW (01700 831224). Traditional, family-run, pet-friendly, licensed Hotel offering superior en suite accommodation. Perfect base for walking, golf, windsurfing and other water sports. Open to non-residents. [🐕]
e-mail: info@stblaneshotel.com website: www.stblaneshotel.com

Loch Goil

Six mile long loch stretching from Lochgoilhead to Loch Long.

DARROCH MHOR, CARRICK CASTLE, LOCH GOIL PA24 8AF (01301 703249; Fax: 01301 703348). Five self-catering Chalets on the shores of Loch Goil in the heart of Argyll Forest Park. Fully equipped except linen. Colour TV, fitted kitchen, carpeted. Pets very welcome. Open all year. [🐕]
e-mail: chalets@murray-s.fslife.co.uk website: www.argyllchalets.com

Oban

Popular Highland resort and port, yachting centre, ferry services to Inner and Outer Hebrides. Sandy bathing beach at Ganavan Bay. McCaig's Tower above town is Colosseum replica built in 1890s.

MRS STEWART, GLENVIEW, SOROBA ROAD, OBAN PA34 4JF (01631 562267). Small family-run guest house, 10 minutes' walk from train, boat and bus terminal. A warm welcome awaits you all year round. [🐕]

COLIN & JO MOSSMAN, LAGNAKEIL HIGHLAND LODGES, LERAGS, OBAN PA34 4SE (01631 562746). Our Timber Lodges and four cottages are set in a tranquil, scenic wooded glen overlooking Loch Feochan, only 3 miles from the picturesque harbour town of Oban: "Gateway to the Isles". Lodges equipped to a high standard, including linen and towels, country pub a short walk. OAP discount. Free loch fishing. Special Breaks from £49 per lodge per night, weekly from £225. Sleep 2-12 comfortably. VisitScotland ★★★/★★★★ Self-Catering. [Pets £15 per week].
e-mail: info@lagnakeil.co.uk website: www.lagnakeil.co.uk

WILLOWBURN HOTEL, CLACHAN SEIL, BY OBAN PA34 4TJ (01852 300276). Peaceful, relaxing, informal and addictive. Superb setting overlooking the Sound of Seil. Walk, fish, birdwatch or simply just laze. Completely non-smoking. Tempted? Bring your owners too! STB ★★★★ Small Hotel, AA ★★ [🐕]
website: www.willowburn.co.uk

MRS LINDA BATTISON, COLOGIN COUNTRY CHALETS, LERAGS GLEN, BY OBAN PA34 4SE (01631 564501; Fax: 01631 566925). Cosy chalets, lodges, cottages and houses, all conveniences. Situated on farm, wildlife abundant. Launderette, licensed bar serving home-cooked food. Free fishing. Playpark. STB ★★★/★★★★ Self-Catering [pw! Pets £20per week.]
e-mail: info@cologin.co.uk website: www.cologin.co.uk

MELFORT PIER AND HARBOUR, KILMELFORD, BY OBAN PA34 4XD (01852 200333; Fax: 01852 200329). Superb Lochside houses each with Sauna, Spabath, Sky TV, Telephone, Wifi, on the shores of Loch Melfort. Excellent base for touring Argyll and the Isles. From £90 to £235 per night. Sleeps 2-6. 2 pets very welcome. Service with a smile. [Pets £15 each per stay]
website: www.mellowmelfort.com

TRALEE BAY HOLIDAYS, BENDERLOCH, BY OBAN PA37 1QR (01631 720255/217). Overlooking Ardmucknish Bay. The wooded surroundings and sandy beaches make Tralee the ideal destination for a self-catering lodge or caravan holiday anytime of the year. STB ★★★★★ [Pets £15 per week]
e-mail: tralee@easynet.co.uk website: www.tralee.com

Well-equipped Scandinavian chalets in breathtaking scenery near Oban. Chalets sleep 4–7, are widely spaced and close to Loch Tralaig. Car parking. From £200 per week per chalet. Available April to October. STB ★★ Self Catering. APPLY – ANNE & ROBIN GREY, ELERAIG HIGHLAND LODGES, KILNINVER, BY OBAN PA34 4UX (01852 200225) [🐕]
e-mail: robingrey@eleraig.co.uk website: www.scotland2000.com/eleraig

Tarbert

Fishing port on isthmus connecting Kintyre to the mainland.

WEST LOCH HOTEL, BY TARBERT, LOCH FYNE PA29 6YF (01880 820283; Fax: 01880 820930). Family-run, 18th century coaching inn, well situated for a relaxing holiday. It is renowned for outstanding food. Excellent for hill-walking and enjoying the wide variety of wildlife. Attractions include castles, distilleries, gardens and sandy beaches. STB ★★ Inn. [🐕]
e-mail: westlochhotel@btinternet.com website: www.westlochhotel.co.uk

BALINAKILL COUNTRY HOUSE, CLACHAN, NEAR TARBERT PA29 6XL (01880 740206; Fax: 01880 740298). Historic award-winning hotel on Kintyre peninsula. Perfect base for touring or just relaxing. En suite rooms, superb cuisine, relaxing therapies, friendly staff, history, romance, wonderful scenery. AA Rosette, Green Tourism Silver Award. [🐕]
website: www.balinakill.com

Taynuilt

Village in Argyll 1km south west of Bonawe.

JENIFER MOFFAT, AIRDENY CHALETS, TAYNUILT PA35 1HY (01866 822648). Three 3-bedroom chalets (STB ★★★★) and four 2-bedroom chalets (STB ★★★), furnished to a very high standard. Ideal for walking, cycling, fishing, bird watching, touring, or just relaxing. Dogs welcome. Open all year. [Pets £10 per week].
e-mail: jenifer@airdenychalets.co.uk website www.airdenychalets.co.uk

Pet-Friendly
Pubs, Inns & Hotels
on pages 424-432
Please note that these establishments may not feature in the main section of this book

Ayr

HORIZON HOTEL Esplanade, Ayr KA7 1DT

A welcome guest. In all my years of experience of this business, I have never received a complaint about a dog slamming bedroom doors late at night, talking loudly in the corridors or driving away noisily from the car park when other guests are trying to sleep. Never has a dog made cigarette burns on the carpets, furniture or in the bath. No dog has ever stolen my towels, sheets or ashtrays. No cheque written by a dog has ever bounced and no dog has ever tried to pay with a stolen credit card. Never has a dog insulted my waitress or complained about food or wine. Neither have we ever had a dog who was drunk. In short you are welcome whenever you wish to come to this hotel and if you can vouch for your master, you are welcome to bring him along too!!

Ayr's only seafront hotel, just five minutes' walk from town centre. Lunches, dinners and bar suppers served.
Phone now for free colour brochure. Under the personal supervision of Mr & Mrs A.H. Meikle.

Tel: 01292 264384 • Fax: 01292 264011
e-mail: reception@horizonhotel.com • www.horizonhotel.com

Ayr

Popular family holiday resort with sandy beaches. Excellent shopping, theatre, racecourse.

HORIZON HOTEL, ESPLANADE, AYR KA7 1DT (01292 264384; Fax: 01292 264011). Highly recommended for golf breaks; special midweek rates. Coach parties welcome. Lunches, dinners and bar suppers served. Phone now for free colour brochure. [🐕]
e-mail: reception@horizonhotel.com website: www.horizonhotel.com

Other specialised holiday guides from FHG

PUBS & INNS OF BRITAIN
COUNTRY HOTELS OF BRITAIN
WEEKEND & SHORT BREAKS IN BRITAIN & IRELAND
THE GOLF GUIDE WHERE TO PLAY, WHERE TO STAY
500 GREAT PLACES TO STAY
SELF-CATERING HOLIDAYS IN BRITAIN
BED & BREAKFAST STOPS IN BRITAIN
CARAVAN & CAMPING HOLIDAYS IN BRITAIN
FAMILY BREAKS IN BRITAIN

Published annually: available in all good bookshops or direct from the publisher:
FHG Guides, Abbey Mill Business Centre, Seedhill, Paisley PA1 1TJ
Tel: 0141 887 0428 • Fax: 0141 889 7204
e-mail: admin@fhguides.co.uk • www.holidayguides.com

Cumbria ~ Scottish Borders

• Superb character cottages set in historic landscape on conservation farm with panoramic views • High quality furnishings • Wood-burning stoves • Stabling facilities - bring your own horse • Great walking, cycling, riding, forest tracks, bridleways, rivers and wooded valleys • Explore the Lake District, Hadrian's Wall, Solway Coast, historic Carlisle and return to a barbecue on your own patio, or relax by the fire. • Sleep up to 7 + cot • Open all year • £250-£450 per week.

Sally Spencer, Saughs Farm & Cottages, Bailey, Newcastleton TD9 0TT (016977 48346/48000; Fax: 016977 48180)
e-mail:kevin.graykm@btopenworld.com website: www.skylarkcottages.co.uk

Ferniehirst Mill Lodge

A chalet-style guest house set in grounds of 25 acres. All rooms en suite with tea/coffee making facilities. Licensed for residents. Well behaved pets (including horses) welcome by arrangement. AA ★★ ALAN & CHRISTINE SWANSTON, FERNIEHIRST MILL LODGE, JEDBURGH TD8 6PQ • 01835 863279
e-mail: ferniehirstmill@aol.com • www.ferniehirstmill.co.uk

Westwood House – Kelso

Overlooking Scotland's famous River Tweed

TOTAL "OFF LEAD" FREEDOM FOR DOGS IN ENCLOSED AND SECLUDED GROUNDS

Renovated riverside cottage with 12 acres of paths, through walled gardens and on own private island.
4 bedrooms sleeping 2 - 8 (+ child), 2 bathrooms, period features, cosy log fire and centrally heated.
• ½ mile Kelso town • one hour Edinburgh/Newcastle • ½ hour Berwick (station) and Northumberland coast

DOGS WELCOME FREE

For Brochure and tariff, from £375 per week fully inclusive of all linen and towels, electricity and heating.
2-person discounts available. Trout fishing also included.

Welcome Host

**Debbie Crawford,
Pippin Heath Farm, Holt,
Norfolk NR25 6SS
Tel: 07788 134 832**

ACHIEVING GOLD IN GREEN TOURISM AND 'HIGHLY COMMENDED' IN SCOTTISH THISTLE AWARDS

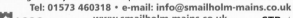

SMAILHOLM MAINS FARM COTTAGES • BY KELSO TD5 7RT

Two cosy farm cottages, each sleeping 5, in a peaceful setting 6 miles from Kelso. Both with open fires, central heating, Sky TV. Close to golf, fishing, walking or a day at the races. Open Jan-Dec. Short Breaks available £150-£250.
Tel: 01573 460318 • e-mail: info@smailholm-mains.co.uk
www.smailholm-mains.co.uk

ASSC STB ★★★★

Delightful 4 bedroomed country house overlooking river in the Cheviot hills. Sleeps up to 10 people in the best standard of self-catering accommodation. Space and relaxing comfort including log fires. Ideal for walking, fishing, golf, shooting, rugby and racing.

STB ★★★

GLEBE HOUSE

Glebe House, Hownam, by Kelso, Scottish Borders TD5 8AL
Tel: 07971 522 040 • Fax: 01896 870 664
e-mail: enquiries@holidayhomescotland.co.uk
www.holidayhomescotland.com

2 large Victorian houses, sleeping 11 and 14,
perfect for large get-togethers.
Original decor, open fires, walking distance to all amenities.
Great walks, golf, fish horses, pubs.
Tel: 018358 24887 • www.lilshouse.com

Selkirk, West Linton

Warm, modern farmhouse B&B set in delightful walled garden in the heart of the Scottish Borders. Spacious bedrooms with private bathrooms. Good home cooking using local produce. Loch fishing; grazing for horses; ideal for walking, cycling and horse riding. Well behaved pets welcome. Open all year.
Whitmuir, Selkirk TD7 4PZ • Tel: 01750 721728 • Fax: 01750 720379
e-mail: whitmuir@btconnect.com • www.whitmuirfarm.co.uk

Slipperfield House

West Linton EH46 7AA

Scottish Tourist Board ★★★★ Self Catering – America Cottage

Scottish Tourist Board ★★★ Self Catering – Loch Cottage

Two well-equipped cottages a mile from West Linton. Set in a hideaway country estate at the foot of the Pentland Hills, 19 miles from Edinburgh city centre, the cottages sleep 4/6, with open fires, digital TV and central heating. Linen and towels can also be supplied.
Lovely walks with the countryside on your doorstep.

Details from Mrs C.M. Kilpatrick

• Dogs welcome (max. 2 per cottage) • Ample parking
• Car essential • Central Edinburgh 19 miles
• Golf, walking and fishing nearby • Available all year

"...thank you for a wonderful family holiday once again, it was perfect."

Tel: 01968 660401 e-mail: cottages@slipperfield.com www.slipperfield.com

Bailey/Newcastleton

Border town of Liddel Water 17 miles South of Hawick.

SALLY SPENCER, SAUGHS FARM COTTAGES, BAILEY, NEWCASTLETON, ROXBURGHSHIRE TD9 0TT (01697 748346/748000; Fax: 01697 748180). Superb character cottages on Cumbrian/Scottish Borders. Panoramic views. Quality furnishings. Stabling facilities. Great for walking, cycling, riding. Children and pets welcome. Open all year. STB ★★★★ SELF CATERING
e-mail: kevin.graykm@btopenworld.com website: www.skylarkcottages.co.uk

Jedburgh

Small town on Jed water, 10 miles north-east of Hawick. Ruins of abbey founded in 1138.

ALAN & CHRISTINE SWANSTON, FERNIEHIRST MILL LODGE, JEDBURGH TD8 6PQ (01835 863279). A chalet style guest house set in grounds of 25 acres. All rooms en suite with tea/coffee making facilities. Licensed for residents. Well behaved pets (including horses) welcome by arrangement. AA ★★. [🐕]
e-mail: ferniehirstmill@aol.com website: www.ferniehirstmill.co.uk

Visit the FHG website

www.holidayguides.com

for details of the wide choice of accommodation

featured in the full range of FHG titles

Kelso

Market town 18 miles north-west of Hawick and 20 miles south-west of Berwick-upon-Tweed.

WESTWOOD HOUSE, OVERLOOKING SCOTLAND'S FAMOUS RIVER TWEED. Enclosed and secluded riverside cottage with walled gardens and own private island. Sleeps 2-8 persons plus child, from £375 per week. 2 person discounts. For brochure contact: DEBBIE CRAWFORD, PIPPIN HEATH FARM, HOLT, NORFOLK NR25 6SS (07788 134832). [🐕]

MRS KIRSTY B. SHAW, SMAILHOLM MAINS FARM COTTAGES, BY KELSO TD5 7RT (01573 460318). Two cosy farm cottages, each sleeping 5, in a peaceful setting 6 miles from Kelso. Both with open fires, central heating, Sky TV. Close to golf, fishing, walking or a day at the races. Short breaks available. STB ★★★★[🐕]
e-mail: info@smailholm-mains.co.uk website: www.smailholm-mains.co.uk

MRS SARAH FRASER-BALLANTYNE, GLEBE HOUSE, HOWNAM, BY KELSO TD5 8AL (07971 522 040; Fax: 01896 870 664). Delightful 4 bedroomed country house overlooking river in the Cheviot hills. Sleeps up to 10 people. Space and comfort. Ideal for walking, fishing, golf, shooting. STB ★★★ *SELF-CATERING.* [🐕]
e-mail: enquiries@holidayhomescotland.co.uk website: www.holidayhomescotland.co.uk

Melrose

Small town on the south side of the River Tweed 4 miles east of Galashiels.

Two large Victorian houses, sleeping 11 and 14, perfect for large get-togethers. Original decor, open fires, walking distance to all amenities. Great walks, golf, fish horses, pubs. MRS L. GOGAN, KIPPILAW HOUSE, KIPPILAW, MELROSE TD6 9HF (018358 24887).
website: www.lilshouse

Selkirk

Town on hill above Ettrick Water, 9 miles north of Hawick.

THE GARDEN HOUSE, WHITMUIR, SELKIRK TD7 4PZ (01750 721728; Fax: 01750 720379). Comfortable, warm modern farm house B&B. Spacious bedrooms, private bathrooms. Good home cooking. Fishing, walking, cycling and horse riding nearby. Grazing available. Open all year. [🐕]
e-mail: whitmuir@btconnect.com website: www.whitmuirfarm.co.uk

West Linton

Village on east side of Pentland hills, 7 miles south-west of Penicuick. Edinburgh 18 miles.

MRS C. M. KILPATRICK, SLIPPERFIELD HOUSE, WEST LINTON EH46 7AA (01968 660401). Two lovely cottages on hideaway country estate near Edinburgh. Sleep 4/6. Available all year. Perfect dog-friendly location. STB ★★★/★★★★ [🐕]
e-mail: cottages@slipperfield.com website: www.slipperfield.com

Please note

All the information in this book is given in good faith in the belief that it is correct. However, the publishers cannot guarantee the facts given in these pages, neither are they responsible for changes in policy, ownership or terms that may take place after the date of going to press. Readers should always satisfy themselves that the facilities they require are available and that the terms, if quoted, still apply.

Auchencairn, Castle Douglas, Drummore, Dumfries, Gatehouse-of-Fleet

Country House Hotel, **Auchencairn, Near Castle Douglas DG7 1QZ**

The hotel offers well appointed bedrooms, all with en suite facilities. Imaginative cuisine is based on local delicacies including seafood. This is an ideal location for exploring the gardens and National Trust properties of South-West Scotland and enjoying walking, birdwatching and golf.

www.balcary-bay-hotel.co.uk • reservations@balcary-bay-hotel.co.uk

Tel: 01556 640217 • Fax: 01556 640272 • STB ★★★ • AA ★★★ 2 Rosettes

Craigadam

Working organic sheep farm. Family-run 18th century farmhouse. All bedrooms en suite. Billiard room/honesty bar. Lovely oak-panelled dining room offering Cordon Bleu cooking using local produce such as venison, pheasant and salmon.

Trout fishing, walking, and golfing available.

Tel & Fax: 01556 650233

Mrs C. Pickup, Craigadam,

Castle Douglas DG7 3HU

www.craigadam.com

Winner Macallan Taste of Scotland

Scottish Tourist Board ★★★★ Farmhouse

AA ★★★★ Guest House

Mull of Galloway • • • • • • • Drummore

Harbour Row Cottages. A few short steps from the beach. STB 3/4-Star cottages. Tranquil and unspoiled village. Logan Botanical Gardens, golf, fishing, birdwatching nearby. Unrestricted beaches. £5 per animal. Contact SALLY COLMAN:

ASSC • Non-smoking properties available • **01776 840631 • www.harbourrow.co.uk**

AE FARM COTTAGES

• Modern accommodation in old stone buildings on a traditional farm, overlooking a peaceful valley, surrounded by hills and forests. Beautiful views, plentiful wildlife and endless paths on the doorstep.

A great country retreat between Dumfries, Moffat and Thornhill.

David & Gill Stewart, GUBHILL FARM, Dumfries DG1 1RL (01387 860648)

e-mail: gill@gubhill.co.uk STB ★★★ *SELF CATERING* **CATEGORY ONE DISABILITY**

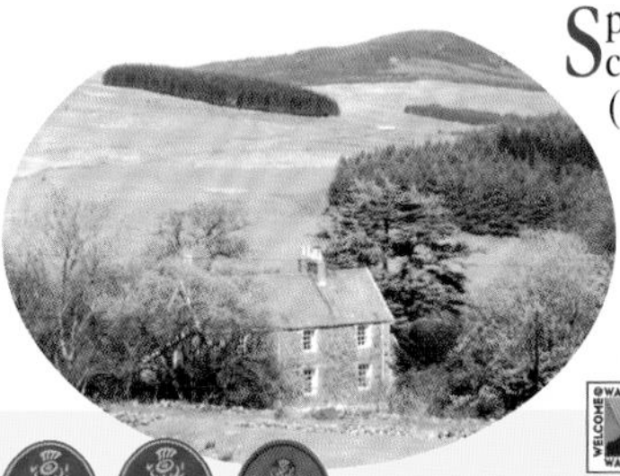

Spacious, beautiful farmhouse and three charming, cosy cottages set amid stunning Scottish scenery near beaches (dogs allowed), hills, forests, castles, gardens and golf course. Loch and river fishing with tuition, free tennis, wonderful walking, cycling and riding country.

Sleep 2-12 • Rates £225-£1329 • Short breaks available.

Pets, including horses, welcome.

info@ruskoholidays.co.uk • www.ruskoholidays.co.uk

Rusko Holidays

Gatehouse of Fleet, Castle Douglas DG7 2BS

Tel: 01557 814215

FREE or REDUCED RATE entry to Holiday Visits and Attractions – see our **READERS' OFFER VOUCHERS** on pages 433-440

Gretna, Moffat, Newton Stewart, Thornhill, Whithorn

SOLWAY LODGE HOTEL

Annan Road, Gretna DG16 5DN

Scottish Tourist Board ★★★ Small Hotel

A small, family-run hotel, where you will be assured of a warm, friendly welcome. The newly refurbished dining room offers an excellent choice of freshly prepared meals, and the lounge bar areas are ideal for relaxing. All hotel bedrooms are en suite and furnished to the highest standards in modern, contemporary style. Ideal for wedddings • Pets welcome by arrangement

Tel: 01461 338266 • Fax: 01461 337791

www.solwaylodge.co.uk

BARNHILL SPRINGS Country Guest House, Moffat DG10 9QS

Early Victorian country house overlooking some of the finest views of Upper Annandale. Comfortable accommodation, residents' lounge with open fire. Ideal centre for touring South-West Scotland and the Borders, or for an overnight stop. Situated on the Southern Upland Way half-a-mile from A74/M74 Moffat Junction. Pets free of charge. Bed & Breakfast from £29; Evening Meal (optional) from £18. *STB ★★ Guest House AA ★★*

Three cottages in the grounds of this historic Scottish estate. 'Bargaly' was once the home of the noted horticulturalist, Andrew Heron, and dates back to 1675.

GATEHOUSE COTTAGE, SQUIRREL COTTAGE and THE GARDENER'S COTTAGE available for holiday lets. Situated in the Bargaly Glen 1½ miles down a scenic country lane, yet only 4 miles from the town of Newton Stewart, 'Gateway to the Galloway Hills', with all facilities. Gentle walks can be taken locally, or a more challenging ramble to the top of Cairnsmore. Cycle hire locally, and the nearby Forest Park Visitor Centre in the Glen has a programme of activities throughout the season. An excellent location for walking, birdwatching, cycling, golf, watersports at Loch Ken, fishing (private 5½ miles stretch for salmon and trout), astronomy (take advantage of our dark skies), horse riding, a plethora of gardens to visit, some fun on the beach, or simply just relaxing. ***Pets welcome.***

Visit our website www.bargaly.com for more information or call us for a brochure - 01671 401048

e-mail: bargalyestate@callnetuk.com ***Galloway's Hidden Retreat***

Hope Cottage, Thornhill, Dumfriesshire DG3 5BJ

Pretty stone cottage in the peaceful conservation village of Durisdeer. Well-equipped self-catering cottage with large secluded garden. Sleeps 6. Towels, linen, heating and electricity included. Pets Welcome.

For brochure telephone: Mrs S Stannett • 01848 331510

Fax: 01848 331810 • e-mail: a.stann@btinternet.com

www.hopecottage.co.uk

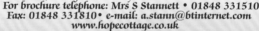

Scottish Tourist Board ★★★★ Self Catering

CRAIGLEMINE COTTAGE B&B

With a rural location and peaceful atmosphere it's a wonderful place to unwind for a short break or a longer holiday. We have one double/family room, one single/twin room and dining room/lounge. Prices from £22. Evening meals available on request, including vegetarian or other dietary needs. Non-smoking. Off-road parking. Children welcome (under six years free). Pets welcome. An ideal base for walkers, cyclists, golf or touring. We also cater for amateur astronomers - call for details. Whether exploring the history, countryside or unspoilt beaches there is something for everyone, you can be sure of a friendly welcome all year round. Contact us for more details, or visit our website.

Glasserton, Near Whithorn, Dumfries DG8 8NE

Tel: 01988 500594

e-mail: cottage@fireflyuk.net

www.startravel.fireflyinternet.co.uk

Wigtown

HILLCREST HOUSE **Maidland Place, Wigtown DG8 9EU Tel: 01988 402018**

Beautiful Victorian character villa set on edge of national book town. Fabulous views over nature reserve. Six bedrooms, residents' lounge. Evening meals using fresh local produce.

e-mail: info@hillcrest-wigtown.co.uk • www.hillcrest-wigtown.co.uk

Auchencairn

Village 7 miles south of Dalbeattie.

BALCARY BAY COUNTRY HOUSE HOTEL, AUCHENCAIRN, NEAR CASTLE DOUGLAS DG7 1QZ (01556 640217: Fax: 01556 640272). Ideal location for exploring South West Scotland. Well appointed bedrooms, all en suite. Imaginative cuisine based on local produce. STB ★★★, AA ★★★, 2 Rosettes. [🐕]
e-mail: reservations@balcary-bay-hotel.co.uk website: www.balcary-bay-hotel.co.uk

Castle Douglas

Old market town at the northern end of Carlingwalk Loch, good touring centre for Galloway

MRS CELIA PICKUP, "CRAIGADAM", CASTLE DOUGLAS DG7 3HU (Tel & Fax: 01556 650233). Family-run 18th century famhouse. All bedrooms en suite. Billiard room/honesty bar. Lovely oak-panelled dining room offering Cordon Bleu cooking using local produce such as venison, pheasant and salmon. Trout fishing, walking and golfing available. STB ★★★★; AA ★★★★ and Breakfast & Dinner Awards. [🐕]
website: www.craigadam.com

Drummore

Coastal location, 4 miles north of Mull of Galloway.

MULL OF GALLOWAY, DRUMMORE. A few short steps from the beach. STB 3/4-Star cottages; non-smoking cottages available. Tranquil and unspoiled village. Logan Botanical Gardens, golf, fishing, birdwatching nearby. Unrestricted beaches. ASSC. Contact SALLY COLMAN (01776 840631). [£5 per pet].
website: www.harbourrow.co.uk

Dumfries

County town of Dumfries-shire and a former seaport. Dumfries contains many interesting buildings including an 18th century windmill containing a camera obscura. Robert Burns lived in the town before his death in 1796.

DAVID & GILL STEWART, AE FARM COTTAGES, GUBHILL FARM, DUMFRIES DG1 1RL (01387 860648). Modern accommodation in old stone buildings on a traditional farm, overlooking a peaceful valley. Beautiful views, plentiful wildlife and endless paths on the doorstep. Between Dumfries, Moffat and Thornhill. STB ★★★ SELF CATERING, CATEGORY ONE DISABILITY. [🐕]
e-mail: gill@gubhill.co.uk

Gatehouse of Fleet

Small town near mouth of Water of Fleet, 6 miles north-west of Kirkcudbright

RUSKO HOLIDAYS, GATEHOUSE OF FLEET, CASTLE DOUGLAS DG7 2BS (01557 814215). Spacious farmhouse and three charming, cosy cottages near beaches, hills, gardens, castles and golf course. Walking, fishing, tennis. Pets, including horses, welcome. Sleep 2-12. Rates £225-£1329. STB ★★ to ★★★★ Self-Catering. Disabled Awards. [Pets £20 each]
e-mail: info@ruskoholidays.co.uk website: www.ruskoholidays.co.uk

Gretna

Village 8 miles East of Annan. Famous for runaway marriages in former times.

SOLWAY LODGE HOTEL, ANNAN ROAD, GRETNA DG16 5DN (01461 338266; Fax: 01461 337791). A small, family-run hotel, where you will be assured of a warm, friendly welcome. Excellent choice of freshly prepared meals. All bedrooms are en suite. Ideal for wedddings. Pets welcome by arrangement. STB ★★★ Small Hotel.
website: www.solwaylodge.co.uk

Moffat

At head of lovely Annandale, grand mountain scenery. Good centre for rambling, climbing, angling and golf. The 'Devil's Beef Tub' is 5 miles, Edinburgh 52, Peebles 33, Dumfries 21.

BARNHILL SPRINGS COUNTRY GUEST HOUSE, MOFFAT DG10 9QS (01683 220580). Early Victorian country house overlooking some of the finest views of Upper Annandale. Comfortable accommodation, residents' lounge with open fire. Situated on the Southern Upland Way half-a-mile from A74/M74 Moffat Junction. Pets free of charge. Bed & Breakfast from £29; Evening Meal (optional) from £18. STB ★★ Guest House, AA ★★. [pw! 🐕]

Newton Stewart

Small town on River Cree 7 miles north of Wigtown.

BARGALY ESTATE COTTAGES, PALNURE, NEWTON STEWART DG8 7BH (01671 401048). Three cottages. The Gatehouse Cottage to the historic Bargaly Estate stands proudly looking over the countryside beyond. Gardener's Cottage was once the home fo the head gardener and lies adjacent to the walled garden. Nestling in a woodland setting lies Squirrel Cottage. Salmon and trout fishing. [Pets £20 per week.].
e-mail: bargalyestate@callnetuk.com website: www.bargaly.com

Thornhill

Small town on River Nith 13 miles north-west of Dumfries. Site of Roman signal station lies to the south.

HOPE COTTAGE, THORNHILL DG3 5BJ (01848 331510; Fax: 01848 331810). Pretty stone cottage in the peaceful conservation village of Durisdeer. Well-equipped self-catering cottage with large secluded garden. Sleeps 6. Towels, linen, heating and electricity included. Phone MRS S. STANNETT for brochure. STB ★★★★ [🐕]
e-mail: a.stann@btinternet.com website: www.hopecottage.co.uk

Whithorn

Small town 9 miles south of Wigtown.

MIKE AND HELEN ALEXANDER, CRAIGLEMINE COTTAGE B&B, GLASSERTON, NEAR WHITHORN DG8 8NE (01988 500594). Our rural location makes this a wonderful place to unwind. Ideal for touring, your dog will love the nearby beaches. Evening meal available. STB ★★ [🐕]
e-mail: cottage@fireflyuk.net website: www.startravel.fireflyinternet.co.uk

Wigtown

Small town on hill above River Cree.

HILLCREST HOUSE, MAIDLAND PLACE, WIGTOWN DG8 9EU (01988 402018). Beautiful character Victorian villa set on edge of national book town. Fabulous views over nature reserve. Six bedrooms, residents' lounge. Evening meals using fresh local produce. [Pets free in kennels, £1 per night indoors]
e-mail: info@hillcrest-wigtown.co.uk website: www.hillcrest-wigtown.co.uk

A useful index of towns/counties appears at the back of this book

Rosewell

Hunter Holiday Cottages Thornton Farm, Rosewell, Edinburgh EH24 9EF

Hunter Holiday Cottages have 2 x two-bedroom and 1 x 3-bedroom cottages situated on our working farm just 20 minutes' drive south of Edinburgh city centre. Pets welcome, great walks on tracks and through woods. For more information visit our website.

Contact Margot Crichton. Telephone for availability for Short Breaks

Tel: 0131-448 0888 • Fax: 0131-440 2082 • e-mail: info@edinburghcottages.com • www.edinburghcottages.com

Rosewell

Village 4 miles south west of Dalkeith.

HUNTER HOLIDAY COTTAGES, THORNTON FARM, ROSEWELL, EDINBURGH EH24 9EF (0131 448 0888; Fax: 0131 440 2082). 2 x two-bedroom cottages and 1 x 3-bedroom cottage on working farm 20 minutes' drive Edinburgh. Great walks on tracks and through woods. Contact MARGOT CRICHTON. [Pets £10 per night/week].

e-mail: info@edinburghcottages.com website: www.edinburghcottages.com

Fife

Lower Largo, St Andrews

Main Street, Lower Largo, Fife KY8 6BT near St Andrews

Old-world ambience with fine harbour views. En suite accommodation, outstanding cuisine, free house. Excellent centre for sailing, golf, birdwatching, wind surfing, coastal walks.

Tel: 01333 320759 • Fax: 01333 320865

email: relax@crusoehotel.co.uk • www.crusoehotel.co.uk

ST ANDREWS COUNTRY COTTAGES

Idyllic Country Cottages and Farmhouses in St Andrews and on a beautiful Country Estate. Perfect for golf, exploring or relaxing. Enclosed gardens, log fires, private walking. Sleep 4 to 14.

Scottish Tourist Board ★★★/★★★★ Self Catering

ASSC

Brochure:- Mountquhanie Estate, FREEPOST, Cupar, Fife KY15 4BR

Tel: 01382 330318 • Fax: 01382 330480

e-mail: enquiries@standrews-cottages.com • www.standrews-cottages.com

COBWEBS in the HEART OF ST ANDREWS

Scottish Tourist Board ★★★ Self Catering

Self catering for five people, opposite the University, at the heart of the Auld Toon.

www.heartofstandrews.co.uk

Just three minutes from the Castle Sands and ten from the famous links and West Sands, our secluded, secure walled garden is perfect for you and your pets.

Telephone us on 01764 685482 or email Frances from the web page.

Lower Largo

Village on the bay, 2 miles NE of Leven. Birth place of Alexander Selkirk of Robinson Crusoe fame.

THE CRUSOE HOTEL, Main Street, Lower Largo, NEAR ST ANDREWS KY8 6BT. (01333 320759; Fax: 01333 320865). Old-world ambience with fine harbour views. En suite accommodation, outstanding cuisine, free house. Excellent centre for sailing, golf, birdwatching, wind surfing, coastal walks. STB ★★★ Hotel. [ ]
email: relax@crusoehotel.co.uk website: www.crusoehotel.co.uk

St Andrews

Home of golf - British Golf Museum has memorabilia dating back to the origins of the game. Remains of castle and cathedral. Sealife Centre and beach Leisure Centre. Excellent sands. Ideal base for exploring the picturesque East Neuk.

MR & MRS PATRICK WEDDERBURN, ST ANDREWS COUNTRY COTTAGES, MOUNTQUHANIE ESTATE, FREEPOST, CUPAR KY15 4BR (01382 330318; Fax: 01382 330480). Quality self-catering houses and cottages in St Andrews and on a tranquil Country Estate. Central heating, TV. Enclosed gardens. STB ★★★ to ★★★★★ Self Catering. [pw! Dogs £15 per week, Cats F.O.C.].
e-mail: enquiries@standrews-cottages.com website: www.standrews-cottages.com

COBWEBS. Self-catering for five people, situated opposite the University, just 3 minutes from the Castle Sands and 10 from the famous links. Our secluded, secure walled garden is perfect for you and your pets. Telephone 01764 685482 or e-mail Frances from the web page. STB ★★★ Self-catering [Pets £20 per pet per week].
website: www.heartofstandrews.co.uk

Looking for Holiday Accommodation?

FHG
K·U·P·E·R·A·R·D

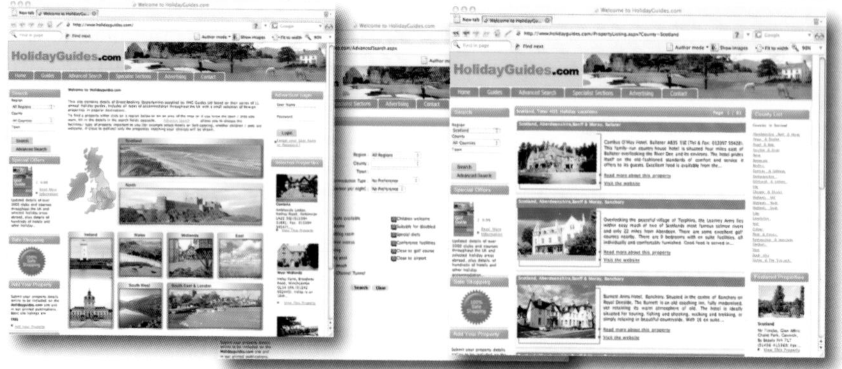

for details of hundreds of properties throughout the UK, visit our website

www.holidayguides.com

Highlands - Wester Ross

COVE VIEW 36 Mellon Charles, Aultbea IV22 2JL

Wester Ross is ideal for a quiet restful holiday. Detached chalet, available all year, has two small bedrooms, sitting area with mini kitchen, bathroom with shower. Ideal for two persons. Terms from £200 to £250 per week. Your dog is welcome free. Contact Mrs P. MacRae. Tel: 01445 731351

Cairngorm Highland Bungalows

Glen Einich, 29 Grampian View,
Aviemore, Inverness-shire PH22 1TF

Tel: 01479 810653 • Fax: 01479 810262

e-mail: linda.murray@virgin.net
www.cairngorm-bungalows.co.uk

Beautifully furnished and well-equipped bungalows ranging from one to four bedrooms. All have colour TV, video, DVD, microwave, cooker, washer-dryer, fridge and patio furniture. Some have log fires. Leisure facilities nearby include golf, fishing on the River Spey, swimming, sauna, jacuzzi, tennis, skating and skiing. Within walking distance of Aviemore. Ideal touring base. Children and pets welcome. Phone for colour brochure. Open all year.

Scottish Tourist Board ★★★ Self Catering

Scottish Tourist Board ★★★★ Self Catering

For the very best in Highland Holidays

ASSC

AVIEMORE PINE BANK CHALETS

Enjoy the stunning beauty of the Highlands and the Cairngorm Mountains from our choice of superbly appointed log cabins and chalets. Great location – close to Spey River. Peaceful and relaxing setting. Friendly service staff, selected Sky TV, video, barbecue, mountain bikes. Many activities available. Leisure pool and restaurants nearby. Large choice of style and price.

5 log cabins, 6 chalets, 2 Flats, sleeping up to 6
Open all year £390-£725 per week • Pets Welcome

Dalfaber Road, Aviemore, Inverness-shire PH22 1PX
Tel: 01479 810000
e-mail: pinebankchallets@btopenworld.com
website: www.pinebankchalets.co.uk

CULLIGRAN COTTAGES • GLEN STRATHFARRAR

Pure magic! Come for a spell in a chalet or cottage and this glen will cast one over you!

Nature Reserve with native woodlands and wildlife. 15 miles of private road. Bikes for hire. Fly fishing (salmon and trout) on the rivers Farrar and Glass. Watch the wild deer from your window. Feed the farm deer.

Brochure • Open March-November • Prices from £199-£529

FRANK & JULIET SPENCER-NAIRN, STRUY, NEAR BEAULY, INVERNESS-SHIRE IV4 7JX • Tel/Fax: 01463 761285
e-mail: info@culligrancottages.co.uk
www.culligrancottages.co.uk

An individual hotel for individual guests in the Cairngorms National Park.
Award-winning 2 AA Rosette cuisine. Pets welcome.
The Boat, Boat of Garten, Inverness-shire PH24 3BH
Telephone: (01479) 831258
Fax: (01479) 831414
email: info@boathotel.co.uk www.boathotel.co.uk

the boat

AA ★★★

The Treehouse

Self-catering Lodge, Boat of Garten

Unique lodge in woodland setting, yet minutes from local amenities. Fully equipped, superb log-burning fire. Perfect for an active or a relaxing break, with woodland walks and cycle tracks nearby. Pets welcome. Sleeps 7.

www.treehouselodge.co.uk
Tel: Anne Mather 0131-337 7167
e-mail: fbg@treehouselodge.plus.com

Privately owned and operated 20-bedroom Country House Hotel with miles of forest walks, many log fires, and great food.
Both you and your dog are made to feel most welcome.

Coul House Hotel, Contin, By Strathpeffer Ross-shire IV14 9ES
Tel: 01997 421487 • Fax: 01997 421945
e-mail: stay@coulhousehotel.com • www.coulhousehotel.com

DORNOCH CASTLE

An idyllic retreat in the Scottish Highlands

Dornoch Castle is set in the beautiful, historic town of Dornoch, directly opposite the inspiring 12th century Dornoch Cathedral in the quaint Market Square, a dramatic backdrop for an overnight stay. This impressive Castle offers a cosy and comfortable stay, and is renowned for the best in Scottish hospitality. Dornoch Castle makes an ideal base for touring in the area, providing information such as local maps, walks, heritage trails and visitor attractions. As a family-run Castle, Dornoch offers a friendly and relaxed atmosphere for guests to soak in the tranquillity and delight of the Highlands.
Pets welcome by arrangement.

Dornoch Castle Hotel, Castle Street, Dornoch, Sutherland IV25 3SD
Tel: 01862 810216 • Fax: 01862 810981
e-mail: enquiries@dornochcastlehotel.com • www.dornochcastlehotel.com

AA ★★★ HOTEL

GLENURQUHART LODGES Situated between Loch Ness and Glen Affric in a spectacular setting ideal for walking, touring or just relaxing in this tranquil location. Four spacious chalets all fully equipped for six people, set in wooded grounds. Owner's hotel adjacent where guests are most welcome in the restaurant and bar. **Near Drumnadrochit, Inverness IV63 6TJ • Tel: 01456 476234 • Fax: 01456 476286**
www.glenurquhart-lodges.co.uk • e-mail: carol@glenurquhartlodges.co.uk

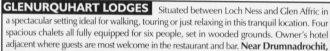

Fort William, Inverness-shire PH33 6RW
Tel: (01397) 702341 • Fax: (01397) 706174
reception@clanmacduff.co.uk • www.clanmacduff.co.uk

Small, well behaved pets are always welcome at the Clan MacDuff. This family-run hotel overlooks Loch Linnhe, two miles south of Fort William. Situated in its own grounds in a quiet and peaceful location with a large car park, the hotel is in an excellent location for touring and experiencing the rugged mountains and enchanting coastline of the West Highlands. All bedrooms have colour TV, hair dryer and hospitality tray, all with private facilities. The hotel offers great value hospitality.

Scottish Tourist Board ★★★ HOTEL

Bed and Breakfast in an en suite room from £27.50 per person per night.
Spring and Autumn Special Offer - 3 Nights Dinner, Bed & Breakfast from £119.50pp.
Please phone or write for our colour brochure & tariff.

Fort William, Glencoe, Glen Shiel

Linnhe LOCHSIDE HOLIDAYS

Corpach, Fort William, Inverness-shire PH33 7NL

Almost a botanical garden, Linnhe is unique and one of the most beautiful Lochside parks in Britain. Close to Ben Nevis and Fort William. Excellent facilities including licensed shop, bakery, playgrounds, private beach and free fishing. Pets welcome.

Luxury Holiday Caravans (from £220 per week)

Short Breaks from £135

Tent & Touring Pitches also available • Open mid March - end October • Colour Brochure

Tel: 01397 772376 • Fax: 01397 772007
www.linnhe-lochside-holidays.co.uk
e-mail: relax@linnhe-lochside-holidays.co.uk

LOCH LEVEN HOTEL

On the banks of beautiful Loch Leven, near Glencoe, Fort William and the famous mountain, Ben Nevis, this small, informal, family-run hotel would like to welcome you.

There is a lounge bar, the Loch View Restaurant for a bit of comfort and luxury, and a friendly public bar with an open fire. The games room/family room opens out onto the decking, the garden, the scenery – and no traffic. Children and pets welcome. B&B from £35pp, Dinner,B&B from £45pp

Tel: 01855 821236
reception@lochlevenhotel.co.uk • www.lochlevenhotel.co.uk
Old Ferry Road, North Ballachulish, Near Fort William PH33 6SA

Great Glen Holidays

Torlundy, Fort William PH33 6SW
Tel/Fax: 01397 703015

Eight spacious, 2-bedroom, timber chalets situated in woodland with spectacular mountain scenery. On working Highland farm. Riding, fishing and walking on farm. Ideal for family holidays, excellent base for touring; four miles from town. Sleep 4-6. Prices from £250 to £510 per week.

e-mail: chris.carver@btconnect.com • www.fortwilliam-chalets.co.uk

Inchree Centre

Tel/Fax: 01855 821287
e-mail: reception@inchreecentre.co.uk
www.inchreecentre.co.uk

Onich, Near Fort William PH33 6SE

Eight self-catering chalets situated between Ben Nevis and Glencoe in peaceful and spacious grounds. Fully refurbished within, 4 to 6 berth in size. Each chalet has panoramic mountain and loch views. Enjoy forest and waterfall walks from the door. On-site pub and restaurant serving good food and real ales. Short-stay breaks available most of the year. Discount for couples.

Glenshiel, Ross shire IV40 8HL
Tel: 01599 511275

Kintail Lodge Hotel – Shiel Bridge

Beautifully situated on the shores of Loch Duich
6 miles south of Eilean Donan Castle

Spring, Autumn and Winter Short Breaks
Special Offer for 3, 4, or 5 Days – Dogs Welcome

Candlelit Dinners, Log Fires, Big Sofas and fabulous views, whatever the weather! We guarantee your comfort and we promise you the best of Highland food and hospitality.

e-mail: kintaillodgehotel@btinternet.com
www.kintaillodgehotel.co.uk

Spectacular location by Loch Ness at the heart of the Highlands of Scotland. Comfortable, well equipped self catering chalets in spacious grounds, alongside enchanting River Moriston Falls and bridges. Only a few minutes' walk to the village and amenities. Excellent base to explore, hill walk, fish, cycle and much more. Pets welcome in some chalets. Launderette and children's games areas on site.

Glenmoriston, Highlands IV63 7YF
Tel: 01320 351254 • Fax: 01320 351343
www.invermoriston-holidays.co.uk
e-mail: info@invermoriston-holidays.co.uk

Let us spoil you...

It's the little things which matter most to my team at Dunain Park Hotel; our stunning Georgian Country House is surrounded by 6 acres of parkland just outside Inverness. Warm welcomes, discreet and attentive service and going the extra mile for guests is all part of the experience.

Outstanding menu of seasonal dishes using the finest local produce and influenced by their wide international experience. We have 2 charming Garden Cottages to which we warmly welcome pets.

DUNAIN PARK
HOTEL & RESTAURANT

Inverness IV3 8JN • Tel: 01463 230 512 / Fax: 01463 224 532
info@dunainparkhotel.co.uk • www.dunainparkhotel.co.uk

COLUMBA HOUSE
HOTEL & GARDEN RESTAURANT

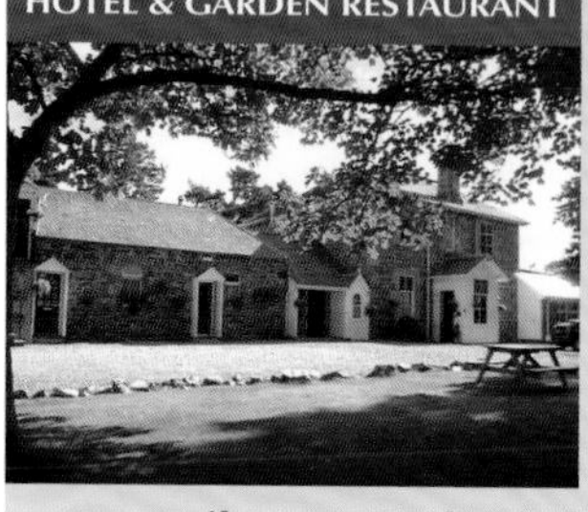

In an area of oustanding natural beauty. An oasis amidst the magnificent scenery, stunning landscapes and tranquillity, in the foothills of snow-capped peaks of the Cairngorm and Monadhliath mountains. Quiet Highland retreat, nestling in a secluded, landscaped, walled garden with patio for summer time dining. Offering the highest standards of welcoming hospitality, accommodation and customer care, friendly atmosphere. Rooms with their own front doors, perfect for doggie holidays. Candlelit Garden Restaurant, renowned for excellent cuisine and attentive service. Homely, enchanting lounge and cosy bar, offering modern facilities while retaining their original charm. Wireless internet. Nearby Leisure Club free. Wheelchair friendly; wet room. Suberb Penthouse Suite. **B&B from £35.**

Scottish Tourist Board ★★★ SMALL HOTEL

Manse Road, Kingussie PH21 1JF • Tel: 01540 661402
e-mail: myra@columbahousehotel.com • www.columbahousehotel.com

Lairg, Loch Ness, Nethy Bridge, Poolewe

Lairg Highland Hotel

Lying in the centre of the village, Lairg Highland Hotel is an ideal base from which to tour the North of Scotland. Superb, home-cooked food is served in the restaurant and lounge bar. All bedrooms are furnished to a high standard, with en suite facilities, colour TV and tea/coffee.

Main Street, Lairg, Sutherland IV27 4DB • 01549 402243 • Fax: 01549 402593
www.highland-hotel.co.uk • e-mail: info@highland-hotel.co.uk

WILDERNESS COTTAGES, LOCH NESS, WEST COAST & PERTHSHIRE

Open all year · Sleep 2-16 · Pets welcome

Escape to the country with Wilderness Cottages and leave behind the hectic lifestyle you lead today. We have a selection of quality self-catering cottages, from rustic appeal to 5-star luxury, from countryside to seashore. Whatever your pastime, be it walking, Munro bagging, cycling, sailing, fishing, birdwatching, or just chilling, we have a cottage for you. Pets with responsible owners are very welcome. Visit our website or phone for our brochure.

www.wildernesscottages.co.uk

Mr & Mrs G. Roberts, Roebuck Cottage, Errogie, Inverness IV2 6UH
Tel: 01456 486358
e-mail: corinne@wildernesscottages.co.uk

• LOCH NESS •

Wildside, Whitebridge, Inverness IV2 6UN

Exceptional riverside lodges close to the spectacular Loch Ness. Mountains, lochs, waterfalls and wildlife abound.

Charming riverside lodges with private lawns, log fires and mountain views. Lodges range from 1, 2 & 3 bedrooms, sleeping from 2 to 8 people. All lodges are non-smoking and enjoy magnificent views. Quiet location with excellent walks from your lodge. Pets welcome. Free fishing.

Tel: 01456 486 373 • Fax: 01456 486 371
e-mail: info@wildsidelodges.com • www.wildsidelodges.co.uk

Nethy Bridge, Highlands • Balnagowan Mill and Woodlark

Comfortable, modern 3 bedroom cottages in secluded locations in the Cairngorms National Park with extensive network of woodland and riverside walks on the doorstep, which is ideal for pets. Furnished to a high standard with full central heating.
£250 - £550 per week inclusive of electricity, bed linen and towels.
Contact Paula Fraser, 33 Argyle Grove, Dunblane, Perthshire FK15 9DT
Tel: 01786 824957 email: paulajfraser@aol.com

MONDHUIE CHALETS & B&B, NETHY BRIDGE, INVERNESS-SHIRE PH25 3DF • Tel: 01479 821062

Situated in the country between Aviemore and Grantown-on-Spey, two comfortable, self-catering chalets, or you can have Dinner, B&B in the house. A warm welcome awaits you. Pets welcome. Red squirrels seen daily. Free internet access.
e-mail: david@mondhuie.com • www.mondhuie.com

Innes-Maree BUNGALOWS

Self-catering bungalows in Wester Ross

Poolewe, By Gairloch IV2 2JU
Tel & Fax 01445 781454

Only a few minutes' walk from the world-famous Inverewe Gardens. A purpose-built complex of six superb modern bungalows, all equipped to the highest standards of luxury and comfort. Each bungalow sleeps six with main bedrooms en suite. Children and pets welcome. *Terms from £205 to £495 inclusive of bed linen and electricity.*

info@poolewebungalows.com • www.poolewebungalows.com

Crofter's Cottages

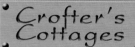

Mr Alexander Urquhart

15 Croft, Poolewe, Ross-shire IV22 2JY
Tel: 01445 781268

Two traditional cottages sleeping 4 and 5 persons. Situated in a scenic and tranquil area, ideal for a "get away from it all" holiday. Crofters Cottages are comfortably furnished, some with antiques and all the essential modern gadgets of today, such as auto-washer/dryer, microwave, fridge, bath and shower. Poolewe is a good base to tour the North West Highlands or for those who enjoy walking, fishing, climbing, golf or maybe just a stroll along one of the many sandy beaches. There are also indoor activities to be enjoyed such as the heated pool and leisure and fitness areas. Close by lie the famous Inverewe Gardens. Pets made welcome.

Low season from £120 – £230 • High season from £250 – £490
Midweek and short breaks available from November – March
e-mail: croftcottages@btopenworld.com
www.crofterscottages.co.uk

Gull Cottage • The Barn •
Rhiconich, Sutherland

Situated on the wild and unspoilt west coast of Scotland overlooking Loch Inchard, the last sea loch on the north west coast. Superb scenery with excellent walks on mountains, moors, and the many beaches in the area. High quality accommodation with full central heating. Gull Cottage sleeps 4, both bedrooms ensuite. The Barn sleeps 2. Pets welcome; secure dog run accessed from cottage.

All enquiries to: **Lynn and Graham, Gull Cottage, Achriesgill, Rhiconich, Lairg, Sutherland IV27 4RJ**
Telephone: 01971 521717

RIVERSIDE LODGES Invergloy, Spean Bridge PH34 4DY • Tel: 01397 712684

The ultimate Highland location, set in 12 acres of grounds, just three uniquely designed lodges sleeping six comfortably. Private beach with free fishing, spectacular river gorge, specimen trees and plants. Ideal for all outdoor pursuits, or for just relaxing. Tariff from £420-£750 per week - discounts for small parties/long stay. Proprietors: Steve & Marilyn Dennis. **Pets welcome • Linen included • Open all year**
e-mail: enquiries@riversidelodge.org.uk • www.riversidelodge.org.uk

Borgie Lodge Hotel

Skerray, Tongue, Sutherland KW14 7TH

Set in a secluded Highland glen by the stunning River Borgie lies Borgie Lodge, where mouthwatering food, fine wine, roaring log fires and a very warm welcome awaits after a day's fishing, hill walking, pony trekking or walking on the beach.Relax after dinner with a good malt and tales of salmon, trout and deer.

Tel: 01641 521 332
www.borgielodgehotel.co.uk
e-mail: info@borgielodgehotel.co.uk

WHITEBRIDGE HOTEL WHITEBRIDGE, SOUTH LOCH NESS IV2 6UN • 01456 486226 • Fax: 01456 486413

Peaceful location with magnificent mountain views and excellent walks. Friendly locals' bar with home-cooked food. 12 en suite rooms. B&B from £30pppn.

e-mail: info@whitebridgehotel.co.uk • www.whitebridgehotel.co.uk

Aultbea (Ross-shire)

Village on east shore of Loch Elve 5 miles north of Poolewe..

MRS P. MACRAE, COVE VIEW, 36 MELLON CHARLES, AULTBEA IV22 2JL (01445 731351). Wester Ross is ideal for hill walking or a quiet restful holiday. Detached chalet, available all year, with two small bedrooms, sitting area with mini kitchen, bathroom with shower. From £200 to £250 per week. A warm welcome awaits you and your pet. [ ]

Aviemore (Inverness-shire)

Scotland's leading ski resort in Spey valley with superb sport and entertainment facilities. All-weather holiday centre.

CAIRNGORM HIGHLAND BUNGALOWS, GLEN EINICH, 29 GRAMPIAN VIEW, AVIEMORE PH22 1TF (01479 810653, Fax: 01479 810262). Well equipped bungalows ranging from one to four bedrooms. Open all year. Leisure facilities nearby. Children and pets welcome. Phone for brochure. STB ★★★-★★★★★ [ ]
e-mail: linda.murray@virgin.net website: www.cairngorm-bungalows.co.uk

PINE BANK CHALETS, DALFABER ROAD, AVIEMORE PH22 1PX (01479 810000). Cosy Log Cabins and 6 Quality Chalets, situated near the River Spey. Superb Family/Activity Holidays by mountains. Ideal skiing, walking, fishing and golf. Sky TV. Short breaks available. Pets welcome. Open all year. ASSC Member. Brochure. [Pets £10 per week.]
e-mail: pinebankchallets@btopenworld.com website: www.pinebankchalets.co.uk

Beauly (Inverness-shire)

Town at head of Beauly Firth, 11 miles west of inverness.

FRANK & JULIET SPENCER-NAIRN, CULLIGRAN COTTAGES, GLEN STRATHFARRAR, STRUY, NEAR BEAULY IV4 7JX (Tel & Fax: 01463 761285). Pure magic! Come for a spell in a chalet or cottage and this glen will cast one over you! Nature Reserve with native woodlands and wildlife. Brochure. (March - November). Terms from £199-£529. [ ]
e-mail: info@culligrancottages.co.uk website: www.culligrancottages.co.uk

Boat of Garten (Inverness-shire)

Village on River Spey, 5 miles north east of Aviemore.

THE BOAT, BOAT OF GARTEN PH24 3BH (01479 831258; Fax: 01479 831414). An individual hotel for individual guests in the Cairngorms National Park. Award-winning cuisine. Pets welcome. AA ★★★ and Two Rosettes for food. [Pets £5 per night.]
e-mail: info@boathotel.co.uk website: www.boathotel.co.uk

ANNE MATHER, THE TREEHOUSE SELF-CATERING LODGE, BOAT OF GARTEN (0131-337 7167). Unique lodge in woodland setting, yet minutes from local amenities. Fully equipped, superb log-burning fire. Sleeps 7. Perfect for an active or a relaxing break. Pets welcome.
e-mail: fhg@treehouselodge.plus.com website: www.treehouselodge.co.uk

Contin (Ross-shire)

Village 2 miles south west of Strathpeffer.

COUL HOUSE HOTEL, CONTIN, BY STRATHPEFFER IV14 9ES (01997 421487; Fax: 01997 421945). Privately owned and operated 20-bedroom Country House Hotel with miles of forest walks, many log fires, and great food. Both you and your dog are made to feel most welcome.
e-mail: stay@coulhousehotel.com website: www.coulhousehotel.com

Dornoch (Sutherland)

Small town in Sutherland 12 miles East of Bonar Bridge.

DORNOCH CASTLE HOTEL, CASTLE STREET, DORNOCH IV25 3SD (01862 810216; Fax: 01862 810981). This impressive Castle offers a cosy and comfortable stay, and is renowned for the best in Scottish hospitality. It makes an ideal base for touring in the area . Pets welcome by arrangement. AA ★★★ and Rosette. [Pets £10 per week].
e-mail: enquiries@dornochcastlehotel.com website: www.dornochcastlehotel.com

Drumnadrochit (Inverness-shire)

Village on the shores of Loch Ness with "Monster" visitor centre. Sonar scanning cruises.

CAROL HUGHES, GLENURQUHART LODGES, BY DRUMNADROCHIT IV63 6TJ (01456 476234; Fax: 01456 476286). Situated between Loch Ness and Glen Affric in a spectacular setting ideal for walking, touring or just relaxing in this tranquil location. Four spacious chalets all fully equipped for six people, set in wooded grounds. Owner's hotel adjacent where guests are most welcome in the restaurant and bar. [Pets £10 per week.]
e-mail: carol@glenurquhartlodges.co.uk website: www.glenurquhart-lodges.co.uk

Fort William (Inverness-shire)

Small town at foot of Ben Nevis, ideal base for climbers and hillwalkers.

THE CLAN MACDUFF HOTEL, FORT WILLIAM PH33 6RW (01397 702341; Fax: 01397 706174). This family-run hotel overlooks Loch Linnhe, two miles south of Fort William, excellent for touring the West Highlands. All rooms have TV, hairdryer, hospitality tray and private facilities. B&B from £27.50pppn. Three nights DB&B from £119.50pp (Spring/Autumn). STB ★★★ Hotel. Phone or write for colour brochure and tariff. [🐕]
e-mail: reception@clanmacduff.co.uk website: www.clanmacduff.co.uk

LINNHE LOCHSIDE HOLIDAYS, CORPACH, FORT WILLIAM PH33 7NL (01397 772376; Fax: 01397 772007). Linnhe is unique and one of the most beautiful lochside parks in Britain. Close to Ben Nevis and Fort William. Excellent facilities. Pets welcome. Open mid March–end October. Colour brochure. (Pets £5 per night, £25 per week).
e-mail: relax@linnhe-lochside-holidays.co.uk website: www.linnhe-lochside-holidays.co.uk

LOCH LEVEN HOTEL, OLD FERRY ROAD, NORTH BALLACHULISH, NEAR FORT WILLIAM PH33 6SA (01855 821236). En suite rooms with lovely views. Meals using freshly prepared Scottish produce. Secluded garden. Safe, private parking. Extensive grounds. Great walks. [pw! 🐕]
e-mail: reception@lochlevenhotel.co.uk website: www.lochlevenhotel.co.uk

GREAT GLEN HOLIDAYS, TORLUNDY, FORT WILLIAM PH33 6SW (Tel/Fax: 01397 703015). Sleep 4-6. Eight spacious, two-bedroom, timber chalets on working Highland farm. Riding, fishing and walking on farm. Ideal for family holidays, excellent touring base. [Pets £15 per week]
e-mail: chris.carver@btconnect.com website: www.fortwilliam-chalets.co.uk

Glencoe (Inverness-shire)

Valley in Lochaber District 3 miles East of Ballachulish.

INCHREE CENTRE, NEAR FORT WILLIAM PH33 6SE (Tel & Fax: 01855 821287). Between Ben Nevis and Glencoe. 8 self-catering chalets, 4 or 6 berth. Pub and Restaurant on site. Discount for couples. Short-stay breaks available most of the year. [Pets £2.50 per night, £15 per week]
e-mail: reception@inchreecentre.co.uk website: www.inchreecentre.co.uk

Glen Shiel (Inverness-shire)

Valley on River Sheil in Skye & Lochalsh district .

KINTAIL LODGE HOTEL, SHIEL BRIDGE, GLENSHIEL IV40 8HL (01599 511275). Beautifully situated on the shores of Loch Duich 6 miles south of Eilean Donan Castle. We guarantee your comfort and we promise you the best of Highland food and hospitality. Dogs welcome.
e-mail: kintaillodgehotel@btinternet.com website: www.kintaillodgehotel.co.uk

Invermoriston (Inverness-shire)

Village on River Moriston, running from Loch Cluanie to Loch Ness.

INVERMORISTON HOLIDAY CHALETS, Glenmoriston IV63 7YF (01320 351254; Fax: 01320 351343). Spectacular location by Loch Ness. Comfortable, well equipped self catering chalets in spacious grounds. Few minutes' walk to the village. Excellent base for touring, walking, fishing etc. Pets welcome in some chalets (max. 2 per chalet). [Pets £20 per week]
e-mail: info@invermoriston-holidays.co.uk website: www.invermoriston-holidays.co.uk

Inverness (Inverness-shire)

A city 113 miles north-west of Edinburgh..

DUNAIN PARK HOTEL & RESTAURANT, LOCH NESS ROAD, INVERNESS IV3 8JN (01463 230512; Fax: 01463 224 532. Stunning Georgian Country House surrounded by 6 acres of parkland. Warm welcome, discreet and attentive service. Two garden cottages welcome pets.
e-mail: info@dunainparkhotel.co.uk website: www.dunainparkhotel.co.uk

Kincraig (Inverness-shire)

Attractive Highland village close to Loch Insh and Glenfeshie, midway between Aviemore and Kingussie.

NICK & PATSY THOMPSON, INSH HOUSE GUESTHOUSE AND SELF-CATERING COTTAGES, KINCRAIG, NEAR KINGUSSIE PH21 1NU (01540 651377). B&B in 1827 Telford Manse and two timber s/c cottages in superb rural location. Ideal for many outdoor activities and good touring base. Dogs and children welcome. STB ★★★ [🐕]
e-mail: inshhouse@btinternet.com website: www.kincraig.com/inshhouse

Kingussie (Inverness-shire)

Tourist centre on the River Spey 48 miles south of Inverness.

COLUMBA HOUSE HOTEL AND GARDEN RESTAURANT, MANSE ROAD, KINGUSSIE PH21 1JF (01540 661402). Quiet Highland retreat offering highest standards of hospitality, care and accommodation. Candlelit Garden Restaurant. Ground-floor rooms with own front doors, perfect for doggie holidays. STB ★★★ [pw! Pets £3 per night, £10 per week]
e-mail: myra@columbahousehotel.com website: www.columbahousehotel.com

Lairg (Sutherland)

Village 17 miles west of Golspie..

LAIRG HIGHLAND HOTEL, MAIN STREET, LAIRG IV27 4DB (01549 402243; Fax: 01549 402593). An ideal base from which to tour the North of Scotland. Superb, home-cooked food is served in the restaurant and lounge bar. All bedrooms are furnished to a high standard, with en suite facilities, colour TV and tea/coffee. STB ★★★ [🐕]
e-mail: info@highland-hotel.co.uk website: www.highland-hotel.co.uk

Lochcarron (Ross-shire)

Village on north shore of Loch Carron 2 miles below the head of the loch. Known for its ties and tartans.

THE COTTAGE, STROMECARRONACH, LOCHCARRON WEST, STRATHCARRON. Small, stone-built Highland cottage, double bedroom, shower room, open plan kitchen/living room, fully equipped. Panoramic views over Loch Carron and the mountains. For further details please phone. MRS A.G. MACKENZIE, STROMECARRONACH, LOCHCARRON WEST, STRATHCARRON IV54 8YH (01520 722284) [🐕]
website: www.lochcarron.org

A useful index of towns/counties appears at the back of this book

Loch Ness (Inverness-shire)

Home of 'Nessie', extending for 23 miles from Fort Augustus to south of Inverness.

WILDERNESS COTTAGES. Self-catering cottages all around Loch Ness plus small selection of West coast properties. Pets welcome. Please see website for details or for a brochure contact: GORDON & CORINNE ROBERTS, ROEBUCK COTTAGE, ERROGIE IV2 6UH (01456 486358). [1 dog free, extra dogs £10 each per week] STB★★★/★★★★/★★★★★ SELF CATERING
e-mail: corinne@wildernesscottages.co.uk website: www.wildernesscottages.co.uk

JUSTINE HUDSON, WILDSIDE HIGHLAND LODGES, WILDSIDE, WHITEBRIDGE, INVERNESS IV2 6UN. (01456 486373; Fax: 01456 486371). Charming riverside lodges. Log fires and mountain views. Sleep 2 to 8 people. Pets welcome. Free fishing. STB ★★★★ Self-catering. [Pets £15 per booking].
e-mail: info@wildsidelodges.com website: www.wildsidelodges.com

Nethy Bridge (Inverness-shire)

Popular Strathspey resort on River Nethy with extensive Abernethy Forest to the south. Impressive mountain scenery. Grantown-on-Spey 5 miles.

BALNAGOWAN MILL AND WOODLARK, NETHY BRIDGE. Comfortable, modern 3 bedroom cottages in secluded locations in the Cairngorms National Park. Woodland and riverside walks on the doorstep. Ideal for pets. Furnished to a high standard with full central heating. £250-£550 per week incl. of electricity, bed linen and towels. VisitScotland ★★★/★★★★. ASSC MEMBER. Contact PAULA FRASER, 33 ARGYLE GROVE, DUNBLANE FK15 9DT (01786 824957) [🐕]
e-mail: paulajfraser@aol.com

MONDHUIE CHALETS & B&B, NETHY BRIDGE PH25 3DF (01479 821062). Situated in the country between Aviemore and Grantown-on-Spey, two comfortable, self-catering chalets, or you can have Dinner, B&B in the house. A warm welcome awaits you. Pets welcome. Red squirrels seen daily. Free internet access. [🐕]
e-mail: david@mondhuie.com website: www.mondhuie.com

Poolewe (Ross-shire)

Village lying between Lochs Ewe and Maree with the river Ewe flowing through.

MR A. URQUHART, CROFTERS COTTAGES, 15 CROFT, POOLEWE IV22 2JY (01445 781 268). Two traditional cottages situated in a scenic and tranquil area, ideal for a "get away from it all" holiday. Comfortably furnished with all mod cons. [🐕]
e-mail: croftcottages@btopenworld.com website:www.crofterscottages.co.uk

INNES-MAREE BUNGALOWS, POOLEWE, BY GAIRLOCH IV2 2JU (Tel & Fax 01445 781454). Six superb modern bungalows, all equipped to the highest standards of luxury and comfort. Each sleeps 6, with main bedrooms en suite. Children and pets welcome. ASSC. STB ★★★ Self Catering. [Pets £15 per week]
e-mail: info@poolewebungalows.com website: www.poolewebungalows.com

Visit the FHG website

www.holidayguides.com

for details of the wide choice of accommodation

featured in the full range of FHG titles

Rhiconich (Sutherland)

Locality at the head of Loch Inchard on west coast of Sutherland District.

LYNN & GRAHAM, GULL COTTAGE, ACHRIESGILL, RHICONICH, SUTHERLAND IV27 4RJ (01971 521717). High quality accommodation on the wild and unspoilt west coast. Superb scenery and excellent walks on mountains, moors and beaches. Pets welcome; secure dog run. STB ★★★ Self-Catering. [🐕]

Spean Bridge (Inverness-shire)

Village on River Spean at foot of Loch Lochy. Site of WWII Commando Memorial.

RIVERSIDE LODGES, INVERGLOY, SPEAN BRIDGE PH34 4DY (01397 712684). The ultimate Highland location. Three lodges, each sleep 6 in 12 acres of woodland garden on Loch Lochy. Free fishing. Open all year. Pets welcome. Brochure on request. [🐕]
e-mail: enquiries@riversidelodge.org.uk website: www.riversidelodge.org.uk

Tongue (Sutherland)

Village near north coast of Caithness District on east side of Kyle of Tongue.

BORGIE LODGE HOTEL, SKERRAY, TONGUE KW14 7TH (Tel & Fax: 01641 521332). Set in a secluded Highland glen lies Borgie Lodge. Try pony trekking, fishing and forest walks. Open fires and fine dining. STB ★★★★ [🐕]
e-mail: info@borgielodgehotel.co.uk website: www.borgielodgehotel.co.uk

Whitebridge (Inverness-shire)

Hamlet in the heart of the Scottish Highlands, 4 miles from Loch Ness and 9 miles from Fort Augustus.

WHITEBRIDGE HOTEL, WHITEBRIDGE, SOUTH LOCH NESS IV2 6UN (01456 486226; Fax: 01456 486413). Peaceful location with magnificent mountain views and excellent walks. Friendly locals' bar with home-cooked food. 12 en suite rooms. B&B from £30pppn. AA ★★[🐕]
e-mail: info@whitebridgehotel.co.uk website: www.whitebridgehotel.co.uk

Pet-Friendly
Pubs, Inns & Hotels
on pages 424-432
Please note that these establishments may not feature in the main section of this book

Symbols

🐕 Indicates that pets are welcome free of charge.

£ Indicates that a charge is made for pets: nightly or weekly.

pw! Shows some special provision for pets; exercise facility, feeding or accommodation arrangement.

⌂ Indicates separate pets accommodation.

CARMICHAEL COUNTRY COTTAGES

Westmains, Carmichael, Biggar ML12 6PG • Tel: 01899 308336 • Fax: 01899 308481

200 year old stone cottages in this 700 year old family estate. We guarantee comfort, warmth and a friendly welcome in an accessible, unique, rural and historic time capsule. We farm deer, cattle and sheep and sell meats and tartan - Carmichael of course. Open all year. Terms from £225 to £595. 15 cottages with a total of 32 bedrooms. Private tennis court and fishing loch, cafe, farm shop and visitor centre

ASSC

e-mail: chiefcarm@aol.com • www.carmichael.co.uk/cottages

Blairmains Farm, Harthill ML7 5TJ Tel: 01501 751278

Attractive farmhouse on small farm of 72 acres. Immediately adjacent to Junction 5 of M8 motorway. Ideal centre for touring, with Edinburgh, Glasgow, Stirling 30 minutes' drive. One double, three twin, one single (three en suite); bathroom; sittingroom, diningroom; sun porch. Central heating. Children welcome. Pets welcome. Ample grounds for walking. Car essential – parking. Bed and Breakfast from £20; weekly rates available. Reduced rates for children. Open all year. **e-mail: heather@blairmains.freeserve.co.uk • www.blairmains.co.uk**

Biggar

Small town set round broad main street. Gasworks museum, puppet theatre seating 100, street museum displaying old shop fronts and interiors. Peebles 13 miles.

CARMICHAEL COUNTRY COTTAGES, CARMICHAEL ESTATE, BY BIGGAR ML12 6PG (01899 308336; Fax: 01899 308481). Our stone cottages nestle in the woods and fields of our historic family-run estate. Ideal homes for families, pets and dogs. 15 cottages, 32 bedrooms. STB ★★/★★★★ Self catering. Open all year. £225 to £595 per week. [pw!]
e-mail: chiefcarm@aol.com website: www.carmichael.co.uk/cottages

Harthill

Village 5 miles south-west of Bathgate.

MRS STEPHENS, BLAIRMAINS FARM, HARTHILL ML7 5TJ (01501 751278; Fax: 01501 753383). Attractive farmhouse on small farm. Ideal for touring. Children welcome. Bed and Breakfast from £20; weekly rates available. Reduced rates for children. Open all year. [ ]
e-mail: heather@blairmains.freeserve.co.uk website: www.blairmains.co.uk

Other specialised holiday guides from FHG

PUBS & INNS OF BRITAIN • **COUNTRY HOTELS** OF BRITAIN

WEEKEND & SHORT BREAK HOLIDAYS IN BRITAIN

THE GOLF GUIDE WHERE TO PLAY, WHERE TO STAY

500 GREAT PLACES TO STAY • SELF-CATERING HOLIDAYS IN BRITAIN

BED & BREAKFAST STOPS • CARAVAN & CAMPING HOLIDAYS

FAMILY BREAKS IN BRITAIN

Published annually: available in all good bookshops or direct from the publisher:

FHG Guides, Abbey Mill Business Centre, Seedhill, Paisley PA1 1TJ

Tel: 0141 887 0428 • Fax: 0141 889 7204

e-mail: admin@fhguides.co.uk • www.holidayguides.com

Aberfeldy

Luxury accommodation with panoramic views in 2 pine lodges on small farm near Aberfeldy. Fully equipped, well maintained; completely fenced. Touring, walking, fishing, golf or simply enjoy the peace and tranquillity. Prices from £170 per week. Short Breaks available.

DULL FARM HOLIDAY LODGES

Aberfeldy, Perthshire, PH15 2JQ • Tel: 01887 820270
E-mail: info@dullfarm.freeserve.co.uk • www.self-cateringperthshire.com

Acharn, By Aberfeldy

Escape the rat race in comfort, peace and tranquillity.
Loch, woodlands and mountains.
Ideal for walking around farmland in majestic scenery.
Each lodge has own enclosed garden.
Self-catering. £220-£590.

Tel: 01887 830209

Fax: 01887 830802

e-mail: remony@btinternet.com
www.lochtaylodges.co.uk

LOCH TAY LODGES

Fortingall Hotel

The award-winning four star Fortingall Hotel is set in the heart of the enchanting thatched village of Fortingall, in stunning Highland Perthshire. From the graceful surroundings of the dining room, to the luxury and comfort of the eleven en suite bedrooms, the Hotel offers 21st century comfort and service, whilst retaining its Victorian style and heritage. Combined with the peace and tranquillity of the area, the friendliness of the staff, and the delicious food, the Fortingall Hotel offers first class facilities in a fabulous setting, ensuring you have a memorable stay.

Best Small Country Hotel 2007

Fortingall, Aberfeldy, Perthshire PH15 2NQ
Tel/Fax: 01887 830367 • e: hotel@fortingallhotel.com
www.fortingallhotel.com

FREE or REDUCED RATE entry to Holiday Visits and Attractions – see our **READERS' OFFER VOUCHERS** on pages 433-440

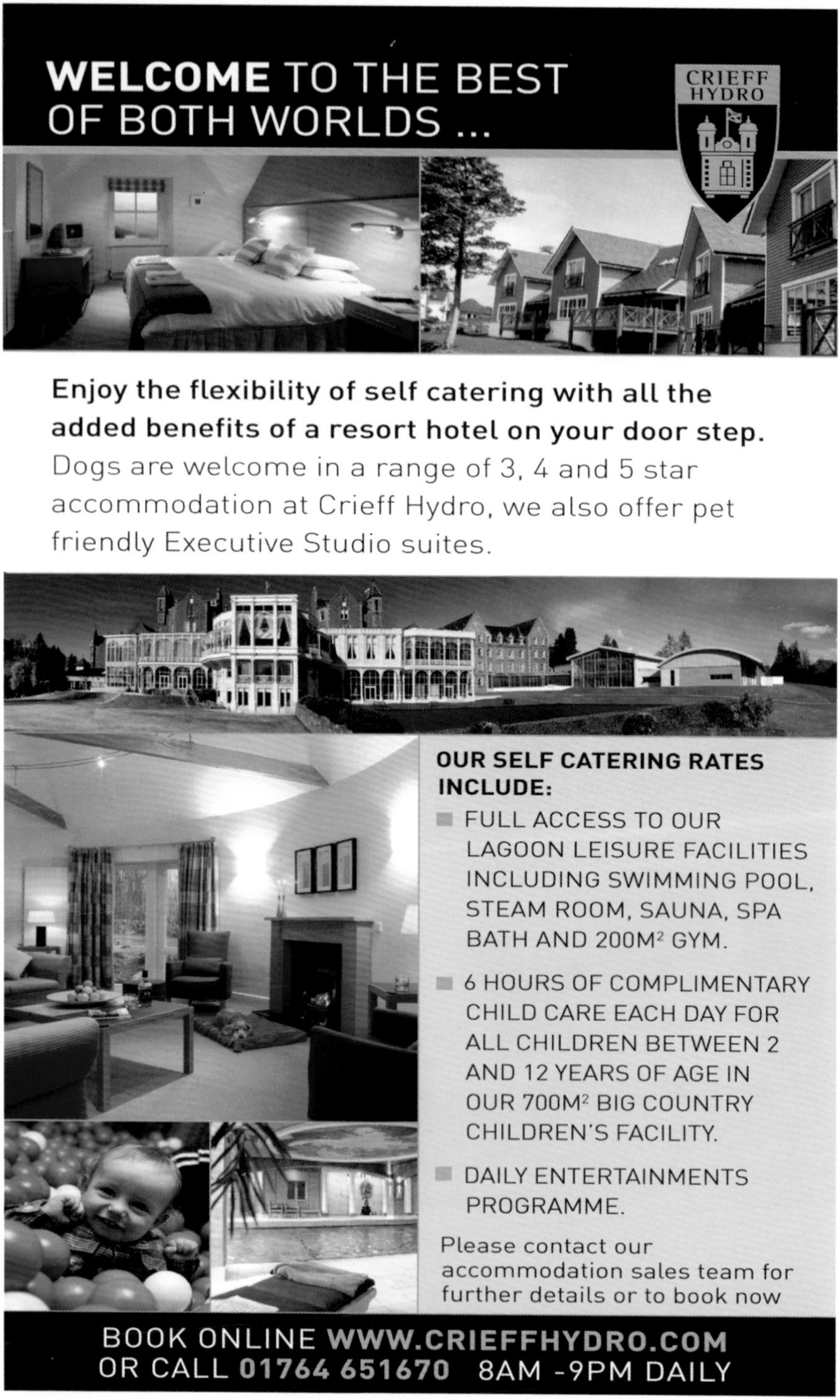
WELCOME TO THE BEST OF BOTH WORLDS ...
CRIEFF HYDRO
Enjoy the flexibility of self catering with all the added benefits of a resort hotel on your door step.
Dogs are welcome in a range of 3, 4 and 5 star accommodation at Crieff Hydro, we also offer pet friendly Executive Studio suites.
OUR SELF CATERING RATES INCLUDE:
FULL ACCESS TO OUR LAGOON LEISURE FACILITIES INCLUDING SWIMMING POOL, STEAM ROOM, SAUNA, SPA BATH AND 200M² GYM.
6 HOURS OF COMPLIMENTARY CHILD CARE EACH DAY FOR ALL CHILDREN BETWEEN 2 AND 12 YEARS OF AGE IN OUR 700M² BIG COUNTRY CHILDREN'S FACILITY.
DAILY ENTERTAINMENTS PROGRAMME.
Please contact our accommodation sales team for further details or to book now
BOOK ONLINE WWW.CRIEFFHYDRO.COM
OR CALL 01764 651670 8AM -9PM DAILY

Killin, Lochearnhead, St Fillans

WESTER LIX

Jonna's Cottage has been refurbished and redecorated. It is family-run, in a rural location set in 7 acres with private lochan. Excellent base for walking, hill climbing and all outdoor sports, including water sports, as well as being central for touring and sightseeing. Jonna's offers Sky TV, sauna, wood-burning stove etc, and all the comforts of home. Well behaved pets by arrangement.

Gill & Dave Hunt, The Steading, Wester Lix, Killin, Perthshire FK21 8RD

Tel: 01567 820990 or 07747 862641 • e-mail: gill@westerlix.net • www.westerlix.net

CLACHAN COTTAGE HOTEL

Lochearnhead, Perthshire FK19 8PU

- Friendly, family-run hotel in spectacular lochside setting.
- Well placed in central Scotland for touring.
- Excellent walking, mountain biking and fishing.
- Water-sports available from the hotel.

AWARD-WINNING TASTE OF SCOTLAND RESTAURANT

GROUP/SOCIETY RATES •PETS WELCOME•

Tel: 01567 830247 • Fax: 01567 830300

www.clachancottagehotel.com

The finest lochside setting in the Southern Highlands

Fine dining to Two AA Red Rosettes or informal Bar Meals, both offering imaginative modern cuisine using only the best fresh Scottish produce. Centrally placed to enjoy many of Scotland's best sights. For the energetic there is a wide variety of walks, from the scenic lochside to the wide open spaces of a Munro. Individually decorated hotel bedrooms, and four-poster rooms, many with loch views, or secluded hillside chalets.

Hi there fellow four-leggers, *well the big news is that at last Andrew has now got a companion for me, being young she is a bit too much at times, and of course far too immature to write or even enjoy our great walks. YOU are of course most welcome (and do bring your charges) and as usual I have insisted that you stay free, so drop me a an email or come and see me.* ***Sham*** *(Resident Reservations Munsterlander) and* ***Pagne*** *(understudy).*

The Four Seasons Hotel

St Fillans, Perthshire PH6 2NF

Tel: 01764 685333 e-mail: sham@thefourseasonshotel.co.uk

AA ★★★ · Scottish Tourist Board ★★★ Small Hotel · Best Loved Hotels · Scotland's Hotels of Distinction

Readers are requested to mention this FHG guidebook when seeking accommodation

Strathyre

ARDOCH LODGE

A haven for nature lovers.

The perfect place to relax and unwind.
Beautiful large grounds with great walking straight from the door and cycle path nearby.
Good local restaurants and pubs.
Pets welcome. Short breaks available.

Telephone 01877 384666 or email ardoch@btinternet.com for a brochure on our two log cabins and cottage.

Ardoch Lodge, Strathyre,
near Callander FK18 8NF
www.ardochlodge.co.uk

Aberfeldy

Small town standing on both sides of Uriar Burn near its confluence with the River Tay. Pitlochry 8 miles.

SHEILA AND PETER CAMPBELL, DULL FARM HOLIDAY LODGES, ABERFELDY PH15 2JQ (01887 820270). Luxury accommodation in 2 pine lodges on small farm. Fully equipped, well maintained; completely fenced. Panoramic views. Touring, walking, fishing, golf. Short Breaks available.
e-mail: info@dullfarm.freeserve.co.uk website: www.self-cateringperthshire.com

LOCH TAY LODGES, REMONY, ACHARN, ABERFELDY PH15 2HR (01887 830209). Enjoy hill walking, golf, sailing or touring. Salmon and trout fishing available. Log fires. Pets welcome. Walks along loch shore from house. STB ★★★ SELF CATERING in village close to Loch. For brochure, contact MRS P. W. DUNCAN MILLAR at above address. [🐕]
e-mail: remony@btinternet.com website: www.lochtaylodges.co.uk

FORTINGALL HOTEL, ABERFELDY PH15 2NQ (Tel/Fax: 01887 830367). Award winning hotel set in thatched village of Fortinghall, Perthshire. With 11 luxury en suite bedrooms the hotel offers first class 21st century facilities in a Victorian setting. STB ★★★★ Hotel. [Pets £15 per night, £50 per week].
e-mail: hotel@fortinghallhotel.com website: wwwfortinghallhotel.com

Crieff

Town and resort 16 miles west of Perth.

CRIEFF HYDRO, CRIEFF PH7 3LQ. Enjoy the flexibility of self-catering with all the benefits of a resort hotel on your doorstep. Dogs are welcome in a range of 3-5 Star acccommodation and there are also pet-friendly Executive Studio suites. Call 01764 651670 (8am-9pm daily).
website: www.crieffhydro.com

Killin

Village at confluence of Rivers Dochart and Lochay at head of Loch Tay.

GILL & DAVE HUNT, THE STEADING, WESTER LIX, KILLIN FK21 8RD (01567 820990 & 07747 862641). Jonna's Cottage has been refurbished and redecorated and has washing machine, freezer, oven, Sky TV, sauna, wood-burning stove. Well behaved pets welcome by arrangement. [Pets £15 per week for first pet, then £5 per pet]
e-mail: gill@westerlix.net website: www.westerlix.net

Kinloch Rannoch

Village at foot of Loch Rannoch.

KILVRECHT CAMP SITE, KINLOCH RANNOCH, PERTHSHIRE (01350 727284; Fax: 01350 727811). Secluded campsite on a level open area in quiet, secluded woodland setting. Fishing available for brown trout on Loch Rannoch. Several trails begin from campsite. Please write, fax or telephone for further information. [🐕]
e-mail: hamish.murray@forestry.gsi.gov.uk

Lochearnhead

Village at head of Lochearn 6 miles South of Killin.

CLACHAN COTTAGE HOTEL, LOCHEARNHEAD FK19 8PU (01567 830247; Fax: 01567 830300). Well placed in central Scotland for touring. Excellent walking, mountain biking and fishing. Water-sports available from the hotel. Award-winning "Taste of Scotland" restaurant. [🐕]
website: www.clachancottagehotel.com

St Fillans

Village at foot of Lochearn, 5 miles west of Comrie.

THE FOUR SEASONS HOTEL, ST FILLANS PH6 2NF (01764 685333). Ideal holiday venue for pets and their owners. Spectacular Highland scenery, walking, fishing, watersports. Wonderful food. Full details on request. STB ★★★ Hotel, AA ★★★ and 2 Red Rosettes, Which? Hotel Guide, Johansens, Best Loved Hotels. [🐕]
e-mail: sham@thefourseasonshotel.co.uk website: www.thefourseasonshotel.co.uk

Strathyre

Village set in centre of Strathyre State Forest.

YVONNE & JOHN HOWES, ARDOCH LODGE, STRATHYRE FK18 8NF (01877 384666). Two log cabins and cottage in wonderful mountain scenery, excellent touring base. Comfortably furnished and well equipped. Pets most welcome. STB ★★★★ SELF CATERING. [pw! 🐕]
e-mail: ardoch@btinternet.com website: www.ardochlodge.co.uk

Symbols

🐕 Indicates that pets are welcome free of charge.

£ Indicates that a charge is made for pets: nightly or weekly.

pw! Shows some special provision for pets; exercise facility, feeding or accommodation arrangement.

⌂ Indicates separate pets accommodation.

THE BELLACHROY
The Oldest Inn on Mull — Est. 1608

e-mail: info@thebellachroy.co.uk
www.thebellachroy.co.uk

The Bellachroy is the oldest Inn on Mull, an historic drovers' Inn renowned for quality home cooked food, where you will receive a warm welcome and genuine hospitality. 6 en suite bedrooms and characterful bars. Stunning location for exploring and touring. Open all year round. Well behaved dogs welcome.

The Bellachroy, Dervaig, Isle of Mull PA75 6QW • Tel: 01688 400314

"Torlochan", Isle of Mull

Torlochan is a small croft situated in the centre of the Isle of Mull, with views over Loch na Keal. It is an ideal base from which to explore all of Mull.

We have two comfortable spacious log cabins, which are well fitted out. They can sleep 4 people and cost from £350 per week; short winter breaks from £60 per night.

The Farmhouse has a lounge, kitchen/dining room, two sitting rooms with open fire and log stove. It sleeps 6 people from £595 per week and can sleep 8 when using a separate log cabin with twin bedroom for an additional £200 per week.

More information from: ***Hylda Marsh, Baliscate House, Tobermory, Isle of Mull PA75 6QA***
Tel: 01688 302048 • Fax: 01688 302251
e-mail: info@islandholidaycottages.com • www.torlochan.com

Dervaig

Village on Mull 5 miles west of Tobermory.

THE BELLACHROY, DERVAIG, MULL PA75 6QW (01688 400314). The oldest Inn on Mull, renowned for quality home cooked food, a warm welcome and genuine hospitality. 6 en suite bedrooms and characterful bars. Open all year round. Well behaved dogs welcome. STB ★★★ Inn [🐕]
e-mail: info@thebellachroy.co.uk website: www.thebellachroy.co.uk

Torlochan

Situated in the centre of Mull, 20 minutes from Tobermory and 25 minutes from Craignure.

TORLOCHAN, GRULINE, ISLE OF MULL. Situated in centre of Mull with views over Loch na Keal, two log cabins and a farmhouse for self-catering. [£10 per dog per week; other pets free]
e-mail: info@islandholidaycottages.com www.torlochan.com/www.islandholidaycottages.com

Other specialised holiday guides from FHG

PUBS & INNS OF BRITAIN • **COUNTRY HOTELS** OF BRITAIN
WEEKEND & SHORT BREAK HOLIDAYS IN BRITAIN
THE GOLF GUIDE WHERE TO PLAY, WHERE TO STAY
500 GREAT PLACES TO STAY • SELF-CATERING HOLIDAYS IN BRITAIN
BED & BREAKFAST STOPS • CARAVAN & CAMPING HOLIDAYS
FAMILY BREAKS IN BRITAIN

Published annually: available in all good bookshops or direct from the publisher:
FHG Guides, Abbey Mill Business Centre, Seedhill, Paisley PA1 1TJ
Tel: 0141 887 0428 • Fax: 0141 889 7204
e-mail: admin@fhguides.co.uk • www.holidayguides.com

Kirkwall, South Ronaldsay, Stenness

Point of Ness Caravan & Camping Site • Stromness

Stromness is a small, picturesque town with impressive views of the hills of Hoy. The site is one mile from the harbour in a quiet, shoreline location. Many leisure activities are available close by, including fishing, sea angling, golf and a swimming & fitness centre. For details contact: Department of Education & Recreation Services, Orkney Islands Council, Kirkwall, Orkney KW15 1NY • Tel: 01856 873535 ext. 2415

Graded "Very Good" by VisitScotland

BLINKBONNY SELF-CATERING HOLIDAY HOMES, NEAR KIRKWALL

3-bedroom houses • 2-bedroom houses

Superb views of Scapa Flow • Fully fitted modern kitchens • Well behaved dogs welcome • Open all year.

For details phone 07796 858569 (day)
01856 870208 (evenings/weekends)
enquiries@blinkbonny.com • www.blinkbonny.com

Banks of Orkney Self-catering and B&B

Two cottages (STB ★★★) and converted barn (STB ★★★★). Located close to ferries, with stunning views over the Pentland Firth. Each cottage sleeps up to 4, and the barn sleeps 5/7. Licensed restaurant on site. For details contact:
Carole & Malcolm, Banks of Orkney, South Ronaldsay KW17 2RW
Tel: 01856 831605 • www.banksoforkney.co.uk

Outbrecks in Orkney offer exceptional and unique self-catering cottages. Open all year – dogs welcome

Within an outstanding National Scenic Area, unwind and relax in comfort, explore the spectacular surrounding countryside and view incredible skies and sunsets. All our non-smoking accommodation is situated within its own private acres of dog-walking fields, in fabulous sea and loch locations by the archaeological World Heritage Site in Stenness. Each cottage is within 200 metres of the shore, except for Harefields (which nestles in its own land). Please check our website for availability.

Harefields (sleeping up to 8) **Raingoose** (sleeping up to 5) and **Pine Trees** (sleeping 2) are all superbly finished, individually designed and spacious. Each, with its own garden, commands fabulous views and has plenty of space to exercise your dog. (£220 - £600 per week inclusive of electricity and linen).

Selkiebay, **Teeo** and **Scootie** Cottages at Outbrecks (each sleeping up to 4) are delightfully converted from late 19th Century farm buildings, set in stunning scenery and with large private lawn and dog-walking fields. (£190 - £330 per week)

Contact: Adrian and Lesley Francis, Outbrecks, Stenness, Orkney, KW16 3EY

Tel: 01856 851 223 • E-mail: accommodation@outbreckscottages-orkney.co.uk • www.outbreckscottages-orkney.co.uk

Kirkwall

An old traditional stone built port and Orkney's second main town, situated on the south western tip of the mainland on the shores of Hamnavoe.

POINT OF NESS CARAVAN & CAMPING SITE, STROMNESS. The site is one mile from the harbour in a quiet, shoreline location. Many leisure activities are available close by, including fishing, sea angling, golf and a swimming & fitness centre. For details contact: DEPARTMENT OF EDUCATION & RECREATION SERVICES, ORKNEY ISLANDS COUNCIL, KIRKWALL, ORKNEY KW15 1NY (01856 873535 ext. 2415. [🐕]

BLINKBONNY SELF-CATERING HOLIDAY HOMES, NEAR KIRKWALL. 3-bedroom houses, 2-bedroom houses. Superb views of Scapa Flow. Fully fitted modern kitchens. Well behaved dogs welcome. Open all year. For details phone 07796 858569 (day); 01856 870208 (evenings/weekends). [Pets £15 per week.]
e-mail: enquiries@blinkbonny.com website: www.blinkbonny.com

South Ronaldsay

Most southerly of the main islands of Orkney .

BANKS OF ORKNEY SELF-CATERING AND B&B. Two cottages (STB ★★★) and converted barn (STB ★★★★). Located close to ferries, with stunning views over the Pentland Firth. Each cottage sleeps up to 4, and the barn sleeps 5/7. Licensed restaurant on site. For details contact: CAROLE & MALCOLM, BANKS OF ORKNEY, SOUTH RONALDSAY KW17 2RW (01856 831605).
website: www.banksoforkney.co.uk

Stenness

Locality on mainland at SE of Loch Steness 4 miles west of Finstown.

ADRIAN AND LESLEY FRANCIS, OUTBRECKS, STENNESS KW16 3EY (01856 851 223) Exceptional self-catering cottages in fabulous sea and loch locations in outstanding National Scenic Area. Sleep 2-8. Open all year. Non-smoking. Dogs welcome. STB ★★★/★★★★.
e-mail: accommodation@outbreckscottages-orkney.co.uk
website: www.outbreckscottages-orkney.co.uk

Outer Hebrides

Isle of Harris

Carminish House Bed and Breakfast

Secluded, spacious, traditionally built B&B, with one double and two twin en suite rooms, lounge with panoramic views over the Sound of Harris. Payphone, satellite TV, Wi-Fi. Ideal place to explore the Western Isles. Garden and parking. Full Scottish breakfast. Excellent local places to eat. Non-smoking. Children and pets welcome.
Contact Howard and Sallie Lomas, 1A Strond, Leverburgh, Isle of Harris HS5 3UD
Tel: 01859 520400 • E-mail: info@carminish.com • www.carminish.com

Leverburgh

Village on S.W. Coast of Harris 4 miles N.W. of Rennish Point.

HOWARD AND SALLIE LOMAS, CARMINISH HOUSE, 1A STROND, LEVERBURGH HS5 3UD (01859 520400) Secluded, spacious, traditionally built B&B, one double and two twin en suite rooms. Panoramic views. Payphone, satellite TV, Wi-Fi. Garden and parking. Non-smoking. Children and pets welcome. STB ★★★★.
e-mail: info@carminish.com website: www.carminish.com

Visit the FHG website

www.holidayguides.com

for details of the wide choice of accommodation

featured in the full range of FHG titles

Wales

Conwy Valley, Snowdonia, p394

Self-catering woodland lodges in Pembrokeshire, p405

Narrowboats in the Brecon Beacons National Park. p418

Looking for Holiday Accommodation?

FHG
K·U·P·E·R·A·R·D

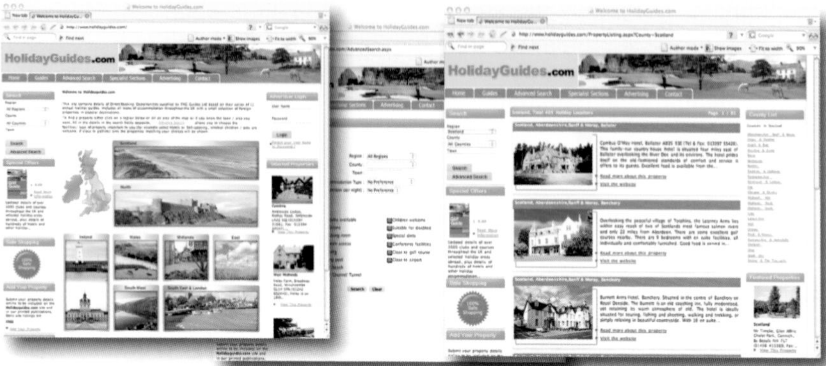

for details of hundreds of properties throughout the UK, visit our website

www.holidayguides.com

Symbols

🐕 Indicates that pets are welcome free of charge.

£ Indicates that a charge is made for pets: nightly or weekly.

pw! Shows some special provision for pets; exercise facility, feeding or accommodation arrangement.

⌂ Indicates separate pets accommodation.

"QUALITY COTTAGES', CERBID, SOLVA, HAVERFORDWEST, PEMBROKESHIRE SA62 6YE (01348 837871). Cottages set in all coastal areas, enjoy unashamed luxury, highest residential standards. Log fires. Linen supplied. Pets welcome, free. [pw! 🐕]
website: www.qualitycottages.co.uk

Around the magnificent coast of Wales
Pembrokeshire, Cardigan Bay, Snowdonia, Anglesey, Lleyn Peninsula, Borders
Choose from over 300
Quality Cottages

Pets Welcome Free

A small specialist agency with over 40 years experience letting quality cottages.

Enjoy unashamed luxury in traditional Welsh Cottages. Situated near safe sandy beaches and in the heart of Wales — famed for scenery, walks, wild flowers, birds, badgers and foxes.

Pets welcome FREE at most of our properties

Leonard Rees, Quality Cottages, Cerbid,
Solva, Haverfordwest, Pembrokeshire.
SA62 6YE

Telephone: (01348) 837871
for our FREE Colour Brochure

QUALITY COTTAGES
CERBID

www.qualitycottages.co.uk

100s of pictures of quality cottages
and beautiful Wales

Around the magnificent coast of Wales
Pembrokeshire, Cardigan Bay, Snowdonia, Anglesey, Lleyn Peninsula, Borders
Choose from over 300
Quality Cottages

Pets Welcome Free

A small specialist agency with over 40 years experience letting quality cottages.

Enjoy unashamed luxury in traditional Welsh Cottages. Situated near safe sandy beaches and in the heart of Wales — famed for scenery, walks, wild flowers, birds, badgers and foxes.

Pets welcome FREE at most of our properties

Leonard Rees, Quality Cottages, Cerbid, Solva, Haverfordwest, Pembrokeshire. SA62 6YE

Telephone: (01348) 837871
for our FREE Colour Brochure

QUALITY COTTAGES
CERBID

www.qualitycottages.co.uk

100s of pictures of quality cottages and beautiful Wales

• TY GWYN • two-bedroomed luxury caravan in private grounds. Situated just two miles from Bala in beautiful country area, ideal for walking, sailing, fishing and canoeing. Only 30 miles from seaside.

Contact: **MRS A. SKINNER, TY GWYN, RHYDUCHAF, BALA LL23 7SD**

Tel: 01678 521267

OGWEN VALLEY HOLIDAYS

1 PENGARREG, NANT FFRANCON, BETHESDA, BANGOR LL57 3LX

Spectacular Snowdonia

Ty Pengarreg Cottage Flat for two, £169-£319pw.
Pen y Graig Old Farm Cottage for six, £259-£599pw.
Comfortable and welcoming with spectacular views.

Tel: 01248 600122

e-mail: jilljones@ogwensnowdonia.co.uk www.ogwensnowdonia.co.uk

Llwyndu Farmhouse

Llanaber, Barmouth, Gwynedd LL42 1RR

16th century farmhouse hotel. Stunning location with views over Cardigan Bay and its huge sandy beaches. All bedroom en suite and very individual, some in converted granary. Super food, local beers and good wine list. Cosy, informal atmosphere amidst oak beams, inglenooks and history.

Tel: 01341 280144

e-mail: intouch@llwyndu-farmhouse.co.uk

www.llwyndu-farmhouse.co.uk

- Comfortable three-bedroomed house
- Enclosed garden • Near beaches, common, forest
- Fully equipped; bedding and electricity inclusive
- Colour TV/video, microwave • Dogs and children welcome. WTB ★★★

Croeso

£220 to £410 per week

MRS J. GUNDRY, FARMYARD LODGE, BODORGAN, ANGLESEY LL62 5LW • Tel: 01407 840977

Plas-Y-Bryn Chalet Park

Bontnewydd, Near Caernarfon LL54 7YE

Tel: 01286 672811

Our small park is situated two miles from the historic town of Caernarfon. Set into a walled garden it offers safety, seclusion and beautiful views of Snowdonia. It is ideally positioned for touring the area. Shop and village pub nearby.

A selection of chalets and caravans available at prices from £195 (low season) to £445 (high season) per week for the caravans and £140 (low season) to £580 (high season) per week for the chalets. Well behaved pets always welcome.

WTB ★★★★ **www.plasybrynholidayscaernarfon.co.uk**

Criccieth, Dulas Bay

❖ Rhos Country Cottages ❖

A superb collection of secluded country cottages with private gardens, surrounded by wildflower meadows. Chill out, relax and listen to birdsong; walk the Lleyn Coastal Path from the garden gate or explore the Snowdonia National Park. Private fishing and rough shooting by arrangement.

The cottages are heated and really warm in winter.

Open all year. VisitWales ★★★★★ Quality Award

Rhos Country Cottages, Criccieth, Porthmadog LL52 0PB

Telephone: 0776 986 4642 or 01758 720047

e-mail: cottages@rhos.freeserve.co.uk www.rhos-cottages.co.uk

PARC WERNOL PARK • Chwilog, Pwllheli LL53 6SW • 01766 810506

- Panoramic views • Peaceful and quiet
- Ideal for touring Lleyn and Snowdonia
- 4 miles Criccieth and Pwllheli
- 3 miles beach • Cycle route
- Free coarse fishing lake • Safe children's play area
- Games room • Footpaths • Dog exercise field
- Self-catering holidays • 1,2 & 3 bedroom cottages
- 2 and 3 bedroom caravans and chalets
- Colour brochure • Personal attention at all times
- A truly Welsh welcome.

www.wernol.co.uk

A warm welcome awaits you in comfortable self-catering cottages. Easily accessible to numerous attractions, or enjoy tranquillity of countryside.

From £125-£400. Short breaks (min 2 nights) from £80. Pets welcome.

MRS M. WILLIAMS, GAERWEN FARM, YNYS, CRICCIETH, GWYNEDD LL52 0NU
Tel: 01766 810324
e-mail: gaerwen@btopenworld.com
www.gaerwenfarmcottages.co.uk

TYDDYN HEILYN

CHWILOG, CRICCIETH LL53 6SW • Tel: 01766 810441

Comfortably renovated Welsh stone cottage with character. Cosy, double-glazed, centrally heated and enjoying mild Gulf Stream climate with holiday letting anytime. Two bedrooms with sea views. Ample grounds with enclosed garden with doggy walk. Positioned on Llyn Peninsula, 3 miles Criccieth, on edge Snowdonia, with 1½ mile tree-lined walk to beach. Very central for touring.

Tai Gwyliau DWYFACH Country Cottages

Tel: 01766 810208 • *5 Star cottages near Criccieth.*

Luxury cottages, superbly equipped. Ideal place to unwind and relax. Special rates off season. Exciting choice of eating places nearby. Brochure.

S. Edwards, Pen-y-Bryn, Chwilog, Pwllheli, Gwynedd LL53 6SX

e-mail: info@dwyfach.co.uk • www.dwyfach.co.uk

Beautiful Victorian Country House standing in 20 acres of woodland, gardens and fields. High standard of accommodation in family, twin and double rooms, all en suite. Pets welcome. Stabling/grazing available.

★★★★

MRS G. McCREADIE, DERI ISAF, DULAS BAY LL70 9DX

Tel: 01248 410536 • Mobile: 07721 374471

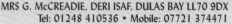

e-mail: mccreadie@deriisaf.freeserve.co.uk • www.angleseyfarms.com/deri.htm

Dyffryn Ardudwy, Holyhead, Pentraeth, Trearddur Bay

Pentre Mawr Farm ❖

Relax in the peace and quiet of this working farm situated between Barmouth and Harlech. Inglenook fireplaces, spacious en suite bedrooms, and a homely atmosphere. Village shops, pubs. Cambrian Coast station and beach all within walking distance. Ample parking. Pets welcome. No children under 12. Phone Sue Owen for a colour brochure.

Dyffryn Ardudwy, Gwynedd LL44 2ES

Tel: 01341 247 413 www.pentre-mawr.co.uk

WALKERS WELCOME CROESO CERDDWYR · CYCLISTS WELCOME CROESO BEICWYR

★★★★ Farmhouse

Boathouse Hotel

Tranquil setting overlooking the harbour • Ferry terminal 4 minutes On the edge of country park and marina • Luxury en suite bedrooms at affordable prices • Seafood a speciality • Bar snacks and chef's specials • Lunches and afternoon teas • Ample free parking

BOATHOUSE HOTEL • NEWRY BEACH • HOLYHEAD • ANGLESEY LL65 1YF

Tel: 01407 762094 • www.boathouse-hotel.co.uk

e-mail: boathousehotel@supanet.com

Pen-y-Garnedd Farm Cottage

Near Pentraeth, Isle of Anglesey. Telephone bookings: 01248 450580

Fully refurbished detached cottage on a working smallholding. Electric heating and logburner in lounge. TV/DVD, stereo. One double bedroom; second bedroom with bunk beds and single bed. Fully equipped kitchen. Bathroom with power shower. Enclosed garden. Close to beaches and coastal walks. Low Season Short Breaks. Caravan Club Approved Site (CCL5)

Well behaved children and pets welcome. Open all Year.

Cliff Cottages and Plas Darien Apartments

All year round holidays and short breaks in a choice of centrally heated apartments with wonderful sea views or stone-built cottages in village-like situation very near sea.

Own private indoor heated swimming pools, saunas, snooker, table tennis. Outdoor heated pool, tennis courts, badminton, small golf, bowls. Adjacent 18-hole golf course, horse riding, windsurfing, canoeing, fishing.

Phone or write for brochure:
Plas Darien
The Cliff
Trearddur Bay
Anglesey LL65 2UR

Tel: 01407 860789
Fax: 01407 861150
www.plasdarien.com

Trearddur Bay

Comfortable self-catering holiday bungalows sleeping 2-7 near Trearddur's lovely beaches. Indoor heated swiming pool, licensed club, tennis court. Local, beautiful headland walks, fishing, golf and horse riding.Ideal location to explore Anglesey and the North Wales coast; near Holyhead.

TREARDDUR HOLIDAY BUNGALOWS

LON ISALLT TREARDDUR BAY ANGLESEY LL65 2UP

Tel: 01407 860494 • e-mail: trearholiday@btconnect.com • www.holiday-bungalows.co.uk

"QUALITY COTTAGES', CERBID, SOLVA, HAVERFORDWEST, PEMBROKESHIRE SA62 6YE (01348 837871). Cottages set in all coastal areas, enjoy unashamed luxury, highest residential standards. Log fires. Linen supplied. Pets welcome free. [pw!]
website: www.qualitycottages.co.uk

Bala

Natural touring centre for Snowdonia. Narrow gauge railway runs along side of Bala lake, the largest natural lake in Wales. Golf, sailing, fishing, canoeing.

TY GWYN - two-bedroomed luxury caravan in private grounds. Situated just two miles from Bala in beautiful country area, ideal for walking, sailing, fishing and canoeing. Only 30 miles from seaside. Contact: MRS A. SKINNER, TY GWYN, RHYDUCHAF, BALA LL23 7SD (01678 521267). [ ]

Bangor

Cathedral town and resort on Menai Strait.

OGWEN VALLEY HOLIDAYS, 1 PENGARREG, NANT FFRANCON, BETHESDA, BANGOR LL57 3LX (01248 600122). Spectacular Snowdonia. Cottage flat for two, cottage for six. Comfortable and welcoming with spectacular views. Superb walking. Near River Ogwen, cycle track and dog-walking lane. WTB ★★★★. [Pets £30 per week].
e-mail: jilljones@ogwensnowdonia.co.uk website: www.ogwensnowdonia.co.uk

Barmouth

Modern seaside resort with two miles of sandy beaches. Surrounding hills full of interesting archaeological remains.

LAWRENNY LODGE, BARMOUTH LL42 1SU (01341 280466). Eight bedroom guest accommodation (seven en suite) overlooking the harbour and estuary and only five minutes from beach. Perfect area for long walkies. Evening meal available. Varied restaurant menu, residential licence and private car park. [ ]
e-mail: enquiries@lawrennylodge.co.uk website: www.lawrennylodge.co.uk

MRS PAULA THOMPSON, LLWYNDU FARMHOUSE, LLANABER, BARMOUTH LL42 1RR (01341 280144). Converted 16th century farmhouse retaining many original features. Cosy lounge and character dining room. Bedrooms are modern and well equipped, some with four-poster beds. WTB ★★★★ [ ]
e-mail: intouch@llwyndu-farmhouse.co.uk website: www.llwyndu-farmhouse.co.uk

Beaumaris

Elegant little town dominated by castle built by Edward I in 13th century. Museum of Childhood has Victorian toys and music boxes.

'QUALITY COTTAGES', CERBID, SOLVA, HAVERFORDWEST, PEMBROKESHIRE SA62 6YE (01348 837871). Cottages set in all coastal areas, enjoy unashamed luxury, highest residential standards. Log fires. Linen supplied. Pets welcome free. [pw!]
website: www.qualitycottages.co.uk

Bodorgan

A rural area in South West Anglesey.

CROESO. Comfortable three-bedroomed house. Enclosed garden. Near beaches, common, forest. Fully equipped, bedding and electricity inclusive. Colour TV/video, microwave. Dogs and children welcome. £220-£410 per week. WTB ★★★ [🐕] Contact: MRS J. GUNDRY, FARMYARD LODGE, BODORGAN, ANGLESEY LL62 5LW (01407 840977).

Caernarfon

Historic walled town and resort, ideal for touring Snowdonia. Museums, Segontium Roman Fort, magnificent 13th century castle. Old harbour, sailing trips.

PLAS-Y-BRYN CHALET PARK, BONTNEWYDD, NEAR CAERNARFON LL54 7YE (01286 672811). Two miles from Caernarfon. It offers safety, seclusion and beautiful views of Snowdonia. Ideally positioned for touring. Well behaved pets always welcome. WTB ★★★★ [Pets £20 per week].
website: www.plasybrynholidayscaernarfon.co.uk

Criccieth

Popular family resort with safe beaches divided by ruins of 13th century castle. Salmon and sea trout fishing. Festival of Music and Arts in the summer.

MRS A. M. JONES, RHOS COUNTRY COTTAGES, CRICCIETH, PORTHMADOG LL52 0PB (01758 720047 or 0776 986 4642). Superb collection of secluded country cottages with private gardens. Private fishing and rough shooting by arrangement. Open all year. VisitWales ★★★★★ [🐕]
e-mail: cottages@rhos.freeserve.co.uk website: www.rhos-cottages.co.uk

PARC WERNOL PARK, CHWILOG, PWLLHELI LL53 6SW (01766 810506). Peaceful and quiet, ideal for touring. Self-catering holidays – 1,2 & 3 bedroom cottages, 2 and 3 bedroom caravans and chalets. Colour brochure. [Pets £10 per week.]
website: www.wernol.co.uk

A warm welcome awaits you in comfortable self-catering cottages. Easily accessible to numerous attractions, or enjoy tranquillity of countryside. Short breaks available. Pets welcome. MRS M. WILLIAMS, GAERWEN FARM, YNYS, CRICCIETH LL52 0NU (01766 810324).[🐕]
e-mail: gaerwen@btopenworld.com website: www.gaerwenfarmcottages.co.uk

MRS ANN WILLIAMS, TYDDYN HEILYN, CHWILOG, CRICCIETH LL53 6SW (01766 810441). Comfortably renovated Welsh stone cottage. Double-glazed, centrally heated and enjoying mild Gulf Stream climate. Ample grounds with enclosed garden with doggy walk. 1½ mile tree-lined walk to beach. [🐕]

'QUALITY COTTAGES', CERBID, SOLVA, HAVERFORDWEST, PEMBROKESHIRE SA62 6YE (01348 837871). Cottages set in all coastal areas, enjoy unashamed luxury, highest residential standards. Log fires. Linen supplied. Pets welcome free. [pw! 🐕]
website: www.qualitycottages.co.uk

TAI GWYLIAU DWYFACH COUNTRY COTTAGES. 5 Star cottages near Criccieth. Luxury cottages, superbly equipped. Ideal place to unwind and relax. Special rates off season. Exciting choice of eating places nearby. Contact S. EDWARDS, PEN-Y-BRYN, CHWILOG, PWLLHELI, GWYNEDD LL53 6SX (01766 810208). [One dog free.]
e-mail: info@dwyfach.co.uk website: www.dwyfach.co.uk

Dulas Bay

On north-east coast of Anglesey, between Amlwch and Moelfre.

MRS G. McCREADIE, DERI ISAF, DULAS BAY LL70 9DX (01248 410536; Mobile: 07721 374471). Victorian Country House in 20 acres of woodland, gardens and fields. Family, twin and double rooms, all en suite. Pets welcome. Stabling/grazing available. WTB ★★★★ Country House [Dogs £2.50 per night]
e-mail: mccreadie@deriisaf.freeserve.co.uk website: www.angleseyfarms.com/deri.htm

Dyffryn Ardudwy

Village 5 miles north of Barmouth.

SUE OWEN, PENTRE MAWR FARM, DYFFRYN ARDUDWY LL44 2ES. (01341 247413). Working farm between Barmouth and Harlech. Inglenook fireplaces, spacious en suite bedrooms, and a homely atmosphere.Village shops, pubs, beach all within walking distance. Ample parking. No children under 12. WTB ★★★★ Farmhouse [Pets £10 per stay].
website: www.pentre-mawr.co.uk

Harlech

Small stone-built town dominated by remains of 13th century castle. Golf, theatre, swimming pool, fine stretch of sands

'QUALITY COTTAGES', CERBID, SOLVA, HAVERFORDWEST, PEMBROKESHIRE SA62 6YE (01348 837871). Cottages set in all coastal areas, enjoy unashamed luxury, highest residential standards. Log fires. Linen supplied. Pets welcome free. [pw!]
website: www.qualitycottages.co.uk

Holyhead

Port & industrial town on Holy Island, Anglesey.

BOATHOUSE HOTEL, NEWRY BEACH, HOLYHEAD, ANGLESEY LL65 1YF (01407 762094). Tranquil setting overlooking the harbour; on edge of country park and marina. Luxury en suite bedrooms. Seafood a speciality. Ample free parking.
e-mail: boathousehotel@supanet.com website: www.boathouse-hotel.co.uk

Llanddona

Village on Anglesey 3 miles north west of Beaumaris.

'QUALITY COTTAGES', CERBID, SOLVA, HAVERFORDWEST, PEMBROKESHIRE SA62 6YE (01348 837871). Cottages set in all coastal areas, enjoy unashamed luxury, highest residential standards. Log fires. Linen supplied. Pets welcome free. [pw!]
website: www.qualitycottages.co.uk

Morfa Nefyn

Picturesque village 2 miles west of Nefyn.

'QUALITY COTTAGES', CERBID, SOLVA, HAVERFORDWEST, PEMBROKESHIRE SA62 6YE (01348 837871). Cottages set in all coastal areas, enjoy unashamed luxury, highest residential standards. Log fires. Linen supplied. Pets welcome free. [pw!]
website: www.qualitycottages.co.uk

Pentraeth

Village on Anglesey, near Red Wharf Bay.

PEN-Y-GARNEDD HOLIDAY COTTAGE, PENTRAETH. (01248 450580). Cosy cottage on friendly working small-holding. Sleeps 5, log burner and heating. Well behaved children and pets welcome. Close to beaches and coastal Wales. Low Season Short Breaks. Caravan Club Approved Site. WTB ★★★ [Pets £10 per week].

Symbols

Indicates that pets are welcome free of charge.

£ Indicates that a charge is made for pets: nightly or weekly.

pw! Shows some special provision for pets; exercise facility, feeding or accommodation arrangement.

⌂ Indicates separate pets accommodation.

Porthmadog

Harbour town with mile-long Cob embankment, along which runs Ffestiniog Narrow Gauge Steam Railway to Blaenau Ffestiniog. Pottery, maritime museum, car museum. Good beaches nearby.

'QUALITY COTTAGES', CERBID, SOLVA, HAVERFORDWEST, PEMBROKESHIRE SA62 6YE (01348 837871). Cottages set in all coastal areas, enjoy unashamed luxury, highest residential standards. Log fires. Linen supplied. Pets welcome free. [pw!]
website: www.qualitycottages.co.uk

Red Wharf Bay

Deep curving bay with vast expanse of sand, very popular for sailing and swimming.

'QUALITY COTTAGES', CERBID, SOLVA, HAVERFORDWEST, PEMBROKESHIRE SA62 6YE (01348 837871). Cottages set in all coastal areas, enjoy unashamed luxury, highest residential standards. Log fires. Linen supplied. Pets welcome free. [pw!]
website: www.qualitycottages.co.uk

Trearddur Bay

Attractive holiday spot set amongst low cliffs on Holy Island, near Holyhead. Golf, sailing, fishing and swimming.

CLIFF COTTAGES AND PLAS DARIEN APARTMENTS, TREARDDUR BAY LL65 2UR (01407 860789; Fax: 01407 861150). Fully equipped holiday cottages, sleeping 4/8 plus cot. Near sea. Indoor and outdoor heated pools. Colour television. Choice of centrally heated apartments or stone-built cottages. Own private leisure complex with bowls, saunas, snooker, table tennis; tennis courts. Adjacent golf course. [ ]
website: www.plasdarien.com

TREARDDUR HOLIDAY BUNGALOWS, LON ISALLT,TREARDDUR BAY, ANGLESEY LL65 2UP (01407 860494). Comfortable self-catering holiday bungalows sleeping 2-7 near Trearddur's lovely beaches. Locally, beautiful headland walks, fishing, golf and horse riding. Ideal location to explore Anglesey and the North Wales coast. Terms from £100-£580 per week.
e-mail: trearholiday@btconnect.com website: www.holiday-bungalows.co.uk

Tywyn

Pleasant seaside resort, start of Talyllyn Narrow Gauge Railway. Sea and river fishing, golf.

'QUALITY COTTAGES', CERBID, SOLVA, HAVERFORDWEST, PEMBROKESHIRE SA62 6YE (01348 837871). Cottages set in all coastal areas, enjoy unashamed luxury, highest residential standards. Log fires. Linen supplied. Pets welcome free. [pw!]
website: www.qualitycottages.co.uk

Pet-Friendly
Pubs, Inns & Hotels
on pages 424-432
Please note that these establishments may not feature in the main section of this book

Around the magnificent coast of Wales
Pembrokeshire, Cardigan Bay, Snowdonia, Anglesey, Lleyn Peninsula, Borders
Choose from over 300
Quality Cottages

Pets Welcome Free

A small specialist agency with over 40 years experience letting quality cottages.

Enjoy unashamed luxury in traditional Welsh Cottages. Situated near safe sandy beaches and in the heart of Wales — famed for scenery, walks, wild flowers, birds, badgers and foxes.

Pets welcome FREE at most of our properties

Leonard Rees, Quality Cottages, Cerbid,
Solva, Haverfordwest, Pembrokeshire.
SA62 6YE

Telephone: (01348) 837871
for our FREE Colour Brochure

QUALITY COTTAGES
CERBID

www.qualitycottages.co.uk

100s of pictures of quality cottages and beautiful Wales

Seaside Cottages

In Idyllic North Wales – www.waleshols.com

We have a large selection of self-catering seaside and country cottages, bungalows, farmhouses, caravans etc. offering superb, reasonably priced accommodation for owners and their pets. Our brochures contain details of all you need for a wonderful holiday - please telephone for your FREE copies now.

Mann's Holidays, Shaw's Holidays & Snowdonia Tourist Services

01758 701 702 (24 hrs)

www.mannsholidays.com www.shawsholidays.com www.snowdoniatourist.com

Betws-y-Coed, Colwyn Bay, Conwy

Hill farm in Wales. TV, teamaking, en suite. Set in National Park/ Snowdonia. Very quiet and well off the beaten track. A great welcome and good food. Many return visits. £22 B&B.

MISS MORRIS, TY COCH FARM-TREKKING CENTRE, PENMACHNO, BETWS-Y-COED LL25 0HJ
01690 760248 • e-mail: cindymorris@tiscali.co.uk

NORTH WALES HOLIDAYS

Cedarwood Chalets • Cottages • Coach House

High quality cottages, cosy chalets and large coach house for 2-9, overlooking sea at Bron-Y-Wendon or in picturesque valley at Nant-Y-Glyn. 16 units in total. Wide range of facilities with many leisure activities nearby. Short breaks all year. Pets welcome. VisitWales 2-5 Stars.

Bron-Y-Wendon & Nant-Y-Glyn Holiday Parks, Wern Road, Llanddulas, Colwyn Bay LL22 8HG
e-mail: stay@northwales-holidays.co.uk
www.northwales-holidays.co.uk

For colour brochures telephone: 01492 512903/ 512282 or visit our website

Tyn-y-Groes, Near Conwy

Homely Victorian stone cottage in picturesque Conwy valley. Mountain views. Enjoy walking, mountains, beaches, bird watching. Bodnant Gardens, RSPB reserve and Conwy castle, harbour and marina close by. Victorian Llandudno, Betws-y-Coed, Anglesey, Caernarfon and Snowdon easy distance. Good local food and pubs. Enclosed garden, patio furniture. Parking. Gas fired central heating. Lounge with gas fire, dining room, kitchen, utility.

Brongain

Two double bedded rooms, one small single; blankets/duvet provided. Bathroom with bath, shower, toilet and basin. Colour TV, electric cooker, fridge, microwave, washing machine and tumbler dryer. Terms £240-£350; heating, electricity included. Linen extra. Pets welcome. Open all year. No children under five years..

Mrs G. Simpole, 105 Hay Green Road, Terrington-St-Clement, King's Lynn, Norfolk PE34 4PU

Tel: 01553 828897
Mobile: 0798 9080665

Secluded cottages, log fire and beams
Dogs will love it – a place of their dreams
Plenty of walks around mountains and lakes
Cosy and tranquil – it's got what it takes.
It's really a perfect holiday let
For up to 2-7 people, plus their pet(s).

Apply: Mrs Williams
Tel: 01724 733990 or 07711 217 448 (week lets only)

Conwy, Llandudno, Llandyrnog

Sychnant Pass House

Sychnant Pass Road, Conwy LL32 8BJ
Tel: 01492 596868 • Fax: 01492 585486
e-mail: bre@sychnant-pass-house.co.uk
www.sychnant-pass-house.co.uk

Millie and Maisie, our lovely collies, would love to welcome your four-legged friends to their home in the hills above Conwy. Sychnant Pass House is a lovely Victorian House set in two acres with a little pond and stream running through it. Step out of our garden and straight onto Snowdonia National Park land where you can walk for miles with your dogs. Just over two miles from the beach and one-and-a-half miles from Conwy, it is an ideal base from which to tour Wales. All our rooms are en suite, our garden rooms have French windows opening into the garden which are ideal for pets. We have a lovely sitting room that you can share with your best friends after dinner which is served in our informal, friendly restaurant, doggie bags are always available. Your four-legged friends and their folk are most welcome here. ***Bed & Breakfast from £50 per person***

AA ★★★★★ Guest Accommodation

Tal-y-Fan Cottage and Alltwen Cottage

We have two luxurious self-catering country cottages for rental. Newly developed and well appointed, these properties can accommodate up to four people comfortably. They are located nearby the sleepy village of Dwygyfylchi, with spectacular views. Ideal touring centre for Snowdonia, two and a half miles to Conwy, five to Llandudno and Colwyn Bay; three minutes' walk to the village. Pony trekking, golf and fishing locally.

Terms from £395. Suitable for disabled access.
Pets and children welcome. Short Breaks available.
Non-smoking.

Mr John Baxter, Glyn Uchaf,
Conwy Old Road, Dwygyfylchi,
Penmaenmawr, Conwy LL34 6YS
Tel & Fax: 01492 623737/622053

★★★★★

Vine House Bed & Breakfast

23 Church Walks, Llandudno LL30 2HG

Tel: 01492 876493 • www.vinehouse-llandudno.co.uk

Molly (our Cocker Spaniel) will welcome you with a happy bark to our comfortable family-run guest house.

We are situated opposite the Great Orme Tramway, as well as being close to the town centre, Promenade and beach. There are views to the Great Orme or the sea from all rooms.

Pentre Mawr House

Llandyrnog, Denbigh, North Wales LL16 4LA
Tel: 01824 790732
e-mail: info@pentremawrcountryhouse.co.uk
www.pentremawrcountryhouse.co.uk

Molly and Millie, our lovely collies, would love to welcome your four-legged friends to their family's ancestral home of 400 years with woodland, park and riverside meadows, all within easy reach of Chester and the coast. The en suite bedrooms have all the little extras to make your stay special. Two new suites have hot tubs. There is a heated swimming pool in the walled garden and lovely sittingrooms where you can sit with your best friends after dinner. Furry folk and their families are most welcome here. B&B from £50.00

Dinner Award

AA ★★★★★ Guest Accommodation

Llangollen, Rhos-on-Sea

Standing in the glorious and hidden Ceiriog Valley, The Hand at Llanarmon radiates charm and character.

The Hand at Llanarmon

With 13 comfortable en suite bedrooms, roaring log fires, and fabulous food served with flair and generosity, this is a wonderful base for most country pursuits, or just relaxing in good company.

Llanarmon D.C., Ceiriog Valley, Near Llangollen, North Wales LL20 7LD
reception@thehandhotel.co.uk • www.TheHandHotel.co.uk • Tel: 01691 600666

Ted, Fred and Megan are waiting to greet new friends!

The Golden Pheasant is an 18th Century Hotel & Inn ideally situated for pets, especially dogs. The old world charm bar has an open range fire, pews and slate floor and real ale; comfortable lounges and two restaurants which have extensive and imaginative menus, all freshly prepared by our chef.

Accommodation ranges from cosy Inn rooms located in the older part of the building to superior larger bedrooms and four-poster rooms with whirlpool baths, which have wonderful views of the valley.

Situated in the beautiful Ceiriog Valley, which is a heaven for walking, with its unspoilt country lanes, paths with wild flower banks and verges, all with panoramic views of the valley.

2 nights D,B&B from £135 pp. B&B from £90, two sharing. Pets from £5 per night.

Llwynmawr, Glyn Ceiriog, Near Llangollen LL20 7BB

Tel: 01691 718281 • Fax: 01691 718479

AA ★★★

e-mail: info@goldenpheasanthotel.co.uk website: www.goldenpheasanthotel.co.uk

THE GOLDEN PHEASANT Country Hotel & Inn

★★★

Sunnydowns Hotel

★★★ *Quality Hotel*

66 Abbey Road, Rhos-on-Sea, Colwyn Bay, Conwy, North Wales LL28 4NU

Tel: 01492 544256 Fax: 01492 543223

(Proprietor: Mike Willington)

A Non-Smoking Hotel

A 3 star family-run hotel situated in a quiet area and just a two minute level walk to the beach & shops. High standard of comfort and cleanliness, car park, bar, games room with pool table, Nordic sauna, restaurant, TV lounge.

Our restaurant is non-smoking, serving freshly prepared good home cooking. The towns of Llandudno, Colwyn Bay & Conwy are only five minutes' drive away and just ten minutes to the mountains and castles of Snowdonia and the Isle of Anglesey.

OAP discounts, large family rooms & family suites available. All en suite bedrooms have remote control TV (teletext, video & satellite), clock radio, tea/coffee making facilities, hairdyer, mini-bar, refrigerator, telephone and central heating. Available on request are irons, trouser press, room service and laundry service. Broadband internet access available throughout the hotel.

New this year all rooms fitted with personal digital room safe. Microwave available for guests' use. Also a fitness/exercise machine in games room all available free of charge for all our guests.

Dogs are very welcome and can stay at a small charge. They are allowed in your bedroom with you and in the hotel except the restaurant. Meals also served in the bar where dogs are allowed.

For further information, please phone or write for our colour brochure.

e-mail: sunnydowns-hotel@tinyworld.co.uk • www.hotelnorthwales.co.uk

FREE or REDUCED RATE entry to Holiday Visits and Attractions – see our **READERS' OFFER VOUCHERS** on pages 433-440

Rhos-on-Sea

The Northwood

47 Rhos Road, Rhos-on-Sea, Colwyn Bay LL28 4RS

The Northwood is a family-run guesthouse in the heart of Rhos-on-Sea 175 yards from high class shops, promenade & sea. The en suite single, double, twin and family bedrooms are tastefully furnished. All have colour television and hospitality tray with tea/coffee/drinking chocolate, and biscuits. Dinners are available from May to October, vegetarian meals and special dietary needs are available. The menu is changed daily. Dogs get a Welsh sausage for breakfast.

AA ★★★ Guest House

Telephone: 08450 533105
E-mail: welcome@thenorthwood.co.uk
www.thenorthwood.co.uk

'QUALITY COTTAGES', CERBID, SOLVA, HAVERFORDWEST, PEMBROKESHIRE SA62 6YE (01348 837871). Cottages set in all coastal areas, enjoy unashamed luxury, highest residential standards. Log fires. Linen supplied. Pets welcome free. [pw!]
website: www.qualitycottages.co.uk

SEASIDE COTTAGES. MANN'S, SHAW'S AND SNOWDONIA TOURIST SERVICES (01758 701 702). Large selection of self-catering seaside and country cottages, bungalows, farmhouses, caravans etc. offering superb, reasonably priced accommodation for owners and their pets. Please telephone for brochure.
websites: www.mannsholidays.com www.shawsholidays.com www.snowdoniatourist.com

Betws-y-Coed

Popular mountain resort in picturesque setting where three rivers meet. Trout fishing, craft shops, golf, railway and motor museums, Snowdonia National Park Visitor Centre. Nearby Swallow Falls are famous beauty spot.

MISS MORRIS, TY COCH FARM-TREKKING CENTRE, PENMACHNO, BETWS-Y-COED LL25 0HJ (01690 760248). Hill farm in Wales. TV, teamaking, en suite. Set in National Park/Snowdonia. Very quiet and well off the beaten track. A great welcome and good food. Many return visits. £22 B&B. [ ]
e-mail: cindymorris@tiscali.co.uk

Colwyn Bay

Lively seaside resort with promenade amusements. Attractions include Mountain Zoo, Eirias Park; golf, tennis, riding and other sports. Good touring centre for Snowdonia. The quieter resort of Rhos-on-Sea lies at the western end of the bay.

NORTH WALES HOLIDAYS, BRON-Y-WENDON AND NANT-Y-GLYN HOLIDAY PARKS, WERN ROAD, LLANDDULAS, COLWYN BAY LL22 8HG (01492 512903/512282). Cottages with sea views at Bron-Y-Wendon or chalets, cottages and coach house in picturesque valley at Nant-Y-Glyn. 16 units in total. VisitWales 2-5 Stars [Pets £10 per week].
e-mail: stay@northwales-holidays.co.uk website: www.northwales-holidays.co.uk

Conwy

One of the best preserved medieval fortified towns in Britain on dramatic estuary setting. Telford Suspension Bridge, many historic buildings, lively quayside (site of smallest house in Britain). Golf, pony trekking, pleasure cruises.

BRONGAIN, TY'N-Y-GROES, CONWY. Homely Victorian stone cottage, picturesque Conwy Valley. Snowdonia Mountain views. Enjoy lakes, mountains, walking, bird watching, beaches, Bodnant, RSPB, Conwy Castle. £240-£350. Contact: MRS G. M. SIMPOLE, 105 HAYGREEN ROAD, TERRINGTON ST CLEMENT, KINGS LYNN, NORFOLK PE34 4PU (01553 828897; Mobile: 0798 9080 665) [pw!]

SYCHNANT PASS HOUSE, SYCHNANT PASS ROAD, CONWY LL32 8BJ (01492 596868: Fax: 01492 585486). A lovely Victorian House set in two acres with a little pond and stream. Step out of our garden and straight onto Snowdonia National Park land. Walk for miles with your dogs. All rooms en suite. B&B from £50. AA ★★★★★ and Rosette. [ ]
e-mail: bre@sychnant-pass-house.co.uk website: www.sychnant-pass-house.co.uk

TAL-Y-FAN COTTAGE AND ALLTWEN COTTAGE. Two luxurious self-catering country cottages accommodateing up to four people. Spectacular views. Ideal touring centre for Snowdonia. Pony trekking, golf and fishing locally. Pets and children welcome. Short Breaks available. Non-smoking. Contact: Mr John Baxter, Glyn Uchaf, Conwy Old Road, Dwygyfylchi, Penmaenmawr, Conwy LL34 6YS (Tel & Fax: 01492 623737/622053) WTB ★★★★★. [🐕]
website: www.glyn-uchaf.co.uk

Conwy Valley

Fertile valley with wood and moor rising on both sides. Many places of interest in the area.

Secluded cottages with log fire and beams. Dogs will love it. Plenty of walks around mountains and lakes. For 2 - 7 people plus their pet(s). MRS WILLIAMS (01724 733990 or 07711 217 448) week lets only. [🐕]

Llandudno

Coastal resort at base of Peninsula running out to Great Ormes Head.

VINE HOUSE BED & BREAKFAST, 23 CHURCH WALKS, LLANDUDNO LL30 2HG (01492 876493). Molly (our Cocker Spaniel) will welcome you with a happy bark to our comfortable family-run guest house. Opposite the Great Orme Tramway, and close to the town centre, Promenade and beach. [Pets £3 per night]
website: www.vinehouse-llandudno.co.uk

Llandyrnog

Village 4 miles east of Denbigh.

PENTRE MAWR COUNTRY HOUSE, LLANDYRNOG LL16 4LA (01824 790732) Ancestral home of 400 years with woodland, park and riverside meadows, within easy reach of Chester and coast. Heated swimming pool. All rooms en suite. Pets most welcome. AA ★★★★★ and Dinner Award [🐕]
e-mail: info@pentremawrcountryhouse.co.uk www.pentremawrcountryhouse.co.uk

Llangollen

Famous for International Music Eisteddfod held in July. Plas Newydd, Valle Crucis Abbey nearby. Standard gauge steam railway; canal cruises; ideal for golf and walking.

THE HAND AT LLANARMON, LLANARMON D.C., CEIRIOG VALLEY, NEAR LLANGOLLEN LL20 7LD (01691 600666). Standing in the glorious Ceiriog Valley, The Hand at Llanarmon radiates charm and character. 13 comfortable en suite bedrooms, log fires, and fabulous food, a wonderful base for most country pursuits. [🐕]
e-mail: reception@thehandhotel.co.uk website: www.TheHandHotel.co.uk

GOLDEN PHEASANT COUNTRY HOTEL, GLYN CEIROG, NEAR LLANGOLLEN LL20 7BB (01691 718281; Fax: 01691 718479). Situated in the beautiful Ceiriog Valley. All 19 rooms en suite, colour TV and tea/coffee making facilities. Pets welcome in all rooms (except restaurant and lounge). WTB/AA ★★★ [pw! £5 per night per pet, £35 per week]
e-mail: info@goldenpheasanthotel.co.uk website: www.goldenpheasanthotel.co.uk

Rhos-on-Sea

Popular resort at east end of Penrhyn Bay, adjoining Colwyn Bay to the north-west.

SUNNYDOWNS HOTEL, 66 ABBEY ROAD, RHOS-ON-SEA, CONWY LL28 4NU (01492 544256; Fax: 01492 543223). A 3 star luxury family hotel just two minutes' walk to beach and shops. All rooms en suite with colour TV, video & satellite channels, tea/coffee facilities and central heating. Hotel has bar, pool room and car park. A non-smoking hotel. [pets £4.50 per night]
e-mail: sunnydowns-hotel@tinyworld.co.uk website: www.hotelnorthwales.co.uk

THE NORTHWOOD, 47 RHOS ROAD, RHOS-ON-SEA, COLWYN BAY LL28 4RS (08450 533105). Family-run guesthouse in the heart of Rhos-on-Sea 175 yards from high class shops, promenade & sea. Tastefully furnished bedrooms. Vegetarian meals and special dietary needs are available. AA ★★★.
e-mail: welcome@thenorthwood.co.uk website: www.thenorthwood.co.uk

SIR JOHN'S HILL FARM HOLIDAY COTTAGES
Laugharne, Carmarthenshire SA33 4TD

Old Stables Cottage • Tel: 01994 427001
Wren Cottage & The Farmhouse • Tel: 01994 427667

In one of the finest locations in West Wales with spectacular views of coast and countryside, the three very comfortable cottages are the perfect place for a relaxing break. Here at Sir Johns Hill Farm we specialise in dog-friendly holidays and aim to make their holiday just as good as yours. They will have a great time at the farm which is well away from the main road, and there are lots of great country walks and long sandy beaches nearby too.

www.sirjohnshillfarm.co.uk

WTB ★★★★ - ★★★

Relax in The Farmhouse, one of six traditional cottages set within two acres of secure gardens at **MAERDY COTTAGES.** From this idyllic centre enjoy local walks and famous gardens and discover the beautiful coast and countryside of Carmarthenshire. Each cottage is equipped to give maximum comfort...two cottages are fully wheelchair accessible, and all are ideal for families of all ages. Home cooked evening meals available. Open all year. Brochure and enquiries:
Maerdy Cottages, Taliaris, Llandeilo, Carmarthenshire SA19 7DA • Tel: 01550 777448
e-mail: enquiries@maerdyholidaycottages.co.uk • www.maerdyholidaycottages.co.uk

The Diplomat Hotel Felinfoel Road, Aelybryn, Llanelli SA15 3PJ
Tel: 01554 756156 • Fax: 01554 751649 • AA/WTB ★★★
The Diplomat Hotel offers a rare combination of charm and character, with excellent well appointed facilities to ensure your comfort. Explore the Gower Peninsula and the breathtaking West Wales coastline. Salmon & trout fishing, horse riding, golf, and motor racing at Pembrey are all within reach.
e-mail: reservations@diplomat-hotel-wales.com • www.diplomat-hotel-wales.com

Laughlarne

Village on the River Taf estuary, 4 miles south of St Clears, burial place of Dylan Thomas.

SIR JOHN'S HILL FARM HOLIDAY COTTAGES, LAUGHARNE SA33 4TD. OLD STABLES COTTAGE 01994 427001, WREN COTTAGE & THE FARMHOUSE 01994 427667. Specialising in dog-friendly holidays, three very comfortable cottages. In one of the finest locations in West Wales, with spectacular views, lots of great country walks, and long sandy beaches nearby. [pw! £15 per week.]
website: www.sirjohnshillfarm.co.uk

Llandeilo

Town on River Towy, 14 miles east of Carmarthen.

MAERDY COTTAGES, TALIARIS, LLANDEILO, CARMARTHENSHIRE SA19 7DA (01550 777448). Six traditional cottages set within two acres of secure gardens. Each cottage is equipped to give maximum comfort, two cottages are fully wheelchair accessible, and all are ideal for families of all ages. Home cooked evening meals available. Open all year. WTB ★★★★ - ★★★. [First pet free, others £5 per night, £20 per week].
e-mail: enquiries@maerdyholidaycottages.co.uk website: www.maerdyholidaycottages.co.uk

Llanelli

Village on the River Taf estuary, 10 mile north-west of Swansea.

THE DIPLOMAT HOTEL, FELINFOEL ROAD, AELYBRYN, LLANELLI SA15 3PJ (01554 756156; Fax: 01554 751649). Privately owned and operated with warmth and generous hospitality. The Diplomat Hotel offers a rare combination of charm and character with excellent well appointed facilities to ensure your comfort and convenience. WTB/AA ★★★ [Pets £5 per night]
e-mail: reservations@diplomat-hotel-wales.com website: www.diplomat-hotel-wales.com

Around the magnificent coast of Wales
Pembrokeshire, Cardigan Bay, Snowdonia, Anglesey, Lleyn Peninsula, Borders
Choose from over 300
Quality Cottages

Pets Welcome Free

A small specialist agency with over 40 years experience letting quality cottages.

Enjoy unashamed luxury in traditional Welsh Cottages. Situated near safe sandy beaches and in the heart of Wales — famed for scenery, walks, wild flowers, birds, badgers and foxes.

Pets welcome FREE at most of our properties

Leonard Rees, Quality Cottages, Cerbid, Solva, Haverfordwest, Pembrokeshire. SA62 6YE

Telephone: (01348) 837871
for our FREE Colour Brochure

QUALITY COTTAGES CERBID

www.qualitycottages.co.uk

100s of pictures of quality cottages and beautiful Wales

Devil's Bridge, Aberystwyth SY23 3JL • 01970 890232
Fax: 01970 890394 • e-mail: hafodhotel@btconnect.com
Standing at the head of the Mynach Falls, perfect for exploring some of Wales' most spectacular scenery. Most bedrooms enjoy superb views. The restaurant offers a range of traditional fare, and there is a delightful Victorian Tea Room. WTB ★★ AA ★★★

Quality self-contained cottage, stunning views over Cardigan Bay, peaceful location, garden, close to dog friendly beach. Parking. Sleeps 4/5. Pets welcome. Terms from £265 to £445 per week.

MR & MRS MILLAR, PARC NEWYDD FACH, PARCLLYN, ABERPORTH, CARDIGAN SA43 2DR (01239 811325)

'QUALITY COTTAGES', CERBID, SOLVA, HAVERFORDWEST, PEMBROKESHIRE SA62 6YE (01348 837871). Cottages set in all coastal areas, enjoy unashamed luxury, highest residential standards. Log fires. Linen supplied. Pets welcome free. [pw! 🐕]
website: www.qualitycottages.co.uk

Aberporth

Popular seaside village offering safe swimming and good sea fishing. Good base for exploring Cardigan Bay coastline.

'QUALITY COTTAGES', CERBID, SOLVA, HAVERFORDWEST, PEMBROKESHIRE SA62 6YE (01348 837871). Cottages set in all coastal areas, enjoy unashamed luxury, highest residential standards. Log fires. Linen supplied. Pets welcome free. [pw! 🐕]
website: www.qualitycottages.co.uk

Aberystwyth

Resort at mouth of Rivers Rheidol and Ystwyth on Cardigan Bay, 82 miles from Cardiff.

THE HAFOD HOTEL, DEVIL'S BRIDGE, ABERYSTWYTH SY23 3JL (01970 890232; Fax: 01970 890394). At the head of the Mynach Falls, perfect for exploring some of Wales' most spectacular scenery. Most bedrooms enjoy superb views. Restaurant and a delightful Victorian Tea Room. WTB ★★, AA ★★★ [🐕] pw!
e-mail: hafodhotel@btconnect.com website: www.thehafodhotel.co.uk

Ciliau Aeron

Village in undulating country just inland from the charming Cardigan Bay resorts of New Quay and Aberaeron. New Quay 12 miles, Aberaeron 6.

'QUALITY COTTAGES', CERBID, SOLVA, HAVERFORDWEST, PEMBROKESHIRE SA62 6YE (01348 837871). Cottages set in all coastal areas, enjoy unashamed luxury, highest residential standards. Log fires. Linen supplied. Pets welcome free. [pw! 🐕]
website: www.qualitycottages.co.uk

Pet-Friendly
Pubs, Inns & Hotels
on pages 424-432
Please note that these establishments may not feature in the main section of this book

Llangrannog

Pretty little seaside village overlooking a sandy beach. Superb cliff walk to NT Ynys Lochtyn, a secluded promonto

'QUALITY COTTAGES', CERBID, SOLVA, HAVERFORDWEST, PEMBROKESHIRE SA62 6YE (01348 837871). Cottages set in all coastal areas, enjoy unashamed luxury, highest residential standards. Log fires. Linen supplied. Pets welcome free. [pw!]
website: www.qualitycottages.co.uk

Parcllyn

Located one mile west of Aberporth.

MR & MRS MILLAR, PARC NEWYDD FACH, PARCLLYN, ABERPORTH, CARDIGAN SA43 2DR (01239 811325). Quality self-contained cottage, stunning views over Cardigan Bay, peaceful location, garden, close to dog friendly beach. Parking. Sleeps 4/5. Pets welcome. Terms from £265 to £445 per week. []

Monmouthshire

Monmouth

Robin's Barn WTB ★★★★ **www.robinsbarn.co.uk**

Attractive converted stone barn set amidst 12 acres of beautiful, unspoilt countryside, with spectacular views over the Wye Valley and the Forest of Dean. Close to Offa's Dyke and Wye Valley Walk.• Sleeps 2-4 • Open all year • Spiral staircase, woodburner • Tennis court • Pretty patio • Pub nearby • Contact:
Robin's Nest Farm, Tregagle, Penallt, Monmouth NP25 4RY (01600 860058) • jane@robinsbarn.co.uk

Monmouth

Market town 20 miles NE of Newport.

ROBIN'S BARN. Attractive converted stone barn in 12 acres of beautiful, unspoilt countryside, with spectacular views over the Wye Valley and the Forest of Dean. Sleeps 2-4. Open all year. Tennis court. Pretty patio. Pub nearby. WTB ★★★★ Contact: ROBIN'S NEST FARM, TREGAGLE, PENALLT, MONMOUTH NP25 4RY (01600 860058) [Pets £10 per week.]
e-mail: jane@robinsbarn.co.uk website: www.robinsbarn.co.uk

Please note

All the information in this book is given in good faith in the belief that it is correct. However, the publishers cannot guarantee the facts given in these pages, neither are they responsible for changes in policy, ownership or terms that may take place after the date of going to press. Readers should always satisfy themselves that the facilities they require are available and that the terms, if quoted, still apply.

Around the magnificent coast of Wales
Pembrokeshire, Cardigan Bay, Snowdonia, Anglesey, Lleyn Peninsula, Borders
Choose from over 300
Quality Cottages

Pets Welcome Free

A small specialist agency with over
40 years experience letting quality cottages.

Enjoy unashamed luxury in traditional Welsh Cottages. Situated near safe sandy beaches and in the heart of Wales — famed for scenery, walks, wild flowers, birds, badgers and foxes.

Pets welcome FREE at most of our properties

Leonard Rees, Quality Cottages, Cerbid,
Solva, Haverfordwest, Pembrokeshire.
SA62 6YE

Telephone: (01348) 837871
for our FREE Colour Brochure

QUALITY COTTAGES
CERBID

www.qualitycottages.co.uk

100s of pictures of quality cottages
and beautiful Wales

Cottage Retreats in Pembrokeshire

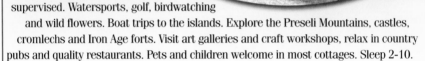

Charming, individual cottages situated near sandy beaches, rocky bays and spectacular cliff walks. Traditional stone-built cottages or modern properties, many with central heating and wood-burning stoves. All furnished to high residential standards, fully equipped and personally supervised. Watersports, golf, birdwatching and wild flowers. Boat trips to the islands. Explore the Preseli Mountains, castles, cromlechs and Iron Age forts. Visit art galleries and craft workshops, relax in country pubs and quality restaurants. Pets and children welcome in most cottages. Sleep 2-10.

Please contact Carole Rogers on
01348 875318 for a brochure
e-mail: carole.rogers@talktalk.net
www.cottageretreats.net

Broad Haven , Croft

PEMBROKESHIRE NATIONAL PARK. Three-bedroom fully furnished holiday house, within easy walking distance of sandy beaches and the Coastal Footpath. Ideal centre for family holidays, walking, birdwatching. Sleeps 6 + cot. From £140 to £360 per week.

MRS L.P. ASHTON, 10 ST LEONARDS ROAD, THAMES DITTON, SURREY KT7 0RJ
020-8398 6349 • e-mail: lejash@aol.com • www.33timberhill.com

Croft Farm & Celtic Cottages
• Pembrokeshire •

Croft makes the ideal place for a main holiday or short break. Delightful barn conversions provide superbly comfortable accommodation. Enjoy the luxury indoor heated pool, sauna, spa pool and gym facilities. Close to sandy beaches, bays and coastal National Park. Good walking country. Indoor and outdoor play areas. Colourful gardens. Friendly farm animals. Pets welcome.

For a brochure please contact Andrew and Sylvie Gow,
Croft Farm & Celtic Cottages, Croft, Near Cardigan, Pembrokeshire SA43 3NT
Tel: 01239 615179 • www.croft-holiday-cottages.co.uk
e-mail: info@croft-holiday-cottages.co.uk

★★★★ ★★★★★

Readers are requested to mention this FHG guidebook when seeking accommodation

Fishguard, Haverfordwest, Llanteg, Llechryd, Moylegrove

Welcome to Ivybridge, where your pet is as welcome as you are!

Situated down a leafy lane, Ivybridge is a modern guesthouse waiting to welcome you. All rooms en suite with TV/hot drinks tray. Swim in our indoor pool, relax in our lounge/bar. Good home cooking. Ample off-road parking. Close by are quiet walks to the sea which you and your pet will enjoy.

Ivybridge, Drim Mill, Dyffryn, Goodwick SA64 0JT • 01348 875366
Fax: 01348 872338 • e-mail: ivybridge5366@aol.com • www.ivybridgeleisure.co.uk

HAVEN COTTAGES

A Relaxing Coastal Break

Haven Cottages

Sycamore Lodge, Nolton Haven SA62 3NH
Tel: 01437 710200
e-mail: info@havencottages.co.uk
www.havencottages.co.uk

Cottages sleeping 2-8 persons. All fully equipped. Children and pets welcome.
Sympathetically converted cottages occupying beach front.

Scamford Caravan Park • Peaceful family-run park

Close to the Coastal Path and lovely sandy beaches. 25 luxurious caravans with Four Star Tourist Board grading. Playground. Pets welcome.

Richard & Christine White Tel/Fax: 01437 710304
www.scamford.com • e-mail: holidays@scamford.com
SCAMFORD CARAVAN PARK, KEESTON, HAVERFORDWEST SA62 6HN

NOLTON HAVEN QUALITY COTTAGES

Ideal for out of season breaks. Most with sea views, some 30 yards from safe, sandy beach. Central heating, open fires. Sleep 2 to 20. 8-bedroom farmhouse sleeps 20.

Contact: Jim & Joyce Canton, Nolton Haven Farmhouse, Nolton Haven, Haverfordwest SA62 6NH (01437 710263)
e-mail: PW8@noltonhaven.com
www.noltonhaven.com
WTB ★★★-★★★★★

LLANTEGLOS ESTATE 01834 831677/831371 VisitWales 3/4 Stars

Charming self-contained Woodland Lodges in quiet estate. Wonderful views of coast and country. Safe children's play area. Fully licensed clubhouse. Miles of sandy beaches. Attractions for all ages and interests. For further details/colour brochure: **TONY & JANE BARON, LLANTEGLOS ESTATE, LLANTEG, NEAR AMROTH, PEMBROKESHIRE SA67 8PU**
e-mail: llanteglosestate@supanet.com • www.llanteglos-estate.com

Castell Malgwyn Country House Hotel

Llechryd, Cardigan, Pembrokeshire SA43 2QA

Well behaved dogs welcome. Set on the banks of the River Teifi in large grounds. Excellent food in Lily's Restaurant.

Tel: 01239 682382 • www.castellmalgwyn.co.uk
e-mail: reception@malgwyn.co.uk

ENJOY THE BEAUTY OF THE NORTH PEMBROKESHIRE COAST WITH YOUR DOGS

3 WELSH COTTAGES *with enclosed gardens. Pets free of charge. Paddock for exercise. Dog- friendly bay and beaches within walking distance, with spectacular views. Bed linen included.* ***Tel: 01239 881 280***

Tynewydd Cottages, Ceibwr Lane, Moylegrove, Pembrokeshire SA43 3BU

Lochmeyler Farm Guesthouse

Cymru Wales Gwobr Aur Gold Award

Tel: 01348 837724
Fax: 01348 837622
e-mail: stay@lochmeyler.co.uk
www.lochmeyler.co.uk

Mrs Morfydd Jones
Llandeloy,
Pen-y-Cwm,
Near Solva,
St Davids,
Pembrokeshire
SA62 6LL

A warm welcome awaits you at Lochmeyler, a 220 acre dairy farm in the centre of the St Davids Peninsula.
It is an ideal location for exploring the beauty of the coast and countryside.
There are 12 bedrooms, four of them in the adjacent cottage suites. All are en suite, non-smoking, luxury rooms with colour TV, video and refreshment facilities. Rooms serviced daily. Children 14 years and over are welcomed. Well behaved dogs are welcome in some of our rooms. Dogs are not permitted to be left unattended in the rooms. There are kennel facilities for owners wishing to leave their dogs during the day. We do not charge for dogs or the kennel facilities.

Open all year round.
Credit cards accepted.
Colour brochure on request.

AWARD AA ★★★★★ WTB ★★★★★ FARM GOLD

DAILY RATES

Bed & Breakfast per person per night £30.00 - £40.00
Optional Dinner every night @ £17.50 per person
10% discount on advance bookings of
Bed, Breakfast and Evening Dinner for 7 nights or more

St Brides, St Davids, Saundersfoot, Whitland

SELECT QUALITY SELF-CATERING HOLIDAYS IN NORTH PEMBROKESHIRE

VW Graded. Pet Welcome. Sleeping 2-11 Short Breaks available

01437 720027 www.sbbc.uk.com

St BRIDES BAY COTTAGES Pembrokeshire

---

www.ffynnonddofn.co.uk

FFYNNON DDOFN

Delightful cottage in quiet lane between St Davids and Fishguard, with panoramic views over spectacular coastline. Ideal for walking; rocky coves and safe, sandy beaches nearby. The cottage is fully carpeted, warm, comfortable and very well-equipped, sleeping six in three bedrooms, plus cot. Washing machine, tumble dryer, freezer, microwave, DVD/video. Large games room, children's toys, pleasant secure garden. Perfect for early or late holidays, with central heating and double glazing. Parking. Shop one mile. Footpath to beach. Open all year. Terms from £320, including heating and electricity. Brochure on request.

Mrs B. Rees White, Brickhouse Farm, Burnham Road, Woodham Mortimer, Maldon, Essex CM9 6SR (01245 224611)

Vine Cottage
GUEST HOUSE

The Ridgeway,
Saundersfoot SA69 9LA

(Non-smoking)

Coastal village outskirts.

AA ★★★★ Guest House

Sandy beaches and coast path nearby. Award-winning garden for guests' and dogs' relaxation and exercise.

Tel: 01834 814422 • www.vinecottageguesthouse.co.uk ★★★★

A country estate of over 450 acres, including 2 miles of riverbank. See a real farm in action, the hustle and bustle of harvest, newborn calves and lambs. Choose from 6 character stone cottages, lovingly converted traditional farm buildings, some over 200 years old.

www.davidsfarm.com

Each cottage is fully furnished and equipped, electricity and linen included, with all year round heating. Children welcome. Brochure available. Contact: **Mrs Angela Colledge, Gwarmacwydd, Llanfallteg, Whitland, Pembrokeshire SA34 0XH**

Self Catering ★★★★ Cottages t **0800 321 3699**

Pet-Friendly
Pubs, Inns & Hotels

on pages 424-432

Please note that these establishments may not feature in the main section of this book

'QUALITY COTTAGES', CERBID, SOLVA, HAVERFORDWEST, PEMBROKESHIRE SA62 6YE (01348 837871). Cottages set in all coastal areas, enjoy unashamed luxury, highest residential standards. Log fires. Linen supplied. Pets welcome free. [pw!]
website: www.qualitycottages.co.uk

Pembrokeshire Coast - Newport to St Davids. Charming, individual cottages situated near sandy beaches, rocky bays and spectacular cliff walks. All furnished to high residential standards and fully equipped. Pets and children welcome. Sleep 2-10. Details from CAROLE ROGERS, COTTAGE RETREATS IN PEMBROKESHIRE, 29 HEOL GLYNDWR, FISHGUARD SA65 9LN (01348 875318). [ ]
e-mail: carole.rogers@talktalk.net website: www.cottageretreats.net

Bosherton

Village 4 miles south of Pembroke, bordered by 3 man-made lakes, a haven for wildlife and covered in water lilies in early summer.

'QUALITY COTTAGES', CERBID, SOLVA, HAVERFORDWEST, PEMBROKESHIRE SA62 6YE (01348 837871). Cottages set in all coastal areas, enjoy unashamed luxury, highest residential standards. Log fires. Linen supplied. Pets welcome free. [pw!]
website: www.qualitycottages.co.uk

Broad Haven

Inlet one mile north of St Govan's Head..

PEMBROKESHIRE NATIONAL PARK. Sleeps 6 + cot. Three-bedroom fully furnished Holiday House. Walking distance sandy beaches and coastal footpath. £140 to £360 per week. MRS L.P. ASHTON, 10 ST LEONARDS ROAD, THAMES DITTON, SURREY KT7 0RJ (020-8398 6349). [ ]
e-mail: lejash@aol.com website: www.33timberhill.com

Croes Goch

Hamlet 6 miles north east of St Davids

'QUALITY COTTAGES', CERBID, SOLVA, HAVERFORDWEST, PEMBROKESHIRE SA62 6YE (01348 837871). Cottages set in all coastal areas, enjoy unashamed luxury, highest residential standards. Log fires. Linen supplied. Pets welcome free. [pw!]
website: www.qualitycottages.co.uk

Other specialised holiday guides from FHG

PUBS & INNS OF BRITAIN • **COUNTRY HOTELS** OF BRITAIN

WEEKEND & SHORT BREAK HOLIDAYS IN BRITAIN

THE GOLF GUIDE WHERE TO PLAY, WHERE TO STAY

500 GREAT PLACES TO STAY • **SELF-CATERING HOLIDAYS** IN BRITAIN

BED & BREAKFAST STOPS • **CARAVAN & CAMPING HOLIDAYS**

FAMILY BREAKS IN BRITAIN

Published annually: available in all good bookshops or direct from the publisher:

FHG Guides, Abbey Mill Business Centre, Seedhill, Paisley PA1 1TJ

Tel: 0141 887 0428 • Fax: 0141 889 7204

e-mail: admin@fhguides.co.uk • www.holidayguides.com

Croft

Located 2 miles SW of Cardigan.

CROFT FARM & CELTIC COTTAGES, CROFT NEAR CARDIGAN SA43 3NT (01239 615179). Featured in Daily Mail. Stone barn conversions with luxury indoor heated pool, sauna, spa pool and gym. Colourful gardens, indoor and outdoor play areas. VisitWales ★★★★★/★★★★ *SELF CATERING*. Pets welcome. [Pets £4 per night, £28 per week, pw!]
e-mail: info@croft-holiday-cottages.co.uk website: www.croft-holiday-cottages.co.uk

Fishguard

Small town at end of Fishguard Bay

IVYBRIDGE, DRIM MILL, DYFFRYN, GOODWICK SA64 0FT (01348 875366, Fax: 01348 872338). Stay at Ivybridge, swim in our heated pool or relax in our comfortable guest lounge. En suite rooms, home cooking, large off road carpark. Pets welcome! [Pets £5 per stay].
e-mail: ivybridge5366@aol.com website: www.ivybridgeleisure.co.uk

Haverfordwest

Administrative and shopping centre for the area; ideal base for explorIng National Park. Historic town of narrow streets; museum in castle grounds; many fine buildings.

HAVEN COTTAGES. Quality beachfront cottages, sleep 2-8, adjacent sandy beach. Well equipped. Open all year. Winter breaks. Contact: SYCAMORE LODGE, NOLTON HAVEN SA62 3NH (01437 710200). [Pets £10 per week].
e-mail: info@havencottages.co.uk website: www.havencottages.co.uk

SCAMFORD CARAVAN PARK, KEESTON, HAVERFORDWEST SA62 6HN (Tel & Fax: 01437 710304). 25 luxurious caravans (shower, fridge, microwave, colour TV). Peaceful park near lovely sandy beaches. Playground. Launderette. Pets welcome. WTB ★★★★ Holiday Park.
e-mail: holidays@scamford.com website: www.scamford.com

NOLTON HAVEN QUALITY COTTAGES. Sleep 2 to 20. 3,4 & 5 star cottages, some with sea view, some just 30 yards from the beach. Children and pets welcome. 8-bedroom farmhouse sleeps 20. WTB ★★★/★★★★/★★★★★ Self-Catering. Contact: JIM & JOYCE CANTON, NOLTON HAVEN FARMHOUSE, NOLTON HAVEN, HAVERFORDWEST SA62 6NH (01437 710263).
e-mail: PW8@noltonhaven.com website: www.noltonhaven.com

Lawrenny

Village near River Cresswell estuary, 8 miles south-west of Narberth

MRS VIRGINIA LORT PHILLIPS, KNOWLES FARM, LAWRENNY SA68 0PX (01834 891221). Come and relax with us in our lovely south-facing farmhouse. Listen to the silence and spoil yourselves and your dogs whilst discovering the delights of hidden Pembrokeshire. Walk along the shores of the Estuary which surrounds our organic farm. B&B from £30 to £36pppn, Dinner on request. WTB ★★★ [First pet free, others £2 per pet per night.]
e-mail: ginilp@lawrenny.org.uk

Llanteg

Hamlet 4 miles south of Whitland.

TONY & JANE BARON, LLANTEGLOS ESTATE, LLANTEG, NEAR AMROTH SA67 8PU (01834 831677 /831371). Self-contained Woodland Lodges. Sleep 6. Children's play area. Licensed bar. Visitor attractions. Open all year. Call for brochure. VisitWales ★★★/★★★★ Self Catering [Pets £6 per night, £35 per week.]
e-mail: llanteglosestate@supanet.com website: www.llanteglos-estate.com

Readers are requested to mention this FHG guidebook when seeking accommodation

Llechryd

Village on the A484 3 miles from Cardigan.

CASTELL MALGWYN COUNTRY HOUSE HOTEL, LLECHRYD, CARDIGAN SA43 2QA (01239 682382) Well behaved dogs welcome. Set on the banks of the River Teifi in large grounds. Excellent food in Lily's Restaurant. [Pets £10 per night]
e-mail: reception@malgwyn.co.uk website: www.castellmalgwyn.co.uk

Moylegrove

Village 4 miles west of Cardigan..

NORTH PEMBROKESHIRE COAST. 3 WELSH COTTAGES with enclosed gardens. Paddock for exercise. Dog-friendly bay and beaches within walking distance, with spectacular views. Bed linen included. TYNEWYDD COTTAGES, CEIBWR LANE, MOYLEGROVE SA43 3BU (01239 881 280). []

Newgale

On St Bride's Bay 3 miles east of Solva. Long beach where at exceptionally low tide the stumps of a submerged forest may be seen.

'QUALITY COTTAGES', CERBID, SOLVA, HAVERFORDWEST, PEMBROKESHIRE SA62 6YE (01348 837871). Cottages set in all coastal areas, enjoy unashamed luxury, highest residential standards. Log fires. Linen supplied. Pets welcome free. [pw!]
website: www.qualitycottages.co.uk

Newport

Small town at mouth of the River Nyfer, 9 miles south west of Cardigan. Remains of 13th-century castle.

'QUALITY COTTAGES', CERBID, SOLVA, HAVERFORDWEST, PEMBROKESHIRE SA62 6YE (01348 837871). Cottages set in all coastal areas, enjoy unashamed luxury, highest residential standards. Log fires. Linen supplied. Pets welcome free. [pw!]
website: www.qualitycottages.co.uk

St Brides

Located on St Bride's Bay 7 miles north west of Milford Haven.

ST BRIDE'S BAY COTTAGES (01437 720027). Select quality self-catering holidays in North Pembrokeshire. Sleep 2-11. Short Breaks available. Pet welcome. VisitWales graded.
website: www.sbbc.uk.com

St Davids

Smallest cathedral city in Britain, shrine of Wales' patron saint. Magnificent ruins of Bishop's Palace. Craft shops, farm parks and museums; boat trips to Ramsey Island.

MRS M. JONES, LOCHMEYLER FARM GUEST HOUSE, LLANDELOY, PEN-Y-CWM, NEAR SOLVA, ST DAVIDS, PEMBROKESHIRE SA62 6LL (01348 837724; Fax: 01348 837622). Welcome Host Gold Award. 12 en suite luxury bedrooms, four in the cottage suites adjacent to the house. All bedrooms non-smoking, with TV, video and refreshment facilities. Children 14 years and over welcomed. WTB ★★★★★ *FARM*, AA★★★★★ [pw!]

PEMBROKESHIRE SHEEPDOGS, TREMYNYDD FACH, ST DAVID'S SA62 6DB (01437 721677; Fax: 01437 720308). A working sheep farm, whose fields extend down to the sea. Farm B&B (in cosy cottages) and Self-catering (in farmhouse and chalet) available. Spectacular and unspoilt stretch of coastal path abounding with rare species of plants and wildlife. [Pets £10 per week]
e-mail: sheepdog_training@lineone.net website: www.sheepdogtraining.co.uk

FFYNNON DDOFN, LLANON, LLANRHIAN, NEAR ST DAVIDS. Comfortable, well-equipped cottage with panoramic coastal views. Sleeps 6. Fully carpeted with central heating. Large games room. Open all year. Pets welcome free of charge. Brochure on request from: MRS B. REES WHITE, BRICKHOUSE FARM, BURNHAM RD, WOODHAM MORTIMER, MALDON, ESSEX CM9 6SR (01245 224611). [🐕]
website: www.ffynnonddofn.co.uk

'QUALITY COTTAGES', CERBID, SOLVA, HAVERFORDWEST, PEMBROKESHIRE SA62 6YE (01348 837871). Cottages set in all coastal areas, enjoy unashamed luxury, highest residential standards. Log fires. Linen supplied. Pets welcome free. [pw! 🐕]
website: www.qualitycottages.co.uk

Saundersfoot

Popular resort and sailing centre with picturesque harbour and sandy beach. Tenby 3 miles

VINE COTTAGE GUEST HOUSE, THE RIDGEWAY, SAUNDERSFOOT SA69 9LA (01834 814422). Coastal village outskirts. Sandy beaches and coast path nearby. Award-winning garden for guests' and dogs' relaxation and exercise. Non-smoking throughout. WTB/AA ★★★★ [pw! Pets £5 per stay.]
e-mail: enquiries@vinecottageguesthouse.co.uk website: www.vinecottageguesthouse.co.uk

Solva

Picturesque coastal village with sheltered harbour and excellent craft shops. Sailing and watersports; sea fishing, long sandy beach.

'QUALITY COTTAGES', CERBID, SOLVA, HAVERFORDWEST, PEMBROKESHIRE SA62 6YE (01348 837871). Cottages set in all coastal areas, enjoy unashamed luxury, highest residential standards. Log fires. Linen supplied. Pets welcome free. [pw! 🐕]
website: www.qualitycottages.co.uk

Tenby

Popular resort with two wide beaches. Fishing trips, craft shops, museum. Medieval castle ruins, 13th-century church. Golf, fishing and watersports; boat trips to nearby Caldy Island with monastery and medieval church.

'QUALITY COTTAGES', CERBID, SOLVA, HAVERFORDWEST, PEMBROKESHIRE SA62 6YE (01348 837871). Cottages set in all coastal areas, enjoy unashamed luxury, highest residential standards. Log fires. Linen supplied. Pets welcome free. [pw! 🐕]
website: www.qualitycottages.co.uk

Whitland

Village 6 miles east of Narberth. Whitland Abbey 2 km.

MRS ANGELA COLLEDGE, GWARMACWYDD FARM, LLANFALLTEG, WHITLAND SA34 0XH (0800 321 3699). Country estate with six character stone cottages, fully furnished and equipped. All linen and electricity included; heated for year-round use. WTB ★★★★ [pw! Pets £10 per pet per week]
website: www.davidsfarm.com

Symbols

🐕 Indicates that pets are welcome free of charge.

£ Indicates that a charge is made for pets: nightly or weekly.

pw! Shows some special provision for pets; exercise facility, feeding or accommodation arrangement.

⌂ Indicates separate pets accommodation.

Castle Dell Cottage Castle View, Brecon, Powys LD3 9BU

Tucked away under the 200 year old town house of Castle View, Castle Dell Cottage is only 200 yards from Brecon's town centre. Quality accommodation, home from home, sleeps four (1 double bedroom/1 double sofa bed). Secure private garden, ideal for bringing your pets!. Non smoking. Weekly breaks available all year. Short Breaks outside peak season.

Kathy and Kizzy Edgson Tel: 01874 624110 www.castledellcottage.co.uk

---

AA ★★★

Caer Beris Manor

WALES TOURIST BOARD GWESTY ★★★ HOTEL

Family-owned three star Country House Hotel set in 27 acres of parkland. Free salmon and trout fishing on River Wye (two rods) and on River Irfon. Superb walking and touring. 18 hole Golf Course nearby. Excellent cuisine. All rooms en suite with telephone, TV and tea making.

DOGS WELCOME!

DB&B from £70.95pppn, from £425.70 weekly

B&B from £57.95pppn. Terms based on 2 sharing

Mrs Katharine Smith, Caer Beris Manor, Builth Wells
Powys LD2 3NP • Tel: 01982 552601 • Fax: 01982 552586
e-mail: caerberis@btconnect.com • www.caerberis.com

• ERWOOD, BUILTH WELLS LD2 3SZ • Tel: 01982 560680 •

Situated in secluded grounds with glorious views of the beautiful Wye Valley. Attractive spacious rooms (one en suite, two sharing guests' own bathroom), have TV, drinks tray, fridge, wash basin. Bacon and sausage from locally reared pigs, free range eggs and home made preserves for breakfast. Two bedrooms with double aspect. FHG Diploma Winner 2004.

e-mail: linda@oldvicwyevalley.co.uk • www.oldvicwyevalley.co.uk WTB ★★ Farm

---

Visit the FHG website

www.holidayguides.com

for details of the wide choice of accommodation

featured in the full range of FHG titles

Garthmyl, Hay-on-Wye, Llandrindod Wells

A Superb Holiday Setting for all Seasons

USet in a 30-acre woodland, all our lodges are individually designed and fully fitted throughout, including colour TV, DVD, microwave, full kitchen, bath/shower room, and include all bedding. 19 lodges sleeping 2 – 8 people and one cottage which sleeps six. Fishing on the Montgomery canal, River Severn and our own private lake. 9-hole golf course opening May 2008. Quad trekking and pony trekking nearby.
Pets welcome in certain cabins,

From £185 to £692 per cabin per week inc. VAT • Short Breaks • Open all year round

Tel/Fax 01686 640269 for a colour brochure
Penllwyn Lodges, Garthmyl, Powys SY15 6SB
e-mail: daphne.jones@onetel.net
www.penllwynlodges.co.uk

17th century farm in rural Radnorshire, five miles Hay-on-Wye.
Wonderful walking country. Self-catering apartments sleeping 2-14.
A warm welcome for you and your pet(s). WTB ★★★

MRS E. BALLY, LANE FARM, PAINSCASTLE, BUILTH WELLS LD2 3JS
Tel & Fax: 01497 851605 • e-mail: lanefarm@onetel.com

TROWLEY FARMHOUSE. Detached farmhouse in unspoilt location on 400-acre working farm. Views of Black Mountains and Brecon Beacons. Oak beams, stone walls and large farmhouse kitchen retain much of the 16th century character, with every modern convenience to make your stay comfortable.

- En suite family room, two twin rooms, one double room, en suite room with bunk bed (sleeps 4)
- All fuel and linen (except towels) incl. Home-cooked meal service.
- Ample parking, garden with barbecue.
- A warm welcome for you and your pets.

Mr Ben Lewis, LLanbedr Hall, Painscastle, Builth Wells, Powys LD2 3JH
01497 851665 • e-mail: ruth@trowleyfarmhouse.co.uk

The Park House Motel
Crossgates, Llandrindod Wells LD1 6RF

Set in 3 acres of beautiful Welsh countryside and close to the famous Elan Valley. Accommodation includes static caravans, touring pitches and fully equipped motel units which have either a twin or double bedroom, shower room, and kitchen with a dinette that converts to a double bed. Sleeping up to 4, they can be booked for either self-catering or B&B. On-site facilities include restaurant, bar and snug. Well behaved pets are very welcome.

Tel: (01597) 851201 • www.parkmotel.co.uk

The Forest Country Guest House

Wales Cymru ★★★★

Hidden in the beautiful Vale of Kerry, The Forest offers 4 star luxury bed and breakfast in 5 charming en suite rooms. Four acres of gardens, tennis court, games room, kennels and stables, owner is a veterinarian. Perfect to explore many attractions of Mid Wales.
Paul & Michelle Martin, The Forest, Gilfach Lane, Kerry, Newtown, Powys SY16 4DW
Tel: 01686 621 821 • E-mail: info@theforestkerry.co.uk • www.bedandbreakfastnewtown.co.uk

Cosy cottage in lovely Border countryside. 2 miles from Offa's Dyke • Central heating, washing machine, microwave, dishwasher, colour TV, inglenook, woodburner, linen included; power shower over bath • Sleeps 4 plus cot • Ample parking • Sun-trap garden • On working farm in peaceful hamlet • Children and pets welcome • WTB 4 Stars. MRS R. L. JONES, UPPER HOUSE, KINNERTON, NEAR PRESTEIGNE LD8 2PE • Tel: 01547 560207

Oak Wood LODGES

Llwynbaedd, Rhayader, Powys LD6 5NT

Luxurious Self Catering Log Cabins situated at approximately 1000ft above sea level with spectacular views of the Elan Valley and Cambrian mountains. Enjoy pursuits such as walking, pony trekking, mountain biking, fishing, and bird watching in the most idyllic of surroundings. Excellent touring centre. Dogs welcome. Short breaks as well as full weeks. Open all year round

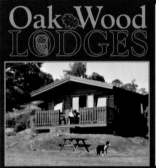

For more information and brochure call:

01597 811422

www.oakwoodlodges.co.uk

Brecon

Market town 14 miles north of Merthyr Tydfil.

KATHY & KIZZY EDGSON, CASTLE DELL COTTAGE, CASTLE VIEW, BRECON LD3 9BU (01874 624110) Quality accommodation only 200 yards from Brecon's town centre Sleeps 4. Private garden. Non smoking. Weekly breaks available all year. Short Breaks outside peak season. [🐕]
website: castledellcottage.co.uk

Builth Wells

Old country town in lovely setting on River Wye amid beautiful hills. Lively markets; host to Royal Welsh Agricultural Show

MRS KATHARINE SMITH, CAER BERIS MANOR, BUILTH WELLS LD2 3NP (01982 552601; Fax: 01982 552586). Family-owned country house hotel set in 27 acres of parkland. Free salmon and trout fishing; golf nearby, superb walking and touring. All rooms en suite. WTB/AA ★★★ [Pets £5 per night, £30 per week].
e-mail: caerberis@btconnect.com website: www.caerberis.com

MRS LINDA WILLIAMS, OLD VICARAGE, ERWOOD, BUILTH WELLS LD2 3SZ (01982 560680). Situated in secluded grounds with glorious views of the beautiful Wye Valley. Attractive spacious rooms (one en suite, two sharing guests' own bathroom), have TV, drinks tray, fridge, wash basin. Bacon and sausage from locally reared pigs, free range eggs and home made preserves for breakfast. Two bedrooms with double aspect. WTB ★★ Farm, FHG Diploma Winner 2004.[🐕]
e-mail: linda@oldvicwyevalley.co.uk website: www.oldvicwyevalley.co.uk

Garthmyl

Situated on A483 between Welshpool and Newtown in unspoilt countryside.

Self-catering log cabins set in 30 acres of unspoilt woodland teeming with wildlife. Central heating, colour TV/DVD, microwave etc. Pets welcome in certain cabins. From £185-£692 per cabin per week breaks. Apply PENLLWYN LODGES, GARTHMYL, POWYS SY15 6SB (Tel & Fax: 01686 640269) for colour brochure. [Pets £15 breaks, £20 week.]
e-mail: daphne.jones@onetel.net website: www.penllwynlodges.co.uk

Hay-on-Wye

Small market town at north end of Black Mountains, 15 miles north-east of Brecon.

MRS E. BALLY, LANE FARM, PAINSCASTLE, BUILTH WELLS LD2 3JS (Tel & Fax: 01497 851605). 17th century farm in rural Radnorshire, five miles Hay-on-Wye. Wonderful walking country. Self-catering apartments sleeping 2-14. A warm welcome for you and your pet(s). WTB ★★★ [🐕]
e-mail: lanefarm@onetel.com

TROWLEY FARMHOUSE. Detached farmhouse in unspoilt location. Sleeps up to 14 – family room, two twin, one double and one room with bunk beds. All fuel and linen (except towels) incl. Home-cooked meal service. A warm welcome for you and your pets. MR B. LEWIS, LLANBEDR HALL, PAINSCASTLE, BUILTH WELLS LD2 3JH (01497 851665) [Pets £20 per week]
e-mail: ruth@trowleyfarmhouse.co.uk website: www.trowleyfarmhouse.co.uk

Llandrindod Wells

Popular inland resort, Victorian spa town, excellent touring centre. Golf, fishing, bowling, boating and tennis. Visitors can still take the waters at Rock Park Gardens.

THE PARK HOUSE MOTEL, CROSSGATES, LLANDRINDOD WELLS LD1 6RF (01597 851201). In three acres, amidst beautiful countryside near Elan Valley. Static caravans, touring pitches and fully equipped motel units. Licensed restaurant, bar. Pets welcome. [Pets £3 per night, £20 per week. Guide dogs free). [🐕]
e-mail: barr560@btinternet.com website: www.parkmotel.co.uk

Llangurig

Village on River Wye, 4 miles south-west of Llanidloes. Ideal walking countryside.

MRS J. BAILEY, GLANGWY, LLANGURIG, LLANIDLOES SY18 6RS (01686 440697). Bed, breakfast and evening meals in the countryside. Plenty of walking locally. Also caravan and campsite. Prices on request. [🐕]

Newtown

Town on River Severn 12 miles SW of Welshpool.

PAUL & MICHELLE MARTIN, THE FOREST, KERRY, NEWTOWN SY16 4DW (01686 621821). Luxury bed and breakfast with five en suite rooms. Four acres of gardens, tennis court, games room, kennels and stables, owner is a veterinarian. WTB ★★★★. [Pets £5 per night]
e-mail: info@theforestkerry.co.uk website: www.bedandbreakfastnewtown.co.uk

Presteigne

Attractive old town with half timbered houses. Ideal for hillside rambles and pony trekking.

MRS R. L. JONES, UPPER HOUSE, KINNERTON, NEAR PRESTEIGNE LD8 2PE (01547 560207). Cosy cottage two miles from Offa's Dyke. Central heating, washing machine, dishwasher, microwave, colour TV, inglenook, woodburner, linen included. Power shower over bath. Sleeps 4 plus cot. Children and pets welcome. WTB ★★★★ [🐕].

Rhayader

Small market town on River Wye north of Builth Wells. Popular for angling and pony trekking

OAK WOOD LODGES, LLWYNBAEDD, RHAYADER LD6 5NT (01597 811422). Luxurious self-catering log cabins with spectacular views of the Elan Valley and Cambrian Mountains. Walking, pony trekking, mountain biking, fishing and bird watching in idyllic surroundings. Phone for brochure. [Dog £20 per week, £13 per short break; additional dogs half price].
website: www.oakwoodlodges.co.uk

HALF MOON INN Llanthony, Abergavenny NP7 7NN

Set amidst the beautiful scenery of the Vale of Ewyas and dominated by the slopes of the Black Mountains, this attractive inn is a welcome sight, serving traditional ales, cider and good food. The Offa's Dyke and Beacons Way footpaths are only half a mile away. Bed and Breakfast accommodation is available. Dogs welcome. **Tel: 01873 890611**

e-mail: halfmoon@llanthony.wanadoo.co.uk • www.halfmoon-llanthony.co.uk

The Haybarn and The Bull Pen • ★★★★ Self-Catering

Stone barn conversion, nestling high on hillside with outstanding views. Equipped to high standard with all bedrooms en suite. Sleeps 6 & 4. Pets free. 3 or 4 night short breaks.

Terms: Min. £305 per week (4 people) Bull Pen. Min. £375 per week (6 People) Haybarn.

Tor-y-Mynydd Farm, Devauden, Chepstow NP16 6NU • Tel: 01600 860887 Fax: 01600 860869
e-mail brian.tor-y-mynydd@virgin.net • www.tor-y-mynydd.co.uk

18th Century luxury Guest House where our aim is to ensure a peaceful, comfortable and relaxing stay. Guest rooms are all en suite and spacious, with views over the Vale of Neath. Licensed bar and restaurant • Vegetarian & other diets catered for • Children welcome • • Parking • Non-smoking rooms • Pets welcome by arrangement

Mrs C. Jones, Green Lanterns Guest House, Hawdref Ganol Farm, Cimla, Neath SA12 9SL • 01639 631884 • www.greenlanterns.co.uk

BEST WESTERN ABERAVON BEACH HOTEL

Modern seafront hotel. A warm Welsh welcome awaits you and your pets. 2 miles of flat promenade and a pet friendly beach. Pets Paradise!! And for you..... comfortable rooms, fine cuisine, leisure centre and many local attractions. Tel: 01639 884949

AA ★★★

Neath Port Talbot, Swansea Bay SA12 6QP • www.aberavonbeach.com

Cwrt-y-Gaer in the Vale of Usk and Wye Valley

www.cwrt-y-gaer.co.uk

One, four or more dogs welcome FREE. Three self-catering units in well converted stone Welsh Longhouse, set in old hilltop fort in 20 acres with fine views across to mountains. Quiet area with good access to many places of interest. Good walking. Open all year. Brochure from:

Sue & John Llewellyn, Cwrt-y-Gaer, Wolvesnewton, Chepstow, Monmouthshire NP16 6PR

Tel: (01291) 650700 • e-mail: john.llewellyn11@btinternet.com

All units are WTB ★★. One unit is Grade 1 access for the disabled.

Please note

All the information in this book is given in good faith in the belief that it is correct. However, the publishers cannot guarantee the facts given in these pages, neither are they responsible for changes in policy, ownership or terms that may take place after the date of going to press. Readers should always satisfy themselves that the facilities they require are available and that the terms, if quoted, still apply.

CASTLE NARROWBOATS CHURCH ROAD WHARF, GILWERN NP7 0EP (01873 830001). The Monmouthshire & Brecon Canal in South Wales. Discover the beauty of Wales onboard one of our excellent narrowboats. 2-8 berth boats, short breaks available. Pets welcome.For a free colour brochure call Castle Narrowboats:
website: www.castlenarrowboats.co.uk

Abergavenny

Historic market town at south-eastern gateway to Brecon Beacons National Park. Pony trekking, leisure centre; excellent touring base for Vale of Usk.

HALF MOON INN, LLANTHONY, NEAR ABERGAVENNY NP7 7NN (01873 890611). B&B, good food and real ale in 17thC inn. Wonderful scenery of Black Mountains. Good base for walking, pony trekking, birdwatching. Dogs welcome.[Pets £1.50 per night]
e-mail: halfmoon@llanthony.wanadoo.co.uk website: www.halfmoon-llanthony.co.uk

Chepstow (Monmouthshire)

Town on River Wye 15 miles east of Newport.

THE HAYBARN AND THE BULL PEN. Stone barn conversion, nestling high on hillside with outstanding views. Equipped to high standard with all bedrooms en suite. Peaceful and relaxing. Sleeps 6 & 4. Linen and towels included. TOR-Y-MYNYDD FARM, DEVAUDEN, CHEPSTOW NP16 6NU (01600 860887; Fax: 01600 860869) WTB ★★★★ [🐕]
e-mail: brian.tor-y-mynydd@virgin.net website: www.tor-y-mynydd.co.uk

Mumbles

Seaside resort of Swansea to west and north west of Mumbles Head.

MUMBLES & SWANSEA. Seafront ground floor flat. Well-equipped modern conveniences. Ideal for beaches, countryside and local amenities. Personally supervised. Plenty of dog walks! WTB ★★★. MRS JEAN GRIERSON, 112 MUMBLES ROAD, BLACKPILL, SWANSEA SA3 5AS (01792 402278). [🐕]

Neath

Town on River Neath 8 miles NE of Swansea.

MRS C. JONES, GREEN LANTERNS GUEST HOUSE, HAWDREF GANOL FARM, CIMLA, NEATH SA12 9SL (01639 631884). 18th Century luxury Guest House with spacious en suite rooms, all with views over the Vale of Neath. Licensed bar and restaurant. Vegetarian & other diets catered for. Pets welcome by arrangement. WTB ★★★★.
website: www.greenlanterns.co.uk

Swansea

*Second largest city in Wales with a wide variety of leisure activities and excellent shopping.*e

BEST WESTERN ABERAVON BEACH HOTEL, NEATH PORT TALBOT, SWANSEA BAY SA12 6QP (01639 884949). Modern seafront hotel. A warm Welsh welcome awaits you and your pets. 2 miles of flat promenade and a pet friendly beach. Pets Paradise!! And for you..... comfortable rooms, fine cuisine, leisure centre and many local attractions. AA ★★★.[🐕]
website: www.aberavonbeach.com

Wye Valley

Scenic area, ideal for relaxation.

MR & MRS J. LLEWELLYN, CWRT-Y-GAER, WOLVESNEWTON, CHEPSTOW NP16 6PR (01291 650700). 1, 4 or more dogs welcome free. Self-catering, attractively converted stone buildings of Welsh Longhouse. 20 acres, super views of Usk Vale. Brochure. Three units (one suitable for disabled). WTB ★★, Welcome Host Gold Award. [pw! 🐕]
e-mail: john.llewellyn11@btinternet.com website: www.cwrt-y-gaer.co.uk

1000 Inspected Cottages
Sun-Fri 9am to 9pm
Sat 9am to 7pm

IMAGINE IRELAND
Coastal Holiday Cottages
IRELAND IN ONLY 99 MINS BY FAST FERRY!
NEW!
PETS WELCOME & GO FREE
Smaller party prices
Low car hire & ferry inc prices

from **£13** pppn inc. superferry
FREE 100 Page BROCHURE **01756 707764**
www.petsandselfcatering.co.uk

IMAGINE IRELAND, COASTAL HOLIDAY COTTAGES (01756 707764). 1000 inspected coastal Holiday Cottages. From £13 per person per night, inc. ferry. Pets go free. Low car hire and ferry inc. prices. Smaller party prices. Free 100 page brochure.
website: www.petsandselfcatering.co.uk

Co Kerry

Lauragh

Creveen Lodge

Immaculately run small hill farm overlooking Kenmare Bay in a striking area of County Kerry. Reception is found at the Lodge, which also offers guests a comfortable sitting room, while a separate block has well-equipped and immaculately maintained toilets and showers, plus a communal room with a large fridge, freezer and ironing facilities. The park is carefully tended, with bins and picnic tables informally placed, plus a children's play area with slides and swings.

There are 20 pitches in total, 16 for tents and 4 for caravans, with an area of hardstanding for motor caravans. Electrical connections are available. Fishing, bicycle hire, water sports and horse riding available nearby. SAE please, for replies.

Mrs M. Moriarty, Creveen Lodge, Healy Pass Road, Lauragh
00 35364 83131 • 00 353 64 66 83131 from June 2009
e-mail: info@creveenlodge.com • www.creveenlodge.com

Lauragh

Rural location on Ring of Beara.

MRS M. MORIARTY, CREVEEN LODGE, HEALY PASS ROAD, LAURAGH (00 35364 83131; 00 353 64 66 83131 from June 2009). Small, carefully tended, well equipped park, 16 pitches for tents, 4 for caravans, with hardstanding for motor caravans. Fishing, bicycle hire, water sports and horse riding available nearby. [🐕]
e-mail: info@creveenlodge.com website: www.creveenlodge.com

NARROWBOATS

Discover the beauty of Wales
on board one of our excellent narrowboats
Cruising along the Monmouth and Brecon Canal, through the Brecon Beacons National Park, you can take a short break, week or longer.

We have boats for 2-8 people and pets are welcome.
Visit our website for up to date availability.
www.castlenarrowboats.co.uk
or call 01873 830001 for a brochure
Castle Narrowboats, Church Road Wharf, Gilwern, Monmouthshire NP7 0EP

Holidays with Horses

A selection of accommodation where horse and owner/rider can be put up at the same address – if not actually under the same roof! We would be grateful if readers making enquiries and/or bookings from this supplement would mention **Pets Welcome!**

England

Devon

SPIRIT OF EXMOOR
(01598 753318).
e-mail: stephany@spiritofexmoor.fsnet.co.uk website: www.spiritofexmoor.com

Exhilarating riding across miles of untamed moorland in small groups. Fit, friendly, forward going well schooled horses. Non-riders, own horses and pets welcome. Delicious home cooked cuisine, vegetarians welcome. Special winter breaks available. Colour brochure. Contact: Stephany Pettinger.

WESTERMILL FARM
EXFORD, MINEHEAD TA24 7NJ
(01643 831238; Fax: 01643 831216)
e-mail: pw@westermill.com website: www.westermill.com

Cottages (Disabled Catergory 2) in grass paddocks. Ideal for children. Stabling and fields for horses. Wonderful for dogs and owners. Separate campsite by river.

LEONE & BRIAN MARTIN,
RISCOMBE FARM HOLIDAY COTTAGES, EXFORD,
EXMOOR NATIONAL PARK TA24 7NH
(Tel: 01643 831480)
website: www.riscombe.co.uk (with up-to-date vacancy info.)

Four self-catering stone cottages in the centre of Exmoor National Park. Excellent walking and riding country. Dogs and horses welcome. Stabling available. Open all year. VB ★★★★

Oxfordshire

JUNE AND GEORGE COLLIER
55 NETHERCOTE ROAD, TACKLEY, KIDLINGTON, OXFORD OX5 3AT
(01869 331255; mobile: 07790 338225)
website: www.colliersbnb.co.uk

An ideal base for riding - superb network of Bridleways. Stop-over for Claude Duval route. Close to Blenheim. Regular train and bus service. Local Hostelries serve excellent food. ETC ★★★

Suffolk

MRS JANE BREWER,
LODGE COTTAGE, LAXFIELD ROAD, CRATFIELD, HALESWORTH IP19 0QG
(01986 798830 or 07788 853884)
e-mail: janebrewer@ukonline.co.uk

Pretty 16C thatched cottage retaining some fine period features. Sleeps 4. Pets welcome. Fenced garden. One mile from village. 30 minutes to Southwold and coast. Rural, quiet and relaxing. Brochure.

Shropshire

THE ANCHORAGE
ANCHOR, NEWCASTLE on CLUN, CRAVEN ARMS SY7 8PR
(Tel: 01686 670737)

Two well-equipped modern caravan holiday homes in Area of Outstanding Natural Beauty. Perfect for walking, cycling, riding, or just unwinding! Each has three bedrooms, TV, shower room with flush toilet, and kitchen with fridge and microwave. Well behaved pets and children welcome, horses also accommodated. Open Easter to October.

East Yorkshire

PAWS-A-WHILE
KILNWICK PERCY, POCKLINGTON YO42 1UF
(01759 301168; Mobile: 07711 866869)
e-mail: paws.a.while@lineone.net • website: www.pawsawhile.net

Small family B & B set in forty acres of parkland twixt York and Beverley. Golf, walking, riding. Pets and horses most welcome. Brochure available. ETC ★★★★

South Yorkshire

PENNINE EQUINE HOLIDAY COTTAGES
COTE GREEN FARM, WORTLEY, SHEFFIELD
(0114 284 7140; Mobile: 07939 906523)
website: www.pennine-equine.co.uk

Two comfortably furnished cottages attached to main stable building (each sleeps 6/8). Dogs not allowed, but kennels available. Livery and stabling for visitors' horses. 3-mile cross country course within grounds. Riding lessons available. Ample parking for trailers, horse boxes etc. Contact: Bromley Farm, Wortley, Sheffield S35 7DE

FARLAM HALL HOTEL
BRAMPTON CA8 2NG.
(016977 46234; Fax: 016977 46683)
e-mail: farlam@relaischateaux.com • website: www.farlamhall.co.uk

Standing in four acres of gardens, with its own lake, Farlam Hall offers fine quality cuisine and individually decorated guest rooms. Ideal touring centre for the Lakes, Borders and hadrian's Wall. AA Three Stars Inspectors' Choice and Two Rosettes, Relais & Chateaux.

Scotland

Dumfries & Galloway

AE FARM COTTAGES
GUBHILL FARM, DUMFRIES DG1 1RL
(01387 860648)
e-mail: gill@gubhill.co.uk

Modern accommodation in old stone buildings on a traditional farm, overlooking a peaceful valley. Beautiful views, plentiful wildlife and endless paths on the doorstep. Between Dumfries, Moffat and Thornhill. STB ★★★ SELF CATERING, CATEGORY ONE DISABILITY.

RUSKO HOLIDAYS,
GATEHOUSE OF FLEET, CASTLE DOUGLAS DG7 2BS
(01557 814215)
e-mail: info@ruskoholidays.co.uk • website: www.ruskoholidays.co.uk

Spacious, traditional farmhouse and three charming, cosy cottages near beaches, hills and forest park. Lots of off-road riding amid stunning scenery. Stabling and grazing available for your own horse. Beautiful walking and riding country, fishing and tennis. Rates £225-£1329. STB ★★ to ★★★★

MR P. JONES
BARGALY ESTATE COTTAGES
PALNURE, NEWTON STEWART,
DUMFRIES & GALLOWAY DG8 7BH
(Tel: 01671 401048)
e-mail: bargalyestate@callnetuk.com website:www.bargaly.com

Three cottages available all year on Historic Estate. Paddocks available close to cottages. Safe riding, forest trails from the Estate. Local Equestrian centre.

Wales

Anglesey & Gwynedd

MRS ANN WILLIAMS
TYDDYN HEILYN, CHWILOG, CRICCIETH LL53 6SW
(Tel: 01766 810441)

Comfortably renovated Welsh stone cottage; two bedrooms with sea views. Ample grounds with enclosed garden. On Llyn Peninsula, on edge Snowdonia. Very central for touring.

North Wales

MIS MORRIS
TY COCH FARM-TREKKING CENTRE
PENMACHNO, BETWS-Y-COED
NORTH WALES LL25 0HJ
(Tel: 01690 760248)
e-mail: cindymorris@tiscali.co.uk

Hill farm in Wales. TV, teamaking, en suite. Set in National Park/Snowdonia. Very quiet and well off the beaten track. A great welcome and good food. Many return visits. £22 B&B.

Carmarthenshire

SIR JOHN'S HILL FARM HOLIDAY COTTAGES
LAUGHARNE
CARMARTHENSHIRE SA33 4TD
Old Stables Cottage (Tel: 01994 427001)
Wren Cottage & The Farmhouse (Tel: 01994 427667)
website:www.sirjohnshillfarm.co.uk

A great place to come if you want to get away from it all with your horse(s) and your dog(s). Beautiful scenery, relaxing rides, including beach rides, and great accommodation.

Powys

MRS E. BALLY
LANE FARM, PAINSCASTLE, BUILTH WELLS LD2 3JS
(Tel & Fax: 01497 851605)
e-mail: lanefarm@onetel.com

Self-Catering apartments sleeping 2-14. Nine good stables and ample grazing in the heart of rural Radnorshire with wonderful open riding. Some cross-country jumps. WTB ★★★

PURINA winalot

Visit the NEW Winalot website today!

Winalot knows how important giving your dog a balanced diet and plenty of exercise is for their wellbeing, so we've totally re-designed our website to showcase our great balanced range of foods, and the best walks that Britain can offer for you and your furry friend.

www.winalot-dog.co.uk

PURINA
winalot
Roasts
Winalot Roasts -
Mealtimes never tasted so good!
Tender pieces of meat, gently cooked to give that special roasted taste, then smothered in a thick meaty gravy to give your dog that extra taste sensation he deserves!
Available in Chicken, Beef and Lamb varieties.
winalot Roasts with chicken in a delicious gravy
winalot Roasts with beef in a delicious gravy
winalot Roasts
2x with beef in a delicious gravy
2x with chicken in a delicious gravy
2x with lamb in a delicious gravy

Pet-Friendly Pubs
A selection of Pubs and Inns where pets are especially welcome!
The Bell Inn, Adderbury, Oxfordshire

The Hood Arms, Kilve, Somerset

The Greyhound

Eton Wick, Berkshire SL4 6JE • Tel: 01753 863925
www.thegreyhoundetonwick.co.uk
A picturesque pub with plenty of walks close by. Food served daily. Sunday lunch only £5.95 between 12 noon – 3pm.
Pet residents: Tully (Shepherd), Harvey (Retriever), Teeni, Bourbon.

The Springer Spaniel

Treburley, near Launceston, Cornwall PL15 9NS
Tel: 01579 370424 • e-mail: enquiries@thespringerspaniel.org.uk
www.thespringerspaniel.org.uk
Country pub providing a warm welcome and specialising in home cooked, fresh, locally sourced food. Emphasis upon game, with beef and lamb from the owner's organic farm. Dogs can snooze by the fire, water provided (perhaps a biscuit if especially good) or lounge in the beer garden.
Pet Regulars: some very regular customers and their accompanying owners.

Cumberland Inn

Tel: 01434 381875
Townfoot, Alston, Cumbria CA9 3HX
stay@cumberlandinnalston.com • www.cumberlandinnalston.com
A comfy retreat in the secluded North Pennines. Real beer, real fires and real hospitality await your arrival. Home-made hearty fare available all day to revive flagging spirits. Our 5 recently refurbished rooms are all en suite. Muddy dogs and boots welcome.
Dog bowls filled with water (or even beer).
Pets welcome in bedrooms and bar. No charge for pets.

the mardale inn @ st patrick's well

Bampton, Cumbria CA10 2RQ Tel: 01931 713244
www.mardaleinn.co.uk info@mardaleinn.co.uk
Always open • fresh local produce • open fires
fine cask beers • warm beds • Haweswater location.
Daily Telegraph '50 Best Pubs' - May 2008.
Children and dogs welcome
(children must be kept on a short leash at all times!)

Tower Bank Arms

Near Sawrey, Ambleside, Cumbria LA22 0LF • Tel: 015394 36334
enquiries@towerbankarms.com • www.towerbankarms.co.uk

17thC Inn situated in the village of Near Sawrey, next to Hilltop, Beatrix Potter's former home. With many original features, and offering fresh local food and traditional local ales.

Water and treats provided • Dogs allowed in bar and accommodation

The Coledale Inn

Braithwaite, Near Keswick, Cumbria CA12 5TN
Tel: 017687 78272
e-mail: info@coledale-inn.co.uk • www.coledale-inn.co.uk

Friendly, family-run Victorian inn in peaceful location. Ideally situated for touring and walking direct from the hotel grounds. Fine selection of wines and local real ales. Families and pets welcome.

Outgate Inn

Outgate, Ambleside, Cumbria LA22 0NQ • Tel: 015394 36413
e-mail: outgate@outgate.wanadoo.co.uk • www.outgateinn.co.uk

A traditional 17thC Lakeland inn. Log fire and oak beams; beer garden at rear. Serves well kept Robinson's real ales and home-cooked meals.
Bed and Breakfast available in three en suite letting bedrooms.
One bedroom (largest double) is dog-friendly
Dogs allowed in bar area on lead • Water bowls front and back.
Pet Residents: Yellow Labrador (Beefy) and Scottish Terrier (Millie)

the greyhound @ shap

Shap, Cumbria CA10 3PW • Tel: 01931 716474
www.thegreyhoundshap.co.uk info@greyhoundshap.co.uk

15thC coaching inn • handpulled real ales plus extensive wine list • traditional local food served daily • bedrooms with en suite facilities • families, walkers and dogs welcome • fantastic Sunday lunch • M6 J39 only 5 minutes.

Brown Cow Inn

Tel: 01229 717243
Waberthwaite, Near Ravenglass, Cumbria LA19 5YJ
e-mail: browncowinn@btconnect.com

Home-cooked food at prices you can afford. Four real ales. Open fire. Four en suite rooms available. Wheelchair access. Food served daily from 11.30am to 8.30pm. Beer garden.

Pets welcome in bar area and rooms.

The Bullers Arms

Chagford, Newton Abbot, Devon
Tel: 01647 432348 • www.bullersarms.co.uk

Home-made food, lunchtime and evening dinner. Casque Marque accredited real ales. En suite accommodation. Dogs allowed throughout pub, except dining room/kitchen. "More than welcome".

PORT LIGHT Hotel, Restaurant & Inn

Bolberry Down, Malborough, Near Salcombe, Devon TQ7 3DY
Tel: (01548) 561384 or (07970) 859992 • Sean & Hazel Hassall
e-mail: info@portlight.co.uk • www.portlight.co.uk

Luxury en suite rooms, easy access onto the gardens. Close to secluded sandy cove (dogs permitted). No charge for pets which are most welcome throughout the hotel. Outstanding food and service. Winner 2004 "Dogs Trust" Best Pet Hotel in England. Self-catering cottages also available.

Pets may dine in bar area • Pet food fridge available

THE LAMB INN

Sandford, Crediton, Devon EX17 4LW • 01363 773676
thelambinn@gmail.com • www.lambinnsandford.co.uk

16thC pub in beautiful village, 8 miles from Exeter. Beautiful gardens, function rooms, cinema, and stunning new en suite rooms. Very luxurious but reasonably priced, with good food cooked by our French chef, and some great local ales.

Pet Regulars: Tiny (Jack Russell), Bob (Collie Cross Alsatian), Copper (intruding cat).

The Trout & Tipple

Julie and Shaun invite you to

Dogs welcome, bowls of water and treats available on request. Children welcome. Dining room and games room. Real Ales include locally brewed Jail Ale and Dartmoor Best. Lunch on Sunday.

Parkwood Road, Tavistock, Devon PL19 0JS

Tel: 01822 618886 **www.troutandtipple.co.uk**

Fisherman's Haunt Inn

Salisbury Road, Winkton, Christchurch, Dorset BH23 7AS
Tel: 01202 477283 • www.fullershotels.co.uk

Traditional coaching inn with 11 stylishly refurbished bedrooms, some adapted for disabled access. Good food, wine and Fuller's cask ales. Close to Bournemouth Airport and many places of interest. Pets welcome.

Pets allowed in main bar and lounge for dining.
Two pet-friendly rooms in accommodation block.

The Brewers Arms

Martinstown, Dorchester, Dorset DT2 9LB • 01305 889361
e-mail: jackie_smith54@hotmail.com • www.thebrewersarms.com

Country pub with a lovely garden. Pub food. Amenities include a skittle alley, big car park and a large grassed area (which may be suitable for tents).

Chews, water bowls and areas out of the sun
Area in the pub where customers can eat and sit with their dogs.

Pet residents: Jodie and Poppy (both lurchers)

The European Inn

www.european-inn.co.uk

Piddletrenthide, Dorchester, Dorset DT2 7QT
Tel: 01300 348308 • info@european-inn.co.uk

Small country pub with two sumptuous bedrooms.
Taste of the West South West Dining Pub of the Year 2007.
Sister pub to The Gaggle of Geese at Buckland Newton.
Pets welcome throughout • Water/food; fire in winter • Good local walks.

Pet Residents: Summer and her daughters Minnie and Maude (Cocker Spaniels)

Powerstock, Bridport, Dorset DT6 3TF • 01308 485328
info@threehorseshoesinn.com
www.threehorseshoesinn.com

'The Shoes' is a Victorian inn tucked away in a peaceful part of West Dorset. The Inn boasts a great reputation for excellent cuisine. An à la carte menu with specials board is served daily, plus lunchtime snacks. Dogs and children welcome.

Pets welcome in bar, garden and accommodation.

Pet Residents: JJ and Piglet. Pet Regular: Guinness

The White Swan

The Square, 31 High Street, Swanage, Dorset BH19 2LJ • 01929 423804
e-mail: info@whiteswanswanage.co.uk • www.whiteswanswanage.co.uk

A pub with a warm and friendly atmosphere, three minutes from the beach. Traditional pub food, Sunday roasts. Large beer garden. En suite accommodation with parking. Free wifi and internet access. TV and pool table. Children and dogs welcome.

Water, treats • Dogs allowed in beer garden, bar area and accommodation.

Pet resident: Bagsy (Sharpei). Regulars: Meg, Liddy and Em (Black Labradors), Sally and Sophie (Jack Russells), Ruby (English Bulldog), Patch (Jack Russell), Prince (King Charles Spaniel.

The Silent Woman Inn

Bere Road, Coldharbour, Wareham, Dorset BH20 7PA
Tel: 01929 552909 • www.thesilentwoman.co.uk

Traditional country inn nestling in the heart of Wareham Forest. Beautiful gardens, log fires in winter. All fresh ingredients, wonderful food. Real ales, good wines. Adults-only inside.

Water bowls and treats - and affection • Dogs allowed in bar areas and all outside areas except children's play areas.

Pet Residents: Rosie and Ellie (Labs). Regulars: Bruno, Tilly and many others.

Fuller Street, Fairstead, Essex CM3 2BB • 01245 361477
info@thesquareandcompasses.co.uk • www.thesquareandcompasses.co.uk

Independently owned 17thC freehouse in a small sleepy village surrounded by picturesque countryside and near Essex Way long distance footpath. Only a short drive from new Great Leighs racecourse. Food is simple and straightforward, with daily changing chalkboard menus and traditional classic dishes, freshly prepared using local produce. Private dining room. Real ales. Garden and terrace.

Dogs welcome in bar area and garden. Water bowl available.

The Whalebone Freehouse

Chapel Road, Fingringhoe, Colchester, Essex CO5 7BG
Tel/Fax: 01206 729307 • e-mail: fburroughes307@aol.com

Only minutes from Colchester, the Whalebone offers a wide range of excellent food and real ales. Pets are most welcome inside the pub and in the beer garden. Excellent dog-walking trails in and around Fingringhoe. Water bowls provided on request.

Pet Residents: Rosie and Poppy (Basset Hounds)

The Tunnel House Inn

Coates, Cirencester, Gloucestershire GL7 6PW • 01285 770280
e-mail: bookings@tunnelhouse.com • www.tunnelhouse.com

A traditional Cotswold pub set on the edge of a wood. The perfect haven for pets, families, in fact everyone. Home-cooked pub food, traditional ales and ciders. Endless walks lead off from the pub in all directions.

Pets are welcome in all areas inside and out

Plenty of space; water and occasional treats provided.

Pet Regulars: Madge, very friendly Patterdale terrier - loves other dogs too!

White Buck Inn • 01425 402264

Bisterne Close, Burley, Ringwood, Hampshire BH24 4AZ

Victorian Inn blending tradition with modern comfort, located in the heart of the New Forest, with 7 stylish bedrooms, excellent restaurant and bar. Play area and log trail available for children. Pets welcome.

Dogs are permitted in the bar area and bedrooms 1,3 and 8 only.

The Victory Inn,

High Street, Hamble SO31 4HA • Tel: 02380 453105

Grade II Listed family pub. Enjoy a fine and inexpensive meal or simply enjoy a drink.
All food is home-made - à la carte menu and chef's specials.
There are no strangers at The Victory, just friends you have yet to meet.
Viv and Debs and all the staff welcome you to Hampshire's Finest.

Pet Regular - Oscar (Labrador)

The Compass Inn

Winsor Road, Winsor, Southampton, Hants SO40 2HE
Tel: 023 808 12237 • e-mail: mop.draper@btopenworld.com

A proper village pub serving good pub food and real ale.
Award-winning garden. 2 miles from M27 J1.
Twice yearly Beer Festivals (late May and August Bank Holiday).

Pets made very welcome

Pet Residents: Hugo (Jack Russell) and Murphy (Cocker Spaniel)

Trooper Road, Aldbury, Near Tring, Herts HP23 5RW
info@thevalianttrooper.co.uk • www.thevalianttrooper.co.uk

A traditional 18thC pub in a picturesque village. Home-cooked food served all day every day, wide selection of real ales. Children's play area. Large beer garden. Close to many fantastic Ridgeway walks. Group bookings always welcome.

Water bowl • Doggy treats • Dogs allowed in bar area

Pet Residents: Millie and Lucky (Jack Russells).
Pet Regulars: Kyra (Alsatian), Curbs (Jack Russell), Tarn (Border Collie), Jenson (Spaniel), Dickie (Black Lab)

The White Lion Tel: 01494 758387

Jenkins Lane, St Leonards, Near Tring, Herts HP23 6NW

Large secret garden, real fire in winter. Traditional village pub.

Food served lunchtime and evenings.

CAMRA recommended, Cask Marque accreditation for Real Ale.

Fresh water and biscuits always available

Resident Pets: Barney Rubble and My Scrumpy (both Terriers)

Cock Inn Heath Road, Boughton Monchelsea,

Maidstone, Kent ME17 4JD • Tel: 01622 743166
e-mail: cockinnboughtonmonchelsea@hotmail.com

Glorious 16thC timbered black and white inn. Patio and outside eating area. Inglenook fireplace and oak-beamed bar and restaurant.

Dogs are treated and watered, while their owners are cossetted and pampered!

BLACK HORSE INN

Pilgrims Way, Thurnham, Kent ME14 3LD

Tel: 01622 737185 • info@wellieboot.net • www.wellieboot.net

A homely and welcoming inn with its origins in the 18thC, The Black Horse is adorned with hops and beams, and has an open log fireplace to welcome you in winter. A separate annexe has 16 beautiful en suite bedrooms.

Pets can stay in B&B rooms • Welcome in bar on lead
Dog bin and poop bags provided • Maps of local walks available.

The Inn at Whitewell • Forest of Bowland

Near Clitheroe, Lancs BB7 3AT • Tel: 01200 448222
reception@innatwhitewell.com • www.innatwhitewell.com

14thC inn in the beautiful Forest of Bowland.
7 miles fishing from our doorstep - trout, sea trout and salmon.
23 glamorous bedrooms, award-winning kitchen.
Voted by *The Independent* "One of the 50 Best UK Hotels"
Pets welcome in all areas except the kitchen!

The Red Lion 01254 830378

196 Blackburn Road,Wheelton, Near Chorley, Lancs PR6 8EU
info@redlionwheelton.com • www.redlionwheelton.com

A traditional village pub, where we pride ourselves on our wide selection of cask-conditioned ales, cider, quality wines and spirits. Our menu features a wide range of delicious home-cooked meals, using, where possible, the best of local produce.

Dogs welcome inside during trading hours and in beer garden; water always available.

The Hoste Arms

The Green, Burnham Market,
King's Lynn, Norfolk PE31 8HD
Tel: 01328 738777 • www.hostearms.co.uk

Stylish hotel with individually designed bedrooms. Fabulous food. Cosy bar, pretty garden and terraced dining area. Dogs allowed throughout the pub, except restaurant.

Stiffkey Red Lion Tel: 01328 830552

44 Wells Road, Stiffkey, Norfolk NR23 1AJ
e-mail: redlion@stiffkey.com • www.stiffkey.com

5 ground floor en suite bedrooms, 5 on first floor;
all with their own external door.
Pets warmly welcomed

The Bell Inn

High Street, Adderbury, Oxon
Tel: 01295 810338 • www.thebell-adderbury.com

Pretty inn with warm and welcoming atmosphere, good food, fine wines and great company. Dogs allowed throughout the pub and accommodation rooms.

Pet Residents: Murphy and Dizzy (Lancashire Heelers) and Rika (Rottweiler)..

The Bell Hotel & Restaurant

Church Street, Charlebury OX7 3PP • Tel: 01608 810278

www.bellhotel-charlbury.com • reservations@bellhotel-charlebury.com

Vibrant and stylish 18th Century hotel in the heart of the Oxfordshire Cotswolds. Situated in the Centre of Charlebury, we pride ourselves on a warm welcome and excellent food.

• Pets welcome in double/twin en suite rooms in our Cornbury annexe as well as the public areas, excluding the restaurant. Extensive grounds and many local walks.

The Salthouse Pub & Restaurant

Salthouse Road, Clevedon, Somerset BS21 7TY • 01275 343303

info@thesalthousepub.co.uk • www.thesalthousepub.co.uk

Large pub and restaurant with a patio seating 250.
Fantastic views of Clevedon Pier and Severn Estuary.
Large gardens, and to rear of pub are woods and Poets' Walk.

Pets are welcome in the main bar (not restaurant) and patio area. We supply fresh water and comfort. Dogs must be kept on lead.

The Lion Hotel

01398 324437

2 BANK SQUARE, DULVERTON, SOMERSET TA22 9BU

www.lionhoteldulverton.com • lionatdulverton@btconnect.com

Traditional old English market town inn, Grade II Listed, with 14 comfortable en suite rooms. Local produce, home-cooked food, real ales, log fires, and a warm welcome!

Water and dog treats in the bar (by reception).

22 Silver Street, Ilminster, Somerset TA19 0DR • 01460 57904

Cosy, friendly atmosphere. Fully stocked bar, serving a good selection of real ales, lagers, spirits, and fine wines. Excellent home-cooked food served daily. Families welcome. Pool table. Parking nearby. Good walks close by.

Clean water • Dog treats • Pets allowed inside and outside

The Hood Arms

01278 741210

Kilve, Somerset TA5 1EA • www.thehoodarms.com

17th century coaching inn with comfortable dining areas and real ales. 12 en suite bedrooms.
Dogs allowed throughout and in guests' rooms.

Uckfield Road, Ringmer, East Sussex BN8 5RP • 01273 814223

e-mail: info@oldshippub.co.uk • www.oldshippub.co.uk

On the A26 between Lewes and Uckfield, this family-run 17thC inn is the perfect place to relax, with food served from 12 to 9.30pm daily. The charming oak-beamed bar and restaurant is set in one acre of well tended, enclosed gardens. Well behaved dogs welcome inside.

Pet Resident: Marley (Bernese Mountain Dog)

The Broadway

112 London Road, East Grinstead, West Sussex RH19 1EP
Tel: 01342 410306 • e-mail: the-broadway@btconnect.com
www.myspace.com/thebroadwayeg

The Broadway is a large town centre pub, where you will always receive a warm welcome from our friendly staff. Two real ales on tap; Cask Marque accredited. Large front patio with car park at rear of pub.

Well behaved dogs on leash allowed in pub at any time of day.

The Lamb Inn

High Street, Hindon, Wiltshire SP3 6DP
Tel: 01747 820573 • Fax: 01747 820605
www.lambathindon.co.uk

12th Century historic inn with bedrooms full of character. Outstanding food and great wine selection. Pets welcome in the bar and bedrooms. ETC/AA ★★★★

The Castle Inn

7 Wistowgate, Cawood
Selby, North Yorkshire YO8 3SH **Tel: 01757 268324**
info@castleinncawood.co.uk • www.castleinncawood.co.uk

18thC village pub with a 60-seat restaurant and an 18-pitch caravan site. All food is local and fresh. Water bowls outside.

Pet Resident: Elvis (9-year old Springer Spaniel)

Old Hall Inn

Tel: 01756 752441
Main Street, Threshfield, Grassington, N, Yorks BD23 5HB
oldhallinn@fsmail.net • www.oldhallinnandcottages.co.uk

18thC Inn, renowned for fine ales and award-winning cuisine. Large beer garden. Children's outdoor play area. B&B in four en suite bedrooms; quality self-catering available in adjacent cottages.

Well behaved dogs welcome.

Simonstone Hall

Hawes, North Yorkshire DL8 3LY
Tel: 01969 667255 • www.simonstonehall.com

Welcoming bar with great atmosphere.
Wide range of bar meals from snacks to Sunday Lunch.
Comfortable accommodation.
Dogs of all shapes sizes and breeds welcome.

The West Arms Hotel

Llanarmon Dyffryn Ceiriog, Nr Llangollen, Denbighshire North Wales LL20 7LF • Tel: 01691 600665
e-mail: gowestarms@aol.com • www.thewestarms.co.uk

16th century Hotel full of charm and character. Award winning restaurant, bar meals lunchtime and evening. En suite bedrooms. Welcome Pets.

Ballachulish Hotel

Ballachulish, Argyll PA39 4JY
Tel: 01855 811606 • www.ballachulishhotel.com

Stay, refuel, relax and refresh in this historic hotel in a lochside setting. Bar and Bistro serving market fresh produce. Dogs allowed in the lounge and guests' bedrooms, excluding food areas.

THE MUNRO INN

Strathyre, Perthshire FK18 8NA• Tel: 01877 384333
www.munro-inn.com

Chilled out Robbie warmly welcomes doggy friends to the Munro Inn in beautiful highland Perthshire. Perfect base for walking, cycling, climbing, water sports, fishing or relaxing! Great home cooking, lively bar, luxurious en suite bedrooms, drying room, broadband internet.

Four Seasons Hotel

St Fillans, Perthshire • Tel: 01764 685333

Hotel in picturesque setting offering comfortable bedrooms, chalets and apartment. Fine dining restaurant and bar. Dogs allowed in all non-food areas.

Looking for Holiday Accommodation?

FHG
K·U·P·E·R·A·R·D

for details of hundreds of properties throughout the UK, visit our website

www.holidayguides.com

FHG
K·U·P·E·R·A·R·D
READERS' OFFER 2009

LEIGHTON BUZZARD RAILWAY

Page's Park Station, Billington Road,
Leighton Buzzard, Bedfordshire LU7 4TN
Tel: 01525 373888
e-mail: station@lbngrs.org.uk
www.buzzrail.co.uk

One FREE adult/child with full-fare adult ticket
Valid 15/3/2009 - 8/11/2009

NOT TO BE USED IN CONJUNCTION WITH ANY OTHER OFFER

FHG
K·U·P·E·R·A·R·D
READERS' OFFER 2009

BUCKINGHAMSHIRE RAILWAY CENTRE

Quainton Road Station, Quainton,
Aylesbury HP22 4BY
Tel & Fax: 01296 655720
e-mail: office@bucksrailcentre.org
www.bucksrailcentre.org

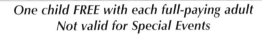

One child FREE with each full-paying adult
Not valid for Special Events

NOT TO BE USED IN CONJUNCTION WITH ANY OTHER OFFER

FHG
K·U·P·E·R·A·R·D
READERS' OFFER 2009

THE RAPTOR FOUNDATION

The Heath, St Ives Road,
Woodhurst, Huntingdon, Cambs PE28 3BT
Tel: 01487 741140 • Fax: 01487 841140
e-mail: heleowl@aol.com
www.raptorfoundation.org.uk

TWO for the price of ONE
Valid until end 2009 (not Bank Holidays)

NOT TO BE USED IN CONJUNCTION WITH ANY OTHER OFFER

FHG
K·U·P·E·R·A·R·D
READERS' OFFER 2009

ANSON ENGINE MUSEUM

Anson Road, Poynton,
Cheshire SK12 1TD
Tel: 01625 874426
e-mail: enquiry@enginemuseum.org
www.enginemuseum.org

Saturdays - 2 for 1 entry (when one of equal or greater value is purchased). Valid 12 April-30 Sept 2009

NOT TO BE USED IN CONJUNCTION WITH ANY OTHER OFFER

A 70-minute journey into the lost world of the English narrow gauge light railway. Features historic steam locomotives from many countries.

PETS MUST BE KEPT UNDER CONTROL AND NOT ALLOWED ON TRACKS

Open: Sundays and Bank Holiday weekends 22 March to 25 October. Additional days in summer.

Directions: on south side of Leighton Buzzard. Follow brown signs from town centre or A505/ A4146 bypass.

FHG GUIDES, ABBEY MILL BUSINESS CENTRE, PAISLEY PA1 1TJ • www.holidayguides.com

A working steam railway centre. Steam train rides, miniature railway rides, large collection of historic preserved steam locomotives, carriages and wagons.

Open: daily April to October 10.30am to 4.30pm. Variable programme - check website or call.

Directions: off A41 Aylesbury to Bicester Road, 6 miles north west of Aylesbury.

FHG GUIDES, ABBEY MILL BUSINESS CENTRE, PAISLEY PA1 1TJ • www.holidayguides.com

Birds of Prey Centre offering audience participation in flying displays which are held 3 times daily. Tours, picnic area, gift shop, tearoom, craft shop.

Open: 10am-5pm all year except Christmas and New Year.

Directions: follow brown tourist signs from B1040.

FHG GUIDES, ABBEY MILL BUSINESS CENTRE, PAISLEY PA1 1TJ • www.holidayguides.com

As seen on TV, this multi award-winning attraction has a great deal to offer visitors. It houses the largest collection of engines in Europe, local history area, craft centre (bodging and smithy work), with changing exhibitions throughout the season.

Open: Easter Sunday until end October, Friday to Sunday and Bank Holidays, 10am to 5pm.

Directions: approx 7 miles from J1 M60 and 9 miles J3 M60. Follow brown tourist signs from Poynton traffic lights.

FHG GUIDES, ABBEY MILL BUSINESS CENTRE, PAISLEY PA1 1TJ • www.holidayguides.com

FHG
·K·U·P·E·R·A·R·D·
READERS' OFFER 2009

CHINA CLAY COUNTRY PARK

Wheal Martyn, Carthew, St Austell,
Cornwall PL26 8XG
Tel & Fax: 01726 850362
e-mail: info@chinaclaycountry.co.uk
www.chinaclaycountry.co.uk

TWO for ONE adult entry, saving £7.50.
One voucher per person. Valid until July 2009.

NOT TO BE USED IN CONJUNCTION WITH ANY OTHER OFFER

FHG
·K·U·P·E·R·A·R·D·
READERS' OFFER 2009

NATIONAL LOBSTER HATCHERY

South Quay, Padstow,
Cornwall PL28 8BL
Tel: 01841 533877 • Fax: 0870 7060299
e-mail: info@nationallobsterhatchery.co.uk
www.nationallobsterhatchery.co.uk

TWO for the price of ONE
Valid November 2008 to March 2009

NOT TO BE USED IN CONJUNCTION WITH ANY OTHER OFFER

FHG
·K·U·P·E·R·A·R·D·
READERS' OFFER 2009

NATIONAL SEAL SANCTUARY

Gweek, Helston,
Cornwall TR12 6UG
Tel: 01326 221361
e-mail: seals@sealsanctuary.co.uk
www.sealsanctuary.co.uk

TWO for ONE - on purchase of another ticket of equal or greater value. Valid until December 2009.

NOT TO BE USED IN CONJUNCTION WITH ANY OTHER OFFER

FHG
·K·U·P·E·R·A·R·D·
READERS' OFFER 2009

CARS OF THE STARS MOTOR MUSEUM

Standish Street, Keswick,
Cumbria CA12 5HH
Tel: 017687 73757
e-mail: cotsmm@aol.com
www.carsofthestars.com

One child free with two paying adults
Valid during 2009

NOT TO BE USED IN CONJUNCTION WITH ANY OTHER OFFER

The Country Park covers 26 acres and includes woodland and historic trails, picnic sites, children's adventure trail and award-winning cycle trail. Remains of a Victorian clay works complete with the largest working water wheel in Cornwall. Shop, cafe, exhibitions, museum.	**Open:** 10am-6pm daily (closed Christmas Day) **Directions:** two miles north of St Austell on the B3274. Follow brown tourist signs. 5 minutes from Eden Project.

FHG GUIDES, ABBEY MILL BUSINESS CENTRE, PAISLEY PA1 1TJ • www.holidayguides.com

A unique conservation programme - see our fisheries at work and find out everything there is to know about the European lobster.	**Open:** from 10am seven days a week. **Directions:** right on the water's edge, in the South Quay car park, right opposite Rick Stein's fish & chip shop.

FHG GUIDES, ABBEY MILL BUSINESS CENTRE, PAISLEY PA1 1TJ • www.holidayguides.com

Britain's leading grey seal rescue centre	**Open:** daily (except Christmas Day) from 10am **Directions:** from A30 follow signs to Helston, then brown tourist signs to Seal Sanctuary.

FHG GUIDES, ABBEY MILL BUSINESS CENTRE, PAISLEY PA1 1TJ • www.holidayguides.com

A collection of cars from film and TV, including Chitty Chitty Bang Bang, James Bond's Aston Martin, Del Boy's van, Fab1 and many more. PETS MUST BE KEPT ON LEAD	**Open:** daily 10am-5pm. Open February half term, lst April to end November, also weekends in December. **Directions:** in centre of Keswick close to car park.

FHG GUIDES, ABBEY MILL BUSINESS CENTRE, PAISLEY PA1 1TJ • www.holidayguides.com

FHG
K·U·P·E·R·A·R·D
READERS' OFFER 2009

THE GRASSIC GIBBON CENTRE

Arbuthnott, Laurencekirk,
Aberdeenshire AB30 1PB
Tel: 01561 361668
e-mail: lgginfo@grassicgibbon.com
www.grassicgibbon.com

TWO for the price of ONE entry to exhibition (based on full adult rate only). Valid during 2009 (not groups)

NOT TO BE USED IN CONJUNCTION WITH ANY OTHER OFFER

FHG
K·U·P·E·R·A·R·D
READERS' OFFER 2009

SCOTTISH MARITIME MUSEUM

Harbourside, Irvine,
Ayrshire KA12 8QE
Tel: 01294 278283
Fax: 01294 313211
www.scottishmaritimemuseum.org

TWO for the price of ONE
Valid from April to October 2009

NOT TO BE USED IN CONJUNCTION WITH ANY OTHER OFFER

FHG
K·U·P·E·R·A·R·D
READERS' OFFER 2009

BO'NESS & KINNEIL RAILWAY

Bo'ness Station, Union Street,
Bo'ness, West Lothian EH51 9AQ
Tel: 01506 822298
e-mail: enquiries.railway@srps.org.uk
www.srps.org.uk

FREE child train fare with one paying adult/concession. Valid 29th March-26th Oct 2009. Not Thomas events or Santa Steam trains

NOT TO BE USED IN CONJUNCTION WITH ANY OTHER OFFER

FHG
K·U·P·E·R·A·R·D
READERS' OFFER 2009

MYRETON MOTOR MUSEUM

Aberlady,
East Lothian
EH32 0PZ
Tel: 01875 870288

One child FREE with each paying adult
Valid during 2009

NOT TO BE USED IN CONJUNCTION WITH ANY OTHER OFFER

Visitor Centre dedicated to the much-loved Scottish writer Lewis Grassic Gibbon. Exhibition, cafe, gift shop. Outdoor children's play area. Disabled access throughout.	**Open:** daily April to October 10am to 4.30pm. Groups by appointment including evenings. **Directions:** on the B967, accessible and signposted from both A90 and A92.

FHG GUIDES, ABBEY MILL BUSINESS CENTRE, PAISLEY PA1 1TJ • www.holidayguides.com

Scotland's seafaring heritage is among the world's richest and you can relive the heyday of Scottish shipping at the Maritime Museum.	**Open:** 1st April to 31st October - 10am-5pm **Directions:** situated on Irvine harbourside and only a 10 minute walk from Irvine train station.

FHG GUIDES, ABBEY MILL BUSINESS CENTRE, PAISLEY PA1 1TJ • www.holidayguides.com

Steam and heritage diesel passenger trains from Bo'ness to Birkhill for guided tours of Birkhill fireclay mines. Explore the history of Scotland's railways in the Scottish Railway Exhibition. Coffee shop and souvenir shop.	**Open:** weekends Easter to October, daily July and August. **Directions:** in the town of Bo'ness. Leave M9 at Junction 3 or 5, then follow brown tourist signs.

FHG GUIDES, ABBEY MILL BUSINESS CENTRE, PAISLEY PA1 1TJ • www.holidayguides.com

On show is a large collection, from 1899, of cars, bicycles, motor cycles and commercials. There is also a large collection of period advertising, posters and enamel signs.	**Open:** March-November - open daily 11am to 4pm. December-February - weekends 11am to 3pm or by special appointment. **Directions:** off A198 near Aberlady. Two miles from A1.

FHG GUIDES, ABBEY MILL BUSINESS CENTRE, PAISLEY PA1 1TJ • www.holidayguides.com

FHG

·K·U·P·E·R·A·R·D·

READERS' OFFER 2009

SPEYSIDE HEATHER GARDEN & VISITOR CENTRE

Speyside Heather Centre, Dulnain Bridge,
Inverness-shire PH26 3PA
Tel: 01479 851359 • Fax: 01479 851396
e-mail: enquiries@heathercentre.com
www.heathercentre.com

Speyside HEATHER GARDEN

FREE entry to 'Heather Story' exhibition
Valid during 2009

NOT TO BE USED IN CONJUNCTION WITH ANY OTHER OFFER

FHG

·K·U·P·E·R·A·R·D·

READERS' OFFER 2009

LLANBERIS LAKE RAILWAY

Gilfach Ddu, Llanberis,
Gwynedd LL55 4TY
Tel: 01286 870549
e-mail: info@lake-railway.co.uk
www.lake-railway.co.uk

RHEILFFORDD LLYN PADARN LLANBERIS LAKE RAILWAY

One pet travels FREE with each full fare paying adult
Valid Easter to October 2009

NOT TO BE USED IN CONJUNCTION WITH ANY OTHER OFFER

FHG

·K·U·P·E·R·A·R·D·

READERS' OFFER 2009

FELINWYNT RAINFOREST CENTRE

Felinwynt, Cardigan,
Ceredigion SA43 1RT
Tel: 01239 810882/810250
e-mail: dandjdevereux@btinternet.com
www.butterflycentre.co.uk

TWO for the price of ONE (one voucher per party only)
Valid until end October 2009

NOT TO BE USED IN CONJUNCTION WITH ANY OTHER OFFER

FHG

·K·U·P·E·R·A·R·D·

READERS' OFFER 2009

NATIONAL CYCLE COLLECTION

Automobile Palace, Temple Street,
Llandrindod Wells, Powys LD1 5DL
Tel: 01597 825531
e-mail: cycle.museum@powys.org.uk
www.cyclemuseum.org.uk

NATIONAL CYCLE COLLECTION

TWO for the price of ONE
Valid during 2009 except Special Event days

NOT TO BE USED IN CONJUNCTION WITH ANY OTHER OFFER

Award-winning attraction with unique 'Heather Story' exhibition, gallery, giftshop, large garden centre selling 300 different heathers, antique shop, children's play area and famous Clootie Dumpling restaurant.	**Open:** all year except Christmas Day and New Year's Day. **Directions:** just off A95 between Aviemore and Grantown-on-Spey.

FHG GUIDES, ABBEY MILL BUSINESS CENTRE, PAISLEY PA1 1TJ • www.holidayguides.com

A 60-minute ride along the shores of beautiful Padarn Lake behind a quaint historic steam engine. Magnificent views of the mountains from lakeside picnic spots. **DOGS MUST BE KEPT ON LEAD AT ALL TIMES ON TRAIN**	**Open:** most days Easter to October, and some dates from mid-February and to mid-December. Free timetable leaflet on request. **Directions:** just off A4086 Caernarfon to Capel Curig road at Llanberis; follow 'Country Park' signs.

FHG GUIDES, ABBEY MILL BUSINESS CENTRE, PAISLEY PA1 1TJ • www.holidayguides.com

Mini-rainforest full of tropical plants and exotic butterflies. Personal attention of the owner, Mr John Devereux. Gift shop, cafe, video room, exhibition. Suitable for disabled visitors. VisitWales Quality Assured Visitor Attraction. **PETS NOT ALLOWED IN TROPICAL HOUSE ONLY**	**Open:** daily Easter to end October 10.30am to 5pm **Directions:** West Wales, 7 miles north of Cardigan off Aberystwyth road. Follow brown tourist signs on A487.

FHG GUIDES, ABBEY MILL BUSINESS CENTRE, PAISLEY PA1 1TJ • www.holidayguides.com

Journey through the lanes of cycle history and see bicycles from Boneshakers and Penny Farthings up to modern Raleigh cycles. Over 250 machines on display **PETS MUST BE KEPT ON LEADS**	**Open:** 1st March to 1st November daily 10am onwards. **Directions:** brown signs to car park. Town centre attraction.

FHG GUIDES, ABBEY MILL BUSINESS CENTRE, PAISLEY PA1 1TJ • www.holidayguides.com

Index of Towns and Counties

FHG Guides

Visit the FHG website

www.holidayguides.com

for details of the wide choice of accommodation

featured in the full range of FHG titles

www.holidayguides.com

Other FHG titles for 2009

FHG Guides Ltd have a large range of attractive
holiday accommodation guides for all kinds of holiday opportunities throughout Britain.
They also make useful gifts at any time of year.
Our guides are available in most bookshops and larger newsagents but we will be happy to post you a copy direct if you have any difficulty. POST FREE for addresses in the UK.
We will also post abroad but have to charge separately for post or freight.

FHG
K·U·P·E·R·A·R·D

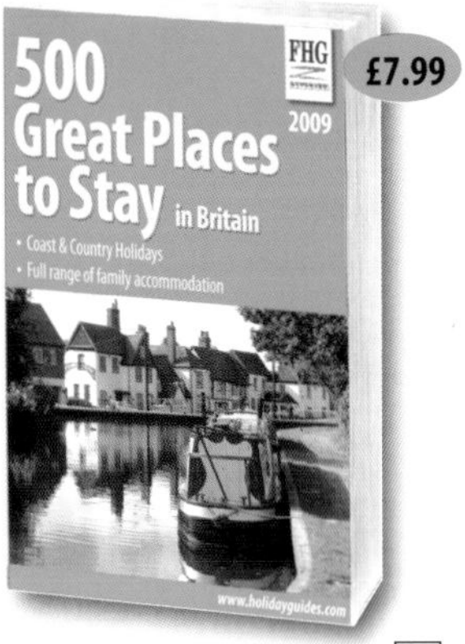

500
Great Places to Stay
in Britain
- Coast & Country Holidays
- Full range of family accommodation

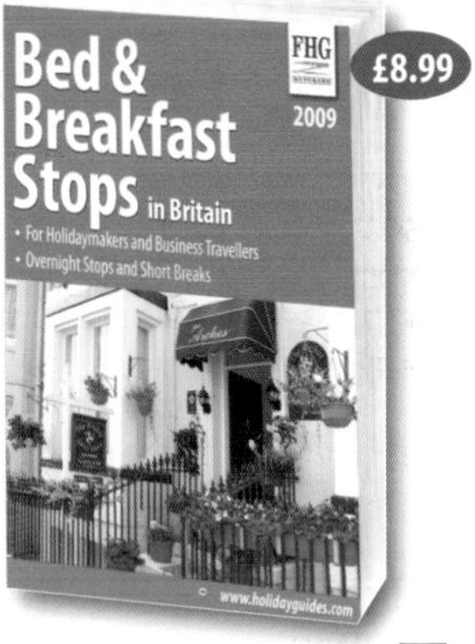

Bed &
Breakfast Stops
in Britain
- For holidaymakers and business travellers
- Overnight stops and Short Breaks

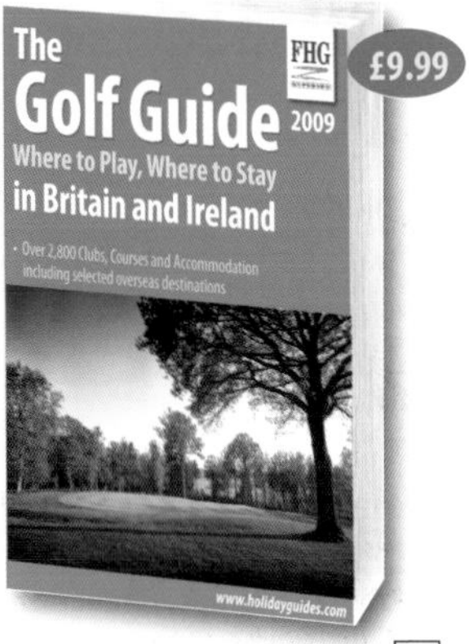

The Golf Guide
Where to play, Where to stay.
- Over 2800 golf courses in Britain with convenient accommodation.
- Holiday Golf in France, Portugal, Spain, USA and Thailand.

Pubs
& Inns
of Britain
- Including Dog-friendly Pubs
- Accommodation, food and traditional good cheer

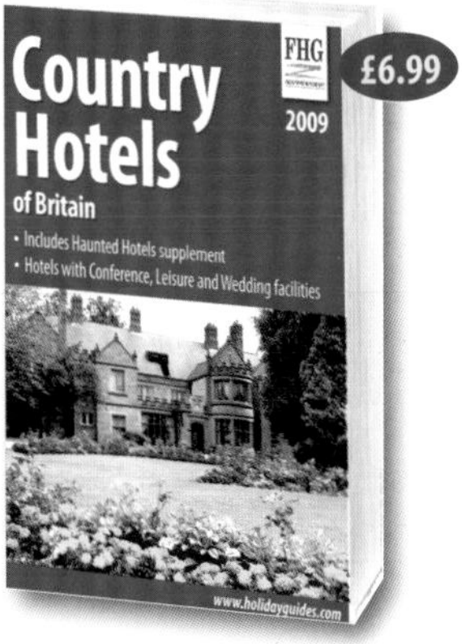

Country
Hotels
of Britain
- Hotels with Conference, Leisure and Wedding Facilities

Caravan
& Camping Holidays
in Britain
- Campsites and Caravan parks
- Facilities fully listed

Family Breaks
in Britain
• Accommodation, attractions and resorts
• Suitable for those with children and babies

☐

Self-Catering Holidays
in Britain
• Cottages, farms, apartments and chalets
• Over 400 places to stay

☐

Weekend & Short Breaks
in Britain
• Accommodation for holidays and weekends away

☐

Tick your choice above and send your order and payment to

FHG Guides Ltd. Abbey Mill Business Centre
Seedhill, Paisley, Scotland PA1 1TJ
TEL: 0141- 887 0428 • FAX: 0141- 889 7204
e-mail: admin@fhguides.co.uk

FHG
·K·U·P·E·R·A·R·D·

Deduct 10% for 2/3 titles or copies; 20% for 4 or more.

Send to: NAME..

ADDRESS ....

....

....

POST CODE ....

I enclose Cheque/Postal Order for £ ....

SIGNATURE ....DATE ....

Please complete the following to help us improve the service we provide.

How did you find out about our guides?:

☐ Press ☐ Magazines ☐ TV/Radio ☐ Family/Friend ☐ Other